MEXICO

THE COOKBOOK

MARGARITA CARRILLO ARRONTE

MEXICO

THE COOKBOOK

My earliest and fondest memories of food are from my childhood, when my grandmother would prepare sweet things for us in the afternoons. On one of those occasions, when she was making *buñuelos* (page 593), she gave me a little ball of dough and first taught me to shape the dough over my knee. Of course, I made big holes in the dough. She placed her hand over my small fingers and showed me how to mend it.

When I behaved well, she'd let me "clean" the paddle of the beater with my fingers and then lick my fingers, until my face was grubby with delicious sweet dough or chocolate. She taught me that cooking for family and friends was a joy, and that teaching with love and patience made the pupil learn easier.

Family tradition, my love for Mexico, and respect for ancestral culture and food have all contributed to my love of food. Family values that revolve around cooking and enjoying food together with your loved ones—in my family the taste for good food was always nourished from mother to daughter and cultivated and encouraged by my father.

You are holding in your hands a cookbook in which you will find a delicious collection of recipes that will take you on a voyage of discovery through the different cuisines of Mexico. You will also find in its pages the ingredients, utensils, techniques, and historical background that have made traditional Mexican cuisine an invaluable representation of a nation with a rich cultural identity.

The world of Mexican food is labyrinthine. Dishes like tacos, tamales, and moles fork off in many different directions, in endless variations. Tortillas—the corn flatbreads that have been the staple of Mexico since ancient times—are used in hundreds of ways. Chiles, that famed Mexican ingredient, are not simply distinguished by being red or green, long or small, but come in around 300 different varieties and not only add heat but flavor.

Mexican food is a marriage of not only of Spanish and indigenous flavors but also the cooking techniques, which belong to both cultures. In fact, Spanish culinary customs of the 16th century were the result of Mediterranean, Arab and Jewish influences and regional variants of the Iberian Peninsula.

When I cook Mexican food, especially with those who are unfamiliar with the cuisine, it makes me feel very proud that the food is sophisticated, the flavors are refined, and the ingredients are fresh and nutritious. I like to think my guests leave my table satisfied.

I hope to introduce readers to Mexican food, culture and tastes and to show that Mexican food is extremely varied and rich, with quality ingredients, unique techniques and surprising flavors. I encourage you to try a culinary adventure and cook the simpler dishes first and the challenge yourself with more elaborate ones such as Chicken Stuffed with Huitalacoche (page 326) or "Day of the Dead" Bread (page 556).

The most important thing is enjoy and *buen provecho*!

THE FOOD OF MESOAMERICA

Mexican cuisine, of course, cannot be separated from its context of geography, people and history. From the border with the United States, Mexico begins in tracts of arid desert silhouetted with giant cacti at dusk—where wheat almost reigns over corn as the major grain and where beef and goat loom large on the menu. Crossing the Tropic of Cancer and heading south to Guatemala, it becomes green, tropical and abundant with produce, with indigenous ingredients that date back to the early people of Mesoamerica—a cuisine that was already rich and developed and of which I am very proud. Adding to this landscape are Mexico's two long coastlines to the east and west, and the mountain ranges that cut through the country from north to south, putting many areas at high elevation (even the capital, Mexico City, is more than 2000 metres above sea level).

Mesoamerica roughly encompassed the southern half of Mexico through to Central America. It was home to one of the world's six great ancient civilisations.

Mesoamerica was in fact a web of civilisations. The Mayan civilisation began around 2000 BC on Mexico's Yucatan Peninsula and in ancient Belize and Guatemala. It was actually in decline in the centuries before Spanish

colonisation for reasons not entirely clear, but research shows that overpopulation, deforestation and drought were factors.

Compared to the Mayans, the Aztecs were a comparatively young civilisation of Mesoamerica, settling in central Mexico on the site of current-day Mexico City in the 13th century after migrating from the north. It was a short but intense period before Spanish colonisation as the Aztecs built impressive cities and rose to wealth and greatness.

The major food that the Mayans, Aztecs and other Mesoamerican people shared was corn. The first farming of corn was around 5500 BC (for more on corn, see page 19).

Other pre-Columbian foods of Mexico are chiles, beans, tomatoes, avocados and pumpkin, with pumpkin agriculture beginning even before corn. It is not only the pumpkin itself but the flowers and seeds that are much used in Mexican cooking.

Mesoamerican farmers devised a way of growing corn, beans and pumpkin (the 'three sisters') together in an early form of companion planting that is still practiced today and known as *milpa*. The corn plant grows first, shooting skyward; the bean plant climbs up the corn and fixes nitrogen in the soil; and the pumpkin plant covers the ground, allowing the soil to retain moisture and suppressing weeds. This method of farming is no less than 5,000 years old.

When you add chocolate and vanilla beans to Mexico's list of indigenous ingredients, it is fair to say that the country's culinary gifts to the world have been more than most making it a richer and more delicious place. Chocolate has been traced back to 1900 BC with the discovery of drinking vessels containing chocolate residue in the ancient land of the Olmecs and pre-Olmecs. The Olmec people lived from around 1500 BC to 400 BC in a small region on the south coast of the Gulf of Mexico, west of the Mayans on the Yucatan Peninsula. Chocolate soon spread to the Mayans and later to the Aztecs, and Christopher Columbus and Hernándo Cortés both noted how valuable the cacao bean was. The Aztecs used them as currency and collected them as taxes.

Powerful Aztecs were fond of drinking spiced hot chocolate with foam on the top, and their ruler Moctezuma was the greatest xocóatl indulger of them all. Cortés and his party were served the drink at one of his feasts. It was not to their taste, being bitter, but they soon began to appreciate it when they added sugar.

Meats eaten in Mexico before the Spanish arrived included deer, turkey, dog, iguana, armadillo and rabbit. But in the Aztec world, meat was an unobtainable delicacy unless you were a member of the elite or a warrior.

Lesser known indigenous ingredients of Mexico that remain important in cooking today include cactus paddles (*nopales*), which are used in many vegetable dishes. Only tender young paddles are used, and their thorns must be sliced off first. Their flavor is like lemony green beans and goes well with most ingredients. They are very healthy and are often used during Lent as a meat replacement. From the same family of cactus plants comes the prickly pear and the xoconostle—two similar looking but different tasting fruits. The prickly pear is very sweet, while the xoconostle is prized for its more acidic flesh and the fact that the seeds are clustered in the centre of the fruit rather than scattered through it. Epazote is one of Mexico's important herbs along with coriander and oregano, called for in soups, with beans or in quesadillas, among other dishes. It has pointed, serrated leaves and is known for its pungence and lemony flavor.

Agave is another Mexican food plant from the arid areas. This succulent resembles a thick-bladed grass, shaped in a neat rosette and offers food in four ways—its leaves in winter and spring; its flowers that grow on a long central stalk; the stalk itself, eaten before the flowers blossom; and the sap tapped from the stalk, which is a natural sweetener and has recently made inroads into the international health-food market as agave syrup, an alternative to sugar. Left to ferment, the sap becomes pulque, a milky colored alcoholic drink that has been made for thousands of years. (A related plant, the blue agave, is what tequila is made from.

This clear alcohol, that has found its way all over the world, was produced soon after the Spanish arrived

in Mexico in the 16th century, when they applied their knowledge of distillation.)

INGREDIENTS

Christopher Columbus led four exploratory voyages in the Atlantic Ocean on behalf of Spain from 1492 until 1502. His intention was to find a route to Asia quicker than going overland from Europe, which would help Spain gain control of the spice trade. Instead, he found a new continent.

Columbus's voyages honed in on the West Indies, only touching on South and Central America. He didn't go as far north as Mexico, stopping at Honduras, where he is believed to have come across Mayans in a large canoe with goods to trade including cacao beans, pottery, and textiles.

Following Columbus' voyages, the Spanish began colonizing the West Indies and eventually set out for Mexico in 1519 with Hernándo Cortés as the commander. He soon conquered the Aztec empire through brute force, some luck, and by appealing to the Aztec people who were disgruntled with their leaders.

Mexican history since Cortés amounts to almost 500 years of Spanish presence and influence. In the realm of food, the ingredients that arrived with the Spanish were wheat flour; meat including beef, pork, lamb, goat and chicken; milk and cheese; rice; citrus; and garlic. Mexican food would forever more be culturally mixed.

Meat is now a big part of the Mexican diet, from barbacoa (literally "barbecue," but traditionally a method of steaming and smoking), to *carnitas* ("little meats"), which are tender braised morsels perfect for wrapping a tortilla around, to abundant dishes with tripe, tongue, and trotters. Mexican styles of cheese are essential in dishes such as quesadillas and empanadas, and milk is celebrated in desserts and sweets such as the rich reduced milk concoction called *cajeta* and in Three Milk Cake (page 612).

Mole (literally, "sauce") is a classic dish that blends indigenous and Spanish ingredients, said to have been invented in the 17th century (its more rustic cousin is stew). Instead of meat being cooked in a sauce, a smooth sauce is poured over the cooked meat, and the spicing and flavoring is more complex with ingredients such as nuts, seeds, and dried fruit, and famously including a little bit of dark chocolate such as in mole poblano.

CORN

Without corn we have no country. Corn is the staple food throughout the country and especially in the Central and Southern regions where it is consumed by all Mexicans virtually every day of their lives. It is eaten "on the cob" as well as in kernel form, ground, dried, used in soups and stews, and to make a variety of "corn food" including tortillas, gorditas, huarachas, tlacoyos, sopes, tamales, and even cakes and sweets!

Delving into the beliefs of the Mayans and Aztecs, it is easy to see how fundamental corn has always been to life in Mexico. The Mayan creation story involves the people being made from corn. The gods used a bolt of lightning to access some corn seeds hidden deep inside a mountain, then they ground the corn and made dough, and fashioned the Mayan people with it. Both the Mayans and the Aztecs worshipped corn gods, and the Aztecs practiced human sacrifice to keep their gods happy and their corn harvest plentiful, just as they did in many other rituals.

Dried corn saw the people of Mesoamerica through their year. The dough or masa made from ground corn kernels was pressed flat, cooked on a small pan called a *comal*, and eaten daily as tortillas. Directly connected to the corn is a very important process called nixtamalisation.

Thousands of years ago it was discovered that water made alkaline with ground limestone or wood ashes loosened the skins of corn kernels when they were boiled in it. This not only made the corn easier to digest and grind, but caused chemical changes in the corn that some say the success of ancient Mexico is founded on. Ground nixtamalised corn is able to be made into a soft, pliable dough necessary for making tortillas. The nutrient content of the corn is also greatly enhanced as the alkaline solution frees nutrients otherwise locked and inaccessible within the corn, while also adding nutrients of its own. Other countries with a diet based on cornmeal in parts of Europe and Africa have suffered deficiencies and disease due to their corn not being nixtamalised.

In Mexico it is not just the cob or kernels of corn that are used in cooking, but the husks too. Far too useful to be discarded, they are nature's natural wrappers and essential for dishes such as tamales (although other leaves such as banana leaves are employed too). Tamales are a mixture of masa dough and meat, seafood, cheese, vegetables or fruit, with herbs, spices and seasonings, steamed in small parcels.

Pozole, a soup of nixtamalised corn kernels, is to Mexico what minestrone is to Italy or borscht is to Russia—a hearty, warming meal in a bowl usually made with pork, accented with garlic and mild dried chiles, and topped with garnishes such as cabbage, radish, avocado and crisp tortilla pieces. In some parts of the country it is eaten on Thursdays and Saturdays, and it is also served at festivals.

THE ANCIENT ART OF THE TORTILLA

Mexico has long been fuelled by corn tortillas. It is not known exactly when the first of these flatbreads were made, but archaeological evidence showing nixtamalisation (see Corn, page 19) practiced at 1500–1200 BC points to the fact that it is undoubtedly an ancient art.

Traditionally there were many stages in the cooking process to get to the simple end result of a thin, round, flexible bread. Making tortillas took up a large part of a woman's day—and in some areas, it still does.

First the dried corn kernels were nixtamalised, a relatively easy process where the corn was boiled briefly in water mixed with powdered lime, or calcium hydroxide, called *cal* in Mexico—then left to cool and soak overnight. Then the corn was rinsed and the skins of the kernels, loosened by the lime, were rubbed off.

Grinding the kernels was the next and most laborious part of making tortillas, done with a *metate*—a large stone base with a shallow depression in it—and a *mano*—a cylinder of stone for grinding, like a horizontal mortar and pestle (The more traditional-shaped mortar and pestle is also used in Mexican cooking and is called a *molcajete*).

Once the corn was ground, water was added to make the mixture into dough, and small portions were deftly patted out to thin discs in the hands. The tortillas were cooked on a comal over an open fire.

In the late 19th century and throughout the 20th century, the tortilla-making process was industrialised. Electric corn grinding machines were invented and from the 1920s through to the 1950s, thousands of mills (molinos) opened in neighbourhoods and villages. Women would take their pre-soaked and washed corn to the mill, have it ground, and then return home to make their tortillas. In the 1960s, Mexico's tortillerias (shops to buy tortillas, for those who preferred not to make them at home) started using machines to roll out and cook tortillas. And then instant masa flour—nixtamalised and ground corn, returned to a dry flour state—hit the market in the 1970s, for people who still wanted to make tortillas but wanted a shortcut. In a century the art of the tortilla had been altered completely. As a result, there is a big difference in the quality of tortillas available today, but many people still favour the taste of those made from freshly ground nixtamalised corn and are versatile enough to be used in everything from tacos to tostadas (see glossary, page 686).

CHILES

Chile is celebrated in so many parts of world, from blow-your-head-off green papaya salads on street sides in Thailand, to chicken stir-fries laden with astounding amounts of dried chiles in Sichaun province, China, to the harissa pastes of north Africa that fire up meat, vegetables or couscous. But nowhere celebrates the nuances of chile like Mexico, its homeland.

There are hundreds of varieties of chiles of which about 12 are most commonly used. Some chiles—such as poblano, cuaresmeño (jalapeño), serrano, and arbol—are used fresh, while others—such as ancho, guajillo, cascabel, mulato, and pasilla—are only ever used dried. Others such as chipotle are smoked and used dry or "wet." Chiles do not necessarily impart heat to a dish, but they always give their own unique flavor.

Each region of Mexico has its favorite palette of chiles—orange habaneros and tiny piquin chiles are used on the Yucatán Peninsula, while large and mild green poblano chiles and round yellow manzano chiles are used around central Mexico, to name but a few. Chiles in their dried forms have different names—the poblano chile becomes the ancho chile when ripened and dried, and very closely related is the almost-black dried mulato chile. Fresh tapering green chilaca chiles become dried pasilla chiles; the jalapeño becomes the chipotle. Many dried chiles are smoked, adding another dimension of flavor.

While some chiles are extremely hot, many others are mild, sweet and fruity, and well-cooked Mexican food is not meant to burn, but be nicely balanced. Partly it is the role of salsas on the table (in their infinite variations) to spice your meal up to your taste.

Many Mexican dishes do not restrict themselves to using just one variety of chile, but blend several for depth of flavor. Moles often feature a "holy trinity" of three dried chiles—ancho, mulato, and pasilla.

There are many different types of beans eaten in Mexico. Throughout the country, beans form an essential part of the daily diet. Served cooked and whole or mashed and "refried," they accompany dishes served at any time of day. They are also used to stuff chiles, tortillas, or tamales. Dried beans should be soaked for 12 hours before being drained and simmered in fresh water until they are thoroughly cooked. A change of water during cooking helps to reduce the gassiness some people experience when they eat beans.

Cooked in various ways, rice accompanies many main dishes in Mexico. It is also used as the basis for countless "one-dish meals."

Salsa just means sauce and there are hundreds of sauces made of all sorts of ingredients from vegetables and fruit to chiles and beans. Salsas can be boiled, raw, roasted, or fried and are not necessarily spicy.

REGIONS

The traditional cuisine of each region of the country is not just the ingredients, preparation methods and utensils; it is the rich legacy of its history and cultural identity. The wealth of indigenous roots, the product of cultural fusion and racial integration and the influence of other countries have all contributed to create a cuisine that today distinguishes each region; Mexican food is my country's heritage and it is an element of identity and of social cohesion. This differentiation and regionalization arose from pre-Hispanic times, while at the same time a culinary variety gained impetus from the intense trade thriving along the length and breadth of Mesoamerica and beyond its borders.

In the North, Mexico widens like a funnel, opening out into a long border with the United States. The landscape is large with dry plains and mountain ranges and the states include Sonora, Chihuahua and Coahuila. In the east is the long, skinny peninsula of Baja California, completely separated from the rest of Mexico.

The food of the north may not be the riot of ingredients and flavors found in the south, but specialities such as beef, goat and cheese make it unique. Steaks have a reputation for being large, and other beef dishes include machaca, shredded dried beef that is used as a filling for tacos or stirred through scrambled eggs. Monterrey in the state of Nuevo Leon specialises in roasted kid, while the state of Chihuahua has cheese-making traditions dating back to the Mennonites who migrated from Holland in the 19th century. Here you can dine on authentic Chile Pasilla Con Queso (page 459)—local cheese is melted into a mixture of fried onion, tomato and lots of mild chiles, a kind of fondue to be accompanied by tortillas. For another cheese dish from the north, see Sonora-style Cheesy Broth (page 198).

Northern Mexico is beyond the natural range of corn, and is suited to wheat-growing instead, so the tortillas are made from wheat flour. Ciudad Juarez in Chihuahua is the birthplace of the burrito, which is a wheat tortilla containing simple fillings.

In Central Mexico, some of the food highlights occur in the state of Puebla, southeast of Mexico City. The country's most famous mole, mole poblano, originates here—a careful blend of dried chiles, spices, nuts, seeds, dried fruit, tomatoes and chocolate that traditionally takes days to prepare. Another celebrated dish is Chiles in Walnut Sauce (page 396), poblano chiles stuffed with a complex meat, fruit and nut filling, with fresh walnut sauce and sprinkled with pomegranate seeds. Due to the pomegranates, it's an autumn dish, and one that is served at Mexican Independence Day in September as it features the green (chile), red (pomegranate seeds) and white (sauce) of the Mexican flag.

Of course, Mexico City abounds with great food, with restaurants hailing from across the country, and indeed, the world. The range of street stalls selling *antojitos* ("little cravings") such as tacos, tamales, tostadas and endless others can keep you entertained for months.

Jalisco and Oaxaca are two states on the Pacific Coast well known for their food. Jalisco is the home of tequila, made from the heart of the blue agave plant. It is also where Birria (page 232) originates, a stew made with goat, lamb or beef, and dried chiles, cinnamon and other spices. The meat is traditionally roasted before it is combined with a tomato-based broth and then served with tortillas.

Oaxaca is the "land of seven moles," covering the color spectrum from black, through shades of brown and red, to green, to yellow. See Party Chicken with Yellow Mole (page 304), Beef in Yellow Mole (page 375), and Pork in Red Mole (page 407). *Chapulines*—grasshoppers—are a popular local snack, fried or toasted and seasoned with garlic, lime and salt. Markets in Oaxaca have grasshoppers displayed in brick-red piles. I love the food from this area because it has held on to its authentic roots with its ancient flavours despite all the influences of globalization.

Like Mexico's Pacific coast states, the states that curve around the Gulf Coast have many fish dishes. The Gulf is particularly abundant with shellfish such as prawns, oysters, mussels and crabs. A signature dish of the long state of Veracruz is whole snapper baked in a tomato sauce flavored with capers and olives. Veracruz is also known for its rice and seafood dishes that are reminiscent of Spanish paella—see the Rice and Beans chapter (pages 518–47) for several recipes. And of course, seafood finds its way into combinations with tortillas, such as in Tabasco-style Seafood Tortillas (page 63).

In the South, the Yucatán Peninsula has unique food thanks to the Mayan people whose history stretches back to ancient Mesoamerica, but who also have a strong presence in the states of the peninsula today. Yucatán was isolated from the center for a long period of time and thus has a unique cuisine that was heavily influenced by the European ships that stopped by for fresh water. Turkey and venison are two popular indigenous meats—see Turkey with Black Stuffing (page 341) and Venison Dzik (page 438). Yucatán is also known for a method of cooking meat in a pit. A large fire is lit above a hole lined with stones. Once the fire has died down to coals, marinated meat is wrapped in banana leaves and buried under a layer of earth. The famous dish is cochinita pibil: *cochinita* means suckling pig, while *pibil* means buried. Modern recipes use the same marinade for smaller cuts of meat. Two key ingredients of the marinade are annatto seeds, which color the meat red, and the sour juice of Seville oranges. See Slow-Cooked Pork (page 403).

Other flavors of the Yucatán Peninsula are habanero chiles, the world's hottest chiles, although generally confined to side dishes such as salsas; and papadzules, which are like an enchilada filled with chopped boiled egg smothered in a pumpkin seed sauce (see page 493).

MEALS

There can be up to five meals in a Mexican day, beginning with *desayuno* (breakfast). For most, breakfast is a quickly consumed meal of coffee and bread or other baked goods, or perhaps an *atole* (pages 577–8), a sustaining hot drink stretching back to pre-Columbian times. The drink is based on masa dough—the same masa used for tortillas—with water to thin it out. It is boiled for a short time to a soup-like consistency, akin to the traditional oat drinks of Scotland. There are many kinds of *atole*, such as with fruit, chocolate or spices, all generally sweetened with sugar. Another drink consumed at breakfast is a *licuado*, a blend of milk and fruit.

The next meal of the day is *almuerzo* in the mid to late morning, especially important for those who didn't have much breakfast. Eggs are a common feature of this meal—dishes include egg versions of chilaquiles and, of course, Huevos Rancheros (page 179), which are fried eggs on top of a tortilla served with tomato salsa. Tacos and tamales are two other possibilities at this meal that roughly equates to brunch.

The *comida* is the most important meal is the one that begins around 2 pm in the afternoon. This is the time for families to get together and enjoy an unhurried meal of several courses, followed by a siesta. However, both the home-based *comida* and the siesta do not gel in big cities with modern lifestyles and long commute times, which means that working people generally have their *comida* in a restaurant and skip the siesta.

Common courses in a *comida* are soup; *sopa seca* ("dry soup"), a dish that begins with water or broth but is cooked until the liquid evaporates, and may feature rice, pasta or sliced tortillas (see Dry Beef Soup, page 224); the main course, which may be a stew or mole; and dessert. Entrees and salads are often included too, and to drink there might be an *aguas frescas*, a refreshing blend of fruit, water and sugar (see Fresh Fruit Water, page 574). Some restaurants specialise in *comida corrida*—a daily set menu.

The next meal, if necessary, is *merienda*—like afternoon tea—although for most people the *comida* is enough to carry them through to *cena*, the evening meal. *Cena* functions like a supper, although it has become the main meal for modern Mexicans to share with their families. It might consist of leftovers from *comida*, a hot chocolate and bread, or a drink such as *atole*.

MASA

MASA DOUGH

4⅓ cups (1 lb/450 g) masa
harina

REGION: ALL REGIONS
PREPARATION TIME: 5 MINUTES
SERVES: 6

Combine the masa harina and ½ cup (4 fl oz/120 ml)
water with your hands until it forms a moist, but not
sticky, dough. Add more water if necessary.

Note: The dough can be covered and stored in
the refrigerator for 4–5 days or in the freezer for a
month. If frozen, allow the dough to defrost, add
a little all-purpose (plain) flour and water, and knead.

TORTILLAS

CORN TORTILLAS

5 cups (1 lb/450 g) masa harina
¼ teaspoon sea salt

REGION: ALL REGIONS
PREPARATION TIME: 10 MINUTES
COOKING TIME: 15 MINUTES
SERVES: 6

Combine the masa harina, salt, and about 1 cup
(9 fl oz/250 ml) water and stir until it becomes
a moist, but not sticky, dough.

Using your hands, shape the dough into balls
the size of golf balls. Line a tortilla press with two
sheets of plastic wrap (clingfilm). Put the ball of
dough between the sheets of plastic and press to
make a tortilla. Alternatively, roll out each ball on
the lightly floured surface, keeping an even round
shape, to make a paper-thin disk about 5 inches
(12 cm) in diameter (alternatively, make a smaller
tortilla by making the disks about 4 inches/10 cm
in diameter). As they are rolled, stack them up
interleaved with sheets of wax (greaseproof) paper.

Heat a comal or flat grill (griddle) pan and cook
the tortillas, one at a time, for 2–3 minutes or until
the dough becomes opaque. Then turn and cook for
an additional 2–3 minutes.

Note: To make tortilla strips, simply cut the cooked
tortillas into ½-inch (1-cm) strips. Preheat oven
to 375°F (190°C/Gas Mark 5). Spread tortilla strips
in a single layer on a baking sheet and bake for
5–10 minutes, or until just golden. Remove from
the oven and let cool. Store in an airtight container
at room temperature for up to 2 days.

TORTILLAS DE HARINA

✺

FLOUR TORTILLAS

4 cups (1 lb 2 oz/500 g)
   all-purpose (plain) flour
½ tablespoon sea salt
½ tablespoon baking powder
   (optional)
2 oz/70 g vegetable shortening
2 oz/70 g lard

REGION: ALL REGIONS
PREPARATION TIME: 10 MINUTES, PLUS
15 MINUTES RESTING
COOKING TIME: 40 MINUTES
SERVES: 4

In a medium bowl, combine the flour, salt, and baking powder, if using, and stir to combine. Add the vegetable shortening and lard and rub it in with your fingertips until thoroughly incorporated. Add 1½ cups (12 fl oz/350 ml) lukewarm water and knead softly for 2–3 minutes, then cover with a dish towel, and allow to rest for 15 minutes.

Using your hands, shape the dough into balls the size of golf balls. Roll out each ball on the lightly floured surface, keeping an even round shape, to make a thin disk about 5 inches (12 cm) in diameter. As they are rolled, stack them up, interleaved with sheets of greaseproof paper.

Heat a comal or flat grill (griddle) pan and cook the tortillas for 1 minute, or until the dough blisters. Turn and cook for another 30 seconds.

GORDITAS

✺

BASIC GORDITAS

4⅓ cups (1 lb/450 g) masa
   harina
1 cup (4½ oz/125 g) all-purpose
   (plain) flour
½ teaspoon sea salt
2 cups (16 fl oz/475 ml) corn oil
sea salt

REGION: ALL REGIONS
PREPARATION TIME: 5 MINUTES
COOKING TIME: 40 MINUTES
SERVES: 6–8

Combine the masa harina, flour, and salt, and add water, 1 tablespoon at a time, to make a soft and supple dough. With floured hands, shape pieces of the dough into 2-inch (5 cm) balls, then flatten into little circles ½ inch (1 cm) thick.

Heat the oil in a saucepan over medium heat. Add the gorditas in batches and cook over medium-low heat for about 5 minutes, turning frequently, until they are golden brown. Remove with a slotted spoon and drain on paper towels.

When all the gorditas have been cooked, and while they are still warm, use a small, sharp knife to open them up from the side to make a deep pocket. Cover them with a dish towel to keep them warm until serving.

CHINTEXTLE
✺
SMOKED CHILE PASTE

5 Oaxacan pasilla or other
  smoked dried chiles,
  dry-roasted
3½ oz/100 g dried shrimp
  (prawns)
6 avocado leaves
½ head garlic, roasted
½ cup (4 fl oz/120 ml) pineapple
  vinegar or apple cider
  vinegar
½ cup (4 fl oz/120 ml) olive oil
sea salt

REGION: OAXACA
PREPARATION TIME: 20 MINUTES
COOKING TIME: 10 MINUTES
SERVES: 6

Preheat the broiler (grill), then broil (grill) the chiles, turning frequently, for 5 minutes. Remove and set aside. Broil the shrimp (prawns) under low heat for 2 minutes—broiling for longer will make them bitter. Remove and set aside.

Dry-roast the avocado leaves in a heavy frying pan or skillet over low heat for 2–3 minutes, until the leaves are a little shiny.

Put the chiles, shrimp, avocado leaves, and garlic into a food processor or blender and process until thoroughly combined. With the motor running, add the vinegar and enough oil to make a spreadable paste. Season with salt.

Variation: You can add dry-roasted pumpkin seeds, pecans, almonds, guajillo chile, and cooked black beans.

ESQUITES
✺
CORN KERNELS

3⅓ cups (1 lb 2 oz/500 g) corn
  kernels
2 sprigs epazote
salt

To garnish:
1 mild red chile
epazote leaf
¾ cup (6 fl oz/175 ml) sour
  cream or mayonnaise
chili pequin powder, to taste
sea salt

REGION: ALL REGIONS
PREPARATION TIME: 10 MINUTES
COOKING TIME: 15 MINUTES
SERVES: 6

Pour 8¾ cups (3½ pints/2 liters) water into a large pan, add the corn kernels, and a pinch of salt, and bring to a boil. Cook for 5 minutes, then add the epazote. Continue cooking for an additional 4 minutes.

Spoon the kernels into bowls with some of the cooking liquid. Top with a chile and epazote leaf. Serve the sour cream or mayonnaise and the pequin powder on the side.

Note: If you plan on using fresh white corn, add a teaspoon of sugar to the saucepan and cook for an additional 15 minutes.

Corn Kernels

GUACAMOLE

GUACAMOLE

1 tomato, seeded and chopped
 (optional)
½ red onion, finely chopped
1 serrano chile, finely chopped
juice of 1 lime
2 tablespoons finely chopped
 cilantro (coriander)
1 avocado, diced
4 tablespoons olive oil
sea salt
tortilla chips, to serve

REGION: ALL REGIONS
PREPARATION TIME: 15 MINUTES
SERVES: 4

Put the tomato, if using, onion, chile, lime juice, and cilantro (coriander) in a bowl, stir well to mix, and season with salt. Gently fold in the avocado, then taste and adjust the seasoning, if necessary. Add the olive oil and mix. Serve with tortilla chips.

Note: It is best to prepare guacamole minutes before serving to avoid discoloration. Instead of incorporating the chopped tomato you can use it as a garnish, arranging it around the edge of the serving bowl.

ENMOLADAS

ENMOLADAS

3 cups (1¼ pints/750 ml)
 Chicken Stock (page 184)
11 oz/300 g black mole paste
⅔ cup (5 fl oz/150 ml) corn oil,
 for frying
18 day-old Corn Tortillas
 (page 36)
2 chicken breasts, cooked and
 shredded
½ cup (4 fl oz/120 ml) sour
 cream
1 small onion, diced
⅓ cup (2 oz/50 g) queso fresco
 or feta cheese, crumbled
Refried Beans (page 532),
 to serve
sea salt

REGION: ALL REGIONS
PREPARATION TIME: 20 MINUTES
COOKING TIME: 15 MINUTES
SERVES: 6

Pour the chicken stock into a saucepan and heat. Stir in the black mole paste and continue stirring until it has dissolved. Season to taste with salt, then remove the pan from the heat and set aside.

Heat the oil in a large frying pan or skillet. One at a time, add the tortillas and cook briefly on both sides, for less than 10 seconds, making sure they do not turn brown and stiff.

Immediately, dip each cooked tortilla in the warm mole sauce to coat. Place it on a plate, put some shredded chicken on one half and fold it up so it looks like a half moon.

Put 3 enmoladas on each plate. Pour the extra sauce over the emmoladas on all the plates. Drizzle sour cream over them. Sprinkle with diced onion and cheese and serve with refried beans.

Guacamole

TZIRITA DE CILANTRO YERBABUENA

PUMPKIN SEED DIP

3½ oz/100 g dried chiles,
   dry-roasted
1 onion, dry-roasted
1 small bunch mint
1 bunch cilantro (coriander)
2 tomatillos
1 cup (3½ oz/100 g) pumpkin
   seeds, hulled and dry-roasted
sea salt
totopos, to serve

REGION: MICHOACÁN
PREPARATION TIME: 20 MINUTES
SERVES: 6

Put the chiles, onion, mint leaves, cilantro (coriander), tomatillos, and pumpkin seeds into a food processor or blender and process until smooth. Add a little water, if necessary. Season to taste with salt.

Serve as an appetizer with totopos.

PLANTANOS FRITOS

PLANTAIN CROQUETTES

3 ripe plantains, unpeeled
1 cup (5 oz/150 g) raisins
1¾ cup (7 oz/200 g) all-purpose
   (plain) flour
4 eggs
2 tablespoons milk
3½ cups (7 oz/200 g) bread
   crumbs
4¼ cups (34 fl oz/1 litre) corn
   oil for deep frying
sea salt and pepper

REGION: YUCATÁN
PREPARATION TIME: 15 MINUTES, PLUS
OVERNIGHT MARINATING
COOKING TIME: 1 HOUR
SERVES: 6

To make the croquettes, put the plantains in a pan, pour enough water to cover, and bring to a boil. Reduce the heat and simmer for 30 minutes.

Remove the pan from the heat and drain. When cool, peel the plantains and mash in a bowl, then add the raisins, and season with salt and pepper. Using your hands, shape some mashed plantain into a small sausage. Put the croquette on a plate and repeat until all the mixture is used up.

Spread the flour out on a plate. Spread the bread crumbs out on another. Lightly beat the egg and the milk in a shallow dish. Heat the oil in a deep-fryer to 350°F (180°C), until a cube of day-old bread browns in 30 seconds.

Roll the croquettes in the flour, dip them in egg and roll them in bread crumbs. Lower them gently into the hot fat until they are browned. Remove with a spatula and drain on paper towels.

PLATANOS RELLENOS

✸

STUFFED PLANTAINS

For the bean paste:
1 cup (5 oz/130 g) black bean
    paste
epazote, chopped (optional)
1 chipotle chile, chopped

For the plantains:
3 ripe plantains, unpeeled
pinch of sea salt
1 tablespoon sugar
1 egg
5 tablespoons flour
4 tablespoons fresh bread
    crumbs
2 cups (16 fl oz/475 ml)
    safflower oil, for deep-frying

To serve:
1 banana leaf
1 cup (9 oz/250 g) panela
    cheese, grated
1 cup (9 fl oz/250 ml) sour
    cream

REGION: GULF
PREPARATION TIME: 1 HOUR
COOKING TIME: 1 HOUR
MAKES: 16

For the bean paste, put all the ingredients in a food processor or blender and process until smooth. Season with salt.

Cook the plantains and let cool. Once cool, peel them, put them into a large bowl, and crush into a fine paste with a fork. Add the salt, sugar, egg, and flour, and mix well, then add the bread crumbs and mix until a firm paste forms.
It shouldn't be too dry. Divide the mixture into 16 portions, then roll into balls about 2 inches (5 cm) in diameter. Flatten the balls on wax (greaseproof) paper into disks about 3 inches (7.5 cm) in diameter and put a teaspoon of the bean mixture in the center, then fold the dough around the filling to completely enclose it.

Heat the oil for deep-frying in a deep-fryer to 350°F (180°C), or until a cube of day-old bread browns in 30 seconds. Deep-fry the plantains, a few at a time, for 2 minutes, or until golden brown. Remove with a slotted spoon and drain on paper towels. Serve immediately.

Serve on a banana leaf with grated cheese and sour cream.

TIRITAS PESCADO

✸

FISH MARINATED IN LIME

1 lb 2 oz/500 g snapper fillets,
    skinned
¾ cup (6 fl oz/175 ml) lime juice
3 serrano chiles, sliced
2 onions, halved and sliced
¼ teaspoon pepper
4 tablespoons chopped cilantro
    (coriander), to serve
sea salt
tortilla chips, to serve

REGION: GUERRERO
PREPARATION TIME: 20 MINUTES, PLUS
1 HOUR MARINATING
SERVES: 4

Cut the fish into strips about 1½ inches (4 cm) long and ½ inch (1 cm) wide. Put them in a dish and add the lime juice, chiles, onion, pepper, and salt to taste. Mix well and cover. Let marinate for 1 hour.

Drain the lime juice, taste and adjust the seasoning, if necessary. Put the fish in a serving bowl and sprinkle the chopped cilantro (coriander) on top. Serve with tortilla chips.

Three-Chile Dry Noodle

FIDEO SECO TRES CHILES

✳

THREE-CHILE DRY NOODLES

4¼ cups (1¾ pints/1 liter)
  Chicken Stock (page 184)
2 poblano or Anaheim chiles,
  dry-roasted
2 guajillo or ancho chiles,
  dry-roasted
2 moritas or other smoked
  chiles, dry-roasted
4 tablespoons corn oil
1 lb 2 oz/500 g dry noodles
2 cloves garlic
½ onion
¼ teaspoon dried oregano
1 tablespoon apple cider
  vinegar
sea salt

To serve:
1 cup (9 fl oz/250 ml) sour
  cream
3½ oz/100 g cotija or feta
  cheese, diced
1 avocado, peeled, pitted,
  and diced

REGION: MEXICO CITY
PREPARATION TIME: 20 MINUTES, PLUS
10 MINUTES SOAKING
COOKING TIME: 30 MINUTES
SERVES: 6

Pour 2 cups (16 fl oz/475 ml) of the chicken stock
into a saucepan and bring to a boil. Remove the pan
from the heat. Put the chiles to a heatproof bowl and
pour the hot chicken stock over them.
Let soak for 10 minutes or until tender.

Heat the oil in a small saucepan. Add the noodles
and cook according to the package directions, gently
stirring occasionally, until lightly golden. Remove
from the pan with a slotted spoon and drain on
paper towels.

Put the chiles, together with their soaking liquid,
garlic, onion, oregano, the remaining chicken stock,
and vinegar into a food processor or blender and
process until thoroughly combined. Drain the liquid
into a bowl and reserve the vegetables.

Put the vegetables into a saucepan and set over
low heat. Cook, stirring gently, for 5 minutes, then
season to taste with salt. Add the noodles and
the stock from the bowl, cover, and simmer over
low heat for an additional 10 minutes or until the
noodles are cooked. Taste and adjust the seasoning,
if necessary.

Serve immediately with sour cream, grated
cheese, and avocado.

CHILAQUILES VERDES CON POLLO

✳

GREEN CHILAQUILES WITH CHICKEN

30 tomatillos, dry-roasted
1 poblano chile, dry-roasted
4 serrano chiles, dry-roasted
1 onion, quartered
2 cloves garlic
3 tablespoons chopped cilantro (coriander), plus extra to serve
3 tablespoons corn oil
12 Corn Tortillas (page 36), cut into squares or triangles
1 large cooked chicken breast, shredded
½ red onion, sliced
sea salt
½ cup (4 fl oz/120 ml) sour cream, plus extra to serve
1¾ cups (7 oz/200 g) grated queso fresco or feta cheese, plus extra to serve

REGION: ALL REGIONS
PREPARATION TIME: 25 MINUTES
COOKING TIME: 20–25 MINUTES
SERVES: 6

Put the tomatillos, chiles, onion, garlic, and cilantro (coriander) into a food processor or blender and process until thoroughly combined. Strain into a bowl.

Heat 1 tablespoon oil in a saucepan and add the tomatillo sauce. Simmer for 10–15 minutes, until thick. Add salt to taste.

Heat the remaining oil in a heavy frying pan or skillet. Add the tortilla pieces and cook over a medium heat, turning occasionally, until golden brown on both sides. Remove from the pan and drain on paper towels.

Preheat the oven to 400°F (200°C/Gas Mark 6). Put the tortilla pieces into an ovenproof dish and add the tomatillo sauce. Gently stir to coat all the fried tortilla pieces. Top with the chicken and onion slices. Pour the cream over the top, sprinkle with the cheese, and bake for 10 minutes. Top with cilantro (coriander) and serve.

Note: Chilaquiles can be served with beans and chicken, beef, or fried eggs.

Green Chilaquiles with Chicken

CHILAQUILES ROJOS

✽

CHILAQUILES IN RED SAUCE

4 tomatoes, dry-roasted
2 serrano chiles, dry-roasted
1 small onion, quartered and
  dry-roasted
1 clove garlic, dry-roasted
3 tablespoons corn oil
3 Flour Tortillas (page 37),
  cut into squares or triangles
2 tablespoons sour cream
sea salt
grated cotija, Pecorino, or
  Grana Padano cheese,
  to serve

REGION: ALL REGIONS
PREPARATION TIME: 30 MINUTES
COOKING TIME: 15 MINUTES
SERVES: 6

Put the tomatoes, chiles, onion, and garlic into a food processor or blender and process until thoroughly combined. Strain into a bowl.

Heat 1 tablespoon oil in a saucepan. Add the tomato mixture and cook over low heat, stirring occasionally, for 10–15 minutes, until thickened. Add salt to taste.

Heat 2 tablespoons oil in a frying pan or skillet and add the tortilla pieces. Cook over medium heat, turning occasionally, until they are golden brown on both sides. Transfer to paper towels to drain, then put them in a big serving dish or divide equally among individual plates.

Preheat the oven to 400°F (200°C/Gas Mark 6). Spoon the mixture over the pieces of tortilla, turning them until they are thoroughly coated with the sauce. Drizzle sour cream on top. Sprinkle on the cheese and bake for 8 minutes or until the cheese is melted, then serve immediately.

ENCHILADAS DIVORCIADAS

✽

DIVORCED ENCHILADAS

1 tablespoon lard or corn oil
18 Corn Tortillas (page 36)
1 (2¼-lb/1-kg) chicken, poached
  and shredded
1 quantity Stewed Tomatillo
  Salsa (page 510)
1 quantity Roast Tomatillo
  Salsa (page 510)
sour cream, grated panela
  or feta cheese, and cooked
  beans, to serve

REGION: ALL REGIONS
PREPARATION TIME: 30 MINUTES
COOKING TIME: 1 HOUR
SERVES: 6

Preheat the oven to 225°F (110°C/Gas Mark ¼).

To make the enchiladas, heat the lard in a small frying pan or skillet. Add the tortillas, one at a time, and cook briefly on each side until golden. Transfer to paper towels and fill them with shredded chicken. Fold in half, put them in a large serving dish, and put in the oven to keep warm. Make all the enchiladas in the same way, then spoon the green and red salsa over them, in two stripes. Serve immediately with sour cream, grated panela or feta cheese, and a side of beans.

ENCHILADAS COLONIALES

✻

COLONIAL ENCHILADAS

butter, for greasing

15 ancho chiles, seeds removed

1 white onion, quartered and
   dry-roasted

2 cloves garlic, dry-roasted

3 ripe tomatoes, dry-roasted
   and peeled

4 tablespoons corn oil or lard

12 Corn Tortillas (page 36)

1 (2¼ lb/1 kg) chicken, poached
   and shredded

1 cup (9 fl oz/250 ml) heavy
   (double) cream

1 cup (3½ oz/100 g) grated
   Chihuahua or cheddar
   cheese

sea salt and pepper

cooked red or black beans,
   to serve

REGION: CHIHUAHUA
PREPARATION TIME: 40 MINUTES
COOKING TIME: 30 MINUTES
SERVES: 6

Preheat the oven to 375°F (190°C/Gas Mark 5) and grease a large ovenproof dish with butter.

Put the chiles, onion, garlic, and tomatoes into a food processor or blender and process until smooth. Strain into a saucepan. Add 1 tablespoon corn oil and bring to a boil over medium heat. Boil for 5 minutes, then season with salt and pepper.

Heat a little of the oil in a frying pan or skillet and add the tortillas one at a time, cooking for about 15 seconds per side to soften them. Add more oil as required. Place them on paper towels to drain, then cover them with a dish towel to keep them warm and soft while heating the remainder. Add more oil as needed.

Spread the chili sauce over the tortillas, put some shredded chicken on one half, then fold them over like a half moon. Arrange in a single layer in the prepared ovenproof dish. Pour over the cream and sprinkle with a generous amount of cheese. Bake in the oven for 30 minutes, until golden brown and bubbles appear on top. Serve immediately with beans.

ENCHILADAS DE CAMARON

✾

SHRIMP ENCHILADAS

2 potatoes, diced
2 tomatoes
1 onion
3 tablespoons corn oil
14 oz/400 g baby shrimp
  (prawns) peeled
12 Corn Tortillas (page 36)
sea salt and pepper

For the salsa:
5 ancho chiles, dry-roasted
2 tomatoes
1 onion, thickly sliced
1 large clove garlic
1 tablespoon apple cider
  vinegar
½ teaspoon dried oregano
sea salt

To garnish:
2 onions, finely sliced,
  marinated in a mild vinegar
  lettuce, shredded
6 radishes, thinly sliced

REGION: NORTH PACIFIC AND GULF
PREPARATION TIME: 1 HOUR
COOKING TIME: 1¼ HOURS
SERVES: 6

Bring a saucepan of water to a boil over high heat, add the potatoes and cook for 10 minutes. Strain and set aside.

To make the salsa, put the chiles in a bowl, add enough hot water to cover, and soak for 10 minutes. Drain and set aside.

Put the tomatoes and onion into a food processor or blender and process until thoroughly combined. Heat 1 tablespoon of the oil in a saucepan. Add the tomato and onion mixture and cook, stirring frequently, for a few minutes. Add the potatoes and cook, stirring occasionally, for 10 minutes, until thickened. Add the shrimp (prawns), season with salt and pepper to taste, and cook for an additional 3 minutes, until the shrimp are pink and cooked through. Remove from the heat.

To make the salsa, preheat the oven to 400°F (200°C/Gas Mark 4). Put the tomatoes, onion, and garlic into a roasting pan and roast for 30 minutes. Remove the pan from the oven. Put the roasted vegetables, chiles, vinegar, oregano, and a pinch of salt into a food processor or blender and process until thoroughly combined. Pass the mixture through a strainer (sieve) into a bowl.

Heat 1 tablespoon oil in a saucepan. Add the shrimp mixture and cook on medium heat, stirring occasionally, for 10 minutes, until thickened. Remove the pan from the heat.

Heat the remaining oil in a frying pan or skillet. Dip a tortilla in the salsa to coat, then add to the skillet and cook briefly on both sides. Remove from the pan, put a heaping tablespoon of the shrimp filling in the center, fold in half, and place on a serving plate. Repeat with the remaining tortillas and filling. Pour over the remaining sauce and garnish with the marinated onion, lettuce, and radishes. Serve immediately.

ENCHILADAS POTOSINAS

❋

SAN LUIS POTOSI ENCHILADAS

For the filling:
1 tablespoon lard or corn oil
3 cloves garlic, minced
4 tomatoes, finely chopped
3 serrano chiles, finely chopped
2¾ cups (11 oz/300 g) grated Chihuahua, Monterey Jack, or mild white cheddar cheese

For the enchiladas:
4 ancho chiles
1 quantity Masa Dough (page 36)
⅓ cup (1½ oz/40 g) all-purpose (plain) flour
1 teaspoon sea salt
2 cups (16 fl oz/475 ml) corn oil or lard

To serve:
4 scallions (spring onions), finely chopped
2 avocados, pitted and sliced
⅔ cup (5 oz/150 g) crumbled feta, ricotta, or farmer's (curd) cheese

REGION: SAN LUIS POTOSÍ
PREPARATION TIME: 1 HOUR
COOKING TIME: 1 HOUR
SERVES: 6

Put the ancho chiles for the enchilada in a bowl, add enough hot water to cover, and soak for 10 minutes.

To make the filling, melt the lard or corn oil in a saucepan. Add the garlic, tomatoes, and chiles, season with salt, and cook over medium heat for about 15 minutes, until thickened. Stir in the grated cheese, then remove from the heat and let cool.

To make the enchiladas, put the soaked chiles into a food processor or blender with ½ cup (4 fl oz/120 ml) of the soaking water and process to a paste. Mix together the flour and salt in a bowl. Knead the chili paste and flour mixture into the dough.

Preheat a flat skillet, griddle pan, or heavy frying pan over medium-high heat. With a tortilla press, shape a heaping tablespoon of dough into small tortillas and put them on the pan. Flip them over a couple of times and when they start to cook, add a spoonful of the filling, enough to thinly cover half of each tortilla. Fold each tortilla in half, and cook for another minute, flipping once or twice.

Line in a basket or a bowl with a napkin and transfer the enchiladas into it, covering with paper towels to prevent them from hardening. Garnish with the scallions (spring onions), avocado, and cheese.

Note: The enchiladas can also be deep-fried. Heat a little of the oil in a frying pan or skillet and add the enchiladas one at a time, cooking for about 1 minute per side to soften them. Add more oil as required. Place them on paper towels to drain, then serve immediately.

Swiss Enchiladas

ENCHILADAS SUIZAS

✺

SWISS ENCHILADAS

30 tomatillos
½ onion
2 cloves garlic
2 serrano chiles
1¼ cups (½ pint/300 ml)
  sour cream
butter, for greasing
2 tablespoons corn oil
18 Corn Tortillas (page 36)
4 cups (1 lb 5 oz/600 g) chicken,
  cooked and shredded
1¼ cups (5 oz/150 g) grated
  Swiss or Gruyère cheese

To serve:
sour cream
cilantro (coriander), to garnish

REGION: MEXICO CITY
PREPARATION TIME: 25 MINUTES
COOKING TIME: 40-50 MINUTES
SERVES: 6

Put the tomatillos, onion, garlic, and chiles in a saucepan, add enough water to cover, and bring to a boil over medium-high heat. Reduce heat and simmer for 30 minutes. Transfer to a food processor or blender and process until thoroughly combined. Pour the tomatillo mixture and sour cream into a saucepan and simmer for 3 minutes.

Preheat the oven to 400°F (200°C/Gas Mark 6). Grease an ovenproof dish with butter.

Heat the oil in a frying pan or skillet over high heat. Dip the tortillas into the oil, one at a time, for about 10 seconds, then remove and drain on paper towels. Keep warm under a piece of aluminum foil.

Fill the tortillas with shredded chicken, roll them, and put them into the prepared dish. Pour the tomatillo sauce over the enchiladas to cover completely, sprinkle with the cheese, and bake for 5–7 minutes or until cheese has melted. Serve with sour cream and cilantro (coriander), to garnish.

CARNE ENCHILADA

✺

MEAT ENCHILADAS

3 tablespoons (1½ oz/40 g)
  butter
2¼ lb/1 kg pork tenderloin
  (fillet), cut into 6 pieces
1 tablespoon apple cider
  vinegar
3 cloves garlic, finely chopped
1 sprig oregano
4 serrano chiles, dry-roasted
1 teaspoon all-purpose (plain)
  flour
sea salt
Flour Tortillas (page 37), to
  serve

REGION: SONORA
PREPARATION TIME: 15 MINUTES
COOKING TIME: 1 HOUR
SERVES: 6

Melt 2 tablespoons of the butter in a frying pan or skillet. Add the pork and cook over medium heat, turning once, for about 10 minutes, until evenly browned. Add the vinegar, garlic, oregano, and a pinch of salt and pour in 2 cups (16 fl oz/475 ml) water. Bring to a boil, then reduce the heat and simmer for 20 minutes.

Put the chiles into a food processor or blender and process until finely ground. Sprinkle them over the meat.

Melt the remaining butter in a small saucepan. Add the flour and cook, stirring continuously, for 2 minutes. Stir the flour paste into the pan of meat, cover, and simmer for about 30 minutes or until the meat is tender. Remove the pan from the heat and serve immediately with warm tortillas.

GORDITAS CHICHARRON

✺

PORK RIND GORDITAS

1 tablespoon corn oil
3 tablespoons finely chopped
    red onion
9 oz/250 g pork rinds
    (scratchings), crumbled
1 quantity Basic Gorditas
    (page 37)

To serve:
lettuce, shredded
sour cream
Salsa of choice (pages 496–514)

REGION: FEDERAL DISTRICT
PREPARATION TIME: 25 MINUTES
COOKING TIME: 15 MINUTES
MAKES: 18

Heat the oil in a medium saucepan. Add the onion and cook over low heat, stirring occasionally, for 5 minutes or until translucent. Add the pork rinds (scratchings) and cook for about 5 minutes, then remove from the pan with a slotted spoon and drain on paper towels.

Fill the gorditas with the pork rind mixture, lettuce, salsa, and sour cream, and serve immediately.

GORDITAS GUANAJUATO

✺

GUANAJUATO GORDITAS

3½ oz/100 g dried guajillo
    chiles, dry-roasted
sea salt
1 lb 2 oz/500 g fresh cheese
    or feta
½ cup (3½ oz/100 g) lard
1 quantity Masa Dough
    (page 36)

To serve:
2 tomatoes, diced
½ romaine (Cos) lettuce,
    shredded
1 cooked potato, diced
pickled jalapeño chiles

REGION: BAJIO CENTER
PREPARATION TIME: 40 MINUTES, PLUS
30 MINUTES SOAKING
COOKING TIME: 1½ HOURS
SERVES: 15 PIECES

Put the chiles in a bowl, add enough hot water to cover, and soak for 10 minutes. Drain and put them in a food processor with salt and a little soaking water and process until smooth. Transfer the mixture to a large bowl, add the cheese, and, using clean hands, knead until a smooth dough is formed. Mix the masa into the dough until it is well incorporated, season with salt, and mix in well.

To make the gorditas, using your hands, divide the dough into 15 portions, then shape each portion into a tortilla about 2 inches (5 cm) in diameter and ¼ inch (5 mm) thick. Cover and set aside. Continue until you have made 15 tortillas.

Heat a heavy frying pan or skillet over medium-high heat, add a little lard, and cook the gorditas, one at a time, for 3 minutes on each side, or until crisp and golden brown. Serve with sliced tomato, lettuce, potato, and jalapeño chiles on top.

Pork Rind Gorditas

GORDITAS NORTEÑAS DE CARNE MOLIDA

NORTHERN MEAT GORDITAS

4 tablespoons corn oil
3 oz/80 g guajillo or red chiles,
    dry-roasted and coarsely
    chopped
4 tomatillos, diced
3 cloves garlic, minced
1 lb 2 oz/500 g ground
    (minced) beef
½ teaspoon ground cumin
sea salt
1 quantity Basic Gorditas
    (page 37)

To serve:
sour cream
lettuce, shredded
queso fresco or feta cheese,
    grated
Salsa of choice (pages 496–514)

REGION: COAHUILA, DURANGO
PREPARATION TIME: 35 MINUTES
COOKING TIME: 25 MINUTES
SERVES: 6–8

Heat 2 tablespoons of the oil in a frying pan or skillet. Put the chiles, tomatillos, garlic, and ½ cup (4 fl oz/120 ml) water into the pan and cook over low heat for 5 minutes. Transfer the mixture to a food processor or blender and process until thoroughly mixed. Pass the contents through a strainer (sieve) and set aside.

Heat the remaining oil in a clean frying pan or skillet. Add the beef, stir in the cumin, and cook over medium-high heat, stirring frequently, for 10 minutes until evenly browned. Stir in the chile and tomatillo mixture and simmer for an additional 10 minutes until the mixture is dry. Remove the pan from the heat, season with salt, and set aside.

Fill the gorditas with the beef mixture, add the sour cream, lettuce, cheese, and salsa, and serve immediately.

GORDITAS DE REQUESÓN

CHEESE GORDITAS

1 cup (7 oz/200 g) requesón
    or ricotta cheese
¼ onion, finely chopped
2 epazote leaves, finely
    chopped
sea salt
1 quantity Basic Gorditas
    (page 37)

REGION: FEDERAL DISTRICT
PREPARATION TIME: 25 MINUTES
COOKING TIME: 8–10 MINUTES
SERVES: 6

Combine the cheese, onion, and epazote in a bowl and season with salt.

Fill the gorditas with the cheese mixture and serve immediately.

Note: You can also added shredded lettuce and salsa of your choice (pages 496-514).

Cheese Gorditas

GORDITAS DE PAPAS CON CHORIZO

❋

POTATO AND CHORIZO GORDITAS

1 tablespoon corn oil
5 oz/150 g chorizo, crumbled
2 potatoes, peeled, parboiled, and diced
sea salt
1 quantity Basic Gorditas (page 37)

To serve:
lettuce, shredded
queso fresco or feta cheese, crumbled
Salsa of choice (pages 496–514)

REGION: FEDERAL DISTRICT
PREPARATION TIME: 35 MINUTES
COOKING TIME: 15–20 MINUTES
MAKES: 18

Heat the oil in a saucepan over medium heat. Add the chorizo and cook, stirring frequently, for 5–8 minutes, until it begins to brown. Add the potatoes, reduce the heat, and cook for an additional 15 minutes, until the potatoes are cooked. Season with salt, remove the pan from the heat, and set aside.

Fill the gorditas with the potato and chorizo mixture, and add the lettuce, crumbled cheese, and salsa. Serve immediately.

QUESADILLAS DE FLOR DE CALABAZA

❋

ZUCCHINI FLOWER QUESADILLAS

1 tablespoon olive oil
¼ onion, finely chopped
1 clove garlic, crushed
1 lb 2 oz/500 g zucchini (courgette) flowers, pistils removed, chopped
4 tablespoons finely chopped epazote
12 Corn Tortillas (page 36)
2 cups (9 oz/250 g) grated quesillo or mozzarella cheese
sea salt
Salsa of choice (pages 496–514), to serve

REGION: MEXICO CITY
PREPARATION TIME: 20 MINUTES
COOKING TIME: 20 MINUTES
SERVES: 6

Heat the oil in a frying pan or skillet over medium heat. Add the onion and garlic and cook over low heat, stirring occasionally, for 5 minutes, until translucent. Add the zucchini (courgette) flowers and epazote, season with salt to taste, and cook for an additional 2–3 minutes. Remove the pan from the heat and let cool completely.

Warm the tortillas in a dry frying pan or skillet, flipping them over until they are soft. Fill the tortillas with the flower mixture and the cheese and fold them into a half moon shape. Serve with salsa.

Note: You can serve them as is or deep-fried at 350°F (180°C) until golden brown.

Zucchini Flower Quesadillas

QUESADILLAS DE HONGOS

✺

MUSHROOM QUESADILLAS

2 tablespoons olive oil
1 onion, chopped
4 cloves garlic, crushed
2 serrano chiles, chopped
2¼ lb/1 kg assorted
   mushrooms, sliced
½ cup (1 oz/25 g) chopped
   epazote leaves
sea salt
18 Corn Tortillas (page 36)
vegetable oil, for frying
   (optional)
Salsa of choice (pages 496–514),
   to serve

REGION: MEXICO CITY
PREPARATION TIME: 15 MINUTES
COOKING TIME: 20 MINUTES
SERVES: 6

To make the filling, heat the oil in a large frying pan or skillet over medium heat. Add the onion and garlic and cook over low heat, stirring occasionally, for 5 minutes, until the onion is translucent. Add the chiles and mushrooms and cook until the mushrooms release their juices. Season with salt and stir in the epazote. Taste and adjust the seasoning, if necessary, remove from the heat, and let cool completely.

Warm the tortillas in a dry frying pan or skillet, flipping them over until they are soft. Fill the tortillas and fold them into half moon shapes. You can serve them as is or deep-fried at 350°F (180°C) until golden brown. Serve with salsa.

QUESADILLAS DE MINILLA

✺

FISH QUESADILLAS

1 lb 2 oz/500 g white fish fillets
mixed herb sprigs, such as
   oregano, thyme, bay leaf, and
   marjoram
1¼ onion, chopped
1 ancho chile, dry-roasted
3 serrano chiles, chopped
2 tomatoes, peeled and
   coarsely chopped
3 tablespoons olive or corn oil
1 tablespoon capers, rinsed
   and coarsely chopped
3 tablespoons chopped cilantro
   (coriander)
sea salt
8 Corn Tortillas (page 36)
vegetable oil or lard, for frying
   (optional)
Salsa of choice (pages 496–514),
   to serve

REGION: VERACRUZ
PREPARATION TIME: 30 MINUTES
COOKING TIME: 25 MINUTES
SERVES: 4

Put the fish, herbs, and ¼ onion into a saucepan, pour in water to cover, and bring just to a boil. Immediately reduce the heat and let stand for 10 minutes. Remove the fish with a spatula and flake the flesh.

Put the chiles and tomatoes into a food processor or blender and process until combined. Heat the oil in a frying pan or skillet, add the chopped onion, and cook over low heat, stirring occasionally, for 10 minutes, until translucent. Add the tomato mixture and season with salt. Add the flaked fish and capers, mix well, and cook until the sauce has reduced. Stir in the chopped cilantro (coriander), then remove the pan from the heat and let cool completely.

Warm the tortillas in a dry frying pan or skillet, flipping them over until they are soft. Fill the tortillas and fold them into half moon shapes. You can serve them as is or deep-fried at 350°F (180°C) until golden brown. Serve immediately with salsa.

QUESADILAS DE JAIBA

✺

CRAB QUESADILLAS

6 tablespoons olive oil
½ small carrot, finely chopped
4 tablespoons finely chopped onion
4 tablespoons finely chopped leek (white part only)
2 cloves garlic, crushed
5 tablespoons tomato paste (puree)
11 oz/300 g crabmeat
½ cup (4 fl oz/120 ml) dry white wine
1 teaspoon capers, chopped
3 tablespoons (1½ oz/40 g) butter, diced
12 Corn Tortillas (page 36)
sea salt and pepper
vegetable oil or lard, for frying (optional)
Salsa of choice (pages 496–514), to serve

REGION: TAMAULIPAS, VERACRUZ
PREPARATION TIME: 30 MINUTES
COOKING TIME: 15 MINUTES
SERVES: 6

Heat the oil in a medium saucepan. Add the carrot, onion, leek, and garlic and cook over low heat, stirring occasionally, for 5–8 minutes. Stir in the tomato paste (puree) and cook for an additional few minutes. Add the crabmeat and wine, stir gently, and cook until reduced. Add the capers and butter and season to taste with salt and pepper. Remove the pan from the heat and let cool completely.

Warm the tortillas in a dry frying pan or skillet, flipping them over until they are soft. Fill the tortillas and fold them into half moon shapes. You can serve them as is or deep-fried at 350°F (180°C) until golden brown. Serve with salsa.

QUESADILLAS DE TINGA

✺

TINGA QUESADILLAS

For the filling:
½ onion
2 cloves
1 lb 2 oz/500 g stewing beef,
  chicken, or pork
4 cloves garlic
1 bay leaf
1 sprig thyme
1 sprig marjoram
sea salt

For the salsa:
2 dried chipotle chiles,
  dry-roasted
4 tablespoons olive oil
3½ oz/100 g chorizo, peeled
  and sliced
1 onion, sliced
3 cloves garlic, finely chopped
3 large tomatoes, dry-roasted,
  peeled, and ground
1½ teaspoons raw sugar
2 bay leaves
2 sprigs thyme
1½ teaspoons dried oregano
pinch of ground cloves
1 teaspoon pepper
2 smoked chipotle chiles in
  adobo
sea salt
12 Corn Tortillas (page 36)
vegetable oil or lard, for frying
  (optional)
Salsa of choice (pages 496–514),
  to serve

REGION: ALL REGIONS
PREPARATION TIME: 30 MINUTES, PLUS
10 MINUTES SOAKING
COOKING TIME: 2½ HOURS
SERVES: 6

For the filling, pour 6¼ cups (2½ pints/1.5 liters) water into a saucepan. Stud the onion half with the cloves and add to the pan with the meat, garlic, bay leaf, thyme, marjoram, and a pinch of salt. Bring to a boil, lower the heat, and simmer for 2 hours or until the meat is tender. Remove the pan from the heat and let the meat cool in the cooking liquid. Lift out the cooled meat and shred it.

In a small bowl, combine the chiles and enough hot water to cover and soak for 10 minutes. Transfer to a food processor or blender and process until smooth. Strain and set aside.

Heat the oil in a saucepan. Add the chorizo and cook over medium heat, stirring frequently, for 7 minutes. Reduce the heat to low, add the onion and garlic, and cook, stirring occasionally, for 6–7 minutes, until the onion is translucent. Add the tomatoes and sugar and cook for 10 minutes. Stir in the bay leaves, thyme, oregano, cloves, pepper, chipotle chiles, and pureed chiles. Cook until the sauce has thickened, then add the shredded meat and season with salt.

Warm the tortillas in a dry frying pan or skillet, flipping them over until they are soft. Fill the tortillas and fold them into half moon shapes. You can serve them as is or deep-fried at 350°F (180°C) until golden brown. Serve with salsa.

POTATO AND CHORIZO QUESADILLAS

2 tablespoons corn oil
7 oz/200 g chorizo, peeled and
  chopped
1 onion, chopped
3 smoked chipotle chiles in
  adobo, chopped, plus extra
  for garnish
1½ cups (11 oz/300 g) mashed
  potatoes
12 Corn Tortillas (page 36)
vegetable oil or lard, for frying
  (optional)
sea salt
Salsa of choice (pages 496–514),
  to serve

REGION: ALL REGIONS
PREPARATION TIME: 15 MINUTES
COOKING TIME: 10 MINUTES
SERVES: 6

To make the filling, heat the oil in a frying pan or skillet. Add the chorizo and cook over medium heat, stirring and turning occasionally, for 5 minutes, until almost cooked. Add the onion and cook, stirring occasionally, for an additional 5 minutes, until it is translucent. Add the chiles and mashed potatoes and season with salt. Stir well to coat everything and remove the pan from the heat. Let cool completely.

Warm the tortillas in a dry frying pan or skillet, flipping them over until they are soft. Fill the tortillas and fold them into half moon shapes. You can serve them as is or deep-fried at 350°F (180°C) until golden brown. Serve with salsa, garnished with chopped chipotle.

TORTILLA RELLENAS DE MARISCOS

✺

SEAFOOD TORTILLAS

2 tablespoons olive oil
¼ white onion, chopped
2 cloves garlic, crushed
3 large tomatoes, finely chopped
2 mild green chiles, finely chopped
2 banana peppers, finely chopped
2¼ lb/1 kg prepared mixed seafood (shrimp/prawns, mussels, calamari)
1–2 tablespoons corn oil
6 Corn Tortillas (page 36)
1–1½ cups (3–4½ oz/ 80–130 g) grated Manchego cheese (optional)
sea salt and pepper
Salsa of choice (pages 496–514), to serve

REGION: TABASCO
PREPARATION TIME: 15 MINUTES
COOKING TIME: 40 MINUTES
SERVES: 6

Heat the olive oil in a saucepan. Add the onion and cook over low heat, stirring occasionally, for 5 minutes. Add the garlic and cook for another minute. Add the tomatoes, chiles, and banana peppers and cook for an additional 10 minutes. Add the seafood and season with salt and pepper. Remove the pan from the heat.

Preheat the oven to 350°F (180°C/Gas Mark 4).

Heat half the corn oil in a frying pan or skillet. Add the tortillas, one at a time, and cook over medium-high heat until browned on both sides. Add more oil as necessary. Open them carefully with a knife and fill with the seafood mixture. Top with grated cheese, if using, and put the tortillas on a baking sheet. Bake for 10–12 minutes, until the cheese has melted.

Remove from the oven, cut the tortillas into triangles, and serve immediately with salsa.

SOPES

✺

BASIC SOPES

1 lb/450 g masa harina
½ teaspoon sea salt

REGION: ALL REGIONS
PREPARATION TIME: 25 MINUTES
COOKING TIME: 25 MINUTES
SERVES: 6

Combine the masa harina and salt. Gradually, add ¼ cup (2 fl oz/60ml) of water and mix until you have a soft and supple dough. With floured hands, shape pieces of dough into 2-inch (5-cm) balls, then flatten into little rounds about ½ inch (1 cm) thick. Heat a frying pan or skillet over medium-high heat, add the dough to the pan, and cook for 2 minutes. Flip and cook over for an additional 2 minutes. Take each sope and make a slightly raised border by pressing the edge between your thumb and index finger. This edge will prevent the filling from leaking out. Put the sopes into a bowl and cover with a clean dish towel until required.

SOPES DE CARNE

✺

MEAT SOPES

1–2 tablespoons corn oil
1 quantity Basic Sopes
  (page 65)
1 quantity Refried Beans
  (page 532)
1 quantity Raw Tomatillo
  Salsa (page 512) or Roast
  Tomato Salsa (page 509)
2 cups (4 oz/120 g) shredded
  romaine (Cos) lettuce
1 cup (6 oz/175 g) shredded,
  cooked chicken, pork,
  beef, or chorizo
1 large onion, finely chopped
1 cup (4 oz/120 g) grated queso
  fresco or feta cheese
1 cup (9 fl oz/250 ml) heavy
  (double) cream

REGION: ALL REGIONS
PREPARATION TIME: 25 MINUTES
COOKING TIME: 30 MINUTES
SERVES: 6

Heat the oil in a large frying pan or skillet. Add the sopes, concave side uppermost, and cook for 2 minutes. Turn them over and put enough refried beans into each one to cover the entire surface inside the border. Add a little salsa, lettuce, and some meat. Finally, add a little onion, cheese, and heavy cream, then remove the pan from the heat. You can also assemble the sopes on a plate over paper towels once they are cooked and then carefully transfer them to the serving plates.

Serve immediately.

JAIBA SOPES

✳

CRAB SOPES

½ cup (4 fl oz/120 ml) olive oil
1 small carrot, finely chopped
4 tablespoons finely chopped
    onion, plus extra for topping
4 tablespoons finely chopped
    leek
2 cloves garlic, minced
5 tablespoons tomato paste
    (puree)
11 oz/300 g crabmeat
½ cup (4 fl oz/120 ml) dry white
    wine
1 tablespoon capers
1½ tablespoons (¾ oz/20 g)
    butter
3 tablespoons corn oil
1 quantity Basic Sopes
    (page 65)
1 quantity Refried Beans
    (page 532)
1 quantity Raw Tomatillo
    Salsa (page 512) or Roast
    Tomato Salsa (page 509)
2 cups (4 oz/120 g) shredded
    lettuce
1 large onion, finely chopped
½ cup (3 oz/80 g) grated queso
    fresco or feta cheese
½ cup (4 fl oz/120 ml) heavy
    (double) cream
sea salt and pepper
1 lime, cut into wedges,
    to serve

REGION: GULF
PREPARATION TIME: 40 MINUTES
COOKING TIME: 30 MINUTES
SERVES: 6

To make the filling, heat the olive oil in a saucepan. Add the carrot, onion, leek, and garlic and cook over low heat, stirring occasionally, for 5–8 minutes, until the onion is translucent. Stir in the tomato paste (puree) and cook for a few minutes, then add the crabmeat. Pour in the wine and cook until it has evaporated. Stir in the capers and butter and season to taste with salt and pepper.

To finish the sopes, heat the corn oil in a large frying pan or skillet. Add the sopes, concave side uppermost, and cook for 3 minutes. Turn them over and put enough refried beans into each one to cover the entire surface inside the border. Add some salsa, lettuce, and crab mixture. Finally, add some onion, cheese, and cream, then remove the pan from the heat.

You can assemble the sopes on a plate over paper towels once they are hot and then carefully transfer them to the serving plates. Serve hot with lime wedges.

TACOS DE CARNE Y CHILE TATEMADO

❋

CHILE BEEF TACOS

1 (1 lb 2-oz/500-g) beef short
  plate (skirt), trimmed of fat
1½ lb/700 g) beef bones
  (optional)
1 white onion, quartered
½ head garlic
sea salt

For the sauce:
20 tomatillos
7 cloves garlic
1½ small white onions,
  quartered
8–12 morita or chipotle chiles,
  lightly dry-roasted
1 tablespoon corn oil
sea salt

For the tacos:
18 Corn Tortillas (page 36)
corn oil, for brushing
  (optional)
6 (6-inch/15-cm) squares of
  banana leaves, lightly
  dry-roasted

REGION: ZACATECAS
PREPARATION TIME: 50 MINUTES
COOKING TIME: 1 HOUR 35 MINUTES
SERVES: 6

Put the meat, bones, onion, garlic, and a pinch of salt into a saucepan, pour in enough water to cover, and bring to a boil. Reduce the heat and simmer for 1 hour, until the beef is tender. Remove the pan from the heat, transfer the beef to a cutting (chopping) board, and let cool. Discard the beef bone, strain the cooking liquid into a bowl, and lift off the grease with paper towels. Once cooled, shred the beef.

To make the sauce, put the tomatillos, 4 cloves garlic, 4 onion quarters, and chiles into a pan, add in ½ cup (4 fl oz/120 ml) of the reserved beef cooking liquid, and bring to a boil. Reduce the heat and simmer for 15 minutes. Remove the pan from heat and let cool.

Transfer the vegetables to a food processor or blender and reserve the cooking liquid. Add the remaining onion quarters and the 3 cloves garlic, then process until smooth and season with salt.

Heat the oil in a saucepan. Add the tomatillo and chile mixture and cook over low heat, stirring occasionally, for 10 minutes. Add the shredded beef and the reserved tomatillo cooking liquid. Bring to a boil, reduce the heat, and simmer for 15 minutes or until thickened and nearly dry. Season with salt and remove the pan from the heat.

To prepare the tacos, quickly heat the tortillas, one at a time, in a heavy frying pan or skillet and keep hot.

Put a tablespoon of the meat and sauce in the center of each tortilla, fold over, and brush with a little oil (optional).

Place 3 tacos on each banana leaf square and fold in the sides to make packages. Put them into a steamer and cook for 10 minutes. The tacos should be soft and steamy.

Remove the steamer from the heat and serve the tacos immediately with the remaining sauce.

TACOS DE CECINA ENCHILADA

✸

GRILLED ADOBO PORK TACOS

5 guajillo chiles, dry-roasted
4 ancho chiles, dry-roasted
6 cloves garlic, dry-roasted
4 tablespoons apple cider vinegar
½ teaspoon dried oregano
10 black peppercorns
1 small cinnamon stick
1 clove
1 (2½-lb/1.2-kg) boneless pork loin
sea salt

To serve:
12 small scallions (spring onions), white parts only
12 mild red chiles
2–3 tablespoons corn oil
18 Corn Tortillas (page 36)
4 limes, quartered
2 avocados, peeled, pitted, and sliced
Green Salsa with Avocado (page 512)
Pico de Gallo with Jicama and Pineapple (page 496)

REGION: OAXACA
PREPARATION TIME: 40 MINUTES, PLUS 2 HOURS MARINATING
COOKING TIME: 30 MINUTES
SERVES: 6

Put the chiles in a bowl, add enough hot water to cover, and soak for 15 minutes. Drain the chiles and reserve the soaking liquid.

Put the chiles, garlic, vinegar, oregano, peppercorns, cinnamon, clove, and a pinch of salt into a food processor or blender and process to a smooth, thick puree. Add a little of the reserved soaking liquid if needed.

With a sharp knife, slice the pork in half horizontally without cutting all the way through and open out like a book. Rub the chile mixture all over it and close it up to its original shape.

Put the meat into a plastic bowl and add the remaining chile mixture. Cover with plastic wrap (clingfilm) and let marinate in the refrigerator for at least 2 hours.

Preheat the broiler (grill). Put the meat on the broiler rack and broil (grill), turning occasionally, for 20 minutes, until cooked through. Add the scallions (spring onions) and chile to the grill rack about 10 minutes before the end of the cooking time and broil until they are just beginning to char, or cook them in a frying pan or skillet until golden brown. Transfer the pork to a plate.

Heat the oil in a frying pan or skillet over medium heat. Add the tortillas, one at a time, turning once, until they are hot on both sides. Put in a basket lined with paper towels.

Serve the hot tortillas with the pork, scallions, chiles, lime wedges, avocado slices, and salsas.

TACOS DE CHAPULINES

GRASSHOPPER TACOS

corn oil, for brushing
5 oz/150 g grasshoppers
juice of ½ lime
12 small Corn Tortillas
  (page 36)
1 quantity Guacamole
  (page 40)
1 quantity Red Pipian Sauce
  (page 498)
1 banana leaf, cleaned

REGION: SOUTH
PREPARATION TIME: 5 MINUTES
COOKING TIME: 12 MINUTES
SERVES: 6

Heat a heavy frying pan or skillet over medium heat, then brush with a little oil, add the grasshoppers, and cook lightly for 5–10 minutes. Sprinkle with lime juice.

Warm the tortillas in the grill (griddle) pan for 1 minute, then remove and spread with guacamole. Add the grasshoppers and chili sauce to taste over the top.

Transfer to a plate and serve.

TACOS FRIJOLES CON QUESO COTIJA

BEAN AND CHEESE TACOS

4 ancho chiles, dry-roasted
4 tablespoons corn oil
2 tablespoons chopped onion
2 cloves garlic, finely chopped
½ teaspoon cumin seeds
  (optional)
3 cups (1 lb/450 g) cooked black
  or red beans
12 Corn Tortillas (page 36)
sea salt

To garnish:
1 cup (2 oz/50 g) shredded
  lettuce
1 cup (5 oz/150 g) grated cotija
  or feta cheese

REGION: ALL REGIONS
PREPARATION TIME: 20 MINUTES, PLUS
15 MINUTES SOAKING
COOKING TIME: 20 MINUTES
SERVES: 6

Put the chiles in a small bowl, add enough hot water to cover, and soak for 15 minutes. Heat 2 tablespoons of the oil in a saucepan. Add the onion and cook over low heat, stirring occasionally, for 5 minutes. Add the garlic, chiles, and cumin seeds, if using, and cook for another few minutes.

Add the beans, mash well, and cook, stirring occasionally, for another 5 minutes. Remove the pan from the heat.

Heat the remaining oil in a frying pan or skillet. Fold the tortillas in half and add to the pan, in batches, if necessary. Cook on both sides until they are a little crispy, then remove with a spatula, opening them up a little so the sides don't stick together, and drain on paper towels. Add more oil to the pan between batches, if necessary. Fill the tortillas with the beans and garnish with lettuce and cheese. Serve immediately.

TACOS DE ALCOCILES

✳

CRAYFISH TACOS

½ cup (4 fl oz/120 ml) olive oil
  or ½ cup (3½ oz/100 g) lard
1½ white onions, finely chopped
4 cloves garlic, finely chopped
5 serrano chiles, finely
  chopped
1 lb 10 oz/750 g crayfish or
  baby shrimp (prawns)
½ cup (2 oz/50 g) finely
  chopped epazote leaves
1 bunch cilantro (coriander),
  chopped, plus extra, to
  garnish
½ cup (4 fl oz/120 ml) Chicken
  Stock (page 184), optional
sea salt
24 blue Corn Tortillas (page
  36), to serve

REGION: PUEBLA, FEDERAL DISTRICT
PREPARATION TIME: 10 MINUTES
COOKING TIME: 25 MINUTES
SERVES: 6

Heat the oil or lard in a large saucepan over low heat, add the onions, and cook for 5 minutes, or until light brown. Season with salt, then add the garlic and cook for an additional 2 minutes or until golden brown. Add the chiles and cook for an additional 3 minutes.

Increase the heat to medium, add the crayfish or baby shrimp (prawns), stir, and cook for 3 minutes. Add the epazote and cilantro (coriander), season with salt, reduce the heat to low, cover the pan, and continue cooking for 10 minutes. If the mixture is too dry, add the chicken stock.

Transfer the crayfish onto a serving plate, sprinkle with chopped cilantro, and serve with blue corn tortillas.

TACOS DE PAPA

✳

POTATO TACOS

3 tablespoons corn oil
1 onion, chopped
6 chipotle chiles in adobo,
  chopped
2½ cups (1 lb 2 oz/500 g)
  mashed potatoes
12 Corn Tortillas (page 36)

To serve:
Green Salsa with Avocado
  (page 512)
sour cream
grated queso fresco or feta
  cheese

REGION: FEDERAL DISTRICT
PREPARATION TIME: 10 MINUTES
COOKING TIME: 25 MINUTES
SERVES: 6

Heat 2 tablespoons of the oil in a saucepan over medium heat. Add the onion and cook over low heat, stirring occasionally, for 10 minutes or until translucent. Add the chiles and cook for another few minutes, then add the mashed potatoes and heat through. Season with salt to taste and remove the pan from the heat.

Warm the tortillas by placing them in a dry frying pan or skillet and flipping them continuously until they are soft. Place them in a basket and cover with a dish towel to keep warm. Fill each tortilla, fold in half, and lightly cook on a grill (griddle) pan or heavy saucepan over medium heat. Serve with sides of salsa, sour cream, and cheese.

TACOS GOBERNADOR

✳

GOVERNOR'S TACOS

2 tablespoons (1 oz/25 g) butter

1 tablespoon corn oil

3 tomatoes, seeded and finely chopped

½ onion, finely chopped

14 oz/400 g raw shrimp (prawns), peeled and chopped

2 tablespoons chopped cilantro (coriander)

2¾ cups (11 oz/300 g) grated Chihuahua, Monterey Jack, or mild cheddar cheese

12 Corn Tortillas (page 36)

melted butter, for brushing

sea salt and pepper

To serve:

medium-hot chili sauce

3 limes, cut into wedges

REGION: SINALOA
PREPARATION TIME: 10 MINUTES
COOKING TIME: 20 MINUTES
SERVES: 6

Heat the butter and oil in a saucepan. Add the tomatoes and onion and cook over medium heat until dry. Add the shrimp (prawns), season with salt and pepper, and stir in the cilantro (coriander). Once it has cooled down, add the cheese and stir.

Warm the tortillas by placing them in a dry frying pan or skillet and flipping them over continuously until they are soft. Place them in a basket and cover them with a dish towel to keep warm. Fill each tortilla with the shrimp and cheese mixture, fold in half, brush with butter, and lightly cook on a ridged grill (griddle) pan or in a heavy saucepan over medium heat.

Serve with the chili sauce and lime wedges.

TACOS DE CARNE SECA

✳

BEEF TACOS

1 tablespoon corn oil

16 oz/450 g ground (minced) beef

1 white onion, finely chopped

2 poblano chiles, dry-roasted and chopped

2 tomatoes, finely chopped

12 small Flour Tortillas (page 37)

sea salt and pepper

Salsa of choice (pages 496–514), to serve

REGION: CHIHUAHUA
PREPARATION TIME: 5 MINUTES
COOKING TIME: 25 MINUTES
SERVES: 6

Heat the oil in a medium pan over high heat. Add the meat and cook, stirring frequently, for 3 minutes or until lightly browned. Lower the heat and add the onion and cook, stirring occasionally, for 10 minutes until translucent. Add the chiles and tomatoes and cook for 10 minutes or until everything is cooked through and tender. Remove the pan from the heat and season with salt and pepper.

Warm the tortillas by placing them in a dry frying pan or skillet and flipping them over continuously until they are soft. Place them in a basket and cover them with a dish towel to keep warm. Serve the filling in a separate bowl and the salsa on the side.

Potato and Chorizo Tacos

TACOS DE PAPA Y CHORIZO

POTATO AND CHORIZO TACOS

4 potatoes, diced
2 tablespoons corn oil, plus
  extra for frying
1 onion, finely chopped
1 lb 2 oz/500 g chorizo,
  skinned and diced
6 smoked chipotle chiles in
  adobo, chopped
12 blue Corn Tortillas (page
  36)
sea salt

To serve:
lettuce, shredded (optional)
grated queso fresco or feta
  cheese (optional)
Salsa of choice (pages 496–514)

REGION: ALL REGIONS
PREPARATION TIME: 20 MINUTES
COOKING TIME: 50 MINUTES
SERVES: 6

Bring a saucepan of water to a boil over high heat, add the potatoes, and cook for 7 minutes. Strain and set aside.

Heat the oil in a saucepan. Add the onion and cook over medium heat, stirring occasionally, for 7 minutes. Add the chorizo and cook, stirring occasionally, for 5 minutes, until browned. Add the chiles and cook for a few minutes, then add the diced potatoes and stir everything together well. Season to taste with salt, then remove the pan from the heat.

Warm the tortillas by placing them in a dry frying pan or skillet and flipping them over continuously until they are soft. Place them in a basket and cover with a dish towel to keep warm. Fill each tortilla and fold in half. Garnish with lettuce and cheese, if using, and serve immediately with salsa.

TACOS DE CAMARON

SHRIMP TACOS

2 tomatoes, dry-roasted
1 onion, dry-roasted
3 tablespoons corn oil
2 potatoes, blanched and diced
14 oz/400 g small shrimp
  (prawns), peeled, heads and
  tails removed, and coarsely
  chopped
12 Flour Tortillas (page 37)
sea salt and pepper
Cooked Tomato Salsa
  (page 501)

To garnish:
2 pickled onions, thinly sliced
shredded lettuce
thinly sliced radishes

REGION: BAJA CALIFORNIA, BAJA CALIFORNIA SUR
PREPARATION TIME: 20 MINUTES
COOKING TIME: 20 MINUTES
SERVES: 6

Put the tomatoes and onion into a food processor or blender and process until thoroughly combined. Heat 1 tablespoon oil in a frying pan. Add the tomato mixture and cook, stirring frequently, for a few minutes. Add the potatoes and cook, stirring occasionally, for 10 minutes until thickened. Add the shrimp (prawns), season with salt and pepper, and cook for an additional 5 minutes until the shrimp are pink and cooked through. Remove the pan from the heat.

Heat the remaining oil in a skillet (frying pan). Dip a tortilla in the salsa to coat, then add to the pan, and cook briefly on both sides. Remove from the pan, put a heaping tablespoon of the shrimp filling in the center, fold in half, and place on a serving platter. Repeat with the remaining tortillas and filling. Garnish with the onion, lettuce, and radishes. Serve immediately.

TACOS DE MINILLA

✺

MINILLA TACOS

1 (2¼-lb/1-kg) mackerel or
  pompano, cleaned
1 bouquet garni
¼ onion, plus 1 onion,
  chopped
1 ancho chile, dry-roasted and
  chopped
3 serrano chiles, chopped
2 tomatoes, peeled
4 tablespoons corn oil
1 tablespoon capers
3 tablespoons chopped cilantro
  (coriander)
12 Corn Tortillas (page 36)
sea salt

To serve:
1 tablespoon corn oil
Salsa of choice (pages 496–514)
sour cream
grated queso fresco or feta
  cheese

REGION: VERACRUZ
PREPARATION TIME: 40 MINUTES
COOKING TIME: 50 MINUTES
SERVES: 6

Put the fish, bouquet garni, and ¼ onion into a saucepan and pour in enough water to cover. Bring to a boil, then reduce to a gentle simmer for 10–15 minutes.

Remove the pan from the heat and lift out the fish. Flake the flesh, discarding the bones and skin.

Put the chiles and tomatoes into a food processor or blender and process until thoroughly combined.

Heat 3 tablespoons of the oil in a saucepan. Add the chopped onion and cook over medium heat, stirring occasionally, for 5–8 minutes, until lightly browned. Add the tomato and chile mixture, reduce the heat to low, and simmer for about 10 minutes. Season to taste with salt, add the fish and capers, and mix well. Simmer for another 10 minutes, until the sauce has reduced. Stir in the cilantro (coriander) and remove the pan from the heat.

Warm the tortillas by placing them in a dry frying pan or skillet and flipping them over continuously until they are soft. Place them in a basket and cover with a dish towel to keep warm. Fill each tortilla with the fish mixture, fold in half, and lightly cook on a ridged grill (griddle) pan or in a heavy saucepan over medium heat.

Put the hot tacos on a serving dish and garnish with salsa, sour cream, and cheese. Serve immediately.

TACOS DE PICADILLO

✻

MEAT TACOS

1 small potato, diced
2 tablespoons corn oil
1 lb 2 oz/500 g ground (minced) beef
1 onion, chopped
1 small tomato, peeled and chopped
¼ teaspoon ground cinnamon
2 tablespoons chopped walnuts
2 tablespoons raisins
12 Corn Tortillas (page 36)
sea salt and pepper
lettuce, shredded
1 quantity Raw Tomato Salsa (page 499) or Michoacan Avocado Salsa (page 507), to serve

REGION: ALL REGIONS
PREPARATION TIME: 15 MINUTES
COOKING TIME: 50–60 MINUTES
SERVES: 6

Bring a saucepan of water to a boil over high heat, add the potatoes, and cook for 7 minutes. Strain and set aside.

To prepare the filling, heat 1 tablespoon oil in a saucepan. Add the ground (minced) beef and 1 tablespoon water and cook over medium-high heat, stirring frequently, for about 10 minutes, until evenly browned and without any lumps. Reduce the heat, stir in the onion, and cook, stirring occasionally, for 5 minutes. Add the tomato, cinnamon, walnuts, raisins, and potato, season with salt and pepper to taste, and cook for an additional 5–10 minutes, until everything is heated well and any liquid has evaporated. Remove the pan from the heat.

Warm the tortillas by placing them in a dry frying pan or skillet and flipping them over continuously until they are soft. Fill them with the mixture and secure with a toothpick or cocktail stick.

Heat the remaining oil in a frying pan or skillet. Add the tortillas, in batches, and cook, turning once, until golden on both sides. Remove with a spatula and drain on paper towels. Garnish with lettuce and salsa and serve immediately.

TACOS AL PASTOR

✸

SHEPHERDS' TACOS

5 guajillo chiles, membranes
 and seeds removed
5 tablespoons apple cider
 vinegar
3 cloves garlic, peeled
pinch of ground cumin
2 cloves
2 tablespoons pineapple juice
 (optional), plus extra for
 serving
1 (1 lb 2-oz/500-g) pork leg or
 rump, thinly sliced
2–3 tablespoons corn oil
1 large onion, thinly sliced
sea salt

To serve:
12 small Corn Tortillas
 (page 36)
½ pineapple, peeled, quartered,
 cored, and sliced
1 small onion, finely chopped
4 tablespoons finely chopped
 cilantro (coriander)
Salsa of choice (pages 496–514)

REGION: FEDERAL DISTRICT
PREPARATION TIME: 30 MINUTES, PLUS
5 HOURS MARINATING
COOKING TIME: 35 MINUTES
SERVES: 6

Put the chiles into a saucepan, add the vinegar, and simmer for 15 minutes, until the chiles are soft. Add the garlic, cumin, and cloves, then transfer the mixture to a food processor or blender and process to a paste. Add more vinegar, if necessary, and pineapple juice, if using, and strain.

Transfer the paste to a saucepan and cook over low heat for 10 minutes, stirring constantly to prevent it from sticking. Remove from the heat and let cool.

Spread a thin layer of chili paste over the slices of meat. Stack them on a plate, cover them with plastic wrap (clingfilm), and let marinate in the refrigerator for 5 hours or overnight.

Heat the oil in a frying pan or skillet. Add the pork slices and cook for 2 minutes, turn them over, and cook for an additional 2 minutes, until partially cooked. Remove from the pan, cut into bite-sized pieces, and return to the pan. Add the onion and cook for another 3 minutes. Transfer the meat to a serving plate.

Put the tortillas, one at a time, into the pan and cook for 20–30 seconds on both sides. Remove from the pan and drain on paper towels.

Divide the pork among the tortillas, add the pineapple slices, onion, and cilantro (coriander), and top with salsa. Serve immediately.

Shepherds' Tacos

TAQUITOS DE REQUESON CON CHILE VERDE

CURD CHEESE AND GREEN CHILE TACOS

6 serrano chiles
2 tablespoons corn oil
1 white onion, chopped
2 cloves garlic, minced
2¼–2⅔ cups (1 lb 2 oz–1 lb 5 oz/
   500–600 g) crumbled curd
   cheese or ricotta
2 tablespoons finely chopped
   epazote leaves
18 Corn Tortillas (page 36)
sea salt
banana leaf, cut into 4-inch
   (10-cm) squares, to garnish

REGION: NORTHWEST
PREPARATION TIME: 10 MINUTES
COOKING TIME: 20 MINUTES
SERVES: 6

Put the chiles in a small bowl, add enough hot water to cover, and soak for 15 minutes. Heat the oil in a small saucepan over medium heat. Add the onion and garlic and sauté for 3 minutes, or until translucent. Add the crumbled cheese, stir well, then add the chiles and epazote. Mix well, then check the seasoning, adding salt to taste. Remove the pan from the heat.

Warm the tortillas, then spread a little of the cheese mixture over the tortillas to make taquitos. Place in a large basket or on a serving plate lined with the banana leaf squares or paper towels, or aluminum foil, and keep warm.

CHILAPITAS DE CHAPULINES

GRASSHOPPER CHILAPITAS

5 tablespoons olive oil
¼ cup (2¼ oz/60 g) butter
2 large onions, sliced
1 lb/580 g grasshoppers, rinsed
½–¾ cup (4–6 fl oz/120–175 ml)
   lemon juice
½ cup (4 fl oz/120 ml) mild chili
   sauce
sea salt
18 chilapitas or 6 tostadas
Guacamole (page 40)

REGION: OAXACA
PREPARATION TIME: 10 MINUTES
COOKING TIME: 15 MINUTES
SERVES: 6

Heat the oil and butter in a large saucepan over medium heat. Add the onion and cook for 5 minutes or until golden brown, then add the grasshoppers and cook for 5 minutes, or until they are slightly browned.

Mix the lemon juice and mild chili sauce together in a bowl, then pour into the pan. Season with salt to taste and cook for 5 minutes, or until the grasshoppers are crisp. Serve in chilapitas with guacamole.

GRINGA

PORK AND CHEESE TACOS

8 pasilla or ancho chiles,
   membranes and seeds
   removed
20 dried guajillo or 4 oz/120 g
   other chiles, membranes and
   seeds removed
6 tablespoons apple cider
   vinegar
6 tablespoons pineapple juice
1 head garlic, cloves separated
pinch of ground cumin
pinch of ground cloves
1 lb 2 oz/500 g lean pork, cut
   into cutlets about ¼ inch
   (5 mm) thick
1 large onion, finely chopped
16 Flour Tortillas (page 37)
14 oz/400 g Chihuahua or
   gouda cheese, sliced into
   8 pieces
sea salt
Salsa of choice (pages 496–514),
   to serve

REGION: FEDERAL DISTRICT
PREPARATION TIME: 25 MINUTES, PLUS
5 HOURS MARINATING
COOKING TIME: 30 MINUTES
SERVES: 4

Put the chiles, vinegar, and pineapple juice into a saucepan over medium heat and cook for 10 minutes, until the chiles have softened. Add the garlic, cumin, and cloves, transfer the mixture to a food processor or blender, and process to a spreadable paste. Add a little more vinegar, if necessary.

Transfer the paste to a frying pan or skillet, season with salt, and cook over low heat, stirring constantly, for 5 minutes. If it begins to stick, add a little water to prevent it from sticking. Remove the pan from the heat and let cool.

Lightly coat the pork with the paste, then stack the cutlets up on a plate, cover with plastic wrap (clingfilm) and marinate for at least 5 hours in the refrigerator.

Heat a heavy frying pan or skillet, add a pork cutlet, and cook for 2–3 minutes on each side. Remove the cutlet from the pan and cut into small pieces. Repeat with the remaining cutlets. Return all the pieces of pork to the pan, add the onion and cook for an additional 5 minutes. Transfer the pork to a large plate and clean the pan with paper towel.

Heat the pan again over low heat and place a tortilla in the pan, put a slice of cheese on top, and when it has melted, add one-eighth of the pork mixture, spreading it out over the cheese. Cover this with another tortilla and press down slightly so they stick together. Flip the taco over and cook it for 30 seconds or so. Remove it from the pan and put on a large plate. Cover it with a dish towel so it stays soft. Repeat with the remaining tortillas, cheese, and pork mixture. Cut each one into 4 pieces and serve immediately with salsa.

CARNITAS

✻

CARNITAS

1 cup (9 fl oz/250 ml) vegetable
   oil
3¼ lb/1.5 kg pork loin, cut into
   bite-size pieces
½ onion
1 cup (9 fl oz/250 ml) milk
1 small bunch aromatic herbs
thinly pared zest of 1 orange
sea salt and pepper

To serve:
Flour Tortillas (page 37)
Salsa of choice (pages 496–514)

REGION: BAJIO, MICHOACAN, MEXICO STATE
PREPARATION TIME: 10 MINUTES
COOKING TIME: 2 HOURS
SERVES: 4

Heat the oil in a saucepan. Add the meat and onion
and cook over medium heat, stirring occasionally,
for about 8 minutes, until evenly browned.

Remove the onion. Pour in the milk and ½ cup
(4 fl oz/120 ml) water, add the herbs and orange zest,
and season with salt and pepper. Reduce the heat to
low and cook, stirring occasionally, for 2 hours or
until all the liquid has evaporated.

Remove the meat from the pan and serve
immediately with warm flour tortillas and salsa.

TAMAL BRAZO DE REINA

✻

QUEEN'S ARM TAMAL

For the chiltomate:
4 ripe tomatoes
½ onion, chopped
1 habanero chili, membrane
  and seeds removed and finely
  chopped
1 sprig epazote leaves
sea salt

For the dough:
1 cup (7 oz/200 g) lard or
  vegetable shortening
8¾ cups (2¼ lb/1 kg) masa
  harina
½ cup (4 fl oz/120 ml) Chicken
  Stock (page 184)
1 tablespoon sea salt
2¼ lb/1 kg chaya, Swiss chard,
  or spinach leaves, finely
  chopped

For the assembly:
1 cup (7 oz/200 g) pumpkin
  seeds, hulled, plus extra to
  serve
12 (6-inch/15-cm) squares
  banana leaves
1 teaspoon sea salt
8 hard-boiled eggs, shelled and
  chopped
2–3 habanero or Morita
  chiles, membranes and seeds
  removed, finely chopped
queso fresco or feta cheese, to
  serve

REGION: YUCATÁN
PREPARATION TIME: 50 MINUTES
COOKING TIME: 1 HOUR 10 MINUTES
SERVES: 6

For the chiltomate, combine the tomatoes, onion, chile, and epazote leaves in a saucepan and cook over medium heat for 10 minutes. Season to taste, discard the epazote, and process the mixture in a food processor or blender. Season and transfer to a serving bowl.

For the dough, whip the lard for 5 minutes until it whitens and becomes fluffy. Add the masa harina in small amounts, letting it blend with the lard, alternating with the chicken stock and salt. Continue beating for an additional 5 minutes. Taste the dough; it should be slightly salty. Add the chaya and mix well to incorporate.

To assemble, put the pumpkin seeds and salt into a mortar and grind. Set aside. Place a ball of dough (the amount that fits in your hand) in the center of the dull side of a banana leaf and spread it out to form a 4 x 3-inch (10 x 7.5-cm) rectangle about ⅛ inch (2 mm) thick. Cover with a thin layer of pumpkin seed powder and chiles to taste. Place ½ cup hard-boiled egg and a little chile along one shorter end of the rectangle and, roll the masa over to cover the egg. Give it another turn, then add some more egg, trying to make it as compact as possible without pressing too much. Close the tamal and wrap it into a cylinder, tying the ends with thin strings of the banana leaves or kitchen string. Make the rest of the tamales in the same way until you use up the ingredients.

Place the tamales horizontally in a prepared steamer and cook over high heat for 1 hour or until the dough can be easily separated from the leaf. Remove the steamer from the heat and let them rest for 20 minutes before eating.

To serve, cut each tamal into round slices about ¾ inch (2 cm) thick. Spoon a small amount of chiltomate over them, and sprinkle with chopped pumpkin seeds and cheese.

TAMALES ROJOS
※
RED PORK TAMALES

1 lb 2 oz/500 g boneless
   pork leg
1 sprig thyme
1 bay leaf
1 onion, halved
4 cloves garlic
1 teaspoon salt
2 ancho chiles
1 guajillo chile
2 tomatoes
1 cup (9 fl oz/250 ml) Chicken
   Stock (page 184)
½ teaspoon dried oregano
¼ teaspoon black peppercorns
1 tablespoon vegetable
   shortening, lard, or corn oil
sea salt

For the dough:
1 cup (7 oz/200 g) lard or
   vegetable shortening
4⅓ cups (1 lb 2 oz/500 g) masa
   harina
1½ teaspoons sea salt
1½ teaspoons baking powder
12 corn husks, soaked in hot
   water for 20 minutes and
   drained thoroughly

REGION: ALL REGIONS
PREPARATION TIME: 1½ HOURS, PLUS
15 MINUTES SOAKING
COOKING TIME: 2 HOURS
SERVES: 6

Put the pork, thyme, bay leaf, ½ onion, 2 cloves garlic, and salt into a saucepan, add 6¼ cups (2½ pints/1.5 liters) water, and bring to a boil. Reduce the heat and simmer for 1 hour or until the meat is tender. Set aside.

Meanwhile, put the chiles, tomatoes, remaining onion half, and remaining cloves garlic into a frying pan or skillet and roast for 15 minutes over medium-high heat.

Pour the stock into a saucepan and bring to a boil. Put the chiles in a small bowl, add enough hot stock to cover them, and soak for 15 minutes. Put the chiles, oregano, peppercorns, tomatoes, roasted onion half, and roasted garlic and some of the soaking liquid in a food processor or blender, and process until smooth. Strain into a saucepan, add the vegetable shortening over medium heat, and cook, stirring frequently, for 5–10 minutes. Season with salt.

When the meat is cooked, remove the pan from the heat and lift out the pork. Reserve the cooking liquid and strain into a bowl. Let cool, then shred and chop the meat. Add the pork to the reserved chile mixture and simmer for an additional 2–3 minutes. Taste and adjust the seasoning, if necessary, remove the pan from the heat, and let cool.

To prepare the dough, beat the lard until creamy and fluffy, add the masa harina in four additions, add the salt and the baking powder and beat well. Add 1 cup (9 fl oz/250 ml) reserved cooking liquid to make a smooth, soft dough. Spread out the corn husk leaves. Spread 1 heaping tablespoon of dough on the widest part of each leaf and place a tablespoon of the cooled meat filling in the center. Fold the leaf over, without pressing, then fold in the ends.

Stand the tamales vertically in a prepared steamer and cook over high heat for about 1 hour or until the dough can be easily separated from the husks. Remove the steamer from the heat and let the tamales rest for 20 minutes before serving.

TAMALES DE CAMARON Y POBLANO

✻

SHRIMP AND POBLANO TAMALES

For the filling:
3 ancho chiles, dry-roasted and
    cut into strips
2 poblano chiles
1 lb 5 oz/600 g fresh shrimp
    (prawns), unpeeled
2 tablespoons lard or corn oil
1 onion, finely chopped
4 cloves garlic, finely chopped
2 ripe tomatos, chopped
1–2 serrano chiles, membranes
    and seeds removed and cut
    into strips
1 teaspoon dried oregano
sea salt, to taste

For the dough:
9 oz (250 g) lard or oil
4⅓ cups (1 lb 2 oz/500 g) masa
    harina
1½ tablespoon salt

For the assembly:
15 dry corn husks, soaked in
    boiling water for 15 minutes,
    well drained
15 thin dry corn husks, strips

REGION: OAXACA
PREPARATION TIME: 1 HOUR, PLUS
25 MINUTES SOAKING
COOKING TIME: 1¼ HOURS
SERVINGS: 15 TAMALES

Put the chiles in a small bowl, add enough hot water to cover them, and soak for 15 minutes.

For the filling, bring 2 cups (16 fl oz/475 ml) water and a teaspoon of salt to a boil in a saucepan and add the shrimp (prawns). Cover the pan and cook for 1 minute. Remove the shrimp, strain, and reserve the cooking liquid. Peel the shrimp, place in a food processor or blender and process with 1 cup (9 fl oz/250 ml) of cooking liquid until smooth. Strain.

In a bowl, combine the ancho chiles and 1½ cups (12 fl oz/350 ml) soaking liquid in a food processor or blender, and process until smooth. Set aside, reserving 4 tablespoons of chile paste for the dough. Heat some lard or oil in a saucepan and cook the onion and the garlic. Add the tomatoes, the serrano chile, and half the shrimp liquid, stir, then add the chopped shrimp and the reserved blended ancho chili paste. Simmer for 5 minutes, add the oregano, season with salt to taste, stir, remove from the heat and set aside.

For the dough, whip the lard or vegetable shortening for 5 minutes or until it whitens and becomes fluffy. Add small amounts of masa harina and the salt, and continue whipping for an additional 5 minutes until you have a smooth and homogeneous mix. Slowly add 2 spoonfuls of ancho chili paste, alternating with the rest of the blended shrimp liquid. The masa should taste slightly salty.

To assemble, place 2 tablespoon of the masa on each corn husk. Hollow the center and add a heaping spoonful of filling, cover the filling with the masa, and close the leaf, compacting it and tying the ends with the strings of corn leaves to form a cylinder. Make the rest of the tamales in the same way until all the dough and filling have been used.

Place the tamales horizontally in a prepared steamer and cook at high heat 1 hour or until the dough is easily separated from the husk. Remove the tamales from the heat and let rest for 20 minutes before eating.

TAMALES DE ESPINACA Y QUESO

✳

SPINACH AND CHEESE TAMALES

For the filling:
1 tomato, dry-roasted
lard or corn oil, for frying
3 tablespoons chopped onion
1 clove garlic, finely chopped
7 oz/200 g ground (minced)
   pork
2 tablespoons raisins
2 tablespoons chopped
   almonds
sea salt and pepper

For the dough:
1 cup (5 oz/150 g) lard or
   vegetable shortening
4⅓ cups (17 oz/500 g) masa
   harina
1 teaspoon sea salt
2 cups (10 oz/300 g) grated
   Monterey Jack or white
   cheddar cheese
3½ cups (3½ oz/100 g) large
   spinach leaves
slices cheese, to serve

For the salsa:
2–3 tomatoes, dry-roasted
½ onion, coarsely chopped
lard or oil for frying
3 poblano chiles, dry-roasted
   and cut into thin strips
sea salt and pepper

REGION: ALL REGIONS
PREPARATION TIME: 1¼ HOURS
COOKING TIME: 1½ HOURS
SERVES: 6

To make the filling, put the tomato into a food processor or blender and process, then pass through a strainer (sieve) into a bowl. Heat the lard or oil in a large frying pan or skillet. Add the onion and cook over medium heat, stirring occasionally, for about 7 minutes, until translucent. Add the garlic and sauté until aromatic.

Add the meat and cook, stirring frequently, for about 8 minutes, until evenly browned. Add the tomato, raisins, and almonds, season with salt and pepper, and simmer over low heat for 15 minutes or until almost dry. Remove the pan from the heat and let cool.

For the dough, beat the lard or vegetable shortening until fluffy, add the masa harina in 4 batches with the salt, and beat until thoroughly combined. Fold in the grated cheese, then adjust the seasoning.

Lay out a moistened piece of cheesecloth (muslin) or dish towel on a work surface, then spread the dough into a 12½ x 8 inch (35 x 20 cm) rectangle. Cover with the cooled filling, starting at the long side, carefully to roll it up into a cylinder; cut the roll into ¾ inch (2 cm) thick slices. Wrap each slice securely in 2–3 spinach leaves, the wrap in plastic wrap (clingfilm) or aluminum foil. Place them in a steamer and steam over high heat for 1 hour or until the dough can easily be separated from the husk.

Meanwhile, make the salsa. Put the tomatoes and onion into a food processor or blender and process until smooth, then pass through with a sieve (strainer) into a bowl. Heat the lard in a saucepan. Add the chile strips and cook over medium heat, stirring frequently, for 5 minutes. Pour in the tomato and onion mixture, season with salt and pepper, and simmer for 5–10 minutes, until thickened.

Serve the hot tamales, unwrapped, with salsa and sliced cheese.

TAMALES NORTEÑO DE FRIJOL

✸

NORTHERN BEAN TAMALES

2 teaspoons lard or corn oil
1½ cups (7 oz/200 g) cooked
flor de mayo or pinto beans
sea salt
25–30 corn husks, soaked in
boiling water for 15 minutes,
drained, and leaves cut in
half lengthwise if they are
too wide

For the sauce:
1 cup (9 fl oz/250 ml) Beef
Stock (page 185)
2 ancho chiles, dry-roasted
1–2 cloves garlic
¼ teaspoon ground cumin
¼ teaspoon crushed black
peppercorns

For the dough:
17 oz/500 g masa harina
¾ cup (5 oz/150 g) lard or
vegetable shortening
2 teaspoons sea salt
1½ teaspoons baking powder
½–1 cup (4–8 fl oz/120–250 ml)
Beef Stock (page 185)

REGION: NUEVO LEON
PREPARATION TIME: 50 MINUTES, PLUS
15 MINUTES SOAKING
COOKING TIME: 1¼ HOURS
SERVES: 6

To make the sauce, pour the stock into a saucepan and bring to a boil, then remove the pan from the heat. Put the chiles into a small bowl, and enough hot stock to cover them, and soak for 15 minutes.

Put the chiles and soaking liquid, garlic, cumin, and crushed peppercorns into a food processor or blender and process until smooth.

Heat the lard in a saucepan. Add the beans and cook over medium heat, mashing them to a thick paste. Set aside 3 tablespoons of the chili sauce and stir the remainder into the pan with the beans. Season with salt to taste.

Continue cooking the beans, stirring frequently to prevent them from sticking, until they become thick. Taste and adjust the seasoning, if necessary. Remove the pan from the heat and let cool.

To make the dough, beat the lard in a bowl until fluffy and creamy, add the dough in four parts, the reserved sauce, the salt, and baking powder. Gradually beat in up to 1 cup (9 fl oz/250 ml) stock or water, if necessary. Continue beating until a piece of the mixture will float in a glass of water. Spread out the leaves of the drained corn husks.

Spread a generous tablespoon of the dough on the wide side of the corn husk, leaving a thin margin. Top with a spoonful of the bean paste and fold one end of the leaf over the other to form a thin tamal. The overlapping dough helps the leaves stay in place. Stand the tamales vertically in a steamer and cook over high heat for 1 hour or until the dough can easily be separated from the husk. Remove the steamer from the heat and let the tamales rest, covered, for 20 minutes, before serving.

TAMALES DE CAPITAS O SIETE CUEROS

❁

SEVEN-LAYER TAMALES

For the filling:

5 oaxacan pasilla or morita
  chiles, dry-roasted
2 tablespoons lard or corn oil
1 white onion, sliced
6 avocado leaves, dry-roasted
  (optional)
4 cloves garlic, dry-roasted
3½ cups (1 lb 5 oz/600 g)
  cooked black beans, cooking
  liquid reserved

For the dough:

1 lb 2 oz/500 g masa harina
¾ cup (5 oz/150 g) lard or oil
¼ teaspoon sea salt
3 tablespoons Chicken Stock
  (page 184) (optional)
10 hoja santas, central stems
  removed
10 banana leaves

REGION: OAXACA
PREPARATION TIME: 1 HOUR, PLUS
15 MINUTES SOAKING
COOKING TIME: 1 HOUR 20 MINUTES
SERVES: 12

For the filling, combine the chiles and enough hot water to cover them in a small bowl, and soak for 15 minutes.

Heat 1 tablespoon of the lard or oil in a saucepan over medium heat, add the onion, and sauté for 5 minutes. Put the onion into a food processor or blender, add the avocado leaves, if using, garlic, and chiles with the soaking water, and process to a smooth paste. Mix in the black beans gradually, adding some of the cooking liquid, if necessary, to make a smooth paste.

For the dough, combine the masa harina, oil, and salt in a large bowl and mix well, adding some chicken stock, if necessary.

Lay out a piece of double cheesecloth (muslin) and arrange a layer of hoja santa. Put the dough on top to form a rectangle, then cover with a layer of the bean paste. From one long end, roll the tamal, using the cheesecloth to help form a cylinder, without trapping the cheesecloth inside.

Remove the cheesecloth and carefully cut slices about 1 inch (2.5 cm) thick, then arrange each slice inside a banana leaf. Close, fold, and put the tamales vertically into a steamer. Cover the tamales with a damp dish towel and the lid to make sure that the steam doesn't escape. Steam over high heat for 1 hour, or until the dough can easily be separated from the husk. Let stand for 20 minutes before serving them.

Seven-Layer Tamales

TAMALES PESCADO

✳

FISH TAMALES

10 guajillo or other dried chile,
 dry-roasted
20–25 corn husks
5 tomatoes, chopped
½ onion, coarsely chopped
3 cloves garlic
1 tablespoon epazote leaves
1 lb 2 oz/500 g white fish fillets
¾ cup (5 oz/150 g) vegetable
 shortening or lard
4⅓ cups (1 lb 2 oz/500 g) masa
 harina
1½ teaspoons salt
½ cup (4 fl oz/120 ml) Fish
 Stock (page 184) (optional)
sea salt

REGION: OAXACA
PREPARATION TIME: 40 MINUTES, PLUS
15 MINUTES SOAKING
COOKING TIME: 1 HOUR 10 MINUTES
SERVES: 6

Put the chiles in a small bowl, add enough hot water to cover them and soak for 15 minutes. Soak the corn husks in hot water for 15 minutes, then drain.

Put the chiles, their soaking liquid, tomatoes, onion, garlic, and epazote leaves into a food processor or blender and process until thoroughly ground, then pass through a strainer (sieve). Season to taste.

Transfer the mixture to a saucepan and cook for about 10 minutes or until thickened. Remove the pan from the heat and let cool.

Rinse the fish and pat dry, then cut into small cubes and put into a bowl. Add the cooled sauce and mix gently. Store in the refrigerator until required.

Beat the lard until fluffy and creamy, add the masa harina in four batches, add salt and enough of the fish stock to make a smooth, soft dough. Test by dropping a small piece into a glass of water—it is ready when it floats. Spread out the corn husks. Spread 1 heaping tablespoon of dough on the broad side of every leaf, add 1 tablespoon of the fish mixture, then fold up. Stand the tamales vertically in a steamer and cook for 1 hour or until the tamal separates easily from the husk. Remove the steamer from the heat and let the tamales rest for 20 minutes before serving.

TAMALES VERDES DE PUERCO

✳

GREEN PORK TAMALES

20–25 corn husks

9 oz/250 g boneless pork leg or shoulder

4 cloves garlic

½ white onion, halved

1 bouquet garni

⅔ cup (4 oz/125 g) lard or vegetable shortening

4⅓ cups (1 lb 2 oz/500 g) masa harina

1½ teaspoons sea salt

3 tomatillos

2–3 green chiles

2 sprigs cilantro (coriander)

1 tablespoon corn oil

REGION: ALL REGIONS
PREPARATION TIME: 1 HOUR, PLUS
15 MINUTES SOAKING
COOKING TIME: 1½ HOURS
SERVES: 6

Soak the corn husks in hot water for 15 minutes, then drain.

Put the pork, 2 cloves garlic, onion, bouquet garni, and just enough water to cover in a large saucepan. Bring to a boil over medium-high heat, then reduce to a simmer and cook for 30 minutes or until the meat is tender. Remove the pan from the heat, take out the pork, and let cool. Reserve and strain the cooking liquid into a bowl. Shred the pork.

Beat the fat until fluffy and creamy, add the masa harina in four batches, add the salt and enough of the reserved cooking liquid to make a smooth, soft dough. Test by dropping a small piece into a glass of water—it is ready when it floats.

Put the tomatillos into a saucepan, pour in just enough water just to cover, and cook for 10 minutes. Drain and put the tomatillos into a food processor or blender, add the remaining onion and garlic, the chiles, and cilantro (coriander) and process until thoroughly combined.

Heat the oil in a saucepan. Add the tomatillo and chile mixture and cook over medium heat, stirring occasionally, for 5 minutes. Remove the pan from the heat and stir in the shredded pork. Spread out the corn husk leaves. Spread 2 heaping tablespoons of the dough on the broad side of each leaf, add 1 heaping tablespoon of the pork filling, and close and fold. Stand the tamales vertically in a steamer and steam over high heat for 1 hour or until the dough separates easily from the husk. Remove the steamer from the heat and let the tamales rest for 20 minutes before serving.

TAMALES DE MOLE CON POLLO

✳

TAMALES WITH CHICKEN MOLE

9–12 plantain leaves
¾ cup (5 oz/150 g) lard or
   vegetable shortening
4⅓ cups (1 lb 2 oz/500 g)
   masa harina
1½ teaspoon sea salt
3½ cups (1 lb 2 oz/500 g)
   cooked chicken, shredded

For the sauce:
1 cup (9 fl oz/250 ml) Chicken
   Stock (page 184)
1¼ cups (11 oz/300 g)
   concentrated mole paste
sea salt

REGION: OAXACA
PREPARATION TIME: 45 MINUTES
COOKING TIME: 1¼ HOURS
SERVES: 6

Using a sharp knife, remove the thick vein of the plantain leaves. Wipe clean with damp paper towels. Cut into 8-inch (20-cm) squares and roast lightly over a gas flame.

Beat the fat until fluffy and creamy, add the masa harina in four batches, add the salt and enough of the reserved cooking liquid to make a smooth, soft dough. Test by dropping a small piece into a glass of water—it is ready when it floats.

To make the sauce, pour the stock into a saucepan, stir in the mole paste, and cook over medium-low heat, stirring constantly, until thickened. Remove from the heat and let cool.

Spread 2 tablespoons of the dough on the dull side of each plantain leaf square, and add a generous tablespoon of the cooked chicken and a generous tablespoon of the mole. Roll up the leaves, lay them in a steamer, and steam over high heat for 1 hour or until the dough can easily be separated from a leaf and remain firm. Remove the steamer from the heat and let the tamales rest for 20 minutes before serving.

TLACOYOS DE HABAS

✳

FAVA BEAN TLACOYOS

1⅔ cups (9 oz/250 g) shelled
   fava (broad) beans
3 chipotle chiles in adobo
1 avocado or spearmint leaf,
   dry-roasted (optional)
4⅓ cups (1 lb 2 oz/500 g) Masa
   Dough (page 36)
sea salt

To serve:
Salsa of choice (pages 496–514)
1 cup (8 oz/225 g) queso fresco
   or ricotta cheese, beaten

REGION: CENTRAL MEXICO
PREPARATION TIME: 20 MINUTES
COOKING TIME: 1¼ HOURS
SERVES: 6

If the fava (broad) beans are mature, pop them out of their skins by squeezing gently between your index finger and thumb. If they are young, this is not necessary.

Bring a saucepan of water to a boil with a pinch of salt. Add the beans and cook for 15–25 minutes until soft. Drain well.

Put the beans, chiles, and avocado or spearmint leaf, if using, into a food processor or blender and process to a paste. Season to taste with salt.

Shape the masa dough into balls the size of golfball and flatten with your hand to make thick tortillas. Put a tablespoon of the bean paste in the center of each one and fold the sides into the center, making an oval shape.

Heat a heavy frying pan or skillet. Add the tlacoyos in batches, if necessary, and cook over low heat for 5 minutes on each side, or until lightly browned and cooked through.

Serve immediately, topped with salsa and cheese.

TLACOYOS DE REQUESÓN

✳

CHEESE TLACOYOS

1 cup (9 oz/250 g) requesón,
   farmers' (curd) cheese, or
   ricotta cheese
3 chipotle chiles in adobo,
   finely chopped
2–3 tablespoons chopped
   epazote
4⅓ cups (1 lb 2 oz/500 g) Masa
   Dough (page 36)
sea salt
Salsa of choice (pages 496–514),
   to serve
cotija or feta cheese, crumbled,
   to serve

REGION: CENTRAL MEXICO
PREPARATION TIME: 15 MINUTES
COOKING TIME: 1¼ HOURS
SERVES: 4

Combine the cheese, chiles, and epazote in a bowl and season to taste with salt.

Shape the dough into balls the size of golf balls and flatten with your hand to make thick tortillas. Put a tablespoon of the cheese mixture in the center of each and fold the sides into the center, making an oval shape.

Heat a heavy frying pan or skillet. Add the tlacoyos in batches, if necessary, and cook over medium-low heat for 4 minutes on each side.

Line a bread basket with a napkin. Remove the tlacoyos with a spatula, put them into the basket, and keep warm. Serve topped with salsa and crumbled cheese.

TLACOYOS DE FRIJOLES

✱

BEAN TLACOYOS

2 cups (14 oz/400 g) cooked
  black beans, drained, with
  the liquid reserved
3 smoked chipotle chiles in
  adobo
1 avocado leaf, dry-roasted
  lightly
4⅓ cups (1 lb 2 oz/500 g) Masa
  Dough (page 36)
sea salt

To serve:
½ cup cotija or feta cheese,
  shredded
avocado, peeled, pitted and
  diced
½ red onion, thinly sliced
Salsa of choice (pages 496–514)
  (optional)

REGIONS: FEDERAL DISTRICT, CENTRAL MEXICO
PREPARATION TIME: 20 MINUTES
COOKING TIME: 1¼ HOURS
SERVES: 4

Put the beans into a food processor or blender with the chiles and avocado leaf, if using, and process into a fine paste. Use a little bean liquid to thin it if necessary. Taste and season with salt. Transfer to a bowl and set aside.

Shape the dough into balls about double the size of golf balls and flatten with your hand to make disks about ¼ inch (5 mm) thick. Put a tablespoon of the bean paste in the center of each, spread it out into a strip and fold the top and bottom sides of the disks into the center so they slightly overlap. Press gently to make a stuffed, oval-shaped tortilla.

Heat a heavy frying pan or skillet. Add the tlacoyos, in batches if necessary, and cook over medium-low heat for 5 minutes on each side, flipping them from time to time to make sure they don't burn.

Line a basket with a napkin. Remove the tlacoyos with a spatula, put them into the basket, and cover them with a dish towel to keep them warm.

Plate the tlacoyos and scatter over the cheese, avocado, sliced, and salsa, if using.

Note: The masa harina can be any color for this recipe.

Bean Tlacoyos

TOSTADAS DE PUERCO

✻

PORK TOSTADAS

1 lb 2 oz/500 g boneless pork

2–3 large tomatoes

3 cloves garlic, crushed

2 tablespoons olive oil

1 onion, thinly sliced

3 smoked chipotle chiles in adobo, chopped

2 bay leaves

2 sprigs thyme

2 teaspoons dried oregano, crushed

sea salt

1 bag tostadas (14 oz/400 g) or 18 small Corn Tortillas (page 36), fried or dry-roasted until they are crispy

To serve:

1 cup (9 fl oz/250 ml) sour cream

2 cups (4 oz/120 g) finely shredded lettuce

1 cup (5 oz/150 g) crumbled queso fresco or feta cheese

REGION: CENTRAL MEXICO
PREPARATION TIME: 30 MINUTES
COOKING TIME: 2 HOURS
SERVES: 6

Place the pork in a large saucepan and add enough water to cover. Bring it to a boil, then reduce the heat and simmer for 1½ hours, until it is completely cooked. Remove the pork from the water and let it cool. Shred it with 2 forks and set it aside. Reserve the cooking liquid.

Preheat the oven to 400°F (200°C/Gas Mark 6). Put the tomatoes and 1 clove garlic into a roasting pan and roast for 30 minutes. Remove the pan from the oven, transfer the tomatoes and garlic to a food processor or blender, and process.

Heat the oil in a medium saucepan. Add the onion and 2 crushed cloves garlic and cook over low heat, stirring occasionally, for about 8 minutes until lightly browned. Add the tomato mixture, chiles, bay leaves, thyme, and oregano, season with salt, and simmer, stirring occasionally, for about 10 minutes, until thickened.

Add the shredded pork and simmer for an additional 10 minutes. The mixture should be thick but if it is sticking to the bottom of the pan, add some of the cooking liquid. Taste and adjust the seasoning, if necessary, and remove the pan from the heat.

Put the tostadas on a serving plate and spread sour cream over them. Add 2–3 tablespoons of the pork mixture. Garnish with the lettuce and a sprinkle of cheese and serve immediately.

TORTA DE JAMÓN Y QUESO

✳

HAM AND CHEESE SANDWICH

6 bolillos or crusty white rolls
1 cup (7 oz/200 g) Refried
  Beans (page 532)
1 cup (9 fl oz/250 ml) sour
  cream or mayonnaise
1 lb 2 oz/500 g ham, sliced
2 tomatoes, sliced
1 small onion, sliced
1 avocado, peeled, pitted, and
  sliced
6–12 pickled jalapeños, sliced
6 lettuce leaves
7 oz/200 g fresh farm cheese or
  feta cheese, sliced thinly
sea salt

REGION: ALL REGIONS
PREPARATION TIME: 15 MINUTES
SERVES: 6

Cut the rolls in half horizontally and remove some of the crumb. Spread the bottom halves of the bread with beans and the top halves with sour cream. Divide the ham, tomatoes, onion, and avocado among the bottom halves of the bread and season with salt to taste. Add the pickled jalapeños, lettuce, and cheese and cover with the other halves of the bread. Press down lightly. Cut in half diagonally. Serve immediately.

"Drowned" Sandwiches

TORTAS AHOGADAS

✺

"DROWNED" SANDWICHES

2 cups (16 fl oz/475 ml)
  Chicken Stock (page 184)
6 tomatoes, peeled
¼ cup (2 fl oz/60 ml) medium-
  hot chili sauce
6 bolillos or crusty white rolls
1 cup (7 oz/200 g) Refried
  Beans (page 532)
1 cup (7 oz/200 g) Carnitas
  (page 80), coarsely chopped
2 onions, finely chopped, to
  serve (optional)

REGION: JALISCO
PREPARATION TIME: 15 MINUTES
SERVES: 6

Combine the chicken stock and tomatoes in saucepan, bring to a boil, and simmer for 15 minutes. Put the mixture into a food processor or blender and pulse until combined and chunky. Return to the saucepan, add the chili sauce, and stir. Set aside.

Cut the bread in half and scoop out the insides. Spread the beans over one half of each roll, then add the pork. Close the sandwich, dip the entire sandwich in the sauce, and serve sprinkled with chopped onion, if using.

TORTA PIERNA

✺

ROASTED PORK SANDWICH

6 bolillos or crusty white rolls
1 cup (7 oz/200 g) Refried
  Beans (page 532)
½ cup (4 fl oz/120 ml) sour
  cream
1 lb 5 oz/600 g roasted pork
  leg, thinly sliced
1 large tomato, thinly sliced
½ small onion, thinly sliced
1 avocado, peeled, pitted, and
  sliced
6–12 pickled jalapeños, sliced
7 oz/200 g fresh farm or feta
  cheese, sliced
6 lettuce leaves
sea salt

REGION: GUANAJUATO, HIDALGO, QUERÉTARO
PREPARATION TIME: 20 MINUTES
SERVES: 6

Slice the bread in half horizontally and scoop out the insides. Spread the bottom halves with the beans and the other halves with the sour cream. Divide the pork slices, tomato, onion, and avocado among the bottom halves and season with salt to taste. Add the chiles, cheese, and lettuce and cover with the other halves of the bread. Flatten slightly, cut in half diagonally, and serve on a plate.

Pulled Pork Sandwiches

TORTAS DE COCHINITA PIBIL

PULLED PORK SANDWICHES

6–12 bolillos or crusty white
  bread rolls
1 quantity Slow-Cooked Pork
  (page 403)
1 quantity Red Onion
  Escabeche (page 478)
1½ cups (12 oz/350 g) Refried
  Beans (page 532)

REGION: YUCATÁN
PREPARATION TIME: 30 MINUTES, PLUS
OVERNIGHT MARINATING
COOKING TIME: 3 HOURS
SERVES: 6

Slice open the bolillos and pull out some of the
crumb. Top with the slow-cooked pork and add
some of the red onion escabeche. Serve immediately.

Note: This dish is traditionally served for breakfast.

TOSTADAS DE ATÚN

TUNA TOSTADAS

1 red bell pepper
½ cup (4 fl oz/120 ml)
  mayonnaise
2 tablespoons smoked chipotle
  chiles in adobo
1 (14-oz/400-g) can tuna,
  drained
3½ oz/100 g small shrimp
  (prawns)
3 scallions (spring onions),
  finely chopped, including the
  green parts
¼ cup (1 oz/25 g) pitted black
  olives, sliced
1 teaspoon dried oregano,
  crushed

To serve:
½ bag (7 oz/200 g) tostadas
½ romaine (Cos) lettuce
  washed and cut into fine
  strips

REGION: FEDERAL DISTRICT, MEXICO STATE
PREPARATION TIME: 10 MINUTES
SERVES: 4

Preheat the oven to 350°F (180°C/Gas Mark 4).
Put the bell pepper into a roasting pan and roast,
turning occasionally, for 15 minutes or until the
skin is beginning to char. Remove the pan from the
oven, transfer the bell pepper to a plastic bag and
tie the top.
  Combine the mayonnaise, chiles, and the juice
from the chipotles in a small bowl.
  When the bell pepper is cool enough to handle,
remove it from the bag and rub off the skin with
your fingers, then halve, seed, and chop. Flake
the tuna.
  Combine the tuna, shrimp (prawns), scallions
(spring onions), bell pepper, olives, and oregano in
another bowl.
  Divide the tostadas among 4 serving plates, add
2–3 tablespoons of the tuna mixture to each, top
with the mayonnaise, and garnish with the lettuce.
Serve immediately.

TOSTADAS DE JAIBA

✺

CRAB TOSTADAS

4 tomatoes
3 cloves garlic
1 white onion
2 bay leaves
pinch of dried oregano
3 peppercorns
4 tablespoons corn oil
3½ tablespoons capers, rinsed
  and chopped
1 cup (3½ oz/100 g) green
  olives, chopped
2 tablespoons chopped cilantro
  (coriander)
1 lb 10 oz/750 g crabmeat
sea salt
1 bag tostadas (14 oz/400 g) or
  20–24 small Corn Tortillas
  (page 36), fried or dry-roasted
  until they are crispy

For the sauce:
1¼ cup (10½ oz/300 g)
  mayonnaise
4–6 smoked chipotle chiles in
  adobo

To garnish:
lettuce, finely chopped
ripe avocado, peeled, pitted,
  and diced
Red Onion Escabeche
  (page 478), to garnish

REGION: GULF
PREPARATION TIME: 20 MINUTES
COOKING TIME: 15 MINUTES
SERVES: 10–12

Put the tomatoes, garlic, onion, bay leaves, oregano, and peppercorns in a food processor or blender and process until it is smooth and strain into a bowl. Heat the oil in a saucepan over medium heat. Add the tomato mixture and cook for 10 minutes over low-medium heat. Add the capers, olives, cilantro (coriander), and crabmeat, mix well, then season with salt to taste. Remove from the heat and set aside.

For the sauce, put the mayonnaise and chipotle chiles in a food processor or blender and process until smooth. Put in a serving bowl and set aside.

Spread the sauce over the tostada shells and put the crab mixture on top. Garnish with some lettuce, avocado, and red onion escabeche. Serve immediately.

Note: Tostadas should be served immediately, otherwise they turn soggy.

Crab Tostadas

TOSTADAS DE TINGA DE POLLO

✵

CHICKEN TINGA TOSTADAS

½ onion

2 cloves

1 (3-lb/1.4-kg) whole chicken

2 cloves garlic

1 bay leaf

1 sprig thyme

1 sprig marjoram

1 teaspoon sea salt

For the tinga sauce:

3 large tomatoes

2 dried chipotles chiles, soaked and drained

4 tablespoons olive oil

3 tablespoons diced chorizo, fried

1 onion, sliced horizontally

3 cloves garlic, finely chopped

2 smoked chipotles chiles in adobo, sliced

3 tablespoons piloncillo or packed brown sugar

2 bay leaves

2 thyme sprigs

1 teaspoon dried oregano, crushed

sea salt

1 (14 oz/400 g) bag tostadas or 20–24 Corn Tortillas (page 36), fried or dry-roasted

To serve:

sour cream

¼ romaine (Cos), shredded (optional)

1 cup (4 oz/120 g) grated queso fresco or feta cheese

REGION: PUEBLA
PREPARATION TIME: 1 HOUR, PLUS 15 MINUTES SOAKING
COOKING TIME: 2–2½ HOURS
SERVES: 8

Pour 6¼ cups (2½ pints/1.5 liters) water into a saucepan. Stud the onion half with the cloves. Add the chicken, onion, garlic, bay leaf, thyme, marjoram, and salt to the pan. Bring to a boil, reduce the heat and simmer for 1–1½ hours or until the chicken is cooked.

Remove the pan from the heat and lift out the chicken. Reserve the cooking liquid. Let cool, then take the meat off the bones. Discard the skin and the bones and shred the meat finely.

Meanwhile, make the tinga sauce. Preheat the oven to 400°F (200°C/Gas Mark 6). Put the chiles and enough hot water to cover them and soak for 15 minutes. Put the tomatoes into a roasting pan and roast for 30 minutes. Remove the pan from the oven. Put the tomatoes and soaked chipotle chiles into a food processor or blender and process to a smooth consistency, then strain the mixture into a bowl and set aside, discarding the skin and seeds.

Heat the olive oil in a medium saucepan. Add the chorizo and cook over low heat for 5 minutes. Add the onion and continue to cook for an additional 8 minutes, until lightly browned. Add the garlic, tomato and chipotle mixture, sliced chipotles with their liquid, the bay leaves, thyme, and oregano. Season with salt and cook, stirring occasionally, until the sauce has thickened. Add the shredded chicken, 1 cup (9 fl oz/250 ml) of the reserved cooking liquid and the sugar and cook for an additional 10 minutes, until the sugar has completely dissolved and the chicken has warmed through.

Divide the tostadas among serving plates and spread them with sour cream. Add 2–3 tablespoons of the chicken mixture to each, garnish with the lettuce, if using, and cheese. Serve immediately.

Chicken Tinga Tostadas

Tomato and Pumpkin Seed Dip

CHORIZO CON QUESO Y TEQUILA

CHEESE WITH CHORIZO AND TEQUILA

1 lb 10 oz/750 g good-quality
   chorizo, crumbled
2 white onions, finely chopped
7 poblano chiles, dry-roasted
   and sliced
½ cup (4 fl oz/120 ml) tequila
3 cups (14 oz/400 g) Oaxaca,
   gouda, or cheddar cheese,
   shredded
Corn Tortillas (page 36),
   to serve

REGION: CENTRAL MEXICO
PREPARATION TIME: 10 MINUTES
COOKING TIME: 20 MINUTES
SERVES: 6

Put the chorizo into a large frying pan or skillet and cook over medium heat for 5 minutes, or until the oil from the chorizo is released. Add the onions and chiles and stir until everything is well combined. Add the tequila, increase the heat, and boil for 8–10 minutes until all the alcohol has evaporated. Put the shredded cheese over the top of the chorizo mixture in a single layer and cook for 1–2 minutes, until it is melted. Serve immediately with hot tortillas.

SIKIL PAK

TOMATO AND PUMPKIN SEED DIP

3 ripe tomatoes
1 habanero chile
1 white onion, halved
¾ cup (5 oz/150 g) pumpkin
   seeds, hulled and ground
⅔ cup (1 oz/25 g) finely
   chopped cilantro (coriander)
4 tablespoons sour orange juice
sea salt
tortilla chips, to serve

REGION: YUCATÁN
PREPARATION TIME: 10 MINUTES
COOKING TIME: 15 MINUTES
SERVES: 6

Preheat the oven to 350°F (180°C/Gas Mark 4). Put the tomatoes, chile, and onion into a roasting pan and roast for 15 minutes. Meanwhile, grind the pumpkin seeds in a blender or spice grinder. Remove the pan from the oven.

Transfer the roasted ingredients into a food processor or blender, add the cilantro (coriander) and orange juice, and process until you get a smooth consistency. Transfer the mixture to a bowl, stir in the ground seeds, season to taste with salt, and mix well. Serve with tortilla chips on the side.

EMPANADAS DE REQUESON
✵
EMPANADAS WITH RICOTTA

REGION: CENTRAL MEXICO AND GULF
PREPARATION TIME: 25 MINUTES
COOKING TIME: 25 MINUTES
SERVES: 6

For the dough:
4⅓ cups (1 lb 2 oz/500 g) masa
  harina
4 tablespoons whole-wheat
  (wholemeal) flour
1 tablespoon butter, softened
½ teaspoon sea salt

For the filling
2¼ cups (1 lb 2 oz/500 g) ricotta
  cheese
3 serrano chiles, finely
  chopped
1 sprig epazote, chopped
¼ white onion, diced
corn oil, for deep-frying

To make the dough, put the masa harina, flour, butter, and salt in a large bowl, gradually add 2½ cups (18 fl oz/550 ml) water and mix until you have a soft and manageable dough. Knead, then cover with plastic wrap (clingfilm) and set aside at room temperature.

For the filling, put the ricotta, chiles, epazote, and onion into a bowl and mix well.

With clean hands, divide the dough into 16 small portions, then roll each portion into a ball between the palms of your hands and set aside, covered loosely in plastic wrap (clingfilm). Continue until you have used up all the dough.

Using a tortilla press or a rolling pin, flatten a dough ball until it is ¼ inch (5 mm) thick, then place on a piece of baking parchment. Put 1 tablespoon of the filling in the center, then fold one side of the dough over, enclosing the filling to make a half-moon shape and press down with your fingers to seal the edges. Do not overfill.

Heat the oil for deep-frying in a deep-fryer to 350°F (180°C), or until a cube of day-old bread browns in 30 seconds. Deep-fry the empanadas, a few at a time, for 8 minutes or until golden brown, then remove with a slotted spoon and drain on paper towels. Serve immediately.

ENJOCADAS

✳

TORTILLA IN CREAM AND GREEN SAUCE

For the green sauce:
15 tomatillos
2 serrano chiles
1 clove garlic
½ onion, chopped
1½ tablespoons corn oil
sea salt

For the filling:
3½ oz/100 g chorizo
5 tablespoons vegetable oil
18 small Corn Tortillas
  (page 36)
2 cups (16 fl oz/475 ml) sour
  cream
2 cups (12 oz/350 g) cooked
  chicken, shredded

REGION: ALL REGIONS
PREPARATION TIME: 30 MINUTES
COOKING TIME: 35–45 MINUTES
SERVES: 6

Preheat oven to 350°F (180°C/Gas Mark 4).

To make the green sauce, put the tomatillos and chiles into a saucepan, pour in just enough water to cover, and bring to a boil. Reduce the heat and simmer for 10 minutes. Remove from the heat and let cool slightly, then transfer to a food processor or blender with a slotted spoon. Add the garlic and onion and process until smooth.

Heat the oil in a saucepan, add the tomatillo mixture, and cook over high heat, stirring occasionally, for 3–4 minutes, until reduced. Season with salt and set aside to cool.

To make the filling, heat a frying pan or skillet over medium heat. Crumble in the chorizo and cook, stirring frequently, for 3–4 minutes, until fat is released. Remove from the heat, and set aside to cool.

Heat the oil in another pan. Dip the tortillas into the oil, one at a time, for less than 10 seconds, then remove and drain on paper towels. Do not let the tortillas brown.

Pour the sour cream into a saucepan and bring just to a boil. Reduce the heat immediately and simmer for 5 minutes, until reduced. Dip each tortilla into the cream to coat lightly.

Fill and roll half the tortillas with shredded chicken and the other half with the chorizo mixture. Put half of them into an ovenproof dish in a single layer, alternating the fillings. Cover with half the green sauce and half the remaining sour cream. Make another layer of rolled tortillas in the same way and cover with the remaining sauce and sour cream. Bake for 15–20 minutes. Serve immediately.

MOLLETES

✲

CHEESE AND BEANS ON TOAST

2 tablespoons corn oil
2 onions, chopped
2 cups (10 oz/275 g) cooked
  kidney or black beans,
  drained and mashed
4 tablespoons olive oil, plus
  extra for brushing
4 ciabatta rolls or 4 small
  baguettes, halved lengthwise
1 cup (4 oz/120 g) crumbled or
  grated oaxaca, chihuahua, or
  mild cheddar cheese
2 cups (16 fl oz/475 ml) Raw
  Tomato Salsa (page 499)
sea salt

REGION: ALL REGIONS
PREPARATION TIME: 20 MINUTES
COOKING TIME: 30 MINUTES
SERVES: 4

Heat the oil in a frying pan or skillet. Add the onion and cook over medium-low heat, stirring occasionally, for 15 minutes or until caramelized.

Add the beans to the skillet and cook, stirring and mashing, gradually adding the olive oil until it becomes a thick puree. Add some water, if necessary. Season with salt. Remove from the heat and keep warm.

Preheat the oven to 400°F (200°C/Gas Mark 6).

Put the halved rolls or baguettes on a baking sheet, cut sides uppermost. Remove some of the crumb, brush the insides with olive oil and heat in the oven until lightly toasted. Remove from the oven, spread the bean mixture over each roll and sprinkle with the cheese. Return to the oven for 5 minutes until the cheese has melted. Serve immediately with the salsa.

CHARALES TOSTADOS A LA MEXICANA

✲

TOASTED CHARALES

2 tablespoons corn oil
7 oz/200 g dried charales
juice of 1 lemon

To serve:
Green Salsa with Avocado
  (page 512)
Corn Tortillas (page 36)

REGION: ALL REGIONS
PREPARATION TIME: 5 MINUTES
COOKING TIME: 5 MINUTES
SERVES: 6

Rinse the charales quickly to remove the excess salt and dry well. Heat the oil in a saucepan over medium heat. Add the charales and cook for 5 minutes, stirring constantly, until light brown. Remove from the heat and stir in the lemon juice. Serve with the salsa and warm tortillas.

Cheese and Beans on Toast

ALITAS EXTRA PICANTES

✺

EXTRA-SPICY WINGS

1 tablespoon ground black
  pepper
½ teaspoon garlic powder
2 cloves garlic, crushed
4 egg yolks
½ cup (4 fl oz/120 ml) hot chili
  sauce
¼ cup (2 fl oz/60 ml) Tabasco
  sauce
1 teaspoon apple cider vinegar
1 cup (4 oz/120 g) all-purpose
  (plain) flour
36 chicken wings
corn oil, for deep-frying
sea salt

For the cheese sauce:
½ cup (4 fl oz/120 ml) heavy
  (double) cream
7 oz/200 g blue cheese,
  crumbled
1 tablespoon apple cider vinegar
black pepper

REGION: ALL REGIONS
PREPARATION TIME: 30 MINUTES
COOKING TIME: 1 HOUR
SERVES: 6

For the chicken wings, mix the pepper, garlic powder, crushed garlic, and salt together in a large bowl. Add half the egg yolks, the chile and Tabasco sauces, and vinegar and mix well to a thick consistency. If not, add the remaining egg yolks.

Spread the flour out on a large plate. Put the chicken wing pieces into the bowl and coat with the mixture, then add them to the flour and toss until coated all over.

Heat the oil for deep-frying in a deep fryer to 375°F (180°C), or until a cube of day-old bread browns in 30 seconds. Carefully lower the chicken pieces, a few at a time, into the hot oil, and deep-fry for 8 minutes, or until cooked through and golden brown. Remove and drain on paper towels. Continue with the remaining chicken wings.

Meanwhile, for the cheese sauce, mix the cream, blue cheese, and vinegar together in a bowl until combined. Season with pepper. Serve the wings with the cheese sauce.

ELOTES

✺

CORN ON THE COB

6 corn on the cobs
sea salt

To serve:
1 cup (5 oz/150 g) queso fresco
  or feta cheese, finely grated
3 limes, halved
1 cup (8 oz/225 g) mayonnaise
chili powder

REGIONS: FEDERAL DISTRICT, MEXICO STATE,
MORELOS, PUEBLA
PREPARATION TIME: 10 MINUTES
COOKING TIME: 10–30 MINUTES
SERVES: 6

Put the corn on the cobs into a saucepan, add enough water to cover and a pinch of salt to taste, and bring to a boil. Cook for about 25 minutes, until tender. If you are using yellow corn, only cook for 5 minutes. Drain and pierce the cobs in the fat end with a wooden skewer so that you can hold them.

Spread the cheese out on a plate. Rub a lime half over each cob and use a spatula to spread them with mayonnaise. Roll them in grated cheese and season with salt and chili powder.

ENFRIJOLADAS DE POLLO

✳

CHICKEN ENFRIJOLADAS

1 clove garlic
½ onion
1 pasilla or ancho chile,
  membranes and seeds
  removed
2 morita or other smoked
  chile, membranes and seeds
  removed
2 avocado leaves (optional)
1½ cups (7 oz/200 g) cooked
  black beans, drained, with
  cooking liquid reserved
⅔ cup (5 fl oz/150 ml) corn oil
  or lard
18 day-old Corn Tortillas
  (page 36)
1½ lb/700 g chicken breasts,
  cooked and shredded

To garnish:
½ cup (4 fl oz/120 ml) sour
  cream
10½ oz/300 g chorizo, sliced

REGION: ALL REGIONS
PREPARATION TIME: 30 MINUTES
COOKING TIME: 30 MINUTES
SERVES: 6

Preheat the oven to 350°F (180°C/Gas Mark 4).
Put the garlic, onion, chiles, and avocado leaves, if
using, into a roasting pan and roast for 15 minutes
Remove the leaves, if using, after 3 minutes. Remove
the pan from the oven.

Put the beans, garlic, onion, chiles, avocado
leaves, if using, a pinch of salt, and the reserved
cooking liquid into a food processor or blender
and process until thoroughly combined. You may
need a little of the bean cooking liquid to do this.
Strain into a bowl.

Heat 2 tablespoons of the oil in a shallow
saucepan. Add the bean mixture and cook over
low heat, stirring occasionally, for 10 minutes, until
it thickens.

Heat the rest of the oil in a large frying pan or
skillet. One at a time, add the tortillas and cook
briefly on both sides, for no more than 10 seconds,
making sure they do not turn brown and stiff.

Dip the cooked tortillas immediately into the
warm bean sauce to coat. Place each one on a plate,
put some shredded chicken on one half, and fold it
up so it looks like a half moon.

Put 3 enfrijoladas on each plate. Pour the extra
sauce over the enfrijoladas. Drizzle sour cream over
them and top with chorizo slices.

Note: They can also be garnished with sliced red
onion and cotija cheese.

Chicken Enfrijoladas

SALADS AND STARTERS

RED CORN SALAD

2 tablespoons extra virgin
  olive oil
4 cups (1 lb 5 oz/600 g) red
  corn kernels
1½ teaspoons sugar (optional)
1½ teaspoons lemon juice
2 tablespoons chopped cilantro
  (coriander)
4 tablespoons crumbled cotija
  or feta cheese
sea salt and pepper

REGION: MICHOACÁN
PREPARATION TIME: 10 MINUTES
COOKING TIME: 20 MINUTES
SERVES: 6

Heat the olive oil in a large saucepan. Add the corn kernels, sprinkle with the sugar, if using, and cook over medium heat, stirring frequently, for 8–10 minutes or until the corn is lightly golden brown. Stir in the lemon juice, season with salt and pepper, and cook for 2–3 minutes. Stir in the cilantro (coriander) and cook for an additional 2 minutes, then remove the pan from the heat.

Gently stir in the cheese. Taste and adjust the seasoning, if necessary, and serve immediately.

Note: This salad can be made with any type of fresh corn or a combination.

BEAN AND MUSHROOM SALAD

3⅔ cups (9 oz/250 g)
  mushrooms
1 (7-oz/200-g) jar roasted red
  bell peppers, drained and
  chopped
2 cups (11 oz/300 g) cooked
  kidney beans
2 cups (11 oz/300 g) cooked
  purple ayocote beans
2 cups (11 oz/300 g) cooked
  black beans
2 celery stalks
1 cup (80 g/3 oz) grated
  Parmesan cheese
¾ cup (6 fl oz/175 ml) Shallot
  Vinaigrette (page 513)
½ cup (1 oz/25 g) finely
  chopped parsley

REGION: FEDERAL DISTRICT
PREPARATION TIME: 5 MINUTES
SERVES: 6

Combine the mushrooms, roasted bell peppers, all the beans, the celery, and half the cheese in a large bowl. Add the vinaigrette and mix well, then sprinkle with the parsley, garnish with the remaining cheese, and serve.

Note: Diced chicken or Serrano ham may also be added to this salad.

ENSALADA DE AMARANTO

AMARANTH SALAD

⅔ cup (¼ pint/150 ml) sherry
vinegar
½ teaspoon sea salt
2 tablespoons agave syrup
6 tablespoons extra virgin
olive oil
½ cucumber, seeded and diced
3 plum tomatoes, skinned,
seeded, and diced
⅔ cup (1 oz/25 g) finely
chopped cilantro (coriander)
2 teaspoons finely diced green
chiles
4 cups (1 lb/450 g) amaranth
pepper

REGION: PUEBLA
PREPARATION TIME: 10 MINUTES
SERVES: 6

Combine the vinegar, salt, agave syrup, olive oil,
and a pinch of pepper in a bowl. Add the cucumber,
tomatoes, cilantro (coriander), and chile and mix
well. Finally, add the amaranth, mix, check the
seasoning, and serve immediately.

ENSALADA DE TOMATE, QUESO Y CILANTRO

TOMATO, CHEESE, AND CILANTRO SALAD

1 small white onion, thinly
sliced
½ cup (4 fl oz/120 ml) sherry
vinegar
½ cup (4 fl oz/120 ml) extra
virgin olive oil
12 celery stalks, chopped
8 tomatoes, cut into wedges
⅔ cup (1 oz/25 g) finely
chopped cilantro (coriander)
1–1½ cups (4–6 oz/120–175 g)
crumbled feta cheese
sea salt and pepper

REGION: FEDERAL DISTRICT
PREPARATION TIME: 10 MINUTES, PLUS
15–20 MINUTES STANDING
SERVES: 6

Put the onion in a bowl, sprinkle with salt, add the
vinegar, and let stand for 15–20 minutes. Season
with pepper and stir in the oil.

Combine all the remaining ingredients in a bowl,
pour the dressing over them, mix well, and serve
immediately.

ENSALADA DE BETABELES ROSTIZADOS Y PEPITA

ROAST BEET AND PUMPKIN SEED SALAD

10 beets (beetroots)
⅔ cup (¼ pint/150 ml) agave
  syrup
6 tablespoons sherry or apple
  cider vinegar
3 cloves garlic, crushed
6 tablespoons extra virgin
  olive oil
1 cup (4 oz/120 g) pumpkin
  seeds, toasted
½ cup (1 oz/25 g) chopped
  parsley
2 cups green beans, cooked
3½ cups (3½ oz/100 g) spinach
sea salt and pepper

REGION: FEDERAL DISTRICT
PREPARATION TIME: 30 MINUTES
COOKING TIME: 60–90 MINUTES
SERVES: 6

Preheat the oven to 400°F (200°C/Gas Mark 6).

Wrap each beet (beetroot) separately in aluminum foil. Bake for 60–90 minutes, or until soft when pricked with the point of a sharp knife.

Remove the beets from the oven and let cool. When cooked, their skins will slip off, or use a paring knife to remove. Cut the beets into wedges.

Combine the agave syrup, vinegar, garlic, and oil in a bowl and season with salt and pepper to taste. Stir in the beets, pumpkin seeds, parsley, green beans, and greens. Taste and adjust the seasoning.

Divide the salad among 6 individual plates, garnish with sesame seeds, and serve immediately.

ENSALADA DE BERROS

WATERCRESS SALAD

7 oz/200 g bacon, diced
2¼ lb/1 kg watercress
2 avocados, halved, pitted,
  peeled, and sliced
4½ cups (11 oz/300g) sliced
  white mushrooms
2 large tomatoes, cut into
  wedges

For the dressing:
4 tablespoons red wine vinegar
1 teaspoon sea salt
½ teaspoon pepper
1 tablespoon Dijon mustard
¾ cup (6 fl oz/175 ml) extra
  virgin olive oil

REGION: FEDERAL DISTRICT
PREPARATION TIME: 25 MINUTES
COOKING TIME: 15 MINUTES
SERVES: 6

To make the dressing, whisk together the vinegar, salt, and pepper in a bowl until the salt has dissolved. Whisk in the mustard and gradually whisk in the olive oil until fully combined. Taste and adjust the seasoning, if necessary. Set aside.

Add the bacon to a frying pan or skillet over high heat and cook until it releases its fat. Reduce the heat to low and cook the bacon, stirring occasionally, for 5–7 minutes, until browned. Remove the pan from the heat and transfer the bacon to paper towels to drain.

Divide the watercress among 6 dishes and add the avocados, mushrooms, and tomatoes. Sprinkle with the bacon and serve immediately with the dressing on the side.

Roasted Beet Salad

Mexican Salad

ENSALADA MEXICANA

✳

MEXICAN SALAD

4 cups (8 oz/225 g) spinach
   leaves or any salad greens
10½ oz/300 g cherry tomatoes,
   halved
2 tablespoons chili flakes
Corn Tortilla Strips (page 36)
3 tablespoons sliced almonds,
   toasted

For the dressing:
juice of 1 lemon
¾ cup (6 fl oz/180 ml) extra-
   virgin olive oil
½ teaspoon salt
ground pepper

REGION: FEDERAL DISTRICT
PREPARATION TIME: 15 MINUTES
SERVES: 6

For the dressing, whisk the lemon juice with the salt and pepper, add the olive oil, and adjust seasoning if needed. Set aside.

Combine the spinach, cherry tomatoes, chili flakes, and almonds in a bowl and toss lightly. Pour over the dressing, toss again, and garnish with the tortilla strips.

ENSALADA DE GARBANZOS

✳

CHICKPEA SALAD

5 oz (150 g) creamy white
   cheese, diced
1 poblano chile, dry-roasted
   and sliced
1 large red bell pepper, seeded
   and cut into thin strips
2 (14–15-oz/400–425-g) cans
   chickpeas
juice of 5 lemons
2 tablespoons finely chopped
   cilantro (coriander)
1 small onion, finely chopped
3 tablespoons extra virgin
   olive oil
1 lettuce, leaves separated
sea salt and pepper

REGION: FEDERAL DISTRICT
PREPARATION TIME: 20 MINUTES, PLUS
2 HOURS STANDING
SERVES: 6

Put the cheese, chile, bell pepper, and chickpeas into a salad bowl.

Whisk together the lemon juice, cilantro (coriander), onion, and olive oil in a bowl. Season with salt and pepper to taste and mix again. Let stand for 2 hours.

Stir the dressing and pour it into the salad bowl. Lay the lettuce leaves on a serving platter, add the chickpea salad, and serve.

BETABELES

BEET SALAD

14 beets (beetroots)
¾ cup (5 oz/150 g) sugar
1 tablespoon cornstarch
 (cornflour)
juice of 3 oranges
juice of 1½ lemons
2 teaspoons grated orange zest
sea salt and pepper

REGION: FEDERAL DISTRICT
PREPARATION TIME: 15 MINUTES
COOKING TIME: 45 MINUTES
SERVES: 6

Put the beets (beetroots) into a saucepan, add enough water to cover, and bring to a boil. Reduce the heat and simmer for 30 minutes or until skin begins to blister. Remove the pan from the heat, drain, and once cooled, peel off the skin.

Combine the sugar, cornstarch (cornflour), orange and lemon juice, and orange zest in a saucepan and mix until the cornstarch and sugar are dissolved. Bring to a boil over medium heat, stirring constantly, and boil for 4 minutes.

Slice the beets, add them to the pan with the sugar, season with salt and pepper to taste, and heat through, stirring gently, until the beets are hot. Serve immediately.

ENSALADA DE CHAYOTE EN ESCABECHE

PICKLED CHAYOTE SALAD

5 chayotes
½ teaspoon sea salt
½ teaspoon pepper
2 tablespoons red wine vinegar
1 teaspoon dried oregano
⅔ cup (¼ pint/150 ml) extra
 virgin olive oil
½ cup (4 oz/120 g) red onion,
 thinly sliced

REGION: FEDERAL DISTRICT, TLAXCALA
PREPARATION TIME: 20 MINUTES, PLUS
10 MINUTES STANDING/CHILLING
COOKING TIME: 40 MINUTES
SERVES: 6

Put the chayotes into a saucepan, add enough water to cover, and bring to a boil. Reduce the heat and simmer for 20–35 minutes until tender.

Remove the pan from the heat and drain. Peel the chayotes and quarter them lengthwise, discarding the pits. Put them into a bowl.

In a small bowl, combine the vinegar, salt, and pepper and mix well. Add the oregano, then whisk in the oil.

Pour the dressing over the chayotes and toss lightly to coat. Let stand in the refrigerator for at least 10 minutes.

Toss the salad again and transfer to a serving platter. Garnish with the onion and serve.

ENSALADA DE MANGO

✷

MANGO SALAD

6 ripe mangoes, peeled
1 (5-oz/150-g) bag mixed salad
　greens
2 avocados, peeled, pitted,
　and sliced
½ cup (2½ oz/65 g) thinly
　sliced jicama
2 red onions, thinly sliced

For the dressing:
⅔ cup (¼ pint/150 ml) apple
　cider vinegar
1 clove garlic, finely chopped
½ small onion, finely chopped
½ cup (1 oz/25 g) chopped
　parsley
1¼ cups (2 oz/50 g) chopped
　cilantro (coriander)
1 teaspoon sugar
1 teaspoon sea salt
½ teaspoon pepper
1 cup (9 fl oz/250 ml) extra
　virgin olive oil
2 arbol or serrano chiles,
　seeded and chopped
orange juice (optional)

REGION: VERACRUZ
PREPARATION TIME: 25 MINUTES
SERVES: 6

Put all the dressing ingredients into a food processor or blender and process until smooth. Add orange juice to thin out if necessary.

　Cut each mango into 2 slices, cutting down on each side of the pit. Brush each slice with about 1½ teaspoons of dressing and put them into a dish. Store in the refrigerator until required.

　Slice the mangoes. Divide the salad greens among 6 individual plates and put 2 slices of mango on top or beside them. Garnish with sliced avocado, jicama, and onion. Serve immediately with the dressing on the side.

ENSALADA DE HABAS DESCALZAS

✷

FAVA BEAN SALAD

1 teaspoon apple cider vinegar
pinch of sea salt
1 tablespoon extra virgin
　olive oil
1 teaspoon oregano
3 cups (1 lb/450 g) fava (broad)
　beans, cooked

REGION: FEDERAL DISTRICT
PREPARATION TIME: 10 MINUTES, PLUS
1 HOUR MARINATING
SERVES: 6

Whisk together the vinegar and salt in a bowl, then gradually whisk in the oil and add the oregano, crushing it between the palms of your hands.

　Add the beans and stir well. Taste and adjust the seasoning, if necessary.

　The salad can be served immediately, or let it marinate for 1 hour in the refrigerator. It is best served at room temperature or chilled.

Cactus Paddle Salad

ENSALADA DE NOPALES

※

CACTUS PADDLE SALAD

1⅓ tablespoon sea salt
pinch of baking soda
  (bicarbonate of soda)
1 lb 5 oz/600 g cactus paddles,
  cut into strips
4 tablespoons chopped cilantro
  (coriander)
1 tomato, chopped
1 small red onion, thinly
  sliced, plus extra to serve
4 tablespoons extra virgin
  olive oil
1 teaspoon dried oregano
1 tomato, sliced, to serve
4 oz/120 g Parmesan, grated

REGION: FEDERAL DISTRICT, TLAXCALA
PREPARATION TIME: 45 MINUTES
COOKING TIME: 25 MINUTES
SERVES: 6

Bring some water to a boil in a stockpot over high heat. Add the salt, baking soda (bicarbonate of soda), and cactus paddles and cook for about 20 minutes, until tender but not limp. Remove the pan from the heat, drain well, and refresh in cold water until the slime they produce is lost. Drain again.

In a large bowl, combine the cactus paddles, 1 teaspoon salt, cilantro (coriander), tomatoes, sliced onion, and olive oil. Add the oregano, crushing it between the palms of your hands or with your fingers. Let stand for a few minutes.

Put the salad on a serving platter and top with a layer of sliced of tomato. Garnish with the grated cheese and sliced onion and serve.

ENSALADA DE NOPALITOS PICANTE

※

SPICY CACTUS PADDLE SALAD

1 tablespoon corn oil
2¼ lb/1 kg cactus paddles,
  diced
2 tablespoons finely chopped
  white onion
1 tomato, chopped
⅔ cup (1 oz/25 g) chopped
  cilantro (coriander)
1½ tablespoons lime juice
3 chiles, finely chopped
1 tablespoon extra virgin
  olive oil
3 oz/80 g pork rinds
  (scratchings), crumbled
sea salt

REGION: MICHOACÁN
PREPARATION TIME: 15 MINUTES, PLUS
30 MINUTES STANDING
COOKING TIME: 15 MINUTES
SERVES: 6

Heat the corn oil in a heavy saucepan. Add the cactus paddles, 4 tablespoons water, and a pinch of salt. Cover and cook over medium heat for 5 minutes, until tender but not slimy. Uncover the pan and cook, stirring slowly from the bottom so they don't stick, for about 10 minutes. Remove the pan from the heat and let cool.

Combine the cactus paddles, onion, tomato, cilantro (coriander), lemon juice, chiles, and olive oil in a bowl, season with salt, and let stand for at least 30 minutes.

Just before serving, sprinkle the salad with the pork rinds (scratchings).

ENSALADA
DE SANDÍA
Y JÍCAMA

✺

WATERMELON AND JICAMA SALAD

For the vinaigrette:

4 tablespoons lemon juice

2 tablespoons tequila

2 tablespoons packed brown
  sugar

6 tablespoons extra virgin
  olive oil

sea salt and pepper

For the salad:

2 cups (10 oz/275 g) sliced
  watermelon

2 cups (10 oz/275 g) sliced jicama

10 cups (11 oz/300 g) mixed
  salad greens

1 avocado, peeled, seeded,
  and diced

REGION: JALISCO
PREPARATION TIME: 15 MINUTES
SERVES: 6

Combine the lemon juice, tequila, and sugar in a
bowl, season with salt and pepper, and stir in the
olive oil until thoroughly combined.

   In a large bowl, combine the watermelon, jicama,
and salad greens. Add the avocado and mix gently.
Add the dressing to taste and serve immediately.

ENSALADA
DE VERANO

✺

SUMMER SALAD

4 tablespoons extra virgin
  olive oil

2 smoked chipotle chiles in
  adobo

1 teaspoon packed brown
  sugar

24 tomatillos, seeded and diced

½ red onion, finely chopped

3 tablespoons finely chopped
  cilantro (coriander)

1 cup (4 oz/120 g) grated cotija
  or cheddar cheese

Corn Tortilla Strips (page 36)

sea salt and pepper

REGION: MICHOACÁN, JALISCO, FEDERAL DISTRICT
PREPARATION TIME: 15 MINUTES
SERVES: 6

To make the dressing, put the olive oil, chiles, and
sugar in a food processor or blender, season with salt
and pepper, process until combined, and season to
taste.

   Combine the tomatillos, onion, and cilantro in
a bowl, add the dressing, and toss gently.

   Divide the salad among 6 serving plates, sprinkle
with the cheese and tortillas, and serve immediately.

Watermelon and Jicama Salad

ENSALADA DE TOMATES ORGANICOS

✳

HEIRLOOM TOMATO SALAD

2¼ lb/1 kg heirloom tomatoes
1 clove garlic, finely chopped
30 basil leaves, torn
juice of 2 limes
⅔ cup (¼ pint/150 ml) extra
    virgin olive oil
1 teaspoon packed brown
    sugar
grated zest of 1 lemon
1½ cups (6 oz/175 g) pitted
    Kalamata olives, chopped
1½ cups (6 oz/175 g) pitted large
    green olives, chopped
sea salt and pepper

REGION: ALL REGIONS
PREPARATION TIME: 15 MINUTES
SERVES: 6–8

Cut the tomatoes into bite-size chunks.
    Combine the tomatoes, garlic, basil, lime juice, and olive oil in a medium bowl, add the sugar, season with salt and pepper, and mix well. Stir in the lemon zest and add the tomatoes and olives. Put the salad into a serving bowl and serve immediately.

ENSALADA DE POLLO

✳

CHICKEN SALAD

10 oz/275 g beets (beetroots)
1 lb 10 oz/750 g skinless
    boneless chicken breasts
2 cups (10 oz/275 g) diced
    chayotes, cooked
1½ cups (8 oz/225 g) thinly
    sliced carrots, cooked
sea salt

REGION: ALL REGIONS
PREPARATION TIME: 20 MINUTES
COOKING TIME: 55 MINUTES
SERVES: 6

Put the beets (beetroots) into a saucepan, add enough water to cover, and bring to a boil. Reduce the heat and simmer for 30 minutes or until skin begins to blister. Remove the pan from the heat, drain, and once cooled, peel, skin and dice.
    Put the chicken into a saucepan, add water to cover, add a pinch of salt, and bring to a boil. Reduce the heat and simmer for 15–20 minutes until tender. Remove the pan from the heat, lift out the chicken breasts with a slotted spoon, put them on a cutting (chopping) board, and let cool. Cut the chicken breasts into thin strips.
    Combine the chicken, chayotes, carrots, and beets (beetroots) in a bowl and season with salt to taste. Serve immediately.

WARM SEAFOOD SALAD

1½ tablespoons extra virgin
olive oil
1½ tablespoons chipotle chiles
in adobo, pureed
1 lb 10 oz/750 g cooked squid,
mussels, and shrimp (prawns)
juice and grated zest of
3 lemons
2 cups (11 oz/300 g) soybeans
1½ cucumbers, diced
¾ cup (1½ oz/40 g) mint, cut
into thin strips
6 cups (12 oz/350 g) shredded
lettuce
sea salt and pepper

REGION: BAJA CALIFORNIA
PREPARATION TIME: 10 MINUTES
COOKING TIME: 10 MINUTES
SERVES: 6

Heat the oil in a deep pan. Add the pureed chiles
and the shellfish and cook over medium heat for
2–3 minutes. If the mixture is too thick, add a little
water. Stir in the lemon juice and zest, and season
with salt and pepper. Remove the pan from the
heat. Add the soybeans, cucumbers, and mint
and mix well.

Divide the lettuce among 6 plates and put the
shellfish mixture on top. Serve warm or cold.

LOBSTER SALAD

3 cups (12 oz/350 g) cooked
lobster
1 clove garlic, finely chopped
4 tablespoons jalapeño chile,
seeded and chopped
½ cup (80 g/3 oz) cooked peas
1½ cups (11 oz/300 g) good-
quality mayonnaise
¾ cup (3 oz/80 g) pitted
kalamata olives
3 carrots, chopped or shredded
1 lettuce, leaves separated
1 (4-oz/110-g) can pimientos,
drained and sliced
sea salt and pepper

REGION: BAJA CALIFORNIA
PREPARATION TIME: 15 MINUTES
SERVES: 6

Combine the lobster, garlic, chile, peas, mayonnaise,
olives, and carrots in a bowl and season to taste
with salt and pepper.

Make a bed of lettuce on a serving platter, top
with the lobster salad, and garnish with pimiento
strips. Serve immediately.

Jicama and Orange Salad

CITRUS SALAD

REGION: ALL MEXICO
PREPARATION TIME: 15 MINUTES
SERVES: 6

2 oranges, peeled and cut into
    segments
1 pink grapefruit, peeled and
    cut into segments
6 cups (4¼ oz/120 g) wild
    greens, watercress, or arugula
    (rocket)
2 tablespoons toasted sesame
    seeds
1 green apple, finely sliced

For the dressing:
4 tablespoons lemon juice
⅔ cup (5 fl oz/150 ml) extra
    virgin olive oil
salt and pepper to taste

To make the dressing, combine all the ingredients in a bowl and whisk together. Season to taste.

Arrange the orange and grapefruit segments on serving plates, then add the salad greens and apple slices. Add the dressing and sprinkle with sesame seeds. Serve immediately.

TRICOLOR SALAD

REGION: FEDERAL DISTRICT
PREPARATION TIME: 20 MINUTES
COOKING TIME: 25–30 MINUTES
SERVES: 6

1 teaspoon baking soda
    (bicarbonate of soda)
3 cups (10 oz/275 g) cactus
    paddles, diced
2 small jicamas, peeled and
    diced
2 heirloom tomatoes, peeled,
    seeded, and diced
3–4 tablespoons extra virgin
    olive oil
3 tablespoons sesame seeds
sea salt

Bring a saucepan of water with the baking soda (bicarbonate of soda) and a pinch of salt to a boil. Add the cactus paddles and simmer gently for 20–25 minutes, until they are soft but still have a bite, then drain, and let cool.

To make the dressing, combine the lime juice and a pinch of salt in a bowl and gradually whisk in the oil. Add the toasted sesame seeds, then pour into a food processor or blender and process until thoroughly combined.

Put the cactus paddles, jicamas, and tomatoes into a salad bowl, pour over the dressing, toss lightly, and serve immediately.

AGUACATES RELLENOS DE ALUBIAS Y CAMARONES

✳

AVOCADOS STUFFED WITH BEANS AND SHRIMP

16 shrimp (prawns), peeled and deveined
1 cup (5 oz/150 g) cooked navy (haricot) beans
1 tablespoon finely chopped parsley
5 tablespoons extra virgin olive oil
1 large red bell pepper, dry-roasted, seeded, and cut into thin strips
½ red onion, thinly sliced
¾ cup (1¼ oz/35 g) fresh bread crumbs
2 tablespoons chopped chives or basil
3 large ripe avocados
6 cups (6 oz/175 g) mesclun or other mixed salad greens
sea salt

For the simple vinaigrette:
2 tablespoons Dijon mustard
4 tablespoons apple cider vinegar
½ cup (4 fl oz/120 ml) extra virgin olive oil

REGION: FEDERAL DISTRICT
PREPARATION TIME: 20 MINUTES
COOKING TIME: 5 MINUTES
SERVES: 6

Bring a large saucepan of lightly salted water to a boil over medium-high heat. Add the shrimp (prawns) and cook for 1–3 minutes, or until they are pink and opaque. Drain and rinse the shrimp in a colander under cold running water.

Set aside 8 shrimp for the garnish and chop the remainder. Combine the shrimp, beans, parsley, olive oil, bell pepper, onion, and bread crumbs in a bowl and mix well. Season with salt and add the chives or basil.

To make the vinaigrette, combine all the ingredients together and whisk until emulsified.

Halve, pit, and peel the avocados. Make a bed of salad greens on each of 6 individual plates and top with the avocado halves. Fill the cavities with a generous portion of the salad, garnish with the reserved shrimp, pour a little vinaigrette over the salad, and serve immediately.

QUESO DE CABRA, FLOR DE CALABAZA CHILE POBLANO

GOAT CHEESE CHARLOTTES

4 cambray onions
2 cloves garlic, crushed
2 tablespoons finely chopped
   cilantro (coriander)
1 tablespoon finely chopped
   parsley
2 tablespoons finely chopped
   mint
2 tablespoons finely chopped
   chives, plus extra to garnish
14 oz/400 g goat cheese
3 tablespoons sour cream
16 zucchini (courgette) flowers,
   stamens removed
sea salt and pepper
butter, for greasing
chopped black olives
toasted baguette, to serve

For the sauce:
¾ cup (6 fl oz/175 ml) extra
   virgin olive oil
1 white onion, finely chopped
2 cloves garlic, finely chopped
6 large poblano chiles,
   dry-roasted
1 bouquet garni
1 cup (9 fl oz/250 ml) Chicken
   Stock (page 184)
sea salt and pepper

REGION: FEDERAL DISTRICT
PREPARATION TIME: 25 MINUTES
COOKING TIME: 20 MINUTES
SERVES: 6

Bring a saucepan of salted water to a boil over high heat and add the onions. Boil for 4–5 minutes, then remove them with a slotted spoon and transfer them to a bowl of ice water. When the onions have cooled completely, pat them dry, and chop.

Combine the garlic, onion, cilantro (coriander), parsley, mint, chives, goat cheese, and cream in a bowl, season with salt and pepper and mix well. Cover the bowl with plastic wrap (clingfilm) and chill in the refrigerator.

Steam the zucchini (courgette) flowers over boiling water for 1 minute until they wilt. Remove and use half of the flowers to line 6 greased ramekins. Fill the ramekins with the cheese mixture and cover with the remaining petals.

To make the sauce, heat the olive oil in a saucepan over medium heat. Add the onion and garlic, reduce the heat to medium-low, and sauté for 5 minutes. Add the chiles, bouquet garni, and stock, cover, and simmer for 5 minutes.

Remove the pan from the heat and discard the bouquet garni. Pour the mixture into a food processor or blender and process until smooth, then strain into a bowl. Season to taste with salt and pepper, let cool, and store in the refrigerator.

Turn the charlottes out onto 6 individual plates, drizzle with the sauce, and garnish with the chives and chopped olives. Serve with toasted baguette.

MIXIOTES DE NOPALES Y CAMARONES

✳

CACTUS PADDLE AND SHRIMP PACKAGES

6 maguey leaves, soaked and
  cut into 10-inch (25-cm)
  squares (optional)
1 tablespoon corn oil
3½ oz/100 g chorizo, skinned
  and crumbled
1 bay leaf
2 sprigs thyme
1 large white onion, finely
  chopped
5 oz/150 g raw shrimp
  (prawns), peeled and
  deveined
8 cactus paddles, cooked and
  cut into thin strips
3 smoked chipotle chiles in
  adobo, chopped
sea salt
Roast Tomatillo Salsa (page
  510), to serve (optional)

REGION: CENTRAL MEXICO AND GULF
PREPARATION TIME: 20 MINUTES
COOKING TIME: 40 MINUTES
SERVES: 6

Spread out the leaf squares or cut six 10-inch (25-cm) squares of parchment paper. Set aside.

Heat the oil in a saucepan. Add the chorizo and cook, stirring frequently, for 5–6 minutes. Add the bay leaf, thyme, and onion and sauté, stirring frequently, for an additional 5–6 minutes until the chorizo is browned.

Add the shrimp (prawns) and stir. Then add the cactus paddles and chipotle chiles, and cook for an additional 2–3 minutes. Season to taste with salt and remove the pan from the heat. Remove and discard the bay leaf.

Put 1 tablespoon of the mixture into the center of each wrapper. Fold in the sides of the wrappers to make packages and tie with kitchen string.

Put the packages in the top of a steamer and cook for 20 minutes. Remove the pan from the heat and transfer the packages to a serving platter. Serve immediately with the salsa, if using.

Cactus Paddle and Shrimp Packages

ITACATE DE QUELITES

MEDLEY OF WILD GREENS

4 teaspoons safflower oil
2 white onions, finely chopped
2 cloves garlic, finely chopped
4 tomatoes, peeled, seeded, and
  finely chopped
2¼ lb/1 kg wild greens
3 tablespoons finely chopped
  fresh chiles
6 oz/180 g goat cheese
½ cup (3½ fl oz/100 ml) heavy
  (double) cream
2 hoja santa leaves
6 corn husks, soaked in boiling
  water
sea salt and pepper
Pot Beans (page 533), to serve

REGION: PUEBLA
PREPARATION TIME: 25 MINUTES
COOKING TIME: 35 MINUTES
SERVES: 6

Heat the oil in a saucepan. Add the onions and garlic and cook over low heat, stirring occasionally, for 5 minutes, until translucent. Add the tomatoes and cook for an additional 5 minutes, then add the wild greens and cook for 2 minutes. Season with salt and pepper, remove the pan from the heat, and drain as much as possible.

Combine the chiles, cheese, and cream in a bowl. Divide into 6 elongated portions, wrap in pieces of hoja santa, and put aside.

Drain the corn husks. Spread a layer of the wild greens mixture over the wide part of the husks, put a goat cheese package in the center, and cover with more wild greens. Fold the leaf to close and tie with kitchen string. Repeat with the rest of the leaves and cheese mixture packages.

Put the packages into the top of a steamer and cook over high heat for 20 minutes or until warmed through. Remove from the heat, lift out the packages, and serve with pot beans.

AGUACATES MEXICANOS

MEXICAN AVOCADOS

3 large ripe avocados
1¼ cups (7 oz/200 g) cooked
  peas
1 cooked boneless chicken
  breast, shredded
4 tablespoons chipotle chiles
  in adobo
1 teaspoon extra virgin olive
  oil
1 iceberg lettuce, shredded
1 cup (3½ oz/100 g) grated
  Manchego cheese
sea salt
sliced radishes and parsley,
  to garnish

REGION: ALL REGIONS
PREPARATION TIME: 20 MINUTES
SERVES: 6

Halve, pit, and peel the avocados.

Combine the peas, chicken, chiles, oil, and a pinch of salt in a bowl and mix well. Fill the cavities in the avocado halves with the mixture.

Make a bed of the lettuce on 6 individual plates, then top with the filled avocado halves. Sprinkle the cheese on top, garnish with radishes and parsley sprigs, and serve immediately.

CREPAS DE FLOR DE CALABAZA, CHAPULINES, Y QUESO

❋

GRASSHOPPER, ZUCCHINI FLOWER, AND CHEESE CREPES

3 tablespoons (1½ oz/40 g)
  butter, room temperature,
  plus extra for greasing
4 tablespoons chopped white
  onion
1 clove garlic, chopped
1 lb 10 oz/750 g zucchini
  (courgette) flowers, pistils
  removed
2½ oz/65 g grasshoppers,
  chopped
2 smoked chipotle chiles in
  adobo, finely chopped
2 sprigs epazote, chopped
sea salt and pepper
6 sprigs parsley, to garnish

For the crepes:
1¼ cups (½ pint/300 ml) milk
1½ tablespoons (¾ oz/20 g)
  melted butter, plus extra for
  greasing
3 eggs
1¼ cups (5 oz/150 g) all-purpose
  (plain) flour
sea salt

For the cheese sauce:
1¼ cups (½ pint/300 ml) heavy
  (double) cream
3 oz/80 g cotija or Parmesan

REGION: OAXACA
PREPARATION TIME: 25 MINUTES, PLUS
5 MINUTES STANDING
COOKING TIME: 45 MINUTES
SERVES: 6

To make the crepes, add the the milk, melted butter, and eggs and mix well. Sift in the flour and a pinch of salt and mix well. Let stand for 5 minutes. If necessary, add more milk or cold water until the batter has the consistency of a thin cream.

Grease a heavy frying pan or skillet with butter and heat until very hot. Add a small ladleful of the batter and tilt the pan so that it covers the bottom. Cook over medium heat for a couple of minutes until the underside is lightly browned, then flip over with a spatula and cook the other side. Slide the crepe out of the pan. Repeat, greasing the pan as necessary, until all the batter has been used. Put the cooked crepes in a tortilla container or stack them interleaved with wax (greaseproof) paper on a plate and wrap them in a dish towel to prevent them from drying out.

To make the filling, melt the butter in a saucepan. Add the onion and garlic and cook over low heat, stirring occasionally, for 5 minutes, until translucent. Add the flowers and cook for 5 minutes or until dry, season with salt and pepper, and add the grasshoppers. Remove the pan from the heat.

To make the sauce, pour the cream into a saucepan, add the cheese, and heat gently, stirring constantly. As soon as the cheese has melted and is fully incorporated, remove the pan from the heat. Season to taste with salt and pepper.

Put a crepe on each of 6 plates, add some filling, then place another crepe on top. Continue stacking the crepes and filling until all the ingredients have been used. Pour the sauce over the crepes. Sprinkle with chiles and epazote, garnish with parsley, and serve immediately.

Note: The crepes can be kept warm in the oven for 10–15 minutes before serving. Preheat the oven to 200°F (110°C/Gas Mark ¼).

QUESO CORAZON EN SALSA VERDE

※

CHEESE IN GREEN SALSA

1 lb 4 oz/600 g fresh cheese,
  cut into 1 inch (2.5 cm) slices
16 tomatillos, dry-roasted
1 large clove garlic, dry-roasted
1 white onion, dry-roasted
1–2 dried chipotles chiles,
  dry-roasted

To serve:
Tortilla Strips (page 36)
chives, cut into 1-inch (2.5 cm)
  lengths
fried tomato skin
sea salt

REGION: FEDERAL DISTRICT
PREPARATION TIME: 25 MINUTES
COOKING TIME: 7 MINUTES
SERVES: 6

Put the tomatillos, garlic, onion, and chiles into a food processor or blender and process until smooth. Pour the sauce into a saucepan and simmer for 7 minutes.

Heat a grill (griddle) or frying pan over high heat. Using a heart-shaped cookie cutter, cut the cut the slices of cheese. Add the cheese and fry for 3 minutes on each side, or until until brown.

Ladle the sauce onto a plate, position the cheese, and garnish with tortilla strips, chives and fried tomato skins. Serve immediately.

MIXIOTE DE HONGOS

※

MIXED MUSHROOMS

6 maguey leaves, soaked and
  cut into 10-inch (25-cm)
  squares (optional)
2 pasilla chiles, seeded and
  soaked in 1 cup (9 fl oz/
  250 ml) pulque or beer
2¼ lb/1 kg assorted
  mushrooms, coarsely
  chopped
2 cloves garlic, finely chopped
40 epazote leaves, coarsely
  chopped
2 green chiles, chopped
6 tablespoons corn or extra
  virgin olive oil (optional)
sea salt

REGION: GUANAJUATO
PREPARATION TIME: 30 MINUTES
COOKING TIME: 15 MINUTES
SERVES: 6

Spread out the maguey leaves or cut 6 x 10-inch (25-cm) squares of parchment paper.

Put the pasilla chiles with their soaking liquid in a food processor or blender and process, then put 1 tablespoon of the mixture in the center of each wrapper.

Combine the mushrooms and garlic in a bowl and divide the mixture among the wrappers. Top with the epazote, green chiles, and a pinch of salt. Add 1 tablespoon of oil to each if you like. Fold in the sides of the wrappers to make packages and tie with kitchen string.

Put the packages into the top of a steamer and cook for 15 minutes. Remove the steamer from the heat. Transfer the packages to a serving platter and serve immediately.

Cheese in Green Salsa

ALAMBRE A LA MEXICANA

✳

MEXICAN-STYLE SKEWERS

1½ lb/700 g boneless beef
  round or tenderloin (fillet),
  cut into bite-size pieces
2 poblano chiles, seeded and
  chopped
1 white onion, diced
5 oz/150 g bacon, sliced
vegetable oil, for brushing
coarse sea salt and pepper
12 wooden skewers

To serve:
Guacamole (page 40)
Charros Beans (page 534)

REGION: FEDERAL DISTRICT
PREPARATION TIME: 30 MINUTES, PLUS
25 MINUTES STANDING
COOKING TIME: 15 MINUTES
SERVES: 6

Thread a piece of meat, chile, onion, and bacon onto each of the skewers. Season with salt and pepper. Let stand for 25 minutes.

Heat a ridged grill (griddle) pan and brush with oil. Brush the skewers with oil, add to the pan, and cook over medium heat, turning frequently, for 15 minutes.

Remove the pan from the heat and transfer the skewers to individual plates. Serve immediately with guacamole and charros beans.

QUESILLO EN SALSA DE EPAZOTE

✳

CHEESE IN EPAZOTE SAUCE

9 chilaca or any mild chiles,
  dry-roasted
1–1½ cups (2–3 oz/50–80 g)
  epazote leaves
3 tablespoons corn oil
1 lb 10 oz/750 g Oaxaca
  quesillo or mozzarella cheese,
  diced
sea salt
8 Corn Tortillas (page 36)

REGION: VERACRUZ
PREPARATION TIME: 10 MINUTES
COOKING TIME: 15 MINUTES
SERVES: 6–8

Put the chiles and epazote into a food processor or blender and process to a puree.

Heat the oil in a saucepan. Add the chile mixture and cook over medium heat, stirring constantly, for 3 minutes. Add 1 cup (9 fl oz/250 ml) water and simmer for a few minutes until the mixture has the consistency of a light sauce. Add the cheese and cook for only a few minutes, until heated through but not melted. Taste and adjust for salt if necessary.

Serve immediately with warm tortillas.

BOCADOS DE POLLO A LA PARRILLA

✻

CHICKEN SANDWICHES

1 tablespoon lemon juice

2 teaspoons soy sauce

½ teaspoon chili oil (optional)

1 lb 10 oz/750 g skinless boneless chicken breasts or thighs

½ cup (4 fl oz/120 ml) rice vinegar

1 tablespoon sugar

½ teaspoon sea salt

2 large carrots, cut into thin strips

corn oil, for brushing

1 large baguette

1–2 jalapeño chiles, seeded and finely chopped (optional)

12 sprigs cilantro (coriander)

REGION: ALL REGIONS
PREPARATION TIME: 30 MINUTES, PLUS UP TO 2 HOURS MARINATING
COOKING TIME: 10 MINUTES
SERVES: 4

Combine the lemon juice, soy sauce, and chili oil, if using, in a dish. Add the chicken, turning it to coat, cover with plastic wrap (clingfilm) and let marinate in the refrigerator for at least 30 minutes and up to 2 hours.

Meanwhile, whisk together the vinegar, sugar, and salt in a bowl. Add the carrots and set aside for 30 minutes at room temperature.

Preheat the broiler (grill) to medium-high heat and brush the rack with oil. Remove the chicken from the marinade and broil (grill) for 4–5 minutes on each side, until tender. Remove the chicken from the broiler, let rest for 5 minutes, and then cut it into thin slices.

Slice the baguette in half lengthwise without cutting all the way through. Cut into 4 pieces. Put the chicken slices on the bottom of the baguette and top with the carrot salad. Add the chiles, if using, and cilantro (coriander) sprigs. Close the baguette and press gently so the bread absorbs the juices. Serve immediately.

EMPANADAS DE PLATANO MACHO RELLENAS DE PICADILLO

✳

PLANTAIN AND MEAT EMPANADAS

1 lb 2 oz/500 g firm ripe
plantains
3½ oz/100 g boneless pork loin
3½ oz/100 g boneless beef
tenderloin (fillet)
2 tablespoons corn oil, plus
extra for oiling and deep-
frying
1½ onions, chopped
2 cloves garlic, crushed
2 tomatoes, chopped
½ cup (2 oz/50 g) pitted green
olives
½ cup (2 oz/50 g) capers
⅓ cup (2 oz/50 g) raisins
½ cup (2 oz/50 g) blanched
almonds
sea salt
Pozole Salsa (page 508),
to serve
sliced plantain, to serve

REGION: VERACRUZ
PREPARATION TIME: 45 MINUTES, PLUS
CHILLING OVERNIGHT
COOKING TIME: 1½ HOURS
MAKES: 12

The day before serving, preheat the broiler (grill). Put the unpeeled plantains on the rack and broil (grill), turning frequently, for 8–12 minutes. Remove from the heat. Allow to cool, then peel and put them into a bowl. Cover with plastic wrap (clingfilm) and chill in the refrigerator.

The next day, put the pork and beef into a saucepan, add enough water to cover, and bring to a boil. Reduce the heat and simmer for 30 minutes or until tender and cooked through. Remove the pan from the heat, lift out the meat and chop finely. Reserve the cooking liquid.

Heat the oil in a large frying pan or skillet. Add the onions and cook over low heat, stirring occasionally, for 5 minutes. Add the garlic and when fragrant, add the tomatoes, and cook for 10 minutes.

Add the meat, olives, capers, raisins, and almonds, season with salt, and simmer, adding a little of the reserved cooking liquid if necessary, for 30 minutes. Remove the pan from the heat.

The next day, put the plantains into a food processor or blender and process to a "dough." Coat your hands with oil or dip them in water and shape small balls from the plantain dough. Put each ball between 2 sheets of plastic wrap and flatten in a tortilla press or with a rolling pin.

Put a tablespoon of the meat mixture in the middle of each tortilla, fold them over, and press the edges to seal to create an empanada. Repeat until all the dough has been used.

Heat the oil for deep-frying to 350°F (180°C) or until a cube of day-old bread browns in 30 seconds. Add the empanadas, in batches, and cook until they are dark golden, then remove and drain on paper towels. Serve immediately with dry chile salsa.

Plantain and Meat Empanadas

EMPANADAS DE MINILLA DE CAZÓN

※

DOGFISH EMPANADAS

2–3 dried chipotle chiles, dry-roasted
3 ancho chiles, dry-roasted
2 tablespoons extra virgin olive oil
2 white onions, finely chopped
4–5 cloves garlic, finely chopped
2 small tomatoes, chopped
1 lb 2 oz/500 g dogfish, cooked and flaked
3 tablespoons chopped mixed aromatic herbs
½ teaspoon dried oregano, crushed
sea salt
Green Salsa with Avocado (page 512)

For the dough:
3¼ cups (14 oz/400 g) all-purpose (plain) flour
1 teaspoon baking powder
1 teaspoon sea salt
½ cup (4 oz/120 g) butter or lard
2 eggs
½ cup (120 ml/4 fl oz) milk
1 egg yolk, lightly beaten

REGION: VERACRUZ
PREPARATION TIME: 40 MINUTES, PLUS 15 MINUTES SOAKING AND 10 MINUTES RESTING
COOKING TIME: 55 MINUTES
SERVES: 6

Combine the chiles and enough hot water to cover them and soak for 15 minutes. Put the chiles and their soaking water into a food processor or blender and process until smooth. Strain and set aside.

Heat the oil in a large frying pan or skillet. Add the onions, garlic, tomatoes, and fish and cook over low heat, stirring occasionally, for 5 minutes. Add the chiles, aromatic herbs, and oregano and cook, stirring occasionally, for an additional 2–3 minutes until slightly dried. Season to taste with salt and remove the pan from the heat.

To make the dough, sift together the flour, baking powder, and salt and make a well and in the center. Put the fat, eggs, and milk in the well and mix together, gradually incorporating the dry ingredients. Knead lightly, shape into a ball, cover with plastic wrap (clingfilm), and let rest for 10 minutes.

Meanwhile, preheat the oven to 350°F (180°C/ Gas Mark 4) and line a baking sheet with nonstick parchment paper.

Take pieces of the dough, shape into small balls, and roll out with a rolling pin into circles about ⅛ inch (3 mm) thick. Divide the filling among the circles, fold them in half, and pinch the edges firmly to seal. Put them onto the baking sheet. Beat the egg yolk with 2 teaspoons water and brush it over the empanadas to glaze.

Bake the empanadas for 40 minutes or until golden brown, then remove from the oven and serve.

Dogfish Empanadas

EMPANADAS DE SARDINAS

SARDINE EMPANADAS

1 (8-oz/230-g) can sardines in tomato sauce
1 large tomato, seeded and finely chopped
2 pickled jalapeño chiles, finely chopped
1 white onion, finely chopped
10 pitted olives, chopped
1½ cups (3½ oz/100 g) mushrooms, cooked and finely chopped
butter, for greasing
2 sheets (1 lb 2 oz/500 g) puff pastry dough
all-purpose (plain) flour, for dusting
2 egg yolks, lightly beaten
sea salt and pepper

REGION: YUCATÁN
PREPARATION TIME: 40 MINUTES
COOKING TIME: 30 MINUTES
SERVES: 6

Preheat the oven to 350°F (180°C/Gas Mark 4). Grease a baking sheet with butter.

Combine the sardines, tomato, chiles, onion, olives, and mushrooms in a bowl and season with salt and pepper to taste.

Roll out the dough on a lightly floured surface. Stamp out 4-inch (10-cm) circles with a plain cookie cutter. Put 1 tablespoon of the sardine mixture in the center of each, fold it over, and press the edges with the tines of a fork to seal. Place the pies on the prepared baking sheet and brush with the egg yolk to glaze. Make a small hole in the center of each empanada to let the steam escape during cooking.

Bake for about 30 minutes, until golden brown. Remove from the oven and let cool before serving.

DZIK DE PESCADO

FISH DZIK

1 red onion, finely diced
5 radishes, finely diced
2 slices habanero chile, finely diced
1 handful cilantro (coriander), finely chopped
juice of 3 oranges
juice of 2 lemons
3 tablespoons apple cider vinegar
1½ lb/700 g fresh white fish fillets, diced
sea salt and pepper
tostadas, to serve

REGION: YUCATÁN
PREPARATION TIME: 15 MINUTES
SERVES: 6

Combine the onion, radishes, chile, cilantro (coriander), orange juice, lemon juice, and vinegar in a bowl, mixing well. Add the fish, gently mix, and season with salt and pepper.

Spoon the fish salad on the tostadas.

EMPANADAS DE JAIBA

✳

CRAB EMPANADAS

3 tablespoons extra virgin
   olive oil
½ onion, finely chopped
2 cloves garlic, finely chopped
3 large tomatoes, peeled,
   seeded, and finely chopped
finely chopped jalapeño chiles,
   to taste
9 oz/250 g crabmeat
8 olives, pitted and finely
   chopped
8 capers, finely chopped
2 tablespoons finely chopped
   parsley
apple cider vinegar, to taste
sea salt and pepper

For the dough:
3⅔ cups (1 lb/450 g) all-purpose
   (plain) flour
1½ teaspoons baking powder
1 teaspoon sea salt
1 cup (7 oz/200 g) lard or
   vegetable oil
3 eggs
¾ cup (6 fl oz/175 ml) milk
1 egg yolk

REGION: VERACRUZ
PREPARATION TIME: 40 MINUTES, PLUS
10 MINUTES STANDING
COOKING TIME: 1 HOUR
SERVES: 6

Heat the olive oil in a saucepan. Add the onion and cook over low heat, stirring occasionally, for 5 minutes. Add the garlic, then stir in the tomatoes and chiles and cook for about 10 minutes. Add the crabmeat, olives, capers, and parsley, and season with vinegar, salt, and pepper. Cook gently for a few more minutes until the filling dries slightly.

To make the dough, sift together the flour, baking powder, and salt into a mound and make a well and in the center. Add the fat, eggs, and milk into the well and mix together, gradually incorporating the dry ingredients. Knead very lightly and let stand for 10 minutes.

Meanwhile, preheat the oven to 350°F (180°C/ Gas Mark 4).

Break off small pieces of the dough, shape into balls, and roll out into circles about 6 inches (15 cm) in diameter. Divide the crab filling among them, brush the edge with water, fold over, and pinch to seal. Put the empanadas on a baking sheet. Beat the egg yolk with 2 teaspoons water in a small bowl and brush the mixture over the empanadas to glaze.

Bake for 40 minutes or until golden brown. Remove the baking sheet from the oven and serve the empanadas immediately.

CEVICHE VERDE

✼

GREEN CEVICHE

2¼ lb/1 kg fresh white fish fillets, diced
juice of 8 lemons
5 tablespoons apple cider vinegar
2 bay leaves
½ teaspoon oregano
1 teaspoon sea salt
½ tomato, chopped
tortilla chips, to serve

For the dressing:
1 cup (2½ oz/65 g) coarsely chopped parsley
4 tablespoon coarsely chopped basil
10 green olives, pitted
1 serrano or habanero chile, membranes and seeds removed
1 cup (9 fl oz/250 ml) extra virgin olive oil
sea salt, to taste

REGION: FEDERAL DISTRICT
PREPARATION TIME: 20 MINUTES, PLUS 30 MINUTES MARINATING
SERVES: 6

In a glass or plastic container with airtight lid, add the diced fish, lemon juice, vinegar, bay leaves, oregano, tomato, and sea salt. Mix gently, cover, and let marinate in the refrigerator for 30 minutes.

To make the dressing, combine all the ingredients in a blender or food processor and process until well mixed. Add the dressing to the fish, mix gently, and season to taste.

Strain the fish from the marinade and add the dressing. Garnish with tomatoes and serve with tortilla chips.

Green Ceviche

ACAPULCO-STYLE CEVICHE

2¼ lb/1 kg swordfish, skinned
  and diced
1 bay leaf
juice of 5 lemons
½ teaspoon dried oregano
1 onion, finely chopped
4 tomatoes, seeded and
  chopped
3 tablespoons finely chopped
  cilantro (coriander)
6 pickled chiles, finely chopped
⅔ cup (2½ oz/65 g) pitted green
  olives, chopped
½ cup (2 oz/50 g) capers,
  chopped
4¼ cups (1¾ pints/1 liter)
  tomato juice
1½ cups (12 fl oz/350 ml) white
  wine
½ cup (2 oz/60 ml) extra virgin
  olive oil
sea salt
1 avocado, peeled, pitted,
  halved, and sliced, to garnish

REGION: GUERRERO
PREPARATION TIME: 30 MINUTES, PLUS
2 HOURS MARINATING
COOKING TIME: 10 MINUTES
SERVES: 6

Put the fish into a saucepan, add the bay leaf and enough water to cover the fish, and bring to a boil. Reduce the heat and simmer for 2 minutes. Remove the pan from the heat and drain.

Transfer the fish to a dish. Add the lemon juice, oregano, onion, and a pinch of salt and chill in the refrigerator for at least 2 hours, occasionally stirring the mixture gently.

Add the tomatoes, cilantro (coriander), pickled chiles, olives, capers, and tomato juice to the fish, and mix together, gradually incorporating the wine and olive oil. Taste and adjust the seasoning, if necessary.

Transfer the mixture to a serving platter and garnish with the avocado.

COLIMA-STYLE CEVICHE

1½ lb/750 g fresh white fish
   fillets, skinned and finely
   chopped
juice of 8 limes
1½ white onions, finely
   chopped
2½ carrots, finely chopped
2 small tomatoes, finely
   chopped
3–4 serrano chiles, seeded and
   finely chopped
2 cups (7 oz/200 g) green olives,
   pitted and finely chopped
1 cup (9 fl oz/250 ml) white
   wine vinegar
⅔ cup (¼ pint/150 ml) extra
   virgin olive oil
3 tablespoons finely chopped
   cilantro (coriander)
¼ teaspoon dried marjoram,
   crushed
sea salt and pepper

To serve:
6 Corn Tortillas (page 36), cut
   into ¾-inch (2-cm) disks and
   toasted
hot chili sauce

REGION: COLIMA
PREPARATION TIME: 30 MINUTES, PLUS
2½ HOURS MARINATING
SERVES: 6

In a medium bowl, combine the fish, lime juice, and a pinch of salt, stir, and let stand for 1 hour.

Add the onion and let marinate for 1½ hours in the refrigerator. Strain most of the liquid from the fish, then add the carrots, tomatoes, chiles, olives, vinegar, olive oil, cilantro (coriander), and marjoram, season with salt and pepper to taste, and mix well. Let stand for an additional 15 minutes.

Serve with toasted tortillas and hot chili sauce.

CEVICHE ESTILO SINALOA

SINALOA-STYLE CEVICHE

1½ lb/700 g red snapper fillets, skinned and diced
juice of 8 limes
2 tomatoes, seeded and finely chopped
¾ white onion, finely chopped
1 large cucumber, seeded and finely chopped
3 pickled jalapeño chiles, membranes and seeds removed and finely chopped
3 tablespoons finely chopped cilantro (coriander)
sea salt and pepper
extra virgin olive oil, for drizzling
tostadas, to serve
1 avocado, peeled, pitted, and sliced, to serve

REGION: SINALOA
PREPARATION TIME: 30 MINUTES, PLUS 3 HOURS MARINATING
SERVES: 6

Put the fish into a bowl, add the lime juice, and let marinate in the refrigerator for about 3 hours or until the flesh changes color without losing its texture. Drain off the liquid.

Combine the tomatoes, onion, cucumber, and chiles in another bowl and season with salt and pepper. Gently fold in the cilantro (coriander) and fish and drizzle with olive oil. Taste and adjust the seasoning, if necessary.

Serve on tostadas covered with sliced avocado.

CEVICHE DE LA SIERRA

SWORDFISH CEVICHE

1½ lb/700 g swordfish fillets, skinned and diced
1 white onion, finely chopped
juice of 8 lemons
30 tomatillos, finely chopped
2 jalapeño chiles, finely chopped
24 green olives, pitted and finely chopped
1 cup (1½ oz/40 g) finely chopped cilantro (coriander)
2 avocados, sliced
1 cup (9 fl oz/250 ml) extra virgin olive oil
sea salt

REGION: SINALOA
PREPARATION TIME: 30 MINUTES, PLUS 1 HOUR MARINATING
SERVES: 6

Put the fish and onion into a bowl, add the lemon juice, season with salt, and let marinate in the refrigerator for 1 hour or until the flesh changes color without losing its texture. Drain off the liquid.

Combine the tomatillos, chiles, olives, and ⅔ cup (1 oz/25 g) of the cilantro (coriander) in another bowl and mix well. Peel, halve, and pit the avocados. Dice 1½ avocados and cut the remaining half into thin strips.

Pour the olive oil into the tomatillo mixture, fold in the diced avocado and fish, and taste and adjust the seasoning, if necessary.

Serve in bowls, garnished with the remaining cilantro and sliced avocado.

MIXIOTES DE ESCAMOLES

✺

ANT EGG PACKAGES

5 tablespoons (2½ oz/65 g)
 butter
4 teaspoons corn oil
1 white onion, finely chopped
8 serrano chiles, membranes
 and seeds removed and finely
 chopped
1⅓ cups (2¾ oz/70 g) finely
 chopped epazote or cilantro
 (coriander)
14 oz/400 g ant eggs
6 (6-inch/15-cm) squares
 maguey leaves (optional)
sea salt and pepper
Corn Tortillas (page 36),
 to serve

REGION: HIDALGO
PREPARATION TIME: 15 MINUTES
COOKING TIME: 20 MINUTES
SERVES: 6

Melt the butter with the oil in a saucepan. Add the onion and cook over low heat, stirring occasionally, for 5 minutes. Add the chiles and epazote or cilantro (coriander), season with salt and pepper, and remove the pan from the heat. Gently stir in the ant eggs and mix carefully.

Divide the mixture among the squares of maguey leaves or six 6-inch (15-cm) squares of parchment paper. Fold in the sides of the wrappers to make packages and tie with kitchen string.

Put the packages in the top of a steamer and cook for 10 minutes, then remove from the heat.

Put the packages onto a serving platter and serve immediately with warm tortillas.

QUESO PANELA MARINADO

✺

MARINATED PANELA CHEESE

12 oz/350 g panela or any fresh
 cheese, cut into ¾-inch
 (1.5-cm) cubes
1 tablespoon dried oregano
1 teaspoon chopped cilantro
 (coriander)
1 teaspoon finely chopped
 pequin pepper
3–4 sprigs rosemary, finely
 chopped
1 teaspoon sea salt
½ cup (4 fl oz/120 ml) extra
 virgin olive oil
1 (8-oz/225-g) can pitted black
 olives, coarsely chopped

REGION: FEDERAL DISTRICT
PREPARATION TIME: 15 MINUTES, PLUS
24 HOURS MARINATING
SERVES: 6

Put the cubes of cheese into a dish and sprinkle with the oregano, cilantro (coriander), pequin pepper, rosemary, and salt. Add the olive oil and let marinate for at least 24 hours in the refrigerator.

Remove the dish from the refrigerator 30–60 minutes before serving to bring the mixture to room temperature. Serve in a big glass dish, garnished with black olives. Provide toothpicks or cocktail sticks for people to pick up the cheese.

CEVICHE DE CALLOS DE ALMEJA

BAY SCALLOP CEVICHE

REGION: BAJA CALIFORNIA
PREPARATION TIME: 20 MINUTES, PLUS 20–30 MINUTES MARINATING
COOKING TIME: 10 MINUTES
SERVES: 6

- 2 cups (16 fl oz/475 ml) mixed orange, grapefruit, and mandarin juice
- 1 lb 2 oz/500 g small fresh bay scallops, shelled
- ¾ cup (6 fl oz/175 ml) lime juice
- 2 bay leaves
- ½ red onion, chopped
- 1 habanero chile, seeded and chopped
- ½ cup (4 fl oz/120 ml) extra virgin olive oil
- 2 tablespoons chopped cilantro (coriander) leaves, plus extra for garnish
- 4 tablespoons chopped peppermint or spearmint leaves
- 1 cup (6 oz/175 g) orange and grapefruit segments, chopped
- sea salt and pepper
- 1 slice lemon, to garnish
- 1 slice lime, to garnish
- tortilla chips, to serve

Pour the mixed citrus juice into a saucepan, bring to a boil, and reduce by half. Set aside.

Put the scallops in a bowl or dish, add enough lime juice to cover, add the bay leaves, cover with plastic wrap (clingfilm), and marinate for 20–30 minutes. Drain, put in a clean bowl, add the onion, chile, reduced citrus juice, olive oil, salt and pepper to taste, and the herbs and mix well. Add the fruit segments. Garnish with a lemon and lime slice and tortilla chips on the side.

Bay Scallop Ceviche

BROCHETAS DE CAMARONES AL PASTOR

✹

SHRIMP BROCHETTES

10 pasilla chiles, lightly
  dry-roasted
10 guajillo chiles, lightly
  dry-roasted
1 cup (9 fl oz/250 ml) apple
  cider vinegar
¼ head garlic
½–1 teaspoon cumin seeds,
  dry-roasted
3 cloves
1 cup (9 fl oz/250 ml) pineapple
  juice
2¼ lb/1 kg large shrimp
  (prawns), peeled and
  deveined
3 tablespoons corn oil, plus
  extra for drizzling
½ fresh pineapple, peeled,
  cored, and cut into triangles
½ white onion, finely chopped
2–3 tablespoons finely chopped
  cilantro (coriander)
sea salt
Roast Chile and Tomato Salsa
  (page 508), to serve

REGION: FEDERAL DISTRICT
PREPARATION TIME: 45 MINUTES, PLUS
OVERNIGHT MARINATING
COOKING TIME: 35 MINUTES
SERVES: 6

Put the chiles into a saucepan, add vinegar to cover, and bring to a boil. Reduce the heat and simmer for 10 minutes, or until softened. Remove the pan from the heat.

Put the chiles, vinegar, garlic, cumin, cloves, and a pinch of salt into a food processor or blender and process, adding as much pineapple juice as necessary to make a smooth paste.

Scrape the mixture into a saucepan and cook over low heat, stirring constantly to prevent it from sticking, for 10 minutes. Remove from heat, taste and adjust the seasoning, if necessary, and let cool.

Lightly coat the shrimp (prawns) with the chile mixture, put them into a bowl, and let marinate in the refrigerator for several hours or overnight.

Heat the oil in a heavy frying pan or skillet. Add the pineapple triangles and cook over medium heat, turning occasionally, for 5 minutes, until lightly browned. Remove the pan from the heat and let cool.

Heat the broiler (grill), barbecue, or a ridged grill pan (griddle). Thread the shrimp and pineapple triangles alternately onto skewers, drizzle with a little oil, and place on the heat. Cook for about 2 minutes, until the shrimp change color, then turn and cook on the other side for about 2 minutes.

Transfer the brochettes to a serving platter, garnish with the onion and cilantro (coriander), and serve immediately with the salsa on the side.

CÓCTEL DE CAMARÓN

SHRIMP COCKTAIL

1 lb 5 oz/600 g fresh shrimp (prawns), peeled

½ cup (4 fl oz/125 ml) ketchup

1–2 smoked chipotle chiles in adobo

1 cup (9 fl oz/250 ml) orange juice

4 tomatoes, seeded and chopped

1¼ cup (2 oz/50 g) finely chopped cilantro (coriander)

1 onion, finely chopped

1 avocado, peeled, pitted, and sliced

extra virgin olive oil, for drizzling

saltine crackers, to serve

lemon juice, to serve

REGION: VERACRUZ
PREPARATION TIME: 25 MINUTES
COOKING TIME: 5 MINUTES
SERVES: 6

Bring a large saucepan of lightly salted water to a boil over medium-high heat. Add the shrimp (prawns) and cook for 1–3 minutes, or until they are pink and opaque. Drain and rinse in a colander under cold running water and chop.

Put the ketchup, chile, orange juice, and 1 cup (9 fl oz/250 ml) water in a food processor or blender and process until thoroughly combined. Pour the mixture into a bowl and fold in the shrimp.

Divide the shrimp mixture among 6 glass dishes, add the tomatoes, cilantro (coriander), and onion, and garnish with sliced avocado. Drizzle with olive oil and serve with saltines and lemon juice.

CALAMARES A LA PARILLA

BROILED SQUID

2¼ lb/1 kg squid, cleaned

juice of 2½ lemons

1½ tablespoons extra virgin olive oil

3 cloves garlic, finely chopped

1 tablespoon finely chopped lemon zest

1½ teaspoons sea salt

pinch of dried thyme

pepper

salad greens and boiled potatoes, to serve

REGION: FEDERAL DISTRICT
PREPARATION TIME: 30 MINUTES, PLUS 30 MINUTES MARINATING
COOKING TIME: 1 MINUTE
SERVES: 6

To prepare the squid, pull the tentacles away from the bodies and remove the quills. Pull the wing-like flaps away and rinse the body under cold running water. Cut the body in half lengthwise, score with a sharp knife, and put them in a glass or ceramic dish.

Combine the lemon juice, olive oil, garlic, lemon zest, salt, and thyme in a a small bowl and pour the mixture over the squid. Season with pepper and let marinate for at least 30 minutes.

Preheat the broiler (grill) to high, put the squid on the rack of the pan, and cook for 20–30 seconds on each side. Remove the squid from the broiler.

Transfer to a platter. Serve immediately with a side of salad greens and potatoes.

Pickled Jalapeños with Vegetables

CHILES JALAPEÑOS ESCURTIDOS CON VERDURAS

✳

PICKLED JALAPEÑOS WITH VEGETABLES

½ cup (4 fl oz/120 ml) extra
  virgin olive oil
24 small scallions (spring
  onions), white part only
8 cloves garlic, halved
12 jalapeño chiles
1 large carrot, peeled and cut
  into strips
1 cup new potatoes, halved
1 cup (5 oz/150 g) cauliflower
  florets
2 cups (16 fl oz/475 ml) apple
  cider vinegar
10 bay leaves
2 tablespoons black
  peppercorns
¾ teaspoon allspice berries
8 cloves
3 sprigs thyme
¼ cup (2 oz/50 g) raw cane
  sugar or white sugar
2 large zucchini (courgettes),
  thickly sliced
sea salt

REGION: ALL REGIONS
PREPARATION TIME: 20 MINUTES
COOKING TIME: 50 MINUTES
SERVES: 4

Heat the olive oil in a frying pan or skillet. Add the scallions (spring onions) and cook over low heat for 4–5 minutes, then remove from pan, and set aside. Add the garlic, chiles, carrot, new potatoes and cauliflower florets to the pan, and cook for 15 minutes over low heat.

Put the vinegar, bay leaves, peppercorns, allspice, cloves, thyme, and sugar into a medium-size pan. Pour in 2 cups (16 fl oz/475 ml) water, season with salt, and bring to a boil over medium heat. Simmer for 20 minutes, add the zucchini (courgettes), reduce the heat, and cook for another 15 minutes. Remove from the heat and let cool.

Pack the cold mixture into a sterilized glass jar and seal. Store in the refrigerator for any occasion.

CHILES EN VINAGRE CON NOPALES Y QUESO FRESCO

✻

PICKLED CHILES WITH CACTUS PADDLES AND CHEESE

9 oz/250 g cactus paddles, diced
pinch of baking soda (bicarbonate of soda)
1 tablespoon extra virgin olive oil
1 white onion, chopped
3 garlic cloves
3 carrots, sliced
9 oz (250 g) serrano chiles
9 oz (250 g) queso fresco or feta cheese, diced
5 black peppercorns
2 cloves
1 cup (9 fl oz/250 ml) sugar cane vinegar
2 bay leaves
1 teaspoon dried oregano
sea salt

REGION: FEDERAL DISTRICT, PUEBLA
PREPARATION TIME: 10 MINUTES, PLUS 1 WEEK STANDING
COOKING TIME: 25 MINUTES
SERVES: 6

Put the cactus paddles into a pan, pour in water to cover, add the baking soda (bicarbonate of soda), and bring to a boil. Reduce the heat and simmer for 25–30 minutes until tender. Remove the pan from the heat, drain the cactus paddles, rinse in cold water, and drain well again.

Heat the oil in a saucepan. Add the onion and cook over low heat, stirring occasionally, for 5 minutes. Add the garlic, carrots, chiles, cactus paddles, cheese, peppercorns, cloves, and a pinch of salt and cook, stirring occasionally, for 10 minutes. Remove the pan from the heat.

Pour the vinegar and 1 cup (9 fl oz/250 ml) water into the pan and add the bay leaves and oregano. Transfer the mixture to a terracotta pot or a stylish bottle, seal, and let stand for a week before eating.

CODORNICES EN ESCABECHE ORIENTAL

✺

YUCATAN-STYLE QUAIL IN VINEGAR

½ cup (4½ fl oz/125 ml) sour
    orange juice
5 tablespoons achiote paste
12 quails, cleaned
1 onion, thinly sliced
¾ cup (6 fl oz/175 ml) pineapple
    vinegar or apple cider
    vinegar
banana leaves, dry-roasted
    (optional)
avocado leaves
2 tablespoons corn oil, plus
    extra for brushing
1 large onion, thinly sliced
1 cup (9 fl oz/250 ml) sugar
    cane vinegar
1 cup (9 fl oz/250 ml) Chicken
    Stock (page 184)
sea salt and pepper

REGION: YUCATAN
PREPARATION TIME: 30 MINUTES
COOKING TIME: 50 MINUTES
SERVES: 6

Combine the orange juice and achiote paste. Spread the mixture over the quails, and put them into a large dish. Cover each bird with sliced onion and 1 tablespoon vinegar, checking that they are completely covered. Cover with the banana leaves, if using, and let marinate overnight.

Light the charcoal on a barbecue. While you are waiting for the coals to turn red, heat the oil in a frying pan or skillet, add the onion, and cook over medium-low heat, stirring occasionally, for 5 minutes. Remove the pan from the heat.

When the charcoal is red, cover it with avocado leaves. Top with the quails and cook, brushing frequently with vegetable oil and some of the marinade.

When the quails are just browned, put the remaining marinade in a large pan or flameproof casserole dish, add the cooked onion slices and vinegar, and season with salt and pepper. Simmer over low heat for 3 minutes, adding the stock. Transfer the quails to the pan or casserole, cover, and cook over low heat for 15 minutes or until they are cooked through.

ESCABECHE TIBIO PESCADO

✳

FISH ESCABECHE

2¼ lb/1 kg fresh white fish fillets, sliced

1 cup (9 fl oz/250 ml) extra virgin olive oil, plus extra for drizzling

2 guajillo chiles, seeded, sliced

3 cloves garlic, thinly sliced

1 large white onion, sliced

3–4 sprigs thyme

3–4 sprigs marjoram

2 bay leaves

2 cloves

1 small cinnamon stick

10 black peppercorns

1–2 tablespoons American mustard

1 cup (9 fl oz/250 ml) apple cider vinegar

1 tablespoon sugar

sea salt

tortilla chips, to serve

REGION: VERACRUZ
PREPARATION TIME: 25 MINUTES
COOKING TIME: 35 MINUTES
SERVES: 6

Preheat the oven to 350°F (180°C/Gas Mark 4).

Put the fish into an ovenproof dish, drizzle with olive oil, and sprinkle with salt. Cover the dish with aluminum foil and bake for 15 minutes.

Meanwhile, heat half the oil in a large frying pan or skillet. Add the chile rings and cook, stirring frequently, for 1 minute, then remove from the pan with a slotted spoon. Add the sliced garlic and cook, stirring frequently, for 2–3 minutes until lightly golden. Do not let it brown or it will become bitter. Remove the pan and set aside.

Add the remaining olive oil to the pan. Add the onion, thyme, marjoram, bay leaves, cloves, cinnamon, and peppercorns, and cook over low heat, stirring occasionally, for about 5 minutes until the onion is translucent. Stir the mustard into the vinegar in a small bowl, then stir into the pan. Pour in 1 cup (9 fl oz/250 ml) water and simmer for 5 minutes. Stir in the sugar and season to taste with salt.

Plate the fish, scatter over the onions and spoon over the cooking liquid. Sprinkle with the sliced garlic and sliced chile. Serve immediately with tortilla chips.

CAMARONES EN ESCABECHE

✺

SHRIMP ESCABECHE

50 g/2 oz ancho chiles,
 cleaned, dry-roasted
1 cup (9 fl oz/250 ml) apple
 cider vinegar
10 black peppercorns
½ cinnamon stick
½ teaspoon cumin seeds
4 whole cloves
1 onion, coarsely chopped
3 cloves garlic, coarsely
 chopped
3 tablespoons corn oil
3 bay leaves
2¼ lb/1 kg shrimp (prawns),
 peeled and deveined
1 avocado, cut into wedges
Corn Tortillas (page 36),
 to serve

REGION: VERACRUZ
PREPARATION TIME: 20 MINUTES, PLUS
2 HOURS MARINATING
COOKING TIME: 30 MINUTES
SERVES: 6

Put the chiles in a small bowl, mix the vinegar with ½ cup (4½ fl oz/125 ml) boiling water, pour the mixture over the chiles, and let soak for 15 minutes or until soft.

In a skillet, add the peppercorns, cinnamon, cumin seeds, and cloves and dry-roast, stirring frequently, for a few minutes until fragrant. Put the spices into a food processor or blender, add the chiles, some of the diluted vinegar, onion, and garlic, and process until thoroughly combined and smooth,

Heat 1 tablespoon of the oil in a heavy pan. Add the bay leaves, and chile escabeche and cook over low heat, stirring occasionally, for 20 minutes.

Heat the remaining oil in a skillet. Add the shrimp (prawns), in batches if necessary, and cook over high heat for 4–5 minutes until just cooked, then transfer to a nonmetallic dish. Add the escabeche, mix well, and let marinate for 2 hours.

Serve warm or at room temperature garnished with avocado wedges, with fresh tortillas.

Pickled Pigs' Feet

PICKLED PIGS' FEET

6 pig' feet (trotters), cleaned
3 tablespoons extra virgin
  olive oil
1 white onion, sliced
2 carrots, sliced
2 cuaresmeño chiles
aromatic herbs
pinch of dried oregano
2 cups (16 fl oz/475 ml) sugar
  cane vinegar
sea salt and pepper

REGION: CENTRAL MEXICO
PREPARATION TIME: 20 MINUTES
COOKING TIME: 1 HOUR
SERVES: 6

Bring 6 cups (48 fl oz/1.5 liters) salted water to a boil, add the pigs' feet (trotters), and simmer, covered, for 40 minutes.

In the meantime, heat the olive oil in a frying pan over medium heat, add the onions and sauté for 10 minutes or until translucent. Add the carrots, chiles, aromatic herbs and oregano. Season with salt and pepper. Add the vinegar and the pigs' feet. Cook for 8 minutes until the vegetables are tender. Let stand for 1 hour before serving.

Note: This can be garnished with avocado and tomato slices or served as an appetizer.

CHICKEN ESCABECHE

20 black peppercorns
1 teaspoon oregano leaves
3 cloves garlic
½ teaspoon cumin seeds
1 cinnamon stick
pinch of ground cloves
juice of 3 large sour oranges
6 chicken thighs or
  drumsticks, cut into pieces
6 onions, sliced
1 xcatic, habanero, guero or
  hot yellow wax chile
sea salt and pepper

REGION: YUCATAN
PREPARATION TIME: 30 MINUTES
COOKING TIME: 50 MINUTES
SERVES: 6

Grind the peppercorns, oregano, garlic, cumin, and cinnamon in a mortar with a pestle or a spice grinder. Stir the spice mixture and the ground cloves into two-thirds of the orange juice. Season with salt.

Spread the mixture over the chicken pieces, put them in a saucepan, pour in 2 cups (16 fl oz/475 ml) water and bring to a boil over medium heat. Reduce the heat to low, cover, and simmer for 35 minutes or until the chicken is tender.

Remove the pan from the heat, lift out the chicken, and set aside. Return the pan to the heat, add the onions, chile, and remaining orange juice, and season with salt to taste. Bring to a boil and cook for 5 minutes.

Serve the chicken with the onions and chile on top and sprinkled with pepper. Spoon over the cooking liquid.

HUEVOS MOTULENOS

✳

EGGS FROM MOTUL

4 tablespoons corn oil or lard

6 Corn Tortillas (page 36)

9 tomatoes

1 onion, coarsely chopped

2 cloves garlic, coarsely chopped

2 serrano chiles, membranes and seeds removed, coarsely chopped

6 eggs

sea salt

1–2 ripe plantains, cut into ½-inch (1-cm) slices

To garnish:

2 cups (1 lb 2 oz/500 g) Refried Beans (page 532)

½ cup (3½ oz/100 g) finely chopped ham

⅔ cup (3½ oz/100 g) grated queso fresco, panela, or mild feta cheese

⅓ cup (2 oz/50 g) peas

REGION: YUCATAN
PREPARATION TIME: 15 MINUTES
COOKING TIME: 20 MINUTES
SERVES: 6

Heat 2 tablespoons of the corn oil in a frying pan or skillet. Add the tortillas, one at a time, and fry for a few seconds on each side until golden, then transfer to paper towels to drain. Cover with a clean dish towel to keep them warm and set aside. Add more oil to the pan as you work, if necessary.

Put the tomatoes into a medium saucepan, pour in water to come about halfway up the sides, and bring just to a boil. Reduce the heat, cover, and poach for about 5 minutes. Remove, and when they are cool enough to handle, peel off the skins.

Put the tomato flesh, onion, garlic, and chiles into a food processor or blender and process until thoroughly combined. Strain the tomato mixture into a saucepan and heat over medium heat for 5 minutes.

Heat a tablespoon of fat or oil in a skillet. Fry the eggs, keeping the yolk runny.

Heat a tablespoon of oil in a frying pan or skillet over medium heat, add the sliced plaintains and sauté until golden for 10 minutes.

Put a fried tortilla on each of 6 plates. Put an egg on top of the tortilla and divide the sauce, ham, cheese, and peas among them. Serve immediately.

HUEVOS A LA ALBAÑIL

✺

ALBANIL EGGS

1 tablespoon corn oil
12 eggs, lightly beaten
sea salt

For the sauce:
3 tomatoes, dry-roasted
¼ onion, dry-roasted
1 clove garlic, dry-roasted
2 dried árbol chiles,
   dry-roasted
2 tablespoons corn oil
1 sprig epazote
sea salt

To serve:
6 Corn Tortillas (page 36)
Refried Beans (page 532)
queso fresco or feta cheese,
   crumbled

REGION: MEXICO CITY
PREPARATION TIME: 25 MINUTES
COOKING TIME: 10 MINUTES
SERVES: 6

To make the sauce, put the tomatoes, onion, garlic, and chiles into a food processor or blender, add 1 cup (9 fl oz/250 ml) water and process until smooth. Strain into a bowl.

To cook the eggs, heat the oil in a frying pan or skillet. Scramble the eggs until they are nearly done, so they are still slightly runny. Season with salt and remove the eggs from the pan. Cover them to keep warm and set aside.

Pour the sauce into the pan, add the epazote, and cook for 5 minutes. Season with salt, add the scrambled eggs, and cook for an additional 1–2 minutes, stirring gently, until the eggs are cooked.

Serve the eggs immediately with warm tortillas, refried beans, and cheese.

Drowned Eggs

HUEVOS AHOGADOS

✳

DROWNED EGGS

6 tomatoes, dry-roasted
½ onion, quartered and
    dry-roasted
2 cloves garlic, dry-roasted
4¼ cups (1¾ pints/1 liter)
    Chicken Stock (page 184)
1 tablespoon corn oil
1 sprig epazote, chopped
12 eggs
½ cup peas
sea salt and pepper
Refried Beans (page 532),
    to serve
6 Corn Tortillas (page 36),
    to serve

REGION: ALL REGIONS
PREPARATION TIME: 30 MINUTES
COOKING TIME: 25 MINUTES
SERVES: 6

Put the tomatoes, onion, and garlic into a food processor or blender and process until smooth. Set aside.

Heat the oil in a large, deep frying pan or skillet, add the tomato mixture and epazote, and cook over medium heat for 10 minutes. Taste and adjust the seasoning, if necessary.

Reduce the heat to low. Add the eggs to the pan, one at a time, being careful not to break the yolks. Season the eggs with salt and pepper. Add the stock and simmer for about 3 minutes, covered, until the egg whites are beginning to set. Add the peas, cover, and cook until the egg whites have set and the yolks are still runny.

Remove the pan from the heat, and spoon 2 eggs into each of 6 deep plates or wide, shallow bowls. 'Drown' the eggs in the sauce and serve with refried beans and warm tortillas on the side.

HUEVOS RABOS DE MESTIZA

✻

MESTIZAN EGGS WITH CHILE

2 small scallions (spring onions), chopped

3 ancho chiles, membrane and seeds removed

9 tomatoes, chopped

2–3 cloves garlic

1¼ cups (2 oz/50 g) chopped cilantro (coriander)

9 tomatillos, chopped

1 bay leaf

¼ teaspoon dried marjoram

1 tablespoon lard or corn oil

3 poblano chiles, dry-roasted and cut into strips

12 eggs

⅔ cup (¼ pint/150 ml) sour cream

5 oz/150 g panela or ricotta cheese, thinly sliced

sea salt

REGION: YUCATAN
PREPARATION TIME: 20 MINUTES
COOKING TIME: 50 MINUTES
SERVES: 6

Pour 2 cups (16 fl oz/475 ml) water into a large saucepan, add the scallions (spring onions), chiles, tomatoes, garlic, cilantro (coriander), tomatillos, bay leaf, marjoram, and a pinch of salt, and bring just to a boil. Reduce the heat and simmer for 30 minutes. Remove the pan from the heat. Discard the bay leaf.

Transfer the mixture to a food processor or blender and process until thoroughly combined. Strain into a bowl.

Heat the lard in a large frying pan or skillet, add the sauce and half the poblano chile strips, and cook for 5 minutes. Add the eggs, then add the remaining poblano strips and sour cream. Carefully stir in the cheese, and cook over medium-low heat until the eggs are cooked.

Serve immediately in wide, shallow bowls, drizzled with sour cream.

Mestizan Eggs with Chile

HUEVOS DIVORCIADOS

✳

DIVORCED EGGS

vegetable oil, for frying
12 eggs
sea salt
1 cup (7 oz/200 g) Raw
   Tomatillo Salsa (page 512)
1 cup (7 oz/200 g) Raw Tomato
   Salsa (page 502)
Refried Beans (page 532)
grated cheddar cheese
tortilla chips, to garnish

REGION: ALL REGIONS
PREPARATION TIME: 15 MINUTES
COOKING TIME: 15 MINUTES
SERVES: 6

Heat 2 teaspoons of the oil in a nonstick frying pan or skillet. Fry the eggs over medium-low heat until the white is set. Season with salt and transfer 2 eggs to each plate.

Put a generous spoonful of green salsa over the white of one egg and another spoonful of red salsa over the other. Put a spoonful of refried beans between the eggs and garnish with grated cheese and tortilla chips. Serve immediately.

OMELETTE SALSA HUITLACOCHE

✳

HUITLACOCHE AND GOAT CHEESE OMELET

12 eggs
4 tablespoons corn or olive oil
sea salt and pepper
Chiltomate Salsa (page 509),
   to garnish

For the filling:
2 tablespoons corn oil or
   butter
½ onion, finely chopped
9 oz/250 g huitlacoche
2 tablespoons chopped
   epazote leaves
2 serrano chiles, membranes
   and seeds removed, and
   finely chopped
5 oz/150 g fresh goat cheese,
   crumbled
sea salt

REGION: MEXICO CITY
PREPARATION TIME: 10 MINUTES
COOKING TIME: 40 MINUTES
SERVES: 6

To make the filling, heat the oil in a saucepan. Add the onion and cook over low heat, stirring occasionally, for 5 minutes, until translucent. Add the huitlacoche, epazote, and chiles and season with salt. Cook for 15 minutes, then taste and adjust the seasoning, if necessary, and fold in the cheese until it is completely incorporated. Remove the pan from the heat.

To make the omelets, beat the eggs with salt and pepper until fluffy. Heat 1 tablespoon of the oil in a frying pan or skillet over low heat. Pour in a small ladle of the beaten egg and tilt the pan to coat evenly. When the egg is just beginning to set, add a little of the filling on one half of the egg. Fold the empty half of the omelet over the filling and finish cooking. Transfer to a serving plate, add chiltomate salsa. Repeat with the remaining eggs. Serve immediately.

Divorced Eggs

ENVUELTOS CON CHIPOTLE MECO

✻

HEARTY SCRAMBLED EGGS

7 oz/200 g boneless pork
   leg, diced
¼ onion
2 cloves garlic
sprigs of herbs such as
   oregano, thyme, marjoram,
   and bay leaves
7 tablespoons corn oil
3½ oz/100 g chorizo, finely
   chopped
6 eggs
1 tablespoon butter
12 Corn Tortillas (page 36)
¾ cup (3 oz/80 g) grated cotija
   or feta cheese
sea salt
Refried Beans (page 532),
   to serve

For the sauce:
1 chipotle chiles, dry-roasted
1 mulato chiles, dry-roasted
2 pasilla chiles, dry-roasted
2 tomatoes, dry-roasted
4 cloves garlic, dry-roasted
½ onion, dry-roasted
4¼ cups (1¾ pints/1 liter)
   Beef Stock (page 185)
1 tablespoon butter

REGION: OAXACA
PREPARATION TIME: 1 HOUR 10 MINUTES, PLUS
15 MINUTES SOAKING
COOKING TIME: 1¾ HOURS
SERVES: 4

Put the pork, onion, garlic, sprigs of herbs, and
a pinch of salt into a saucepan, add enough water to
cover, and bring to a boil over medium heat. Reduce
the heat, cover, and simmer for 1 hour. Remove from
the heat and transfer the meat to a plate to cool.
Discard the liquid.

To make the sauce, in a small bowl, combine the
chiles and enough water to cover them and soak for
15 minutes.

Put the tomatoes, garlic, onion, and chiles into a
food processor or blender and process until smooth.
Add 1 cup (9 fl oz/250 ml) of beef stock and process.
Strain the sauce into a bowl.

Pour the sauce into a saucepan, add the butter,
and simmer until the sauce has thickened. Gradually
stir in the remaining beef stock and simmer gently
for 10–15 minutes, until thickened. Taste and adjust
the seasoning, if necessary, and remove the pan
from the heat.

Heat 1 tablespoon of the corn oil in a frying
pan or skillet over medium heat. Add the pork and
cook, stirring frequently, until it browns. Transfer
the meat to a plate, cover, and set aside. Add the
chorizo to the pan and cook, stirring frequently, for
5 minutes. Remove the pan from the heat and, using
a slotted spoon, transfer the chorizo to a paper towel
to drain, cover, and set aside.

Beat the eggs with a pinch of salt in a bowl. Melt
the butter in a saucepan. Pour in the eggs and cook,
stirring until scrambled. Remove from the heat and
set aside.

Heat the remaining corn oil in the frying pan.
Add the tortillas, one at a time, and cook for a few
seconds on both sides to soften them. Transfer to
a plate lined with paper towels to drain and cover
with paper towels to keep them warm and soft.

Spread the sauce on a tortilla, add some
scrambled egg, roll it up, and put on a serving
platter. Repeat. Spoon the remaining sauce over
them. Garnish with the pork, chorizo, and grated
cheese and serve immediately with refried beans.

bread or 1-day-old baguette
4¼ cups (1¾ pints/1 liter)
  Chicken Stock (page 184) or
  Beef Stock (page 185)
8 tomatoes, dry-roasted
¼ onion, dry-roasted
2–3 cloves garlic, dry-roasted
2 arbol chiles, dry-roasted
5 guajillo or ancho chiles,
  membranes and seeds
  removed
2 tablespoons corn oil
2 sprigs epazote leaves
6 eggs, lightly beaten
sea salt
6 Corn Tortillas (page 36),
  to serve

Dry-roast the guajillo or ancho chiles just until they are shiny. Don't let them turn brown or they will taste bitter. Put the chiles in a bowl and cover them with boiling water. Soak them for 15 minutes, then drain.

Put the dry-roasted tomatoes, onion, garlic, and chiles into a food processor or blender and process until smooth.

Squeeze out the bread and set aside. Add 1 cup (9 fl oz/250 ml) of the bread-soaking liquid to the food processor or blender, with the tomato mixture. Strain into a bowl.

Heat the oil in a saucepan over medium heat. Add the sauce, epazote, and a pinch of salt, and cook for 10 minutes. Add the remaining stock and bring to a boil. Pour the eggs into the pan through a strainer (sieve), stir in the bread, and cook for a few minutes until the eggs are done. Taste and adjust the seasoning, if necessary, discard the epazote sprigs, and remove the pan from the heat. Serve immediately with hot tortillas.

HUEVOS EN CAZUELA

✳

EGGS IN TERRACOTTA POTS

1 large tomato, dry-roasted
2 smoked chipotles chiles in adobo
2⅓ tablespoons corn oil
1 clove garlic, chopped
½ onion, finely chopped
8 eggs
1 scallion (spring onion), chopped
4 tablespoons plain yogurt
sea salt

REGION: MEXICO CITY
PREPARATION TIME: 20 MINUTES
COOKING TIME: 20 MINUTES
SERVES: 4

Put the tomato, chiles, and 2 tablespoons water into a food processor or blender and process until smooth. Strain into a bowl, taste the sauce, and add salt, if necessary.

Heat 1 tablespoon oil in a frying pan or skillet. Pour in the sauce and simmer for 10–15 minutes, until it thickens.

Divide 1 teaspoon oil between 4 individual terracotta pots or flameproof ramekins and heat. Divide the garlic and onion among them and cook over low heat for 5 minutes, until translucent. Crack 2 eggs into each pot, sprinkle with the chopped scallion (spring onion), and cook until the whites are just set. Season with salt.

Serve immediately in the pots, covered with the sauce and a spoonful of yogurt.

HUEVOS CHORIZO

EGGS WITH CHORIZO

8 eggs
7 oz/200 g chorizo, finely chopped
1 tablespoon corn oil (optional)
¼ onion, thinly sliced
sea salt and pepper

To serve:
Salsa of choice (page 496–514)
Corn Tortillas (page 36)
Refried Beans (page 532)

REGION: MEXICO CITY
PREPARATION TIME: 10 MINUTES
COOKING TIME: 15 MINUTES
SERVES: 4

Beat the eggs in a bowl and season with salt and pepper.

Heat a frying pan or skillet over medium-high heat. Add the chorizo, reduce to a low heat, and cook for 3–4 minutes, or until the chorizo has released its fat. Add a little oil if necessary.

Add the onion and cook, stirring constantly, for 3 minutes. Add the eggs and scramble for 3–4 minutes, or until the desired consistency is reached.

Serve immediately with salsa, warm tortillas, and refried beans.

4 tablespoons vegetable oil
6 Corn Tortillas (page 36)
12 eggs
Dry Chile de Arbol Salsa
    (page 502), to serve
bread, to serve

for longer, they will be crispy. Add more oil to the pan as necessary. Transfer to paper towels to drain and cover to keep warm.

Fry the eggs seperately in the same pan.

Place 1 tortilla on each of 6 plates, top with 2 eggs, and spoon the salsa over the top. Serve immediately with bread.

VERACRUZ EGGS

2 tablespoons corn oil
½ onion, finely chopped
4 tomatoes, finely chopped
12 eggs, lightly beaten
½ teaspoon sea salt
12 Corn Tortillas (page 36)
Refried Beans (page 532),
    to serve
Salsa of choice (page 496–514)
    to serve

REGION: VERACRUZ
PREPARATION TIME: 5 MINUTES
COOKING TIME: 15 MINUTES
SERVES: 6

Heat half the oil in a frying pan or skillet. Add the onion and cook over medium heat, stirring occasionally, for 5 minutes. Add the tomatoes and cook for 3 minutes, then add the eggs and salt, and cook until just set. Transfer the mixture to a warm dish.

Add the remaining oil to the pan and reheat. Briefly dip the tortillas into the oil, one at a time, to coat.

Put 2 tortillas on each of 6 individual plates and top each with the scrambled eggs. Serve with refried beans and salsa.

HUEVOS REVUELTOS MACHACA

SCRAMBLED EGGS WITH MACHACA

3 tablespoons corn oil
2 cups (8 oz/225 g) shredded
   machaca*
2 tomatoes, finely chopped
1 onion, finely chopped
1 clove garlic, finely chopped
2–3 serrano chiles, membranes
   and seeds removed, finely
   chopped
12 eggs, lightly beaten
Refried Beans (page 532),
   to serve
6 Flour Tortillas (page 37),
   to serve

STATES: COAHUILA, CHIHUAHUA, DURANGO
PREPARATION TIME: 10 MINUTES
COOKING TIME: 20 MINUTES
SERVES: 6

Heat the oil in a frying pan or skillet. Add the machaca and cook over medium heat, stirring frequently, for 8–10 minutes, until golden brown. Remove the meat from the pan with a slotted spoon.

Add the tomatoes, onion, garlic, and chiles and cook, stirring occasionally for 5 minutes. Return the machaca to the pan, reduce the heat to low, and cook for a few more minutes. Pour the eggs over the machaca, mix well, and stir until lightly scrambled.

Serve immediately with refried beans and warm flour tortillas.

*Note: Machaca is a marinated beef that is similar to jerky. As a rule, machaca is salted, so do not add extra salt. Shredded beef may also be used as a substitute.

HUEVOS TIRADOS

EGGS TIRADOS

2 tablespoons lard or butter
1 small onion, finely chopped
2–4 cuaresmeño or jalapeño
   chiles, membranes and seeds
   removed, and finely chopped
6 eggs, beaten
1½ cups (7½ oz/210 g) Refried
   Beans (page 532)
sea salt
6 Corn Tortillas (page 36),
   to serve

ORIGIN: VERACRUZ
PREPARATION TIME: 15 MINUTES
COOKING TIME: 10 MINUTES
SERVES: 6

Melt the lard in a saucepan over medium heat. Add the onion and chiles, increase the heat, and sauté for 3 minutes.

Season the eggs with salt and add to the pan. Mix well, then quickly stir in the refried beans. Stir with a spoon or spatula until the eggs are done.

Serve immediately with warm tortillas.

2 large tomatoes, coarsely
 chopped
1 clove garlic, chopped
½ onion, chopped
1 can smoked chipotle chiles,
 seeded and chopped
1 tablespoon vegetable oil
3 cactus paddles, cooked and
 cut into thin strips
2 tablespoons chopped cilantro
 (coriander)
2 cups (16 fl oz/475 ml) Chicken
 Stock (page 184), Beef Stock
 (page 185), or vegetable stock
12 eggs
sea salt
cooked black beans, to serve

Heat the oil in a large frying pan or skillet, add the tomato mixture, and cook, stirring occasionally, until it changes color.

Add the cactus paddles, cilantro (coriander), and stock and simmer over medium heat for a few minutes. Season with salt, reduce the heat, and crack the eggs in one by one. When the eggs are just cooked, remove the pan from the heat.

Serve immediately with black beans.

FONDO
BLANCO AVE

CHICKEN STOCK

1 onion
2 cloves
2¼ lb/1 kg chicken bones and giblets
10 chicken feet
1 carrot, sliced
1 leek, sliced
1 celery stalk, chopped
1 head garlic
1 cup (9 fl oz/250 ml) white wine
1 bouquet garni

REGION: ALL REGIONS
PREPARATION TIME: 15 MINUTES
COOKING TIME: 2½ HOURS
SERVES: 4

Stud the onion with the cloves.

Put the chicken bones, giblets, chicken feet, carrot, leeks, celery, garlic, and white wine into a large saucepan, and bring to a boil over high heat. When the wine has evaporated, add 8½ cups (3½ pints/2 liters) water, the onion, and the bouquet garni. Reduce the heat and simmer, frequently skimming the surface, for about 2 hours.

Remove the pan from the heat, strain into a bowl, and let cool. Remove the fat that sets on the surface before using.

All stocks may be stored in the refrigerator for up to 8 days and in the freezer for up to 3 months.

FONDO PESCADO

FISH STOCK

2¼ lb/1 kg sea bass or red snapper scraps or trimmings, bones, and heads
1½ tablespoons (1½ oz/40 g) butter
1½ tablespoons olive oil
1 onion, sliced
2 cloves garlic
2 carrots, sliced
2 celery stalks, chopped
1 cup (9 fl oz/250 ml) dry white wine
1 bouquet garni
sea salt

REGION: ALL REGIONS
PREPARATION TIME: 15 MINUTES
COOKING TIME: 40 MINUTES
SERVES: 4

Remove and discard the gills from the fish heads to prevent the stock from tasting bitter.

Melt the butter with the oil in a large saucepan. Add the fish scraps or trimmings, bones, and heads, the onion, garlic, carrots, and celery, and cook over low heat for 5–8 minutes, until the vegetables are softened but not colored. Add the wine and simmer until it has almost completely evaporated.

Add 8½ cups (3½ pints/2 liters) water, the bouquet garni, and a pinch of salt. Bring to a boil, then simmer over low heat for 15–20 minutes, skimming off any scum that rises to the surface.

Remove the pan from the heat. Strain the stock through a fine-mesh strainer (sieve), and let cool.

All stocks may be stored in the refrigerator for up to 8 days and in the freezer for up to 3 months.

2¼ lb/1 kg beef bones
1 head garlic
2 carrots
1 leek
1 celery stalk
sea salt

Reduce heat and simmer for 6–8 hours.

Remove the pan from the heat, strain into a bowl, and let cool.

All stocks may be stored in the refrigerator for up to 8 days and in the freezer for up to 3 months.

DARK VEAL STOCK

2¼ lb/1 kg veal bones
3–4 carrots, sliced
1 onion, thinly sliced
1 clove garlic
1 bouquet garni

REGION: ALL REGIONS
PREPARATION TIME: 15 MINUTES
COOKING TIME: 4½ HOURS
SERVES: 6

Preheat the oven to 400°F (200°C/Gas Mark 6).

Put the veal bones in a roasting pan and cook in the oven for 45 minutes, or until they brown. Put all the ingredients into a large saucepan and pour over enough water to cover. Bring to a boil over medium heat, skimming off any scum that rises to the surface. Reduce the heat to low and simmer for 3 hours, skimming the surface as necessary and adding cold water to keep the level of the liquid above the bones.

Remove the pan from the heat. Strain the stock through a fine-mesh strainer (sieve). Return the stock to a clean saucepan and bring to a boil. Cook for about 30 minutes until reduced to about 4¼ cups (1¾ pints/1 liter). Remove from the heat and let cool.

All stocks may be stored in the refrigerator for up to 8 days and in the freezer for up to 3 months.

Green Chile Soup with Corn

4 corn on the cobs
1 teaspoon sea salt,
  plus extra to season
2 serrano chiles
1 cup (2 oz/50 g) cilantro
  (coriander)
1 cup (2 oz/50 g) epazote

To garnish:
2 epazote leaves
1 green chile, sliced
juice of 4 limes

add water to cover, add the salt, and bring to a boil. Reduce the heat and simmer for about 20 minutes or until tender. Drain and set aside.

Put the corn kernels into a food processor or blender, add water to cover, and process until milky in appearance. Add the chiles, cilantro (coriander), epazote, and a little more water and process.

Pour 4½ cups (1¾ pints/1 liter) water into a saucepan, add a pinch of salt, and bring to a boil over low heat. Gently stir in the corn and chile mixture until combined. Taste and adjust the seasoning, if necessary, then add the pieces of corn on the cob and heat through.

Serve in bowls, garnished with epazote, green chile, and lime juice.

CHILLED AVOCADO SOUP

2 large ripe avocados, peeled
  and pitted
4¼ cups (1¾ pints/1 liter)
  Chicken Stock (page 184)
2 cups (16 fl oz/475 ml) plain
  yogurt or light (single) cream
grated zest and juice of 1 lemon
sea salt and white pepper

To garnish:
pomegranate seeds
chopped parsley

REGION: MEXICO CITY
PREPARATION TIME: 15 MINUTES, PLUS
1 HOUR CHILLING
SERVES: 6

Put the avocados, stock, yogurt, and lemon zest and juice into a food processor or blender, season with salt and pepper, and process until thoroughly combined. Add to a bowl and taste. Adjust the seasoning if necessary. Cover tightly with plastic wrap (clingfilm) and chill in the refrigerator for at least 1 hour before serving.

Serve cold in soup bowls, sprinkled with pomegranate seeds and chopped parsley.

Note: This soup pairs beautifully with white wine.

TARASCAN SOUP

1 tomato
1 onion, thickly sliced
1 clove garlic
1 ancho chile, seeded
5 avocado leaves (optional)
2 cups (14 oz/400 g) cooked
    pinto beans, cooking liquid
    reserved
2 tablespoons corn oil
4¼ cups (1¾ pints/1 liter)
    Chicken Stock (page 184)
    or water
sea salt

To serve:
Tortilla Strips (page 36)
¾ cup (6 fl oz/175 ml) sour
    cream
1 pasilla chile, seeded, sliced,
    and fried
½ cup (2 oz/50 g) grated cotija
    or feta cheese
½ avocado, peeled, pitted,
    and diced

REGION: MICHOACÁN
PREPARATION TIME: 20 MINUTES
COOKING TIME: 55 MINUTES
SERVES: 6

Preheat the oven to 400°F (200°C/Gas Mark 6).

Put the tomato, onion, garlic, chile, and avocado leaves, if using, into a roasting pan and roast for 30 minutes, removing the leaves and chiles after 2–3 minutes. Remove the pan from the oven.

Put the beans in a food processor or blender and process into a fine paste. Add the reserved liquid if necessary. Remove the beans from the food processor or blender and set aside.

Put the tomato mixture into the food processor or blender, add 1 cup (9 fl oz/250 ml) of bean liquid or water, and process until smooth. Strain into a bowl and set aside.

Heat the oil in a large saucepan. Add the tomato mixture and cook over medium heat, stirring gently, for a few minutes. Add the beans and avocado leaves, if using, and add the stock or water. Simmer over low heat, stirring occasionally, for about 20 minutes. Season to taste with salt, remove the pan from the heat.

Divide some tortilla strips, sour cream, chile, cheese and avocado between 6 bowls and ladle over the soup. Serve immediately.

1 clove garlic

1 ancho chile, seeded

½ teaspoon dried oregano

2 tablespoons chopped cilantro
  (coriander):

3 tablespoons olive oil

1½ lb/700 g catfish fillets, cut
  into bite-size pieces

4¼ cups (1¾ pints/1 liter) Fish
  Stock (page 184)

2 zucchini (courgettes), sliced

2 carrots, diced

1 cup sliced cabbage

sea salt

To serve:

chopped cilantro (coriander)

4 pickled jalapeño chiles,
  chopped

2 limes, cut into wedges

Finely chop the remaining half of the onion. Heat the oil in a medium saucepan. Add the chopped onion and cook over low heat, stirring occasionally, for 5 minutes or until translucent. Add the fish and cook, turning gently, for about 8 minutes, until golden. Remove and set aside.

Stir the tomato into the pan and bring to a boil, then add the fish stock, zucchini (courgettes), carrots, and cabbage, and season with salt. Bring to a boil, then reduce the heat, and simmer for 25 minutes, adding the fish 5 minutes before the end of the cooking time.

Remove the pan from the heat, ladle into soup bowls, garnish with cilantro (coriander) and pickled jalapeños. Serve with lime wedges.

Cactus Paddle Soup

2 tablespoons corn oil
1 onion, finely chopped
2 cloves garlic, finely chopped
5 cups (2 pints/1.2 liters)
  Chicken Stock (page 184)
1 cooked chicken breast,
  shredded
5 cactus paddles, cooked and
  cut into thin strips
1 sprig epazote, finely chopped
3 chipotle chiles in adobo,
  chopped

or blender and process until smooth, then push through a strainer (sieve).

Heat the oil in a large saucepan, add the onion, garlic, and pureed tomatoes and cook over medium heat, stirring occasionally, for 5 minutes. Add the stock, chicken, cactus paddles, epazote, and chiles, and heat through. Serve immediately.

SOPA AJO

GARLIC SOUP

4¼ cups (1¾ pints/1 liter)
  Chicken Stock (page 184)
16 cloves garlic
2 sprigs thyme
2 tablespoons olive oil
1 thick slice bread, crusts
  removed and diced
1 cup (3½ oz/100 g) grated
  Manchego cheese
4 tablespoons finely chopped
  parsley
sea salt and pepper

REGION: MEXICO CITY
PREPARATION TIME: 15 MINUTES
COOKING TIME: 20 MINUTES
SERVES: 4

Pour the stock into a saucepan, add the garlic and thyme, season with salt and pepper, and bring to a boil over medium heat. Reduce the heat and simmer for about 15 minutes or until garlic is tender.

Meanwhile, heat the oil in a frying pan or skillet. Add the diced bread and cook, stirring and tossing frequently, until golden brown all over. Remove with a slotted spoon and drain on paper towels.

Remove the pan from the heat and pour the stock through a chinois (conical strainer or sieve) into a bowl, crushing the garlic with a pestle.

Serve hot in a tureen, with the croutons, cheese, and parsley.

CHILE AND HUITLACOCHE SOUP

2 poblano chiles, seeded
2 cups (16 fl oz/475 ml) sour
   cream
2 tablespoons corn oil
1 onion, finely chopped
1 clove garlic, finely chopped
11 oz/300 g huitlacoche
4¼ cups (1¾ pints/1 liter) Beef
   Stock (page 185)
2 sprigs epazote
4 oz/120 g fresh goat cheese,
   diced
Tortilla Strips (page 36)
sea salt

REGION: MEXICO CITY
PREPARATION TIME: 20 MINUTES
COOKING TIME: 40 MINUTES
SERVES: 6

Heat a ridged grill (griddle) pan over medium heat. Add the chiles and cook, turning frequently, for 8–10 minutes or until lightly charred. Remove the pan from the heat.

Put the chiles and sour cream into a food processor or blender and process until thoroughly combined.

Heat the corn oil in a frying pan or skillet and add the onion and the garlic. Fry gently for 5 minutes or until fragrant, then add the huitlacoche. Continue to cook for another 5–10 minutes, until the fungi are soft.

Pour the stock into a saucepan and bring to a boil over low heat. Stir in the chile mixture and bring back to a boil. Add the epazote, season with salt to taste, and remove the pan from the heat.

Divide the cheese, onion, garlic, and huitlacoche, and tortilla strips among warm soup bowls, then ladle in the soup.

CREAM OF CILANTRO SOUP

2 tablespoons olive oil
½ large onion, coarsely
   chopped
2 cloves garlic, coarsely
   chopped
2 cups (3 oz/80 g) coarsely
   chopped cilantro (coriander)
1 cup (3½ oz/100 g) chopped
   walnuts
6¼ cups (2½ pints/1.5 liters)
   Chicken Stock (page 184)
½ cup (4 fl oz/120 ml) heavy
   (double) cream
Tortilla Strips (page 36)
sea salt and pepper

REGION: MEXICO CITY
PREPARATION TIME: 15 MINUTES
COOKING TIME: 20 MINUTES
SERVES: 6

Heat the oil in a small saucepan. Add the onion and garlic and cook over medium heat, stirring occasionally, for 5 minutes. Add the cilantro (coriander) and cook for 1 minute, then remove the pan from the heat.

Transfer the cilantro mixture to a food processor or blender. Reserve 4 tablespoons of the chopped walnuts for the garnish, add the remainder to the cilantro mixture, together with 1 cup (9 fl oz/250 ml) of the chicken stock, and process until combined.

Heat the mixture in a saucepan over medium heat. Gradually stir in the remaining chicken stock, then the cream. Once heated, adjust the seasoning, if necessary. Serve the soup in bowls and garnish with chopped walnuts and tortilla strips.

MUSHROOM BROTH

2 tablespoons olive oil
2 cloves garlic
1 onion, roughly chopped
½ zucchini (courgette) flower,
   torn into pieces
3⅔ cups (9 oz/250 g)
   white (button) or oyster
   mushrooms, sliced
3 sprigs epazote
8¾ cups (3½ pints/2 liters)
   Chicken Stock (page 184)
1 cup (9 fl oz/250 ml) heavy
   (double) cream
3½ oz/100 g panela or feta
   cheese crumbled or diced
sea salt

translucent. Add the zucchini (courgette) flower, mushrooms, epazote, and the stock, season with a little salt, and bring back to a boil. Remove the pan from the heat, taste and adjust the seasoning, if necessary, and let cool.

Ladle the soup into bowls, swirl the cream into each, sprinkle with the cheese, and serve.

Note: Reserve the chicken when you strain the stock. Pull the meat from the bones and serve it in fried tortillas to make tacos to accompany the soup.

BREAD CRUMB SOUP

3 bread rolls, diced
3 tablespoons olive oil
2 small onions, finely chopped
8 cloves garlic, finely chopped
4¼ cups (1¾ pints/1 liter)
   Chicken Stock (page 184) or
   Beef Stock (page 185)
2 eggs, beaten
sea salt and pepper

REGION: MEXICO CITY
PREPARATION TIME: 20 MINUTES, PLUS
5 MINUTES SOAKING
COOKING TIME: 20 MINUTES
SERVES: 4

Put the rolls into a bowl, add enough hot water to cover, and let soak for 5 minutes. Drain and squeeze out.

Heat the oil in a saucepan. Add the onions and garlic and cook over low heat, stirring occasionally, for 5 minutes, until the onions are translucent. Add the soaked rolls and cook for a few minutes, then add the stock and bring to a boil.

Pour the eggs into the pan through a strainer (sieve), stirring continuously to make threads. Season to taste with salt and pepper. Serve immediately.

SOPA DE NUEZ
DEL PATRON

PECAN SOUP "DEL PATRON"

2 tablespoons (1 oz/25 g) butter

1 leek, white part only, sliced

2 celery stalks, chopped

1 cup (4 oz/120 g) chopped
pecans

2 dried chipotle or other
smoked chiles

1 tablespoon packed brown
sugar

1 clove

1 cinnamon stick

2 dried bay leaves

3 tomatoes, peeled, seeded, and
finely chopped

8¾ cups (3½ pints/2 liters)
Chicken Stock (page 184)

1 cup (9 fl oz/250 ml) heavy
(double) cream

pinch of grated nutmeg

sea salt and pepper

To garnish:

18 pecans, toasted and coarsely
chopped

2 sprigs parsley, finely chopped

REGION: CHIHUAHUA
PREPARATION TIME: 30 MINUTES
COOKING TIME: 40 MINUTES
SERVES: 6

Melt the butter in a medium saucepan over low heat. Add the leek and celery and cook, stirring gently, for 5 minutes. Add the pecans, chiles, sugar, clove, cinnamon stick, bay leaves, and tomatoes and continue stirring gently until fragrant. Add the chicken stock and continue to stir gently until the mixture comes to a boil. Simmer for 20 minutes, then remove from the heat and let cool.

Remove and discard the bay leaves. Pour the mixture into a food processor or blender and process until smooth. Pour the mixture into a clean pan and set over low heat, stirring gently, until warmed through. Add the cream and simmer, stirring constantly, for another 5 minutes, then stir in the nutmeg and season with salt and pepper.

Serve immediately with toasted pecans and sprinkled with parsley.

black beans, drained and
  liquid reserved
1 clove garlic, finely chopped
½ small onion, finely chopped
1 tablespoon corn oil
2 morita chiles, dry-roasted
1 ancho chile, dry-roasted
1 tablespoon butter
1 lb 2 oz/500 g xonequi,
  spinach, or Swiss chard,
  stems removed and chopped
1 cup (4 oz/120 g) grated queso
  fresco, Monterey jack, or
  mild cheddar cheese
1 tablespoon finely chopped
  onion
2 tablespoons chopped cilantro
  (coriander)
Chocoyotes (page 394), to serve
sea salt

it into a large saucepan with the black beans, garlic, onion, and oil. Bring to a boil over high heat, reduce the heat and simmer for 30 minutes.

Measure 1 cup (9 fl oz/250 ml) of the bean cooking liquid from the pan and pour it into a separate saucepan. Add the chiles and bring to a boil over high heat. Reduce the heat and simmer for 10 minutes, then remove the pan from the heat.

Transfer the beans and their cooking liquid to a food processor or blender and process until smooth. Strain through a fine-mesh strainer (sieve) into a bowl.

Melt the butter in a saucepan, add both the chile and bean mixtures, and cook over low heat a few minutes. Add the xonequi, spinach, or Swiss chard. Mix well, and remove the pan from the heat.

Serve immediately with cheese, chopped onion, cilantro (coriander), and chochoyotes.

SOPA ELOTE MEXICANA

CORN SOUP

8 white corn on the cobs
5 tablespoons (2½ oz/60 g)
  butter
½ onion, finely chopped
2 cloves garlic, crushed
3 serrano chiles, seeded and
  chopped
2 poblano chiles, dry-roasted
  and sliced
4¼ cups (1¾ pints/1 liter)
  Chicken Stock (page 184)
pinch of baking soda
  (bicarbonate of soda)
1 cup (9 fl oz/250 ml) milk
1–2 sprigs epazote or oregano
sea salt and pepper

To garnish:
1 cup (8 oz/225 g) cotija or
  queso fresco, diced
2 mild chiles, membrane and
  seeds removed and cut into
  strips

REGION: MEXICO CITY
PREPARATION TIME: 25 MINUTES
COOKING TIME: 35–40 MINUTES
SERVES: 6

Remove and discard the husk from the corn on the cobs and cut off the kernels with a sharp knife. Set aside 6 tablespoons for garnish.

Melt the butter in a large saucepan. Add the onion and garlic and cook over medium heat, stirring occasionally, for 5 minutes. Add the chiles and three-quarters of the remaining corn kernels and cook, stirring constantly, for 3 minutes. Add half the stock, season with salt and pepper, and bring to a boil. Reduce the heat and simmer for 10 minutes, until the corn is tender. Remove the pan from the heat.

Put the remaining corn kernels into a food processor, add the remaining stock, and process until thoroughly combined. Combine the baking soda (bicarbonate of soda) and the milk, and, with the motor running, gradually add the mixture to the food processor through the feeder tube until pureed. Strain into a pan, add the epazote, and bring to a boil over low heat, stirring constantly. Simmer until thickened, then stir in the chile and corn mixture. When the soup is hot, remove the pan from the heat. Remove and discard the epazote, taste, and adjust the seasoning.

Serve in soup bowls with cheese, corn, and strips of chile.

Corn Soup

CALDO QUESO

CHEESY BROTH

2 tablespoons corn oil
2 potatoes, diced
½ onion, diced
2 tomatoes, peeled and diced
1 cuaresmeño or jalapeño
   chile, seeded and cut into
   thin strips
6¼ cups (2½ pints/1.5 liters)
   Chicken Stock (page 184)
2¼ lb/1 kg Chihuahua,
   Monterey Jack, or mild white
   cheddar, diced
sea salt and pepper

REGION: BAJA CALIFORNIA
PREPARATION TIME: 15 MINUTES
COOKING TIME: 25 MINUTES
SERVES: 6

Heat the oil in a medium saucepan. Add the potatoes, onion, tomatoes, and chile and cook over low heat, stirring frequently, for 15 minutes.

Pour the chicken stock into a large saucepan, bring to a boil over medium heat, and season with salt and pepper. Gradually stir in the cheese. Cook for another minute, then remove the pan from the heat.

Serve immediately in soup bowls.

CALDO DE QUESO ESTILO SONORA

SONORA-STYLE CHEESY BROTH

4 potatoes, diced
1 tablespoon corn oil
1 onion, sliced
1 tomato, seeded and chopped
3 serrano chiles, cut in
   thin strips
4¼ cups (1¼ pints/1 liter) milk
pinch of baking soda
   (bicarbonate of soda)
3 cups (1¼ pints/750 ml)
   Chicken Stock (page 184)
1½ lb/700 g Monterey Jack or
   mild cheddar cheese, diced
sea salt
4 Corn Tortillas (page 36),
   to serve

REGION: SONORA
PREPARATION TIME: 15 MINUTES
COOKING TIME: 30 MINUTES
SERVES: 4

Bring a saucepan of water to a boil, add the potatoes, and cook for 10 minutes. Strain and set aside.

Heat the oil in a large saucepan. Add the onion and cook over low heat, stirring occasionally, for 5 minutes until translucent. Add the potatoes, tomato, and chiles. Combine the milk with the baking soda (bicarbonate of soda) and add to the pan. Season with salt and bring to a boil over low heat, stirring gently.

Add the chicken stock and simmer until the potatoes are tender. Gradually stir in the cheese and cook for 1 minute. Remove the pan from the heat, cover, and let stand until all the cheese has melted.

Serve in bowls with hot tortillas.

fava (broad) beans, with their
  cooking liquid reserved
1 large clove garlic, finely
  chopped
1 onion, finely chopped
4 tomatoes, dry-roasted
2 tablespoons olive oil
1 sprig cilantro (coriander),
  finely chopped
5 mint leaves, plus extra,
  chopped, to garnish
sea salt and pepper

heat, reduce the heat and simmer for 30 minutes.
Set aside.

Put the tomatoes into a food processor or blender
and process until smooth, then strain.

Heat the oil in a medium saucepan. Add the
pureed tomatoes and cook over low heat, stirring
occasionally, until thickened. Add the tomatoes to
the beans in the pan. Add the cilantro (coriander)
and the mint leaves, and season to taste with salt
and pepper. Boil for about 15 minutes, until the
stock thickens, remove the pan from the heat, and
taste and adjust seasoning, if necessary.

Serve in bowls and sprinkle with chopped mint.

SOPA DE
VERDURA

VEGETABLE SOUP

2 corn on the cobs, halved
2 carrots, diced
1 potato, diced
¾ cup (3 oz/80 g) sliced green
  beans
⅓ cup (2 oz/50 g) peas
2 tomatoes, coarsely chopped
1 clove garlic, coarsely chopped
½ white onion, coarsely
  chopped
1 teaspoon olive oil
2 tablespoons finely chopped
  parsley
1 serrano chile, chopped
  (optional)
sea salt

REGION: ALL REGIONS
PREPARATION TIME: 20 MINUTES
COOKING TIME: 25 MINUTES
SERVES: 4

Put the corn, carrots, potato, green beans, and peas
into a medium saucepan, add the stock, and bring
to a boil over medium heat. Reduce the heat and
simmer for 15 minutes, until all the vegetables are
tender.

Meanwhile, put the tomatoes, garlic, and onion
into a food processor or blender and process until
combined.

Heat the oil in a small saucepan. Add the tomato
mixture and cook over low heat, stirring frequently,
for 2–3 minutes, then stir into the pan of vegetables.
Season to taste with salt, add the parsley and chile,
and remove the pan from the heat.

Serve immediately in a large tureen.

SOPA DE TORTILLA CON CHILE PASILLA

TORTILLA SOUP WITH PASILLA CHILE

6 pasilla chiles, dry-roasted
4¼ cups (1¾ pints/1 liter)
   Chicken Stock (page 184)
½ cup (4 fl oz/120 ml) corn oil
2 cloves garlic, dry-roasted
½ onion, sliced and dry-roasted
¼ teaspoon baking soda
   (bicarbonate of soda)
1 cup (9 fl oz/250 ml)
   evaporated milk
sea salt
Tortilla Strips (page 36),
   to serve
1 avocado, peeled, pitted,
   and diced
5 oz/150 g panela, cotija,
   or feta cheese, diced

REGION: MEXICO CITY
PREPARATION TIME: 30 MINUTES, PLUS
10 MINUTES SOAKING
COOKING TIME: 15 MINUTES
SERVES: 4

Pour the chicken stock into a saucepan and bring to a boil, then remove from the heat. Add the chiles and let soak for 10 minutes or until plump. Remove the chiles with a slotted spoon and put them in a food processor or blender. Add the garlic, onion, and 1 cup (9 fl oz/250 ml) stock and process until smooth. Strain into the pan with the stock.

Combine the baking soda (bicarbonate of soda) with the evaporated milk, then add the mixture to the pan. Simmer over medium heat for 10 minutes. Season with salt and remove the pan from the heat.

Serve the soup in individual bowls garnished with the tortilla strips, avocado, and cheese.

TOTOCÓXCATL MUSHROOM BROTH

2 tablespoons olive oil
2 cloves garlic, finely chopped
2 poblano chiles, dry-roasted
   and sliced
1 lb 2 oz/500 g assorted
   mushrooms, sliced
4¼ cups (1¾ pints/1 liter)
   Chicken Stock (page 184)
1 sprig epazote
sea salt
Corn Tortillas (page 36),
   to serve

REGION: VERACRUZ
PREPARATION TIME: 15 MINUTES
COOKING TIME: 30 MINUTES
SERVES: 4

Heat the oil in a medium saucepan. Add the garlic and cook over medium heat for 2 minutes, until fragrant, then add the chiles and cook for an additional 2 minutes. Add the mushrooms and cook for 5 minutes.

Add the chicken stock, and the epazote, season with salt, and bring to a boil. Reduce the heat to low and simmer for 20 minutes. Remove the pan from the heat and remove and discard the epazote.

Serve in soup bowls accompanied by warm tortillas.

FLOWER SOUP

4 tablespoons (2 oz/50 g) butter
½ onion, finely chopped
2 cloves garlic, finely chopped
3⅓ cups (1 lb 2 oz/500 g) corn
   kernels
1 ancho chile, dry-roasted
4¼ cups (1¾ pints/1 liter)
   Chicken Stock (page 184)
2 sprigs epazote, finely chopped
pinch of baking soda
   (bicarbonate of soda)
1 cup (9 fl oz/250 ml) milk
10 zucchini (courgette) flowers,
   pistils removed
sea salt

To garnish:
1 tablespoon butter
1 pasilla or ancho chile,
   dry-roasted, and sliced
¾ cup (6 fl oz/175 ml) sour
   cream
1 sprig epazote

onion is translucent. Add the chicken stock and simmer for about 15 minutes.

Season with salt and add the epazote. Stir the baking soda (bicarbonate of soda) into the milk and add to the pan. Simmer, gently stirring occasionally, for 5 minutes. Taste and adjust the seasoning, if necessary. Reserve 4 of the zucchini (courgette) flowers and very gently add the remainder to the soup, and simmer for an additional 5 minutes. Set aside.

To make the garnish, melt the butter in a frying pan or skillet over low heat. Add the reserved flowers and cook for 2 minutes, then remove from the pan with a slotted spoon and drain on paper towels. Add the chile to the pan and cook, stirring occasionally, for 3–5 minutes, then remove from the pan with a slotted spoon and drain on paper towels.

Serve the soup in bowls and garnish with a flower, chile, sour cream, and an epazote leaf.

SOPA DE MILPA

CORN FIELD SOUP

1 tablespoon corn oil
½ small onion, finely chopped
1 clove garlic, finely chopped
2⅔ cups (14 oz/400 g) corn
    kernels
1 lb 2 oz/500 g assorted
    mushrooms, sliced
2 cups (16 fl oz/475 ml)
    Chicken Stock (page 184)
1 sprig epazote, leaves cut into
    thin strips
1 zucchini (courgette), diced
9 oz/250 g zucchini (courgette)
    flowers, pistils removed, torn
sea salt and pepper
Corn Tortillas (page 36),
    to serve

REGION: MEXICO CITY AND TLAXCALA
PREPARATION TIME: 15 MINUTES
COOKING TIME: 35 MINUTES
SERVES: 6

Heat the oil in a medium saucepan. Add the onion and garlic and cook over low heat, stirring occasionally, for 5 minutes. Add the corn and cook for 10 minutes, then add the mushrooms and cook for 2–3 minutes.

Add the stock and epazote, bring to a boil, reduce the heat, and simmer for 5 minutes. Add the zucchini (courgettes) and cook for an additional 5 minutes until tender. Add the flowers, season to taste with salt and pepper, and remove the pan from the heat.

Serve immediately with warm tortillas.

SOPA REQUESON

REQUESON SOUP

5 oz/150 g curd cheese
2 oz/60 g goat cheese
½ cup (4 fl oz/120 ml) light
    (single) cream
2 cups (16 fl oz/475 ml) milk
½ small onion, diced
3 sprigs epazote, leaves only
1 serrano chile
2 cups (16 fl oz/475 ml)
    Chicken Stock (page 184)
2 tablespoons (1 oz/25 g) butter
sea salt and pepper
1 red onion, finely chopped
epazote leaves, to serve

REGION: MEXICO CITY
PREPARATION TIME: 10 MINUTES
COOKING TIME: 10 MINUTES
SERVES: 4

Combine the cheeses, cream, milk, onion, epazote, and chile in a food processor or blender and process until smooth. Add a little of the chicken stock to thin out the consistency, if needed, and season with salt and pepper.

In a saucepan over low heat, melt the butter, add the mixture with the chicken stock, and heat for 10 minutes, until warm. Serve in soup bowls, garnish with the onion and chopped epazote leaves.

Corn Field Soup

CREAM OF LENTIL SOUP

1 cup (8 oz/225 g) green lentils
2 tablespoons olive oil
½ onion, coarsely chopped
2 cloves garlic
1 tomato, chopped
1 sprig epazote
2 tablespoons (1 oz/25 g) butter
1 thick slice bread, crusts
   removed and diced
5 tablespoons heavy (double)
   cream
sea salt and pepper

REGION: MEXICO CITY
PREPARATION TIME: 25 MINUTES
COOKING TIME: 55 MINUTES
SERVES: 4

Put the lentils into a saucepan, add water to cover, and bring to a boil. Cook over medium heat for 30 minutes or until tender. Remove the pan from the heat, but do not drain.

Heat the oil in a saucepan. Add the onion, garlic, and tomato and cook over low heat, stirring occasionally, for 10 minutes. Remove the pan from the heat and strain, reserving the cooking liquid.

Put the onion mixture, lentils, and 1 cup (9 fl oz/250 ml) of the lentil cooking liquid into a food processor or blender and process until smooth. Add the reserved tomato cooking liquid and the epazote, and season with salt and pepper. Simmer gently for 10 minutes.

Meanwhile, melt the butter in a frying pan or skillet. Add the bread and cook, stirring and tossing frequently, for a few minutes until golden brown all over. Remove the pan from the heat and transfer the croutons with a slotted spoon to paper towels to drain.

Remove the pan of soup from the heat and discard the epazote sprig. Divide the croutons and cream among 4 soup bowls, ladle in the soup, and serve immediately.

1¼ cups (9 oz/250 g) green
   lentils
1 tablespoon corn oil
1 onion, finely chopped
1 clove garlic, finely chopped
2 oz/50 g chorizo, finely
   chopped
1 small bell pepper, seeded and
   finely chopped
1 large tomato, finely chopped
2 tablespoons finely chopped
   parsley
olive oil, for drizzling
1 teaspoon balsamic vinegar
sea salt

Remove from the heat and season with salt.

Heat the oil in a saucepan over low heat. Add the onion, garlic, and chorizo and cook over low heat, stirring occasionally, for 5 minutes. Add the bell pepper and tomato and cook for an additional 10 minutes, then stir in the parsley.

Put the onion and chorizo mixture into the pan of lentils and stir well to mix. Taste and adjust the seasoning, if necessary.

Serve the soup in bowls, drizzled with olive oil and a few drops of balsamic vinegar.

TEPARY BEAN SOUP

2 cups (14 oz/40 g) cooked
   tepary or white (haricot)
   beans, with their cooking
   liquid reserved
1 tablespoon corn oil
½ onion, finely chopped
1 tomato, chopped
1 jalapeño chile, seeded and
   finely chopped
1 sprig cilantro (coriander)
sea salt

To garnish:
½ cup (2 oz/50 g) grated cotija
   or feta cheese
2 tablespoons chopped cilantro
   (coriander)

REGION: BAJA CALIFORNIA
PREPARATION TIME: 15 MINUTES
COOKING TIME: 20 MINUTES
SERVES: 4

Measure out 4¼ cups (1¾ pints/1 liter) of the bean cooking liquid. Top it up with water or vegetable stock if necessary.

Put the drained beans into the food processor or blender and process them to a coarse paste. Add some of the reserved liquid if needed.

Heat the oil in a saucepan. Add the onion, tomato, and chile and cook over low heat, stirring occasionally, for 5 minutes, until the onion is translucent. Add the cilantro (coriander) sprig, then gently stir in the beans from the food processor. Cook for 10 minutes, gradually stirring in enough of the reserved water from the beans to obtain the desired consistency. Remove the pan from the heat and taste and adjust the seasoning, if necessary.

Serve in soup bowls, garnished with cheese and cilantro.

BEAN PASCAL

1 cup sesame seeds, toasted

2¼ cups (9 oz/250 g) masa harina

2 cups (14 oz/400 g) cooked great northern or other white beans, drained

½ onion, halved

2 chayotes, peeled, cored, and diced

1 bunch squash flowers, pistils removed

3 tablespoons finely chopped cilantro (coriander)

1 tablespoon finely chopped mint

6 epazote leaves, finely chopped

sea salt

REGION: CHIAPAS
PREPARATION TIME: 30 MINUTES
COOKING TIME: 40 MINUTES
SERVES: 6

Grind the sesame seeds in a blender or spice grinder. Put the masa harina and ½ cup (4 fl oz/120 ml) water into a food processor or blender and process until smooth. Add the ground sesame seeds and process until thoroughly combined.

Pour 4¼ cups (1¾ pints/1 liter) water into a saucepan, add the beans and onion, bring to a boil, and simmer for 20 minutes.

Add the masa harina mixture and cook for an additional 10 minutes, stirring constantly to thicken the soup. Add the chayotes, squash flowers, cilantro (coriander), and mint, season to taste with salt, and cook for an additional 5 minutes. Remove the pan from the heat.

Ladle into soup bowls, sprinkle with epazote, and serve immediately.

3 ancho chiles
1 serrano chile
5 white corn on the cobs
1 (2¼-lb/1-kg) chicken
3 tablespoons masa harina
2 tomatoes
2 tablespoons vegetable
  shortening or lard
1–2 sprigs epazote
1 small piece of raw sugar
sea salt

Remove and discard the husk from the corn on the cobs and cut off the kernels with a sharp knife. Put the corn kernels and chicken into a saucepan, add water to cover, add a pinch of salt, and bring to a boil. Reduce the heat and simmer for 1 hour.

Meanwhile, put the masa harina into a bowl, add ½ cup (4 fl oz/120 ml) water, and mix well, then strain. When the chicken is tender, remove the meat from the bones and return it to the pan, stir in the paste and cook for 10 minutes, until slightly thickened.

Put the tomatoes and chiles into a food processor or blender and process until combined, then pass through a strainer (sieve). Melt the shortening in a frying pan or skillet. Add the tomato and chile mixture and cook, stirring frequently, for 5 minutes. Stir the mixture into the pan with the chicken, add the epazote and raw sugar, and cook for another 10 minutes, until the chicken and the corn are cooked through and the soup has thickened. Serve immediately.

SOPA POBLANA

POBLANO CHILE SOUP

4 tablespoons (2 oz/50 g) butter
½ onion, coarsely chopped
1 large leek, white part only, sliced
2 poblano chiles, dry-roasted and sliced
3 cloves garlic, finely chopped
2 potatoes, diced
4¼ cups (1¾ pints/1 liter) Chicken Stock (page 184)
1 cup (9 fl oz/250 ml) sour cream
sea salt and pepper

To garnish:
Tortilla Strips (page 36)
9 oz/250 g panela or feta cheese, diced
epazote leaves

REGION: PUEBLA
PREPARATION TIME: 20 MINUTES
COOKING TIME: 30 MINUTES
SERVES: 4

Melt the butter in a medium saucepan. Add the onion, leeks, chiles, garlic, and potatoes and cook over low heat, stirring occasionally, for 5–8 minutes, until the onion is translucent.

Pour the stock into the pan with the vegetables, season with salt and pepper, and simmer for 20 minutes, until the potatoes are falling apart. Remove the pan from heat.

Pour the soup into a food processor or blender and process until smooth. Return the soup to the pan, stir in the sour cream, and reheat gently but do not let it boil. Remove the pan from the heat. Taste and adjust the seasoning, if necessary. Serve hot, garnished with tortilla strips, cheese, and epazote.

Poblano Chile Soup

GREEN SOUP WITH SHRIMP AND CHILE

2 large sprigs epazote
2¼ lb/1 kg raw shrimp
  (prawns), peeled
1 teaspoon butter
3 tablespoons coarsely
  chopped cilantro (coriander)
  leaves, plus extra to garnish

2 serrano chiles
¾ cup (3½ oz/100 g) masa
  harina
sea salt
epazote leaves, to serve

REGION: VERACRUZ
PREPARATION TIME: 25 MINUTES
COOKING TIME: 40 MINUTES
SERVES: 6

Reserve 6 epazote leaves. Pour 6¼ cups (2½ pints/ 1.5 liters) water into a saucepan, add the remaining epazote, and bring to a boil over medium heat. Add the shrimp (prawns) and cook for about 4 minutes, then drain, reserving the cooking liquid.

Melt the butter in a saucepan over low heat. Add 1 cup (9 fl oz/250 ml) of the reserved cooking liquid, add the cilantro (coriander) leaves and the chiles, and simmer for 10 minutes.

Meanwhile, combine the masa harina with ½ cup (4 fl oz/120 ml) water in a bowl. Drain off any excess liquid.

Transfer the chile mixture to a food processor or blender and process until thoroughly combined. Strain into a pan, add the shrimp and masa harina, and cook over low heat, stirring constantly, for 20 minutes. Season to taste with salt.

Serve in bowls with the cilantro and epazote.

SHRIMP SOUP

4¼–6¼ cups (1¾–2½ pints/
 1–1.5 liters) Fish Stock
 (page 184) or Chicken Stock
 (page 184)
11 oz/300 g shrimp (prawns),
 peeled and deveined, heads
 and shells reserved
2 ancho chiles, dry-roasted
2 large tomatoes
3 tablespoons olive oil
2 onions, finely chopped
4 poblano chiles, dry-roasted
 and finely chopped
2 cups (11 oz/300 g) corn
 kernels
1 sprig epazote
sea salt
3 tablespoons finely chopped
 parsley, to garnish
Macha Salsa (page 501),
 to serve

simmer for 20 minutes. Remove from the heat and strain into a bowl.

Meanwhile, put the ancho chiles into a bowl, add water to cover, and let soak for 15 minutes. Transfer the ancho chiles to a food processor or blender and process, then strain into a bowl. Put the tomatoes into the food processor or blender and process, then strain into another bowl.

Heat the oil in a saucepan. Add the onions and cook over low heat, stirring occasionally, for 5 minutes. Add the poblano chiles and corn kernels and cook for an additional few minutes. Add the processed tomatoes and simmer over medium heat for 10 minutes, or until the tomatoes change color. Add the ancho chiles and simmer until the mixture has thickened and looks slightly dry.

Add the strained stock and epazote and simmer for 15 minutes, then add the shrimp (prawns) and season to taste with salt. Remove the pan from the heat and discard the epazote.

Serve hot, garnished with parsley, with the salsa on the side.

CHACALES SOUP

REGION: CHIHUAHUA
PREPARATION TIME: 30 MINUTES, PLUS
15 MINUTES SOAKING
COOKING TIME: 50 MINUTES
SERVES: 6

3½ oz/100 g mirasol chiles,
  dry-roasted
9 oz/250 g chacales
1 head garlic, halved
1 clove garlic, dry-roasted
2 tablespoons corn oil
1 small white onion, finely
  chopped
sea salt

To garnish:
cilantro (coriander) leaves
grated Chihuahua, Monterey
  Jack, or mild cheddar cheese
2 limes, cut into wedges

In a small bowl, combine the chiles and enough hot water to cover them and soak for 15 minutes.

Soak the chacales in a bowl filled with plenty of cold water for 5–10 minutes and skim off any debris that floats to the top. Drain and rinse well, then put them in a saucepan with plenty of water and the garlic head halves. Bring to a boil, then reduce the heat and simmer for 30 minutes or until tender.

Put the chiles with their soaking water and the garlic clove into a food processor or blender and process, then strain and set aside.

Heat the oil in a saucepan. Add the onion and cook over low heat, stirring occasionally, for 5 minutes, until translucent. Add the chile mixture and simmer for 5 minutes.

Remove the pan of chacales from the heat and strain the contents into a bowl. Discard the garlic and add the chacales to the onion and chile mixture. Add enough of the chacale cooking liquid to create a soupy consistency. Simmer for an additional 8 minutes, season to taste with salt, and remove the pan from the heat.

Pour into bowls and garnish with cilantro (coriander) leaves and grated cheese. Serve immediately with lime wedges.

CHILL SOUP

2 tablespoons corn oil
1 white onion, chopped
1½ poblano chiles, dry-roasted, and finely diced
2 cups (5 oz/150 g) sliced mushrooms
⅔ cup (3½ oz/100 g) corn kernels
2 cloves garlic, finely chopped
9 tomatoes, dry-roasted, peeled, and chopped
2 chipotle chiles in adobo, sliced
4 tablespoons chopped epazote
8¾ cups (3½ pints/2 liters) Chicken Stock (page 184)
3½ oz/100 g zucchini (courgette) flowers, shredded
sea salt and pepper

5–6 minutes. Add the tomatoes, chipotle chiles, and epazote and cook for an additional 10 minutes. Add the stock and simmer gently for 15 minutes. Season to taste with salt and pepper and remove the pan from the heat.

Put the shredded zucchini (courgette) flowers into a tureen, add the soup, and serve immediately.

✳

CATFISH AND
CRAB IN BROTH

2 oz/50 g guajillo chiles,
dry-roasted
2 oz/50 g puya chiles,
dry-roasted
2 cloves garlic
1 tablespoon olive oil
½ onion, sliced
½ cup (2 oz/50 g) masa harina,
diluted in ½ cup (4 fl oz/
120 ml) water and strained
1 lb 5 oz/600 kg catfish,
cleaned
7 oz/200 g blue crabmeat
2 sprigs epazote
1 green chile, finely chopped
1 onion, finely chopped
sea salt
Corn Tortillas (page 36),
to serve
2 limes, cut into wedges

REGION: GUERRERO
PREPARATION TIME: 30 MINUTES, PLUS
10 MINUTES SOAKING
COOKING TIME: 25 MINUTES
SERVES: 6

In a small bowl, combine the chiles and enough hot
water to cover them and soak for 10 minutes. Drain.

Put the chiles and garlic into a food processor or
blender and process to a smooth consistency, then
strain into a bowl and set aside.

Heat the oil in a saucepan over medium-low heat.
Add the onion and cook over low heat, stirring
occasionally, for 5 minutes. Stir in the chile and
garlic mixture and cook for a few minutes. Add
the masa harina and 6½ cups (50 fl oz/1.5 liters)
water and bring to a boil. Add the fish, crabmeat,
and epazote, season with salt to taste and cook for
another 10 minutes, until the fish is cooked.

Remove the pan from the heat and ladle the soup
into bowls. Garnish with chopped green chile and
chopped onion, and serve immediately with hot
tortillas and lime wedges.

SOPA JAIBA

✳

CRAB SOUP

18 cascabel chiles, dry-roasted
3 ancho chiles, dry-roasted
1 clove garlic
2 tablespoons olive oil
1 onion, finely chopped
9 oz/250 g crabmeat
5 cups (2 pints/1.2 liters) Fish
Stock (page 184)
4½ lb/2 kg crabs, halved
1 sprig epazote, plus extra,
chopped, to garnish
sea salt and pepper

REGION: TAMAULIPAS
PREPARATION TIME: 25 MINUTES, PLUS
15 MINUTES SOAKING
COOKING TIME: 35 MINUTES
SERVES: 4

Put the chiles into a heatproof bowl, add boiling
water to cover, and let soak for 15 minutes.

Put the chiles and their soaking water with the
garlic into a food processor or blender and process
until thoroughly combined. Strain.

Heat the oil in a large saucepan. Add the onion
and cook over low heat, stirring occasionally, for
5 minutes, until translucent. Add the crabmeat,
increase the heat to medium, and cook for 5 minutes.
Add the chile mixture and cook, stirring occasionally,
for 10 minutes, then add the stock. Add the crabs
and epazote and simmer for 15 minutes. Season to
taste and remove the pan from the heat. Discard the
epazote sprig. Serve in soup bowls, garnished with
chopped epazote.

dry-roasted
4 tomatoes, dry-roasted
4 cups (1⅔ pints/950 ml) fish
  stock
1 lb 2 oz/500 g raw or dried
  shrimp (prawns), shelled
1⅓ cups (5 oz/150 g) masa
  harina
½ oz/13 g epazote
sea salt

and reserve the soaking liquid.

Put the chiles and tomatoes into a food processor or blender and process until smooth, adding some of the soaking liquid if necessary.

Bring the fish stock to a boil over medium heat, add the shrimp (prawns), and cook for 5 minutes. Drain and set aside, reserving the stock and the shrimp.

Pour 1 cup (9 fl oz/250 ml) water over the masa harina and stir until it is well incorporated. Strain into a bowl.

Pour the fish stock into a large saucepan. Add the tomato and chile sauce and the epazote and bring to a boil over medium heat. Add the masa harina and cook, stirring constantly for 10 minutes, until the soup thickens. Add the shrimp, season with salt, and cook for 4 minutes or until cooked through. Serve immediately in soup bowls.

✷

RED SEAFOOD
SOUP

1 white onion, halved

2 cloves garlic

3 tomatoes

3 guajillo or ancho chiles,
  seeded

1 chipotle chile

1 cinnamon stick

4 peppercorns

4 tablespoons corn oil

7 oz/200 g blue crabmeat

2 potatoes, diced

4¼ cups (1¾ pints/1 liter)
  Fish Stock (page 184)

1 sprig epazote, chopped, plus
  extra for garnish

4 oz/120 g cooked baby shrimp
  (prawns), peeled

4 tablespoons Masa Dough
  (page 36)

10 oz/275 g fresh oysters

salt

REGION: VERACRUZ
PREPARATION TIME: 45 MINUTES, PLUS
15 MINUTES SOAKING
COOKING TIME: 45 MINUTES
SERVES: 4

Dry-roast half an onion, garlic, and tomatoes in
a frying pan or skillet for 15 minutes, then add the
guajillo or ancho chiles, and roast for an additional
5 minutes. In a small bowl, combine the chipotle
chiles and enough hot water to cover them and soak
for 15 minutes.

Put the dry-roasted ingredients, chiles and their
soaking liquid, cinnamon stick, and peppercorns
into a food processor or blender and process until
smooth. Strain and set aside.

Finely chop the other half of the onion. Heat
1 tablespoon oil in a frying pan or skillet over
medium heat, add the onion, and cook for 5 minutes
until fragrant. Add the crabmeat and cook for an
additional 5 minutes.

Heat 1 tablespoon oil in a large saucepan. Add
the potatoes and cook, stirring frequently, for
5 minutes, then stir in the tomato mixture, fish
stock, and epazote. Cook for a few minutes, then
add the shrimp (prawns). Mix the masa dough with
½ cup (4 fl oz/120 ml) water in a bowl, stir it into the
pan, and boil the mixture, stirring constantly for
2 minutes. Season to taste, add the oysters, and cook
for another 2 minutes, then remove the pan from
the heat and set aside.

Heat the remaining oil in a frying pan or skillet,
add the epazote leaves, and cook for 1 minute.
Remove the pan from the heat.

Divide the hot soup evenly among 4 serving
bowls, garnish with the fried epazote leaves, and
serve immediately.

Red Seafood Soup

HUATAPE
CAMARON SECO

DRIED SHRIMP SOUP

2 poblano or Anaheim chiles
7 oz (200 g) dried shrimp
  (prawns), shells reserved
1 onion, sliced
1 clove garlic
4 tomatoes
¾ cup (3½ oz/100 g) masa
  harina
2 tablespoons corn oil
2 sprigs epazote, plus extra
  finely chopped, to serve
sea salt
Corn Tortillas (page 36),
  to serve
2 limes, cut into wedges,
  to serve

REGION: VERACRUZ
PREPARATION TIME: 20 MINUTES, PLUS
10 MINUTES SOAKING
COOKING TIME: 55 MINUTES
SERVES: 6

Preheat the oven to 350°F (180°C/Gas Mark 4).

Put the chiles, shrimp (prawn) shells, onion, garlic, and tomatoes into a roasting pan and roast for 15 minutes.

Put the chiles into a heatproof bowl, add boiling water to cover, and let soak for 10 minutes or until softened, then drain.

Meanwhile, pour 4½ cups (1¾ pints/1 liter) water into a saucepan and bring to a boil over high heat. Add the shrimp and cook for 10 minutes, then strain, reserving the cooking liquid.

Put the roasted chile and shrimp shell mixture, and 1 cup (9 fl oz/250 ml) of the reserved cooking liquid into a food processor or blender and process until smooth. Strain into a bowl.

Add ½ cup (4 fl oz/120 ml) water to the masa harina in a bowl and mix well.

Heat the oil in a medium saucepan. Add the processed tomato mixture and cook over medium heat, stirring frequently, for 10 minutes. Season with salt, add the remaining cooking liquid, and bring to a boil over high heat. Stir in the masa harina mixture and epazote, then add the shrimp. Cook, stirring frequently, for another 10 minutes. Taste and adjust the seasoning, if necessary, and remove the pan from the heat. Remove and discard the epazote.

Ladle the soup into bowls, sprinkle with epazote, and serve immediately with warm tortillas and lime wedges

4 tomatoes
1 onion, diced
1 clove garlic, peeled
1 serrano chile, halved and
seeded
1 jalapeño chile, halved and
seeded
1 cinnamon stick
2 peppercorns
3 tablespoons olive oil
1 Corn Tortilla (page 36)
8 oz (400 g) shrimp (prawns),
peeled
sea salt and pepper
5 epazote leaves, finely
chopped, to garnish
1 lime, cut into wedges,
to serve

Combine the tomatoes, onion, garlic, chiles, cinnamon, and peppercorns in a food processor or blender, add 1 cup (9 fl oz/250 ml) water, and process to a smooth consistency. Add the tortilla and process briefly again to thicken, then set aside.

Heat the oil in a saucepan. Add the shrimp (prawns) and cook over medium heat for 3 minutes. Add 4¼ cups (1¾ pints/1 liter) water, stir in the tomato mixture, and season to taste with salt. Reduce the heat, cover, and cook for 20 minutes, then add ½ cup (4 fl oz/120 ml) water. Stir and cook for 5 minutes.

While still very hot, transfer to a soup tureen, sprinkle with the epazote leaves, and serve with lime wedges.

6 ancho chiles, seeded
2 teaspoons oregano
2¼ lb/1 kg hominy corn
1 head garlic
1 small white onion
10 bay leaves
1 lb 2 oz/500 g loin or pork leg
1 lb 2 oz/500 g pig's head
2 pig legs, cleaned and
  quartered
sea salt

To serve:
12 lemons, quartered
oregano, to taste
piquin chile, to taste
1 white onion, finely chopped
½ lettuce, finely shredded
12 radishes, sliced

them with their soaking liquid into a food processor or blender, add 1 teaspoon oregano, and process until smooth. Strain, pour into a frying pan or skillet, and cook over medium heat for 15 minutes, then remove from the heat and set aside.

Put the garlic, onion, bay leaves, remaining oregano, salt to taste, and water into a large saucepan and cook over low-medium heat for 30 minutes. Meanwhile, put the loin, head, and legs in a large saucepan, add enough water to cover, and bring to a boil over medium heat. Boil for 45 minutes, or until soft. Remove the meat and shred it. Cut the meat from the head into bite-size cubes and set aside.

Add the corn to the garlic and onion stock, and cook for 30 minutes, until the corn is fully soft. Add the chile paste and check the seasoning.

Ladle the soup into bowls, dividing the meat generously among each bowl. Serve with lemon, oregano, piquin chile, onion, lettuce, and radishes.

GUERRERO GREEN POZOLE

30 tomatillos

1 prepared ox tongue, skinned and cut into pieces

10 large sorrel leaves, chopped

2–3 serrano chiles

2 tablespoons corn oil

½ cup (2 oz/50 g) pumpkin seeds, dry-roasted and ground

6 cups (2¼ lb/1 kg) cooked hominy, cooking liquid reserved

1 bunch epazote

sea salt

To serve:

1 onion, finely chopped

dried oregano

1 large avocado, peeled, pitted, and diced

2½ oz/65 g fried pork rinds (scratchings)

1 lemon, quartered

1 (4-oz/120-g) can sardines in oil, drained

REGION: GUERRERO
PREPARATION TIME: 25 MINUTES
COOKING TIME: 55 MINUTES
SERVES: 6

Put the tomatillos into a small saucepan, add water to cover, and bring to a boil. Reduce the heat to medium and simmer for about 15 minutes, until softened but not bursting. Remove the pan from the heat.

Put the tomatillos, ox tongue, sorrel, chiles, and all but 4¼ cups (1¾ pints/1 liter) of the hominy cooking liquid into a food processor or blender and process until smooth. Strain the mixture into a bowl.

Heat the oil in a medium saucepan. Add the processed tomatillo mixture and cook over high heat, stirring occasionally, for about 5 minutes. Add the pumpkin seeds and cook for about 10 minutes, until the mixture has thickened. Stir in the hominy and remaining cooking liquid. Add the epazote, season with salt to taste, and cook for an additional 10–15 minutes. Taste and adjust the seasoning, if necessary, and remove the pan from the heat.

Discard the epazote. Serve in bowls with sides of onion, oregano, avocado, fried pork rinds (scratchings), lemon, and sardines.

Note: Cooked, shredded pork may also be served with this soup.

3 cups (1 lb/2 oz/500 g) cooked
  hominy
1 small head garlic
3 onions
11¾ cups (4¾ pints/2.5 liters)
  Fish Stock (page 184)
2 tablespoons corn oil
1 lb 2 oz/500 g soft-shell crabs,
  cleaned
1 lb 2 oz/500 g shrimp
  (prawns), peeled, heads and
  shells reserved
9 oz/250 g white fish fillets, cut
  into pieces
3½ oz/100 g guajillo chile,
  seeded
9 oz/250 g cooked octopus,
  sliced
11 oz/300 g crabmeat
1 lb 2 oz/500 g live clams,
  scrubbed
1 teaspoon dried oregano
sea salt
2 limes, cut into wedges,
  to serve

until tender.

Heat 1 tablespoon of oil in a frying pan or skillet.
Add the soft-shell crabs and shrimp (prawns) and
cook over medium heat for 8 minutes, until the
shrimp change color. Remove the seafood from the
pan and set aside.

Add the fish to the pan and cook over medium
heat, occasionally stirring gently, for 8 minutes.
Remove the pan from the heat.

Chop the remaining onions. Heat the remaining
oil in a saucepan, add the onions, shrimp heads and
shells, and the chile and cook over medium heat,
stirring frequently, for 5 minutes. Add 2 cups
(16 fl oz/475 ml) fish stock and bring to a boil, then
reduce the heat, and simmer for 10 minutes. Remove
the pan from the heat, pour the mixture into a food
processor or blender, and process. Strain it into the
pan of hominy, add the remaining fish stock, stir
well, and simmer for 15 minutes.

Add the octopus, crabmeat, clams, soft-shell
crabs, shrimp, and oregano and simmer for an
additional 5 minutes. Remove and discard any
clams that remain closed.

Remove the pan from the heat, taste and adjust
the seasoning, if necessary, and serve immediately
with lime wedges.

DRY BEEF
SOUP

2 tablespoons olive oil
½ onion, finely chopped
2 cloves garlic, finely chopped
6 oz/165 g beef jerky, shredded
3 serrano chiles, seeded and
  finely chopped
2 tomatoes, skinned, seeded,
  and chopped
2 potatoes, diced
4¼ cups (1¾ pints/1 liter) Beef
  Stock (page 185)
sea salt and pepper
Flour Tortillas (page 37),
  to serve

REGION: CHIHUAHUA
PREPARATION TIME: 15 MINUTES
COOKING TIME: 40 MINUTES
SERVES: 4

Heat the oil in a medium saucepan. Add the onion and cook over medium heat, stirring occasionally, for 5 minutes. Add the garlic and cook, stirring occasionally, for a minute or until fragrant, then add the beef, chiles, and tomatoes, and cook, stirring frequently, for 2 minutes, until the beef has browned. Add the potatoes and cook for 3 minutes, then add the stock, cover, and simmer for 20 minutes or until potatoes are tender. Season with salt and pepper to taste. Cook for another 5 minutes, then remove the pan from the heat.

Taste and adjust the seasoning, if necessary. Serve in soup bowls with warm tortillas.

CHURIPO

CHURIPO

¼ ancho chile, dry-roasted
2¼ lb/1 kg beef shank
1 lb 2 oz/500 g beef neck bones
4 sprigs mint, coarsely chopped
4 prickly pears, peeled, seeded,
  and diced
4 tomatoes, dry-roasted
1 garlic clove, dry-roasted
½ cabbage, diced
sea salt

REGION: MICHOACÁN
PREPARATION TIME: 30 MINUTES, PLUS
15 MINUTES SOAKING
COOKING TIME: 55 MINUTES
SERVES: 6

In a small bowl, combine the chile and enough hot water to cover it and soak for 15 minutes. Drain.

Put the meat, bones, and mint in a saucepan, add water to cover, and bring to a boil. Reduce the heat and simmer for 40 minutes. Add the prickly pears and cabbage and season to taste with salt.

Put the chiles, tomatoes, and garlic into a food processor or blender and process until combine. Strain into the pan and stir. Taste and adjust the seasoning, if necessary, and simmer for an additional 15 minutes.

Remove the pan from the heat and discard the bone. Ladle the soup into bowls and serve.

Churipo

TLALPAN-STYLE CHICKEN IN BROTH

1 large, skinless chicken breast
1 carrot, diced
2 zucchini (courgettes), diced
1 potato, diced
½ cup chopped green beans
1 tablespoon corn oil
1 clove garlic, finely chopped
½ small onion, finely chopped
2 small tomatoes, dry-roasted, peeled, seeded, and chopped
½ sprig epazote
½ cup (3 oz/80 g) cooked chickpeas
sea salt and pepper

To serve:
1 avocado, diced
1 sprig cilantro (coriander), finely chopped
1 serrano chile, finely chopped
1 smoked chipotle chile, seeded and chopped
1 lime, cut into wedges

REGION: MEXICO CITY
PREPARATION TIME: 25 MINUTES
COOKING TIME: 1 HOUR
SERVES: 4

Put the chicken breast into a medium saucepan, add 4½ cups (1¾ pints/1 liter) water or enough water to cover, and bring to a boil over medium heat. Add the carrot, zucchini (courgettes), potatoes, and green beans. Season with sea salt and pepper, then reduce the heat and simmer for 30 minutes or until the chicken is tender.

Heat the oil in a frying pan or skillet. Add the garlic, onion, and tomatoes and cook over low heat, stirring occasionally, for 5 minutes. Transfer this vegetable mixture to the pan of chicken, stir well, and add the chickpeas. Simmer for 15 minutes.

Remove the chicken breast with a slotted spoon and coarsely shred the meat, then stir it back into the pan. Taste and adjust the seasoning and remove the pan from the heat.

Serve the soup in bowls garnished with avocado, cilantro (coriander), and chiles, and lime wedges on the side.

1 (3¼-lb/1.5-kg) chicken, cut
  into 8 pieces
8 saffron threads
¼ teaspoon cumin seeds,
  dry-roasted
4¼ cups (1¾ pints/1 liter)
  Chicken Stock (page 184)
2 tablespoons olive oil
1 onion, finely chopped
sea salt and pepper
4 sprigs parsley, finely chopped,
  to garnish

chicken is tender. Remove the pan from the heat
and allow to cool. Cut the breast meat into bite-size
pieces and set aside.

Put the chicken meat, saffron, and cumin into
a food processor or blender and process briefly.
Add a little chicken stock, and process again, to
make a smooth mixture.

Heat the oil in a saucepan. Add the onion and
cook over low heat, stirring occasionally, for
5 minutes. Stir in the spiced chicken mixture, add the
remaining chicken stock, add the remaining pieces
of chicken, and season with salt and pepper. Simmer
for 5 minutes, then remove the pan from the heat.

Ladle the soup into bowls, add the chicken to
each bowl, sprinkle with the parsley, and serve.

RANCH-STYLE
CHICKEN SOUP

2 Corn Tortillas (page 36),
  toasted, plus extra to serve
1 chicken, cut into 8 pieces
4 cloves garlic, halved
1 onion, halved
1 jalapeño chile, seeded and
  cut into thin strips
1 large tomato, seeded and
  finely chopped
1 sprig peppermint or
  spearmint, finely chopped
¼ teaspoon cumin seeds,
  dry-roasted
3 carrots, diced
3 zucchini (courgettes), diced
3 corn on the cobs, quartered
sea salt

REGION: GUANAJUATO
PREPARATION TIME: 20 MINUTES, PLUS
5 MINUTES SOAKING
COOKING TIME: 1 HOUR 10 MINUTES
SERVES: 6

Put the tortillas into a dish, add water to cover, and
soak for 5 minutes, then drain, transfer to a food
processor or blender, and process.

Put the chicken into a saucepan, add water to
cover, add the garlic, season with salt, and bring
to a boil. Add the onion, chile, tomato, peppermint
or spearmint, cumin, vegetables, and processed
tortillas. Bring back to a boil, then reduce the heat
and simmer for about 1 hour or until the chicken
is tender.

Serve the soup in bowls accompanied by warm
tortillas.

MENUDO

REGION: CHIHUAHUA
PREPARATION TIME: 20 MINUTES, PLUS
15 MINUTES SOAKING
COOKING TIME: 1 HOUR 40 MINUTES
SERVES: 6

2¼ lb/1 kg pigs' feet
4½ lb/2 kg prepared
  honeycomb tripe, chopped
1 head garlic, halved
3 cloves garlic
1 large onion, halved
3 cups (1 lb oz/450 g) hominy
  corn kernels
1⅓ cups (5 oz/150 g) serrano
  chiles, seeded
2 tablespoons corn oil
sea salt

To serve:
chopped oregano
1 onion, finely diced
lime, cut into wedges

Put the pigs' feet, tripe, garlic, and onion into
a heavy saucepan and add enough water to cover.
Bring to a boil, then reduce the heat to medium and
simmer for 30 minutes or until the meat falls off the
bones. Remove from the heat, remove the meat from
the bones, and chop. Discard the bones. Add the
hominy and cook for 20 minutes.

Meanwhile, heat a frying pan or skillet. Add the
chiles and dry-roast over medium heat, stirring and
turning frequently, for 8–10 minutes. Remove from
the pan, put into a heatproof bowl, add warm water
to cover, and let soak for 15 minutes.

Drain the chiles and put them into a food
processor or blender with the garlic. Process until
thoroughly combined, then strain into a bowl, and
season with salt. Heat the oil in a frying pan or
skillet. Add the chile mixture and cook over low
heat, stirring frequently, for 5 minutes, then remove
from the heat.

Put the chile mixture into a large saucepan and
simmer for 20 minutes. Add the hominy and meat,
season to taste with salt, and cook for an additional
10 minutes.

Serve in pozolero or soup bowls and garnish with
chopped oregano. Serve with onion and lime.

Menudo

1 oz/25 g puya or guajillo
  chiles, dry-roasted
4½ lb/2 kg oxtail, cut into
  pieces
13–17½ cups (5¼ –7 pints/
  3–4 liters) Beef Stock
  (page 185)
2 white onions, halved
1 head garlic, halved, plus
  3 cloves
2 sprigs thyme
2 sprigs marjoram
2 bay leaves
1 cup (6 oz/175 g) chacales, rice,
  or pearl barley
½ teaspoon cumin seeds
  roasted
sea salt and pepper
1–2 avocados, peeled, pitted,
  and diced, to serve
3 tablespoons finely chopped
  cilantro (coriander), to serve
½ red onion, finely diced,
  to serve
1 lemon, cut into wedges

Put the oxtail, beef stock, 1 onion, head of garlic, thyme, marjoram, and bay leaves into a pressure cooker, add a pinch of salt, and secure the lid. Bring to high pressure and cook for 45 minutes.

Remove the pan from the cooker and lift out the oxtail, reserving the cooking liquid. Remove the meat from the bones, discarding the bones, skin, and fat. Strain the cooking liquid into a bowl and remove any fat with a skimmer and/or paper towels. Pour the cooking liquid into a saucepan.

Drain the chiles, reserving the soaking liquid. Put them into a food processor or blender, add the cloves of garlic, the remaining onion, and 1–2 tablespoons of the soaking water, and process until combined. Strain the mixture into the pan, stir to mix well, and bring to a boil over medium heat. Add the chacales and bring back to a boil, then reduce the heat and simmer for 15 minutes.

Add the meat and cumin to the saucepan, season with salt and pepper to taste, and simmer another few minutes. Taste and adjust the seasoning, if necessary.

Remove the pan from the heat and ladle the soup into a tureen, garnish with diced avocado, cilantro (coriander), and onion, and serve with lemon.

BIRRIA

REGION: JALISCO
PREPARATION TIME: 1 HOUR, PLUS AT LEAST
5 HOURS MARINATING
COOKING TIME: 3 HOURS 50 MINUTES
SERVES: 6

6 chiles, dry-roasted
5 guajillo chiles, dry-roasted
4 cloves garlic, dry-roasted
¾ cup (6 fl oz/175 ml) apple
  cider vinegar
1 cinnamon stick
½ inch (1 cm) fresh ginger,
  grated
2 teaspoons dried oregano
½ teaspoon ground cumin
½ teaspoon pepper
1 teaspoon sea salt
3¼–4½ lb/1.5–2 kg boneless
  shoulder of lamb, trimmed of
  excess fat
2 tomatoes
1 cup (9 fl oz/250 ml) Beef
  Stock (page 185)
4 tablespoons dry sherry or
  white wine
chopped cilantro (coriander),
  to garnish

Put the chiles into a saucepan, add enough water cover, and bring to a boil. Remove the pan from heat and soak for 20 minutes or until soft. Drain the chiles, reserving the soaking liquid, and put them into a food processor or blender. Add the garlic and vinegar and process to a smooth paste. Add the cinnamon, ginger, 1 teaspoon of the oregano, cumin, pepper, and salt and process again until thoroughly combined and it forms a thick paste. If necessary, add 1 tablespoon of the reserved soaking liquid. Adjust the seasoning and strain the paste into a bowl.

Rub the paste over the lamb, place in a bowl, and cover with plastic wrap (clingfilm). Let marinate in the refrigerator for at least 5 hours, preferably overnight.

Preheat the oven to 350°F (180°C/Gas Mark 4).

Put a rack in a roasting pan and add enough water to reach just below the rack. Put the lamb on the rack and cover the pan completely with aluminum foil, sealing it around the edges. Put the lamb in the oven and bake for 3 hours. Remove from the oven and increase the oven temperature to 375°F (190°C/Gas Mark 5).

Remove the meat from the rack, reserving the liquid in the roasting pan, and cut it into large pieces. Put them on a baking sheet and return to the oven to brown for 15 minutes. Turn the meat at least once. Put the tomatoes in a separate roasting pan and roast for 15 minutes in the oven with the meat.

Skim off any fat from the liquid in the roasting pan and pour the cooking liquid into a large saucepan. Put the tomatoes, the remaining oregano, and the stock into a food processor or blender and process until smooth. Add this liquid and the sherry and bring to a boil. Reduce the heat to low and simmer for 15 minutes. Adjust the seasoning. Divide the meat among 6 bowls and ladle the soup on top. Garnish with chopped cilantro (coriander).

Birria

SALPICON MARINERO

✳

MARINERS' SEAFOOD SALAD

14 oz/400 g sole or any flat fish,
  filleted
1 (3½-oz/100-g) canned tuna
  fish
1⅔ cups (7 oz/200 g) cooked
  shrimp (prawns), finely
  chopped
4 tablespoons olive oil
juice of 3 limes
2 celery stalks, finely chopped
2 cucumbers, peeled, seeded,
  and finely chopped
6 radishes, finely chopped
½ cup (3½ oz/100 g)
  mayonnaise
sea salt and pepper

To serve:
1 romaine (Cos) lettuce
1¼ cups (4 oz/120 g) black
  olives

REGION: GULF
PREPARATION TIME: 20 MINUTES, PLUS
15 MINUTES STANDING
COOKING TIME: 8 MINUTES
SERVES: 6

Put the fish and 1 cup (9 fl oz/250 ml) water into
a large saucepan, bring to a boil, then simmer for
6 minutes. Drain the fish, cut into bite-size pieces,
and put into a bowl with the tuna and shrimp
(prawns). Season with the olive oil and lime juice
and let stand for 15 minutes.

Add the celery, cucumber, and radishes to the
fish, then add the mayonnaise and a little more lime
juice, to taste. Add salt and pepper to taste. Put the
salad in the center of a serving plate, arrange the
lettuce around the outside, and garnish with black
olives. Serve.

5 potatoes
2 ancho chiles, dry-roasted
2 cloves garlic
10 black peppercorns
2 tablespoons olive oil
4 tablespoons (2 oz/50 g) butter
6 (6-oz/180-g) salt cod fillets, desalted
1 white onion, dry-roasted and finely chopped
2 tomatoes, dry-roasted and finely chopped
5 sprigs parsley, finely chopped
2 red bell peppers, broiled (grilled) and cut into strips
sea salt
White Rice (page 521), to serve

Drain, let cool, then slice and set aside.

Put the chiles into a bowl, add just enough boiling water to cover, and soak for 10 minutes. Put the chiles and the soaking liquid into a food processor or blender, add the garlic and peppercorns, and process until smooth. Strain into a bowl.

Heat the oil and butter in a large frying pan or skillet over medium heat. Add the cod and cook for 2 minutes each side, then remove with a slotted spoon and set aside. In the same pan, add the onion and sauté for 2 minutes, then add the tomatoes and parsley.

Add the chili sauce to the onion mixture and bring to a boil. Reduce the heat and simmer for 5–10 minutes until the sauce thickens. Reduce the heat to low, and add the cod, and cook gently for 10 minutes. Add the potato slices and bell peppers, then check seasoning. Serve with white rice.

BACALAO CON CHILES SECOS

✻

SALT COD IN DRIED CHILI SAUCE

4 ancho chiles, lightly
  dry-roasted
3 cloves garlic, dry-roasted
1 cinnamon stick, dry-roasted
¼ teaspoon cumin seeds,
  dry-roasted
3 cloves, dry-roasted
3 tablespoons olive oil
3 tablespoons bread crumbs
1 lb 2 oz/500 g salt cod,
  desalted and cut into squares
  sea salt
White Rice (page 521), to serve

REGION: CENTRAL MEXICO
PREPARATION TIME: 40 MINUTES, PLUS
15 MINUTES SOAKING
COOKING TIME: 35 MINUTES
SERVES: 6

Put the chiles into a heatproof bowl, add just enough hot water to cover, and soak for 15 minutes. Put them in a food processor with the garlic, cinnamon, cumin, and cloves, and process until smooth. Strain into a bowl, discarding the contents of the strainer (sieve).

Heat the oil in a saucepan over medium heat. Add the sauce and heat for 5 minutes. Add the bread crumbs, mix to combine, and bring to a boil. As soon as it is boiling, add the cod with 4 tablespoons of water, then reduce the heat to low, cover, and cook for 20 minutes. Check the seasoning and serve with white rice.

5 oz/150 g chilmole paste
6 tablespoons apple cider
  vinegar
sea salt
6 (2¼-lb/1-kg) grouper fillets
2 tablespoons corn oil
6 tomatoes, seeded and
  chopped
1 white onion, thinly sliced
2 red bell peppers, thinly sliced
3 tablespoons chopped parsley
pinch of ground nutmeg
½ teaspoon ground cumin

To serve:
tacos or tostadas
1 habanero chile, dry-roasted
  and finely chopped
lemon juice

salt, then add the fish and turn until the fish is coated in the mixture. Cover with plastic wrap (clingfilm) and marinate in the refrigerator for 30 minutes.

Heat the oil in a frying pan or skillet over medium heat, add the tomatoes, onion, and bell peppers, and sauté for 2 minutes. Add the chopped parsley, nutmeg, and cumin.

Put the marinated fish in a large saucepan with a lid, pour the sauce over the fish, cover, and simmer for 10 minutes or until the fish is cooked.

Serve with tacos or tostadas, habanero chile, and a squeeze of lemon juice.

PESCADO TIKIN-XIK

✻

"TIKIN-XIK" FISH

3¼ lb/1.5 kg grouper, filleted
juice of 1 orange
1½ teaspoons oregano
2 tablespoons achiote paste
4 tablespoons apple cider
  vinegar
4 tablespoons (2¼ oz/60 g) lard
  or butter
1 large white onion, sliced
3 tomatoes, sliced
2 bay leaves
½–1 habanero chile,
  membrane and seeds
  removed
2 yellow bell peppers, seeded
  and cut into strips
1 banana leaf
sea salt and pepper
fried plantains, to serve
Refried Beans (page 532),
  to serve
Red Onion Escabeche (page
  478), to serve

REGION: YUCATÁN PENINSULA
PREPARATION TIME: 25 MINUTES, PLUS
1 HOUR MARINATING
COOKING TIME: 25 MINUTES
SERVES: 6

Preheat the oven to 350°F (180°C/Gas Mark 4).

Place the fillets in a shallow dish. Add the orange juice and oregano and season with salt and pepper.

Put the achiote and vinegar in a small bowl, and stir until dissolved. Pour the mixture over the fish, cover with plastic wrap (clingfilm), and marinate in the refrigerator for 1 hour.

Grease a large ovenproof dish with some of the lard or butter. Remove the fish from the marinade and place the fish opened out in the dish. Spread with the remaining lard, then put the onion, tomatoes, bay leaves, chile, and bell peppers on top. Wrap the fish with the banana leaf, then cover with aluminum foil and bake in the oven for 25 minutes or until the fish is cooked but not dry.

Serve with plantains and refried beans.

"Tikin-Xik" Fish

SERE DE PESCADO

✺

FISH IN COCONUT SAUCE

6 cloves garlic, dry-roasted
2 tablespoons achiote paste
3 tomatoes, coarsely chopped
½ white onion, coarsely chopped
2 tablespoons corn oil
2 green plantains, diced
2 cups (16 fl oz/475 ml) coconut milk
1 xcatic chile, dry-roasted and chopped
6 (5¼-oz/150-g) grouper fillets
sea salt
White Rice (page 521), to serve

REGION: QUINTANA ROO
PREPARATION TIME: 25 MINUTES
COOKING TIME: 1 HOUR 10 MINUTES
SERVES: 6

Add ¼ cup (2 fl oz/60 ml) water to a saucepan, along with the garlic and achiote paste and bring to a boil over medium heat, stirring continuously. Boil for 5 minutes, then remove from the heat and set aside to infuse.

Put the tomatoes and onion into a food processor or blender and process to a paste. Strain through a strainer (sieve) into a bowl. Heat the oil in a frying pan or skillet over medium heat, add the onion paste, and sauté for 10 minutes, then set aside.

Put the plantains in a large saucepan, pour in enough water to just cover them, and bring to a boil over medium heat. Cook for 10–15 minutes, until soft, then add coconut milk, chopped chile, and tomato paste. Stir to incorporate and then season with salt to taste. Put the fish in a deep sauté pan and pour the sauce on top. Bring to a boil and simmer for 15–20, minutes until the fish is pure white and flakes apart easily. Check the seasoning and serve with white rice.

STUFFED WITH BEANS

For the pasilla sauce:
3 cups (1¼ pints/750 ml)
   Chicken Stock (page 184)
30 tomatillos
10 dried pasilla chiles,
   dry-roasted
1 small white onion,
   dry-roasted and diced
2 cloves garlic, dry-roasted
sea salt and pepper

For the fish:
2 cups (14 oz/400 g) drained,
   cooked black beans, the
   cooking liquid reserved
2 tablespoons corn oil
1 dried avocado leaf, chopped
12 sea bass fillets
juice of 3 limes
sea salt and pepper
White Rice (page 521), to serve

saucepan and cook for 20 minutes. Put the chicken stock mixture into a food processor or blender and process until smooth, then strain into another saucepan and cook over medium heat for 30 minutes, until thick. Season to taste with salt and pepper.

For the fish, put the beans into a food processor or blender and process until smooth. Add reserved bean liquid or a little water, if necessary. Press through a strainer (sieve) or a hand food mill (mouli) and set aside, discarding the contents of the strainer.

Heat the oil in a frying pan or skillet over medium heat, add the avocado leaf, and sauté for 1 minute. Add the beans and cook for 5 minutes, then remove from the heat and set aside.

Lay the fillets out, season with salt and pepper, and squeeze the lime juice over them, and let them rest for 5 minutes. Spread a small amount of the beans on half the fillets, then cover each one with another fillet, pressing them together, to prevent the filling from escaping.

Heat a little oil in a frying pan or skillet with a lid over low heat. Place the stuffed fish fillets in the pan, leaving plenty of room between them so they cook well. Cook in batches if necessary. Cover with a lid and cook for 5 minutes. Turn them over carefully and cook for an additional 5 minutes.

Transfer to a plate. Pour the pasilla sauce over the fish and serve with white rice.

FILETE DE ROBALO RELLENO DE HUITLACOCHE

✳

SEA BASS WITH HUITLACOCHE

2 tablespoons corn oil
1 white onion, sliced
3 cloves garlic, finely chopped
1 lb 8½ oz/700 g huitlacoche, coarsely chopped
1 sprig epazote, chopped
¾ cup (4 oz/120 g) cooked corn kernels
13 sea bass fillets
2 eggs
1 cup (9 fl oz/250 ml) light (single) cream
juice of 1 lime
butter, for greasing
½ cup (4 fl oz/120 ml) white wine
4¼ cups (1¾ pints/1 liter) Fish Stock (page 184)
sea salt and pepper
White Rice (page 521), to serve

For the sauce:
2 tablespoons corn oil
½ white onion, finely chopped
2 cloves garlic, finely chopped
10 tomatoes, peeled, seeded, and finely chopped
2 tablespoons Chicken Stock (page 184) (optional)
sea salt and pepper

REGION: CENTRAL MEXICO
PREPARATION TIME: 30 MINUTES
COOKING TIME: 40 MINUTES
SERVES: 6

Preheat the oven to 400°F (200°C/Gas Mark 6).

Heat the oil in a frying pan or skillet over medium heat. Add half of the onion and the garlic and sauté for 2 minutes, until fragrant. Add the huitlacoche, epazote, corn kernels, salt and pepper to taste and simmer gently with the lid on for 10 minutes. Add a little water if the pan gets dry. Remove from the heat and set aside.

Put one of the sea bass fillets into a food processor or blender with the eggs, cream, and lime juice and process until a thin paste. Stir into the huitlacoche and corn mixture. Set aside.

Flatten the remaining fish fillets gently with a rolling pin. Put a small amount of the huitlacoche mixture onto 6 fillets, then cover with the remaining 6 fillets, pressing them down to prevent the filling from escaping. Grease an ovenproof dish with butter, then add the fish. Pour in the wine, then add the remaining onion, and pour fish stock into the bottom of the pan to a depth of about 1 inch (2.5 cm). Cover the pan with aluminum foil and bake in the oven for 20 minutes.

Meanwhile, to make the sauce, heat the oil in a saucepan over medium heat. Add the onion and garlic and sauté for 2 minutes, until brown. Add the tomatoes, season with salt and pepper to taste, and simmer for 10 minutes. Put the mixture into a food processor or blender and process until smooth. Strain into a saucepan, return to medium heat, and cook for 10 minutes, until it is thick. If you want a lighter sauce, add a little chicken stock.

Pour the tomato sauce over the fish and serve with white rice.

9 oz/250 g candied cactus

6 large sea bass fillets

juice of 8 limes

10 tomatillos

1 white onion

1 clove garlic

4¼ cups (1¾ pints/1 liter) Fish
Stock (page 184)

9 oz/250 g cactus paddles,
cooked and diced

9 oz/250 g prickly pears,
cooked and sliced

9 oz/250 g cactus flowers, cut
into strips

1 tablespooon finely chopped
cilantro (coriander)

¾ cup (3½ oz/100 g) all-purpose
(plain) flour

corn oil

½ cup (4 fl oz/120 ml) white
wine

sea salt and pepper

White Rice (page 521), to serve

sugar. Drain and set aside.

Preheat the oven to 350°F (180°C/Gas Mark 4).

Put the fish in a large bowl, pour over the lime juice, cover with plastic wrap (clingfilm), and let stand for 10 minutes.

Put the tomatillos, onion, and garlic into a frying pan or skillet and dry-roast over medium heat for 10 minutes, stirring constantly, then set aside. Put the garlic, onion, tomatillos, and 1 cup (9 fl oz/250 ml) of the fish stock into a food processor or blender and process until smooth. Strain into a saucepan.

Put the rest of the fish stock into the pan, season with salt and pepper, and bring to a simmer over medium heat for 15 minutes. Add the cactus paddles, prickly pears, cactus flowers, candied cactus, and cilantro (coriander), and let simmer over low heat for 10 minutes, then remove the cilantro (coriander). Set the sauce aside.

Spread the flour out on a large plate. Season the fish fillets with salt and pepper, then toss them in the flour until coated. Heat the oil in a large saucepan over medium heat. When the oil is hot, add the fish and cook for 2 minutes, flip over, and cook for an additional 2 minutes. Arrange the fish in an ovenproof dish, pour the wine over it, then cover with aluminum foil, and bake in the oven for 5 minutes. Remove from the oven, pour the sauce over the fish, and return to the oven for another 10 minutes. Serve with white rice.

PESCADO EN CUÑETE

✻

FISH CONFIT

1 (3¼-lb/1.5-kg) whole white
  fish, filleted and head
  reserved
juice of 10 limes
½ cup (4 fl oz/120 ml) corn oil
1 cup (9 fl oz/250 ml) olive oil
2 small heads garlic, skin on
6 sprigs thyme, plus extra for
  sprinkling
6 bay leaves
1 teaspoon dried oregano, plus
  extra for sprinkling
5 limes, thinly sliced
10 allspice berries
1 cup (9 fl oz/250 ml) apple
  cider vinegar
sea salt

REGION: PACIFIC COAST, MICHOACAN
PREPARATION TIME: 30 MINUTES, PLUS
1 HOUR MARINATING
COOKING TIME: 30 MINUTES
SERVES: 6

Rinse the fish thoroughly under cold running water, then rinse again with the lime juice. Cut the fish into bite-size pieces, put into a bowl, add salt to taste, cover with plastic wrap (clingfilm), and marinate in the refrigerator for 1 hour.

Heat the corn oil in a frying pan or skillet over medium heat. Add the fish pieces and cook for 2–3 minutes on each side, then remove with a slotted spoon and let cool.

Heat the olive oil in another saucepan over medium heat. Add the fish head, garlic heads, thyme, bay leaves, dried oregano, lime slices, and salt to taste and cook for 5 minutes, turning regularly. Remove the fish head and add the allspice and the fish, and let the oil in the pan cool down until it is just warm. Add the vinegar and cook over low heat for 10 minutes, then remove from the heat and let cool for 2 hours. Place a layer of fish in a clamp-lid jar, sprinkle with some oregano and thyme, and add 3 lime slices from the pan. Cover with the cooking liquid, and repeat the layers. Finish by filling the "barrel" with olive oil, then seal with the lid. Serve immediately or store for up to 4 days in the refrigerator.

2 tablespoons olive oil
2 cloves garlic
3 ancho chiles, membranes
  and seeds removed, sliced
4 pasilla chiles, membranes
  and seeds removed, sliced
2 guajillo chiles, membranes
  and seeds removed, sliced
2 cups (16 fl oz/475 ml) Fish
  Stock (page 184)
1 tablespoon Worcestershire
  sauce
⅔ cup (¼ pint/150 ml) dry
  white wine
6 (5¼-oz/150-g) sea bass fillets
1 cup (4 oz/120 g) all-purpose
  (plain) flour, for dusting
sea salt and pepper

To serve:
lemon juice
⅓ cup (¾ oz/20 g) finely
  chopped parsley
1 lb 2 oz/500 g new potatoes,
  unpeeled, cooked, and sliced

chiles and stir-fry quickly for 2 minutes. Add the fish stock, Worcestershire sauce, and white wine and bring to a boil. Reduce the heat and simmer for a few minutes until it is reduced a little, then season with salt and pepper.

Season the fish, then dust with flour. Line the broiler (grill) rack with aluminum foil, then place the fish on it and broil (grill) for 1 minute on each side. Reduce the oven temperature to 350°F (180°C/Gas Mark 4).

Transfer the fish to an ovenproof dish, cover with the sauce, and bake in the oven for 15 minutes, until it is white (not translucent) and flakes apart easily. Sprinkle with lemon juice, parsley and serve with the potatoes.

LOMITO DE ROBALO EN VERDE

※

SEA BASS IN CAPER SAUCE

2¾ lb/1.2 kg sea bass fillets

For the sauce:
4 tablespoons chopped cilantro
  (coriander)
3 tablespoons chopped parsley
3 tablespoons chopped mint
3 cloves garlic, sliced
2–3 serrano chiles, membranes
  and seeds removed
1 tablespoon Dijon mustard
10 anchovy fillets
4 tablespoons capers
½ cup (4 fl oz/120 ml) olive oil
3–4 tablespoons lemon juice
sea salt and pepper

To garnish:
2 tablespoons olive oil
1 clove garlic, crushed
4½ lb/2 kg spinach

REGION: CENTRAL MEXICO, BAJA CALIFORNIA SUR
PREPARATION TIME: 15 MINUTES, PLUS
10 MINUTES STANDING
COOKING TIME: 15 MINUTES
SERVES: 6

Preheat the oven to 400°F (200°C/Gas Mark 6).

For the sauce, put the cilantro (coriander), parsley, mint, garlic, chiles, mustard, anchovies, and capers into a food processor or blender and process until smooth. Add the olive oil, lemon juice, and season to taste and process to combine.

Put the fish into an ovenproof dish and pour half of the sauce over it. Bake in the oven for 10 minutes or until the fish is cooked on the outside but still raw in the center. Remove from the oven, cover with aluminum foil, and let stand for 10 minutes.

For the garnish, heat 2 tablespoons olive oil in a saucepan over medium heat, add the garlic and spinach, and sauté for 2 minutes.

Put the spinach in a pile in the middle of a serving dish, arrange the fish on top, and pour over a little more of the sauce. Serve immediately.

6 tablespoons (3 oz/80 g) butter
1 white onion, finely chopped
2 leeks, white part only, thinly
  sliced
½–1 habanero chile,
  membranes and seeds
  removed
½ cup (4 fl oz/120 ml) white
  wine
½ cup (4 fl oz/120 ml) apple
  cider vinegar
2 ripe mangoes, peeled, seeded,
  and chopped
3 cups (1¼ pints/750 ml)
  Chicken Stock (page 184)
3 purple sweet potatoes,
  unpeeled
6 (5¼-oz/150-g) white fish fillets
sea salt and white pepper

the wine and let simmer for 5 minutes, until it has evaporated. Add the vinegar and cook for an additional 5 minutes until it evaporates, then add the chopped mango and sauté for 5 minutes, until it is partially cooked. Add the stock and bring to a boil. Boil gently for 15 minutes, until it has reduced by half, then season with salt and white pepper. Let cool.

Meanwhile, cook the sweet potatoes in a saucepan over medium heat for 25–30 minutes or until cooked. Drain, peel, and slice, then cover and set aside.

Once the sauce is cool, put it into a food processor or blender, add the cream, and process until smooth. Strain into a clean saucepan, discarding the contents of the strainer (sieve), and cook over low heat for a 5 minutes, until hot. Check the seasoning, adjust if necessary, and set aside.

Broil (grill), poach, or steam the fish to your liking. Plate the fish and cover with the sauce. Serve with sweet potato.

ROBALO EN ESCABECHE BLANCO

✺

MARINATED SEA BASS

½ cup (4 fl oz/120 ml) olive oil
6 (7-oz/200-g) sea bass fillets
2 onions, thinly sliced
10 cloves garlic, thinly sliced
pinch of ground cinnamon
2 sprigs thyme
2 sprigs oregano
4 cloves
3 bay leaves
10 black peppercorns
½ cup (4 fl oz/120 ml) dry white
  wine
4 tablespoons apple cider
  vinegar
sea salt
White Rice (page 521), to serve

REGION: YUCATÁN PENINSULA
PREPARATION TIME: 10 MINUTES
COOKING TIME: 15 MINUTES
SERVES: 6

Heat a little of the oil in a large saucepan over medium heat, add the fish, and cook for about 1 minute on each side. Remove from the pan with a slotted spoon and set aside.

Heat a little more oil in a saucepan over medium heat, add the onions, and sauté for 2 minutes. Add the garlic, cinnamon, thyme, oregano, cloves, bay leaves, and peppercorns. Pour in the wine and vinegar and cook for an additional 2 minutes. Carefully add the fish and cook, covered, for an additional 5 minutes, or until the fish is just cooked. Let it rest, check the seasoning, and serve with white rice and the sauce poured over the fish.

4 slices bread, crusts removed
3 tablespoons apple cider
 vinegar
2½ lb/1.2 kg white fish fillets
1 white onion
3 tablespoons finely chopped
 parsley
5 whole eggs
1 clove garlic, crushed

For the green sauce:
3 tablespoons corn oil
2 tablespoons finely chopped
 onion
2 cloves garlic, finely chopped
6 poblano chiles, dry-roasted
 and cut into thin strips
4 oz/125 g ground pumpkin
 seeds
3 tomatillos, dry-roasted
2 cups (16 fl oz/475 ml) Fish
 Stock (page 184) or water
sea salt and pepper

To serve:
White Rice (page 521)
black beans

Put the bread, whole onion, parsley, eggs, and crushed garlic, into a food processor or blender and season with salt and pepper. Process until thoroughly combined and smooth. Remove from the food processor and, with your hands, make fish balls, about 2 inches (5 cm) in diameter. Put them on a plate, cover, and chill in the refrigerator for at least 2 hours.

For the green sauce, heat the oil in a large frying pan or skillet over medium heat. The pan needs to be deep enough to hold all the fish balls and sauce. Add the onion, garlic, chile, pumpkin seeds, tomatillos, and fish stock and mix well. Reduce the heat and simmer for about 10 minutes, then pour into a food processor or blender and process until smooth. Return the sauce to the pan and bring to a boil over medium heat. Add the fish balls to the sauce and simmer for 8 minutes until cooked. Check the seasoning of the stock and simmer for an additional 2–3 minutes. Transfer the fish balls to individual plates. Ladle the sauce over them and serve with white rice and black beans.

Veracruz-Style Fish

For the spice infusion:
1 cinnamon stick
2 bay leaves
1 thyme sprig
1 teaspoon black pepper
1 sprig epazote

For the fish:
6 (7-oz/200-g) red snapper
   fillets
juice of 3 limes
sea salt and pepper

For the sauce:
1 cup (9 fl oz/250 ml) olive oil
10 cloves garlic, 6 cloves finely
   chopped
1 white onion, finely chopped
4 cups (4½ lb/2 kg) pureed
   tomatoes
4 tomatoes, seeded and
   chopped
2 tablespoons capers
½ cup (2 oz/50 g) olives, pitted
   and halved
sea salt

To serve:
½ cup (2¼ oz/60 g) olives
5 tablespoons (1½ oz/40 g)
   capers
pickled jalepeños
2 sprigs parsley, finely chopped
12 pitted green olives, sliced
1 tablespoon chopped parsley

water to cover, and bring to a boil. Boil for 15 minutes, then strain and set aside.

Clean the fish, then rub with the lime juice, and season with salt and pepper, rubbing them in. Put on a plate, cover with plastic wrap (clingfilm), and place in the refrigerator for 1 hour.

For the sauce, heat the oil in a saucepan over medium heat, add the whole garlic cloves, sauté for 1 minute, then remove them. Add the chopped onion and garlic and sauté for 5 minutes or until transparent. Add the pureed tomatoes and a little salt, then reduce the heat to low and simmer for 10 minutes. Add the chopped tomatoes and cook for an additional 10 minutes or until thick. Add the capers and olives and cook for an additional 10 minutes.

Remove the fish from the refrigerator and put in a large saucepan with a lid, add the sauce, and cover with the lid. Cook over low heat for 10–15 minutes, until the fish is cooked.

To serve, pour the sauce into a deep serving platter, place the fish on top, and garnish with olives, capers, jalapeños, and parsley.

PESCADO "TATEMADO"

FISH IN CHARRED CORN HUSKS

dried corn husks
6 (11½-oz/300-g) whole red
   snappers or any white fish,
   cleaned with heads and
   tails intact
sea salt and pepper

To serve:
Salsa of choice (page 496–514)
2 large limes, cut into wedges
6 Corn Tortillas (page 36)

REGION: PACIFIC COAST
PREPARATION TIME: 20 MINUTES, PLUS
20 MINUTES SOAKING
COOKING TIME: 25–30 MINUTES
SERVES: 6

Heat the barbeque and let the flames die down.

Soak the dried corn husks in a bowl of hot water for 20 minutes, then drain and set aside.

Using a sharp knife, score both sides of the fish, then season with salt and pepper, rubbing it into the slashes. Wrap the fish in the corn husks to cover them completely, tying them with string to secure. Cook on the grill (barbeque) for 25–30 minutes, or until the fish is cooked. Let the outside of the corn husks burn a little while cooking as this will flavor the fish.

Serve with salsa, lime wedges, and hot tortillas.

PESCADO ZARANDEADO

GRILLED FISH IN BANANA LEAF

6 (7-oz/200-g) small red
   snappers, cleaned with heads
   removed
3 tablespoons olive oil
1 banana leaf
juice of 2 limes
sea salt and pepper

To serve:
Salsa of choice (page 496–514)
6 Corn Tortillas (page 36)
Refried Beans (page 532)

REGION: PACIFIC COAST, SINALOA
PREPARATION TIME: 20 MINUTES
COOKING TIME: 10 MINUTES
SERVES: 6

Heat up the barbeque and let the flames die down.

Using a sharp knife, go to the inside of the fish and split the fish along its length from head to tail without going all the way through. Alternatively, ask the fish dealer to butterfly your fish for you. Open the fish out and season both sides with salt and pepper, then rub with the oil.

Put the fish in a fish barbeque basket (so it does not stick) on the rack, flesh side down, and cover with the banana leaf so that the fish gets evenly smoked. Heat for 5 minutes, then remove the banana leaf and turn the fish over, and replace the banana leaf. Grill for for another 5 minutes or until thoroughly cooked. Sprinkle lime juice on top and serve with salsa, hot tortillas, and refried beans.

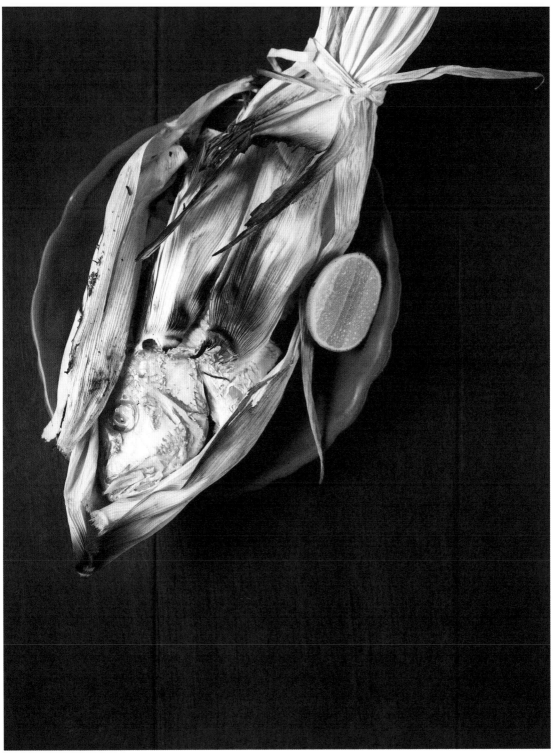

Fish in Charred Corn Husks

PESCADO A LA TALLA

※

GRILLED FISH

5 tablespoons mayonnaise
1 tablespoon lemon juice
3¼ lb/1.5 kg red snapper,
    cleaned
oil, for brushing
sea salt and pepper

For the sauce:
10 guajillo chiles, dry-roasted
5 anchos chiles, dry-roasted
4 tomatoes, dry-roasted,
    peeled, and seeded
4 cloves garlic
1 tablespoon apple cider
    vinegar
3 cloves
½ white onion
½ teaspoon oregano
½ teaspoon thyme
½ teaspoon marjoram
½ teaspoon ground cumin
2 tablespoons olive oil

To serve:
Roast Tomato Salsa (page 509)
1 lime, cut into wedges
Corn Tortillas (page 36)

REGION: PACIFIC COAST, GUERRERO
PREPARATION TIME: 40 MINUTES, PLUS 20 MINUTES
MARINATING AND 15 MINUTES SOAKING
COOKING TIME: 50 MINUTES
SERVES: 6

Combine the mayonnaise, lemon juice, and salt and pepper in a bowl. Rub this mixture over and inside the cavity of the fish. Put the fish on a plate and marinate in the refrigerator for 20 minutes.

For the sauce, put the chiles into a heatproof bowl, add enough boiling water to add cover, and soak for 15 minutes. Put the chiles and the soaking liquid into a food processor or blender and process until smooth. Add the tomatoes, garlic, vinegar, cloves, onion, oregano, thyme, marjoram, and cumin and process until smooth.

Heat the oil in a saucepan over medium heat, add the sauce, and cook for 10 minutes, until thick. Check the seasoning and set aside.

Preheat an outdoor grill (barbeque) or a broiler (grill). Lightly oil the grill and place it 8 inches (20 cm) above the coal. Put the fish on the grill, skin side down, and grill for 10–15 minutes frequently, brushing the fish with the sauce frequently. Turn the fish over, brush with oil, and grill for another 10 minutes, or until the fish is cooked. If you are broiling (grilling) in the oven, put the rack in the top-middle of the oven and broil (grill) the fish for 10 minutes a side, frequently brushing the fish with the sauce during the cooking time.

Serve with tomato sauce, lime wedges, and tortillas.

CRUST

3 smoked chipotle chiles in adobo
⅔ cup (5 oz/150 g) prickly pear honey or molasses
½ cup (2½ oz/70 g) black and white sesame seeds, dry-roasted
2½ tablespoons chile seeds, dry-roasted and crushed
2½ tablespoons coriander seeds, dry-roasted and crushed
3 tablespoons finely chopped parsley
3 tablespoons finely chopped basil
2¼ lb/1 kg fresh tuna steak, cut into 6 thick portions
3 tablespoons olive oil
½ cup (4 fl oz/120 ml) corn oil
sea salt and pepper
1 lb 5 oz/600 g Watercress Salad (page 118) or any green salad, to serve

seeds, parsley, basil, salt, and pepper together in a shallow bowl. Rub the tuna pieces with olive oil and salt and pepper to season. Dip the tuna in the seeds and turn until completely coated.

Heat the corn oil in a frying pan or skillet over medium heat, add the tuna, and cook for a minute on each side, until seared but still rare. Cut each piece of tuna into thin slices and plate it. Serve with the sauce and salad.

PASTEL DE ATUN

✸

TUNA CAKE

6 tablespoons (3 oz/80 g)
  butter, plus extra for greasing
4 slices stale white bread
½ cup (4 fl oz/120 ml) milk
4 eggs
2 (5½-oz/160-g) cans good-
  quality tuna, drained
2 cups (9 oz/250 g) grated
  chihuahua cheese
2 pickled jalapeños, drained
  and chopped
sea salt and pepper
Mexican Salad (page 121),
  to serve

REGION: MEXICO
PREPARATION TIME: 15 MINUTES
COOKING TIME: 1¼ HOURS
SERVES: 6

Preheat the oven to 375°F (190°C/Gas Mark 5) and grease an ovenproof dish with butter.

Cut the crusts off the bread and discard, and crumble the bread into a bowl. Add the milk and stir to form a paste, then add the eggs, tuna, cheese, jalapeños, and salt and pepper to taste, and mix well. Melt the butter in a saucepan over low heat, then add to the mixture and beat until well combined. Pour the mixture into the prepared dish and bake in the oven for about 1 hour 15 minutes, or until golden brown and soft. Let cool, then serve with a Mexican salad.

CAZON A LA CAMPECHANA

✸

CAMPECHE-STYLE DOGFISH

2½ lb/1.2 kg fresh dogfish,
  sliced
8 sprigs epazote
juice of 4 oranges
6 tomatoes
2 tablespoons (1 oz/25 g) butter
2 onions, finely chopped
4 serrano chiles, dry-roasted
  and sliced
sea salt and pepper
White Rice (page 521), to serve

REGION: YUCATAN PENINSULA
PREPARATION TIME: 20 MINUTES
COOKING TIME: 45 MINUTES
SERVES: 6

Pour 5 cups (2 pints/1.2 liters) water into a large saucepan, add the fish, and bring to a boil over medium heat. Boil for 5 minutes, then add the epazote leaves, and orange juice, and boil for an additional 10 minutes. Remove from the heat, taste, and adjust the seasoning. Take the fish out of the pan, and remove the skin.

Put the tomatoes into a saucepan, pour in enough water to just cover them, add 2 pinches of salt, and bring to a boil over medium heat. Boil for 10 minutes, until soft, then remove them from the water with a slotted spoon and put into a food processor or blender. Process until smooth, then set aside.

Heat the butter in a saucepan over medium heat, add the onions, and sauté for 2 minutes. Add the tomatoes and the remaining orange juice and bring to a boil. Add the fish, chile, and salt and pepper to taste, then reduce the heat to low and simmer for 15 minutes or until the sauce thickens and the fish is cooked. Serve with white rice.

2 banana leaves, dry-roasted

6 hoja santas

1 dogfish, cleaned, filleted, and sliced

4 tablespoons (2 oz/50 g) butter or lard, melted

2 green bell peppers, chopped

3 tomatoes, chopped

1 onion, finely chopped

1 clove garlic, crushed

¾ cup (1 oz/30 g) finely chopped cilantro (coriander)

2 güero chiles, sliced

1 plantain, sliced and fried or steamed

sea salt

little warm butter or lard over the top and divide the remaining ingredients between the packages. Wrap the packages well to enclose the filling, secure with kitchen string, and steam for 15 minutes, or until cooked. Serve immediately.

PESCADO EN SALSA DE CIRUELA

❁

FISH IN PLUM SAUCE

7 tablespoons (3½ oz/100 g)
   butter
1 leek, white part only, thinly
   sliced
6 serrano chiles or jalapeños,
   dry-roasted, membranes and
   seeds removed
½ small white onion, dry-
   roasted and chopped
3¼ lb/1.5 kg yellow plums,
   pitted, plus extra to garnish
2 sprigs epazote, 1 whole and
   1 finely chopped
sea salt and pepper
6 (4½-oz/130-g) white fish fillets

To serve:
juice of 1 lemon
2¼ lb/1 kg wild greens,
   spinach, or Swiss chard,
   steamed, drained, and
   seasoned
1 sprig epazote, finely chopped

REGION: CENTER, MORELOS
PREPARATION TIME: 25 MINUTES
COOKING TIME: 25 MINUTES
SERVES: 6

Preheat the oven to 350°F (180°C/Gas Mark 6).
Melt the butter in a saucepan over a medium heat,
add the leek, chiles, onion, plums, and whole
epazote, and heat until the onion and leek are
translucent and fragrant. Let cool, take out the
epazote sprig, and put into a food processor or
blender and process until smooth. Strain and pour
back into the pan. Set aside.

Season the fish, then place on an ovenproof
serving plate. Cover with aluminum foil and bake in
the oven for 5 minutes. Remove from the oven, pour
the sauce over the fish to cover, then bake for an
additional 5–10 minutes.

Serve immediately with lemon juice, wild greens,
garnished with a few fresh plums and epazote.

FISH LOIN WITH CHILI AND ORANGE SAUCE

For the sauce:
10 cascabel chiles,
  membranes and seeds
  removed, dry-roasted
½ cup (4 fl oz/120 ml) apple
  cider vinegar
2 cups (16 fl oz/475 ml) orange
  juice
4 tablespoons packed
  brown sugar
10 allspice berries
2 teaspoons thyme leaves
1 bay leaf
grated zest of 1 orange
sea salt

For the fish:
6 (4½-oz/130-g) white fish fillets
4 tablespoons olive oil
3 tablespoons butter, cut into
  6 pieces
salt and black pepper
orange slices, to garnish

let cool. Pour into a food processor or blender and process until smooth. Strain the sauce and check the seasoning.

Season the fish with salt and pepper. Heat the olive oil in a large frying pan or skillet over medium heat. Add the fish and cook for 3–4 minutes per side, depending on thickness. Put a piece of butter on top of each fish.

Arrange the fish on a serving plate, cover with the sauce, and garnish with orange slices.

PESCADO EN CHILEAJO COLORADO

❄

FISH IN RED GARLIC SAUCE

6 large pasilla chiles,
   dry-roasted
6 cloves garlic, dry-roasted
8 tomatoes, dry-roasted
pinch of cumin seeds,
   dry-roasted
2 cloves, dry-roasted
pinch of ground cinnamon
4 tablespoons (2 oz/50 g) butter
4 tablespoons apple cider
   vinegar
1 (3¼-lb/1.5-kg) fish loin, cut
   into 6 pieces
1 tablespoon oregano
sea salt and pepper
salad, to serve

REGION: CENTRAL MEXICO
PREPARATION TIME: 40 MINUTES, PLUS
15 MINUTES SOAKING
COOKING TIME: 40 MINUTES
SERVES: 6

Add the chiles in a small bowl, add just enough boiling water to cover, and soak for 15 minutes. Put the chiles and the soaking liquid, garlic, tomatoes, cumin, cloves, cinnamon, and pepper into a food processor or blender and process until smooth. Strain into a bowl.

Heat the butter in a frying pan or skillet over medium heat. Add the sauce and heat for 10–15 minutes, until it thickens. Add the vinegar and check the seasoning.

Arrange the fish in a large ovenproof dish, then pour the sauce over the fish to cover. Bake in the oven for 20 minutes, then remove from the oven, and sprinkle with the oregano, and return to the oven for an additional 5 minutes.

Serve with a salad of your choice.

4 tablespoons olive or corn oil

2 large white onions, finely chopped

2–3 serrano chiles, chopped

½ head garlic, peeled and crushed

2 tomatoes, seeded and chopped

5 tablespoons chopped marjoram leaves

5 tablespoons chopped thyme leaves

⅔ cup (1½ oz/40 g) chopped mint leaves

1 cup (2 oz/50 g) chopped parsley leaves

3¼ lb/1.5 kg carp fillets

1 cup (9 fl oz/250 ml) Fish Stock (page 184) or Chicken Stock (page 184)

lime juice, to taste

sea salt and pepper

To serve:
steamed potatoes or White Rice (page 521)
Corn Tortillas (page 36)

Add the tomatoes and season. Bring to a boil, then add all the herbs. Mix well and remove three-quarters of the mixture and set aside. Spread the rest of the mixture onto the bottom of the pan and arrange a layer of the fish on top. Season with salt and pepper, then pour some of the reserved mixture on top, and repeat the layers, finishing with herb mixture on top. Pour in the stock, reduce the heat to low, cover with the lid, and cook for 10–15 minutes. Carefully remove the pieces of fish, then return to the pan, and sprinkle with lime juice to taste.

Serve hot with steamed potatoes or white rice and warm tortillas.

Note: This recipe can be made with fish fillets, with the skin still on, and cut into large pieces. The fish will need less cooking time.

PESCADO ADOBADO ESTILO OAXACA

✳

OAXACA-STYLE FISH

For the marinade:
4 cloves garlic
12 ancho chiles, membranes
  and seeds removed
1 teaspoon oregano
½ teaspoon cumin
½ tablespoon black
  peppercorns
½ teaspoon cloves
1 cup (9 fl oz/250 ml) Fish
  Stock (page 184)
4 tablespoons apple cider
  vinegar
2 tablespoons sugar
sea salt

For the fish:
1 (7-oz/200-g) red snapper,
  cleaned

REGION: OAXACA
PREPARATION TIME: 20 MINUTES
COOKING TIME: 25 MINUTES
SERVES: 6

Preheat the oven to 400°F (200°C/Gas Mark 6).

To make the marinade, put all the ingredients into a food processor or blender and process until smooth. Strain into a saucepan, then sauté over medium heat for 10 minutes. Season and let cool.

Preheat a barbeque grill, brush the fish with the marinade, and grill for 7–10 minutes on each side. Serve immediately.

Oaxaca-Style Fish

SARDINAS CON LONGANIZA

✻

SARDINES WITH LONGANIZA

1 lb 2 oz/500 g longaniza
(Spanish sausage), thinly
sliced

12 fresh sardines, cleaned, with
tails still on

2 cloves garlic, finely chopped

2 tablespoons finely chopped
cilantro (coriander)

juice of 2 limes

1½ teapoons chili powder

pinch of sea salt

2 tablespoons olive oil

½ cup (1 oz/25 g) fresh bread
crumbs

salad, to serve

REGION: GULF, VERACRUZ, TAMAULIPAS
PREPARATION TIME: 25 MINUTES
COOKING TIME: 25 MINUTES
SERVES: 6

Preheat the oven to 375°F (190°C/Gas Mark 5).

Sauté the longaniza in a saucepan over medium heat for 5 minutes. Remove and drain on paper towels.

Rinse the sardines under cold running water. Put the fish on its side and use a sharp knife to cut down each side of the backbone as close as possible to the ribs, starting at the tail, to make pockets between the ribs and the skin on the outside. Turn the fish over and, using your fingers, separate the backbone from the fish, then stuff the pocket with the longaniza. Close the fish.

Mix the garlic, cilantro (coriander), lime juice, chili powder, salt, 1½ tablespoons olive oil, and the bread crumbs together in a bowl. Put the sardines into the mixture and turn until coated, then place them on a baking sheet and sprinkle with the remaining olive oil. Bake in the oven for 20 minutes, until the bread crumbs are lightly brown. Serve with a salad.

1 bunch dried corn husks
1 tablespoon corn oil
1 large white onion, finely
  chopped
3 cloves garlic, finely chopped
3 red chiles, finely chopped
3 prickly pears, peeled, seeded,
  and chopped
4 tablespoons chopped epazote
4 tablespoons chopped cilantro
  (coriander)
6 (5-oz/150-g) trout fillets
sea salt

To serve:
Corn Tortillas (page 36)
Salsa of choice (page 496–514)

30 minutes or until soft. Drain well and set aside.

Heat the oil in a large saucepan over medium heat, add the onion, garlic, chiles, and prickly pears, and sauté for 2 minutes. Add the epazote and cilantro (coriander) and season with salt. Let cool completely.

Season the trout fillets with salt. When the onion and herb mixture is cold, put into a large bowl, add the trout fillets, and mix well to coat the fish.

Place a trout fillet on a corn husk, folding the fillet in half, if necessary. Wrap another leaf around the fillet to enclose it. Continue with all the fish and corn leaves.

Fire up the outdoor grill (barbeque) or heat a ridged grill (griddle) pan (or heavy frying pan or skillet) over low heat, then add the fish packages and cook, turning them over several times when the fish is cooked inside and the outer leaves are charred. Cook for 20 minutes, or until there are no longer any drips from the packages onto the griddle. Serve hot or at room temperature with warm tortillas and salsa.

Note: *Mextlapiques* are considered to be tamales without the masa harina.

ROBALO AL PASTOR

❈

RUSTIC SEA BASS

For the guajillo sauce:
1 tablespoon corn oil
½ white onion, finely chopped
1 clove garlic, finely chopped
2 small tomatoes, seeded and
  finely chopped
8 guajillo chiles, membrane
  and seeds removed
2 cups (16 fl oz/475 ml) Fish
  Stock (page 184)
2 oz/50 g achiote paste
juice of 6 oranges
sea salt and pepper
2 tablespoons apple cider
  vinegar

For the fish:
6 (5¼-oz/150-g) sea bass fillets
juice of 3 limes
14 oz/400 g pineapple, peeled
  and diced
chopped cilantro (coriander),
  to serve
2 limes, quartered
butter, for greasing

REGION: NORTHWEST AND CENTER
PREPARATION TIME: 25 MINUTES, PLUS
1 HOUR 5 MINUTES MARINATING
COOKING TIME: 1 HOUR
SERVES: 6

For the sauce, heat the oil in a frying pan or skillet over medium heat, add the onion and garlic, and sauté for 2 minutes. Add the tomatoes, chiles, and just enough fish stock to cover and bring to a boil. Boil for 15 minutes or until cooked. Transfer the tomato mixture into a food processor or blender, add achiote paste and orange juice, and process until smooth. Strain into a clean saucepan and cook for 10 minutes over medium heat. Season to taste with salt and pepper. Add some more fish stock if the sauce is too thick.

For the fish, combine the fish fillets and lime juice together, stir, cover with plastic wrap (clingfilm), and marinate in the refrigerator for 5 minutes. Add the mixture to the fish, cover, and refrigerate for 1 hours.

Preheat the broiler (grill) to medium. Arrange the pineapple on the broiler rack and cook for 3 minutes per side. Set aside. Preheat the oven to 375°F (190°C/Gas Mark 5).

Grease a deep roasting pan. Place the fish fillets in the pan and lay the pineapple over each fillet, covering only one half. Fold the empty end of the fillet over the pineapple end of the fillet and secure with a toothpick or cocktail stick. Bake in the oven for 25 minutes, until the fish is white and flaky.

Meanwhile, put the remaining marinade into a saucepan and bring to a boil over medium heat. Simmer slowly while the fish is cooking and serve with the fish with chopped cilantro (coriander), lime wedges, and diced pineapple.

1 cup (7 oz/200 g) butter

2 cloves garlic, finely chopped

2 red bell peppers, roasted, peeled, seeded, and cut into thin strips

2 yellow bell peppers, roasted, peeled, seeded, and cut into thin strips

2 green bell peppers, roasted, peeled, seeded, and cut into thin strips

corn oil, for brushing

6 small cactus paddles

2½ lb/1.2 kg large shrimp (prawns), peeled and deveined with tails intact

½ red onion, finely chopped

½ cup (4 fl oz/120 ml) white tequila

1½ cups (12 fl oz/375 ml) light (single) cream

sea salt and pepper

White Rice (page 521), to serve

salt and pepper to taste. Set aside.

Brush the cactus paddles with oil and broil (grill) over high heat for 3 minutes per side.

Thread the shrimp (prawns) onto skewers and set aside.

Melt the remaining butter in a wide frying pan or skillet over medium heat, add the onion and the remaining chopped garlic, and sauté for 2 minutes. Add the shrimp (prawns) skewers and heat, turning the skewers over a couple of times, for 3 minutes. Pour in the tequila and heat it to boiling point. Set it alight and flambé the shrimp. Let the flames die down.

Pour the light (single) cream into the frying pan or skillet and cook over very low heat for 2 minutes, stirring the whole time. Season to taste.

Place a cactus paddle on each serving plate, then add the bell pepper mixture on top, and finish with the shrimp. Drizzle with the sauce and serve with white rice.

CAMARONES EN VERDE

❋

SHRIMP IN GREEN SAUCE

8 cloves garlic
5 tomatillos
3 large jalapeños, halved,
    membrane and seeds
    removed
7 hoja santa, deveined
3 avocado leaves, dry-roasted
¼ cup (2 fl oz/60 ml) olive oil,
    plus extra for drizzling
2½ lb/1.2 kg large shrimp (tiger
    prawns), peeled and deveined
sea salt

To serve:
White Rice (page 521)
Fried plantains
Corn Tortillas (page 36)

REGION: VERACRUZ
PREPARATION TIME: 25 MINUTES
COOKING TIME: 30 MINUTES
SERVES: 6

Put the garlic, a little salt, and a little water into a food processor or blender and process until a paste forms, then put in a bowl and set aside.

Put the tomatillos, jalapeños, hoja santa, and avocado leaves into a small saucepan and add enough water to just cover. Cover and cook over low heat for 10 minutes. Uncover and boil rapidly for an additional 10 minutes until the water has reduced a little. Drain, reserving 1 cup (9 fl oz/250 ml) of the liquid. Put the tomatillo mixture in a food processor or blender, add the reserved water, and process until smooth. Strain and set aside.

Heat a little olive oil in a large frying pan or skillet over very high heat, add the shrimp (prawns), and sauté for 1 minute. Reduce the heat, add the garlic paste and cook for 1 minute, stirring constantly, then add the tomatillo mixture and simmer for 5 minutes. Remove from the heat, check the seasoning, and drizzle a little more olive oil over the shrimp (prawns) just before serving. Serve with white rice, fried plantains and warm tortillas.

CAMARONES AL MOJO DE AJO

❋

GARLIC SHRIMP

20 cloves garlic
1 teaspoon apple cider vinegar
½ cup (4 fl oz/125 ml) olive oil
    or corn oil
5 black peppercorns
2¼ lb/1 kg shrimp (prawns),
    peeled and deveined
sea salt

To serve:
6 slices bread
3 lemons, halved

REGION: ALL REGIONS
PREPARATION TIME: 30 MINUTES, PLUS
MARINATING TIME
COOKING TIME: 10 MINUTES
SERVES: 6

Put the garlic, vinegar, half the oil, peppercorns, and salt into a food processor or blender and process until smooth. Pour into a shallow dish, add the shrimp (prawns), mix well to coat, then cover with plastic wrap (clingfilm), and marinate in the refrigerator for at least 1 hour, preferably overnight.

Pour the remaining oil into a pan with a lid, then heat over medium heat. When the oil is hot, add the shrimp (prawns) and stir well for 3 minutes then add the marinade, and cook for an additional 5 minutes, stirring occasionally, until cooked.

Toast the bread and place on a dish. Add the garlic shrimp and serve with a lemon half.

1 lb 10 oz/750 g shrimp
(prawns)
3 tomatoes, peeled
⅓ white onion, coarsely
chopped
2 cloves garlic
¼ teaspoon dried oregano,
dry-roasted
4 cloves, dry-roasted
¼ teaspoon dried thyme
pinch of ground ginger
4 tablespoons corn oil
¾ white onion, finely chopped
3 bay leaves
6 poblano chiles, dry-roasted
1–2 cups (9–18 fl oz/250–475
ml) olive oil
White Rice (page 521), to serve

For the escabeche:
2 tablespoons olive oil, plus
extra for frying
1 white onion, sliced
1 large cinnamon stick
4 bay leaves
1 carrot, cut into strips and
blanched
1 cup (9 fl oz/250 ml) apple
cider vinegar or rice vinegar
sea salt and pepper

immediately. Peel, clean, and chop them coarsely.

Put the tomatoes, onion, garlic, oregano, cloves, thyme, and ginger into a food processor or blender and process until combined.

Heat the corn oil in a frying pan or skillet. Add the finely chopped onion and cook over low heat, stirring occasionally, for 5 minutes. Add the tomato mixture, increase the heat to medium, and cook, stirring occasionally, for 15 minutes, or until slightly thickened. Add the shrimp and bay leaves, reduce the heat to low, and simmer for 10 minutes. Remove the pan from the heat. Remove and discard the bay leaf.

Carefully fill the chiles with the shrimp mixture and secure with a toothpick or cocktail stick.

To make the escabeche, heat the olive oil in a saucepan. Add the onion and cook over low heat, stirring occasionally, for 5 minutes, then remove the pan from the heat.

Add the cinnamon, bay leaves, carrot, and vinegar, season with salt and pepper, and mix well. Pour the mixture into a preserving jar or other heatproof glass container.

Pour the olive oil into a frying pan or skillet to a depth of about 3 inches (7.5 cm) and heat. Add the stuffed chiles and cook for 2–4 minutes on each side, until lightly browned. Remove the pan from the heat.

Using a slotted spoon, transfer the chiles to the jar of the escabeche. Cover and chill in the refrigerator overnight.

Remove the jar from the refrigerator 30–60 minutes before serving to let the chiles come to room temperature. Serve covered with the escabeche, accompanied by white rice.

ALBONDIGAS DE CAMARON

SHRIMP BALLS

1 lb 10½ oz/750 g shrimp
  (prawns), peeled and
  deveined
2 eggs
¼ cup (2 fl oz/60 g) olive oil
1 sprig cilantro (coriander)
sea salt
White Rice (page 521), to serve

For the stock:
3 guajillo chiles, dry-roasted
1 clove garlic, dry-roasted
pinch of cumin
3 cups (1¼ pints/750 ml) Fish
  Stock (page 184)
1 tablespoon corn oil
1 small white onion, finely
  chopped

REGION: PACIFIC COAST, SINALOA, SONORA
PREPARATION TIME: 25 MINUTES
COOKING TIME: 20 MINUTES
SERVES: 6

Put the shrimp (prawns) into a food processor or blender and process until ground, then put the ground shrimp (prawns) into a bowl, add the eggs, and mix thoroughly. Using damp hands, make balls the size of golf balls.

For the stock, put the chiles, garlic, cumin, and fish stock into a food processor or blender and process until smooth. Strain into a bowl.

Heat the oil in a frying pan or skillet over medium heat, add the onion and sauté for 2 minutes. Add the stock, adjust the seasoning, and heat. Set aside.

In a separate frying pan or skillet, add 2 tablespoons of oil, add the shrimp balls, in batches, if necessary, and cook for 5–7 minutes, or until golden brown. Remove with a slotted spoon and drain on paper towels. Set aside.

Transfer the shrimp balls to a plate, add the sauce and garnish with the cilantro (coriander). Season with salt and serve with white rice.

Shrimp Balls

REVOLTIJO

※

SHRIMP AND WILD GREENS IN MOLE

3 eggs, separated
1 tablespoon all-purpose (plain) flour
2 tablespoons ground dried shrimp (prawns)
1 teaspoon sea salt
2–4 tablespoons corn oil, for frying
1½ cups (9 oz/250 g) diced cactus paddles, cooked
1 cup (9 oz/250 g) cooked romeritos
18 shrimp (prawns), peeled and deveined
2 small potatoes, boiled and peeled

For the mole sauce:
10 pasilla chiles, dry-roasted
2 mulato chiles, dry-roasted
2 ancho chiles, dry-roasted
4 tablespoons sesame seeds, toasted
1 clove garlic, dry-roasted
2 cloves, dry-roasted
3 black peppercorns, dry-roasted
2 tablespoons pumpkin seeds, dry-roasted
5 almonds, unpeeled and toasted
1 Corn Tortilla (page 36), toasted
1 tablespoon chile seeds, dry-roasted
2 tablespoons corn oil
1 square semisweet (dark) chocolate

REGION: CENTRAL MEXICO
PREPARATION TIME: 1 HOUR, PLUS 15 MINUTES SOAKING
COOKING TIME: 1 HOUR 10 MINUTES
SERVES: 6

For the mole sauce, put the chiles into a heatproof bowl, pour in enough hot water just to cover, and soak for 15 minutes. Put the chiles and their soaking liquid, sesame seeds, garlic, cloves, peppercorns, pumpkin seeds, almonds, tortilla, and chile seeds into a food processor or blender and process until a smooth paste forms. Strain into a bowl.

Heat the corn oil in a Dutch oven, casserole dish, or heavy saucepan over medium heat. Add the strained paste and bring to a boil. Boil for 30 minutes. Add the chocolate and stir until it melts and is completely incorporated. Set aside.

Whisk the egg whites until stiff peaks form, then reduce the speed and slowly incorporate the egg yolks, flour, and ground dried shrimp (prawns). Do not overbeat—keep as much air in as you can, so once everything is incorporated, stop mixing. Heat 2 tablespoons oil in a frying pan or skillet over medium heat. Using a big mixing spoon, put spoonfuls of the mixture into the pan to make patties about 2 inches (5 cm) across, making sure you leave room to flip them over, and cook until little bubbles form all over the tops of the pancakes and the edges look a little browned. Turn them over and cook for another minute or so on the other side, then remove and drain on paper towels. Repeat until all the batter is used, adding oil to the pan when necessary. Set aside.

Add the cactus paddles and romeritos to the mole sauce and simmer for another 5 minutes, until they are hot. Add the shrimp (prawns), reduce the heat, and simmer for 4–5 minutes or until the shrimp have turned red and are cooked.

Put the potatoes into a deep, flat bowl, cover with sauce, and serve with the patties.

Shrimp and Wild Greens in Mole

CAMARONES EN SALSA DE ACUYO

✺

SHRIMP WITH HOYA SANTA SAUCE

10 hoja santas, deveined
3 cloves garlic
½ onion, chopped
3 jalapeño chiles, seeded and deveined
sea salt
2 tablespoons corn oil
2¼ lb/1 kg medium shrimp (prawns), peeled and deveined without heads or tails
2¼ oz/60 g Masa Dough (page 36) dissolved in 1 cup (9 fl oz/250 ml) water and strained to get rid of any lumps

To serve:
White Rice (page 521)
Corn Tortillas (page 36)

REGION: GULF
PREPARATION TIME: 15 MINUTES
COOKING TIME: 25–30 MINUTES
SERVES: 6

Put the hoja santa leaves, garlic, onion, chiles, and ½ cup (4 fl oz/120 ml) water into a blender or food processor and process until smooth. Add another ½ cup (4 fl oz/120 ml) water and ½ teaspoon salt.

Heat the oil in a large skillet or frying pan over medium heat, add the sauce, and cook, stirring for about 10 minutes or until thick. Add the dissolved masa and simmer, stirring frequently, for 10–15 minutes or until the sauce is smooth and thick. Add salt to taste.

Add the shrimp (prawns) to the sauce and let simmer about 5 minutes or until the shrimp (prawns) turn pink and are cooked. Check the seasoning and serve hot with white rice and warm tortillas.

3 tomatoes, halved and seeded
½ cup (4 fl oz/120 ml) olive oil
3–5 smoked chipotle chiles in
  adobo
½ cup (2 oz/50 g) grated ginger
2½ lb/1.2 kg shrimp (prawns),
  peeled and deveined
1 tablespoon orange zest
4 cloves garlic, crushed
1 cup (9 fl oz/250 ml) orange
  juice
sea salt and pepper

To serve:
wilted spinach
mashed potatoes or White Rice
  (page 521)

brush with olive oil. Place the tomatoes on a cookie sheet and roast in the oven for 30 minutes.

Put the tomatoes, chipotles, and half the ginger into a food processor or blender. Season with salt and process until smooth. Strain the sauce into a shallow bowl, add the shrimp (prawns), and mix until well coated. Cover with plastic wrap (clingfilm) and marinate in the refrigerator for several hours, or overnight.

Heat the remaining olive oil in a heavy sauté pan over medium heat. Add the remaining ginger, then reduce the heat to low and heat for 2–3 minute, until browned. Add the orange zest and garlic and sauté for about 2 minutes or until the garlic is fragrant. Pour in the orange juice and simmer for an additional few minutes. Add the shrimp (prawns) and marinade and cook for 10 minutes until they are pink. Check the seasoning and serve with spinach and mashed potatoes or white rice.

CAMARONES EN SALSA DE ACUYO

✳

SHRIMP WITH ACUYO SAUCE

½ cup (2¼ oz/60 g) masa harina
10 hoja santa, deveined
3 cloves garlic
½ onion, chopped
3 jalapeño chiles, membrane
  and seeds removed
2 tablespoons corn oil
2¼ lb/1 kg shrimp (prawns),
  peeled and deveined
sea salt

To serve:
White Rice (page 521)
Corn Tortillas (page 36)

REGION: GULF, VERACRUZ
PREPARATION TIME: 25 MINUTES
COOKING TIME: 30 MINUTES
SERVES: 6

In a small bowl, dissolve the masa harina in 1 cup (9 fl oz/250 ml) water, and then strain to get rid of any lumps.

Put the hoja santa, garlic, onion, chiles, and ½ cup (4 fl oz/120 ml) water into a food processor or blender and process until smooth. Add another ½ cup (4 fl oz/120 ml) water and the salt.

Heat the oil in a large frying pan or skillet over medium heat, add the sauce and cook, stirring constantly for about 10 minutes or until thick. Add the dissolved masa harina and simmer, stirring frequently, for 10–15 minutes or until the sauce is smooth and thick. Add salt to taste.

Add the shrimp (prawns) to the sauce and let simmer about 5 minutes or until the shrimp (prawns) turn pink and are cooked. Check the seasoning and serve hot with white rice and warm tortillas.

CAMARONES EN ESCABECHE

✳

PICKLED SHRIMP

50 g/2 oz ancho chiles,
  cleaned, dry-roasted
1 cup (9 fl oz/250 ml) apple
  cider vinegar
10 black peppercorns
½ cinnamon stick
½ teaspoon cumin seeds
4 whole cloves
1 onion, coarsely chopped
3 cloves garlic, coarsely
  chopped
3 tablespoons corn oil
3 bay leaves
2¼ lb/1 kg shrimp (prawns),
  peeled and deveined
1 avocado, cut into wedges
Corn Tortillas (page 36),
  to serve

REGION: VERACRUZ
PREPARATION TIME: 25 MINUTES, PLUS 15 MINUTES
SOAKING AND 2 HOURS MARINATING
COOKING TIME: 25 MINUTES
SERVES: 6

Put the chiles in a small bowl, mix the vinegar with ½ cup (4½ fl oz/125 ml) boiling water, pour the mixture over the chiles, and let soak for 15 minutes or until soft.

In a skillet, add the peppercorns, cinnamon, cumin seeds, and cloves and dry-roast, stirring frequently, for a few minutes until fragrant. Put the spices into a food processor or blender, add the chiles, some of the diluted vinegar, onion, and garlic, and process until thoroughly combined and smooth,

Heat 1 tablespoon of the oil in a heavy pan. Add the bay leaves, and chile escabeche and cook over low heat, stirring occasionally, for 20 minutes.

Heat the remaining oil in a skillet. Add the shrimp (prawns), in batches if necessary, and cook over high heat for 4–5 minutes until just cooked, then transfer to a nonmetallic dish. Add the escabeche, mix well, and let marinate for 2 hours.

Serve warm or at room temperature garnished with avocado wedges, with fresh tortillas.

PADDLES AND CILANTRO

1 bay leaf
½ white onion, sliced
18 large shrimp (prawns)
1 lb 2 oz/500 g small shrimp
1 cup (9 fl oz/250 ml) apple
  cider vinegar
2 tablespoons Dijon mustard
4 cloves garlic, crushed
1 cup (9 fl oz/250 ml) olive oil
2 red bell peppers, finely
  chopped
2¼ lb/1 kg cactus paddles,
  diced and cooked
sea salt and pepper
3 tablespoons finely chopped
  scallions (spring onions), to
  garnish
3 tablespoons chopped cilantro
  (coriander), to garnish

heat. Add the shrimp (prawns) and as soon as they change color, drain and plunge them into a bowl of cold water to stop them cooking. Let cool and then peel and devein.

In a bowl, combine the vinegar, mustard, garlic, and olive oil and mix well. In a separate bowl, add the cactus paddles, bell peppers, shrimp, salt and pepper. Pour the vinaigrette over the salad, stir, and let stand in the refrigerator for 1 hour.

To serve, stir the mixture, then remove the large shrimp, and set aside. Plate the salad and garnish with 3 large shrimp, scallions (spring onions) and cilantro (coriander). Drizzle with a little vinaigrette and serve.

CAMARONES EN SALSA DE TAMARINDO

✺

SHRIMP IN TAMARIND SAUCE

3 tablespoons butter
24 jumbo shrimp (tiger prawns), peeled, head and tails intact, and shells reserved
1 small onion, sliced
2 dried chipotle chiles
2 cloves garlic, dry-roasted
5 oz/150 g tamarind paste
1 cup (9 fl oz/250 ml) Veal Stock (page 185)
sea salt
cilantro (coriander), to garnish

REGION: CENTRAL MEXICO
PREPARATION TIME: 20 MINUTES
COOKING TIME: 30 MINUTES
SERVES: 6

In a large frying pan or skillet over medium heat, add 2 tablespoons butter, jumbo shrimp (tiger prawn) shells, onion, garlic, chile, and tamarind paste and cook for 7 minutes. Add the veal stock, bring to a boil, reduce the heat and simmer for 15 minutes.

Transfer the mixture to a food processor or blender and process until smooth. Strain through a fine-mesh strainer (sieve) and set aside.

Met the remaining butter in a frying pan or skillet, add the jumbo shrimp (tiger prawn), and cook for 5 minutes. Add the sauce, cook for an additional minute, and remove from the heat.

Transfer to a plate and garnish with coriander (cilantro).

CAMARONES A LA DIABLA

✺

DEVILLED SHRIMP

1 cup (10 fl oz/275 ml) ketchup
4 black peppercorns
1 teaspoon apple cider vinegar
1 tablespoon corn oil
5 tablespoons (2¾ oz/70 g) butter
1 lb/450 g shrimp (prawns), peeled and deveined
4 arbol chiles, membranes and seeds removed and finely chopped
sea salt and pepper
Corn Tortillas (page 36), or crusty bread, to serve

REGION: FEDERAL DISTRICT
PREPARATION TIME: 15 MINUTES
COOKING TIME: 15 MINUTES
SERVES: 6

Put the ketchup, peppercorns, and vinegar into a food processor or blender and process until smooth. Strain into a bowl.

Heat the oil and butter in a large saucepan over medium heat, add the shrimp (prawns), and cook for 2 minutes. Add the sauce together with the chiles and salt and pepper to taste, then cover, reduce the heat to low and simmer for 10 minutes. Serve with warm tortillas or crusty bread.

Shrimp in Tamarind Sauce

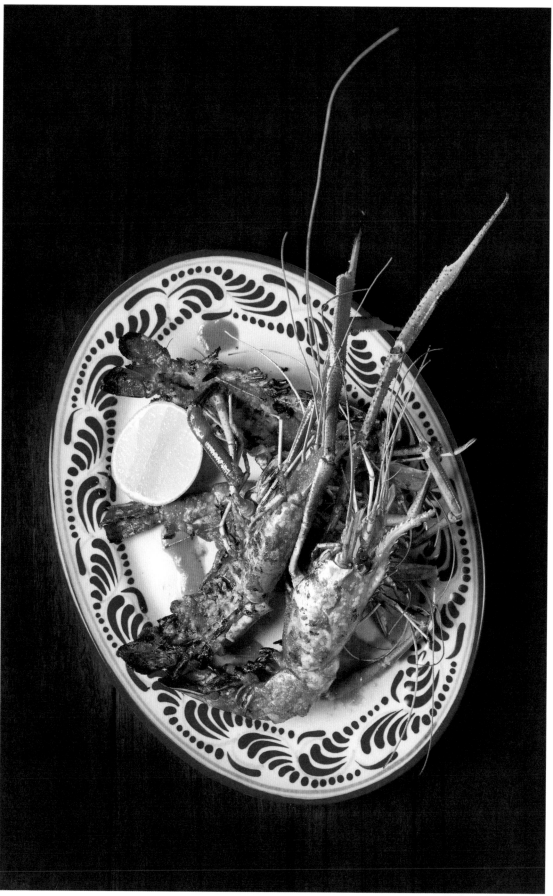

Barbequed Langoustines

4 ancho chiles, lightly
   dry-roasted
2 mulato chiles, lightly
   dry-roasted
3 tomatoes, dry-roasted
1 white onion, dry-roasted
14 garlic cloves
8 black peppercorns
4 cloves
1 cinnamon stick
¼ teaspoon cumin
½ cup (4 fl oz/120 ml) olive oil
1 tablespoon apple cider
   vinegar
2¼ lb/1 kg langoustines,
   cleaned and peeled
4 avocado leaves
sea salt
1 lime, cut into wedges

cover, and soak for 10 minutes. Drain and set aside.

Put the tomatoes, onion, dry-roasted garlic cloves, 5 peppercorns, 2 cloves, the cinnamon stick, cumin, and the chiles into a food processor or blender and process until smooth. Heat 3 tablespoons of the oil in a saucepan over medium heat, add the sauce, and heat for 20 minutes. Season and set aside.

Put the remaining whole garlic cloves, cloves, peppercorns, and vinegar in a food processor or blender, season with salt, and process until smooth but not a liquid. Put into a bowl.

Cut the langoustines in half lengthwise, add to the mixture in the bowl, coat, then cover with plastic wrap (clingfilm) and marinate in the refrigerator for 1 hour.

Heat the remaining oil in a large frying pan or skillet over medium heat. Add the langoustines and cook for 4–5 minutes. Add the avocado leaves and reserved sauce, then reduce the heat to low and simmer for 15 minutes. Check the seasoning and remove from the heat. Serve immediately with lime wedges.

Note: This recipe can be made with diced fish fillets, or jumbo shrimp (tiger prawns).

LANGOSTINOS EN MOLE DE XOCONOSTLE

LANGOUSTINES IN XOCONOSTLE MOLE

18 langoustines or jumbo shrimp (tiger prawns), peeled and cleaned
1 cup (9 fl oz/250 ml) sangria
½ cup (4 fl oz/120 ml) tequila
4 tablespoons corn oil or olive oil
sea salt and pepper

For the xoconostle mole:
6 anchos chiles, dry-roasted
3 tablespoons olive oil
6 cloves garlic
3 tomatoes, dry-roasted
1–2 teaspoons oregano, to taste
2 bay leaves
1 lb 2 oz/500 g xoconostle, peeled
sea salt and pepper

To serve:
6 prickly pears in syrup or brine
Corn Tortilla Strips (page 36)
4 tablespoons chopped chives

REGION: CENTRAL MEXICO
PREPARATION TIME: 35 MINUTES, PLUS 15 MINUTES SOAKING AND 30 MINUTES MARINATING
COOKING TIME: 30 MINUTES
SERVES: 6

Put the chiles in a bowl with enough boiling water to just cover and soak for 15 minutes. Set aside.

Heat the olive oil in a pan over medium heat. Add the garlic and sauté for about 2 minutes. Add the tomatoes, oregano, bay leaves, and xoconostle. Transfer the mixture to a food processor or blender and process with the chiles until smooth. Strain back into the pan, heat over medium heat, and season to taste with salt and pepper. Cook, stirring, for 10 minutes.

Season the langoustines, then place in a shallow dish, pour in the sangria and tequila, cover with plastic wrap (clingfilm), and marinate in the refrigerator for 30 minutes.

Heat the oil in a large saucepan over high heat, add the langoustines, and sauté for 4–5 minutes or until they are cooked and have turned pink. Serve with the mole, garnished with the prickly pears, tortillas, and chives.

5 large guajillo chiles,
  dry-roasted
3 ancho chiles, dry-roasted
4 costeños chiles
2–4 arbol chiles, membranes
  and seeds removed and
  chopped (optional)
1 white onion, chopped
4 cloves garlic
1 teaspoon oregano
4 tablespoons olive oil
sea salt
4½ lb/2 kg langoustines
  or jumbo shrimp (tiger
  prawns), cleaned, peeled, and
  deveined
White Rice (page 521), to serve

Put the chiles with their soaking water into a food processor or blender. Add the onion, garlic, oregano, and olive oil, and process until smooth. Strain and season with salt to taste. Put into a shallow bowl or dish. Add the langoustine, cover with plastic wrap (clingfilm), and marinade in the refrigerator for 1 hour.

Heat a frying pan or skillet over medium heat. Remove the langoustine from the marinade and fry them for 5 minutes until red and cooked through. Serve with white rice.

Note: Cook the langoustines with the marinade for a more intense flavor.

PLATANOS RELLENOS DE JAIBA

✺

CRAB-STUFFED PLANTAINS

3 ripe plantains, unpeeled
pinch of sea salt
1 tablespoon sugar
1 egg, beaten
5 tablespoons all-purpose
  (plain) flour
4 tablespoons fresh bread
  crumbs
1 lb/450 g crabmeat
2 cups (16 fl oz/475 ml) corn oil

To garnish:
1 banana leaf, lightly
  dry-roasted
1 cup (8 oz/225 g) sour cream
1 cup (4 oz/120 g) crumbled
  panela

REGION: GULF, TAMAULIPAS
PREPARATION TIME: 30 MINUTES, PLUS
10 MINUTES STANDING
COOKING TIME: 40 MINUTES
SERVES: 6

Put the unpeeled plantains into a large saucepan, pour in enough water to cover, and simmer for 25 minutes, then drain and let stand cooling.

Peel the plantains, put the flesh into a bowl, and mash with a fork until smooth. Stir in the salt and sugar, then stir in the egg and flour and mix. Add the bread crumbs and mix until the dough is firm but not dry. With your hands, roll the mixture into balls, 2 inches (5 cm) in diameter. Oil the palm of your hands to prevent the dough from sticking. Flatten each ball between 2 pieces of plastic wrap (clingfilm) into a thin circle, put a teaspoon of crabmeat in the center, then bring the dough up and around the crabmeat to form a little round package. Seal it well with your fingers and set aside. Repeat until you have run out of dough or filling.

Heat the oil in a deep fryer or deep saucepan to 350°F (180°C) or until a cube of day-old bread browns in 30 seconds. Carefully lower the crab-filled balls into the hot oil and deep-fry for 5 minutes or until they are golden brown. Remove with a slotted spoon and drain on paper towels.

Put the banana leaf on a serving plate, arrange the crab balls in the center, and serve drizzled with sour cream and covered with crumbled cheese.

2 tomatoes, coarsely chopped
4 tablespoons olive oil
1 small carrot, diced
½ leek, finely chopped
½ small onion, finely chopped
½–1 habanero chile, finely
  chopped
3 cloves garlic, crushed
14 oz/400 g crabmeat
11 oz/300 g fresh clams,
  (optional)
½ cup (4 fl oz/120 ml) dry white
  wine
2 teaspoons capers, chopped
4 tablespoons butter, diced
6 poblano chiles, dry-roasted
sea salt and pepper

To serve:
finely chopped epazote
1 tablespoon olive oil
White Rice (page 521)

heat, add the carrots, leek, onion, habanero chile, garlic, and pureed tomatoes, and sauté for 2–3 minutes until it dries out a little. Add the crabmeat and clams, then pour in the wine and reduce for 10 minutes. Turn off the heat and stir in the chopped capers. Add the butter pieces and just tilt the pan around slowly to melt the butter and incorporate itself into the ingredients. Season to taste with salt and pepper.

Peel the poblano chiles and then split them down one side, leaving the stem intact and making sure you don't go all the way through. Carefully open them up, remove the membranes and seeds, and fill the chiles with the stuffing. This is most easily done with wet hands, so keep a bowl of water on hand and keep dipping your working hand in it while you clean and stuff.

Put the chiles on a serving plate, sprinkle with epazote and a little oil, and serve with white rice.

MEDALLONES DE CAMARON

✳

SHRIMP MEDALLIONS

3¼ lb/1.5 kg large shrimp
  (prawns), peeled and
  deveined
11 oz/300 g sea bass fillet
2 eggs
¾ cup (6 fl oz/175 ml) light
  cream
juice of 1½ limes
scant ¼ cup (3¼ oz/90 g) butter,
  plus extra for greasing
½ cup of bread crumbs
pinch sea salt and freshly
  ground black pepper
White Rice (page 521), to serve

For the sauce:
2 cups (14 oz/400 g) sugar
juice of 1 lime
¾ cup (6 fl oz/175 ml) apple
  cider vinegar
1 cup (9 fl oz/250 ml) Fish
  Stock (page 184) (optional)

REGION: FEDERAL DISTRICT, BAJA CALIFORNIA
PREPARATION TIME: 30 MINUTES, PLUS 1 HOUR
SETTING TIME
COOKING TIME: 35 MINUTES
SERVES: 6

Put half of the shrimp (prawns), sea bass, cream, and eggs into a food processor or blender and process to a fine paste. Season with salt and pepper and stir in the lime juice. Put the remaining shrimp (prawns) in a bowl and add the paste. Stir well to coat.

Take six 4-inch (10-cm) ring molds and distribute the mixture among them, pressing down firmly. Cover with plastic wrap (cling film) and put them in the fridge for one hour to set.

Preheat the oven to 350°F (180°C/Gas Mark 4) and grease a baking sheet. Place the molds onto the baking sheet, then carefully remove the molds, cutting around the side to free the medallion, if needed. Bake for 25–30 minutes.

To make the sauce, put the sugar, ⅔ cup (5 fl oz/ 150 ml) water, and lime juice in a saucepan and bring to a simmer over low heat, until golden. Add the vinegar, bring to a boil over medium heat, and boil for 5 minutes. Add a little fish stock if you prefer a thinner sauce.

Plate the medallions, ladle over the sauce, and serve with white rice.

12 fresh crabs with large claws, about 3¼ lb/1.7 kg in total weight
6 tomatoes
1 white onion, chopped
4 cloves garlic
1 cinnamon stick
2 jalapeño chiles
3 tablespoons corn oil
10 cups (4¼ pints/2.4 liters) Fish Stock (page 184)
1 large sprig epazote
1 lb 10 oz/750 g crabmeat
sea salt

To serve:
Chochoyotes (page 394)
Macha Salsa (page 501)

chiles in a dry frying pan or skillet and heat over medium heat for 5–10 minutes, turning them over and taking them out as they blister and brown. Put the tomato mixture into a food processor or blender and process until smooth. Strain into a bowl.

Heat the oil in a heavy saucepan over medium heat, add the tomato sauce, and heat for 10 minutes. Add the crabs, fish stock, epazote, and salt to taste, reduce the heat to low and cook, covered, for 30 minutes, or until the crabs are cooked and pink.

Remove the crabs from the pan. Leave the pan on low heat to keep the sauce piping hot.

Remove the claws from the crabs, crack them open but don't take the meat out. Distribute the crab claws, the halved crabs (without their claws), and the crabmeat among the serving bowls. Ladle the sauce over the crabs. Dumplings and serve the macha sauce on the side.

PULPOS AL AJILLO Y CHILACAS

✻

OCTOPUS WITH GARLIC AND CHILACAS

8 sprigs parsley
8 sprigs thyme
5½ lb/2.5 kg octopus
1 white onion, thinly sliced
10 cloves garlic
1 teaspoon black peppercorns

For the garlic sauce:
1 cup (9 fl oz/250 ml) olive oil
1 large white onion, finely
    sliced
15 cloves garlic, crushed
12 chilacas, dry-roasted
juice of 5 limes
4 tablespoons Worcestershire
    sauce
4 tablespoons Maggi sauce
sea salt and pepper

REGION: GULF
PREPARATION TIME: 20 MINUTES
COOKING TIME: 1 HOUR
SERVES: 6

Tie the parsley and thyme sprigs together with kitchen string.

Clean the octopus by turning the inside out and rinsing well under warm running water. Remove the beak (small hard ball found in the middle of the octopus), the eyes, and the ink sack. Set the ink sack aside. Turn the octopus the right way out again and put in a large pan, with enough water to cover, together with the onion, garlic, peppercorns, and the bundle of herbs. Simmer for about 45 minutes, or until tender. Remove from the heat and take the octopus out of the pan, and then cut into 1½-inch (4-cm) pieces and set aside.

For the sauce, heat the oil in a frying pan or skillet over medium heat, add the onion, and sauté for a minute. Add the garlic and sauté for about 1 minute, or until fragrant. Add the chiles, lime juice, Worcestershire sauces, and all-purpose liquid seasoning. Reduce the heat to low, check the seasoning, and simmer gently for 10 minutes.

Add the octopus to the sauce, mix well and serve on individual plates.

3¼ lb/1.5 kg cooked octopus,
  cut into bite-size pieces

For the sauce:
4 tablespoons olive oil
½ onion, finely chopped
2 cloves garlic, finely chopped
3 tomatoes, peeled, seeded, and
  finely chopped
½ cup (4 fl oz/120 ml) dry white
  wine
2 bay leaves
2 cups (16 fl oz/475 ml) Fish
  Stock (page 184)
4 tablespoons finely chopped
  parsley
2½ cups (9 oz/250 g) almonds,
  blanched, toasted, and
  coarsely chopped
5 tablespoons golden raisins
  (sultanas), chopped
12 black olives, pitted and
  finely sliced
black pepper

To serve:
White Rice (page 521)
fried plantains, sliced

let simmer to evaporate the alcohol, then add the
bay leaves and fish stock and cook for 10 minutes.
Remove the bay leaves, add the parsley, almonds,
raisins, olives, and black pepper to taste, then
add the octopus, stir, and cook for an additional
5 minutes, or until the octopus is hot. Serve with
white rice and plantains.

PULPOS COLORADOS

✻

STEWED OCTOPUS

6 tomatoes, dry-roasted
4 cloves garlic, dry-roasted
½ teaspoon cumin seeds,
  dry-roasted
1 tablespoon olive oil, plus
  extra for greasing
3¼ lb/1.5 kg octopus, sliced
2 large poblano chiles,
  dry-roasted and sliced
1 cup (3½ oz/100 g) olives,
  sliced
6 tablespoons capers
oregano, to taste
sea salt and pepper
½ cup (4 fl oz/120 ml) red wine
2 tablespoons chopped parsley,
  to garnish
White Rice (page 521), to serve

REGION: GULF
PREPARATION TIME: 40 MINUTES, PLUS
15 MINUTES SOAKING
COOKING TIME: 35 MINUTES
SERVES: 6

Preheat the oven to 350°F (180°C/Gas Mark 4).

Put the ancho chiles into a small bowl with enough hot water to cover them and soak for 15 minutes. Put the chiles and their water into a food processor or blender. Add the tomatoes, garlic, and cumin, and process until smooth. Strain into a bowl.

Heat the oil in a frying pan or skillet over medium heat. Add the strained sauce and simmer for 10 minutes until the sauce has thickened.

Grease an ovenproof dish and arrange a layer of sliced octopus on the bottom. Scatter some of the poblano chile, olives, capers, and oregano, and season with salt and pepper. Pour over some of the wine and then some of the chili sauce. Repeat the layers, beginning with the octopus and ending with the sauce. Cover with aluminum foil and bake for about 20–25 minutes.

Garnish with parsley and serve with white rice.

Stewed Octopus

PULPOS A LA ANTIGUA

✴

OLD-FASHIONED OCTOPUS

5½ lb/2.5 kg octopus
1 clove garlic, peeled
½ onion
2 bay leaves

For the sauce:
½ cup (4 fl oz/120 ml) olive oil
2 onions, chopped
1 clove garlic, finely chopped
4 cups (3¼ lb/1.5 kg) tomato
   puree (passata)
zest of 1 orange, grated
1 teaspoon aromatic herbs
1 cup (4 oz/125 g) olives, finely
   chopped
½ cup (4 fl oz/120 ml) red wine
sea salt
White Rice (page 521), to serve

To garnish:
toasted almonds, chopped
raisins, chopped
toasted pine nuts
toasted pecans, chopped
güero chiles (if available)

REGION: GULF
PREPARATION TIME: 20 MINUTES
COOKING TIME: 1 HOUR 30 MINUTES
SERVES: 6

Clean the octopus by turning it inside out and rinsing well under warm running water. Remove the beak (small hard ball found in the middle of the octopus), the eyes, and the ink sac. Set the ink sac aside. Turn the octopus the right way out again and put into a large saucepan with the garlic, onion, bay leaves, and just enough water to cover. Cook over low heat for 1½ hours, topping up with the water if necessary. Drain and set aside.

Meanwhile, heat the olive oil in a large saucepan over medium heat, add the onions and garlic, and sauté for 2 minutes. Add the tomato puree (passata), orange zest, aromatic herbs, and olives. Stir the ink from the ink sac into the red wine until combined, then add the mixture to the pan. Check the seasoning.

Put a portion of octopus on each serving plate, then garnish with almonds, raisins, pine nuts, pecans, and chiles, and serve with white rice.

Old-Fashioned Octopus

CALDO ISTMEÑO DE NOPALES Y CAMARÓN

❋

SHRIMP AND CACTUS PADDLE STEW

3⅓ cups (1 lb 2 oz/500 g) peas
5 cups (1 lb 2 oz/500 g) green
  beans
1 lb 2 oz/500 g cooked cactus
  paddles, diced
2 sprigs purple epazote plus
  6 epazote leaves, finely
  chopped
6 guajillo chiles, dry-roasted
1 lb 2 oz/500 g small shrimp
  (prawns), peeled and
  deveined, heads and shells
  reserved
2 tablespoons olive oil
1 onion, finely chopped
1 clove garlic, finely chopped
2 small tomatoes, seeded and
  finely chopped
sea salt

To serve:
cilantro (coriander), finely
  chopped
1 serrano chile, finely chopped

REGION: OAXACA
PREPARATION TIME: 25 MINUTES, PLUS
20 MINUTES SOAKING
COOKING TIME: 40 MINUTES
SERVES: 6

Bring a large saucepan of water to a boil over medium heat, add the cactus paddle, peas, and beans, and cook for 10 minutes, or until cooked but still crisp. Drain and set aside.

Bring 2 cups (16 fl oz/475 ml) water to a boil in a pan over medium heat. Add the epazote sprigs. Remove the pan from the heat, add the chiles, and soak for 20 minutes. Remove the epazote.

Put the reserved heads and shells of the shrimp (prawns) with the soaked chiles and some of the soaking water into a food processor or blender and process until smooth. Strain, then return the mixture to the epazote stock.

Heat the olive oil in a saucepan over medium heat, add the onion, garlic, and tomatoes, and cook for 15 minutes, until well combined. Add the epazote stock and bring to a simmer. Season, add the shrimp (prawns), and simmer for 3–4 minutes or until the shrimp are pink, then add the vegetables just to reheat. Add the remaining epazote, then season with salt. Sprinkle with cilantro (coriander) and serve with the chile on the side.

1 tablespoon butter
1 tablespoon vegetable oil
1 white onion, finely chopped
2 cloves garlic, finely chopped
3 tomatoes, seeded and finely
  chopped
3 jalapeños, dry-roasted
36 fresh oysters, shucked
1 tablespoon corn oil
1 tablespoon all-purpose
  (plain) flour
4 tablespoons white wine
sea salt and pepper
2 tablespoons finely chopped
  parsley, to serve

jalapeños, and oysters, then season and add water to make a thin sauce. Mix lightly, and set aside.

In a separate saucepan, heat the corn oil over medium heat, then add the flour and cook for 1 minute or until golden. Pour in the wine, and stir until the flour has dissolved. Add the oysters with the sauce and bring to a boil. Boil for 3–4 minutes, then taste and adjust seasoning, if necessary. Sprinkle with chopped parsley and serve.

CALAMARES A LOS TRES CHILES

❋

SQUID WITH CHILES

1¾ lb/800 g squid, cleaned
4 tablespoons olive oil
3 cloves garlic, finely chopped
1 mulato chile, membrane and
   seeds removed and sliced
1 pasilla chile, membrane and
   seeds removed and sliced
1 ancho chile, membrane and
   seeds removed and sliced
sea salt and pepper
White Rice (page 521), to serve

REGION: CENTRAL MEXICO
PREPARATION TIME: 15 MINUTES
COOKING TIME: 10 MINUTES
SERVES: 6

Separate the body and the tentacles of the squid. Score the body in a crosscross pattern and leave the tentacles whole.

Heat the oil in a frying pan or skillet over medium heat, add the garlic and chiles, and sauté for 1–2 minutes. Do not let them burn. Remove the mixture from the pan and set aside. Add the squid to the pan, increase the heat to high, and cook for 1 minute on one side, turn, and then cook for an additional minute, until firm and cooked through. Return the garlic and chile mixture to the pan, stir, and serve with white rice.

Squid with Chiles

Mussels with Cilantro

2¼ lb/1 kg fresh mussels

½ teaspoon black peppercorns

1–3 cuaresmeño or serrano chiles, membranes and seeds removed

3 cloves garlic

½ bunch cilantro (coriander)

½ bunch parsley, leaves only

sea salt

4 tablespoons Chicken Stock (page 184)

½ teaspoon sugar

3 tablespoons corn or olive oil

cilantro (coriander) leaves, to garnish

crusty bread, to serve

that are broken or do not close when tapped firmly on the shell. Set aside.

Put the peppercorns, chiles, garlic, cilantro (coriander), parsley, salt, chicken stock, and sugar into a food processor or blender and process until it is a smooth paste. Strain into a bowl.

Heat the oil in a wok or a heavy skillet or sauté pan with a lid over medium heat. When it is hot, add the paste and sauté for 30 seconds. Add the mussels and shake the pan to mix everything together well. Cover with a lid and cook for 5 minutes or until the mussels open. Check the seasoning and discard any mussels that are still closed. Garnish with cilantro leaves and serve immediately with crusty bread.

PARTY CHICKEN WITH YELLOW MOLE

1 white onion, thinly sliced
juice of 6 limes
13 cups (5¼ pints/3 liters)
   Chicken Stock (page 184)
3 tablespoons (1½ oz/45 g)
   achiote paste
7 guajillo chiles, dry-roasted
25 acuyo leaves
1 (4-lb/1.8-kg) whole chicken
4 teaspoons corn oil
1½ cups (6 oz/175 g) Masa
   Dough (page 36)
⅓ cup (2 oz/50 g) green beans
2 zucchini (courgettes)
sea salt and pepper

REGION: OAXACA
PREPARATION TIME: 30 MINUTES
COOKING TIME: 1¼ HOURS
SERVES: 4–6

Preheat the oven to 350°F (180°C/Gas Mark 4).

Put the sliced onion into a bowl, drizzle it with the lime juice, and season to taste with salt. Cover and set aside.

Pour the stock into a saucepan, set over medium heat and stir in the achiote paste until it has dissolved. Add the chiles and acuyo leaves and bring to a boil.

Reduce the heat, add the chicken, and simmer for 15 minutes. Transfer the chicken to a roasting pan, brush with the oil, and roast for about 40 minutes, until cooked through. Remove it from the oven and cover it with aluminum foil to keep it warm.

In the meantime, remove the acuyo leaves from the pan with a slotted spoon, put them into a food processor or blender, and process to a thick paste. Add a little stock to loosen if needed. Transfer the paste to a bowl.

Remove the chiles from the pan with a slotted spoon and put them into the food processor or blender. Add enough of the stock to cover and process until thoroughly combined. Pass through a strainer (sieve) back into the pan with the stock.

Stir the masa dough into the pan and simmer, stirring continuously, for 15 minutes or until the stock has thickened into a sauce. Season to taste with salt and pepper.

Cook the green beans and zucchini (courgettes) in a saucepan of lightly salted boiling water for 5 minutes, then drain and set aside.

To serve, carve the chicken. Ladle a generous portion of mole sauce onto individual plates. Top with the chicken and serve immediately with the vegetables, the marinated onion, and acuyo paste.

2 tablespoons corn oil

1 (8¾-lb/4-kg) chicken,
   cut into 6 pieces

1 lb 2 oz/500 g boneless pork
   shoulder, cut into 6 pieces

½ small head plus 2 cloves
   garlic

1½ onions

15 tomatillos

2 cloves

3 black peppercorns

½ cinnamon stick

⅓ cup (1½ oz/40 g) capers

½ teaspoon oregano

3 tablespoons raisins

pinch of sugar

4 tablespoons pitted green
   olives

2 oz/50 g pickled güero chiles
   (optional), to serve

sea salt

browned. Remove the pan from the heat.

Transfer the meat to a cooking pan, add the garlic cloves, 1 onion, and a pinch of salt, pour in water to cover, and bring to a boil. Reduce the heat and simmer for 35–40 minutes, until the meat is tender and the pan is almost dry.

Meanwhile, dry-roast the tomatillos, onion half, and half a head of garlic in a dry frying pan. Remove them as they begin to blacken. Separate the garlic head into cloves and peel.

Put the cloves, peppercorns, and cinnamon into a spice mill and grind into a powder. Tip the powder, dry-roasted onion, garlic, and tomatillos into a food processor or blender and process into a paste. Add the capers and oregano, and process again until thoroughly combined.

Heat the remaining oil in a saucepan. Add the tomatillo mixture and cook over low heat, stirring occasionally, for 10 minutes, until thickened.

When the meat is ready, remove the pan from the heat. Transfer the chicken and pork to the saucepan of sauce. Strain the cooking liquid into the pan of sauce, add the raisins, sugar, and olives, stir well, and simmer for an additional few minutes.

Remove the pan from the heat and season with sea salt to taste. Divide the meat and sauce among 6 individual plates, garnish with pickled güero chiles, and serve immediately.

QUAIL ATAPAKUA

4 pasilla or ancho chiles,
   membranes and seeds
   removed
4 corn on the cobs
12 quails, cleaned
¼ cup (2 fl oz/60 ml) corn oil
1 onion, quartered
2 cloves garlic
3 guajillo chiles, seeded
2 serrano chiles, membranes
   and seeds removed
4 cloves
2 black peppercorns
2 bell peppers, seeded and
   coarsely chopped
2 sprigs thyme
6 tomatillos
2 tomatoes
sea salt

REGION: MICHOACÁN
PREPARATION TIME: 15 MINUTES, PLUS
15 MINUTES SOAKING
COOKING TIME: 1½ HOURS
SERVES: 6

In a small bowl, combine the pasillo chiles and enough hot water to cover them and soak for 15 minutes. Drain.

Put the corn into a large saucepan, pour in water to cover, and bring to a boil. Cook for 7–10 minutes, or until done. Set aside.

Put the quails in a large saucepan, pour in water to cover, and bring to a boil. Reduce the heat and simmer for 30 minutes, until tender. Remove the pan from the heat and transfer the quails to a plate, reserving the cooking liquid.

Heat the oil in a large saucepan. Add the onion and garlic and cook over low heat, stirring occasionally, for 5 minutes. Add the quails, increase the heat to medium, and cook, turning frequently, for 10 minutes. Pour in the reserved cooking liquid and simmer for 10 minutes.

Using a sharp knife, cut off the kernels from the corn on the cobs and put them into a food processor or blender. Add all the chiles, the cloves, peppercorns, bell peppers, thyme, tomatillos, and tomatoes, and process until thoroughly combined. Add 1 cup (9 fl oz/250 ml) of the cooking liquid and blend again. Pass through a strainer (sieve) into the pan with the quails, and cook, stirring continuously, for an additional 10 minutes until thickened. Season to taste with the salt, remove the pan from the heat, and serve.

Quail Atapakua

BARBECUED CHICKEN

6 ancho chiles, dry-roasted

12 guajillo chiles, dry-roasted

¾ teaspoon black peppercorns,
  dry-roasted

pinch of cumin seeds,
  dry-roasted

pinch of dried oregano,
  dry-roasted

1 cinnamon stick, dry-roasted

1 clove garlic, dry-roasted

6 chicken legs, thighs and
  drumsticks separated

11 oz/300 g banana leaves,
  lightly dry-roasted

6 avocado leaves

12 Corn Tortillas,
  to serve

½ onion, finely diced

chile sauce, to serve

scallions (spring onions),
  to serve

sea salt

REGION: HIDALGO, MEXICO CENTER
PREPARATION TIME: 1 HOUR, PLUS 15 MINUTES
SOAKING AND 24 HOURS MARINATING
COOKING TIME: 1 HOUR
SERVES: 6

In a small bowl, combine the chiles and enough hot water to cover them and soak for 15 minutes.

Put the chiles and their soaking water into a food processor or blender, add the peppercorns, cumin seeds, oregano, cinnamon, and garlic, and process until thoroughly combined. Pass through a strainer (sieve) into a bowl and season with salt to taste.

Spread the chile mixture all over the chicken legs, put them into a dish, cover with plastic wrap (clingfilm), and let marinate in the refrigerator for 24 hours.

Cut the banana leaves into 10-inch (25-cm) squares. Put a chicken leg on a banana leaf square, add an avocado leaf, and cover with another banana leaf square. Fold in the sides tightly to make a package and tie with string. Repeat with the remaining chicken legs.

Put the chicken packages in the top of a steamer and cook for about 1 hour, until tender, replenishing the water as necessary. Remove the pan from the heat and lift out the packages.

Pull the meat off the bone and serve immediately with warm tortillas, onion, chile sauce and scallions (spring onions).

WEDDING VEIL CHICKEN

1 white onion, quartered and
   dry fried
3 jalapeño chiles, dry-roasted
3 cloves garlic, dry-roasted
6 tablespoons olive oil
2¼ cups (9 oz/ 250 g) pine nuts,
   dry-roasted
2 cloves, dry-roasted
2 allspice berries, dry-roasted
4¼ cups (34 fl oz/1 liter)
   Chicken Stock (page 184)
6 chicken breasts
½ cup (2 oz/50 g) Mexican pink
   pine nuts
sea salt

Heat 1 tablespoon of the oil in a large pan. Add chile mixture and cook over, medium-high heat stirring frequently, for 5 minutes.

Put the pine nuts, cloves, and allspice berries into a food processor or blender and process until combined. Again, add a ladleful of the chicken stock. Strain into the pan with the chile mixture. Taste the sauce and season with salt if necessary. Add the rest of the stock, reduce the heat to low and simmer for 30 minutes, stirring occasionally.

Heat the remaining oil in a large skillet or frying pan. Add the chicken and cook over medium heat for 4–5 minutes on each side until golden brown. Remove the pan from the heat.

Transfer the chicken to the pine nut sauce and simmer over low heat for 20 minutes or until cooked through. Remove the pan from the heat.

Divide the chicken and sauce among 6 individual plates, sprinkle with the pink pine nuts, and serve immediately.

✳

GRANDPA'S CHICKEN

18 guajillo chiles, dry-roasted
6 costeño or small guajillo
   chiles, dry-roasted
pinch of cumin seeds,
   dry-roasted
pinch of black peppercorns,
   dry-roasted
2 cloves garlic, dry-roasted
½ onion, dry-roasted
pinch of dried marjoram
2 cloves, dry-roasted
6 large chicken pieces
1 large banana leaf
hoja santa, stem and thick
   central vein removed
2 tablespoons olive oil
1 cup (9 fl oz/250 ml) Chicken
   Stock (page 184) or water
sea salt
White Rice (page 521), to serve
lime wedges, to serve

REGION: GUERRERO
PREPARATION TIME: 50 MINUTES, PLUS 15 MINUTES
SOAKING AND AT LEAST 3 HOURS MARINATING
COOKING TIME: 1½ HOURS
SERVES: 6

In a small bowl, combine the chiles and enough hot water to cover them and soak for 15 minutes.

Place the chiles, cumin seeds, peppercorns, garlic, onion, marjoram, and cloves in a food processor or blender and process until combined. Season with salt and strain into a bowl.

Rub the chile mixture all over the chicken pieces, put them into a dish, cover with plastic wrap (clingfilm), and let marinate in the refrigerator for 3 hours (or overnight).

Line a deep, heavy frying pan or skillet with the banana leaf, letting it overhang the rim. Add a layer of hoja santa on the bottom and add the marinated chicken. Drizzle the remaining hoja santa with the olive oil and cover the chicken with it. Pour in the stock or water and wrap completely with the overhanging banana leaf.

Cover the pan with a lid or aluminum foil and cook over low heat for 1½ hours until the chicken is cooked through and tender.

Divide the chicken among 6 plates and serve with the white rice and a lime wedge.

2 tablespoons olive oil
1 large onion, finely chopped
3 cloves garlic, crushed
1⅓ cups (7 oz/200 g) corn
  kernels
1 lb 10 oz/750 g assorted
  mushrooms, chopped
1 lb 10 oz/750 g zucchini
  (courgette) flowers, pistils
  removed
½ cup (1 oz/25 g) finely
  chopped epazote
7 oz/200 g goat cheese,
  crumbled
6 poblano chiles, roasted
  directly over the flame,
  peeled, and seeded
sea salt and pepper
½ red onion, thinly sliced,
  to garnish

For the sauce:
7 tomatoes, dry-roasted
½ large white onion,
  dry-roasted
2 cloves garlic, dry-roasted
6 ancho chiles, dry-roasted
1–2 chipotle chiles, dry-roasted
1 tablespoon olive oil
1 sprig epazote, finely chopped
sea salt and pepper

for 5 minutes. Add the corn kernels and mushrooms and cook until they have released all their liquid. Set aside a few zucchini (courgette) flowers for garnish and shred the remainder into large pieces. Add the shredded flowers and epazote to the pan, season to taste with salt and pepper, and stir in the goat cheese. Remove the pan from the heat.

Fill the poblano chiles with this mixture. Return the frying pan to the heat and heat the remaining oil. Add the filled chiles to warm for a few minutes, then remove from heat and set aside.

To make the sauce, put the tomatoes, onion, garlic, and chiles into a food processor or blender and process until combined. Strain into a bowl.

Heat the olive oil in a frying pan or skillet over medium heat. Add the tomato mixture and cook, stirring occasionally, for a 2–3 minutes. Stir in the epazote, season with salt and pepper to taste, and remove the pan from the heat.

Place the stuffed chiles on a serving platter, spoon over the hot sauce, and garnish with the reserved zucchini (courgette) flowers and red onion. Serve immediately.

CHILPOZONTES

1 (4-lb/1.8-kg) chicken,
  separated into pieces
½ white onion
4 cloves garlic
3 green chayotes, peeled,
  cored, and quartered
4 zucchini (courgettes), cut
  lengthwise into ⅛-inch
  (3-mm) slices
1 lb/500 g assorted
  mushrooms, coarsely
  chopped
4 sprigs epazote, chopped
sea salt
Corn Tortillas (page 36),
  to serve

For the sauce:
3 dried chipotle chiles,
  dry-roasted
8 morita chiles, dry-roasted
3 pasilla chiles, dry-roasted
4 hoja santas, the central vein
  removed
½ white onion
4 cloves garlic
1½ teaspoons allspice berries
sea salt

REGION: PUEBLA
PREPARATION TIME: 30 MINUTES
COOKING TIME: 1 HOUR 35 MINUTES
SERVES: 6–8

Bring 13 cups (5¼ pints/3 liters) water to a boil in a terracotta pot or a pan. Add all the chicken pieces and the carcass on the bone, onion, garlic and a pinch of salt, and bring back to a boil. Reduce the heat and simmer for 45 minutes. Remove the chicken meat and reserve. Reserve the stock and discard the bones.

To make the sauce, put the chiles and hoja santas into a pan, pour in water just to cover, and bring to a boil. Reduce the heat and simmer for 15 minutes.

Remove the pan from the heat, remove the hoja santas, and put the chiles with the water into a food processor or blender. Add the onion, garlic, and allspice berries and process until thoroughly combined. Taste and add salt if necessary.

Pass the chile mixture through a strainer (sieve) into the chicken stock and bring to a boil. Reduce the heat and simmer for 20 minutes.

Bring the sauce back to a boil, add the chayotes, reduce the heat, and simmer for 10 minutes. Add the zucchini (courgettes) and simmer for 3 minutes, until they are tender but not soggy. Add the mushrooms and then the chicken pieces and epazote, and simmer for an additional few minutes until heated through. Check the seasoning.

Remove the pan from the heat, ladle the chilpozonte into large soup bowls, and serve immediately with hot tortillas.

1 (4-lb/1.8-kg) chicken,
   separated into pieces
2 tablespoons corn oil
1 red onion, chopped
2 cloves garlic
3 tomatoes, chopped
1 güero chile or green chile,
   membrane and seeds
   removed, chopped
2 cloves
1 bay leaf
½ cup (4 fl oz/120 ml) dry
   sherry or dry white wine
2 potatoes, diced
sea salt
White Rice (page 521), to serve

the heat and simmer for 30 minutes. Lift out the chicken meat and reserve. Discard the carcass. Reserve the stock.

Heat the oil in a saucepan. Add the onion, garlic, tomatoes, and chile and cook over medium heat, stirring occasionally, for 5 minutes. Remove the pan from the heat and transfer the mixture to a food processor or blender. Process to a puree, adding 1 cup (9 fl oz/250 ml) of the chicken stock, then strain into a flameproof casserole or saucepan. Discard the contents of the strainer (sieve).

Set the pan over medium-low heat and season with salt. Add the chicken pieces, cloves, bay leaf, sherry, and potatoes. Cook for 20 minutes, until the potatoes are tender and the chicken is heated through.

Remove the pan from the heat and discard the cloves and bay leaf. Serve with white rice.

GALLINAS BORRACHAS

DRUNKEN CHICKEN

2 large tomatoes, chopped
4 tablespoons corn oil
2 (3–4-lb/1.2–1.8-kg) chickens
2 cloves garlic, chopped
2 sprigs parsley, chopped
1 lb 2 oz/500 g chorizo, sliced
3 cups (1 lb 2 oz/500 g)
    chopped ham
4 cups (1⅔ pints/1 liter) dry
    sherry or dry white wine
1 tablespoon sugar
pinch of ground cloves
pinch of ground cinnamon
pinch of black pepper
pinch of ground nutmeg
½ cup (2½ oz/65 g) raisins
½ cup (2 oz/50 g) almonds
sea salt

REGION: COAHUILA
PREPARATION TIME: 15 MINUTES
COOKING TIME: 35 MINUTES
SERVES: 8

Put the tomatoes into a food processor or blender and process to a puree. Heat the oil in a large saucepan. Quarter the chickens and add the pieces, pureed tomatoes, garlic, and parsley and cook over medium heat, turning the chicken pieces occasionally, for 10–15 minutes.

Add the chorizo and ham and cook for an additional 5 minutes, then pour in the sherry and cook for a few minutes until the sherry has mostly evaporated. Add the sugar, cloves, cinnamon, pepper, nutmeg, raisins, and almonds, and season. Reduce the heat and simmer for 15 minutes, until the chicken is cooked through and the cooking liquid has thickened.

Remove the pan from the heat. Put a piece of chicken on each plate, spoon over the sauce, and serve with rice or salad.

MIXIOTES DE NOPALES CON HIGADITOS

CACTUS AND CHICKEN LIVER PACKAGES

4 banana leaves, lightly dry-
    roasted (optional)
24 epazote leaves
2 tablespoons corn oil
10 cactus paddles, diced and
    cooked
2½ tablespoons chopped onion
1 lb 2 oz/500 g chicken livers,
    roughly chopped
9 oz/250 g chicken gizzards,
    chopped (optional)
1–2 green serrano chiles,
    chopped
sea salt

REGION: MEXICO CENTER, NORTH
PREPARATION TIME: 25 MINUTES
COOKING TIME: 45 MINUTES
SERVES: 6

Cut the banana leaves and a sheet of aluminum foil into 6 rectangles about 6 x 8 inches (15 x 20 cm). Finely chop half the epazote leaves. Heat the oil in a saucepan over medium heat. Add the cactus paddles, onion, livers, gizzards (if using), chopped epazote, and chiles and season with salt. Reduce the heat to low and cook, stirring occasionally, for 10 minutes.

Divide the mixture among the banana leaves and add 2 epazote leaves to each. Fold in the sides and tie with kitchen string to make a package, and cover with aluminum foil.

Bring some water to a boil in a steamer. Line the steamer with the banana leaves if you have them, add the packages, and cook for 30 minutes. Remove from the heat. Remove the foil and cut the strings but do not unwrap the packages. Serve immediately.

Drunken Chicken

CHICKEN IN "SANDALS"

3 tablespoons butter or lard
1 white onion, chopped
2 cloves garlic, chopped
2 tomatoes, chopped
⅔ cup (3½ oz/100 g) chopped
  ham
¾ cup (3½ oz/100 g) skinned
  and chopped chorizo
1 apple, cored and sliced
1 pear, cored and sliced
5 pineapple slices, diced
1 sweet potato, peeled and
  sliced
2 tablespoons capers
4 tablespoons almonds
4 tablespoons raisins
pinch of saffron strands,
  lightly crushed
pinch of ground cinnamon
pinch of ground cloves
6 boneless chicken breasts
1 cup (9 fl oz/250 ml) red wine
sea salt and pepper

REGION: AGUASCALIENTES
PREPARATION TIME: 15 MINUTES
COOKING TIME: 1¼ HOURS
SERVES: 6–8

Melt the butter in a flameproof terracotta pot or saucepan. Add the onion and garlic and cook over low heat, stirring occasionally, for 8–10 minutes, until lightly browned. Add the tomatoes, ham, and chorizo and cook for an additional 10 minutes.

Add the apple, pear, pineapple, sweet potato, capers, almonds, raisins, saffron, cinnamon, and cloves. Cover and cook on low heat for 15 minutes. Remove the pot from the heat.

Remove and reserve 2 cups (16 fl oz/475 ml) of this mixture. Cover it so it stays warm and leave the rest in the pot. Add the chicken to the pot, putting it on top of the fruit mixture. Pour in the wine, cover, and simmer for 35 minutes or until the chicken is tender and cooked through. Season with salt and pepper.

Remove the pot from the heat and serve immediately with the reserved ham, vegetable, and fruit mixture.

1 teaspoon sea salt

6 chicken thighs, skin on

2 whole allspice berries

1 clove

6 black peppercorns

1 bay leaf

juice of 2 oranges

6–8 tomatillos

4 tablespoons (1½ oz/40 g)
butter or oil

½ head garlic, dry-roasted
and finely chopped

1 onion, finely chopped

3 red bell peppers, finely
chopped

2 tablespoons apple cider
vinegar

sea salt

White Rice (page 521), to serve

salted water over it, and let stand for 20 minutes.

Meanwhile, grind together the allspice berries, clove, peppercorns, and bay leaf with a mortar and pestle or in a spice grinder. Stir half of this spice mixture into the orange juice in a bowl and pour it into the water with the chicken.

Set the pan over low heat and cook the chicken for 1–½ hours, until it is cooked through and tender and the cooking liquid has reduced.

Meanwhile, put the tomatillos into another saucepan, add a pinch of salt, cover with water, and bring to a boil. Reduce the heat and simmer for 10 minutes. Remove the pan from the heat and drain.

Peel the tomatillos, then put them into a food processor or blender and process. Strain into a bowl and stir in the remaining ground spice mixture.

Remove the pan of chicken from the heat, lift out the chicken, and let cool. When cold, remove the meat from the bones and put it onto a serving platter.

Melt 3 tablespoons of butter in a saucepan. Add the garlic, onion, and bell peppers and cook over medium-high heat, stirring occasionally, for a few minutes. Add the tomatillo mixture, vinegar, and 1 tablespoon butter. Taste, adjust the seasoning, if necessary, and remove the pan from the heat. Pour the sauce over the chicken and serve immediately with white rice.

CHICKEN MEDALLIONS IN MANGO SALSA

3 skinless, boneless chicken
  breasts, halved horizontally
12 slices manchego cheese
all-purpose (plain) flour, for
  dusting
4 tablespoons corn oil
sea salt and pepper

For the mango sauce:
6 mangoes
1½ tablespoons cornstarch
  (cornflour)
1 tablespoon butter
4 tablespoons sugar

To serve:
White Rice (page 521) or
  roasted sweet potato

REGION: FEDERAL DISTRICT
PREPARATION TIME: 30 MINUTES
COOKING TIME: 40 MINUTES
SERVES: 6

For the mango sauce, skin and pit the mangoes and put them into a food processor or blender. Process until smooth and strain into a bowl.

Stir the cornstarch (cornflour) into 4 tablespoons water in a small bowl to make a paste.

Put the pureed mangoes into a saucepan and bring to a boil over medium-low heat, stirring continuously. Stir in the cornstarch paste, butter, and sugar, reduce the heat, and simmer, stirring occasionally, for 10 minutes. Remove the pan from the heat.

Put each chicken piece between 2 sheets of plastic wrap (clingfilm) and flatten slightly with the smooth side of a meat mallet. Season on both sides with salt and pepper. Put 2 slices of cheese on top of each piece of chicken, roll up, and secure with a toothpick (cocktail stick). Dust each chicken roll with flour and shake off the excess.

Preheat the oven to 375°F (190°C/Gas Mark 5). Heat the oil in a large frying pan or skillet. Add the chicken rolls and cook over medium-low heat, with the lid on the pan, turning occasionally, for 15 minutes, until cooked through and golden.

Remove the pan from the heat and transfer the chicken rolls to paper towels to drain. Bake the rolls in the oven, covered with aluminum foil, for 10 minutes. Remove from the oven and pit a roll on each individual plate. Pour the mango salsa over the rolls and serve immediately with white rice or roasted sweet potato.

2 ancho chiles, dry-roasted

8 guajillo chiles, dry-roasted

1 large white onion, sliced and
dry-roasted

2 cloves garlic, dry-roasted

4 tablespoons lard or corn oil

5 tablespoons chopped fresh
or dry epazote

2¾ cups (11 oz/300 g) pumpkin
seeds, dry-roasted and
ground to powder

sea salt

½ cup (3½ oz/100 g) pumpkin
seeds, dry-roasted, to garnish

To serve:

White Rice (page 521)

Refried Beans (page 532)

the heat to a simmer. Cover the pan and simmer for
30 minutes, until the chicken pieces are just cooked.
Remove the chicken from the liquid and set aside,
reserving the cooking liquid.

Put the chiles into a small bowl, pour over
boiling water to cover, and let soak for 15 minutes.
Put the chiles with their soaking water into a food
processor or blender. Add the roasted onion and
garlic and process to a smooth consistency, then
strain into a bowl.

Heat 1 tablespoon of the lard in a pan. Add
the chile and onion mixture and the epazote and
cook over low heat, stirring frequently, for about
10 minutes. Stir in 1 cup (9 fl oz/250 ml) of the
chicken cooking liquid. Add the ground pumpkin
seeds and bring to a boil, stirring continuously,
adding more liquid gradually if needed until it is
a thick sauce. Season with salt to taste and let
simmer for an additional 5 minutes. Add the cooked
chicken and heat gently, with the lid on, until the
chicken is warmed all the way through.

Serve on a hot serving platter garnished
with toasted pumpkin seeds, with white rice and
refried beans.

6 skinless, boneless chicken
  thighs
6 avocado leaves

For the salsa:
1 chipotle chile, dry-roasted
1 morita chile, dry-roasted
2 ancho chiles, dry-roasted
10 guajillo chiles, dry-roasted
2 cloves garlic, dry-roasted
pinch of ground cloves,
  dry-roasted
pinch of cumin seeds,
  dry-roasted
pinch of dried oregano
2 tablespoons white wine
sea salt and pepper

To serve:
White Rice (page 521)
Corn Tortillas (page 36)

Reduce the heat and simmer for 15 minutes. Remove
the pan from the heat and transfer the chiles with
a slotted spoon into the food processor or blender.
Retain the cooking liquid. Add the garlic, cloves,
cumin, oregano, and wine, season with salt and
pepper, and process until thoroughly combined,
adding enough of the cooking liquid to make a thick
sauce. Strain this into a large bowl.

Put all the chicken into the bowl and stir to coat.
Put each piece onto a large square of parchment
paper. Cover with sauce, top with an avocado leaf,
and gather the paper upward to make a package. Tie
with kitchen string.

Bring some water to a boil in a large steamer, put
the packages in the top, and cook for
1 hour. Check the water level occasionally and
add more water, if necessary.

Remove the pan from the heat and lift out the
packages. Serve immediately with white rice and hot
tortillas on the side.

MUC BI CHICKEN

REGION: YUCATAN PENINSULA
PREPARATION TIME: 1 HOUR 10 MINUTES,
PLUS 15 MINUTES MARINATING
COOKING TIME: 1 HOUR 55 MINUTES
SERVES: 6

For the spice mixture:
3 tablespoons achiote paste
4 tablespoons orange juice
2 cloves garlic, dry-roasted
⅛ teaspoon dried oregano,
　dry-roasted
1 clove, dry-roasted
2 allspice berries, dry-roasted
⅛ teaspoon cumin seeds,
　dry-roasted
¾ teaspoon dried chiles,
　dry-roasted
4 tablespoons Chicken Stock
　(page 184)
2 teaspoons butter or lard

For the filling:
9 oz/250 g boneless side (belly)
　of pork
½ head garlic, dry-roasted
½ white onion, dry-roasted
½ chicken breast
2 chicken legs
1 tablespoon olive oil
1 small onion, sliced
9 tomatoes, dry-roasted,
　seeded, and sliced
½ cup (7 oz/200 g) Masa
　Dough (page 36)
1 banana leaf
7 large epazote leaves, chopped
melted lard or oil, for brushing

To make the spice mixture, stir together the achiote and orange juice in a bowl. Combine the remaining herbs and spices and chicken stock in a food processor or blender and process until combined. Stir in the achiote mixture.

Melt the butter in a saucepan over medium heat, add the spice mixture, and reduce the heat to low. Cook for 15 minutes, stirring occasionally.

To make the filling, put the pork, garlic, onion, and tomatoes into a saucepan, pour in enough water to cover, and bring to a boil. Reduce the heat and simmer for 15 minutes. Add the chicken and cook for another 15 minutes or until the chicken is completely cooked. Reserve the cooking liquid. Let cool and then shred the meats. Combine the meat and spice mixture, mix well, and let marinate for 15 minutes.

Heat the olive oil in a saucepan over low heat. Add the onion and cook, stirring occasionally, for 5 minutes. Add the marinated meat, increase the heat to medium, and cook, stirring frequently, for 8 minutes or until lightly browned. Stir in half the tomatoes and bring to a boil.

Meanwhile, combine the masa dough and ¾ cup (6 fl oz/175 ml) of the reserved cooking liquid. Strain into a saucepan to get rid of any lumps and cook over low heat, stirring continuously, for 10–15 minutes, until thickened and the consistency of thin porridge. Add the meat, season with salt, then remove the pan from the heat, and let cool.

Preheat the oven to 350°F (180°C/Gas Mark 4). Line an ovenproof dish with aluminum foil and a banana leaf, making sure it overhangs the rim. Spread out half the masa dough. Spoon in the meat filling, the remaining tomatoes, and sprinkle with epazote leaves. Cover with the remaining masa dough and brush with melted lard. Fold the banana leaf over the top, then cover with aluminum foil.

Bake for 1 hour, remove the foil, and bake for another 15 minutes, until firm to the the touch. Remove from the oven and serve immediately.

⅓ white onion, sliced
3 cloves garlic, crushed
6 large skinless chicken breasts
sea salt

For the sauce:
3 tomatoes
6–7 tablespoons corn oil
3 cloves garlic
1½ cups (8 oz/225 g) raisins
1¼ cups (4 oz/120 g) slivered
  almonds
¼ small white onion, sliced
¼ ripe plantain, peeled and
  sliced
1 slice brioche, diced
5 tablespoons sesame seeds
1 cinnamon stick
2 cloves
2 black peppercorns
1 sprig parsley

To serve:
20 green olives
almonds
4 tablespoons sliced pickled
  jalapeño chiles

5 minutes. Add the chicken and simmer for about 25 minutes or until just tender. Remove the pan from the heat and lift out the chicken. Strain the cooking liquid into a measuring cup, and make up to 7 cups (2¾ pints/1.6 liters) with water, if necessary.

To make the sauce, put the tomatoes into a saucepan, add enough water to cover, and bring to a simmer. Cook for about 10 minutes, until soft, being careful not to let them burst. Remove the pan from the heat and drain. Put the tomatoes into a food processor or blender and process to a puree. Transfer to a bowl.

Heat 1 tablespoon oil in a frying pan or skillet. Add the garlic, sauté for a minute until slightly brown, then add the raisins, almonds, onion, plantain, and brioche to the pan and sauté for several minutes until fragrant. Add more oil if necessary. Transfer to a plate and set aside. Add the sesame seeds and toss in the hot pan until a deep golden brown.

Add the cinnamon, cloves, peppercorns, parsley, and 1 cup (9 fl oz/250 ml) of the cooking liquid to a food processor or blender and process to combine. With the motor running, add the sesame seeds and process until the mixture is fairly smooth.

Add another 1 cup (9 fl oz/250 ml) of the cooking liquid to the food processor or blender, then add all the sautéed ingredients and pulse until combined. Add more stock as needed to make a thick, creamy sauce.

Heat 3 tablespoons oil in a heavy saucepan. Add the contents of the food processor or blender and cook for 5 minutes, stirring occasionally to prevent it from sticking. Add a little more cooking liquid, if necessary. Stir in the pureed tomatoes and continue cooking for about 8 minutes, until the mixture has reduced and thickened. Stir in the remaining cooking liquid and simmer for another 10 minutes.

Put the chicken on plates, pour over the sauce, and garnish with olives, chiles, and almonds.

MOLE FROM QUERETARO

1 cooked chicken, cut into
  pieces
¾ cup (4 oz/100 g) peeled,
  chopped almonds to garnish
cilantro (coriander), to garnish

For the mole:
7 oz/200 g black pasilla chile,
  seeds and membranes
  removed, dry-roasted
1 teaspoon cumin
4 cloves
7 oz/200 g ancho chile, seeds
  and membranes removed,
  dry-roasted
1 teaspoon black pepper
1 tortilla, toasted
2 cups (17 fl oz/475 ml)
  Chicken Stock (page 184) or
  turkey stock
½ teaspoon ground allspice
¼ cup (1¼ oz/35 g) peanuts,
  toasted
1 bolillo or baguette
½ cup (2½ oz/50 g) walnuts
3 tablespoons (2½ oz/50 g) lard
  or corn oil
⅓ cup (2½ oz/50 g) almonds,
  toasted
1 oz/30 g chocolate, chopped
⅓ cup (2½ oz/50 g) raisins
5 garlic cloves, roughly
  chopped
1 small white onion, roughly
  chopped
1 large tomato, dry-roasted
½ marjoram sprig

REGION: QUERETARO
PREPARATION TIME: 30 MINUTES, PLUS
15 MINUTES SOAKING
COOKING TIME: 1 HOUR
SERVES: 6

Put the chiles and enough hot water to cover them
into a small bowl and soak for 15 minutes.

Put the chiles into a food processor or blender,
add 4 tablespoons of the chile-soaking water, and
process to a pulp. Add the other ingredients and
process again. Pass through a strainer (sieve) into
a bowl.

Heat the lard in a saucepan. Add the paste and
cook over low heat for 10 minutes, until the fat rises
to the surface. Add the chicken pieces and cook on a
medium heat until heated through

Divide the chicken and sauce among the serving
plates and sprinkle with the chopped nuts and
cilantro (coriander).

Mole from Queretaro

CHICKEN STUFFED WITH HUITLACOCHE

5 tablespoons (2½ oz/65 g)
  butter
1 small onion, finely chopped
2 cloves garlic, crushed
1 lb 2 oz/500 g huitlacoche,
  chopped
1 lb 2 oz/500 g zucchini
  (courgette) flowers, pistils
  removed, chopped
6 skinless, boneless chicken
  breasts
sea salt and pepper

For the sauce:
4 tablespoons (2 oz/50 g) butter
¼ white onion, chopped
1 clove garlic, crushed
6 poblano chiles, dry-roasted
1 bunch epazote leaves, finely
  chopped
¾ cup (6 oz/175 g) sour cream
cilantro (coriander), to garnish
4 oz/120 g manchego and goat
  cheese, grated or crumbled

REGION: FEDERAL DISTRICT
PREPARATION TIME: 30 MINUTES
COOKING TIME: 40 MINUTES
SERVES: 6

Melt the butter in a frying pan or skillet over low heat. Sauté the onion, stirring occasionally, until translucent. Stir in the garlic and cook for a few minutes until fragrant. Stir in the huitlacoche and cook, stirring occasionally, for 10 minutes. Add the zucchini (courgette) flowers, season, and cook until the flowers wilt. Remove the pan from the heat, taste and adjust the seasoning, if necessary, and let cool.

Put the chicken breasts between sheets of plastic wrap (clingfilm) and flatten evenly with the smooth side of a meat mallet. Put a chicken breast on a piece of plastic wrap, season, and top with 2 tablespoons of the huitlacoche mixture. Roll up the chicken breast tightly in the plastic, twist the ends to secure them, and tuck them under. Repeat with the other chicken breasts and then put them all in large watertight sandwich bags.

Pour 6¼ cups (2½ pints/1.5 liters) water into a large saucepan and bring to a boil. Add the chicken packages and return to a boil. Reduce the heat, cover, and simmer for 30 minutes.

To make the sauce, melt the butter in a saucepan. Add the onion and cook over low heat, stirring occasionally, for 5 minutes, until translucent. Stir in the garlic and cook for a few minutes until it gives off its aroma. Add the chiles and epazote then season with salt. Remove the pan from the heat. Put the contents of the pan into a food processor or blender, add the sour cream, and process. Add a little water if the sauce is too thick. Push through a sieve (strainer) and into the pan. Return to the heat and simmer, stirring occasionally, for 5 minutes, and season.

Transfer the chicken packages to a plate. When they are cool enough to handle, unwrap the chicken rolls and slice diagonally. Put the sliced chicken on individual plates, spoon over the sauce, garnish with cheese and a sprig of cilantro (coriander), and serve immediately.

6 Cornish game hens or
poussins, butterflied
6 tablespoons extra virgin
olive oil, plus extra for
rubbing
3 tablespoons dried arbol
chiles, finely chopped
6 tablespoons grated ginger
3 tablespoons finely chopped
garlic
3 shallots, thinly sliced
1½ cups (12 fl oz/350 ml) white
wine
3 cups (1¼ pints/750 ml)
Chicken Stock (page 184)
5½ tablespoons (2¾ oz/70 g)
unsalted butter
¾ teaspoon red wine vinegar
sea salt and pepper
mashed potatoes, to serve

1 tablespoon of the garlic. Cover tightly with plastic wrap (clingfilm) and let marinate overnight in the refrigerator.

Season the chicken with salt. Heat 2 tablespoons of oil in each of 2 large frying pans or skillets. Add the birds, one at a time in each pan, with the skin side downward, and cook over medium heat, pressing them down slightly, for 15–20 minutes, until they are almost cooked through. Turn them over and cook for another 5–10 minutes, until the skin is crisp and golden. Transfer the birds to a platter and keep warm.

Drain the fat from a pan, add the remaining oil, and heat. Add the remaining ginger and garlic along with the shallots, cook over medium heat for a few minutes, stirring occasionally, until softened and fragrant.

Pour in the wine, deglaze the pan, and cook until it has reduced by three-quarters. Add the stock and cook until it has reduced by half. Whisk in the butter, stir in the vinegar, and season with salt and pepper to taste.

Serve the Cornish game hens on warm individual plates, pour the sauce over them, and serve with mashed potatoes.

CHICKEN IN PINE NUT MOLE

1 white onion, quartered and
   dry-roasted
3 jalapeño chiles, dry-roasted
3 cloves garlic, dry-roasted
4¼ cups (1¾ pints/1 liter)
   Chicken Stock (page 184)
6 tablespoons olive oil
2 cups (9 oz/250 g) pine nuts,
   dry-roasted
2 cloves, dry-roasted
2 allspice berries, dry-roasted
6 chicken breasts
½ cup (2 oz/50 g) pink pine
   nuts, plus extra to garnish
sea salt

REGION: PUEBLA
PREPARATION TIME: 1 HOUR
COOKING TIME: 1 HOUR
SERVES: 6

Put the onion, chiles, and garlic into a food processor or blender, add a ladle of the chicken stock, and process until smooth. Strain into a bowl.

Heat 1 tablespoon oil in a large saucepan over medium heat. Add the chile mixture and cook, stirring frequently, for 5 minutes.

Put the pine nuts, cloves, and allspice berries into a food processor or blender and process until combined. Again, add a ladle of the chicken stock. Strain into the pan with the chile mixture, discarding the contents of the strainer. Taste the sauce and season with salt, if necessary. Add the rest of the stock, reduce the heat to low, and simmer for 30 minutes, stirring occasionally.

Heat the remaining oil in a large frying pan or skillet. Add the chicken and cook over medium heat for 4–5 minutes on each side, until golden brown. Remove the pan from the heat.

Transfer the chicken to the pine nut sauce and simmer over low heat for 20 minutes or until cooked through. Remove the pan from the heat.

Divide the chicken and sauce among individual plates, sprinkle with the pink pine nuts, and serve immediately.

ZUCCHINI FLOWERS AND AMARANTH

6 skinless chicken breasts
1⅔ cups (13 oz/375 g) cream
  cheese
¼ onion, finely chopped
2 sprigs epazote
25 zucchini (courgette) flowers,
  pistils removed
3 eggs
1¾ cups (8 oz/225 g) all-purpose
  (plain) flour
2 cups (11 oz/300 g) amaranth
corn oil, for deep-frying
sea salt and pepper

For the sauce:
3½ cups (1 lb 2 oz/500 g) red
  currants
4 tablespoons red wine
1 teaspoon cornstarch
  (cornflour)
pinch of sugar (optional)
sea salt and pepper

Season the chicken breasts on both sides with salt and pepper.

Mix the cream cheese with the onion and then spread some of this mixture down the middle of each piece of chicken. Top with 2–3 epazote leaves and 3–4 zucchini (courgette) flowers, then roll them up and secure with toothpicks (cocktail sticks) or string.

Beat the eggs with salt and pepper in a shallow dish. Spread out the flour in another shallow dish and the amaranth in a third. Dip the chicken breast first into the flour, shaking off the excess, then dip into the beaten egg and, finally, into the amaranth. Do this twice with each chicken breast.

Heat the oil in a deep fryer or a saucepan to 350°F (180°C) or until a cube of bread browns in 30 seconds. Add the chicken breasts, in batches if necessary, and cook for 10 minutes, until golden. Transfer to a plate lined with paper towels and keep warm.

To make the sauce, put the red currants in a saucepan with the wine and cook over low heat for 15 minutes. Remove the pan from the heat and strain the fruit into another saucepan. Bring to a boil. Stir the cornstarch (cornflour) into 4 tablespoons water, then stir it into the pan. Cook, stirring continuously, until the sauce thickens slightly and becomes shiny and translucent. Season to taste with salt and pepper and, if the sauce seems too acidic, stir in the sugar. Remove the pan from the heat.

Put the chicken breasts on individual plates, drizzle with the sauce, and serve.

✳

STUFFED CHICKEN IN PEANUT SAUCE

4 guajillo chiles, dry-roasted
6 tablespoons (3 oz/80 g) butter
5 tablespoons olive oil
20 mushrooms, sliced
3 tablespoons chopped shallots
2 tablespoons chopped garlic
6 skinless, boneless chicken
  breasts
sifted flour, for dusting
½ cup (3 oz/80 g) peanuts,
  dry-roasted
2 cups (16 fl oz/475 ml) Beef
  Stock (page 185)
3 smoked chipotle chiles in
  adobo
sea salt and pepper

REGION: FEDERAL DISTRICT, PUEBLA
PREPARATION TIME: 50 MINUTES, PLUS 15 MINUTES
SOAKING AND 1 HOUR MARINATING
COOKING TIME: 45 MINUTES
SERVES: 6

Put the chiles in a small bowl, add enough hot water to cover them, and soak for 15 minutes.

Put the chiles into a food processor or blender, add 4 tablespoons of the soaking liquid water, and process to a pulp. Pass through a strainer (sieve) into a bowl.

Melt 3 tablespoons (1½ oz/40 g) butter with 2 tablespoons of the oil in a frying pan or skillet. Add the sliced mushrooms and cook over low heat, stirring occasionally, for 10 minutes. Stir in the chile pulp, shallots, half the garlic, and season. Remove the pan from the heat and let cool.

Put the chicken breasts between 2 sheets of plastic wrap (clingfilm) and flatten evenly with the smooth side of a meat mallet. Uncover the chicken, reserving the plastic wrap, and divide the mushroom mixture among it. Put a chicken breast on the plastic wrap and with one of the long sides facing you, roll up and tie with a string. Repeat with the others, cover with plastic wrap, put them on a plate, and refrigerate for 1 hour.

Spread out some flour on a shallow plate. Unwrap and roll the chicken in it to coat, shaking off any excess.

Preheat the oven to 475°F (240°C/Gas Mark 9). Melt the remaining butter and olive oil in a large ovenproof frying pan or skillet. Add the chicken rolls and cook over medium heat, turning frequently, for 10–12 minutes, until brown on all sides.

Transfer the pan to the oven and bake for 10 minutes or until the chicken is cooked through. Remove from the oven and let stand for 5 minutes.

Put the peanuts into a food processor or blender and process to a powder, then transfer to a bowl. Put the chiles into the food processor and process to a puree. Pour the stock in a saucepan, bring to a boil, and reduce by half. Stir in the ground peanuts and remove the pan from the heat. Stir in the remaining garlic and chile puree.

Slice the chicken rolls. Generously spoon the sauce onto each plate, place a slice of chicken on top, and serve immediately.

6 chicken legs

½ cup (5 oz/150 g) chilmole paste

⅔ cup (¼ pint/150 ml) orange juice

2 tablespoons lemon juice

2 tablespoons apple cider vinegar

3 oz/80 g garlic, dry-roasted

1 huge banana leaf, lightly dry-roasted

2 red onions, sliced

4 red bell peppers, seeded and cut into thin strips

sea salt and pepper

Pot Beans (page 533), to serve

vinegar, and garlic into a food processor or blender and process until thoroughly combined. Rub the mixture all over the chicken.

Line a roasting pan with a banana leaf, make a layer of chicken pieces, and cover with a layer of onion slices and bell pepper strips. Season with salt and pepper. Fold the overhang of the banana leaf over the top, making sure the top is completely covered with banana leaf, and bake for about 1½ hours, until the chicken is tender and cooked through.

Remove the pan from the oven and serve the chicken immediately with pot beans.

YUCATAN-STYLE CHICKEN IN ORANGE SAUCE

REGION: YUCATAN
PREPARATION TIME: 50 MINUTES
COOKING TIME: 1 HOUR
SERVES: 6

6 large chicken pieces
6 tablespoons corn oil or lard
1 large onion, finely chopped
½ small head garlic,
   dry-roasted
3 tomatoes, chopped
1 güero chile, finely chopped
2 bell peppers, chopped
15 raisins
8 pitted green olives, chopped
1 teaspoon grated orange zest
1 cup (9 fl oz/250 ml) orange
   juice
1 tablespoon sugar
sea salt and pepper
1 orange, sliced, to garnish
chopped parsley, to garnish

For the marinade:
4 cloves, dry-roasted
1 cinnamon stick, dry-roasted
¼ teaspoon black peppercorns,
   dry-roasted
pinch of saffron threads
1 teaspoon dried oregano,
   dry-roasted
1 tablespoon apple cider
   vinegar
2 tablespoons sour orange juice
1 small head garlic, dry-roasted
sea salt

To make the marinade, grind together the cloves, cinnamon, peppercorns, saffron, and oregano in a mortar with a pestle or with a spice mill.

Put 1½ tablespoons of the spice mixture into a bowl, stir in the vinegar and orange juice to make a paste, and season with salt. Crush the garlic and stir it into the paste.

Rub the paste all over the pieces of chicken. Heat 4 tablespoons of the corn oil in a frying pan or skillet. Add the chicken and cook over medium heat for about 8 minutes on each side, until golden. Remove the pan from the heat.

Preheat the oven to 375°F (190°C/Gas Mark 5).

Heat the remaining oil in another pan. Add the onion and garlic and cook over low heat, stirring occasionally, for 5 minutes. Add the tomatoes, chile, bell peppers, raisins, olives, orange zest, orange juice, and sugar, and season with pepper and a pinch of the remaining spice mixture. Cook for another few minutes until fragrant. Taste, season with salt, and remove the pan from the heat.

Put the chicken into a ovenproof dish and pour the sauce over it. Cover with aluminum foil and bake for about 40 minutes, until the chicken is cooked through and tender. Remove the dish from the oven.

Divide the orange slices among six individual plates, sprinkle with chopped parsley, and top with the chicken and sauce. Serve immediately.

IN CAPER SAUCE

2 tablespoons corn oil or lard
6 chicken legs
2 cloves garlic, peeled
½ onion, halved
sea salt

For the sauce:
2 cloves garlic, dry-roasted
1 white onion, halved and
　dry-roasted
½ teaspoon cloves, dry-roasted
10 tomatillos, dry-roasted
1 cup (5 oz/150 g) capers
pinch of black pepper
1 teaspoon ground cinnamon
pinch of dried oregano
3 tablespoons corn oil or lard
3 potatoes, cut into match
　sticks
½ cup (2 oz/50 g) pitted green
　olives
sugar
sea salt
pickled guero chiles, to serve

brown. Add the garlic, onion, a little salt, and enough water to cover. Simmer for 20 minutes. Remove the chicken with a slotted spoon and reserve. Strain the cooking liquid into a bowl.

For the sauce, put the garlic, onion, cloves, tomatillos, capers, pepper, cinnamon, and oregano into a food processor or blender and process until thoroughly combined, adding a ladle of the reserved chicken cooking liquid. Strain into a bowl.

Heat the oil in a large saucepan. Add the tomatillo mixture and cook over low heat, stirring occasionally, for about 10 minutes, until thickened. Add the chicken, potatoes, and olives. If the sauce is too thick, add some more chicken cooking liquid. Taste and adjust the seasoning, if necessary, and add a pinch of sugar. Remove the pan from the heat.

Serve immediately with pickled chiles.

✳

CHICKEN
IN CREAMY
TOMATO SAUCE

5 cups (2 pints/1.2 liters)
  Chicken Stock (page 184)
1 white onion, thickly sliced
3 cloves garlic
6 chicken pieces
3 sprigs mint, plus extra
  to garnish

For the sauce:
20 guajillo chiles, dry-roasted
16 puya chiles, dry-roasted
15 allspice berries, dry-roasted
5 cloves, dry-roasted
4 cloves garlic, dry-roasted
3 tomatoes, dry-roasted
2 tablespoons corn oil
2 cups (16 fl oz/475 ml) heavy
  (double) cream or sour cream
sea salt

REGION: MORELOS
PREPARATION TIME: 45 MINUTES, PLUS
15 MINUTES SOAKING
COOKING TIME: 1 HOUR 10 MINUTES
SERVES: 6

Put the chiles in a small bowl, add enough hot water to cover them, and soak for 15 minutes.

Pour the stock into a large saucepan, add the onion and garlic, and bring to a boil. Add the pieces of chicken and the mint, reduce the heat, and simmer for 20 minutes or until just tender. Remove the pan from the heat and lift out the chicken. Strain the cooking liquid into a bowl and reserve.

To make the sauce, put the chiles and their soaking water, allspice, cloves, and garlic into a food processor or blender and process until smooth. Strain into a bowl. Put the tomatoes into the food processor or blender, puree, then strain into another bowl.

Heat the oil in a deep frying pan or skillet. Add the chile mixture and cook, stirring continuously, for 10 minutes. Add the pureed tomatoes and cook over medium heat for another 10 minutes, until slightly reduced. Increase the heat to high, stir in 2½ cups (1 pint/600 ml) of the reserved chicken cooking liquid, and cook for an additional 5 minutes. Add the chicken, season with salt, and simmer for 5 minutes. Stir in the cream, a little at a time, and simmer for an additional few minutes. Do not let it boil. Remove the pan from the heat, taste, and adjust the seasoning, if necessary.

Serve in bowls, garnished with mint.

Chicken in Creamy Tomato Sauce

SAFFRON CHICKEN

½ cinnamon stick
1 black peppercorn
3 achiote seeds
6 chicken legs
2 tablespoons apple cider
  vinegar
1 sprig thyme
1 bay leaf
1 tablespoon oregano
myrtle leaf
1 Corn Tortilla (page 36),
  toasted and ground
1 cup (3½ oz/100 g) green beans
⅔ cup (3½ oz/100 g) peas
2 carrots, sliced
pinch of saffron threads,
  lightly crushed

REGION: CHIAPAS
PREPARATION TIME: 20 MINUTES
COOKING TIME: 40 MINUTES
SERVES: 6

Grind the cinnamon stick, peppercorn, and achiote seeds in a spice grinder or in a mortar with a pestle.

Put the chicken into a saucepan, pour in water to cover, add the vinegar, thyme, bay leaf, oregano, myrtle leaf, and ground spice mixture, and bring to a boil. Reduce the heat and simmer for 20 minutes, until cooked through and tender.

Remove the pan from the heat and lift out the chicken. Remove and discard the skin.

Strain the cooking liquid into a clean saucepan and return to the heat. Add the ground tortilla to the pan and simmer until thickened.

Add the beans and simmer for 5 minutes, then add the peas and carrots and simmer for an additional 5 minutes. Stir in the saffron and the chicken pieces. Simmer for an additional 5 minutes, then remove the pan from the heat.

Place the chicken legs and vegetables on deep individual plates and spoon the sauce over them. Serve immediately.

CILANTRO AND LEMON

3 tablespoons olive oil
3 tablespoons lemon juice
2 cloves garlic, crushed
2 tablespoons chopped cilantro
  (coriander)
½ teaspoon hot chili sauce
6 skinless, boneless chicken
  breasts
2 tablespoons corn oil
sea salt and pepper

salt and pepper. Add the chicken breasts, turning to coat, and let marinate in the refrigerator, turning two or three times, for at least 3 hours.

Preheat the oven to 475°F (240°C/Gas Mark 9). Heat 1 tablespoon corn oil or lard in a heavy frying pan or skillet. Remove the chicken breasts from the marinade and season with salt and pepper. Brush with corn oil and cook for 5 minutes on each side. Transfer to a roasting pan, cover with aluminum foil, and bake for 20 minutes. Remove from the oven, let stand for 5 minutes, then serve.

LUZ CATALINA'S CHICKEN

3 tablespoons corn oil
6 chicken legs
pinch of ground cinnamon
pinch of ground anise seeds
pinch of ground allspice
pinch of dried thyme
20 large scallions (spring
  onions), chopped
7 tablespoons (3½ oz/100 g)
  butter
½ cup (4 fl oz/120 ml) white
  wine or Chicken Stock
  (page 184)
18 small dried chipotle chiles
sea salt and pepper
mashed potatoes, to serve

REGION: CHIHUAHUA
PREPARATION TIME: 10 MINUTES
COOKING TIME: 55 MINUTES
SERVES: 6

Heat the oil in a large saucepan. Add the chicken in only one layer (use two pans if your pan is not big enough) and cook over medium heat, for about 8 minutes on each side, until lightly browned.

Sprinkle with the spices and scallions (spring onions), season with salt and pepper, and dot with the butter. Pour in the wine or stock, add the chiles, cover tightly, and simmer for 30–40 minutes. If the pans get too dry, add some more wine, stock, or just water.

Remove the pan from the heat and serve immediately with mashed potatoes.

CHICKEN WITH ACUYO

3 tablespoons corn oil
2 tablespoon sea salt
6 skinless chicken pieces
6 acuyo leaves
2 tablespoons chopped garlic
1 white onion, chopped
5 serrano chiles
15 tomatillos
1 cup (9 fl oz/250 ml) Chicken
    Stock (page 184)

REGION: VERACRUZ, GULF OF MEXICO
PREPARATION TIME: 20 MINUTES
COOKING TIME: 25 MINUTES
SERVES: 6

Heat 2 tablespoons of the oil in a large frying pan or skillet, sprinkle with the salt, and let smoke, then add the chicken. Cook for 8 minutes, then turn over and cook for another 8 minutes until the chicken is cooked through.

Remove the pan from the heat and lift out the chicken pieces. Wrap them in the acuyo leaves.

Put the garlic, onion, chiles, tomatillos, and stock in a food processor or blender and process until thoroughly combined.

Heat the remaining oil in a pan. Add the contents of the blender and cook over high heat for a few minutes, stirring frequently. Reduce the heat to low and simmer for another 10 minutes.

Put the chicken portions on individual plates, pour over the sauce, and serve immediately. Discard the leaves.

CHICKEN IN LEMON SAUCE

2 large onions, sliced
4 garlic cloves, finely chopped
4 tablespoons coriander seeds
1 bunch parsley, finely chopped
1 chicken, cut in pieces, skin
    removed
1 generous pinch saffron
3 cinnamon stick
zest and juice of 2 lemons
4 preserved lemons, sliced
    (optional)
sea salt and pepper

REGION: FEDERAL DISTRICT
PREPARATION TIME: 10 MINUTES
COOKING TIME: 1½ HOURS
SERVES: 6

In a heavy saucepan or Dutch oven, add the onion, garlic, coriander seeds, parsley, chicken, saffron, cinnamon, and lemon juice and zest. Add 2½ cups (18 fl oz/550 ml) boiling water over the chicken, then add the preserved lemon sliced and 4–6 tablespoons of the preserved lemon oil (alternatively, add slices of regular lemon and olive oil). Season with salt and pepper.

Bring to a boil, reduce the heat, let simmer, covered, for 30 minutes or until chicken is cooked through.

Lemon Chicken

POLLO ENJOCOCADO

CHICKEN IN JOCOQUE SAUCE

REGION: GUERRERO
PREPARATION TIME: 25 MINUTES
COOKING TIME: 40 MINUTES
SERVES: 6

3 tablespoons corn oil
6 chicken legs
3 Anaheim chiles, dry-roasted
2 tomatoes, dry-roasted
small pinch of cumin seeds
2 cloves garlic, dry-roasted
2¼ cups (18 fl oz/500 ml)
   jocoque or thick sour cream
sea salt and pepper

To serve:
Pot Beans (page 533) or
   Refried Beans (page 532)
White Rice (page 521)

Preheat the oven to 350°F (180 °C/Gas Mark 4).

Heat the oil in a large frying pan or skillet. Season the chicken with salt and pepper, add to the pan, and cook over medium heat for about 8 minutes on each side, until lightly golden. Remove the pan from the heat, transfer the chicken to an ovenproof dish, put it in the oven, uncovered, and cook for 20 minutes, then remove.

Put the chiles, tomatoes, cumin, garlic, and jocoque into a food processor or blender and process until smooth. Strain into a bowl. Taste the sauce and season with salt, if necessary.

Pour the sauce over the chicken and stir until well coated. Cover with aluminum foil and return to the oven for 10 minutes.

Remove the dish and transfer the chicken and sauce to individual plates, then serve immediately with beans and white rice.

2 oz/50 g red chiles, seeded
4 tablespoons dried oregano
2 heads garlic, roasted
25 tomatoes
8 Tabasco peppers
1 teaspoon pepper
10 cloves
1 teaspoon achiote
2 green bell peppers, seeded
    and coarsely chopped
6 lb 10 oz/3 kg ground
    (minced) pork
2 sprigs epazote, finely chopped
5 hard-boiled eggs
5 eggs, lightly beaten
1 (8 lb 13-oz/4-kg) turkey
½ cup plus 2 tablespoons
    (5 oz/150 g) butter or ⅔ cup
    (5 fl oz/150 ml) corn oil
sea salt

Garnish:
1 red bell pepper, seeded and
    cut into thin strips
1 green bell pepper, seeded and
    cut into thin strips
2 tomatoes, quartered
2 hard-boiled eggs, sliced

tomatoes into a roasting pan ...
minutes. Remove the pan from the oven. Add the
chiles and enough hot water to cover them to a small
bowl and soak for 15 minutes. Peel and seed the
roasted tomatoes, then chop 5 of them and set aside.

Drain the chiles, rinse well, and drain again.
Put the chiles, oregano, garlic, 10 whole roasted
tomatoes, Tabasco peppers, pepper, cloves, achiote,
and bell peppers into a food processor or blender
and process until smooth. Strain into a bowl.

Put the pork in a bowl and add 1 cup (9 fl oz/
250 ml) of the processed spice mixture, a pinch
of salt, half the epazote, and the roasted chopped
tomatoes. Halve the hard-boiled eggs and set the
yolks aside. Chop the egg whites, add to the mixture,
and mix well. Add the beaten eggs. Stuff the turkey
with the pork mixture and the hard-boiled egg yolks
and sew up with trussing thread.

Pour the remaining spice mixture into a large
saucepan or flameproof casserole, add the stuffed
turkey, and bring to a boil. Reduce the heat and
simmer for 1 hour, until the turkey is tender.

When the turkey is cooked, remove the pan
from the heat and lift out the bird. Put it on a
carving dish and cover with aluminum foil. Slice the
remaining 10 tomatoes. Return the pan to the heat
and stir in the butter or oil, then add the
sliced tomatoes and remaining epazote. Simmer
until thickened.

Carve the turkey and put it onto a large serving
plate. Spoon some of the sauce over it and garnish
with the red and green bell peppers, tomatoes, and
hard-boiled eggs. Serve immediately, handing the
rest of the sauce separately.

Chicken in Avocado Leaves

LEAVES

7 oz/200 g butter
3 large onions, quartered
20 avocado leaves, lightly
  roasted
2 cups (16 fl oz/475 ml)
  Chicken Stock (page 184)
1½ cups (12 fl oz/350 ml) sour
  orange juice
3 young chickens
sea salt and pepper

or blender and process to a paste, and
salt and pepper. Rub about half the paste all over
the chicken and under the skin.

Combine the remaining paste with the 1 cup
(9 fl oz/250 ml) of the orange juice in a bowl.

Cover the bottom of a casserole dish or deep
metal roasting pan with avocado leaves and put the
chicken on top. Pour the orange juice mixture over
and cover with more avocado leaves.

Cover with the lid or cover tightly with foil
and bake for 45 minutes or until the chicken is
tender. Remove the dish from the oven and take off
the lid, then return to the oven for an additional
10–15 minutes until the chicken is lightly browned.
Remove the dish from the oven, transfer the chicken
to a plate, and keep warm. Discard the leaves.

Set the dish or pan over low heat and add the rest
of the stock and orange juice. Deglaze and simmer
until reduced by half. Remove the dish from the
heat, pour the cooking liquid into a food processor
or blender, and process until smooth. Strain into a
bowl, discarding the contents of the strainer (sieve).
Taste and adjust the seasoning, if necessary.

Serve on a platter, spoon over the sauce, and
serve immediately.

CHICKEN IN CASCABEL CHILI SAUCE

35 cascabel chiles, dry-roasted
6 slices smoked bacon, diced
1 white onion, sliced
6 chicken legs
1 sprig epazote
1½ cups (9 oz/250 g) corn
   kernels
sea salt and pepper
6 fried cascabel chiles,
   membrane and seeds
   removed, to garnish
White Rice (page 521), to serve

REGION: MEXICO CITY
PREPARATION TIME: 15 MINUTES, PLUS
15 MINUTES SOAKING
COOKING TIME: 1 HOUR
SERVES: 6

Put the chiles and enough hot water to cover them into a small bowl and soak for 15 minutes.

Preheat the oven to 375°F (190°C/Gas Mark 5). Heat a large frying pan or skillet. Add the bacon slices and cook over medium-low heat until the fat starts to run, then add the onion and cook, stirring occasionally, for 7 minutes, until translucent. Remove the bacon and onion.

Add the chicken to pan, increase the heat to medium-high, and brown for 3–4 minutes per side.

Put the chiles and the soaking liquid in a food processor or blender and process until smooth. Strain into a bowl.

Put the chicken, bacon, and onion into a roasting pan, cover with the chili sauce and epazote, and season with salt and pepper. Cover tightly and bake for 40 minutes.

Remove the pan from the heat. Discard the epazote. Put the chicken legs on 6 individual plates and spoon over the sauce. Garnish with the fried cascabel chiles and serve immediately with rice.

SAUCE

1 (4½-lb/2-kg) duck, neck and
  giblets reserved
1 tablespoon butter or corn oil
1 cup (9 fl oz/250 ml) Chicken
  Stock (page 184), or water
3 tablespoons tequila (optional)
sea salt and pepper
broiled (grilled) cactus paddles,
  asparagus, or green beans, to
  serve

For the xoconostle sauce:
10 xoconostles, halved, peeled,
  seeded, and chopped
¾ cup (6 fl oz/175 ml)
  grenadine
¾ cup (6 fl oz/175 ml) orange
  juice
4 tablespoons apple cider
  vinegar
grated zest of 1 lemon
2 cloves garlic, dry-roasted
¾ onion, dry-roasted
8 bell peppers, roasted, seeded,
  and cut into strips

2 inches (5 cm) above the bottom of a roasting p
Add the stock. Roast for 45 minutes, then turn over,
and roast for another 45 minutes, until tender and
golden brown.

To make the sauce, put the duck neck and giblets
into a saucepan, add enough water to cover, and
bring to a boil. Reduce the heat and simmer for
20 minutes, until the giblets are tender. Remove the
giblets, leaving only the neck in the pan.

Add the xoconostles, grenadine, orange juice,
vinegar, lemon zest, garlic, onion, and bell peppers
to the pan. Pour in 1 cup (9 fl oz/250 ml) of water
and bring to a boil. Reduce the heat and simmer for
15 minutes.

Remove the pan from the heat, carefully lift out
the xoconostles, and set aside for garnish. Remove
and discard the duck neck. Place the remaining
contents of the pan into a food processor or blender
and process until smooth. Strain into a bowl, taste,
and adjust the seasoning, if necessary.

When the duck has finished cooking, remove the
pan from the oven. Transfer the bird to a carving
dish and cover with aluminum foil.

Skim off all the fat from the cooking juices, add
the tequila, if using, and cook over low heat for
5 minutes, scraping up the sediment from the
bottom of the pan.

Strain through a strainer (sieve) into a
saucepan, skim off any remaining fat, and stir in
the xoconostle sauce. Discard the contents of the
strainer. Simmer gently for a few minutes, add any
juices from the carving dish, and remove the pan
from the heat. Add salt if necessary.

Carve the duck and plate it. Spoon the sauce over
it and add your vegetables of choice. Garnish with
the reserved xoconostles and serve immediately.

DUCK IN RED PUMPKIN SEED SAUCE

2 cloves garlic, 1 clove
  dry-roasted
4 tablespoons sea salt
3 tablespoons dried oregano
6 duck breasts
5 tomatoes, dry-roasted
2⅔ cups (1 lb 5 oz/500 g)
  pumpkin seeds, hulled and
  dry-roasted
2 tablespoons Roast Chile and
  Tomato Salsa (page 508)
3 black peppercorns,
  dry-roasted
1 sprig epazote
1 tablespoon masa harina
sea salt
toasted pumpkin seeds, hulled,
  to garnish

REGION: YUCATAN
PREPARATION TIME: 40 MINUTES
COOKING TIME: 1 HOUR
SERVES: 6

With a big wooden spoon, crush a garlic clove with the sea salt and oregano to make a paste and rub the mixture all over the inside and outside of ducks.

Preheat the broiler (grill). Make 3 diagonal slashes with a sharp knife in the fat on each duck breast.

Melt the butter with the oil in a large frying pan or skillet over high heat. Drain the duck breasts, season with salt and pepper, add to the pan, fat side down, and sear for a few minutes to get a really crispy skin.

Put the tomatoes, pumpkin seeds, spicy red salsa, peppercorns, epazote, dry-roasted garlic and 1 cup (9 fl oz/250 ml) chicken stock and process until combined. Strain into a bowl and set aside. Add the tomato mixture to the pan and stir well. Simmer for 5 minutes, then lift out the ducks and set aside. Combine the masa harina with 2 tablespoons water in a bowl, then strain into the pan, getting rid of any lumps. Cook over low heat, stirring continuously, until the sauce thickens. Remove the pan from the heat and season the sauce to taste with salt.

Slice the duck breasts. Ladle the sauce onto a plate, add the duck breast, and drizzle over more sauce. Garnish with pumpkin seeds.

Duck in Red Pumpkin Seed Sauce

DUCK IN GREEN PUMPKIN SEED SAUCE

6 duck breasts
6 tablespoons (3 oz/80 g) butter
½ cup (4 fl oz/120 ml) olive oil
sea salt and pepper

For the pumpkin seed sauce:
4½ white onions, 1½ quartered,
   2 halved, 1 sliced
12 cloves garlic
15 tomatillos
6–8 serrano chiles, seeded
3⅔ cups (1 lb 2 oz/500 g)
   pumpkin seeds, lightly
   toasted
1⅔ cups (250 g) roasted peanuts
1 cup (6 oz/175 g) sesame seeds,
   toasted
4 lettuce leaves
4 radish leaves
¾ bunch cilantro (coriander)
   leaves, coarsely chopped
8 hoja santas, coarsely
   chopped
½ cup (4½ fl oz/125 ml) corn oil
1½–2 tablespoons sea salt

REGION: FEDERAL DISTRICT, MEXICO STATE,
PREPARATION TIME: 55 MINUTES, PLUS
20 MINUTES STANDING
COOKING TIME: 1¼ HOURS
SERVES: 6

To make the pumpkin seed sauce, preheat the oven to 350°F (180°C/Gas Mark 4). Put the quartered onions into a roasting pan with half the garlic, and roast for 15 minutes. Remove from the oven and set aside.

Bring 2 cups (16 fl oz/475 ml) water to a boil in a saucepan. Add the remaining garlic cloves, the 2 halved onions, the tomatillos, and chiles and simmer over medium heat for 25 minutes. Remove the pan from the heat and let cool. Drain it and reserve the cooking liquid in a bowl.

Put the simmered vegetables into a food processor or blender, add the pumpkin seeds, peanuts, sesame seeds, roasted onions and garlic, lettuce leaves, radish leaves, cilantro (coriander), and hoja santa and process to a sauce with the consistency of thick cream. Add some stock from the pan if needed. Strain into a bowl.

Heat the oil in a saucepan over medium heat. Add the sliced onion and cook over medium-low heat, stirring occasionally, for 8–10 minutes, until lightly browned. Add the pumpkin seed sauce, taste, and season. Cook, stirring continuously with a wooden spoon, until the spoon leaves a trail on the bottom of the pan.

Preheat the broiler (grill). Make 3 diagonal slashes with a sharp knife in the fat on each duck breast. Put them on the broiler rack and broil (grill) for 5–10 minutes per side, depending on the desired doneness. Transfer the duck breasts to a pan or heatproof dish, add enough hot water to cover, and let stand for 20 minutes.

Melt the butter with the oil in a large frying pan or skillet over high heat. Drain the duck breasts, season with salt and pepper, add to the pan, fat side down, and sear for a few minutes to get a really crispy skin.

Heat the sauce if necessary. Put the duck breasts on individual plates and spoon the sauce over them.

3 tomatoes, dry-roasted
2 tablespoons chopped white
 onion, dry-roasted
2 cloves garlic, dry-roasted
1 smoked chipotle chile in
 adobo
pinch of cumin seeds
pinch of ground cinnamon
1 clove
6 duck breasts skin on
6 canned or cooked artichoke
 hearts, choke removed
3⅓ cups (1 lb 2 oz/500 g) pitted
 wild cherries, gently stewed
 with a little sugar until soft
sea salt and pepper

Strain into a bowl.

Using a small sharp knife, cut a diamond pattern into the skin of the duck, without cutting into the meat. Heat a frying pan or skillet over medium-high heat, add the duck breasts, skin side down, and cook for about 10 minutes, until golden brown. Turn them over and cook for an additional 5 minutes. Remove the duck from the heat and cover with aluminum foil to keep warm.

Lower the heat and add the tomato mixture to the pan and cook, stirring occasionally, for about 15 minutes. Remove the pan from the heat and season to taste with salt and pepper.

Slice the duck breasts. Fill the hollow in the artichoke hearts with some of the sauce and top with the cherries.

Spoon the sauce onto individual plates and put some slices of duck on one side and a filled artichoke heart on the other. Serve immediately.

DUCK BREAST IN TAMARIND SAUCE

REGION: FEDERAL DISTRICT
PREPARATION TIME: 25 MINUTES
COOKING TIME: 1½ HOURS
SERVES: 6

12 cactus paddles
1 tablespoon olive oil, plus
    extra for brushing
1 tablespoon butter
3 sweet potatoes, thickly sliced
1 teaspoon confectioners'
    (icing) sugar
6 (7-oz/200-g) duck breasts
sea salt and pepper

For the sauce:
2–4 smoked chipotle chiles
    in adobo
4¼ cups (1¾ pints/1 liter)
    orange juice
1¼ cups (5 oz/150 g) tamarind
    pulp
½ cup (3½ oz/100 g) sugar
1 tablespoon tomato paste
    (puree)
1 cup (9 fl oz/250 ml) red wine
    vinegar
4–5 tablespoons Beef Stock
    (page 185)

For the sauce, push the chiles through a strainer (sieve) or a food mill to make a fine paste without skin or seeds.

Pour the orange juice into a saucepan, bring to a boil over medium heat, and boil until reduced by half. Stir in the tamarind pulp and cook for about 20 minutes until reduced to the consistency of jam. Remove the pan from the heat.

Put the sugar into another saucepan, pour in 5 tablespoons water, and heat slowly until the sugar has completely dissolved. Bring to a boil, without stirring, for 6–8 minutes, until golden. Stir in the tomato paste (puree), vinegar, beef stock, and the tamarind and orange mixture, and simmer for 5 minutes. Remove the pan from the heat, strain into a bowl, and stir in the chile puree. Reserve.

Preheat the broiler (grill). Brush the cactus paddles with a little olive oil, and season with salt and pepper. Broil (grill) for 5 minutes on each side, then remove from the heat.

Cut out circles from the sweet potato slices with a 2-inch (5-cm) cookie cutter. Preheat the broiler and heat the butter with the olive oil on a ridged grill (griddle) pan, add the sweet potato circles, and cook for 5–7 minutes on each side, until lightly colored. Sprinkle the confectioners' (icing) sugar on the slices and caramelize them under the broiler.

Preheat the oven to 450°F (230°C/Gas Mark 7). Season the duck with salt and pepper. Using a sharp knife, score the skin of the duck breasts in a diamond pattern without cutting the flesh. Heat a frying pan or skillet, add the duck breasts, skin side down, and cook for about 5 minutes, until they render their fat and the skin is golden brown. Turn off the heat, turn them over, and let stand a few minutes in the pan, then transfer to a roasting pan. Put them in the oven for 5 minutes, then remove and let stand while you reheat the sauce.

Cut the duck breasts into slices and garnish with the sweet potato and cactus paddles. Serve immediately with the sauce.

IN CHIPOTLE SAUCE

2½ lb/1.2 kg beef tenderloin (fillet)

⅔ cup (¼ pint/150 ml) mescal

2 tablespoons black peppercorns, crushed

3 tablespoons corn oil

1 clove garlic, crushed

1 cup (9 fl oz/250 ml) white wine

1½ cups (12 fl oz/375 ml) Beef Stock (page 185)

4 tablespoons sour cream

1 teaspoon strong mustard

2 tablespoons chopped smoked chipotle chiles in adobo

½ white onion, chopped

3 tomatillos, roasted

2¼ lb/1 kg small red potatoes, boiled

sea salt and pepper

3 tomatillos, halved, to serve

2 small red potatoes, cooked, to serve

1 tablespoon oil in a frying pan or skillet over medium-high heat. Add the meat and cook for 3 minutes on each side, until a dark golden brown. Remove from the pan and let stand for 10 minutes on a rack over a plate to reserve the juices.

Meanwhile, add the garlic to the pan and cook, stirring frequently, for a few minutes, then pour in the wine and stock. Cook, stirring with a wooden spoon and scraping up the sediment from the bottom of the pan. Add the remaining mescal and boil for 1 minute over low heat.

Pour the cooking juices from the pan into a food processor or blender and add the sour cream, mustard, chipotle chiles, and the juices that drained from the meat onto the plate, process until combined, and strain.

Pour the mixture into the frying pan, boil for 2 minutes, until thickened, then season with salt.

Heat the remaining oil in a saucepan. Add the onion and cook over low heat, stirring occasionally, for 5 minutes. Add the tomatillos and cook, stirring occasionally, for 8 minutes, until they are half cooked, then add potatoes and cook for another 5 minutes, until the tomatillos are done. Taste and adjust the seasoning, if necessary, and remove the pan from the heat.

Slice the meat. Divide the sauce among individual serving plates and top with the meat. Surround it with the tomatillos and potatoes and serve immediately.

CHIHUAHUA-STYLE PIPIAN

½ cup (3¼ oz/90 g) dry corn
  kernels
2¼ cups (11 oz/300 g) pumpkin
  seeds
4 red chiles, roasted
2 cups (16 fl oz/475 ml)
  Chicken Stock (page 184)
4 cloves garlic
¼ teaspoon cumin seeds,
  dry-roasted
1 tablespoon butter
2¼ lb/1 kg cooked pork, beef,
  or chicken, or 2¼ lb/1 kg
  steamed vegetables
sea salt

To serve:
White Rice (page 521)
Refried Beans (page 532)

REGION: CHIHUAHUA AND MEXICO CENTER, NORTH
PREPARATION TIME: 35 MINUTES, PLUS
10 MINUTES SOAKING
COOKING TIME: 25 MINUTES
SERVES: 6

Roast the corn in a dry frying pan or skillet over medium heat for 5 minutes, stirring continuously, until evenly browned all over. Remove and let cool, then put into a food processor or blender and process to a fine powder. Set aside. Repeat with the pumpkin seeds, roasting them for 5 minutes in the skillet, then letting cool and processing to a powder in a food processor or blender.

Put the roasted chiles in a heatproof bowl, pour in the hot stock, and soak for 10 minutes, or until soft. Transfer with their soaking liquid to a food processor or blender and process until smooth. Strain, then return to the blender or food processor along with the seeds, corn, garlic, cumin, and salt and process until it is a smooth consistency, adding a little more stock if necessary. Strain into a saucepan. Add the butter and cook over medium heat for 10 minutes. Add the meat or vegetables, cook for 5 minutes, then check the seasoning and the thickness of the sauce. If using vegetables, make sure that they are not overcooked. To serve, arrange the meat or vegetables in a serving dish, cover with the sauce, and serve with white rice and refried beans.

3 ancho chiles, membranes
  and seeds removed
3 guajillo chiles, membranes
  and seeds removed
2 mora chipotle chiles,
  membranes and seeds
  removed
2 cloves, crushed
2 small peppercorns
5 cloves garlic, peeled
1 tomato
¼ small onion
1 tablespoon lard
1 teaspoon pineapple cider
  vinegar
3¼ lb/1.5 kg stewing beef
3 large plantain leaves, halved
12 pozol or platanillo leaves
6 avocado leaves
12 bay leaves
sea salt

into a food processor or blender, add the spices,
garlic, tomato, and onion and process well. Drain
the chiles and add to the food processor, adding
1½ cups (12 fl oz/350 ml) water, little by little, until
you obtain a smooth puree consistency.

Heat the lard in a saucepan, add the sauce and
simmer for 5 minutes, until it reduces a little, then
add the vinegar, season with salt, and mix well.
Marinate the beef in the sauce for 24 hours in the
refrigerator.

Lightly pass the plantain and pozol leaves over a
gas flame. Take a plantain leaf, shiny side up, place
a pozol leaf on top, and then a few pieces of beef, an
avocado leaf, and 2 bay leaves. Cover the beef with
a pozol leaf and begin to cover with the plantain
leaf, folding over the sides so you can make a sturdy
package, and tie with the pieces of string. Repeat to
make 6 packages.

Place the prepared packages into a pressure
cooker on top of a metal rack. Add enough water,
making sure it does not cover the meat, and steam
for at least 1½ hours, or 4 hours if using a normal,
covered saucepan on the stove.

BARBECUE BEEF 2

24 chipotle chiles, seeded
5 ancho chiles, membrane and
    seeds removed
½ head garlic
¼ teaspoon ground cumin
5 allspice berries
3 cloves
½ cinnamon stick
½ teaspoon dried oregano
1 sprig thyme
2 bay leaves
1 cup (9 fl oz/250 ml) apple
    cider vinegar
2½ lb/1.2 kg beef tenderloin
    (fillet), diced
24 sheets mixiote
sea salt

For the salsa:
8 tomatillos
3 serrano chiles
1 onion, coarsely chopped
1 tablespoon olive oil

To serve:
4 avocados, peeled, pitted, and
    sliced
lettuce leaves

REGION: FEDERAL DISTRICT, MORELOS,
PUEBLA, TLAZCALA, HIDALGO
PREPARATION TIME: 30 MINUTES, PLUS
15 MINUTES SOAKING
COOKING TIME: 1½ HOURS
SERVES: 6

Put the chiles into a heatproof bowl, pour in boiling water to cover, and let soak for 15 minutes. Drain, reserving the soaking water.

Put the chiles, garlic, cumin, allspice, cloves, cinnamon, oregano, thyme, bay leaves, and a pinch of salt into a food processor or blender, pour in 1 cup (9 fl oz/250 ml) of the reserved soaking water and the vinegar, and process until thoroughly combined.

Put the meat into a dish, add the spice mixture, and toss well to coat. Put ¾ cup (3½ oz/100 g) of the meat on each mixiote sheet. Fold up the sides to make packages and tie with string.

Put the packages into a steamer and cook for 1 hour until the meat is tender. Check the water level in the pan frequently and top up with boiling water when necessary.

Meanwhile, make the salsa. Preheat the oven to 350°F (180°C/Gas Mark 4). Put the tomatillos and chiles in a roasting pan and roast for 15 minutes. Remove the pan from the oven.

Put the tomatillos, chiles, and onion into a food processor or blender and process until thoroughly combined. Heat the oil in pan, add the mixture, and cook, stirring occasionally, for 10 minutes. Remove the pan from the heat.

When the meat is cooked and tender, remove the steamer from the heat and lift out the packages. Put them on a serving plate and serve immediately with the salsa, avocado slices, and lettuce leaves.

removed, dry-roasted

3 serrano chiles, membrane
  and seeds removed

1½ white onions

2¼ lb/1 kg boneless beef
  shanks (shin of beef), diced

6 cloves garlic

6 sprigs mint

6 tomatillos

1⅓ cups (7 oz/200 g) corn
  kernels, blanched

5 sprigs cilantro (coriander),
  chopped

sea salt

Cut 1 onion into quarters and chop the other half onion. Put the meat, 2 garlic cloves, and the onion quarters into a medium saucepan, add enough water to cover, and bring to a boil. Reduce the heat and simmer for 45–60 minutes, until tender. Remove the meat and set aside. Reserve the stock.

Put the remaining onion, remaining garlic, all the chiles, the mint, and tomatillos into a food processor or blender and process until smooth. Add 1 cup (9 fl oz/250 ml) of the stock and process again.

Strain the chile mixture into a saucepan. Simmer for 10 minutes, then add enough of the reserved stock, if necessary, to make a thick sauce and simmer for an additional 5 minutes. Add the beef and corn kernels, season with salt, and simmer until everything is warmed though. Ladle into bowls and top with chopped cilantro (coriander).

COSTILLAS CON LENTEJAS

BEEF RIBS WITH LENTILS

1 ancho chile, dry-roasted

2¼ lb/1 kg beef short (fore)
  ribs, diced

½ onion, coarsely chopped

3 cloves garlic

2½ cups (1 lb 2 oz/500 g)
  cooked lentils

1 bay leaf

1 sprig thyme

2 black peppercorns

1 clove

2 tomatoes, coarsely chopped

sea salt

REGION: CHIHUAHUA AND DURANGO, NORTH
PREPARATION TIME: 15 MINUTES
COOKING TIME: 1½ HOURS
SERVES: 6

Put the chiles into a small bowl, add enough hot water to cover, and soak for 10 minutes. Drain.

Put the meat, onion, and garlic into a medium saucepan, pour water to cover, and bring to a boil. Reduce the heat and simmer for about 30 minutes, until the meat is tender. Remove and discard the onion and garlic. Reserve 2 cups (16 fl oz/475 ml) of the cooking liquid. Add the lentils, bay leaf, and thyme to the pan.

Put the chile, peppercorns, clove, tomatoes, and reserved cooking liquid into a food processor or blender and process until thoroughly combined. Strain into the pan, stir, and simmer for an additional 30 minutes. Season to taste with salt and remove the pan from the heat. Serve immediately.

BEEF TENDERLOIN IN PASILLA SAUCE

14 pasilla chiles
2 cups (16 fl oz/475 ml)
  Beef Stock (page 185)
1 teaspoon ground cumin
1 onion, sliced
3 cloves garlic, dry-roasted
2 cloves, dry-roasted
3 Tabasco peppercorns,
  dry-roasted
3 tablespoons cornstarch
  (cornflour)
1 sprig epazote, plus some
  leaves to garnish
1 tablespoon masa harina
2 tablespoons apple cider
  vinegar
2½ lb/1.2 kg beef tenderloin
  (fillet)
2 tablespoons olive oil
sea salt and pepper

REGION: FEDERAL DISTRICT
PREPARATION TIME: 25 MINUTES
COOKING TIME: 10 MINUTES
SERVES: 4–6

Put the chiles with the beef stock, cumin, onion, garlic, cloves, and peppercorns into a food processor or blender and process until you get a smooth sauce. Combine the cornstarch (cornflour) with 2 tablespoons water and mix well. Add the mixture to the saucepan, then add the epazote and vinegar, and boil for 2 minutes. Strain and reserve.

Rub the beef tenderloins (fillets) with olive oil, salt and pepper. Heat the oil in a saucepan over medium heat, add the onion and cook for 7 minutes, or until translucent. Add the cumin and cook for 2 minutes, or until fagrant. Add the beef, and cook for 3–4 minutes on each side or until it begins to release its juices on top.

Transfer the beef to a large plate, pour some sauce over it, garnish with fresh epazote leaves, and serve immediately.

4 tablespoons lard or corn oil
2 onions, thinly sliced
7 poblano chiles, dry-roasted
2 cups (16 fl oz/475 ml) Stewed
   Tomatillo Salsa (page 510)
12 Corn Tortillas (page 36)
6 oz (175 g) oaxacan cheese (or
   mild cheddar)
2½ lb/1.2 kg beef tenderloin
   (fillet) cut into 6 pieces
4 oz (120 g) queso fresco or
   farmers' (curd) cheese,
   to garnish
sea salt and pepper

chiles, and cook, stirring occasionally, for another 5 minutes. Season with salt and pepper, remove the pan from the heat, and set aside.

For the enchiladas, heat 1 tablespoon of the remaining fat in a saucepan. Add the green sauce and cook for 10 minutes. Take 6 of the tortillas and dip them, one by one, in the sauce, completely coating them. Remove them from the sauce and fold each one up in thirds, and set them aside.

For the quesadillas, heat a frying pan or skillet. Put the remaining tortillas in the dry pan, one at a time, and cook briefly on both sides to warm them. When warm, put enough of the oaxacan cheese in the middle of each, then fold them into a semicircular shape and dry-roast for a bit longer, flipping once or twice, until the cheese has melted.

Preheat the broiler (grill). Thinly slice the steaks lengthwise and broil (grill) for 2–4 minutes on each side, or until cooked to your liking. Season with salt and pepper.

Transfer the steaks to 6 individual plates, add a portion of the chiles, the green enchiladas, and the quesadillas. Sprinkle with the grated cheese and remaining raw onion. Serve immediately.

CARNE EN
SU JUGO

STEWED MEAT

9 oz/250 g lean bacon, diced
1 lb 10 oz/750 g boneless beef
  chuck or round (stewing
  steak), diced
4¼ cups (34 fl oz/1 liter) Beef
  Stock (page 185)
4 chipotle chiles in adobo
2 bay leaves
1 tablespoon sea salt
1½ teaspoons pepper
1 lb 2 oz/500 g Pot Beans
  (page 533)

To garnish:
1 cup (2 oz/50 g) chopped
  cilantro (coriander)
12 scallions (spring onions),
  broiled (grilled)

To serve:
1 oz (25 g) serrano chiles
3 lemons, quartered
Flour Tortillas (page 37)
avocado, peeled, pitted,
  and sliced

REGION: JALISCO
PREPARATION TIME: 20 MINUTES
COOKING TIME: 45 MINUTES
SERVES: 6

Fry the bacon in a heavy frying pan or skillet over medium heat until it renders its fat and is crispy. Remove with a slotted spoon and drain on paper towels.

Increase the heat and add the beef to the pan. Cook, stirring frequently, for a few minutes until browned on all sides. Add 3 cups (25 fl oz/750 ml) of the stock.

Pour the remaining stock into a food processor or blender, add the chipotle chiles, and process to a puree. Stir the chile mixture into the pan, add the bay leaves, salt, and pepper, and bring to a boil. Reduce the heat and simmer for 20 minutes. Taste and adjust the seasoning, if necessary, and remove the pan from the heat.

Divide the beans among 6 bowls, ladle in the meat in its own juices, and garnish with the bacon, cilantro (coriander), and scallions (spring onions). Serve immediately with the serrano chiles and lemon quarters, hot tortillas, and avocado.

1 lb 10 oz/750 g beef short
  (fore) rib, diced
2 corn on the cobs, shucked
1 tomato, chopped
1 white onion, chopped
2 cloves garlic
1 sweet potato, diced
½ cup (8 oz/225 g) chopped
  green beans
1 chayote peeled, cored, and
  chopped into bite-size pieces
2 green plantains, cut into
  ½-inch (1-cm) slices
1 sprig cilantro (coriander)
1 sprig spearmint
sea salt
finely chopped serrano chiles,
  to garnish

30 minutes. Add the sweet potatoes and cook for an additional 15 minutes, then add the green beans, chayote, and plantains and cook for 15 minutes, until everything is cooked through and tender. In the last few minutes, add the cilantro (coriander) and spearmint and stir.

Divide the stew among individual plates, garnish with chiles, and serve.

SINALOA-STYLE BEEF

1½ lb/700 g beef chuck or
   round (stewing beef)
2 cloves garlic
5 black peppercorns
½ red onion, halved
5 tablespoons corn oil
1 potato, cooked and diced
2 tomatoes, coarsely chopped
1 Anaheim chile, membrane
   and seeds removed, and
   finely chopped
10 sprigs cilantro (coriander),
   finely chopped
pinch of dried oregano
2½ cups (1 lb 2 oz/500 g)
   Refried Beans (page 532),
   to serve

To garnish:
½ red onion, sliced
lime juice, for drizzling
1 cup (2 oz/50 g) shredded
   lettuce
½ cucumber, peeled and sliced
2 radishes, sliced
1 avocado, pitted, peeled and
   sliced
5 oz/150 g panela or Monterey
   Jack cheese, grated
sea salt

REGION: SINALOA
PREPARATION TIME: 35 MINUTES
COOKING TIME: 1 HOUR 25 MINUTES
SERVES: 4

Put the beef, garlic, peppercorns, and quartered onion into a saucepan, pour in enough water to cover, and bring to a boil. Reduce the heat and simmer for 1 hour or until the meat is cooked through and tender. Remove the pan from the heat and lift out the meat. Reserve the cooking liquid.

Cut the meat into small pieces. Heat 4 tablespoons of the oil in a frying pan or skillet. Add the beef and potato and cook over medium heat, stirring frequently, for 5 minutes, until evenly golden brown. Remove from the pan and reserve, covering with aluminum foil to keep warm.

Drizzle the sliced red onion with lemon juice and season with salt, then set aside.

Meanwhile, put the tomatoes and boiled onion in a food processor or blender and process until combined. Heat the remaining oil in a saucepan. Add the tomato and onion mixture and the chile and cook over medium-low heat, stirring occasionally, for 10 minutes. Stir in the cilantro (coriander) and enough of the reserved cooking liquid to make a thick sauce and simmer for an additional 5 minutes. Add the oregano and remove the pan from the heat.

Add the meat and potato to the sauce and stir gently to coat. Transfer to serving plates.

Garnish the plates with the red onion, lettuce, cucumber, radishes, avocado slices, and cheese and serve immediately with refried beans.

For the chilmole:
7 tomatillos, peeled
1½ onions, dry-roasted
6 cloves garlic, dry-roasted
6 serrano chiles, dry-roasted
5 oz/150 g chilmole paste
1 cup (2 oz/50 g) chopped
  epazote
5 tablespoons olive oil or lard
2 onion slices
2 cups (16 fl oz/475 ml)
  Chicken Stock (page 184)
2 sprigs epazote
sea salt

For the beef tenderloin:
1 teaspoon peppercorns
1 teaspoon ground allspice
1 teaspoon cumin
1 teaspoon coriander seeds
¼ cinnamon stick
½ onion, dry-roasted
2 cloves garlic
⅔ cup (5 fl oz/150 ml) olive oil
8 (7 oz/200 g) beef tenderloin
  (fillet), sliced
½ cup (4 oz/120 g) butter
1 cup (9 fl oz/250 ml) Chicken
  Stock (page 184)
sea salt

For the garnish:
2 red onions, sliced
¾ cup (6 fl oz/175 ml) sour
  orange juice
2 cloves garlic, minced
½ teaspoon peppercorns
½ teaspoon ground allspice
4–6 manzano chiles
sea salt

into a food processor or blender and process until smooth.

Heat the oil in a frying pan or skillet over medium heat, add the onion and cook for 7 minutes, or until translucent. Add the tomatillo sauce and chicken broth and cook for 30 minutes or until the sauce has thickened.

Heat the oil in a saucepan and sauté the onion. Add the tomatillo sauce, chicken stock, and the epazote sprigs. Cook for about 30 minutes, until the sauce is reduced and thickened. Season to taste with salt.

For the beef tenderloin, heat a frying pan or skillet and roast the peppercorns, allspice, cumin, coriander seeds, and the cinnamon stick. Use a mortar with a pestle or a blender to grind these ingredients together with the onion and garlic, adding the oil and a little salt to form a thick paste. Add a small amount of the stock, if necessary. Rub each beef tenderloin (fillet) with the paste and let marinate for 1 hour.

Preheat a ridged grill (griddle) pan and a small slice of butter and olive oil, and grill the steaks for 3–4 minutes on each side or until they begin to release the juices on top. Add any cooking juices to the chilmole sauce and strain until smooth.

To make the garnish, put the red onions, sour orange juice, garlic, peppercorns, allspice, and salt, and mix well. Pierce the manzano chiles on top and bottom so they can be used as garnishes on the plates.

To serve, place each juicy steak on a large plate, pour over the chilmole sauce, and garnish with the onions and manzano chile.

RANCH-STYLE BEEF

6 tomatoes, dry-roasted
¼ teaspoon ground cumin
4 allspice berries
1½ lb/750 g dry beef or jerky
⅓ cup (2 oz/50 g) vegetable
    shortening or lard
5 green chiles, dry-roasted and
    cut into thin strips
1½ white onions, chopped
3 cloves garlic, finely chopped
2 tablespoons all-purpose
    (plain) flour
sea salt

REGION: COAHUILA
PREPARATION TIME: 20 MINUTES
COOKING TIME: 25 MINUTES
SERVES: 6

Put the tomatoes, cumin, and allspice into a food processor or blender and process until combined. Set aside.

Beat the beef with a meat bat to tenderize, then add it to a food processor or blender, and pulse until coarsely chopped. Melt the fat in a pan. Add the meat and cook over medium heat, stirring occasionally, for 10 minutes until golden brown.

Add the tomato mixture, chiles, onions, garlic, and flour and season to taste with salt. Simmer for 15 minutes until thickened. Serve immediately.

GRIDDLED STEAK

½ cup (4½ fl oz/125 ml) corn oil
½ teaspoon dried oregano
3 bay leaves, crushed
beer
6 x 7 oz/200 g rib-eye, T-bone,
    sirloin, or other steaks
sea salt and pepper

To serve:
onions, dry-roasted
potatoes, cooked
Guacamole (page 40)
Salsa of choice (page 496–514)

REGIONS: CHIHUAHUA AND NORTHERN MEXICO
PREPARATION TIME: 15 MINUTES, PLUS
2 HOURS MARINATING
COOKING TIME: 30 MINUTES
SERVES: 6

Combine the oil, oregano, bay leaves, and beer in a dish and season with salt and pepper. Add the steaks, turning to coat, and let marinate for 2 hours.

Heat a ridged grill (griddle) pan or preheat a barbecue. Add the steaks, in batches if necessary, and cook for 3 minutes, then turn over, and cook for another 3 minutes. Turn over again and also turn the steaks through 45° to create a diamond pattern. Turn again and cook until the steaks are done to your liking. You can brush the steaks with the remaining marinade while they are cooking, if you like.

Serve immediately with the roasted onions, potatoes, guacamole, and salsa.

1 ancho chile, dry-roasted
2½ lb/1.2 kg bone-in beef
  shanks (shin)
2 cloves garlic
1 white onion, dry-roasted
  and halved
1 tomato, dry-roasted
1 cup (4 oz/120 g) pumpkin
  seeds, dry-roasted
1 cup (4 oz/120 g) masa harina
1 tablespoon corn oil
1 sprig epazote
sea salt
White Rice (page 521), to serve

large saucepan, pour in enough water to cover, and bring to a boil. Reduce the heat and simmer for about 1¼ hours, until tender. Remove the beef from the liquid and cut it into small pieces. Retain the beef and the liquid. Discard the bone.

Put the remaining roasted onion, tomato, pumpkin seeds, and chiles in a food processor or blender and process until smooth. Add the masa harina and process, adding enough of the beef stock to the food processor to make a thick sauce. Strain the sauce into a bowl.

Heat the oil in a frying pan or skillet. Add the sauce and simmer for 5 minutes, until it thickens.

Add the sauce and the epazote sprig to the pan of meat and coat the meat well. Add enough of the beef stock to thin the sauce to your liking and cook for 15 minutes. Remove the pan from the heat, season to taste with salt, discard the sprig epazote, and serve immediately with white rice.

ESCALOPAS DE
RES CON FLOR
DE CALABAZA

BEEF SCALLOPS WITH ZUCCHINI FLOWERS

2½ lb/1.2 kg whole beef
  tenderloin (fillet)
5 tablespoons corn oil
1 white onion, cut into fine
  thin strips
2 cloves garlic, finely chopped
2¼ lb/1 kg zucchini (courgette)
  flowers, pistils removed,
  coarsely chopped
1 sprig epazote, chopped
2¼ cups (1 lb 2 oz/500 g) sour
  cream
5 poblano chiles, dry-roasted
  and peeled
9 oz/250 g Oaxaca or
  mozzarella cheese, shredded
sea salt and pepper
White Rice (page 521), to serve

REGION: MEXICO CITY
PREPARATION TIME: 30 MINUTES, PLUS
15 MINUTES RESTING
COOKING TIME: 1 HOUR
SERVES: 6

Preheat the oven to 400°F (200°C/Gas Mark 6).

Cut the beef into about 18 slices and flatten slightly with a meat mallet. Do not make the scallops (escalopes) too thin.

Heat 2 tablespoons of the oil in a small saucepan. Add half the onion and the garlic and cook over medium heat, stirring occasionally, for about 8 minutes, until golden. Add the zucchini (courgette) flowers, epazote, and 2 tablespoons of the sour cream and simmer for 10 minutes. Remove the pan from the heat.

Heat 1 tablespoon of the oil in a small saucepan. Add the remaining onion and cook over low heat, stirring occasionally, for 5 minutes. Add the chiles and the remaining cream and simmer for 15 minutes. Remove the pan from the heat and let cool slightly, then transfer to a food processor or blender and process into a smooth sauce, adding a little water if needed. Strain into a bowl.

Heat the remaining oil in a heavy frying pan or skillet. Add the beef scallops and cook over medium heat for 2 minutes per side. Transfer to a deep baking pan and put a little of the flower mixture on top of each scallop, season with salt and pepper, and divide the cheese among them. Cook in the oven for 5 minutes.

One minute before the beef is ready, spoon a pools of the sauce onto individual plates. Remove the beef scallops from the oven and place one on top of each pool of sauce. Serve immediately with white rice.

½ white onion, halved

2 cloves garlic

1 lb 5 oz/600 g boneless beef chuck or round (stewing beef), diced

6 beef short (fore) ribs

7 hoja santas, central veins cut out

2–3 serrano chiles, membrane and seeds removed

1 tablespoon corn oil or lard

1 corn on the cob, husked and cut into 6 pieces

1 lb 2 oz/500 g cassava, peeled and sliced into ½-inch (1-cm) disks

18 Chochoyotes (page 394)

sea salt

1 hour or until soft. Remove the pan from the heat. Transfer the meat to a bowl with a slotted spoon and reserve the cooking liquid. Cut the meat into bite-size pieces.

Meanwhile, put the hoja santas, onion, garlic, and chiles into a food processor or blender, add 1 cup (9 fl oz/250 ml) of the beef cooking liquid, and process. Strain into a bowl.

Melt the oil in a saucepan. Add the chile mixture and cook over medium heat, stirring occasionally, for 10 minutes. Add the rest of the reserved beef cooking liquid and bring to a boil. Add the slices of corn, and the cassava and season with salt. Add the meat and simmer for 5 minutes to warm it through.

Serve immediately in bowls with pieces of meat and 3 chochoyotes in each.

STUFFED CHILES FROM MONTERREY

½ cup (4½ fl oz/125 ml)
 vegetable oil, plus extra for
 drizzling
2 tablespoons white wine
 vinegar
1 teaspoon salt
½ teaspoon sugar
6 poblano chiles, seeded
1 lb/450 g flank steak
1 white onion, sliced
1 tablespoon corn oil
3 ripe avocados
½ teaspoon lime juice
2 tablespoons finely chopped
 white onion
2 green chiles, finely chopped
sea salt and pepper
rice or salad, to serve

For the bean sauce:
9 oz/250 g cooked beans,
 cooking liquid reserved
1 tomato, dry-roasted
½ onion
1 clove garlic, dry-roasted
1 morita chile, dry-roasted
sea salt

REGION: NUEVO LEÓN
PREPARATION TIME: 20 MINUTES
COOKING TIME: 30 MINUTES
SERVES: 6

Make a vinaigrette by whisking the vegetable oil, white wine vinegar, salt, and sugar together. Pour it into a shallow saucepan. Add the chiles, cover the pan, and simmer on low heat for 3 minutes to soften. Remove the pan from the heat and as soon as they are soft, remove the chiles and let cool.

To make the sauce, put all the ingredients into a food processor or blender and process until smooth, adding the reserved bean liquid if necessary. Strain into a saucepan and simmer for 5 minutes. Season with salt.

Put the beef and sliced onion into a frying pan or skillet, drizzle the corn with oil, season with salt and pepper, and cook for 10–20 minutes, depending on desired doneness.

Chop the meat finely into small pieces.

Halve and pit the avocados, scoop out the flesh into a bowl and chop it. Add the lime juice, chopped onion, and green chiles, and season with salt to taste, then add the meat and mix well.

Carefully fill the chiles with the beef and avocado filling. Ladle the sauce onto serving plates and place the chiles on top. Drizzle with the vinaigrette and serve with rice or salad of your choice.

Stuffed Chiles from Monterrey

1 (2½-lb) ⌐. ⌐.
   cleaned
10 black peppercorns
2 bay leaves
1 sprig marjoram
1 sprig thyme
2 tablespoons apple cider
   vinegar
1 tablespoon corn oil
1 small white onion, finely
   chopped
3 cloves garlic, finely chopped
1 cup (4 oz/120 g) shelled
   pecans
1 tomato, dry-roasted and
   peeled
sea salt and pepper

REGION: CHIHUAHUA
PREPARATION TIME: 30 MINUTES
COOKING TIME: 2 HOURS 40 MINUTES
SERVES: 6

Using a meat mallet, pound the tongue heavily to soften the skin, then rinse under cold running water. Put the tongue, peppercorns, bay leaves, marjoram, thyme, and vinegar into a large saucepan, add a large pinch of salt, and pour in enough water to cover. Bring to a boil, then reduce the heat and simmer for 2 hours, until cooked through and tender.

Remove the pan from the heat, lift out the tongue, and reserve the cooking liquid. When the tongue is cool enough to handle, peel off and discard the skin. Put the tongue on a plate, let cool, and chill in the refrigerator. Thinly slice it.

Heat the oil in a small frying pan or skillet. Add the onion and garlic and cook over medium heat, stirring occasionally, for about 8 minutes, until lightly browned. Remove the pan from the heat. Put the onion and garlic mixture, the nuts, tomato, and ½ cup (4 fl oz/120 ml) of the reserved cooking liquid into a food processor or blender and process until smooth.

Transfer the mixture to a medium saucepan, stir in 1 cup (9 fl oz/250 ml) of the reserved cooking liquid, and bring to a boil. Cook until reduced to 2½ cups (18 fl oz/550 ml).

Season the sauce with salt and pepper, add the slices of tongue, and simmer for about 15 minutes. Remove from the heat and serve immediately.

Note: This is a recipe from my dear grandmother. Make sure that the pecans do not contain any residue of shells, as these will make the sauce taste bitter.

MARINATED OX TONGUE

1 (2½-lb/1.2-kg) ox tongue,
    cleaned
1 bunch aromatic herbs, such
    as thyme, bay leaf, and
    marjoram
5 ancho chiles, dry-roasted
3 cloves garlic
pinch of dried oregano
corn oil, for frying
2 tablespoons apple cider
    vinegar
sea salt and pepper
Corn Tortillas (page 36),
    to serve

REGION: MEXICO STATE
PREPARATION TIME: 20 MINUTES
COOKING TIME: 1 HOUR 5 MINUTES
SERVES: 6

Put the tongue and aromatic herbs into a pressure cooker, add a pinch of salt, pour in enough water to cover, and bring to a boil. Reduce the heat and simmer for about 45 minutes, until the meat is tender. Remove the cooker from the heat, lift out the meat, and allow to cool. Peel off and discard the skin and slice the tongue horizontally.

Put the chiles, garlic, oregano, and 3 tablespoons water into a food processor or blender and process until smooth. Strain into a bowl.

Heat the oil in a large saucepan. Add the chile mixture and cook over low heat, stirring occasionally, for 5 minutes. Add the vinegar and the meat, season with salt and pepper to taste, and simmer for an additional 10 minutes.

Remove the pan from the heat and serve immediately with hot tortillas.

CHORIZO AND PEPPERS

4 oz (120 g) bacon, chopped
1 onion, coarsely chopped
9 oz/250 g chorizo, shredded
2 green bell peppers, seeded
    and diced
1 lb 5 oz/600 g round (rump)
    steak, diced
dash of Worcestershire sauce
sea salt and pepper

To serve:
beans
Roast Chile and Tomato
    Salsa (page 508)
Flour Tortillas (page 37)

REGION: CHIHUAHUA
PREPARATION TIME: 20 MINUTES
COOKING TIME: 45 MINUTES
SERVES: 4

Cook the bacon in a heavy saucepan over medium heat for about 5 minutes or until it has rendered its fat. Add the onion and cook for 5–8 minutes, until golden. Add the chorizo and cook for 3 minutes, then add the bell pepper, steak, and Worcestershire sauce. Season with salt and pepper and cook, stirring occasionally, for 20 minutes, until the meat is tender.

Serve immediately with beans, chili salsa, and hot flour tortillas.

BEEF STEW

1 tablespoon corn oil
3 oz/80 g bacon, diced
2¼ lb/1 kg chuck or eye of
  round (thick flank) steak
9 oz/250 g baby carrots
1 white onion, chopped
pinch of ground mixed spices
  (cloves, cumin, coriander,
  and/or caraway)
2 cloves garlic
3 small tomatoes, chopped
3 small red potatoes
sea salt

REGION: DURANGO
PREPARATION TIME: 15 MINUTES
COOKING TIME: 2 HOURS
SERVES: 4

Heat the oil in a medium saucepan. Add the bacon and cook until the fat is rendered and tender but not crisp. Add the steak, carrots, onion, spices, and garlic and cook over medium heat, stirring occasionally, for 15 minutes, until the meat and vegetables are golden.

Carefully drain off the excess oil and return the pan to the heat. Add the tomatoes and cook for about 5 minutes, then add enough water to cover and season to taste with salt. Cover and cook over medium heat for 50 minutes, until the meat is tender.

Remove the pan from the heat and remove the steak and carrots. Strain into a saucepan. Return to medium heat, add the potatoes, and cook for an additional 15 minutes, until the potatoes are tender.

Slice the meat and put it onto a serving plate. Serve with the potatoes, carrots, and sauce.

STEAK IN POBLANO SAUCE

2¼ lb/1 kg eye of round (thick
  flank) steak
3 tablespoons (1½ oz/40 g)
  butter
8 poblano chiles, dry-roasted
1½ cups (12 fl oz/350 ml)
  evaporated milk
1 teaspoon cornstarch
  (cornflour)
1 cup (4 oz/120 g) grated
  Chihuahua or mozzarella
  cheese
sea salt and pepper

REGION: QUINTANA ROO
PREPARATION TIME: 20 MINUTES, PLUS
10 MINUTES RESTING
COOKING TIME: 30 MINUTES
SERVES: 4

Season the steaks with salt and pepper. Melt 1 tablespoon butter in a frying pan or skillet over medium heat and add the steaks. Cook for 7–8 minutes per side or until the desired level of doneness is reached. Rest for 10 minutes and slice.

Grease an ovenproof dish with the remaining butter and layer in the beef. Put 6 chiles, the evaporated milk, and cornstarch (cornflour) into a food processor or blender and process until combined. Season with salt and pepper and pour this sauce over the meat.

Preheat the oven to 400°F (200°C/Gas Mark 6). Cut the remaining chiles into thin strips and put them on top, then cover with the grated cheese. Bake for 10 minutes, until the cheese has melted and is bubbling. Remove from the oven and serve.

SHORT RIBS IN CHILI AND COFFEE SAUCE

6 beef short (fore) ribs, cut into
  short lengths
2 tomatoes, dry-roasted,
  peeled, and coarsely chopped
sea salt
roasted potatoes, to serve

For the marinade:
7 ancho chiles, dry-roasted,
  and soaked in hot water just
  to cover for 15 minutes
½ white onion, dry-roasted
2 cloves garlic, dry-roasted
1 smoked chipotle chile in
  adobo
1½ teaspoons honey
¾ teaspoon lemon juice
½ teaspoon cumin seeds,
  dry-roasted
1 teaspoon coriander seeds,
  dry-roasted
1 tablespoon black
  peppercorns, dry-roasted
2 tablespoons instant espresso
  powder
sea salt

REGION: CHIHUAHUA, BAJA CALIFORNIA SUR,
FEDERAL DISTRICT
PREPARATION TIME: 25 MINUTES, PLUS
OVERNIGHT MARINATING
COOKING TIME: 2½ HOURS
SERVES: 4

To make the marinade, put the chiles with their soaking water, onion, garlic, chipotle chile, honey, lemon juice, cumin seeds, coriander seeds, peppercorns, and a pinch of salt into a food processor or blender and process until smooth.

Strain the chile mixture into a heavy saucepan, add the coffee, and cook for 2–3 minutes. Remove the pan from the heat and let cool.

Put the ribs into a deep roasting pan and cover generously with the cold marinade. Cover with plastic wrap (clingfilm) and let marinate in the refrigerator overnight.

The following day, preheat the oven to 400°F (200°C/Gas Mark 6).

Remove the ribs from the refrigerator and turn in the marinade so that they are all well coated. Cover tightly with aluminum foil, and cook in the oven for 2–3 hours, until the meat is falling off the bones.

Remove the roasting pan from the oven and lift out the ribs, covering them with the foil to keep them warm. Skim off the fat from the sauce, then add the tomatoes and cook over low heat, stirring occasionally, for 10–15 minutes, until the sauce is gooey.

Remove the pan from the heat. Taste and adjust the seasoning, if necessary. Divide the ribs among 4 plates, cover with the sauce, and serve immediately with roasted potatoes.

BEEF TENDERLOIN WITH CHIPOTLE MAYONNAISE

1 (2½-lb/1.2-kg) beef
  tenderloin (fillet)
1 tablespoon olive oil
sea salt and pepper

For the chipotle mayonnaise:
3 smoked chipotle chiles in
  adobo
2½ teaspoons Worcestershire
  sauce
1½ cups (12 fl oz/350 ml) good-
  quality mayonnaise

To serve:
mixed watercress and arugula
  (rocket)
½ cup (4 fl oz/120 ml) Shallot
  Vinaigrette (page 513)

REGION: FEDERAL DISTRICT
PREPARATION TIME: 30 MINUTES, PLUS
1 HOUR CHILLING
COOKING TIME: 20 MINUTES
SERVES: 6

Season the beef with salt and pepper. Heat the oil in a heavy saucepan. Add the beef and cook over medium heat, turning occasionally, for about 20 minutes, until evenly browned.

Remove the pan from the heat and lift out the beef. Wrap tightly in aluminum foil to give it a neat round shape. Let cool, then chill in the refrigerator for at least 1 hour.

To make the mayonnaise, put all the ingredients into a food processor or blender and process until thoroughly combined. Strain into a bowl, cover, and put in the refrigerator.

Remove the beef from the refrigerator about 15 minutes before serving and unwrap. Using a sharp knife, slice the meat and divide among 6 individual plates.

Put the salad greens into a bowl, add the vinaigrette, toss lightly, and put beside the beef. Drizzle the beef with the chipotle mayonnaise and sprinkle with sea salt. Serve cold.

Note: This is one of my favorite summer dishes to serve to my family on hot days, with a cold beer.

Beef Tenderloin (Fillet) with Chipotle Mayonnaise

MEAT PANCAKES

1¾ lb/800 g skirt steak

2 cloves garlic

3 bay leaves

10 black peppercorns

5 tomatoes

¼ onion

1 jalapeño chile, seeded

5 eggs, separated

2 tablespoons all-purpose
  (plain) flour

1 tablespoon vegetable oil,
  plus extra for brushing

sea salt and pepper

REGION: FEDERAL DISTRICT, MEXICO STATE
PREPARATION TIME: 25 MINUTES
COOKING TIME: 1 HOUR 20 MINUTES
SERVES: 6

Put the meat, 1 clove of garlic, the bay leaves, peppercorns, and a pinch of salt into a large saucepan, pour in enough water to cover, and bring to a boil. Reduce the heat and simmer for about 45 minutes or until the beef is tender. Remove the pan from the heat, lift out the meat, and let cool. Reserve the cooking liquid. When the meat is cool enough to handle, shred it.

Put the tomatoes into the pan of reserved cooking liquid and simmer for 5 minutes. Remove the pan from the heat and lift out the tomatoes with a slotted spoon. Peel them and put them into a food processor or blender with half of the cooking liquid, onion, remaining garlic clove, and the chiles. Process until thoroughly combined.

Whisk the egg whites in a grease-free bowl until stiff peaks form. Fold in the yolks, flour, and season with salt to taste, then gently stir in the shredded meat.

Heat a heavy frying pan or skillet and brush with oil. Scoop up tablespoons of the meat and egg batter, add them to the pan, and cook, turning once, for about 3 minutes, until golden brown on both sides. Remove with a spatula. Do not overcrowd the pan and brush with more oil as necessary.

Heat the oil in a wide saucepan. Add the tomato and chile mixture, season to taste with salt and pepper, and bring to a boil. Reduce the heat, add the pancakes, and simmer for another 3 minutes. Serve immediately.

MOLE AMARILLO
CON RES
✳

BEEF IN YELLOW MOLE

1 lb 2 oz/500 g boneless lean
  beef, diced
1 (3-lb/1.3-kg) chicken, cut into
  pieces, including the carcass
1 large onion, sliced
½ clove garlic
2 bay leaves

For the vegetables:
1 lb 2 oz/500 g chayotes,
  peeled, cored, and cut into
  matchsticks
3 potatoes, cut into
  matchsticks
3 cups (11 oz/300 g) halved
  green beans
sea salt

For the mole:
16 chilcostle or guajillo chiles,
  dry-roasted
½ onion, dry-roasted
1 clove garlic, dry-roasted
6 black peppercorns,
  dry-roasted
6 cloves, dry-roasted
1 teaspoon ground cumin,
  dry-roasted
1 tablespoon oregano leaves
5 tomatoes, dry-roasted
3 tablespoons corn oil or lard
2 cups (9 oz/250 g) Masa
  Dough (page 36)
4 hoja santas, veins removed,
  chopped
sea salt

For the garnish:
Chochoyotes (page 394)
slices of chile de agua

REGION: OAXACA
PREPARATION TIME: 1½ HOURS, PLUS
15 MINUTES SOAKING
COOKING TIME: 1½ HOURS
SERVES: 6

To make the mole, put the chiles into a bowl, add enough hot water to cover them, and soak for 15 minutes.

Put the beef, chicken, onion, garlic, and bay leaves into a large saucepan, add enough water to cover, and bring to a boil. Reduce the heat and simmer for 40 minutes.

Remove the pan from the heat and lift the beef and chicken pieces out. Strain the cooking liquid into a bowl. Cover so the meat does not dry out.

Cook all the vegetables in separate saucepans of boiling water. Strain and reserve the cooking water.

To make the mole, put the chiles, onion, garlic, peppercorns, cloves, cumin, oregano, and tomatoes into a food processor or blender, add 1 cup (9 fl oz/250 ml) of the reserved vegetable cooking liquid, and process until smooth. Strain into a bowl.

Heat the oil in a flameproof earthenware pot or saucepan. Add the chile mixture and cook over low heat for 10 minutes, adding some more of the vegetable cooking liquid if the pan gets too dry.

Meanwhile, put the masa harina and 2 cups (16 fl oz/475 ml) of the reserved meat cooking liquid into a bowl and stir to make a thin paste. Stir, then strain into a bowl.

Add the masa harina paste to the pan with the mole paste, stirring continuously as it quickly thickens. Add all the remaining cooking liquid (both types) and cook over medium heat, stirring continuously. Add the hoja santas and season with salt to taste.

Add the meat and simmer until it is hot all the way through. Add the other vegetables 5 minutes before serving just to warm them through.

Serve in bowls, garnished with the chochoyotes and slices of chile.

MOLE FROM ZACATECAS

6 cloves garlic, crushed
5 dried chipotle chiles,
    dry-roasted
8 ancho chiles, dry-roasted
2¼ lb/1 kg boneless pork
    shoulder, sliced
2 white onions
3 black peppercorns,
    dry-roasted
4 cloves, dry-roasted
½ cinnamon stick, dry-roasted
3 tomatoes, dry-roasted
2 Corn Tortillas (page 36),
    toasted and broken into
    bite-size pieces
7 tablespoons corn oil
1 plantain, peeled and sliced
    into ½-inch (1-cm) disks
1 small cone of piloncillo or
    ½ packed cup (3½ oz/100 g)
    brown sugar
sea salt
White Rice (page 521), to serve

REGION: ZACATECAS
PREPARATION TIME: 1 HOUR, PLUS
15 MINUTES SOAKING
COOKING TIME: 1½ HOURS
SERVES: 6

Dry-roast 2 cloves of garlic. Put the chiles and enough hot water to cover them into a small heatproof bowl and soak for 15 minutes.

Put the meat, an onion, and a pinch of salt into a saucepan, pour in enough water to cover, and bring to a boil. Reduce the heat and simmer, covered, for 60 minutes, until the meat is well cooked.

Meanwhile, put the peppercorns, cloves, and cinnamon into a mortar and grind with a pestle, or grind in a spice mill, then transfer the powder to a food processor or blender. Drain the chiles, reserving the soaking water. Add the chiles, tomatoes, broken tortillas, and dry-roasted garlic to the food processor or blender and process, adding just enough of the reserved chile soaking water to make a thin paste. Strain into a bowl.

Heat frying pan or skillet and add 1 tablespoon of oil. Cut the remaining onion into quarters, add to the pan, and cook, turning occasionally, for about 8 minutes. Remove and set aside. Add another tablespoon of oil to the pan, add the plantain slices, and cook over medium heat, turning once, for 3–4 minutes per side. Remove with a spatula (fish slice) and set aside.

When the meat is done, strain it into a bowl, reserving 2 cups (16 fl oz/475 ml) of the cooking liquid. Top it up with boiling water if necesary. Add the sugar to the liquid, discard the onion, and put the meat back into the pan. Add 4 tablespoons oil to the pan and the remaining garlic cloves and sauté over medium-high heat for 3 minutes, or until the garlic is golden. Remove the meat and garlic.

Add another tablespoon of oil to the pan. Add the chile paste and cook, stirring occasionally, for 5 minutes. Add the reserved cooking liquid and simmer for 10 minutes. Return the plantain slices, the onion, the garlic, and the meat to the pan and simmer over low heat for 30 minutes with the lid on. Remove the pan from the heat and serve immediately with white rice.

NORTHERN BEEF STEW

9 oz/250 g new potatoes

1 tablespoon corn oil

1 lb 2 oz/500 g beef tenderloin (fillet), diced

2 large tomatoes, quartered

½ white onion, quartered

1 clove garlic

2–3 bay leaves

¼ teaspoon ground cinnamon

1 cup (9 fl oz/250 ml) Beef Stock (page 185)

1 tablespoon butter

5 tablespoons (2½ oz/65 g) butter

½ tablespoon all-purpose (plain) flour

½ zucchini courgette, diced

⅓ cup (2 oz/50 g) peas

sea salt and pepper

Flour Tortillas (page 37), to serve

REGION: NUEVO LEON, CHIHUAHUA, DURANGO, COAHUILA
PREPARATION TIME: 20 MINUTES
COOKING TIME: 50 MINUTES
SERVES: 4

Bring a saucepan of water to a boil, add the potatoes, and cook for 10 minutes or until tender.

Heat the corn oil in a large frying pan or skillet over high heat. Add the meat to the pan and brown for 2–3 minutes.

Put the tomatoes, onion, garlic, bay leaves, cinnamon, and stock into a food processor or blender and process until combined. Season with salt and pepper.

Melt the butter in a medium saucepan. Add the flour and cook, stirring continuously, for 2 minutes. Stir in the beer and tomato mixture and bring to a boil, stirring continuously, until it thickens. Add the meat, zucchini (courgette), peas, and potatoes and cook over low heat for 15 minutes, until the meat is tender.

Remove the pan from the heat. Taste and adjust the seasoning, if necessary, and serve immediately with flour tortillas.

ROPA VIEJA

SKIRT STEAK WITH SAUCE

2½ lb/1.2 kg skirt steak
½ white onion
3 cloves garlic
3 sprigs thyme
3 sprigs marjoram
2 bay leaves
sea salt

For the sauce:
4 tomatoes, dry-roasted
¼ white onion, dry-roasted
2 cloves garlic, dry-roasted
½ cinnamon stick, dry-roasted
3 allspice berries
2 tablespoons olive oil
4 whole serrano chiles,
  dry-roasted
½ cup (1 oz/25 g) finely
  chopped cilantro (coriander)
sea salt and pepper

To serve:
Flour Tortillas (page 37)

REGION: FEDERAL DISTRICT
PREPARATION TIME: 40 MINUTES
COOKING TIME: 1¼ HOURS
SERVES: 6

Put the meat, onion, garlic, thyme, marjoram, bay leaves, and a pinch of salt into a pressure cooker, add enough water to cover, close the lid, and bring to high pressure. Cook for 45 minutes, then remove from the heat and let rest until the lid can be released.

Transfer the meat to a cutting (chopping) board and shred. Put it into a bowl and add a little of the cooking liquid. Strain and reserve the remaining cooking liquid.

To make the sauce, put the tomatoes, onion, garlic, cinnamon, and allspice berries into a food processor or blender, season with salt and pepper, and process until thoroughly combined.

Heat the oil in a small saucepan. Add the tomato mixture and cook over medium heat, stirring occasionally, for 15 minutes. Gradually stir in some of the reserved cooking liquid until the mixture has the consistency of a light sauce. Add the chiles and cook for an additional 10 minutes, until they are cooked but not breaking up. Remove the chiles. Add the shredded meat and cilantro (coriander), bring just to a boil, and remove the pan from heat. Serve immediately with hot tortillas.

PACHOLAS CON ESPECIAS

SPICY BEEF PATTIES

2 ancho chiles, dry-roasted
2 cloves garlic
6 peppercorns
2 teaspoons cumin seeds
1 clove
1 teaspoon dried oregano
2 eggs, lightly beaten
10 crackers, crushed
1 lb 2 oz/500 g ground
　(minced) beef
1 lb 2 oz/500 g ground
　(minced) pork
2 tablespoons corn oil
sea salt

To serve:
Salsa of choice (page 496–514)
mixed salad greens

REGION: JALISCO AND GUANAJUATO
PREPARATION TIME: 20 MINUTES, PLUS
15 MINUTES SOAKING
COOKING TIME: 15 MINUTES
SERVES: 6

Put the chiles and enough hot water to cover them into a small heatproof bowl and soak for 15 minutes. Drain.

Put the chiles, garlic, peppercorns, cumin seeds, clove, oregano, and a pinch of salt into a food processor or blender and process. Transfer the mixture to a bowl, add the eggs and crackers, and stir to combine.

Add the meat and mix well, using your hands, then shape into ¾-inch (2-cm) thick patties.

Heat the oil in a heavy frying pan or skillet. Add the patties and cook over medium heat for about 7 minutes on each side, until well browned and cooked through.

Remove the pan from the heat and transfer the patties to individual plates. Serve immediately with salsa and mixed salad greens.

STEAK
NICOLASA

6 ancho chiles, dry-roasted
2 cloves garlic, dry-roasted
4 tablespoons olive oil
6 (6-oz/175-g) beef tenderloin
  (fillet) steaks
sea salt
fried fresh or dried hibiscus
  leaves, to garnish

For the caramelized apples:
5 tablespoons sugar
2 tablespoons (1 oz/25 g) butter
4 tablespoons white tequila
3 yellow or green apples,
  peeled, cored, and each cut
  into 8 wedges

For the salad:
4 tablespoons olive oil
2 tablespoons lemon juice
3½ cups (3½ oz/100 g) tender
  wild greens or baby spinach
3½ cups (3½ oz/100 g) arugula
  (rocket)
sea salt and freshly ground
  white pepper

For the hibiscus sauce:
2 tablespoons sugar
½ cup (4 fl oz/120 ml) red wine
  vinegar
1 cup (9 fl oz/250 ml) hibiscus
  syrup
1 cup (9 fl oz/250 ml) beef stock
  (page 185)
½ teaspoon sea salt

REGION: MEXICO CITY
PREPARATION TIME: 40 MINUTES
COOKING TIME: 40 MINUTES
SERVES: 6

Put the chiles, garlic, 1 tablespoon olive oil, and
a pinch of salt into a food processor or blender
and process to a paste.

To make the caramelized apples, put the sugar,
butter, tequila, and apples into a saucepan and cook
over medium heat, stirring continuously, for
15–20 minutes, until caramelized. Remove the pan
from the heat.

To make the salad, whisk together the oil and
lemon juice in a bowl and season to taste with salt
and white pepper. Mix the wild greens or spinach
with the arugula (rocket) in a bowl, pour the
vinaigrette over them, and toss lightly.

To make the hibiscus sauce, put the sugar
into a saucepan and heat gently until it begins to
caramelize, but do not let it become dark. Stir in the
vinegar until the sugar has dissolved completely,
then stir in the hibiscus syrup and the meat stock
concentrate. Cook until reduced by half. Stir in the
salt and remove the pan from the heat.

Spread the chile paste evenly over the steaks.
Heat the remaining oil in heavy frying pan or skillet.
Add the steaks, in batches if necessary, and cook
over medium-high heat for 2–5 minutes on each side,
depending on how you like your steak.

Put 4 caramelized apple wedges on each plate and
put a steak on top. Put a small mound of salad at the
side. Drizzle the cooking juices over the steaks and
spoon the hibiscus sauce over them. Garnish with
some fried hibiscus leaves and serve immediately.

Note: This is a recipe from my dear friend Gerardo
Vázquez, one of Mexico's top chefs.

Steak Nicolasa

BEEF WITH CHILE AND CHICKPEAS

3 ancho chiles, dry-roasted
1 lb 5 oz/600 g beef brisket
8 cloves garlic
½ white onion
1 green serrano chile,
   membrane and seeds
   removed
2 tomatoes, dry-roasted
1 tablespoon sugar
2 tablespoons corn oil
1½ cups (9 oz/250 g) cooked or
   canned chickpeas, drained
sea salt and pepper

To serve:
Flour Tortillas (page 37)

REGION: BAJA CALIFORNIA SUR
PREPARATION TIME: 20 MINUTES, PLUS
15 MINUTES SOAKING
COOKING TIME: 1 HOUR 25 MINUTES
SERVES: 4

Put the ancho chiles and enough hot water to cover them in a small bowl and soak for 15 minutes.

Put the beef, garlic, and onion into a large saucepan, add a pinch of salt, pour in enough water just to cover, and bring to a boil. Reduce the heat and simmer for 60 minutes, covered, until the meat is tender. Remove the pan from the heat, lift out the beef, and cut it into small cubes. Strain the cooking liquid and reserve.

Put the fresh and dried chiles, tomatoes, sugar, and 1 ladle of the reserved cooking liquid into a food processor or blender, season with pepper, and process until thoroughly combined. Pass the mixture through a strainer (sieve) into a bowl.

Heat the oil in a large saucepan. Add the chile mixture and the rest of the reserved cooking liquid and cook over medium heat, stirring occasionally, for about 10 minutes. Add the meat and chickpeas, stir well to mix, reduce the heat, cover, and simmer for 15 minutes. Add some water, if necessary, so the pan does not dry out.

Remove the pan from the heat, taste and adjust the seasoning, if necessary, and serve immediately with warm flour tortillas.

NORTHERN-STYLE BEEF

⅔ cup (¼ pint/150 ml) corn oil
1 large red bell pepper, seeded and cut into thin strips
1 large yellow bell pepper, seeded and cut into thin strips
1 large green bell pepper, seeded and cut into thin strips
2 white onions, thinly sliced
2½ lb/1.2 kg beef tenderloin (fillet), sliced
½ teaspoon garlic salt
½ teaspoon chili powder
sea salt

To serve:
Flour Tortillas (page 37)
Guacamole (page 40)

REGION: TAMAULIPAS
PREPARATION TIME: 15 MINUTES
COOKING TIME: 35 MINUTES
SERVES: 8

Heat 1 tablespoon of the oil in a heavy saucepan. Add the bell peppers and cook over low heat, stirring occasionally and gradually adding a tablespoon of oil every 5 minutes or so, for 15 minutes. The idea is to slightly caramelize the bell peppers. Remove from the pan and set aside.

Add the onion to the pan and cook over low heat, stirring occasionally and gradually adding an additional 2 tablespoons oil, until translucent. Remove from the pan and set aside.

Season the beef with garlic salt and chili powder. Add 2 tablespoons oil to the pan and heat to medium. Add the strips of beef, and cook, flipping frequently, until evenly browned and cooked to your liking. Season lightly with salt and remove.

Add 1 tablespoon oil to the pan. Return all the vegetables to the pan and mix well. Taste and adjust the seasoning, if necessary.

Remove the pan from the heat and divide among individual plates. Serve immediately with warm tortillas and guacamole.

✳

MARINATED SHORT RIBS

2 pasilla chiles, dry-roasted
3 ancho chiles, dry-roasted
1 head garlic, dry-roasted
¼ teaspoon cumin seeds,
  dry-roasted
¼ teaspoon dried oregano
2 tablespoons apple cider
  vinegar
1 tablespoon corn oil
2¼ lb/1 kg bone-in short
  (fore)ribs
8½ cups (3½ pints/2 liters)
  Beef Stock (page 185)
sea salt and pepper

To serve:
mashed potatoes
Corn Tortillas (page 36)

REGION: ALL REGIONS
PREPARATION TIME: 30 MINUTES, PLUS
15 MINUTES SOAKING
COOKING TIME: 2 HOURS
SERVES: 4

Put the chiles in a small bowl with enough hot water to cover them and soak for 15 minutes.

Put the garlic, chiles, cumin seeds, oregano, and vinegar into a food processor or blender, season with salt and pepper, and process. Add enough of the chile soaking water to make a thick sauce. Strain into a bowl and discard the contents of the strainer (sieve).

Heat the oil in a large saucepan. Add the chile mixture and cook over medium heat, stirring frequently, for a few minutes. Add the ribs and pour in just enough stock to cover them. Bring to a boil, then reduce the heat and simmer for about 2 hours or until the meat is tender and is falling off the bones. Check frequently to add some more water to the pan, if necessary.

Remove the pan from the heat. Taste and adjust the seasoning, if necessary, and serve immediately with mashed potatoes and tortillas.

BEEF WITH CHILES

1 ancho chile, dry-roasted
1 tomato, dry-roasted
1 clove garlic, dry-roasted
1 clove, dry-roasted
½ teaspoon dried oregano
½ cup (4 fl oz/120 ml) corn oil
2½ lb/1.2 kg beef tenderloin (fillet)
2 bay leaves
1 cup (9 fl oz/250 ml) white wine
sea salt and pepper

To serve:
mashed potatoes
green peas
roasted pimiento peppers

REGION: QUERETARO
PREPARATION TIME: 30 MINUTES, PLUS
15 MINUTES SOAKING
COOKING TIME: 25 MINUTES
SERVES: 6

Put the chiles in a small bowl with enough hot water to cover it and soak for 15 minutes.

Put the chile with its soaking water, tomato, garlic, clove, and oregano into a food processor or blender and process until combined. Strain into a bowl and discard the contents of the strainer (sieve).

Heat the oil in a large saucepan. Add the beef and cook, turning it occasionally, for 2 minutes, until evenly browned all over. Add the chile mixture, bay leaves, and 2¼ cups (18 fl oz/500 ml) water and bring to a boil. Add the wine and simmer for 15 minutes, turning the beef regularly. Remove the beef and cover it to keep it warm. Season the sauce with salt and pepper to taste and simmer until it has thickened. Strain the sauce into a sauceboat.

Slice the beef and serve immediately with mashed potatoes, peas and roasted peppers, passing the sauce around separately.

Meatballs with Fried Pork Rinds

ALBONDIGAS DE CHICHARRÓN

MEATBALLS WITH FRIED PORK RINDS

5 oz/150 g fried pork rinds (scratchings)
1½ lb/700 g ground (minced) beef
2 eggs
4 tablespoons cilantro (coriander), finely chopped
2 cloves garlic, finely chopped
2 tablespoons finely chopped onion
2 tablespoons olive oil
4 tomatoes, diced
4 jalapeño chiles, sliced
2 cups (16 fl oz/475 ml) Beef Stock (page 185)
sea salt and pepper

To serve:
White Rice (page 521)
black beans

REGION: MORELOS
PREPARATION TIME: 30 MINUTES, PLUS 15 MINUTES STANDING
COOKING TIME: 30 MINUTES
SERVES: 6

Crush the fried pork rinds (scratchings) to a powder in a mortar with a pestle or in a food processor or blender. Combine it with the beef, eggs, cilantro (coriander), garlic, and onion in a bowl, and season with salt and pepper to taste. With damp hands, shape pieces of the mixture into meatballs, put them onto a plate, and let stand for 15 minutes.

Heat the oil in a saucepan. Add the tomatoes and chiles and cook over low heat, stirring occasionally, for 5 minutes. Pour in the stock and bring to a boil. Add the meatballs, bring back to a boil, reduce the heat, and simmer for 20 minutes. Taste and adjust the seasoning, if necessary.

Remove the pan from the heat and serve in a bowl with white rice and boiled beans.

OX TONGUE
IN PUMPKIN
SEED SAUCE

3½ oz/100 g mirasol or guajillo
  chiles, dry-roasted
1 (2¼-lb/1-kg) ox tongue,
  cleaned
2 bay leaves
2¼ cups (11 oz/300 g) pumpkin
  seeds, dry-roasted
3 cloves garlic
2 cups (9 oz/250 g) cornstarch
  (cornflour)
1¼ cups (5 oz/150 g) ground
  peanuts
sea salt

REGION: CHIHUAHUA
PREPARATION TIME: 25 MINUTES, PLUS
15 MINUTES SOAKING
COOKING TIME: 2 HOURS 20 MINUTES
SERVES: 6

Put the chiles in a small bowl with enough hot water
to cover them and soak for 15 minutes.

Put the tongue, bay leaves, and a pinch of salt
into a large saucepan and pour in enough water to
cover. Bring to a boil, reduce the heat, and simmer
for 3 hours.

Put the pumpkin seeds into a food processor or
blender. Add the chiles and garlic and process until
thoroughly combined. Pour the mixture into a pan.

Put the cornstarch (cornflour) into a bowl and
add just enough water to make a thick paste. Set
the pan of chile and pumpkin seed mixture over
medium heat and stir in the cornstarch paste and
ground peanuts. Cook, stirring continuously, until
the mixture comes to a boil. Reduce the heat to low
and simmer, stirring frequently, for about 2 hours.

Meanwhile, remove the tongue from the pan
and peel off the skin. Let cool and slice. Reserve
the cooking liquid.

When the sauce has finished cooking, stir in
enough of the reserved cooking liquid to make
a sauce with the consistency of gravy. Add the
tongue and heat it through gently for 20 minutes,
until it is piping hot.

BEEF TENDERLOIN STUFFED WITH CABUCHES

REGION: SANS LUIS POTOSI
PREPARATION TIME: 15 MINUTES
COOKING TIME: 25 MINUTES
SERVES: 6

1 (2-lb/900-g) beef
  tenderloin (fillet)
1 egg, lightly beaten
1 tablespoon heavy (double)
  cream
1 lb 2 oz/500 g cabuches or
  asparagus tips
corn oil, for drizzling
sea salt and pepper

For the sauce:
1 tablespoon butter
1 onion, chopped
3 cloves garlic, chopped
1 leek, chopped
5¼ oz/150 g zucchini
  (courgette) flowers
1 cup (9 fl oz/250 ml)
  Chicken Stock (page 184)
1 cup (9 fl oz/250 ml) whipping
  cream

To make the sauce, melt the butter in a frying pan or skillet over medium heat, add the onions, and cook for 7 minutes, or until translucent. Add the garlic and leek and cook for an additional 5 minutes Add the zucchini (courgette) flowers, stock, and cream and simmer for 10 minutes. Transfer the mixture to a food processor or blender and process until smooth. Set aside.

Preheat the oven to 400°F (200°C/Gas Mark 6).

Make an incision along the length of the tenderloin (fillet) to make a deep pocket. Trim some of the meat inside and finely chop. In a large bowl, add the chopped meat, egg, and cream and season with salt and pepper. Add the cabuches.

Fill the pocket in the meat with this mixture and tie securely in several places with kitchen string. Put the meat into a roasting pan, drizzle generously with oil, and roast for 15 minutes. Remove the pan from the oven, carefully turn over the meat, drizzle with oil, and return to the oven for an additional 10 minutes.

Remove the roasting pan from the oven and lift out the meat. Cut into slices and serve immediately with the sauce.

FOUR-CHILE BEEF TENDERLOIN

1 tablespoon black
  peppercorns
2 cloves garlic
4 tablespoons olive oil
4 tablespoons (2 oz/50 g)
  butter, melted
6 (7-oz/200-g) pieces beef
  tenderloin (fillet)
sea salt

For the salsa:
10 tomatillos
½ cup (4 fl oz/120 ml) corn oil
6 ancho chiles, dry-roasted
7 guajillo chiles, membrane
  and seeds removed
3 pasilla chiles, membrane and
  seeds removed
1 onion, quartered and
  dry-roasted, plus 2 slices
4 cloves garlic, dry-roasted
3 cups Pot Beans (page 533)
sea salt

To garnish:
2½ oz/65 g fried pork rinds
  (scratchings)
11 oz/300 g pickled cactus
  paddles
Corn Tortilla Strips (page 36)
4 arbol chiles, dry-roasted

REGION: GUANAJUATO
PREPARATION TIME: 45 MINUTES, PLUS
30 MINUTES MARINATING
COOKING TIME: 1 HOUR
SERVES: 6

Bring a saucepan of water to a boil. Add the tomatillos for the salsa and simmer for 15 minutes, then remove with a slotted spoon and reserve. Reserve the cooking liquid.

Meanwhile, put the peppercorns, garlic, olive oil, melted butter, and a pinch of salt in a food processor or blender and process until thoroughly combined. Put the meat into a dish in a single layer, add the peppercorn mixture, and let marinate for 30 minutes.

To make the salsa, heat half the oil in a saucepan. Add the chiles and cook over low heat, stirring frequently, for a few minutes. Be careful not to burn them because they will become bitter. Remove the pan from the heat and lift out the chiles with a slotted spoon to drain off the oil. Add them to the pan of tomatillo cooking liquid and simmer for 20 minutes or until tender. Remove the pan from the heat and strain into a bowl, reserving the cooking liquid and the chiles.

Put the tomatillos, chiles, onion quarters, garlic, and reserved cooking liquid into a food processor or a blender and process until smooth. Strain into a bowl.

Heat the remaining oil in a saucepan. Add the onion slices and cook over medium heat, stirring occasionally, for 8–10 minutes, until golden brown. Add the tomatillo mixture and season with salt to taste. Bring to a boil over low heat. Add the beans and simmer for 5 minutes with the lid off.

Heat a ridged grill (griddle) pan. Add the beef and cook for 2 minutes on each side, or cook for double the time if you prefer them well done. Transfer to individual plates and spoon the sauce over the meat. Garnish with the fried pork rinds (scratchings), pickled cactus paddles, tortilla strips, and fried arbol chiles, and serve immediately.

FILETE ESTILO MEXICO

MEXICAN BEEF TENDERLOIN

1 ancho chile, dry-roasted
1 tomato, dry-roasted
1 clove garlic, dry-roasted
1 clove, dry-roasted
pinch of oregano
4 tablespoons corn oil
1 (2½-lb/1.2-kg) beef
  tenderloin (fillet)
2 bay leaves
1 cup (9 fl oz/250 ml) pulque or
  1 cup of beer (9 fl oz/250 ml)
  with 1 tablespoon tequila
sea salt and pepper

To garnish:
mashed potatoes
cooked peas

REGION: BAJA CALIFORNIA
PREPARATION TIME: 30 MINUTES, PLUS
15 MINUTES SOAKING
COOKING TIME: 40 MINUTES
SERVES: 6

Put the chiles in a small bowl with enough hot water to cover it and soak for 15 minutes.

Put the chile with the soaking liquid, tomato, garlic, clove, and oregano into a food processor or blender and process until combined. Strain into a bowl.

Heat the oil in a medium saucepan. Add the beef and cook over medium heat for 5 minutes on each side, until golden brown. Add the tomato and chile mixture and cook for an additional few minutes. Add the bay leaves and just enough water to moisten the pan if it starts to get dry. When the mixture comes to a boil, add the pulque, adjust the seasoning if necessary, reduce the heat, and simmer for an additional 15 minutes.

Remove the pan from the heat, transfer the beef to a work surface and let rest. Strain the sauce into a bowl and set aside.

Cut the beef into slices and plate. Pour the sauce over the meat and serve with mashed potatoes and peas.

OAXACA-STYLE BEEF TENDERLOIN

1 (2½-lb/1.2-kg) beef tenderloin (fillet), cut into 6 and butterflied
2 tablespoons corn oil or lard
½ cup (2½ oz/65 g) finely shredded or chopped Oaxaca or mozzarella cheese
sea salt and pepper

For the sauce:
15 pasilla chiles, dry-roasted
1 onion, dry-roasted
3 cloves garlic, dry-roasted
4¼ cups (1¾ pints/1 liter) Chicken Stock (page 184)
5 tomatoes, dry-roasted
1 tablespoon corn oil or lard

To serve:
White Rice (page 521)
Corn Tortillas (page 36)
black beans

REGION: OAXACA
PREPARATION TIME: 40 MINUTES, PLUS 15 MINUTES SOAKING
COOKING TIME: 45 MINUTES
SERVES: 6

Put the chiles for the sauce in a small bowl with enough hot water to cover them and soak for 15 minutes.

To make the sauce, put the chiles with their soaking liquid, the onion, and garlic into a food processor or blender and process until thoroughly combined. Pass through a strainer (sieve) into a bowl.

Pour the stock into a saucepan, add the tomatoes and chile mixture, and bring to a boil. Reduce the heat and simmer for 15–20 minutes.

Heat the oil in a medium saucepan, strain the sauce again into the hot pan and simmer over medium heat for 5–10 minutes, until thickened.

Season the steaks with salt and pepper. Preheat the broiler (grill) to high.

Heat the oil in a frying pan or skillet. Add the steaks and cook for 2–3 minutes on each side; double the time if you prefer them well done. Transfer them to a broiler (grill pan) and sprinkle the cheese on top. Pop them under the broiler so the cheese melts, then transfer to individual plates, and pour the chili sauce over them. Serve immediately with white rice, black beans, and tortillas.

PORK AND AYOCOTE BEANS

3 cups (1 lb 2 oz/500 g) dried
  ayocote or lima (butter)
  beans, soaked in hot water
  to cover for 2 hours and
  drained
½ onion, cut into 3 wedges
3 tablespoons corn oil
1 (1-lb 5-oz/600-g) pork leg, cut
  into 6 pieces
2 cloves garlic
1 lb 5 oz/600 g pork backbone
1 tomato, coarsely chopped
sea salt and pepper

To garnish:
finely chopped green chiles
½ cup (1 oz/25 g) finely
  chopped cilantro (coriander)
½ onion, finely chopped

REGION: PUEBLA, TLAXCALA
PREPARATION TIME: 25 MINUTES
COOKING TIME: 1 HOUR 40 MINUTES
SERVES: 6

Put the beans and 1 onion wedge into a saucepan, pour in enough water to cover, and bring to a boil. Reduce the heat and simmer for 1 hour. Remove the pan from the heat.

Heat 2 tablespoons of the oil in a saucepan, add the back fat and pieces of pork leg, season with salt and pepper, and cook over medium heat for about 10 minutes, until the meat starts to brown. Remove the pan from the heat.

Strain the beans, reserve the cooking liquid, and return it to the pan. Set the beans aside.

Add 2 cups (16 fl oz/475 ml) water, another onion wedge, a clove of garlic, the meat and backbone, and a pinch of salt to the cooking liquid and return it to the heat. Simmer for about 15 minutes, until the meat is tender, then remove the pan from the heat.

Put the tomato, the remaining onion wedge, and the remaining garlic into a food processor or blender and process until thoroughly combined. Heat the remaining oil in a large saucepan. Add the tomato mixture and cook for about 3 minutes, then season to taste with salt and pepper. Add the beans, meat, and cooking liquid and heat through, then remove the pan from the heat.

Serve immediately sprinkled with green chiles, the cilantro (coriander), and chopped onion.

SPICY PORK WITH DUMPLINGS

3 mulato chiles, membrane
and seeds removed, seeds
reserved

6 dried black chiles, membrane
and seeds removed, seeds
reserved

3¼ lb/1.5 kg lean pork, diced

1 white onion, chopped

7 cloves garlic, dry-roasted,
plus 2 additional cloves

2½ cups (9 oz/250 g) sliced
green beans

9 oz/250 g chayotes, peeled,
pitted, and chopped

1 Corn Tortilla (page 36),
toasted

2 cloves

6 allspice berries

pinch of cumin seeds

5 tomatillos, dry-roasted

1 tomato, dry-roasted

3 tablespoons (1½ oz/40 g)
butter

4 avocado leaves, dry-roasted

sea salt

To serve
Flour Tortillas (page 37)

For the chochoyotes:
2¼ cups (9 oz/250 g) Masa
Dough (page 36)
4 tablespoons (2 oz/50 g) butter
sea salt

REGION: OAXACA
PREPARATION TIME: 1 HOUR
COOKING TIME: 1 HOUR 50 MINUTES
SERVES: 6

Dry-roast the chile seeds in a saucepan, tossing and stirring frequently, until charred. Remove the pan from the heat. Put the chile seeds into a bowl, add enough water to cover, and let soak, changing the water several times until you need them.

To make the chochoyotes, knead the masa harina with the butter and a pinch of salt. Shape small pieces of the dough into 1-inch (2.5-cm)-diameter balls and make an indention in the center with your finger.

Bring a saucepan of water to a boil, add the chochoyotes, and cook for 5 minutes. Remove the pan from the heat and drain.

Put the meat, onion, the raw garlic, and a pinch of salt into a large saucepan, pour in enough water to cover, and bring to a boil. Reduce the heat and simmer for 60 minutes, until the meat is tender. Lift out the meat with a slotted spoon and set aside.

In the same pan, add the green beans and cook for 10 minutes, until tender. Lift out the beans with a slotted spoon and set aside. Add the chayotes to the same pan and cook over medium heat for 5 minutes. Lift them out with a slotted spoon and set aside. Reserve the cooking liquid.

Drain the chile seeds. Put the chile seeds, tortilla, cloves, allspice berries, cumin seeds, chiles, tomatillos, tomatoes, and dry-roasted garlic into a food processor or blender and process until thoroughly combined. Add a ladle of cooking liquid, if needed, to make a sauce. Strain into a bowl.

Melt the butter in a saucepan. Add the chile mixture and cook over low heat, stirring frequently, until the spoon leaves a trail on the bottom of the pan.

Add 1 cup (9 oz/250 ml) of the reserved cooking liquid and the avocado leaves and bring to a boil. Reduce the heat to low and add the chochoyotes. Add more reserved cooking liquid, if necessary, then add the green beans, chayotes, and meat. Simmer for a few minutes until heated through, then remove the pan from the heat.

Serve immediately with warm tortillas.

Spicy Pork with Dumplings

✳

CHILES IN WALNUT SAUCE

30 raisins
4 tablespoons corn oil
½ white onion, finely chopped
1 clove garlic, crushed
1 (1-lb 2-oz/500-g) boneless
  pork loin, diced
3 tomatoes, peeled, seeded, and
  diced
2 cups (16 fl oz/475 ml) Beef
  Stock (see page 185)
⅛ teaspoon saffron threads
⅛ teaspoon ground cloves
⅛ teaspoon ground cinnamon
1 yellow apple, cored and diced
2 yellow peaches, peeled,
  pitted, and diced
1 firm pear, cored and diced
1 cup (4 oz/120 g) blanched
  almonds, chopped
1 candied citron, chopped
1 teaspoon sugar
6 large poblano or romano
  chiles, dry-roasted
sea salt and pepper
seeds of 2 large pomegranates,
  to garnish
½ bunch parsley, chopped,
  to garnish

For the walnut sauce:
1 cup (3½ oz/100 g) shelled
  fresh walnuts
½ cup (3½ oz/100 g) cream
  cheese
1 cup (9 fl oz/250 ml) heavy
  (double) cream
1 cup (9 fl oz/250 ml) milk
sea salt

REGION: PUEBLA
PREPARATION TIME: 45 MINUTES, PLUS
15 MINUTES SOAKING
COOKING TIME: 45 MINUTES
SERVES: 6

Soak the raisins in hot water for 15 minutes, then drain.

Heat the oil in a large frying pan or skillet. Add the onion and cook over low heat, stirring occasionally, for 8–10 minutes. Add the garlic. Add the meat, increase the heat to medium, and cook, stirring frequently, for 8–10 minutes, until lightly browned. Add the tomatoes and stock, reduce the heat, and simmer for 15 minutes, until the meat is tender and the cooking liquid has almost all evaporated.

Stir in the saffron, cloves, cinnamon, apple, peaches, pear, raisins, almonds, and the candied citron. Add the sugar, season with salt to taste, and bring to a boil. Reduce the heat and simmer for about 10 minutes, until most of the liquid has evaporated. Remove the pan from heat and let cool slightly.

Carefully stuff the chiles with the mixture and set aside.

To make the walnut sauce—a maximum of 1 hour before serving—put the walnuts, cream cheese, cream, and milk into a food processor or blender and process until thoroughly combined. Season with salt. If the sauce is thick, add a little more milk or cream.

Divide the chiles among individual plates and spoon a little of the walnut sauce over each. Sprinkle with pomegranate seeds and chopped parsley. Serve at room temperature.

Chiles in Walnut Sauce

BEANS AND PORK CHIRMOLE

2¾ cups/500 g dried black
  beans, soaked for 12 hours
  and drained
1 lb 2 oz/500 g boneless pork
  leg, cut into bite-size pieces
14 oz (400 g) ham hock, cut
  into bite-size pieces
1 pig's tail, chopped (optional)
1 pig's ear, chopped (optional)
2 tablespoons corn oil or lard
4 tomatoes, chopped
1 sprig epazote
1 tablespoon black achiote
  paste
1 tablespoon red achiote paste
sea salt
White Rice (page 521), to serve

REGION: YUCATAN PENINSULA
PREPARATION TIME: 20 MINUTES
COOKING TIME: 1 HOUR
SERVES: 6

Put the beans into a big saucepan and add the
pork, ham hock, tail, and ear. Cover with water
and bring to a boil. Reduce the heat and simmer for
60 minutes. Remove from the heat. Take out the tail
and the ear and discard.

Meanwhile, heat the fat in a frying pan or skillet.
Add the tomatoes and epazote and cook over low
heat for 5–8 minutes. Remove the pan from the heat.

Stir both the black and red achiote pastes into
½ cup (4 fl oz/120 ml) water, mix well, and stir into
the pork and beans. Add the tomatoes and epazote
to the pan and cook for an additional 10 minutes.

Mix the cornstarch (cornflour) to a paste with
½ cup (4½ fl oz/125 ml) water and stir into the stew.
Cook, stirring, for 1 minute, until thickened, then
remove the pan from the heat. Serve immediately
with white rice.

ASADO DE PASILLA

STEWED BEEF IN CHILI SAUCE

2¼ lb/1 kg boneless beef chuck
  or round (stewing beef), diced
½ white onion
3 cloves garlic
3 potatoes, cooked and diced
sea salt

For the sauce:
6 large pasilla chiles,
  dry-roasted
3 allspice berries
2 cloves
pinch of cumin seeds
3 cloves garlic, dry-roasted
¼ white onion, dry-roasted
¼ teaspoon ground cinnamon
2 tablespoons olive oil

To serve:
Flour Tortillas (page 37)
White Rice (page 521)

REGION: GUANAJUATO, QUERETARO, MEXICO STATE
PREPARATION TIME: 30 MINUTES, PLUS
15 MINUTES SOAKING
COOKING TIME: 1 HOUR 10 MINUTES
SERVES: 6

Put the meat, onion, garlic cloves, and a pinch of salt into a medium saucepan, add enough water to cover, and bring to a boil. Reduce the heat and simmer for 60 minutes. When the meat is cooked through and tender, remove the pan from the heat. Strain the cooking liquid into a bowl and reserve.

Meanwhile, for the sauce, put the chiles and enough hot water to cover them into a small bowl and soak for 15 minutes. Strain into a bowl, reserving the chiles.

Dry-roast the allspice berries, cloves, and cumin seeds in a frying pan (skillet) over low heat, stirring frequently, for a few minutes until aromatic. Transfer to a small bowl.

Put all the sauce ingredients except the oil into a food processor or blender and process, adding a little of the reserved cooking liquid to make a sauce. Strain into a bowl.

Heat the olive oil in a medium saucepan, add the sauce mixture, and cook for 5 minutes, stirring frequently. Gradually, stir in some more of the reserved cooking liquid, if necessary, until the mixture reaches the consistency of a thick sauce. Remove the pan from the heat, taste, and add salt, if necessary.

Add the potatoes and sauce to the pan with the meat. Stir well to combine and heat for 5 minutes. Taste and adjust the seasoning, if necessary, then serve immediately with warm tortillas and white rice.

BAKED PORK FROM COLIMA

2 guajillo chiles, membrane
  and seeds removed
2½ lb/1.2 kg pork ribs,
  chopped
8 oz/250 g pork leg bones, cut
  into pieces
½ cup (4 fl oz/120 ml) apple
  cider vinegar
3 cloves garlic, peeled
6 allspice berries
3 sprigs thyme
1 small onion, sliced, to garnish
radishes, to garnish
lettuce, finely chopped, to
  garnish
sea salt

REGION: COLIMA, PACIFIC COAST
PREPARATION TIME: 30 MINUTES, PLUS 15 MINUTES
SOAKING AND 3 HOURS STANDING
COOKING TIME: 2 HOURS
SERVES: 6

Put the chiles into a small bowl with enough hot water to cover them and soak for 15 minutes.

Combine the meat, vinegar, and salt in a bowl and let stand for 3 hours.

Drain the chiles, then put them into a food processor or blender and process until well combined with the garlic and allspice. Preheat the oven to 350°F (180°C/Gas Mark 4). Put the meat into a roasting pan with the thyme and put it in the oven for 2 hours, until the meat is tender.

Serve hot, garnished with onion, radishes, and lettuce.

Note: In the North, cinnamon, clove, and a small piece of ginger are added to this dish, and it is served at weddings and baptisms.

PUERCO CON
FRIJOL

PORK AND BEANS

1¾ cups (12 oz/350 g) dried
  black beans
1 lb 5 oz/600 g pork, cut into
  pieces
2 tablespoons (1 oz/25 g) butter
½ white onion
3 clove garlic
sea salt

For the salsa:
1½ white onions, chopped
chopped cilantro (coriander)
3 radishes, chopped
juice of 1 lime
sea salt and pepper

REGION: YUCATAN
PREPARATION TIME: 10 MINUTES, PLUS
12 HOURS SOAKING TIME
COOKING TIME: 1-1½ HOURS
SERVES: 6

Soak the black beans in water overnight and drain.

Put the soaked beans, pork, butter, onion, and garlic into a saucepan, pour in enough water to cover, and bring to a boil. Reduce the heat and simmer for 1–1½ hours, until the beans and meat are tender and the cooking liquid has thickened. Check for seasoning and add salt to taste.

To make the salsa, combine all the ingredients together in a glass bowl and season with salt and pepper.

Remove the pan from the heat and serve immediately with the salsa.

HIDALGO-STYLE CHORIZO

2 tablespoons sea salt

1 teaspoon vinegar

10 ancho chiles, seeded

6 cloves garlic, crushed

2–3 tablespoons cumin seeds

2–3 tablespoons crushed red peppercorns

7 cloves

2–3 cinnamon sticks

1 (3-lb/1.3-kg) boneless pork leg, chopped

3–4 tablespoons dried oregano

intestinal casings, rinsed in salt water

REGION: HIDALGO
PREPARATION TIME: 1 HOUR, PLUS 2 DAYS CHILLING AND STANDING
SERVES: 6

Put the chiles into a bowl with enough hot water to cover, and soak for 15 minutes.

In a small bowl, combine the vinegar and salt and mix well until dissoved. Put the chiles, garlic, cumin seeds, crushed red peppercorns, cloves, cinnamon, and salt mixture into a food processor or blender and process until thoroughly combined. Add the pork and oregano and process again until the meat is finely ground (minced). Transfer to glass or earthenware dish, cover with plastic wrap (clingfilm), and let chill overnight in the refrigerator.

Tie the end of a casing with trussing thread, leaving a 6-inch (15-cm) tail. Fill the casing with the pork mixture using a sausage stuffer or frosting (icing) syringe to avoid air bubbles. Tie with thread at 6–8-inch (15–20-cm) intervals to make links. Repeat with the remaining casings. Hang in a cool, well-ventilated place and let air circulate for a minimum of 24 hours.

PORK WITH CORN AND CHILES

2¼ lb/1 kg boneless pork, diced

6 corn on the cobs, husked

2 cloves garlic, finely chopped

3 tomatoes, finely chopped

1 onion, finely chopped

4 poblanos chiles, dry-roasted

1 cup (9 fl oz/250 ml) Chicken Stock (page 184) or water

sea salt

Corn Tortillas (page 36), to serve

REGION: FEDERAL DISTRICT
PREPARATION TIME: 20 MINUTES
COOKING TIME: 1½ HOURS
SERVES: 6

Put the meat in a saucepan, add enough water to cover, and bring to a boil. Reduce the heat and simmer for 60 minutes, until tender.

Cut the kernels from the corn on the cobs with a sharp knife. Add the corn, garlic, tomatoes, onion, and chiles to the pan, pour in the stock or water, and season with salt. Cover the pan and simmer for an additional 20 minutes with the lid off, until slightly thickened.

Remove the pan from the heat, taste, and adjust the seasoning, if necessary. Serve immediately with warm tortillas.

COCHINITA PIBIL

SLOW-COOKED PORK

½ cup (4 fl oz/120 ml) sour
   orange juice
2¼ lb/1 kg boneless lean leg or
   loin of pork, diced
4 plantain leaves, lightly
   broiled (grilled)
sea salt
Corn Tortillas (page 36),
   to serve
2 cups (16 fl oz/475 ml) Red
   Onion Escabeche (page 478),
   to serve

For the Cochinita Pibil Paste:
3 heads garlic, 2 peeled,
   1 broiled (grilled) and peeled
½ cinnamon stick, dry-roasted
5 tablespoons achiote paste
1½ teaspoons cumin seeds,
   dry-roasted
3 cloves, dry-roasted
4 tablespoons ground dried
   chiles (optional)
4 tablespoons oregano,
   dry-roasted
½ cup (4 fl oz/120 ml) sour
   orange juice
salt

For the spice paste, put all the garlic, the cinnamon stick, achiote paste, cumin seeds, cloves, dried chiles, and oregano into a food processor or blender and process until thick and combined. Transfer to a bowl, stir in the sour orange juice, and add season to taste with salt.

To prepare the meat, measure 4 tablespoons of the spice mixture into a bowl and stir in the sour orange juice until thoroughly mixed. Put the pork into a dish, pour the spice mixture over it, and toss well to coat. Cover with plastic wrap (clingfilm) and let marinate for at least 3 hours, preferably overnight.

Preheat the oven to 400°F (200°C/Gas Mark 6). Put a large heatproof dish of water on the floor of the oven.

Line an earthenware pot or a casserole dish with plantain leaves, spoon in the marinated meat, cover with more leaves, and cover with a lid or aluminum foil. Transfer to the oven and cook for about 3 hours, until the meat is tender and cooked through. Remove the pot or casserole from the oven and let cool without uncovering.

When the meat is cool, remove it from the pot with a slotted spoon, reserving the cooking juices. Shred the meat and put it into an ovenproof dish. Measure the reserved cooking juices and make up to 1 cup (9 fl oz/250 ml) by adding water, if necessary. Pour the liquid over the meat and return to the oven until heated through and evenly colored and flavored.

Remove the dish from the oven. Taste and adjust the seasoning, if necessary, and serve immediately with hot tortillas and the escabeche.

✳

DRUNKEN
PORK LOIN

1 lb 5 oz/600 g boneless lean
   pork loin
5 oz/150 g chorizo, thinly
   sliced
2½ tablespoons corn oil or lard
1 large tomato
4 cloves garlic
1½ cups (13½ fl oz/375 ml)
   pulque (or beer with
   3 tablespoons tequila)
sea salt and pepper
1 onion, thinly sliced,
   to garnish

REGION: CENTRAL MEXICO
PREPARATION TIME: 20 MINUTES
COOKING TIME: 1½ HOURS
SERVES: 4

Using a small sharp knife, cut small pockets all over the meat and fill them with the chorizo, then season with salt and pepper.

Melt the oil in a heavy frying pan or skillet. Add the pork and cook over medium heat, turning frequently, for 8–10 minutes, until evenly browned. Remove the pan from the heat and transfer the pork to an ovenproof casserole dish.

Meanwhile, preheat the oven to 375°F (190°C/ Gas Mark 5).Put the tomato and garlic into a food processor or blender and process until combined. Add the mixture to the pan and cook until it has reduced by half. Add the pulque, cover the pan, reduce the heat, and simmer for 10 minutes.

Pour the sauce over the pork, cover the casserole, and cook in the oven for 45–60 minutes or until the meat has cooked through and the sauce has thickened. Slice the pork and serve with the sauce and sliced onion as a garnish.

✳

AIR-DRIED
MARINATED
PORK

18 guajillo chiles, seeded
3 cloves garlic
pinch of ground cumin
pinch of dried oregano
1 bay leaf
1½ cups (12 fl oz/350 ml) cane
   or apple cider vinegar
2¼ lb/1 kg pork loin, cut into
   thin strips or steaks
sea salt and pepper

REGION: FEDERAL DISTRICT AND MEXICO CENTER
PREPARATION TIME: 5 DAYS OR OVERNIGHT
COOKING TIME: 15 MINUTES
SERVES: 6

Put the chiles, garlic, cumin, oregano, and bay leaf into a food processor or blender, season with pepper, and process until thoroughly combined, adding some water to make a thick paste. Add the vinegar, season with salt and pepper, and blend again.

Rub the meat with the mixture and put it into a deep earthenware or glass bowl. Cover with plastic wrap (clingfilm) and let marinate in the refrigerator for 3 days. Stir once or twice a day, replacing the wrap.

Drain the meat and hang it in a cool place overnight to dry. Cut into pieces and grill, fry, or roast it. It is best eaten with tortillas and beans.

Note: For a quicker version, marinate the meat for 12 hours and cook it fresh without air-drying first.

CHICHARRÓN EN
SALSA VERDE
CON CHORIZO

※

FRIED PORK RINDS IN GREEN SAUCE

2 serrano chiles
2 guajillo chiles
10 tomatillos
11 oz/300 g chorizo, sliced
½ cup (1 oz/25 g) coarsely
  chopped cilantro (coriander)
3 tablespoons corn oil or lard
2 small onions, finely chopped
12 oz/350 g fried pork rinds
  (scratchings), crumbled
sea salt

To serve:
White Rice (page 521)
Refried Beans (page 532)

REGION: CENTRAL MEXICO
PREPARATION TIME: 15 MINUTES
COOKING TIME: 30 MINUTES
SERVES: 6

Put the chiles, tomatillos, and a pinch of salt into a saucepan, add enough water to cover, and bring to a boil. Reduce the heat and simmer for about 10 minutes or until the tomatillos are tender. Remove the chiles and tomatillos from the pan using a slotted spoon and set aside, reserving the cooking liquid.

Heat a heavy frying pan or skillet over medium heat. Add the chorizo and cook for 5 minutes, until the fat has rendered. Remove the pan from the heat.

Put the chiles, tomatillos, and cilantro (coriander) into a food processor or blender and process to combine, adding a little of the reserved cooking liquid, if necessary.

Heat the oil in a pan. Add the onion and cook over low heat, stirring occasionally, for 5 minutes. Add the tomatillo mixture and cook for 5 minutes, then add the fried pork rinds (scratchings) and chorizo, and cook for an additional few minutes. Taste and adjust the seasoning, if necessary, and stir in a little more of the reserved cooking liquid if the mixture is too thick.

Remove from the heat and transfer to a serving dish. Serve immediately with white rice and refried beans.

MEXICAN MEATBALLS

4 thick slices stale baguette
1 cup (9 fl oz/250 ml) milk
1 lb 2 oz/500 g ground
  (minced) beef
1 lb 2 oz/500 g ground
  (minced) pork
1 onion, finely chopped
2 cloves garlic, finely chopped
4 eggs
2 tablespoons chopped
  spearmint leaves
1 hard-boiled egg, diced
2 tablespoons corn oil
1 cup (9 fl oz/250 ml) tomato
  puree or sauce (passata)
3 chipotle chiles in adobo,
  diced
sea salt and pepper
White Rice (page 521), to serve

REGION: PUEBLA
PREPARATION TIME: 35 MINUTES, PLUS
10 MINUTES SOAKING
COOKING TIME: 50 MINUTES
SERVES: 6

Combine the baguette and milk in a bowl and allow to soak for 10 minutes, then gently squeeze out as much milk as possible. Set aside.

Combine the beef, pork, onion, garlic, squeezed-out bread, and uncooked eggs in another bowl and season with salt, pepper and chopped spearmint. Mix well using your hands until thoroughly combined.

With damp hands, shape pieces of the mixture into meatballs, then press the diced hard-boiled egg into the centers. Reshape the meatballs to enclose the egg.

Heat the oil in a saucepan. Add the meatballs and cook over medium heat, turning frequently, for about 10 minutes, until evenly browned. Add the tomato puree (passata) and chiles, pour in 1 cup (9 fl oz/250 ml) water, and season with salt and pepper. Bring to a boil, then reduce the heat and simmer for 35 minutes or until the meatballs are cooked through. Taste and adjust the seasoning, if necessary.

Remove the pan from the heat and serve immediately with white rice.

PORK IN RED MOLE

4½ oz/125 g ancho chiles,
   dry-roasted
4½ oz/125 g pasilla chiles,
   dry-roasted 1 onion
10 cloves garlic
2¼ lb/1 kg pork loin, cut into
   6 pieces
5 tomatoes, dry-roasted and
   chopped
4 tablespoons vegetable
   shortening or lard
sea salt

To serve:
Corn Tortillas (page 36)

REGION: OAXACA
PREPARATION TIME: 30 MINUTES, PLUS
5 MINUTES SOAKING
COOKING TIME: 1½ HOURS
SERVES: 6

Put the chiles and enough hot water to cover them in a small bowl and soak for 15 minutes.

Preheat the broiler (grill). Cut an onion into quarters. Broil (grill) the quartered onion and 6 of the garlic cloves, turning frequently, until browned. Remove from the heat.

Put the pork into a saucepan and add the remaining garlic cloves. Halve the remaining onion, add it to the pan with a pinch of salt, pour in enough water to cover, and bring to a boil. Reduce the heat and simmer for 1 hour, until cooked through and tender. Remove the pan from the heat and lift out the pork, reserving the cooking liquid.

Put the chiles, broiled (grilled) garlic, broiled onion, and roasted tomatoes into a food processor or blender and process until thoroughly combined. Pass the mixture through a strainer (sieve) into a bowl.

Melt the fat in a saucepan. Add the chile mixture and cook over low heat, stirring occasionally, for 5 minutes.

Add the pork and cook for another 5 minutes, then add 1 cup (9 fl oz/250 ml) of the reserved cooking liquid. Season to taste with salt and simmer until thickened, then remove the pan from the heat.

Serve immediately with warm tortillas.

Manchamanteles

MANCHA-MANTELES

1 lb 2 oz/500 g boneless loin
1 bunch aromatic herbs, such
    as thyme, bay, and marjoram
1 lb 2 oz/500 g chicken pieces
8 ancho chiles, dry-roasted
2 tomatoes, dry-roasted
3 cloves garlic, dry-roasted
2 onions, dry-roasted
2 tablespoons apple cider
    vinegar
1 slice stale baguette, toasted
1 cup (3½ oz/100 g) unpeeled
    almonds, toasted
1 tablespoon sugar
¼ teaspoon cumin seeds
½ teaspoon dried oregano
1 cinnamon stick
1 clove
8 black peppercorns
2 slices fresh pineapple, diced
2 pears, diced
2 plantains, sliced
½ cup (3½ oz/100 g) cooked
    chickpeas, drained
1 sweet potato, cooked, peeled,
    and chopped
sea salt
fried plantain slices, to garnish

REGION: PUEBLA, FEDERAL DISTRICT, OAXACA, GUERRERO, TLAXCALA, GUANGUATO, BAJIO
PREPARATION TIME: 35 MINUTES, PLUS 15 MINUTES SOAKING
COOKING TIME: 1 HOUR 25 MINUTES
SERVES: 6

Put the pork, aromatic herbs, and a pinch of salt into a saucepan, pour in enough water to cover, and bring to a boil. Reduce the heat and simmer for 30 minutes. Add the chicken pieces and simmer for another 30 minutes, until the meat is tender.

Put the chiles and enough cooking liquid to cover them in a small bowl add and soak for 15 minutes. Put the chiles and soaking liquid, tomatoes, garlic, onions, vinegar, baguette, and almonds into a food processor or blender and process until thoroughly combined and a smooth consistency.

Strain the mixture into a large saucepan and bring to a boil. Cook for 15 minutes. Stir in the sugar, cumin seeds, oregano, cinnamon, clove, and peppercorns and season with salt. Add the cooked pork and chicken, pineapple, pears, and plantains and cook for an additional few minutes. Add the chickpeas and sweet potato and cook until heated through. Taste and adjust the seasoning, if necessary, and remove the pan from the heat. Serve immediately with plantain slices to garnish.

Note: You could also add 9 oz/250 g chorizo sausages and 12 oz/350 g diced ham.

PIGS' FEET WITH ANCHO CHILE

6 pigs' feet, split in half
  lengthwise
1 small onion
2 cloves garlic, peeled
1 bouquet garni
6 peppercorns
pinch of salt
3 ancho chiles, dry-roasted
4 tablespoons all-purpose
  (plain) flour
3 tablespoons lard or corn oil
3 cloves garlic
1 teaspoon cumin seeds
3 small white onions, cut into
  quarters
1 teaspoon dried oregano
sea salt and pepper

REGION: FEDERAL DISTRICT
PREPARATION TIME: 30 MINUTES, PLUS OVERNIGHT
TO COOL AND 15 MINUTES SOAKING
COOKING TIME: 2 HOURS 40 MINUTES
SERVES: 6

Put the pigs' feet, onion, garlic, bouquet garni, peppercorns and a pinch of salt into a large saucepan, pour in enough water to cover, and bring to a boil. Reduce the heat and simmer for 2 hours, until the meat is falling off the bones. Remove the pan from the heat and lift out the pigs' feet. Let cool completely, then chill in the refrigerator.

In a small bowl, combine the chiles and enough hot water to cover them and soak for 15 minutes. Spread the flour on a plate and season with salt and pepper. Roll the feet in the seasoned flour and shake off any excess.

Melt 2 tablespoons lard in a saucepan. Add the pigs' feet, in batches, and cook over medium heat, for about 7 minutes per side, until golden brown. Remove from heat and set the pigs' feet aside.

Drain the chiles, reserving the soaking liquid. Put the chiles, garlic, and cumin seeds into a food processor or blender and process until thoroughly combined, adding just enough of the soaking liquid to make a thin sauce.

Melt the remaining lard in a wide saucepan. Add the chile mixture and cook over low heat, stirring occasionally, for 10 minutes, until it thickens. Taste and add salt, if necessary. Add the onions and pigs' feet, and simmer for an additional 10–15 minutes.

Remove the pan from the heat and transfer the pigs' feet and sauce to a serving plate. Sprinkle with the oregano and serve immediately.

SLOW-COOKED PORK IN TEQUILA

7 oz/200 g cascabel or
  12 ancho chiles, dry-roasted
2½ tablespoons corn oil or lard
1½ lb/700 g pork leg, diced
1 lb 2 oz/500 g pork ribs,
  chopped
½ teaspoon cumin seeds
½ teaspoon dried oregano
3 cloves garlic
2 white onions, cut into
  chunks
4 tablespoons white tequila
coarse sea salt

To serve:
Flour Tortillas (page 37)
White Rice (page 521)
Pot Beans (page 533)

REGION: TAMAULIPAS
PREPARATION TIME: 15 MINUTES, PLUS
15 MINUTES SOAKING
COOKING TIME: 1 HOUR 10 MINUTES
SERVES: 6

Put the chiles and enough cooking liquid to cover them in a small bowl add and soak for 15 minutes.

Heat the fat in a saucepan. Add the pork leg and ribs and cook over medium heat, stirring and turning frequently, for 10 minutes, until evenly browned. Season with salt and remove the pan from the heat.

Put the chiles with their soaking water, cumin seeds, oregano, garlic, and onion into a food processor or blender and process. Strain into a bowl.

Add the mixture to the pan, return to low heat, cover the pan, and cook, stirring occasionally, for 1 hour, until the meat is tender and has absorbed the sauce. Add a little more water, if necessary, to prevent the meat from drying out.

Pour the tequila into the pan and simmer for another 10 minutes, with the lid off, until the alcohol has evaporated. Remove the pan from the heat.

Serve immediately with warm tortillas, white rice, and pot beans.

CROWN ROAST OF PORK PIBIL

½ cup (4 fl oz/120 ml)
  Cochinita Pibil Paste
  (page 403)
2¼ cups (18 fl oz/500 ml) plus
  8 tablespoons sour orange
  juice
1 (4½-lb/2-kg) crown roast
  of pork
4 banana leaves, lightly
  roasted, center veins
  removed (optional)
sea salt

To serve:
Strained Beans (page 535)
Red Onion Escabeche
  (page 478)

REGION: YUCATAN
PREPARATION TIME: 20 MINUTES,
PLUS 24 HOURS MARINATING
COOKING TIME: 3 HOURS
SERVES: 10

Combine the spice paste and sour orange juice in a saucepan and bring to a boil. Reduce the heat and simmer for 5 minutes. Let cool completely. Put the meat into a large bowl, spoon the cold mixture over it to coat, and let marinate in the refrigerator for 24 hours, covered.

Preheat the oven to 190°C (375°F/Gas Mark 5). Line a roasting pan with aluminum foil, shiny side downward, then cover with banana leaves, if using.

Transfer the meat and all the marinade to the prepared roasting pan and cover with more banana leaves, if using, and then with more aluminum foil. Roast for 2–3 hours, until cooked through and tender.

Remove the pan from the oven. Remove the meat and then carefully remove all the leaves and foil, keeping as much sauce as possible in the pan. Cover the meat to keep warm. Skim the excess fat from the cooking juices. Set the roasting pan over low heat, stir in 8 tablespoons sour orange juice, and heat, scraping up the sediment from the bottom of the pan. Strain into a sauceboat.

Carve the crown roast into separate chops and serve immediately with the sauce, beans, and red onion escabeche.

PORK TENDERLOIN IN PEANUT SAUCE

2 guajillo chiles, dry-roasted

3 ancho chiles, dry-roasted

5 tablespoons corn oil

1 cup (4 oz/120 g) peanuts, peeled

3 thick slices baguette

2¼ lb/1 kg pork tenderloin (fillet)

½ teaspoon ground cinnamon

3 tomatoes, coarsely chopped

1 hoja santa, main vein removed

½ onion

2 cloves garlic

5 black peppercorns

5 whole allspice berries

1 teaspoon sugar

2 chipotle chiles in adobo

2 cups (16 fl oz/475 ml) Chicken Stock (page 184)

2 tablespoons cane or apple cider vinegar

1 cup (9 fl oz/250 ml) red wine

sea salt

REGION: VERACRUZ, GULF OF MEXICO
PREPARATION TIME: 25 MINUTES, PLUS 15 MINUTES SOAKING
COOKING TIME: 1 HOUR
SERVES: 6

Put the chiles and enough hot water to cover them in a small bowl and soak for 15 minutes.

Heat 1 tablespoon oil in a frying pan or skillet. Add the peanuts and cook over low heat, stirring occasionally, for a few minutes, then remove from the pan. Add another tablespoon of oil and the slices of baguette and cook for 2–3 minutes on each side, until golden. Remove from the pan.

Sprinkle the pork with the cinnamon and season with salt. Heat 2 tablespoons oil in the skillet. Add the pork and cook over medium heat, turning occasionally, for about 10 minutes, until evenly browned.

Put the guajillo and ancho chiles with their soaking water, tomatoes, hoja santa, onion, garlic, peppercorns, allspice berries, sugar, chipotle chiles, peanuts, and fried baguette into a food processor or blender and process until thoroughly combined. Add a little water if necessary to make a smooth paste. Pass the mixture through a strainer (sieve) into a bowl.

Heat the remaining oil in a saucepan. Add the chile mixture and cook over low heat, stirring continuously, for about 5 minutes, until thickened. Skim off the oil that rises to the surface or blot it up with paper towels. Stir in the stock, vinegar, and wine, mix well, and simmer for about 30 minutes. Add the pork and cook for 15 minutes or until tender.

Transfer the pork to a board and let rest for 15 minutes. Slice thinly, return the pork to the sauce, and heat through before serving.

PORK LOIN WITH TEJOCOTES

11 oz/300 g ground (minced)
   pork
¾ cup (6 fl oz/175 ml) sour
   cream
1 egg
1¾ lb/800 g tejocotes or plums
1 cup (7 oz/200 g) white sugar
1 cinnamon stick
1 (2¼-lb/1-kg) pork loin
4 tomatoes
1 leek, chopped
1 carrot, chopped
1 white onion, chopped
1 clove garlic, chopped
1 celery stalk, chopped
1 bouquet garni
4¼ cups (1¾ pints/1 liter)
   Chicken Stock (page 184)
juice of 2 lemons
1 cup (9 fl oz/250 ml) white
   wine vinegar
salt and pepper

REGION: FEDERAL DISTRICT, MEXICO CITY
PREPARATION TIME: 1 HOUR
COOKING TIME: 2 HOURS 10 MINUTES
SERVES: 6

Put the ground (minced) meat, cream, and egg into a bowl, season with salt and pepper, and mix well. Set aside.

Put the tejocotes or plums in a small saucepan with enough water to cover them and bring them to a boil. Simmer for 20 minutes, then remove from the heat and drain. When cool, peel and pit them. Return them to the pan, add 2½ cups (1 pint/600 ml) water, ½ cup (3½ oz/100 g) sugar, and the cinnamon stick. Bring to a boil, reduce the heat, and simmer for 30–40 minutes, uncovered, so the mixture thickens. Do not let it burn.

Preheat the oven to 400°F (200°C/Gas Mark 6). Open out and flatten the pork loin. Spread half the stewed tejocotes over the pork loin, roll it up tightly, and tie with kitchen string, then wrap in aluminum foil.

Put the rolled loin in a Dutch oven or casserole dish and add the tomatoes, leek, carrot, onion, garlic, celery, bouquet garni, and chicken stock. Cover and cook in the oven for 1 hour.

Remove from the oven and lift out the pork. Remove and keep it wrapped so it stays warm and moist. Strain the cooking liquid into a bowl. Place the remaining tejocotes into a blender or a food processor. Pour in 1 cup (9 fl oz/250 ml) cooking liquid and blend until smooth. Strain it through a strainer (sieve) back into the bowl of cooking liquid.

Put the remaining sugar, the lemon juice and 1 tablespoon water into a saucepan and bring to a boil over medium heat, stirring continuously until the sugar has dissolved completely. Boil without stirring until the syrup is golden brown, then stir in the vinegar and simmer for an additional few minutes.

Stir in the cooking liquid (with the fruit) and simmer until the caramel has dissolved and thickened. Cut the pork loin into slices, put them onto a serving plate, and spoon the sauce over them. Serve immediately.

PORK IN AGAVE SYRUP

3 dry arbol chiles,
   dry-roasted
4 tablespoons (2 oz/50 g)
   butter
1 (3¾-lb/1.7-kg) pork
   tenderloin (fillet)
¾ cup (6 fl oz/175 ml) agave
   syrup
½ white onion, coarsely
   chopped
1 cup (9 fl oz/250 ml) white
   wine
Plantain Croquettes (page 42),
   to serve
1 scallion (spring onion),
   finely chopped, to serve
sea salt and pepper

Put the chiles and enough hot water to cover them in a small bowl and soak for 15 minutes.

Melt the butter in a saucepan. Season the pork with salt and pepper, add to the pan, and cook over medium heat, turning once, for about 10 minutes, until lightly browned on both sides.

Put the chiles and their soaking water, the agave syrup, onion, and wine into a food processor or a blender and process until thoroughly combined.

Add the chile mixture to the pan and simmer, covered, for 1 hour or until the meat is tender. If necessary, add a little water to prevent the pan from drying out.

Cut the pork into thin slices, transfer to individual plates, and spoon some sauce over them. Add a few croquettes and sprinkle with the scallion (spring onion).

CARNE DE
PUERCO EN
SALSA VERDE

PORK IN GREEN SAUCE

2¼ lb/1 kg lean pork, diced

3 tablespoons corn oil

5 tomatillos

4–6 serrano chiles, membrane and seeds removed

2 cloves garlic

4 sprigs cilantro (coriander)

sea salt

REGION: FEDERAL DISTRICT
PREPARATION TIME: 20 MINUTES
COOKING TIME: 1 HOUR
SERVES: 6

Put the meat into a saucepan, pour in enough water to cover, add a pinch of salt, and bring to a boil. Reduce the heat, cover the pan, and simmer for about 30 minutes or until tender. Remove the pan from the heat and lift out the meat with a slotted spoon. Reserve the cooking liquid.

Heat 2 tablespoons of the oil in a saucepan. Add the pork and cook over medium heat, stirring frequently, for 8–10 minutes, until evenly golden brown. Remove the pan from the heat and set aside.

Put the tomatillos into a saucepan and add enough of the reserved cooking liquid to cover. Bring to a boil, then immediately reduce the heat to low and simmer gently for 15 minutes. Remove the the tomatillos with a slotted spoon and discard the liquid.

Put the tomatillos, chiles, garlic, and cilantro (coriander) into a food processor or blender and process until combined.

Heat the remaining oil in a pan, add the tomatillo mixture, and cook, stirring occasionally, for about 10 minutes. Add the meat and simmer for a few minutes, adding a little of the reserved cooking liquid, if necessary, to make a sauce.

Remove the pan from the heat and taste and adjust the seasoning, if necessary. Transfer the meat and sauce to a serving plate and serve immediately.

PORK WITH PUMPKIN

1 lb 10 oz/750 g boneless pork, diced

1 onion, quartered

2 cloves garlic

1 small pumpkin, or large butternut squash, peeled, seeded, and diced

1 large ear of corn, cut into 6 pieces

3 tomatoes, peeled, seeded, and coarsely chopped

2 serrano chiles, dry-roasted

2 cloves

2 tablespoons chopped cilantro (coriander)

6 mint leaves, chopped

sea salt and pepper

To serve:
White Rice (page 521)

Put the meat, onion, and garlic into a saucepan, pour in enough water to cover, and bring to a boil. Reduce the heat and simmer for 15 minutes.

Remove the pan from the heat, lift out the meat, and let cool. Strain the cooking liquid into a bowl and reserve.

Put the pumpkin into a saucepan, pour in the reserved cooking liquid, and simmer for 15 minutes. Add the meat, corn, tomatoes, chiles, and cloves, and season with salt and pepper. Simmer for 20 minutes or until the meat and vegetables are all tender. If the pan begins to dry out, add some of the reserved cooking liquid.

Remove the pan from the heat. Taste and adjust the seasoning, if necessary, and stir in the cilantro (coriander) and mint. Serve immediately with white rice.

Note: This dish may also be made with beef.

PORK RIBS IN GUAVA AND SMOKED CHILI SAUCE

3¼ lb/1.5 kg meaty pork ribs
sea salt and pepper

For the salsa:
1 white onion, halved and
   dry-roasted
1 clove garlic, dry-roasted
1 tomato, dry-roasted
½ teaspoon ground cumin,
   dry-roasted
2–5 smoked chipotle chiles
   in adobo
2 tablespoons apple cider
   vinegar
1 tablespoon corn oil or lard
¾ cup (6 fl oz/175 ml) light-
   colored Mexican beer
2 tablespoons grated piloncillo
   or brown sugar
3 ripe guavas, seeded and
   sliced
2½ tablespoons guava paste
sea salt and pepper

REGION: SOUTH
PREPARATION TIME: 1 HOUR
COOKING TIME: 2½ HOURS
SERVES: 6

Preheat the oven to 325°F (160°C/Gas Mark 3).

Generously season the ribs with salt and pepper and put them into a roasting pan. Roast, turning once, for about 1½ hours.

Remove the roasting pan from the oven and let cool. Discard the excess fat. When the meat is cool enough to handle, cut the ribs into 6 equal portions and return to the roasting pan. Cover them with aluminum foil so they don't dry out.

Meanwhile, make the sauce. Put the onion, garlic, tomato, cumin, chiles, and vinegar into a food processor or blender and process until smooth, then strain into a bowl.

Heat the oil in a saucepan, add the tomato mixture, and cook over medium-low heat, gradually stirring in the beer and piloncillo. Bring to a boil, then reduce the heat and simmer, stirring occasionally, for about 40 minutes. Add the guava and guava paste and cook for another 20 minutes, until it has reduced by half.

Preheat the oven to 325°F (160°C/Gas Mark 3). Spoon the sauce over the ribs and mix so they are well coated. Cover with foil and cook in the oven for another hour or until the meat is so tender that it falls off the bone. Remove the roasting pan from the oven.

Transfer the ribs to individual plates and spoon some sauce over them to serve.

Pork Ribs in Guava and Chili Sauce

PORK RIBS IN MANGO AND TEQUILA SAUCE

For the sauce:
1 mango
2 tablespoons lemon juice
2 tablespoons honey
2 tablespoons chopped fresh
  ginger
2 tablespoons ketchup
1 clove garlic, chopped
2–3 smoked chipotle chiles in
  adobo
2 tablespoons white tequila

1 tablespoon corn oil or lard
3¼ lb/1.5 kg meaty pork ribs,
  cut into individual ribs
sea salt and pepper
½ cup (1 oz/25 g) finely
  chopped cilantro (coriander),
  to garnish

To serve:
mashed potatoes

Put the mango, lemon juice, honey, ginger, ketchup, garlic, chiles, and tequila into a food processor or blender and process until smooth. Season to taste with salt and pepper and set aside.

Preheat the oven to 375°F (190°C/Gas Mark 5).

Heat the oil in a heavy saucepan. Add the ribs to the pan and sear over high heat. Do this in batches so you only have one layer of ribs in the pan at a time. Transfer the ribs to a roasting pan. When all the ribs have been seared, add half the sauce and mix well.

Put the ribs into the oven, covered with aluminum foil, and cook, basting with the sauce several times, for 1 hour. Remove the roasting pan from the oven and transfer the ribs to a serving plate.

Pour the remaining sauce and a couple of tablespoons water into the roasting pan and set over medium heat, stirring and scraping the sediment on the bottom of the pan. Strain into a sauceboat, discarding the contents of the strainer (sieve).

Sprinkle the ribs with the cilantro (coriander) and serve with mashed potatoes, handing the remaining sauce around separately.

PORK IN CHILE MARINADE

3 large pasilla chiles, lightly
   dry-roasted
1 clove garlic, dry-roasted
1 teaspoon dried oregano
dash of apple cider vinegar
6 pork cutlets or steaks
4 tablespoons corn oil or lard
sea salt
salad, to serve

REGION: PUEBLA, FEDERAL DISTRICT
PREPARATION TIME: 25 MINUTES, PLUS 15 MINUTES
SOAKING AND 1 HOUR MARINATING
COOKING TIME: 20 MINUTES
SERVES: 4

Put the chiles and enough hot water to cover them in a small bowl and soak for 15 minutes.

Put the chiles, garlic, oregano, vinegar, and a pinch of salt into a food processor or blender and process until combined. Add enough chile water to make a thick paste. Strain through a fine-mesh strainer (sieve) into a bowl.

Rub the mixture all over the pork cutlets, put them on a plate, cover with plastic wrap (clingfilm), and let marinate in the refrigerator for 1 hour.

Heat the oil in a frying pan or skillet. Add the pork and cook over medium heat for 5–6 minutes on each side. Remove the pan from the heat and pierce one of the cutlets with the tip of a sharp knife. If the liquid comes out clear, it's done. Let sit on a plate for 2–3 minutes to rest, then serve immediately with salad.

PORK RIBS IN ORANGE SAUCE

4¼ lb/2 kg pork ribs, cut into
   6 portions
1 cup (10 oz/275 g) orange
   marmalade
5 tablespoons Borracha Salsa
   (page 513)
2 tablespoon light Mexican
   beer
2 tablespoons honey
1½ teaspoons grated orange
   zest
sea salt and pepper

REGION: FEDERAL DISTRICT
PREPARATION TIME: 15 MINUTES
COOKING TIME: 1 HOUR
SERVES: 6

Preheat the oven to 350°F (180°C/Gas Mark 4).

Season the ribs generously with salt and pepper and put them into a large roasting pan. Combine the marmalade, Borracha salsa, beer, honey, and orange zest in a large saucepan and cook over low heat, stirring continuously, for 5 minutes.

Pour the hot mixture over the ribs. Cover the pan with aluminum foil, put it in the oven, and cook for about 45 minutes. Remove the foil, return to the oven, and cook for an additional 10–15 minutes, until browned. Serve immediately.

PORK SHANK IN CHILEAJO

3 oz (100 g) costeno chiles,
   lightly dry-roasted
3 guajillo chiles, lightly
   dry-roasted
6 pork shanks (hocks)
2–3 tomatillos, cooked in water
3–4 tomatoes, cooked in water
¼ teaspoon cumin seeds
2 cloves
1 head garlic, dry-roasted
1 slice onion, dry-roasted
1 teaspoon oregano leaves
3–4 tablespoons lard or
   corn oil
sea salt

To serve:
Pot Beans (page 533)

REGION: GUERNERO
PREPARATION TIME: 30 MINUTES, PLUS
15 MINUTES SOAKING
COOKING TIME: 1 HOUR 10 MINUTES
SERVES: 6

Put the chiles and enough hot water to cover them in a small bowl and soak for 15 minutes.

Put the meat into a saucepan, pour in enough water to cover, add a pinch of salt, and bring to a boil. Reduce the heat and simmer over medium heat for 30–40 minutes, until tender. Remove the meat from the liquid with a slotted spoon and put it on a plate. Cover it with aluminum foil. Reserve the cooking liquid.

Meanwhile, put the tomatillos and tomatoes into a saucepan, pour in enough water to cover, and bring to a boil. Reduce the heat and simmer gently for about 8 minutes. Remove the pan from the heat and drain.

Pour 1 cup (9 fl oz/250 ml) of the reserved meat cooking liquid into a food processor or blender, add the cumin seeds, cloves, garlic, onion, oregano, and chiles, and process until thoroughly combined. Strain into a bowl.

Heat the lard in a saucepan. Add the meat and cook over medium heat for a few minutes on each side until evenly browned. Add the chile mixture and the reserved cooking liquid and cook, stirring, for about 20 minutes. Add some water if the pan gets too dry.

Remove the pan from the heat and season to taste with salt. Divide the pork mixture among individual plates and serve immediately with pot beans.

PORK WITH CACTUS PADDLES

3 pasilla chiles, dry-roasted
3 guajillo chiles, dry-roasted
pinch of baking soda
  (bicarbonate of soda)
10 cactus paddles, diced
1 lb 2 oz/500 g boneless pork,
  diced
1 small white onion, halved
2 cloves garlic, 1 clove
  dry-roasted
5 small potatoes
4 tablespoons corn oil or lard
sea salt
Corn Tortillas (page 36)

REGION: FEDERAL DISTRICT
PREPARATION TIME: 40 MINUTES, PLUS
15 MINUTES SOAKING
COOKING TIME: 1 HOUR
SERVES: 6

Put the chiles and enough hot water to cover them in a small bowl and soak for 15 minutes.

Fill a saucepan with water and add a pinch of the baking soda. Bring the water to a boil. Add the cactus paddles and simmer gently for 15–20 minutes. The cactus paddles should be soft but not mushy.

Put the pork, half the onion, 1 unroasted garlic clove, and a pinch of salt into a saucepan, pour in water to cover, and bring to a boil. Reduce the heat and simmer for 30 minutes, until the meat is tender.

Meanwhile, cook the potatoes in boiling water for 20 minutes, until tender. Remove the pan from the heat and drain. When the potatoes are cool enough to handle, peel and dice them.

Remove the pork from the heat and lift out the meat with a slotted spoon. Strain and reserve the cooking liquid. Cut the pork into bite-size chunks.

Heat half the oil in a frying pan or skillet. Add the pork and cook over medium heat, stirring frequently, for 5 minutes, until evenly browned. Remove the pan from the heat.

Put the dry-roasted garlic and remaining onion into a food processor or blender. Add the chiles with their soaking liquid and process until smooth. Strain into a bowl.

Heat the remaining oil in a saucepan. Add the chile mixture and cook over low heat, stirring occasionally, for 10 minutes, until it gets a little thicker. Add the meat, the cooking liquid from the pork, the cactus paddles, and potatoes, and simmer for another 10 minutes, until everything is heated through.

Remove the pan from the heat, transfer the mixture to a tureen or deep serving dish, and serve immediately with hot tortillas.

PORK WITH CASCABEL CHILI SAUCE

REGION: FEDERAL DISTRICT
PREPARATION TIME: 20 MINUTES, PLUS
15 MINUTES SOAKING
COOKING TIME: 1 HOUR
SERVES: 6

10 cascabel chiles, dry-roasted
1 (2¼-lb/1-kg) pork tenderloin
  (fillet)
2 tablespoons corn oil or lard
1 large white onion, quartered
2 cloves garlic
1 tablespoon apricot jam
sea salt and pepper

To serve:
sauteed apricots
mashed potatoes or White Rice
  (page 521)

Put the chiles and enough hot water to cover them in a small bowl and soak for 15 minutes.

Season the pork with salt and pepper. Heat the oil in a frying pan or skillet. Add the pork and cook for about 5 minutes, until evenly browned. Remove the pan from the heat and drain the pork on paper towels.

Put the onion, garlic, and chiles with their soaking water into a saucepan, add enough water just to cover, and bring to a boil. Reduce the heat and simmer for 10 minutes. Pour into a food processor or blender and process until smooth. Strain into a bowl.

Preheat the oven to 400°F (200°C/Gas Mark 6).

Put the pork into a Dutch oven or casserole dish and spoon the chile mixture over it. Stir to coat it well, cover with the lid or with aluminum foil, and bake for about 40 minutes or until tender and cooked through. Taste and adjust seasoning, if necessary.

Remove the casserole from the oven. Remove 4 tablespoons of the sauce and stir into the apricot jam in a bowl.

Slice the pork, put it on a serving plate, and spoon the sauce from the pan over it. Serve immediately with sautéed apricots and mashed potatoes or white rice. Pass the apricot jam and sauce mixture around separately.

PORK WITH PURSLANE

4 morita chiles, dry-roasted
2 lb/900 g pork loin, cut into
  bite-size pieces
10 tomatillos, dry-roated
3 cloves garlic, dry-roasted
½ onion, dry-roasted
4 tablespoons corn oil or lard
2¼ lb/1 kg purslane or any
  other strong-tasting leafy
  green
sea salt

REGION: FEDERAL DISTRICT
PREPARATION TIME: 30 MINUTES, PLUS
15 MINUTES SOAKING
COOKING TIME: 40 MINUTES
SERVES: 6

Put the chiles and enough hot water to cover them in a small bowl and soak for 15 minutes. Put the pork into a saucepan and cover with water. Bring to a boil, then poach gently for 15 minutes. Remove the meat from the water with a slotted spoon and reserve the cooking liquid.

Put the tomatillos, chiles with their soaking liquid, garlic, and onion into a food processor or blender and process until thoroughly combined.

Heat the oil in a frying pan or skillet. Add the meat and cook over medium heat, stirring frequently, for about 5 minutes, until evenly browned. Add the purslane and the tomatillo and chile mixture, reduce the heat, and simmer for 15 minutes. Season to taste with salt, remove the pan from the heat, and serve immediately.

PORK IN
BEET MOLE

7 ancho chiles, dry-roasted
20 guajillo chiles, dry-roasted
2 lbs 10 oz/1.2 kg pork loin
4 beets (beetroots)
2¼ cups (9 oz/250 g) peanuts
5 black peppercorns
1 cinnamon stick
1 onion, coarsely chopped
3 cloves garlic
2 bay leaves
pinch of dried thyme
pinch of dried marjoram
2 tablespoons corn oil or lard
6½ Corn Tortillas (page 36)
1 crusty white roll or
  1 day-old baguette, crusts
  removed
lightly toasted sesame seeds,
  to garnish
1 sprig cilantro (coriander),
  to garnish

To serve:
White Rice (page 521)

REGION: QUERETARO
PREPARATION TIME: 55 MINUTES, PLUS
15 MINUTES SOAKING
COOKING TIME: 1 HOUR 20 MINUTES
SERVES: 6

In a small bowl, add the chiles and enough hot water to cover them and soak for 15 minutes.

Put the pork into a saucepan, add enough water to cover, and bring to a boil. Reduce the heat and simmer for 45–60 minutes, until the pork is done. Remove it from the water and let cool. Reduce the liquid by half and reserve.

Put the beets (beetroots) into a saucepan, add enough water to cover, and bring to a boil. Reduce the heat and cook for 1 hour, until they are tender. Drain, let cool, and then peel them with your hands. Trim off the tops and bottoms and put into a bowl.

Heat a frying pan or skillet over medium heat. Add the peanuts and cook, stirring occasionally, for 1–2 minutes to dry-roast them, without letting them burn. Remove from the pan. One ingredient at a time, dry-roast the peppercorns, cinnamon stick, onion, and garlic, removing them as they begin to darken and are fragrant. Peel the garlic once cooled.

Put the beets, peanuts, peppercorns, cinnamon stick, onion, garlic, bay leaves, thyme, marjoram, and chiles into a food processor or blender and process until thoroughly combined. Add a little meat stock, if needed, to make a thick paste. Strain into a bowl.

Heat the oil in a saucepan. Add the beet mixture and cook over medium-low heat, stirring occasionally, for 10 minutes. Pour in the stock and simmer.

Toast ½ tortilla. Put the bread and tortilla into a food processor or blender and process into fine crumbs, then add them to the pan. Cook, stirring continuously, until the mixture comes to a boil and thickens.

Slice the pork into 1-cm slices and heat gently until the meat is hot all the way through.

Remove the pan from the heat and transfer to a serving dish. Sprinkle with the sesame seeds, garnish with cilantro (coriander), and serve immediately with white rice and tortillas.

Pork in Beet Mole

WEDDING STEW

REGION: ZACATECAS
PREPARATION TIME: 45 MINUTES, PLUS
15 MINUTES SOAKING
COOKING TIME: 45 MINUTES
SERVES: 6

25 guajillo chiles, dry-roasted

9 ancho chiles, dry-roasted

2 tablespoons corn oil

2¼ lb/1 kg boneless lean pork, diced

½ stale baguette, crusts removed, diced and lightly fried in oil

½ cup/100 g almonds, toasted

½ onion, dry-roasted

1 cinnamon stick, dry-roasted

3 large black bell peppers, seeded and dry-roasted

2 cloves, dry-roasted

1 cup (9 fl oz/250 ml) orange juice

thinly sliced onion, to serve

Put the chiles and enough hot water to cover them in a small bowl and soak for 15 minutes.

Heat the oil in a saucepan. Add the pork and cook over medium heat, stirring frequently, for about 10 minutes, until evenly browned.

Meanwhile, put the chiles with their soaking water into a food processor or blender and process. Add the bread, almonds, onion, cinnamon, bell peppers, cloves, and orange juice and process again until smooth.

Strain the mixture into the pan of pork and simmer, covered, for about 30 minutes, until the meat is tender. Serve with the onion.

PORK WITH CACTUS PADDLES IN CHILI SAUCE

2 mulato chiles, dry-roasted
2 ancho chiles, seeded and
  dry-roasted
2 pasilla chiles, dry-roasted
15 cactus paddles
1 lb 5 oz/600 g boneless pork
2 garlic cloves
5 tablespoons corn oil
2 scallions (spring onions),
  sliced
½ cup (2 oz/50 g) grated or
  crumbled queso añejo or
  romano (pecorino) cheese
  to serve
2 hard-boiled eggs, sliced,
  to serve
sea salt

REGIONS: FEDERAL DISTRICT,
EDO. MEX., QUERÉTARO
PREPARATION TIME: 1 HOUR, PLUS
15 MINUTES SOAKING
COOKING TIME: 1 HOUR 35 MINUTES
SERVES: 6

In a small bowl, add the chiles and enough hot water to cover them and soak for 15 minutes.

Cut the cactus paddles into small squares. Bring plenty of water to a boil in a large saucepan. Add the cactus paddles and reduce the heat. Simmer the cactus paddles gently for 20 minutes. Add a pinch of salt and remove the pan from the heat. Drain, rinse, cover with a damp dish towel, and let cool.

Put the chiles with their soaking water into a food processor or blender and process. Pass through a strainer (sieve) into a bowl.

Put the pork, garlic, and a little salt into a saucepan, bring to a boil, reduce the heat, and simmer for 60 minutes. Remove the pan from the heat, lift out the pork, and let cool. Strain the liquid into a bowl and reserve. Discard the contents of the strainer.

When the pork is cold, shred it with 2 forks. Heat the oil in a saucepan. Add the shredded pork and scallions (spring onions) and cook for 5 minutes, then pour in 1 cup (9 fl oz/250 ml) of the reserved cooking liquid and the chili sauce and add the cactus paddles. Season with salt and simmer for 5 minutes.

Remove the pan from the heat and divide the pork among individual plates. Serve immediately with cheese and sliced eggs.

Lamb in Cider Sauce

LAMB IN
CIDER SAUCE

CORDERO A
LA SIDRA

2 cloves garlic
3 tablespoons corn oil
pinch of ground cloves
pinch of ground cinnamon
pinch of black pepper
2¼ lb/1 kg boneless lamb,
   diced
1 teaspoon all-purpose
   (plain) flour
4¼ cups (1¾ pints/1 liter)
   hard (dry) apple cider
3 tablespoons (1½ oz/40 g)
   butter or lard
9 scallions (spring onions),
   chopped
7 oz/200 g chorizo, shredded
   or finely chopped
2¼ cups (18 fl oz/500 ml)
   Beef Stock (page 185)
5 tablespoons slivered (flaked)
   almonds, toasted, to serve
chopped parsley, to serve
sea salt

REGION: MEXICO CITY
PREPARATION TIME: 25 MINUTES
COOKING TIME: 1½ HOURS
SERVES: 6

Put the garlic, 1 tablespoon oil, the cloves, cinnamon, and pepper into a mortar and pound with a pestle to a paste. Spread the paste all over the lamb and dust lightly with the flour. Heat the remaining oil in a frying pan or skillet. Add the meat and cook over medium heat, stirring frequently, for 8–10 minutes, until evenly browned. Remove the pan from the heat and transfer the meat to a plate.

Pour the cider into a saucepan and bring to a boil. Boil until it has reduced by half, then remove the pan from the heat.

Melt the butter in the pan used for the meat. Add the scallions (spring onions) and cook over low heat, stirring occasionally, for about 5 minutes, until translucent. Add the chorizo and cook, stirring frequently, for 10–15 minutes.

Drain off the excess fat and return the pan to the heat. Add the lamb, stock, and cider and season with salt and pepper. Cover and simmer for 45 minutes or until the meat is tender. Taste and adjust the seasoning, if necessary, and remove the pan from the heat.

Transfer to a serving platter and garnish with slivered (flaked) almonds and chopped parsley.

LAMB IN PULQUE

6 chicken feet, cleaned
3 white onions, sliced
1 garlic head, cut in half
  crosswise
6 lb/2.7 kg lamb meat
3½ oz/100 g ancho chile,
  dry-roasted
3½ oz/100 g guajillo chile,
  dry-roasted
2 bay leaves
10 whole allspice berries
15 whole black peppers
2 cinnamon sticks
5 avocado leaves
8½ cups (68 fl oz/2 liters)
  pulque
chopped cilantro, to garnish
mild red chiles, sliced, to
  garnish

REGION: MEXICO CITY
PREPARATION TIME: 35 MINUTES
PLUS 12 HOURS SOAKING
COOKING TIME: 2–3 HOURS
SERVES: 6-8

In a large cazuela or heavy saucepan, place the chicken feet on the bottom of the pan. Then add the remaining ingredients in layers, starting with the sliced onion, garlic, meat, and chiles.

Combine all the spices in a cheesecloth (muslin) bag and add it to the pan. Pour over the pulque and cover with a non-vented lid, to prevent any steam from escaping and bring to a boil over high heat. Reduce the heat to medium and simmer for 2–3 hours, or until the meat falls off the bone.

Let it rest for 30 minutes, then remove the meat and the stock and transfer to separate bowls. Discard the bones, onion, garlic, and spices.

Remove all the meat from the bones, discard the fat, and add it back to the saucepan. Add the sauce and heat through.

Transfer to a serving dish and sprinkle over chopped cilantro and chiles. Serve

Lamb in Pulque

Goat in a Clay Pot

GOAT STEW

REGION: QUERÉTARO
PREPARATION TIME: 50 MINUTES, PLUS 15 MINUTES
SOAKING AND 4 HOURS MARINATING
COOKING TIME: 2¼ HOURS
SERVES: 6

5 guajillo or New Mexican
chiles, dry-roasted
3 ancho chiles, dry-roasted
¼ onion, sliced and dry-roasted
2 cloves garlic, dry-roasted
1 tablespoon apple cider
vinegar
½ bay leaf
1 clove, dry-roasted
½ pinch cumin seeds,
dry-roasted
4 black peppercorns,
dry-roasted
1 teaspoon dried oregano
1 goat leg
toes of 6 prepared chicken feet
4¼ cups (1¾ pints/1 liter) Beef
Stock (page 185) or pulque
Masa Dough (page 36)
1 cup (130g/4 ½ oz) peas
beans, to serve
coarse sea salt

Put the chiles in a bowl, add enough hot water to cover, and soak for 15 minutes. Drain.

Drain the chiles and put them into a food processor or blender, add the onion, garlic, vinegar, bay leaf, clove, cumin seeds, peppercorns, oregano, and a pinch of salt, and process until smooth. Pass the mixture through a strainer (sieve) into a bowl.

Put the meat into a dish, add the chile and spice mixture, and turn the meat to coat. Refrigerate and marinate for 4 hours.

Arrange chicken toes in the bottom of a large flameproof dish or heavy saucepan and add the meat mixture and stock. Cover with a lid and seal the edge with the dough. Cook over medium heat for about 2 hours. Unseal the pan, add in the peas and cook for 2 minutes.

Transfer the meat and sauce to a serving dish. Serve immediately with any type of bean dish.

BABY GOAT WITH CHILI SAUCE

4 ancho chiles, dry-roasted
2 tablespoons apple cider
    vinegar
1 baby goat, cut into pieces
2 cloves garlic, dry-roasted
1 tomato, dry-roasted
⅓ onion, dry-roasted
2 tablespoons corn oil
pinch of ground cumin
sea salt and pepper

To serve:
black beans
Flour Tortilla (page 37)

REGION: TAMAULIPAS
PREPARATION TIME: 35 MINUTES,
PLUS 2 HOURS MARINATING
COOKING TIME: 2 HOURS
SERVES: 4

Put the chiles into a small bowl, add enough hot water to cover, and soak for 15 minutes. Brush the vinegar and salt and pepper all over the meat, put it into a dish, and let marinate for 2 hours.

Preheat the oven to 375°F (190°C/Gas Mark 5).

Put the chiles and their soaking water into a food processor or blender, add the garlic, tomato, onion, oil, and cumin, and process until combined. Strain into a bowl. Brush the meat with the chile mixture, put it into a roasting pan or ovenproof dish, cover with aluminum foil, and bake for about 2 hours.

Remove the meat from the oven and serve immediately with boiled beans and warm tortillas.

QUAIL IN CHILI SAUCE

3 tablespoons lard or corn oil
6 quails, cut in half lengthwise
2¼ lb/1 kg whole yellow
  chanterelle mushrooms
35 guajillo chiles, dry-roasted
1 white onion, quartered and
  dry-roasted
3 cloves garlic, dry-roasted
pinch of dried oregano
sea salt

To serve:
White Rice (page 521)
Flour Tortillas (page 37)

Put the chiles in a bowl, add enough hot water to cover, and soak for 15 minutes. Drain.

Heat the fat in a saucepan. Add the quails in batches, and cook over medium heat, turning occasionally, until lightly browned all over. Remove from the pan and set aside. Put the chanterelles into the pan and sauté for 10 minutes, until they are cooked.

Put the soaked chiles, onion, garlic, and oregano into a food processor or blender with the soaking liquid and process until combined. Pass through a strainer (sieve) into a flameproof casserole dish or large saucepan. Discard the contents of the strainer.

Bring the sauce to a boil over medium heat, add the mushrooms, and cook for an additional 5 minutes. Add the quails, reduce the heat, and simmer for 15 minutes, until the quails are done. Remove the pan from the heat.

Serve immediately with white rice and warm tortillas.

VENISON DZIK

¾ cup (6 fl oz/175 ml) sour
  orange juice
3 tablespoons finely chopped
  chives
½ red onion, finely chopped
½ cup (3½ oz/100 g) finely
  chopped radishes
2¼ lb/1 kg boneless venison,
  roasted and finely shredded
½ cup (1 oz/25 g) finely
  chopped cilantro (coriander)
sea salt

To serve (optional):
tostadas
sliced red onion
pickled chiles

Put the orange juice, chives, onion, radishes, and
a pinch of salt into a glass or ceramic bowl
and let stand for 15 minutes. Add the venison
and cilantro (coriander). Taste and adjust the
seasoning, if necessary.

Serve as an appetizer or on a tostada with red
onion and habanero escabeche.

Note: It can be difficult to find sour orange juice. In
which case, substitute regular orange juice with the
addition of lime juice or white wine vinegar.

Venison Dzik

RABBIT IN PRUNE AND CHILI SAUCE

1 rabbit, cleaned and cut into
   pieces (ask the butcher to do
   this because rabbit bones are
   fragile and splinter easily)
6 slices (rashers) bacon
4 tablespoons olive oil
4¼ cups (1¾ pints/1 liter)
   red wine
2 cloves garlic, finely chopped
1½ cinnamon sticks,
   dry-roasted
1 clove, dry-roasted
5 peppercorns, dry-roasted
1 bay leaf, dry-roasted
1 sprig thyme
1 sprig rosemary
2 sprigs parsley
6 large ancho chiles,
   dry-roasted and sliced in half
2 large onions, sliced
1¾ cups (2¾ cups/500 g) prunes
   soaked in water
sea salt and pepper
chopped parsley, to garnish

To serve
White Rice (page 521)

REGION: MEXICO CITY
PREPARATION TIME: 1½ HOURS, PLUS
2 HOURS MARINATING
COOKING TIME: 1 HOUR 10 MINUTES
SERVES: 6

Season the rabbit pieces all over with salt and pepper, then wrap them in the bacon.

Heat the oil in a large frying pan or skillet. Add the pieces of rabbit, in batches if necessary, and cook over medium heat, turning once, for about 10 minutes, until lightly browned on both sides. Remove the pan from the heat, transfer the rabbit pieces to a dish, and let cool.

Combine the wine, garlic, cinnamon, clove, peppercorns, bay leaf, thyme, rosemary, and parsley in a bowl and mix well. Pour the mixture over the pieces of rabbit, turning to coat. Cover the dish with plastic wrap (clingfilm) and let marinate for at least 2 hours. Drain the rabbit through a strainer (sieve) into a bowl. Reserve the marinade, take the rabbit out of the strainer, and then discard the contents of the strainer.

Spread one-third of the chiles over the bottom of a large saucepan, and put half the pieces of rabbit, half the sliced onions, and half the prunes on top. Cover this with a third of the chiles. Put the rest of the rabbit, onion, and prunes on top and then top with the remaining chiles.

Pour the marinade into the pan and cover. Cook over low heat for about 1 hour or until the rabbit is tender and the sauce has thickened. Remove the pan from the heat and divide everything, including the chiles, among individual plates. Sprinkle with parsley to garnish and serve immediately with white rice.

Rabbit in Prune and Chili Sauce

PACHUQUILLA-STYLE ANT EGGS

½ cup (4 oz/120 g) butter
5 tablespoons olive oil
4 white onions, finely chopped
5 tablespoons chiles,
  membrane and seeds
  removed and finely chopped
½ cup (25 g/1 oz) finely
  chopped epazote or cilantro
  (coriander)
6 cups (2¼ lb/1 kg) fresh
  ant eggs
sea salt
Corn Tortillas (page 36),
  to serve
Guacamole (page 40), to serve

REGION: HIDALGO
PREPARATION TIME: 5 MINUTES
COOKING TIME: 10 MINUTES
SERVES: 6–8

Melt the butter with the oil in a saucepan. Add the onions and chiles and cook over medium heat, stirring occasionally, for 5 minutes. Add the epazote and season with salt. Reduce the heat, add the ant eggs, and cook for 4 minutes.

Remove the pan from the heat and taste and adjust the seasoning, if necessary. Serve immediately with warm tortillas and guacamole.

HIDALGO-STYLE WORMS

¾ cup (6 fl oz/175 ml) corn oil
1 lb 5 oz/600 g maguey worms,
  cleaned
sea salt

To serve:
12 Corn Tortillas (page 36)
2½ cups (1 pint/600ml)
  Guacamole (page 40)
1 cup (9 fl oz/250 ml) Raw
  Tomatillo Salsa (page 512)
6 limes, halved

REGION: HIDALGO
PREPARATION TIME: 5 MINUTES
COOKING TIME: 10 MINUTES
SERVES: 6

Heat the oil in a heavy frying pan or skillet. Add the worms and cook over medium heat, stirring occasionally, for 10 minutes, until they are toasted. Remove the pan from heat.

Remove the worms with a slotted spoon and drain on paper towels. Season with salt to taste. Transfer to a serving dish and serve immediately with warm tortillas, guacamole, green salsa, and limes.

CHILETAS
DE CODERO
MARINADAS

MARINATED LAMB CHOPS

5 ancho chiles, membranes
  and seeds removed
2 mulato chiles, membranes
  and seeds removed
2 pasilla chiles, membranes
  and seeds removed
2 onions, coarsely chopped
2 cloves garlic
1 bay leaf
2 sprigs parsley
pinch of dried oregano
6 black peppercorns
1 clove
½ cups (4 fl oz/120 ml) apple
  cider vinegar
12 (5½-oz/160-g) lamb chops
4 teaspoons vegetable oil
2 cups (16 fl oz/475 ml) white
  wine
1 tablespoon vegetable
  shortening or lard
sea salt

To serve:
grated panela or feta cheese
finely chopped onion
black olives, pitted and
  chopped

REGION: VERACRUZ
PREPARATION TIME: 25 MINUTES, PLUS 15 MINUTES
SOAKING AND 12 HOURS MARINATING
COOKING TIME: 35 MINUTES
SERVES: 6

Put the chiles in a bowl, add enough hot water to cover them, and soak for 15 minutes. Drain.

Put the chiles, onions, garlic, bay leaf, parsley, oregano, peppercorns, clove, and vinegar into a food processor or blender, add a pinch of salt, and process until thoroughly combined.

Put the lamb chops into a dish and pour the chile mixture over them, turning to coat. Cover with plastic wrap (clingfilm) and let marinate for about 12 hours in the refrigerator. Turn the chops over occasionally while they are marinating.

Heat the oil in a small saucepan. Pour in the marinade and the wine and cook, stirring occasionally, for about 20 minutes, until thickened.

Melt the vegetable shortening in a frying pan or skillet. Add the chops and cook for 4–5 minutes, then turn over, and cook for an additional 4 minutes.

Transfer the chops to individual serving plates, pour the sauce over them, and sprinkle with the grated cheese, onion, and olives. Serve immediately.

ROAST GARLIC

4–5 large heads garlic
5 tablespoons olive oil
sea salt and pepper

REGION: ALL REGIONS
PREPARATION TIME: 10 MINUTES
COOKING TIME: 1 HOUR
SERVES: 4

Preheat the oven to 325°F (170°C/Gas Mark 3).

Cut off the tips of the garlic heads, sprinkle with a little olive oil on the cut side, then wrap in aluminum foil and place on a baking sheet. Roast for 1 hour, or until soft when they are gently squeezed.

Note: You can use this as a spread for toasted bread. Squeeze the garlic heads into a bowl, add the remaining olive oil, season with salt and pepper to taste, and mix well to thoroughly combine.

FRESH CHILES

6 tablespoons vegetable oil,
  plus extra for rubbing
1 lb 2 oz/500 g poblano chiles
6 tablespoons olive oil

REGION: ALL REGIONS
PREPARATION TIME: 20 MINUTES, PLUS
20 MINUTES SWEATING
COOKING TIME: 15 MINUTES
SERVES: 6

Rub the chiles with vegetable oil and roast them over direct heat, turning the chiles until evenly charred on all sides. Wrap them in a bag and cover with a damp cloth. Let sweat for 15–20 minutes. Remove them from the bag and peel them with a spoon. Remove the seeds, membrane, and stems.

Note: If you are using them for stuffing, leave the stem attached and open and seed carefully. To make a chile paste, blend in a food processor and pour into a sterilized jar for future uses.

CHIPOTLE CHILES IN ADOBO

REGION: ALL REGIONS
PREPARATION TIME: 15 MINUTES, PLUS
2 HOURS STANDING
COOKING TIME: 35 MINUTES
SERVES: 1 (9-FL OZ/250-ML) JAR

2¼ cups (18 fl oz/500 ml) apple cider vinegar

4 oz/120 g raw sugar

4–5 cloves garlic

1 small bunch of mixed herbs (such as oregano, thyme, marjoram, bay leaf)

4 oz/120 g chipotle, morita, or other smoked chiles

½ cinnamon stick

3 onions, chopped

1 clove

4 allspice berries

4 black peppercorns

2 tablespoons olive oil

oregano

sea salt

Pour 2 cups (16 fl oz/475 ml) water and the vinegar into a saucepan, add the raw sugar and stir over low heat until it has dissolved. Add the garlic, mixed herbs, and chiles and bring to a boil, then reduce the heat and simmer for 15 minutes.

Add the cinnamon, onions, clove, allspice, and peppercorns and simmer for 10 minutes. Add the oil, oregano, and a pinch of salt and simmer for another 10 minutes.

Remove the pan from the heat, remove and discard the mixed herbs and cinnamon stick, and let the sauce stand for 2 hours. Store in the refrigerator.

Stuffed Avocados

STUFFED AVOCADOS

4 ripe avocados
juice of 1 lemon
3½ oz/100 g panela or mild
   feta, diced
⅓ cup (2 oz/50 g) green peas,
   barely cooked
1 tomato, peeled, seeded,
   and chopped
sea salt and pepper

REGION: MICHOACÁN
PREPARATION TIME: 20 MINUTES
SERVES: 4

Cut the avocados in half lengthwise and remove the pit. Scoop out most of the flesh from the avocado halves, leaving a ½-inch (1-cm) layer on the shell. Carefully peel off the skins from the avocados, and sprinkle with lemon juice and salt.

Combine the avocado flesh, cheese, peas, tomato, and mayonnaise in a bowl and season with salt and pepper. Fill the avocado halves with this mixture.

Place the avocado halves on a platter and serve immediately.

REGIONAL WATERCRESS

9 oz/250 g bacon, chopped
6 bunches watercress, washed
   and stems removed
¾ cup (3½ oz/100 g) pine nuts
½ cup (2 oz/50 g) chopped
   walnuts
1½ teaspoons Worcestershire
   sauce
juice of 2 lemons
sea salt

REGION: ALL REGIONS
PREPARATION TIME: 10 MINUTES
COOKING TIME: 7 MINUTES
SERVES: 6

Fry the bacon in a saucepan over medium heat for 7 minutes or until browned and crisp. Drain and set aside.

Put the watercress leaves into a salad bowl, add the bacon, pine nuts, walnuts, Worcestershire sauce, and lemon juice, and mix until everything is combined. Season with salt to taste and serve.

CALABACITAS RELLENAS DE FLOR DE CALABAZA

✺

ZUCCHINI STUFFED WITH FLOWERS

6 zucchini (courgettes)
3 tablespoons (1½ oz/40 g) butter or corn oil
2 white onions, finely chopped
2 cloves garlic, finely chopped
2 small tomatoes, finely chopped
1 lb/450 g zucchini (courgettes) flowers, stems removed and chopped
½ cup (4 fl oz/120 ml) light (single) cream
1 cup (3½ oz/100 g) finely grated Chihuahua cheese
sea salt and pepper

REGION: MICHOACAN, FEDERAL DISTRICT
PREPARATION TIME: 35 MINUTES
COOKING TIME: 40 MINUTES
SERVES: 6

Cut the zucchini (courgette) in half lengthwise and put them into a wide saucepan, cut side facing down. Add enough water to cover, add some salt, bring to a boil and over low heat for 8 minutes. Turn over and cook for an additional 5 minutes or until they are tender. Drain and cool.

Preheat the oven at 375°F (190°C/Gas Mark 5).

Remove the seeds and flesh from the zucchini shells, and set the flesh aside. Put the zucchini shells upside down in a large Dutch oven or casserole dish and set aside.

Heat the oil in a saucepan over medium heat, add the onions and garlic, and sauté for 5 minutes, or until translucent. Add the tomatoes, season with salt, and cook for another 4 minutes. Add the zucchini flesh and stir until the mixture is almost dry. Season to taste with salt and pepper.

Add the chopped zucchini flowers to the pan, then cover, and continue to cook for 2–3 minutes until the mixture is moist but not juicy. Check the seasoning and set aside.

Turn the zucchini around and, using a teaspoon, fill the cavities with the stuffing. Pour the cream over the squash, then sprinkle with the cheese to cover. Bake for 10 minutes, or until the cheese has melted, then serve.

CALABACITAS EN ADOBO

MARINATED SQUASH

5 pasilla chiles, dry-roasted
6 pattypan squash
2 cloves garlic
3 white onions, 2 chopped
1 cinnamon stick
3 cloves
4 black peppercorns
6 tablespoons apple cider
  vinegar
4 tablespoons corn oil
1 avocado
2 tablespoons sesame seeds,
  toasted
salt

REGION: ALL REGIONS
PREPARATION TIME: 20 MINUTES, PLUS 15 MINUTES
SOAKING AND 24 HOURS MARINATING
COOKING TIME: 30 MINUTES
SERVES: 6

In a small bowl, combine the chiles and enough hot water to cover them and soak for 15 minutes.

Bring a medium saucepan of water to a boil, add the squash and a pinch of salt, and cook for 10 minutes. Transfer the vegetables to a dish.

Put the chiles, garlic, chopped onion, cinnamon, cloves, peppercorns, a pinch of salt, 3 tablespoons of the vinegar, and ½ cup (4 fl oz/120 ml) water into a food processor or blender, and process until thoroughly combined. Strain into a bowl.

Scrape the mixture into a saucepan and simmer over medium heat for 10 minutes. Remove the pan from the heat and stir in the oil. Pour the mixture over the squash, cover the dish with plastic wrap (clingfilm), and marinate in the refrigerator for 24 hours.

Slice the remaining onion and put the slices into a small saucepan. Add the remaining vinegar, a pinch of salt, and 3 tablespoons water. Bring to a boil and cook for 2 minutes. Remove the pan from the heat and pour the mixture into a dish. Cover with plastic wrap and set aside until required.

When ready to serve, peel, pit, and slice the avocado. Plate the squash or zucchini and garnish with the avocado slices and the pickled onion. Sprinkle with sesame seeds and serve.

ZUCCHINI WITH SHRIMP

1 lb 2 oz/500 g dried shrimp (prawns)
4 tablespoons corn oil or lard
6 zucchini (courgettes), sliced
3 tomatoes, finely chopped
1 small white onion, finely chopped
1 serrano chile, finely chopped
sea salt and pepper

REGION: ALL REGIONS
PREPARATION TIME: 10 MINUTES, PLUS 15 MINUTES SOAKING
COOKING TIME: 20 MINUTES
SERVES: 6

Put the dried shrimp (prawns) in a bowl, pour in enough warm water to cover, and let soak for 15 minutes. Put the shrimp with the soaking liquid into a food processor or blender and process until smooth.

Heat the oil or lard in a saucepan over medium heat. Add the zucchini (courgettes), shrimp puree, tomatoes, onion, chile, and season with salt and pepper to taste. Cook for 20 minutes, or until the zucchini are tender. Serve hot.

MEXICAN-STYLE ZUCCHINI

2 tablespoons corn oil
½ white onion, finely chopped
¾ cup (4 oz/120 g) corn kernels
4 zucchini (courgettes), chopped
1 chile, finely chopped
1 large tomato, roasted, peeled, seeded, and diced
1 sprig epazote
sea salt

To garnish:
sour cream
grated fresh cheese

REGION: ALL REGIONS
PREPARATION TIME: 10 MINUTES
COOKING TIME: 20 MINUTES
SERVES: 6

Heat the oil in a saucepan over medium heat, add the onion and cook for 5 minutes, or until transparent but not golden. Add the corn, zucchini (courgettes), chile, tomatoes, and epazote, then season to taste with salt. Cook for 15 minutes or until the zucchini are tender. Transfer to a serving dish, pour over the cream, sprinkle the grated cheese over the top, and serve.

ZUCCHINI FROM MICHOACÁN

3 tablespoons corn oil
6 zucchini (courgettes), diced
2 cloves garlic, coarsely
    chopped
1 white onion, coarsely
    chopped
5 tablespoons chopped cilantro
    (coriander)
4 poblano chiles, dry-roasted
    and sliced
1 cup (8 fl oz/225 g) sour cream
½ cup (2 oz/50 g) finely grated
    queso añejo or mild cheddar
    cheese
sea salt

REGION: MICHOACÁN
PREPARATION TIME: 20 MINUTES
COOKING TIME: 25 MINUTES
SERVES: 6

Heat the oil in a heavy saucepan. Add the zucchini (courgettes), sprinkle with salt, and cook over medium heat, stirring occasionally, for 5 minutes, until almost cooked but not soft.

Meanwhile, put the garlic, onion, and cilantro (coriander) into a food processor or blender, add ½ cup (4 fl oz/120 ml) water, and process until smooth. Add the chiles in batches, processing until smooth. Strain into a bowl.

Stir this mixture into the zucchini and simmer for 20 minutes. Taste and adjust the seasoning, if necessary.

Remove the pan from the heat and transfer the mixture to a serving platter. Drizzle with the sour cream and grated cheese and serve immediately.

CALABACITAS RELLENAS DE ELOTE

※

ZUCCHINI STUFFED WITH CORN

6 round zucchini (courgettes)
2 tablespoons corn oil
2 white onions, chopped
1 tablespoon finely chopped
  garlic
2 tomatoes, peeled, poached,
  seeded, and chopped
¼ teaspoon sea salt
1½ cups (6 oz/175 g) corn
  kernels, cooked
pinch of dried oregano
pinch of dried thyme
pinch of dried basil
½ cup (2 oz/50 g) diced panela
  or mozzarella cheese
tomato sauce
sea salt

REGION: CENTRAL MEXICO
PREPARATION TIME: 25 MINUTES
COOKING TIME: 20 MINUTES
SERVES: 3

Bring a saucepan of water with a pinch of salt to a boil over high heat. Meanwhile, cut off the top quarter of each zucchini (courgette). Scoop out as much flesh as possible from both parts of each zucchini with a spoon, without piercing the shells. Reserve the flesh on a plate.

When the water is boiling, add both parts of the zucchini to the pan and cook for 5 minutes. Remove the pan from the heat, drain, and set the zucchini aside.

Heat the oil in a frying pan or skillet over high heat. Add the onion and garlic and cook, stirring frequently, for 2 minutes. Add the tomatoes and salt and cook for 4 minutes. Add the corn kernels, the flesh you removed from the zucchini, oregano, thyme, and basil, and cook for an additional 2 minutes. Stir in the cheese, remove the pan from the heat, and let cool.

Fill the large cavities in the zucchini with the corn stuffing and add the tops. Ladle warm tomato sauce on a plate, then place the zucchinis on top. Serve immediately.

Zucchini Stuffed with Corn

CALABACITAS RELLENAS EN CALDILLO ROJO

✺

STUFFED ZUCCHINI IN BROTH

6 zucchini (courgettes)
1 tablespoon corn oil
1 small onion, finely chopped
14 oz/400 g queso fresco or feta cheese, diced
all-purpose (plain) flour, for dusting
White Rice (page 521) or Corn Tortillas (page 36), to serve

For the sauce:
8 tomatoes, coarsely chopped
1 small onion, finely chopped
2 cloves garlic
1 tablespoon corn oil
2 bay leaves
1 sprig thyme
sea salt

REGION: MEXICO STATE
PREPARATION TIME: 30 MINUTES
COOKING TIME: 35 MINUTES
SERVES: 6

To make the sauce, put the tomatoes, onion, and garlic into a food processor or blender and process until thoroughly combined. Add a little water, if necessary, to get it going and process it into a fine paste. Strain into a bowl. Heat the oil in a large saucepan. Add the tomato mixture, bay leaves, thyme, and 2 cups (16 fl oz/475 ml) water. Simmer over medium heat for 15 minutes. Taste and add salt if necessary.

Cook the zucchini (courgettes) in a large saucepan of boiling water for 5 minutes until tender but not soft. Remove the pan from the heat, remove the zucchini, and let cool.

Cut the zucchini in half lengthwise. Scoop out the seeds and discard, then carefully scoop out most of the flesh, leaving the skin intact, and chop.

Heat the oil in a saucepan over medium heat, add the onion and cook over low heat, stirring occasionally, for 7 minutes, or until translucent. Add the flesh, season with salt and pepper, and cook for an additional 5 minutes. Remove the pan from the heat. Let cool and stir in the cheese.

Fill the cavities of the zucchinis with the cheese and the onion mixture and fit the halves back together.

Serve the stuffed zucchini with the sauce spooned over it. Serve with rice or tortillas.

CALABACITAS RELLENAS DE CARNE

✺

SQUASH STUFFED WITH MEAT

2 tablespoons long-grain rice
1–2 zucchini (courgettes),
   yellow squash, or summer
   squash
9 oz/250 g ground (minced)
   beef
½ teaspoon ground cumin
2 cloves garlic, finely chopped
4 tablespoons butter or corn
   oil
sea salt and pepper
pickled jalapeños, to garnish

For the sauce:
3 tomatoes, coarsely chopped
½ onion, coarsely chopped
2 cloves garlic, chopped
2 tablespoons corn oil
sea salt and pepper

REGION: COAHUILA
PREPARATION TIME: 20 MINUTES, PLUS
15 MINUTES SOAKING
COOKING TIME: 40 MINUTES
SERVES: 6

In a bowl, soak the rice in hot water for 15 minutes and drain.

To make the sauce, put the tomatoes, onion, and garlic into a food processor or blender and process until thoroughly combined. Add 1–2 tablespoons oil to loosen. Strain into a bowl.

Heat the oil in a large saucepan. Add the tomato mixture, season with salt and pepper, and cook over medium heat, stirring occasionally, for 10 minutes.

Pierce the squash several times with the tip of a sharp knife and cook it in a large saucepan of lightly salted, boiling water for 15 minutes, until tender. Remove the pan from the heat and drain the squash. Let cool completely.

Combine the beef, cumin, and garlic in a bowl and season with salt.

Heat the oil in a saucepan. Add the rice and cook over medium heat, gently stirring, for a few minutes until golden. Turn the heat up to medium-high, add the meat mixture, season with salt and pepper, and cook, stirring frequently, for 5 minutes until lightly browned. Remove the pan from the heat.

Cut off a lengthwise slice from each zucchini, deep enough to just expose the seeds. Set this slice aside. Remove the seeds and some of the flesh and discard the seeds. Chop the flesh and put it into the pan with the beef. Give the beef mixture a good stir and then spoon it into the cavity of the zucchini. Put the reserved slice back in position and secure with toothpicks or cocktail sticks through the edges zucchini at all 4 "corners."

Return the zucchini to the pan with the sauce and simmer for 10 minutes, turning it regularly. Remove the pan from the heat.

Transfer the zucchini to a serving plate and open it up, placing the slice on the side to reveal the stuffing. Drizzle with the sauce and serve with pickled jalapeños.

Chilacayotes in Red Pipian

CHILACAYOTES IN RED PIPIAN

3 pasilla chiles, seeded,
 dry-roasted
4 round zucchini (courgettes)
1 cup (4 oz/125 g) pumpkin
 seeds, hulled and toasted
½ cup (3½ oz/50 g) sesame
 seeds, lightly toasted
1 Corn Tortilla (page 36),
 toasted
2 tomatoes, dry-roasted
½ onion, dry-roasted
2 cloves garlic, dry-roasted
1 cinnamon stick
1 tablespoon lard
2 cups (16 fl oz/475 ml) Chicken
 Stock (page 184) (optional)
sea salt and pepper
2 tablespoons sesame seeds,
 lightly toasted, to garnish

REGION: ALL REGIONS
PREPARATION TIME: 50 MINUTES, PLUS
15 MINUTES SOAKING
COOKING TIME: 20 MINUTES
SERVES: 6

In a small bowl, combine the chiles and enough hot water to cover them and soak for 15 minutes.

Cook the zucchini (courgettes) in a saucepan of boiling salted water for 15 minutes, or until tender but not mushy. Drain and set aside.

For the red pipian sauce, put the chiles, pumpkin seeds, sesame seeds, tortilla, tomatoes, onion, garlic, pepper to taste, cinnamon stick, and 1 cup (9 fl oz/250 ml) stock into a food processor or blender and process until smooth.

Put the lard in a pan and heat over medium heat for until brown. Add the paste and cook for another 5 minute, then gradually pour in the chicken stock if needed, to make a sauce. Season with salt, add the zucchini to the sauce, then serve with toasted sesame seeds.

PASILLA CHILES WITH CHEESE

2 tablespoons olive oil
2 white onions, finely chopped
6 tomatoes, seeded and
 chopped finely
22 pasilla chiles, dry-roasted
1½ lb/700 g Oaxaca or
 mozzarella cheese, cut into
 thin strips
salt
Flour Tortillas (page 37),
 to serve

REGION: CHIHUAHUA, OAXACA, PUEBLA
PREPARATION TIME: 15 MINUTES, PLUS
15 MINUTES SOAKING
COOKING TIME: 25 MINUTES
SERVES: 6

In a small bowl, combine the chiles and enough hot water to cover them and soak for 15 minutes.

Heat the oil in a saucepan over low heat. Add the onions and sweat them, with the lid on, for 10 minutes.

Add the tomatoes and chiles, stir, and cook for 5 minutes. Pour in the chile water, bring to a boil, and reduce the heat and season to taste. Lay the cheese on top of the liquid and let simmer until the cheese begins to melt.

Remove the pan from the heat serve immediately with warm tortillas.

CHILES RELLENOS DE UCHEPOS

STUFFED CHILE WITH CORN TAMALES

6 tablespoons (3 oz/80 g) butter
6 pasilla chiles, membranes
  and seeds removed
6 tablespoons corn oil
2 tablespoons apple cider
  vinegar
6 Sweet Corn Tamales (page
  641)
¼ cup (1½ oz/40 g) raisins
12 almonds, blanched and
  ground
3 tablespoons sour cream
6 tablespoons cream mixed
  with 3 drops of red coloring
sea salt and pepper

REGION: MICHOACAN
PREPARATION TIME: 10 MINUTES
COOKING TIME: 20 MINUTES
SERVES: 6

Melt 4 tablespoons butter in a skillet or frying pan over medium heat, add the chiles, and fry for 5 minutes.

Put the oil, vinegar, and salt and pepper to taste into a bowl and stir until combined. Add the vinaigrette to the chiles in the pan, reduce the heat to low, and cook gently for 5 minutes.

Break the corn tamales into uneven pieces. Heat the remaining butter in another frying pan or skillet over medium heat. Add the tamal pieces and cook for 5 minutes, then stir in the raisins, almonds, and sour cream and remove from the heat.

Remove the chiles from the vinaigrette with a slotted spoon and, using a teaspoon, stuff the chiles with the tamal mixture. Serve on a platter, garnished with the pink cream.

CALABACITAS CON HONGOS

ZUCCHINI WITH MUSHROOMS

3½ tablespoons vegetable oil
¼ white onion, finely chopped
1 large poblano chile, dry-
  roasted and cut into strips
3 zucchini (courgettes), diced
4 cups (8 oz/225 g) mushrooms,
  chopped
4 tablespoons cilantro
  (coriander), coarsely chopped
½–¾ cup (4–6 fl oz/120–175 ml)
  light (single) cream
4 oz/115 g fresh cheese, finely
  sliced
sea salt

REGIONS: FEDERAL DISTRICT, PUEBLA
PREPARATION TIME: 15 MINUTES
COOKING TIME: 25 MINUTES
SERVES: 6

Heat 2 tablespoons of the oil in the saucepan over medium heat, add the onion, chile, and a sprinkling of salt, and sauté for 1 minute without browning. Add the zucchini (courgettes), cover, and cook an additional 10 minutes, stirring occasionally, until the zucchini is almost tender.

Meanwhile, mix the mushrooms with the remaining oil in a bowl. Sprinkle with salt and sauté in another saucepan for 5 minutes. Add the mushrooms to the squash, sprinkle with cilantro (coriander), then add the cream and cheese. Cover the pan, reduce the heat to low, and cook for 5 minutes or until the cheese melts. Serve immediately.

CHAYA LEAVES WITH SQUASH

1 lb 2 oz/500 g chaya leaves
3 squash, diced
1 tablespoon corn oil
1 white onion, chopped
1 cup (5 oz/100 g) corn kernels
   cooked
3 tomatillos, chopped
salt and pepper

REGION: ALL REGIONS
PREPARATION TIME: 10 MINUTES
COOKING TIME: 1 HOUR
SERVES: 6

Bring a pan of water to a boil, add the chaya leaves, and simmer for 20 minutes or until the leaves are tender. Remove the pan from the heat, drain the leaves, and chop.

Heat the oil in a medium pan. Add the chaya leaves, squash, onion, corn kernels, and tomatillos, season with salt and pepper, and cook over low heat, stirring occasionally, for 30 minutes or until all the ingredients are cooked through.

Remove the pan from the heat and serve immediately.

PUEBLAN VEGETABLE MEDLEY

1 teaspoon sea salt
½ teaspoon baking soda
   (bicarbonate of soda)
3 potatoes, diced
2¼ cups (9 oz/250 g) shelled
   peas
2 cups (9 oz /250 g) fresh fava
   (broad) beans, peeled
1⅓ cups (9 oz/250 g) green
   beans, cut into ½-inch (1-cm)
   lengths
1 large zucchini (courgette),
   diced
4 poblano chiles, dry-roasted
   and sliced
4 tablespoons olive oil
1 white onion, sliced
1 sprig epazote
sea salt
White Rice (see page 521),
   to serve

REGION: PUEBLA
PREPARATION TIME: 15 MINUTES
COOKING TIME: 30 MINUTES
SERVES: 6

Pour 8¾ cups (3½ pints/2 liters) water into a saucepan, add the salt and baking soda, and bring to a boil. Add the potatoes and simmer for 15 minutes, then add the peas, fava (broad) beans, and green beans. Simmer for an additional 5 minutes, then add the peas and zucchini (courgette), and simmer for an additional 5 minutes. Drain.

Meanwhile, heat the oil in another pan. Add the onion and cook over low heat, stirring occasionally, for 5 minutes. Add the chiles and cook for 5 minutes more.

Add the drained vegetables to the pan of onion and chiles, together with the epazote leaves. Cook for an additional 5 minutes, stirring gently, and remove the pan from the heat.

Taste and adjust the seasoning if necessary, and serve immediately with white rice.

CHAYOTES WITH GUAJILLO SAUCE

4 tablespoons (2 oz/50 g)
   butter, diced, plus extra
   for greasing
4 tomatoes
¼ white onion
2 cloves garlic
6 chayotes, sliced
2 guajillo chiles, seeded and
   deveined
1 tablespoon chopped cilantro
   (coriander), to serve
salt and pepper

REGION: ALL REGIONS
PREPARATION TIME: 15 MINUTES, PLUS
10 MINUTES SOAKING
COOKING TIME: 10 MINUTES
SERVES: 6

In a small bowl, combine the chiles and enough hot water to cover them and soak for 10 minutes.

Put the tomatoes, onion, garlic, and chile into the food processor or blender and process until smooth. Strain into a bowl and reserve.

Preheat the oven to 350°F (180°C/Gas Mark 4). Grease an ovenproof dish with butter.

Put the chayote slices into the prepared dish, season with salt and pepper, and cover with the sauce.

Bake for 10 minutes. Remove from the oven, sprinkle with the cilantro (coriander), and serve immediately.

CHAYOTES WITH CREAM

2 tablespoons corn oil
3 tablespoons finely chopped
   white onion
2 cloves garlic, finely chopped
1 serrano chile, finely chopped
1 lb 5 oz/600 g chayotes, peeled
   and thinly sliced
1 cup (8 fl oz/225 g) cream or
   sour cream
sea salt and pepper

REGION: QUERETARO
PREPARATION TIME: 15 MINUTES
COOKING TIME: 25 MINUTES, PLUS
15 MINUTES STANDING
SERVES: 6

Heat the oil in a pan over medium heat, add the onion, garlic, and chile, sprinkle with salt, and sauté for 1 minute. Add the chayote slices in 2 layers, then season with pepper, pour in ½ cup (4 fl oz/120 ml) water and a pinch of salt. Cover with a lid and cook over medium heat for 8 minutes, or until all the water has evaporated and the chayotes are al dente.

If there is still some liquid left in the pan, remove it, then add the cream. Cover the pan and cook over medium heat for 15 minutes, or until the chayotes are tender. Remove from the heat and let stand for 15 minutes before serving.

Chayotes with Guajillo Sauce

※

PICADILLO-STUFFED JALAPENOS

16 large jalapeño chiles,
  dry-roasted

For the picadillo:
½ cup (4 fl oz/120 ml) olive oil
1 large skinless, chicken breast,
  diced
½ white onion, chopped
1 clove garlic
4 tomatoes, chopped
½ bunch parsley, chopped
¾ cup (2¾ oz/75 g) almonds,
  blanched and chopped
½ cup raisins, chopped
½ cup (2 oz/50 g) green olives,
  chopped
2 large carrots, finely chopped
5 bay leaves
sea salt and pepper

REGION: VERACRUZ
PREPARATION TIME: 50 MINUTES, PLUS
15 MINUTES SOAKING
COOKING TIME: 20 MINUTES
SERVES: 6–8

Peel the chiles, carefully cut a slit along the length of them and remove the seeds.

To make the picadillo, heat 1 tablespoon oil in a frying pan or skillet, add the chicken breast, season with salt and pepper, cook for 7 minutes, and then drain and let cool. Put the chicken in a food processor or blender and process until smooth.

Heat 3 tablespoons oil in a saucepan over medium heat, add the onion and garlic, and sauté for 2 minutes. Add the tomatoes, parsley, almonds, raisins, and olives and cook for 10 minutes, stirring, until fragrant. Add the chicken, then season with salt to taste, and remove from the heat.

Using a teaspoon, fill the chiles with the picadillo mixture and arrange on a platter.

Picadillo-Stuffed Jalapenos

✳

PLANTAIN-STUFFED CHILES

6 pasilla chiles, dry-roasted

3 plantains, unpeeled

2 tablespoons corn oil, plus extra for deep-frying

¼ white onion, finely chopped

1 clove garlic, finely chopped

9 oz/250 g ground (minced) beef

2 tablespoons olives, finely chopped

10 almonds, blanched and finely chopped

2 tablespoons finely chopped parsley

1 cup (5 oz/150 g) tomato paste (puree)

⅛ teaspoon ground cloves

pinch of ground cinnamon

½ cup (2 oz/60 g) all-purpose (plain) flour

sea salt and pepper

REGION: GULF
PREPARATION TIME: 30 MINUTES, PLUS
15 MINUTES SOAKING
COOKING TIME: 1 HOUR
SERVES: 6

Put the chiles in a small bowl, add enough hot water to cover them, and soak for 15 minutes.

Put 2 unpeeled plantains and cook in a saucepan of boiling salted water for 20 minutes, or until the plantains expand by about ¼ inch (4 mm) over the skin. Remove the plantains from the water, peel, put the flesh in a bowl, and crush with a fork to form a paste. Let cool and set aside.

Heat the oil in a frying pan or skillet over medium heat, add the onion, and sauté for 5 minutes, or until translucent. Add the garlic and sauté for an additional minute. Add the meat and sauté for 3–5 minutes, or until is cooked the meat starts to brown. Add the olives and almonds and cook for another 3 minutes. Add the parsley, tomato paste (puree), salt, pepper, cloves, and cinnamon and cook for 15 minutes, stirring occasionally until the mixture is dry. Check the seasoning and remove from the heat.

Using a teaspoon, fill the chiles with the meat mixture, then sprinkle with the flour and coat in with the plantain paste until the chiles are covered.

Heat enough oil for deep-frying or deep heavy saucepan to 375°F (190°C) or until a cube of day-old bread browns in 30 seconds. Carefully lower the stuffed chiles into the hot oil, in batches, and deep-fry for 2 minutes on each side or until brown. Remove with a slotted spoon and drain on paper towels. Keep warm.

Serve the stuffed chiles with refried beans.

CHILES FROM VERACRUZ

6 large dried chipotle chiles,
  membranes and seeds
  removed
2 tablespoons corn oil, plus
  extra for deep-frying
½ white onion, finely chopped
3 cloves garlic, crushed
2 tomatoes, peeled, seeded,
  and finely chopped
10 olives, chopped
6 capers, chopped
4 tablespoons raisins
3½ cups (1 lb 2 oz/500 g)
  cooked meat (beef, pork, or
  chicken), chopped
½ cup (2 oz/60 g) all-purpose
  (plain) flour
3 eggs, separated
sea salt and pepper

To serve:
White Rice (page 521)
Pot Beans (page 533)

REGION: VERACRUZ
PREPARATION TIME: 35 MINUTES, PLUS
20 MINUTES SOAKING
COOKING TIME: 35 MINUTES
SERVES: 6

Put the chiles in a small bowl, add enough hot water to cover them, and soak for 15 minutes.

Heat the oil in a pan over medium heat. Add the onion and sauté for 5 minutes. Add the garlic, tomatoes, olives, capers, and raisins and cook for another 5 minutes. Add the meat, season with salt and pepper, then reduce the heat to low and cook for 15 minutes or until the mixture is slightly dry.

Using a teaspoon, stuff the chiles with the meat mixture, then sprinkle with some flour and set aside.

Heat enough oil for deep-frying to 350°F/180°C or until a cube of day-old bread browns in 30 seconds.

Meanwhile, beat the egg whites in a bowl until soft peaks form. Add the egg yolks and a little salt and pepper and gently fold into the egg whites.

Dip the stuffed chiles into the egg mixture until well coated, then add them to the hot oil and deep-fry for 2 minutes on each side or until pale golden. Remove with a slotted spoon and drain well on paper towels.

Serve with white rice and pot beans.

Cheese-Stuffed Ancho Chile

CHILE ANCHO RELLENO DE QUESO

CHEESE-STUFFED ANCHO CHILE

6 ancho chiles
1 cup (9 fl oz/250 ml) apple
    cider vinegar
1 cup (9 fl oz/250 ml) freshly
    squeezed orange juice
½ lb (250 g) piloncillo or 1
    packed cup (8 oz/220 g)
    packed dark brown sugar
5 cloves garlic
1 bay leaf
1 teaspoon dried oregano
1 teaspoon dried thyme
2 tablespoons vegetable oil
2¼ lb/1 kg grated cheese
sea salt, to taste
1 avocado, peeled, pitted,
    and sliced

REGION: CENTRAL MEXICO
PREPARATION TIME: 20 MINUTES
COOKING TIME: 35 MINUTES
SERVES: 6

Keeping the stem intact, make a lengthwise slit in each chile and remove the seeds and membranes.

In a saucepan over medium heat, combine the vinegar, orange juice, piloncillo or brown suar, garlic, bay leaf, thyme, and oregano and cook until the sugar dissolves. Remove from the heat. Add the chiles and soak for 10–15 minutes, or until soft.

With a slotted spoon, transfer the chiles to a plate lined with paper towels. Strain the cooking liquid and pour it back into the saucepan. Simmer for 5 minutes or until it has the consistency of a light sauce. Remove it from heat and adjust the seasoning, adding some cider vinegar or salt to taste.

Preheat the oven to 375°F (180°C/Gas Mark 4)

Carefully stuff the chiles with the cheese. Arrange the stuffed chiles, seam-side open, in a baking dish, and bake for 15 minutes or until the cheese starts to melt. Reheat the sauce. Serve a chile on each plate and garnish with the avocado slices. Serve the sauce on the side.

ELOTES A LA
PARRILA CON
AJO ASADO

❄

BROILED CORN
WITH GARLIC

2 heads roasted garlic
grated zest of 1 lemon
1 tablespoon butter
4 tablespoons finely chopped
  cilantro (coriander)
4 tablespoons chopped
  tarragon
4 teaspoons extra-virgin
  olive oil
6 corn on the cobs
sea salt and pepper

REGION: FEDERAL DISTRCT
PREPARATION TIME: 20 MINUTES
COOKING TIME: 40 MINUTES
SERVES: 6

Preheat the oven to 350°F (180°C/Gas Mark 4). Squeeze out the garlic cloves into a small bowl and combine with the lemon zest, butter, cilantro (coriander), tarragon, and the remaining oil. Season with salt and pepper.

Preheat the broiler (grill) to low and line a broiler (grill) pan with aluminum foil. Gently pull the husks of the corn back, but do not remove them. Spread the garlic mixture all over the kernels. Wrap the leaves back around the corn and tie with kitchen string, then wrap in aluminum foil.

Broil (grill) the corn on the cobs, turning frequently, for about 30 minutes, until the kernels are tender. Remove the broiler pan from the oven and remove and discard the foil. Return the cobs to the broiler pan, increase the heat slightly, and cook for an additional few minutes until the leaves begin to char. Remove the pan from the heat and serve the corn immediately. You can also do this on the barbeque.

CHILE STRIPS
WITH CORN

6 tablespoons (3 oz/80 g)
  butter, melted
4 tablespoons corn oil
1 clove garlic
1 white onion, thinly sliced
1 cup (6 oz/175 g) corn kernels
14 poblano peppers, dry-
  roasted and cut into strips
¼ cup (2 fl oz/60 ml) milk
1 cup (8 fl oz/225 g) sour cream
1 cup (8 oz/225 g) shredded
  Oaxaca cheese
Corn Tortillas (page 36),
  to serve
sea salt

REGION: FALTA
PREPARATION TIME: 20 MINUTES, PLUS
15 MINUTES SOAKING
COOKING TIME: 30 MINUTES
SERVES: 6

Put the chiles in a small bowl, add enough hot water to cover them, and soak for 15 minutes.

Preheat the oven to 350°F (180°C/Gas Mark 4).

Heat the butter and oil in a large saucepan over medium heat and swirl to mix. Add the garlic and sauté for 1–2 minutes until browned. Add the onion and corn kernels to the pan and cook for 5 minutes, or until the onion is cooked. Add three-quarters of the chile strips and cook for an additional 5 minutes, then remove from the heat and set aside.

Put the remaining chiles into a food processor or blender, add the milk and salt to taste, and process until smooth.

Arrange both mixtures in separate layers in a baking pan. Pour the sour cream over the top and sprinkle the top with the shredded cheese. Bake in the oven for about 15 minutes or until the cheese has melted, then serve with warmed tortillas.

GREEN BEANS
WITH OREGANO

1 lb 8½ oz/700 g green beans
½ cup (2 oz/50g) panela cheese
  or mild feta

For the oregano vinaigrette:
¼ cup (2 fl oz/60 ml) apple
  cider vinegar
½ cup (4 fl oz/120 ml) extra-
  virgin olive oil
½ teaspoon sugar
½ tablespoon dried oregano
¼ teaspoon coarse sea salt
pepper

REGION: ALL REGIONS
PREPARATION TIME: 10 MINUTES
COOKING TIME: 10 MINUTES
SERVES: 6

Put the beans into a pan, pour in enough water to cover, and bring to a boil over medium heat. Reduce the heat to low and simmer gently for 5 minutes, or until tender. Strain.

In a bowl, combine the beans and cheese. Put the vinegar, olive oil, sugar, oregano, salt, and pepper in another bowl and beat well. Pour the vinaigrette over the beans and cheese and mix gently. Serve warm.

EJOTES CON NATA

GREEN BEANS WITH CREAM

2 tablespoons (1 oz/30 g)
   butter, plus extra for greasing
5 cups (1 lb 2 oz/500 g) green
   beans, cut into short lengths
1 cup (8 oz/225 g) sour cream
⅓ cup (2 oz/50 g) panela cheese
   or mild feta, crumbled
1½ teaspoons dried oregano

REGION: ALL REGIONS
PREPARATION TIME: 10 MINUTES
COOKING TIME: 20 MINUTES
SERVES: 6

Preheat the oven to 350°F (180°C/Gas Mark 4).
Grease an ovenproof dish with butter.

Cook the beans in a saucepan of lightly salted
boiling water for 10 minutes. Remove the pan from
the heat and drain well.

Put the beans in the bottom of the prepared
dish, pour the sour cream over them, sprinkle with
crumbled cheese, and dot with butter.

Bake for about 10 minutes and serve immediately.

COLIFLOR CON TOMATE Y ALCARPARRAS

CAULIFLOWER WITH TOMATO AND CAPERS

For the dressing:
1 tablespoon aged mustard
2 tablespoons capers, drained
   and coarsely chopped
2 tablespoons apple cider
   vinegar
2 cloves garlic, crushed
½ cup (4 fl oz/120 ml) olive oil
sea salt and pepper

For the cauliflower:
1 small cauliflower, cut into
   florets
1 tablespoon chopped dill
2 cups (2 oz/50 g) baby
   spinach, coarsely chopped
20 cherry tomatoes, halved

REGION: FALTA
PREPARATION TIME: 20 MINUTES
COOKING TIME: 20 MINUTES
SERVES: 4

For the dressing, mix the mustard, capers, vinegar,
and garlic together in a bowl, then add salt and
pepper to taste. Whisk and gradually add half of the
oil in a thin, steady stream until thick and creamy.
Check the seasoning.

Fill a large bowl with ice water. Cook the
cauliflower florets in a saucepan of boiling water
for 5 minutes. Drain and put in the iced water to
stop the cooking process. Drain again and let dry.

Put the cauliflower into a bowl, add the remaining
olive oil, and season with salt and pepper. Mix well
until everything is combined.

Heat a ridged grill (griddle) pan over high heat
for 5 minutes until it is very hot. Add the cauliflower
florets, in batches, in a single layer, and cook for
12 minutes, turning over, until the cauliflower is
tender and has grill marks from the pan on all sides.
Remove from the pan and put into a bowl, then
repeat until all the cauliflower has been grilled.

Add the dressing, dill, spinach, and tomatoes
to the hot cauliflower and mix carefully. Check the
seasoning and serve at room temperature.

Green Beans with Cream

PASTEL DE MILPA

VEGETABLE CASSEROLE

butter, for greasing
3 zucchini (courgettes), sliced
6 cups (2¼ lb/1 kg) corn
  kernels
⅔ cup (¼ pint/150 ml) corn oil
6 poblano chiles, dry-roasted
  and sliced
18 Corn Tortillas (page 36)
1 lb 2 oz/600 g zucchini
  (courgette) flowers, pistils
  removed, cut into thin strips
20 epazote leaves, chopped
½ cup (4 oz/120 g) sour cream
sea salt

REGION: FEDERAL DISTRICT
PREPARATION TIME: 25 MINUTES
COOKING TIME: 40 MINUTES
SERVES: 6–8

Preheat the oven to 350°F (180°C/Gas Mark 4). Grease a deep ovenproof dish with butter.

Bring a saucepan of water to a boil over high heat. Add the zucchini (courgette) slices and a pinch of salt. Bring back to a boil, then reduce the heat and cook for 5 minutes. Remove the pan from the heat and set aside.

Heat 2 tablespoons of the oil in a frying pan or skillet. Add the chiles and cook over low heat, stirring occasionally, for 5 minutes. Remove the pan from the heat and season with salt.

Heat the remaining oil in a saucepan, then remove from the heat and pass the tortillas through it to soften. Make a layer of tortillas in the bottom of the prepared dish, add a layer of zucchini (courgette) flowers, cover with a layer of corn and zucchini slices, top with chiles, and sprinkle with epazote. Repeat these layers until all the ingredients have been used, ending with a layer of tortillas.

Pour the sour cream over the final layer and bake for 30 minutes. Let cool slightly, then serve warm.

HONGOS AL AJILLO

MUSHROOMS WITH GARLIC

1 cup (9 fl oz/250 ml) olive oil
3 cloves garlic, dry-roasted
  and sliced
5 guajillo chiles, membranes
  and seeds removed and sliced
¼ cup (2 fl oz/60 ml) white
  wine
1 lb 10 oz/750 g assorted
  mushrooms, sliced
2 tablespoons lime juice
sea salt

REGION: OAXACA
PREPARATION TIME: 15 MINUTES
COOKING TIME: 12 MINUTES
SERVES: 6

Heat the olive oil in a frying pan or skillet over medium heat, add the garlic, and sauté for 6 minutes, or until golden and fragrant. Add the sliced chiles and cook for an additional 1 minute, then add the white wine, season with salt and pepper, and cook for another 2 minutes or until the alcohol has evaporated. Add the mushrooms and sauté for an additional 1 minute. Season with lime juice and serve immediately.

Mushrooms with Garlic

CACEROLA DE HONGOS AMARILLOS

✺

CHANTERELLE STEW

3 smoked chipotle chiles
  in adobo
15 tomatillos
1 clove garlic
1 tablespoon lard
4 oz (120 g) masa harina
2 sprigs epazote, chopped
1 lb 2 oz/500 g chanterelles or
  mushrooms, halved
sea salt
White Rice (page 521), and
  Corn Tortillas (page 36),
  to serve

REGION: VERACRUZ
PREPARATION TIME: 15 MINUTES
COOKING TIME: 30 MINUTES
SERVES: 6

Put the chiles, tomatillos, and garlic into a food processor or blender and process until combined.

Melt the lard in a saucepan. Add the chile mixture and 2 cups (16 fl oz/475 ml) water and cook over medium heat, stirring occasionally, for 5 minutes.

Combine the masa harina with 4 tablespoons water in a bowl and mix well. Strain to get rid of any lumps and add to the pan, then add the epazote and mushrooms and season with salt. Cover and cook over medium heat for 25 minutes or until slightly thickened. Taste and add more salt if necessary.

Remove the pan from the heat, transfer to a serving dish, and serve immediately with white rice and warm tortillas.

HONGOS A LA MEXICANA

✺

MEXICAN-STYLE MUSHROOMS

4 teaspoons corn oil or lard
1 small onion, chopped
3 cloves garlic, finely chopped
4 ripe tomatoes, dry-roasted
2 jalapeños, seeded and
  chopped
1 lb 2 oz/500 g assorted
  mushrooms, sliced
1 cup (7 oz/200 g) corn kernels
1 tablespoon chopped cilantro
  (coriander)
sea salt and pepper

REGION: ALL REGIONS
PREPARATION TIME: 10 MINUTES
COOKING TIME: 12 MINUTES
SERVES: 4

Heat the oil in a frying pan or skillet over medium heat, add the onion, and cook for 5 minutes or until soft and translucent. Add the garlic and sauté for 30 seconds, then add the tomatoes and jalapeños and cook for an additional 5 minutes. Season with salt and pepper, then scatter over the cilantro (coriander). Serve immediately.

Mexican-Style Mushrooms

ESCABECHE MORADO

※

RED ONION ESCABECHE

4 tablespoons olive oil
3–4 cloves garlic
½ teaspoon black peppercorns
5 cloves
1 cinnamon stick
2 bay leaves
5 red onions, thinly sliced
2 habanero chiles
½ cup (4½ fl oz/125 ml) apple
  cider vinegar
sea salt

REGION: YUCATAN, CAMPECHE
PREPARATION TIME: 10 MINUTES
COOKING TIME: 15 MINUTES
MAKES: 2 CUPS (16 FL OZ/475 ML)

Heat the olive oil in a pan. Add the garlic, peppercorns, cloves, cinnamon, and bay leaves and cook over low heat, stirring occasionally, until fragrant. Add the red onions and chiles and cook for another 10 minutes. Pour in the vinegar, season to taste with salt, and, if the mixture is too thick, stir in 4 tablespoons water. Remove the pan from the heat and let cool.

CHIPOTLES EN ESCABECHE

※

PICKLED CHIPOTLES

6–7 chipotle chiles
5 allspice berries
1 cinnamon stick
2 bay leaves
1 sprig thyme
2 small cloves garlic
5 scallions (spring onions)
½ teaspoon dried oregano
1 tablespoon sugar
2 cups (16 fl oz/475 ml) apple
  cider vinegar
sea salt

REGION: MEXICO CITY
PREPARATION TIME: 20 MINUTES, PLUS
24 HOURS STANDING
COOKING TIME: 30 MINUTES
MAKES: 4 CUPS (32 FL OZ/950 ML)

Bring 3 cups (1¼ pints/725 ml) water to a boil in a medium saucepan over low heat, add the chiles, and boil for about 20 minutes or until tender. Remove the pan from the heat and set aside for 24 hours.

The next day, drain the chiles. Put them into a pan, pour in 1 cup (9 fl oz/250 ml) water, and bring to a boil over low heat. Add the allspice, cinnamon, bay leaves, thyme, garlic, scallions (spring onions), oregano, and sugar, pour in the vinegar, season with salt, and simmer for about 5 minutes. Remove the pan from the heat and let cool.

When it is cold, transfer the mixture to a large sterilized glass jar, seal tightly with a lid, and set aside for 1 hour.

You can serve this with meat, fish, or poultry.

✺

PICKLED MUSHROOMS

1½ cups (12 fl oz/375 ml) olive oil

2 heads garlic, peeled

1 bunch scallions (spring onions), white part only

7 oz/200 g new potatoes, cooked

3 jalapeño chiles, seeded and cut into thin strips

1 cup (4 oz/125 g) cauliflower florets, blanched

2 green bell peppers, diced

2 red bell peppers, diced

14 oz/400 g mushrooms, cut into quarters

14 oz/400 g crimini (chestnut) or Portobello mushrooms, sliced

½ tablespoon sea salt

5 whole allspice peppers

5 black peppercorns

½ cup (4½ fl oz/125 ml) apple cider vinegar

REGION: CENTER
PREPARATION TIME: 15 MINUTES
COOKING TIME: 35 MINUTES
SERVES: 6

To confit the garlic, heat 1 cup (9 fl oz/250 ml) oil in a heavy pan over low heat, add the garlic and a pinch of salt, and cook gently for about 30 minutes, or until the garlic is tender and cooked. Remove from the heat and let cool. To store, using a slotted spoon, put the garlic into a sterilized jar, cover with the oil, and store in a cool place for up to a month.

Meanwhile, heat the remaining olive oil in a Dutch oven or casserole dish over medium heat. Add the scallions (spring onions), potatoes, chiles, and cauliflower, and sauté for 5 minutes. Add the peppers and mushrooms, and cook for an additional 5 minutes, then add the salt, allspice, black peppercorns, garlic confit, and vinegar. Cook over low heat for another 10 minutes until the vegetables are al dente. Serve at room temperature.

Huauzontles and Chile

HUAUZONTLES AND CHILE

6 pasilla chiles
2¼ lb/1 kg huauzontles
1 tomato
1 small white onion
2 cloves garlic
1½ cups (12 fl oz/350 ml)
  Chicken Stock (page 184)
all-purpose (plain) flour, for
  coating
5 eggs, separated
corn oil, for deep-frying
17½ oz/500 g fresh cheese,
  sliced
sea salt
1 cup (8 fl oz/225 ml) sour
  cream, to serve

REGION: AGUASCALIENTES
PREPARATION TIME: 30 MINUTES, PLUS
15 MINUTES SOAKING
COOKING TIME: 50 MINUTES
SERVES: 6

Put the chiles in a small bowl, add enough hot water to cover them, and soak for 15 minutes. Drain and set aside.

Cook the huauzontles in a saucepan of boiling salted water for 10 minutes, then drain and set aside.

Put the chiles, tomato, onion, and garlic into a food processor or blender and process until smooth, then strain. Put the chile paste into a large saucepan and cook over medium heat for 10 minutes. Add the chicken stock and season with salt to taste.

Spread the flour out on a plate, then put the egg yolks and whites into 2 shallow bowls and beat.

Heat enough oil for deep-frying to 350°F (180°C) until a cube of day-old bread browns in 30 seconds.

Place a slice of cheese in the center of each huauzontle, then dredge in the flour, shake off any excess, and cover with the beaten egg whites, then the egg yolks. Carefully lower the huauzontle into the hot oil and deep-fry for 2 minutes, or until golden brown. Remove with a slotted spoon and drain on paper towels.

Add the huauzontles to the chili sauce and simmer for 15 minutes, or until it thickens slightly. Serve immediately with the cream.

HUITLACOCHE GUISADO

STEWED CORN SMUT

3 tablespoons (1½ oz/40 g)
  butter
3 tablespoons corn oil
3 tablespoons finely chopped
  white onion
4 cloves garlic, finely chopped
1 serrano chile, seeded and
  chopped
2½ cups (1 lb 2 oz/500 g) corn
  smut, cleaned
sea salt

To serve:
12 Corn Tortillas (page 36)
Stewed Tomatillo Salsa
  (page 510)

REGION: CENTER
PREPARATION TIME: 10 MINUTES
COOKING TIME: 15 MINUTES
SERVES: 6

Heat the butter and oil in a saucepan over medium heat. Add the onion and garlic and sauté for 5 minutes. Do not let them brown. Add the chile and cook for 2 minutes. Add the corn smut and salt, stir, taking care not to break the corn smut, and cook for an additional 8 minutes. Cover with a lid and remove from the heat.

Serve with warm tortillas and tomatillo salsa.

NOPALITOS CON FRIJOLES

CACTUS PADDLES WITH BEANS

10 cactus paddles
3 tablespoons corn oil
1 small white onion, sliced
2 tablespoons chopped
  cilantro (coriander)
1 cup (7 oz/200 g) Refried
  Beans (page 532)
½ cup (2 oz/50 g) grated queso
  añejo or pecorino cheese
6–12 pickled jalapeños
sea salt

REGION: FEDERAL DISTRICT
PREPARATION TIME: 15 MINUTES
COOKING TIME: 30 MINUTES
SERVES: 6

Cut the cactus paddles into small squares. Bring plenty of water to a boil in a large saucepan. Add the cactus paddles and reduce the heat. Simmer gently for 20 minutes. Add a pinch of salt and remove the pan from the heat. Drain, rinse, cover with a damp dish towel, and let cool.

Heat the oil in a saucepan. Add the cactus paddles, onion, cilantro (coriander), and a pinch of salt and cook for 5 minutes.

Remove the pan from the heat and transfer the mixture to a serving dish. Serve immediately with refried beans, grated cheese, and pickled jalapeños.

YELLOW
POTATOES

9 oz/250 g beef ribs, cut into
   pieces

2 hoja santas, shredded

1½ potatoes, unpeeled and
   chopped into 1¼-inch (3-cm)
   cubes

5 guajillo chiles, membranes
   and seeds removed

¾ teaspoon cumin seeds,
   lightly ground

1 clove, ground

1 tablespoon dried oregano

6 cloves garlic, dry-roasted

1 cup (9 fl oz/250 ml) Beef
   Stock (page 185)

White Rice (see page 512),
   to serve

sea salt

REGION: OAXACA
PREPARATION TIME: 25 MINUTES, PLUS
15 MINUTES SOAKING
COOKING TIME: 2 HOURS
SERVES: 6

Put the meat into a large saucepan, add 10 cups
(just under 4½ pints/2.5 liters) water, the hoja santas,
and salt to taste, and bring to a boil over medium
heat. Boil for 40 minutes, or until tender. Remove
the meat from the stock with a slotted spoon and
set aside. Strain the stock to measure 8½ cups
(3½ pints/2 liters), adding water, if necessary, to
make up this quantity. Set aside. Return the meat
to the pan and set aside.

Meanwhile, put the potatoes into a saucepan,
cover with water, add salt, and bring to a boil over
medium heat. Cook for 10 minutes, or until tender,
then drain and peel. Return the potatoes to the pan
and mash with a potato masher until smooth. Pour
in 4 cups (1⅔ pints/950 ml) beef stock and stir until
it is a thick consistency, similar to atole (page 577).

Put the chiles in a bowl, pour in enough warm
water to cover, and soak for 15 minutes.

Drain the chiles. Add them, the cumin, clove,
oregano, garlic, and the chicken stock to a food
processor or blender and process until smooth.

Add the paste to the meat with another 1 cup
(9 fl oz/250 ml) beef stock and simmer over low
heat for 10 minutes. Add the potato mixture and
continue cooking, stirring and scraping the bottom
of the pan to make sure it doesn't stick, for another
30 minutes, until it is a thick, gruel-like consistency.
If necessary, add the remaining stock.

Add the meat and cook for an additional
10 minutes. Serve with white rice.

MUSHROOM AND POTATO SALAD

13½ oz/380 g potatoes
4 tablespoons olive oil, plus
  extra for greasing
10½ oz/300 g oyster
  mushrooms
2 poblano chiles, dry-roasted
  and cut into strips
2 tablespoons pumpkin seeds,
  toasted (optional)

For the vinaigrette:
2 pickled jalapeños
3 tablespoon lime juice
½ teaspoon dry oregano
sea salt and black pepper
⅔ cup (5 fl oz/150 ml) olive oil

REGION: ALL REGIONS
PREPARATION TIME: 25 MINUTES
COOKING TIME: 1 HOUR 25 MINUTES
SERVES: 6

Preheat the oven to 375°F (180°C/Gas Mark 5). Coat potatoes in olive oil and salt and pepper, wrap in aluminum foil, and bake for 50 minutes or until tender. Remove from the oven and let cool. Slice into bite-sized chunks.

To make the vinaigrette, combine the pickled jalapeños, lime juice, oregano, salt and pepper in a small bowl and mix well to combine.

In a medium bowl, combine the mushrooms, poblano chiles, potatoes, and vinaigrette and toss well to coat. Garnish with pumpkin seeds, if using, and serve immediately.

Mushroom and Potato Salad

PAPITAS AL AJILLO

✺

POTATOES IN GARLIC

3 tablespoons olive oil
4 cloves garlic, finely chopped
1 lb 10 oz/750 g new potatoes,
  cooked
1 teaspoon ground cumin,
  toasted
mild chile, to serve
sea salt

REGION: ALL REGIONS
PREPARATION TIME: 15 MINUTES
COOKING TIME: 10 MINUTES
SERVES: 6

Heat the olive oil in a pan over medium-low heat. Add the garlic, stirring frequently, for a few minutes until golden. Do not let it brown or it will become bitter.

Put the potatoes into a bowl, add the garlic and the oil from the pan, and mix well. Sprinkle with the cumin and mix again.

Put the potatoes under the broiler (grill) for 5 minutes. Put the potatoes into a serving dish, sprinkle with salt, mix well, and garnish with a chile. Serve immediately.

QUELITES GUISADOS

✺

WILD GREENS

1 tablespoon corn oil
1 white onion, finely chopped
1 serrano or jalapeño chile
  finely chopped
3 tomatoes, chopped
2¼ lb (1 kg) spinach, swiss
  chard, sorrel, or any leafy
  green
sea salt
Corn Tortillas (page 36),
  to serve
cubed panela or mozzarella
  cheese

REGION: ALL REGIONS
PREPARATION TIME: 10 MINUTES
COOKING TIME: 25 MINUTES
SERVES: 6

Heat the oil in a pan. Add the onion and chile and cook over medium heat, stirring occasionally, for 5 minutes. Add the tomatoes, season with salt, and cook for an additional 5 minutes. Reduce the heat, add the spinach, mix well, and cover the pan. Cook for 10 minutes.

Remove the pan from the heat and serve immediately with warm tortillas and cheese.

Potatoes in Garlic

PLANTAIN MOULD

3–4 ripe plantains, unpeeled
2 tablespoons butter
pinch of sugar
1 teaspoon baking powder
1 egg, lightly beaten
2–4 tablespoons all-purpose
  (plain) flour
1½ cup (11 oz/300 g) Refried
  Beans (page 532)
1½ cup (12 oz/350 g) queso
  fresco or mild feta cheese
sea salt
Salsa of choice (page 496–514),
  to serve

REGION: TABASCO
PREPARATION TIME: 25 MINUTES
COOKING TIME: 40 MINUTES
SERVES: 4

Preheat the oven to 400°F (200°C/Gas Mark 6).

Put the plantains into a pan, add enough water to cover, and bring to a boil. Reduce the heat and simmer for 10 minutes until softened. Remove the pan from the heat, drain the plantains, let them cool and peel.

Put the plantains into a bowl and mash well, then add the butter, sugar, baking powder, a pinch of salt, egg and flour, and mix to a paste.

Put half the plantain mixture into a 12 x 9-inch (30 x 23-cm) baking tray. Put the beans on top and spoon the cheese over them. Finally, cover with another layer of the plantain mixture. Bake for 30 minutes.

Remove from the oven and let it settle so the cheese can firm up. Serve it warm with your favorite salsa.

VEGETABLE CASEROLE

5 tablespoons (2½ oz/65 g)
   butter, plus extra for greasing
2 tablespoon olive oil
2 white onions, sliced
3⅔ cups (9 oz/250 g) sliced
   mushrooms
1 large eggplant (aubergine),
   cut into ½-inch (1-cm) thick
   diagonal slices
3 zucchini (courgettes), cut into
   ½-inch (1-cm) thick diagonal
   slices
3 tomatoes, thinly sliced
2 cups (8 oz/225 g) grated
   cheddar or gouda cheese
sea salt and pepper

REGION: ALL REGIONS
PREPARATION TIME: 20 MINUTES
COOKING TIME: 45 MINUTES
SERVES: 6

Preheat the oven to 350°F (180°C/Gas Mark 4). Melt the butter with the oil in the same pan. Add the onions and mushrooms and cook over low heat, stirring, occasionally for 5 minutes or until softened. Remove the pan from the heat.

Grease a large Dutch oven or casserole dish with butter. Make a layer of half the onion and mushroom mixture, then half of the eggplant (aubergine) and zucchini (courgettes), and then half the tomatoes. Season with pepper and sprinkle with half the grated cheese. Repeat the layers.

Cover with the lid or foil and bake for 30 minutes, then remove from the oven, and uncover. Return to the oven and bake for 5–10 minutes more until the cheese is bubbling.

Remove from the oven and let cool to allow the cheese to firm up a bit. Serve cut into squares.

CUCUMBERS STUFFED WITH SHRIMP

6 cucumbers
⅓ cup (2¾ oz/75 g) cream
   cheese
2 tablespoons lemon juice
125 g (4 oz) cooked shrimp
   (prawns)
100 g (3½ oz) red pimiento
   peppers, chopped
8 peppermint leaves, chopped
paprika, to taste
sea salt and pepper

REGION: BAJA CALIFORNIA
PREPARATION TIME: 20 MINUTES
SERVES: 6

Using a teaspoon, scoop out the seeds and flesh from the centers of the cucumbers, and place these vertically on a platter.

Mix the cream cheese and lemon juice together in a medium bowl. Set aside 8 shrimp (prawns), then add the others to the cheese together with the peppers and mint and mix well. Season with salt, pepper, and paprika to taste and mix well.

Using a teaspoon, fill the cucumbers with the mixture, then garnish the platter with reserved shrimp and serve.

SOUFFLÉ DE VERDURAS CON QUESO COTIJA

VEGETABLE SOUFFLE

2 tablespoons corn oil

1 white onion, sliced

5 carrots, cut into thin strips

5 small squash, cut into thin strips

4 chayotes, cut into thin strips

2 poblano chiles, dry-roasted and cut into strips

butter, for greasing

4 eggs, lightly whisked

1 cup (9 fl oz/250 ml) sour cream

3½ oz/100 g cotija cheese, crumbled

1 teaspoon ground nutmeg

1 tablespoon finely chopped parsley

1 tomato, sliced

sea salt

REGION: MICHOACAN
PREPARATION TIME: 25 MINUTES
COOKING TIME: 45 MINUTES
SERVES: 6

Heat the oil in a pan over low heat, add the onion, carrots, squash, chayotes, and chiles, and cook for 10 minutes. Remove from the heat and let cool.

Preheat the oven to 350°F (180°C/Gas Mark 4) and grease a large ovenproof dish with the butter.

Add the eggs, sour cream, cheese, salt, nutmeg, and parsley and mix gently. Arrange the tomato slices
in the bottom of the prepared ovenproof dish, pour in the vegetable mixture, and add the cream and egg mixture. Spread out to cover the bottom, then bake in the oven for 35 minutes.

Remove from the oven and let cool for 10 minutes before serving.

CORN PANCAKES IN SAUCE

6 cups corn kernels
8 tablespoons whipped cream
4 eggs
corn oil, for frying
sea salt

For the sauce:
5 tomatoes, dry-roasted and
 pureed
½ white onion
1 tablespoon corn oil
4 poblano chiles, dry-roasted
 and cut into strips
sea salt and pepper
ranch cheese or panela cheese,
 sliced, to garnish

REGION: CENTRAL MEXICO
PREPARATION TIME: 25 MINUTES
COOKING TIME: 25 MINUTES
SERVES: 6

Put the corn kernels into a food processor and process until ground. Put in a bowl, add the cream, eggs, and salt, and mix together.

Heat the oil in a heavy pan over medium heat. Put tablespoons of the mixture, in batches, into the pan and cook for 4 minutes. Remove and drain on paper towels, then repeat until all the mixture is used.

For the sauce, put the tomatoes and onion into a food processor and process until smooth, then strain. Heat the oil in a medium pan over medium heat. Add the chile strips, and fry for 30 seconds, then add the pureed tomatoes, season with salt and pepper, and cook for 10 minutes until thick. Serve the pancakes with the sauce and sliced cheese.

ROLLOVER PURSLANE

1 lb 2 oz/500 g purslane,
 cleaned
2 Serrano chiles, roughly
 chopped
½ teaspoon finely chopped
 garlic
sea salt

REGION: FALTA
PREPARATION TIME: 15 MINUTES
COOKING TIME: 20 MINUTES
SERVES: 6

Put the purslane in a medium saucepan, add enough water to cover and 2 tablespoons of salt. Cover and cook for 20 minutes, or until the purslane is cooked. Do not overcook. Have a large bowl of iced water nearby. Remove the pan from the heat, then remove the purslane with a slotted spoon and put it into the iced water. Drain, squeezing gently with your hands to remove the excess water, and put into a bowl.

Put the chiles, garlic, and ½ teaspoon salt in a food processor or blender and process until smooth, then add the chili sauce to the purslane and mix until the purslane is covered in the sauce. Serve.

Papadzules

PAPADZULES

2 epazote sprigs

4 tomatoes

1 habanero chile

4½ cups (1 lb 2 oz/500 g) green or white pumpkin seeds, dry-roasted and ground

10 eggs, hard-boiled and chopped

18 Corn Tortillas (page 36)

sea salt, to taste

REGION: GUANAJUATO
PREPARATION TIME: 25 MINUTES
COOKING TIME: 30 MINUTES
SERVES: 6

Put 1½ cups water in a pan and add the epazote sprigs and tomatoes. Reduce the heat to medium-low and simmer for 20 minutes. Remove the pan from the heat, remove the epazote sprigs, transfer the mixture to a food processor or blender and process to a puree. Pour into a bowl.

Put the ground pumpkin seeks into a heatproof bowl and gradually add the epazote puree, working the mixture with your hands to release the oil from the seeds. Set the bowl over a pan of simmering water and cook for 20 minutes. Remove from the heat.

Dip the tortilla in the sauce, one at a time, place a heaping spoonful of the hard-boiled egg in the middle, and roll into a flute shape. Repeat until all the tortillas have been rolled.

Spoon some of the remaining sauce onto individual plates, add 3–4 filled tortillas to each one, and spoon the remaining sauce over them. Garnish with hard-boiled eggs. Serve.

PICO DE GALLO WITH JICAMA AND PINEAPPLE

⁂

REGION: VERACRUZ
PREPARATION TIME: 20 MINUTES
MAKES: 3 CUPS

Put the pineapple, jicama, cucumber, bell peppers, and chile into a bowl. Add the lime juice and pineapple juice and mix gently with your hands. Taste and adjust the seasoning, if necessary, add the olive oil, sprinkle with the cilantro (coriander), and serve with tortilla chips.

⅓ pineapple, cored, diced, and juice reserved
1 jicama, diced
1 large cucumber, peeled and diced
1 red bell pepper, diced
1 yellow bell pepper, diced
1 cuaresmeño or jalapeño chile, seeded and chopped
1 teaspoon lime juice
5 tablespoons extra-virgin olive oil
1 tablespoon finely chopped cilantro (coriander)
sea salt and pepper
tortilla chips, to serve

HABANERO CHILE AND TOMATO SALSA

⁂

REGION: YUCATÁN
PREPARATION TIME: 20 MINUTES
MAKES: 2 CUPS (16 FL OZ/475 ML)

Put the chiles, tomatoes, onions, and cilantro (coriander) into a bowl and mix gently. Add the orange juice and season to taste with salt. Add the olive oil and serve with meat, fish, or poultry.

1 oz/30 g habanero chiles, finely chopped
2 large tomatoes, peeled, seeded, and finely chopped
1 small red onion, finely chopped
¼ cup (½ oz/15 g) finely chopped cilantro (coriander)
juice of 2 sour oranges
2 tablespoons olive oil
sea salt

Pico de Gallo with Jicama and Pineapple

PIPIAN ROSSO

RED PIPIAN SAUCE

1 cup (4 oz/120 g) pumpkin
  seeds, lightly toasted
3 pasilla or ancho chiles,
  dry-roasted
½ cup (4 oz/120 g) sesame
  seeds, lightly toasted
1 Corn Tortilla (page 36),
  toasted
2 tomatoes, dry-roasted
½ onion, dry-roasted
2 cloves garlic, dry-roasted
1 cinnamon stick
1 tablespoon vegetable
  shortening, lard, or corn oil
1–2 cups (8–16 fl oz/250–475 ml)
  Chicken Stock (page 184)
sea salt

REGION: ALL REGIONS
PREPARATION TIME: 35 MINUTES
COOKING TIME: 15 MINUTES
SERVES: 4

Put the chiles into a small bowl, add enough boiling water to cover, and soak for 15 minutes.

Put the pumpkin seeds, drained chiles, sesame seeds, tortilla, tomatoes, onion, garlic, cinnamon, and pepper to taste into a food processor or blender and process to a uniform paste. Heat the fat or oil in a pan, add the paste, and gradually add the chicken stock as required, and cook, stirring constantly, to make a thick sauce. Season with salt.

SALSA PARA BARBACOA

BARBECUE MARINADE

6 ancho chiles, dry-roasted
6 guajillo chiles, dry-roasted
¼ teaspoon cumin seeds,
  dry-roasted
¾ teaspoon dried oregano
5 allspice berries, dry-roasted
3 whole cloves, dry-roasted
2–3 cloves garlic, dry-roasted
sea salt

REGION: OAXACA
PREPARATION TIME: 35 MINUTES, PLUS
15 MINUTES SOAKING
MAKES: 2 CUPS (16 FL OZ/475 ML)

Put the chiles into a small bowl, add enough boiling water to cover, and soak for 15 minutes. Drain and reserve the cooking liquid.

Put the chiles into a food processor or blender with the cumin seeds, oregano, allspice berries, cloves, and garlic. Process until smooth, adding soaking liquid as required.

Use to marinate lamb, poultry or beef for the barbecue.

ANCHO CHILE SALSA

1 cup (9 fl oz/250 ml) orange
  juice
4 ancho chiles, dry-roasted
4 teaspoons white wine
  vinegar
¼ teaspoon chopped fresh
  marjoram
¼ bay leaf
⅛ teaspoon anise seeds
½ small onion, coarsely
  chopped
1 clove garlic
4 tablespoons olive oil
sea salt

REGION: ALL REGIONS
PREPARATION TIME: 15 MINUTES
COOKING TIME: 15 MINUTES
MAKES: 2 CUPS (16 FL OZ/475 ML)

Pour the orange juice into a small saucepan, add the chiles, 2 teaspoons vinegar, marjoram, bay leaf, anise seeds, onion, garlic, and ½ cup (4½ fl oz/125 ml) water, and bring to a boil. Simmer over medium heat for 3 minutes or until the chiles are soft, then remove the pan from the heat.

Pour the mixture into a food processor or blender, add the remaining vinegar, and process until smooth. Season to taste.

Heat the oil in a pan over medium heat. Pour the chile mixture into the pan and cook for 5 minutes over very low heat. Season with salt and if it is too thick, add a little more orange juice. Serve immediately at room temperature.

RAW TOMATO SALSA

3 tomatoes, finely chopped
2 tablespoons finely chopped
  onion
5 green serrano chiles,
  seeded and finely chopped
6 tablespoons cilantro
  (coriander), finely chopped
sea salt

REGION: ALL REGIONS
PREPARATION TIME: 5 MINUTES
SERVES: 4

Combine the tomatoes, onion, chiles, and cilantro (coriander) in a small bowl and season with salt to taste.

Serve with meat, fish, or poultry, or with tacos.

Note: This salsa may also be processed in a food processor or blender, but reserve the cilantro to sprinkle over it when serving.

SPICY SESAME SEED SAUCE

3½ oz/100 g serrano chiles,
dry-roasted

7 tablespoons sesame seeds,
dry-roasted

1 large tomato, dry-roasted
and peeled

2 tablespoons finely chopped
cilantro (coriander)

sea salt

REGION: PUEBLA
PREPARATION TIME: 20 MINUTES
MAKES: 1½ CUP (12 FL OZ/350 ML)

Put the chiles, sesame seeds, tomatoes, and cilantro (coriander) into a food processor or blender and process until smooth. If necessary, add ½ cup (4 fl oz/120 ml) water. Season to taste with salt and pour into a jar.

Serve with meat, fish, or poultry, or use in tacos.

CHILACA CHILE SALSA

6 chilaca chiles, dry-roasted
2 cloves garlic, chopped
½ small onion, chopped
½ teaspoon dried oregano
sea salt

REGION: ALL REGIONS
PREPARATION TIME: 15 MINUTES
MAKES: 1½ CUPS (13½ FL OZ/375 ML)

Put the chiles, garlic, onion, and 1 cup (9 fl oz/250 ml) water into a food processor or blender and process until thoroughly combined. Transfer to a serving bowl, season to taste with salt, and sprinkle with the oregano.

Serve with meat, chicken, or fish.

JALAPEÑO SALSA

5 jalapeño chiles, seeded
2 cloves garlic
½ small onion
juice of 3 limes
sea salt

REGION: MORELOS
PREPARATION TIME: 5 MINUTES
MAKES: ½ CUP (4 FL OZ/120 ML)

Put the chiles, garlic, onion and lime juice into a food processor or blender and process until thoroughly combined. Transfer to a bowl, season to taste with salt, and stir.

Serve this salsa with meat, fish, or poultry, or use with tacos.

MACHA SALSA

1 cup (9 fl oz/250 ml) olive oil
9 oz/250 g dried arbol chiles
3–4 cloves garlic, coarsely
   chopped
sea salt

REGION: CENTRAL MEXICO
PREPARATION TIME: 10 MINUTES
COOKING TIME: 5 MINUTES
MAKES: 2 CUPS (16 FL OZ/ 475 ML)

Heat the oil in a pan. Add the garlic and cook over medium heat until the oil starts to bubble, then add the chiles. Cook for a few seconds, then remove from the heat, and let cool.

Put all the ingredients into a food processor or blender and process until thoroughly combined. Season to taste with salt.

Serve with meat, fish, or poultry, or use with tacos.

COOKED
TOMATO SALSA

3 tomatoes
2 tablespoons coarsely
   chopped onion
3 green serrano chiles, seeded
6 tablespoons finely chopped
   cilantro (coriander)
sea salt

REGION: ALL REGIONS
PREPARATION TIME: 10 MINUTES
COOKING TIME: 15 MINUTES
SERVES: 4

Pour ½ cup (4½ fl oz/125 ml) water into a saucepan. Add the tomatoes, onion, and chiles and simmer for about 15 minutes. Remove from the heat.

Put the mixture and half the cilantro (coriander) into a food processor or blender and process until thoroughly combined. Transfer to a bowl, season to taste with salt, and sprinkle with the remaining cilantro.

Serve with meat, fish, or poultry, or with tacos.

TOMATILLO AND
CHILI SAUCE

7 tomatillos, finely chopped
1 oz/25 g serrano chiles,
   seeded and finely chopped
1 teapoon white sugar
½ small onion, finely chopped
2 tablespoons finely chopped
   cilantro (coriander)
sea salt

REGION: ALL REGIONS
PREPARATION TIME: 10 MINUTES
MAKES: 1½ CUPS (13½ FL OZ/375 ML)

Put the tomatillos, chiles, sugar, onion, and cilantro (coriander) into a bowl and gently stir to combine. Season to taste with salt. Serve with seafood.

DRIED ARBOL
CHILE SALSA

3–5 dry arbol chiles, dry-
  roasted
½ small onion, dry-roasted
1 clove garlic, dry-roasted
7 tomatillos, dry-roasted
sea salt

REGION: ALL REGIONS
PREPARATION TIME: 5 MINUTES
COOKING TIME: 20 MINUTES
MAKES: 1 CUP (9 FL OZ/250 ML)

Put the chiles, onion, garlic, and tomatillos into
a food processor or blender and process until
smooth. If necessary, add a little water. Season
to taste with salt.

Serve with meat, fish, or poultry or use with tacos.

CHILE AND
GARLIC ADOBO

3–4 costeño chiles, dry-roasted
9–10 guajillo chiles, dry-roasted
3–4 morita chiles, dry-roasted
3–4 ancho chiles, dry-roasted
4 tomatoes, chopped
3 cloves garlic
½ onion, finely chopped
3 whole cloves, dry-roasted
6 black peppercorns,
  dry-roasted
3 tablespoons olive oil
2 tablespoons pineapple
  vinegar or apple
  cider vinegar
sea salt

REGION: OAXACA
PREPARATION TIME: 40 MINUTES, PLUS
15 MINUTES SOAKING
COOKING TIME: 10 MINUTES
SERVES: 6

Combine the chiles and enough hot water to cover
and soak for 15 minutes. Put the chiles with some
of their soaking water into a food processor or
blender, add the tomatoes, garlic, onion, cloves, and
peppercorns, and process until a smooth consistency.

Heat the oil in a medium pan, add the chile
mixture, and cook over low heat until it starts to dry
out. Stir in the vinegar, a little at a time, and season
with salt. Remove the pan from the heat and let cool
before serving.

You can use this adobo to prepare shrimp
(prawns), lobster, or pork. Cook according to
the instructions in the recipe.

Dried Arbol Chile Salsa

SALSA DE CHILE ANCHO Y TUÉTANO

✻

BONE MARROW AND ANCHO CHILE SALSA

1 tomato, dry-roasted
3 ancho chiles, dry-roasted
1 onion, sliced and dry-roasted
1 clove garlic, dry-roasted
1 lb 2 oz/500 g marrow bones
2 tablespoons olive oil
sea salt and pepper

REGION: ALL REGIONS
PREPARATION TIME: 25 MINUTES, PLUS
15 MINUTES SOAKING
COOKING TIME: 20 MINUTES
MAKES: 1½ CUPS (13½ FL OZ/375 ML)

Put the tomatoes, chiles, onion, and garlic in a food processor or blender and process until thoroughly combined.

Put the marrow bones and a pinch of salt into a heatproof bowl, pour in boiling water to cover, and let soak for 15 minutes until the marrow softens. Lift out the bones, scoop out the marrow with a long thin spoon, and chop.

Heat the oil in a pan. Add half the marrow and cook over low heat for 5 minutes. Season with salt and pepper and cook for another 5 minutes. Gently stir in the chile mixture and cook for another 5 minutes, then add the remaining marrow, and cook for 5 minutes. Taste and adjust the seasoning, if necessary, and remove the pan from the heat.

Serve warm with any kind of meat, or use with tacos.

SALSA DE CHILE TATEMADO

✻

CHARRED CHILE SALSA

9 oz/250 g dried chipotle chiles
2–3 cloves garlic
1 small onion
9 tomatillos
9 oz/250 g smoked chipotle chiles in adobo
sea salt

REGION: MEXICO CITY
PREPARATION TIME: 10 MINUTES
COOKING TIME: 15 MINUTES
MAKES: 2 CUPS (16 FL OZ/475 ML)

Preheat the oven to 350°F (180°C/Gas Mark 4). Put the dried chipotles, garlic, onion, and tomatillos into a roasting pan and roast for about 15 minutes until the chile seeds turn black and the chiles break when pulled apart. Remove from the oven.

Put the roasted chipotles, smoked chipotle chiles in adobo, garlic, onion, and tomatillos into a food processor or blender and process until smooth. If necessary, add a little water. Season to taste with salt.

Serve with meat, fish, or poultry or use with tacos.

SALSA RANCHERA

RANCH-STYLE SALSA

2 poblano chiles, dry-roasted
1 jalapeño chile, dry-roasted
2 tomatoes, chopped
½ onion, sliced
2 cloves garlic, chopped
¼ teaspoon cumin seeds,
  dry-roasted
¼ teaspoon dried oregano
4 tablespoons Chicken Stock
  (see page 184)
1 teaspoon olive oil
sea salt

REGION: PUEBLA
PREPARATION TIME: 30 MINUTES
MAKES: 1½ CUPS (13½ FL OZ/375 ML)

Peel and seed the poblano chiles with a spoon, and seed the jalapeño.

Put the chiles, tomatoes, onion, garlic, cumin seeds, and oregano into a food processor or blender and process until thoroughly combined. Pour in the chicken stock and olive oil, season to taste with salt, and blend briefly again. If the mixture is too thick, add a little water. Taste and adjust the seasoning, if necessary.

Serve with meat, fish, or poultry or use with tacos.

SALSA CRUDA

FRESH SALSA

½ small onion, finely chopped
1½ oz/40 g serrano chiles,
  seeded, finely chopped
2 small tomatoes, finely
  chopped
3 tablespoons finely chopped
  cilantro (coriander)
4 tablespoons olive oil
juice of 1 lime
sea salt

REGION: ALL REGIONS
PREPARATION TIME: 10 MINUTES
MAKES: 2 CUPS (16 FL OZ/475 ML)

Put the onion, chiles, tomatoes, and cilantro (coriander) into a bowl, pour in the olive oil and lime juice, and stirring gently, stirring the ingredients from underneath to combine thoroughly. Season to taste with salt.

Serve with any savory Mexican dish.

SALSA MORITA

MORITA SALSA

20 tomatillos
3 cloves garlic, coarsely
chopped
4 tablespoons coarsely
chopped onion
10 morita or chipotle chiles
sea salt

REGION: ALL REGIONS
PREPARATION TIME: 5 MINUTES
COOKING TIME: 20 MINUTES
MAKES: 2 CUPS (16 FL OZ/475 ML)

Put the tomatillos, garlic, onion, and chiles into a saucepan, pour in ½ cup (4½ fl oz/125 ml) water, and bring to a boil. Reduce the heat and simmer for 20 minutes or until tender. Remove the pan from the heat.

Put the mixture into a food processor or blender and process until thoroughly combined and smooth. Season with salt and, if necessary, add 4 tablespoons water, and process again. Taste and adjust the seasoning, if necessary.

Serve with meat, fish, or poultry or use with tacos.

SALSA MOLCAJETEADA

STONE-GROUND SALSA

2 ripe tomatoes
2–3 serrano chiles
1 clove garlic
sea salt

REGION: ALL REGIONS
PREPARATION TIME: 10 MINUTES
COOKING TIME: 15 MINUTES
MAKES: 1 CUP (9 FL OZ/250 ML)

Preheat the oven to 350°F (180°C/Gas Mark 4). Put the tomatoes, chiles, and garlic into a roasting pan and roast for 15 minutes. Remove the pan from the oven.

Peel the tomatoes. Put the chiles and garlic into a mortar and sprinkle with salt, then pound with a pestle. Add the tomatoes and pound a little more. Taste and adjust the seasoning, if necessary. Put the mortar in the center of the table to serve.

Serve with meat, fish, or poultry or use with tacos.

SALSA MICHOACANA DE AGUACATE

MICHOACAN AVOCADO SALSA

3 small tomatillos

1 oz/25 g serrano chiles

2 cloves garlic

2 small avocados, peeled and pitted

1 onion, finely chopped

2 tablespoons finely chopped cilantro (coriander)

sea salt

REGION: MICHOACAN
PREPARATION TIME: 15 MINUTES
COOKING TIME: 5 MINUTES
MAKES: 2 CUPS (16 FL OZ/475 ML)

Put the tomatillos and chiles into a small saucepan, pour in water just to cover, and bring to a boil for 5 minutes. Remove the pan from the heat and drain, reserving the cooking liquid.

Put the tomatillos, chiles, and garlic into a food processor or blender and process until combined. Add the avocado and process again until smooth. If necessary, add a little of the reserved cooking water.

Season to taste with salt, pour into a bowl, add the onion and cilantro (coriander), and stir well to mix.

SALSA TRES CHILES CON CACAHUATE

THREE-CHILE SALSA WITH PEANUTS

5 ancho chiles, dry-roasted

3 pasilla chiles, dry-roasted

3 costeño chiles, dry-roasted

½ large onion

4 cloves garlic

2 cups (8 oz/225 g) unsalted peanuts

1 cup (9 fl oz/250 ml) Chicken Stock (see page 184)

1 teaspoon olive oil

sea salt

REGION: GUERRERO
PREPARATION TIME: 25 MINUTES,
PLUS 20 MINUTES SOAKING
MAKES 4½ CUPS (36 FL OZ/1 LITER)

Put the chiles, onion, and garlic into a heatproof bowl, pour in 2 cups (16 fl oz/475 ml) boiling water, and let soak for 20 minutes or until soft.

Put the chiles, peanuts, garlic, onion and chicken stock into a food processor or blender, and process until thoroughly combined and smooth. Season with salt and drizzle with olive oil.

Serve this salsa at room temperature or cold with meat, fish, or poultry or use with tacos.

POZOLE SALSA

7–10 arbol chiles
2 clove garlic
½ onion, coarsely chopped
½ cup (4½ fl oz/125 ml) apple
   cider vinegar
sea salt

REGION: ALL REGIONS
PREPARATION TIME: 10 MINUTES, PLUS
15 MINUTES SOAKING
MAKES: 1 CUP (9 FL OZ/250 ML)

Put the chiles, garlic and onion into a heatproof bowl, pour in 1 cup (9 fl oz/250 ml) boiling water, and let soak for 10–15 minutes, then drain.

Put the chiles, garlic, onion, and vinegar into a food processor or blender and process until thoroughly combined. Pass the mixture through a strainer (sieve) into a bowl and season with salt.

Note: If you want this salsa less spicy, use guajillo chiles instead.

RANCH SALSA

1½ lb/700 g poblano chiles
3 tomatoes
2 cloves garlic
2⅓ cups (7 oz/200 g) finely
   chopped scallions (spring
   onions)
sea salt

REGION: ALL REGIONS
PREPARATION TIME: 10 MINUTES
COOKING TIME: 15 MINUTES
MAKES: 2 CUPS (16 FL OZ/475 ML)

Preheat the oven to 350°F (180°C/Gas Mark 4). Put the chiles and tomatoes into a roasting pan and roast for 15 minutes. Remove the pan from the oven.

Peel and seed the chiles and put them into a food processor or blender with the tomatoes and garlic. Process until combined, then pour into a bowl. Season to taste with salt, add the scallions (spring onions), and stir well.

Serve this salsa with meat, fish, or poultry or use with tacos.

YUCATAN TACO SAUCE

2 tablespoons olive oil
½ onion, sliced
4 tomatoes, finely chopped
2 habanero chiles, seeded and
   cut into fine strips
coarse sea salt

REGION: YUCATÁN
PREPARATION TIME: 5 MINUTES
COOKING TIME: 10 MINUTES
MAKES: 2½ CUPS (20½ FL OZ/600 ML)

Heat the olive oil in a pan. Add the onion and cook over low heat, stirring occasionally, for 5 minutes. Add the tomatoes and chiles, season with salt, and cook, stirring occasionally to prevent sticking, for another 5 minutes or until it is slightly reduced.

Serve with any savory dish from Yucatán as well as with tacos.

ROASTED TOMATO SALSA

6 tomatoes
2 tablespoons chopped onion
3 green serrano chiles, seeded
  and chopped
5 tablespoons cilantro
  (coriander), finely chopped
sea salt

REGION: ALL REGIONS
PREPARATION TIME: 10 MINUTES
COOKING TIME: 15 MINUTES
MAKES: 2 CUPS (16 FL OZ/475 ML)

Preheat the oven to 350°F (180°C/Gas Mark 4). Put the tomatoes, onion, and chiles into a roasting pan and roast for 15 minutes. Remove the pan from the oven.

Put the vegetables into a food processor or blender and process until thoroughly combined. Season to taste with salt and serve sprinkled with cilantro (coriander).

Serve this salsa with meat, fish, poultry, or with tacos.

CHARRED SALSA

2¾ oz/70 g jalapeño chiles
1 clove garlic
1 small white onion, chopped
2 tomatoes
¼ teaspoon dried oregano
¼ teaspoon cumin seeds,
  dry-roasted
sea salt

REGION: ALL REGIONS
PREPARATION TIME: 15 MINUTES
COOKING TIME: 10 MINUTES
MAKES: 1½ CUPS (13½ FL OZ/375 ML)

Preheat a ridged grill (griddle) pan. Add the chiles, garlic, onion, and tomatoes and cook over medium heat, turning frequently, for about 10 minutes or until charred. Remove the pan from the heat.

Put the chiles, garlic, onion, tomatoes, oregano, and cumin seeds into a food processor or blender and process until thoroughly combined. Season to taste with salt.

Serve with meat, fish, or poultry or use with tacos.

CHILTOMATE SALSA

4 large tomatoes
1 habanero or serrano chile
1 onion
2 cloves garlic
1 sprig epazote
sea salt

REGION: ALL REGIONS
PREPARATION TIME: 10 MINUTES
COOKING TIME: 15 MINUTES
MAKES: 2 CUPS (16 FL OZ/475 ML)

Put the tomatoes, chile, onion, and garlic into a saucepan, pour in 1 cup (9 fl oz/250 ml) boiling water, and simmer for 15 minutes. Remove from the heat.

Put all the ingredients into a food processor or blender and process until combined. Season to taste. Return the mixture to the saucepan and cook for another 10 minutes. Add epazote and serve.

ROASTED TOMATILLO SALSA

18 tomatillos
2 tablespoons chopped onion
2 cloves garlic
4 serrano chiles, seeded
pinch of sugar (optional)
6 tablespoons cilantro
  (coriander), chopped
sea salt

REGION: ALL REGIONS
PREPARATION TIME: 10 MINUTES
COOKING TIME: 15 MINUTES
SERVES: 4

Preheat the oven to 350°F (180°C/Gas Mark 4). Put the tomatillos, onion, garlic, and chiles into a roasting pan and roast for 15 minutes. Remove the pan from the oven.

Put the vegetables and sugar into a food processor or blender and process until thoroughly combined. Transfer to a small bowl, season to taste with salt, and sprinkle with cilantro (coriander) before serving.

Serve with meat, fish, or poultry, or with tacos.

STEWED TOMATILLO SALSA

18 tomatillos
½ onion, coarsely chopped
2 cloves garlic
4 serrano chiles, seeded
6 tablespoons cilantro
  (coriander), finely chopped
pinch of sugar (optional)
sea salt

REGION: ALL REGIONS
PREPARATION TIME: 10 MINUTES
COOKING TIME: 15 MINUTES
SERVES: 4

Put the tomatillos into a small saucepan, pour in water just to cover, add the onion, garlic, and chiles, and bring to a boil. Reduce the heat and simmer for 15 minutes, then remove the pan from the heat.

Put vegetables, half the cilantro (coriander), and sugar into a food processor or blender and process until thoroughly combined. Transfer to a small bowl, season to taste with salt, and sprinkle with the remaining cilantro.

Serve with meat, fish, or poultry, or with tacos.

Roasted Tomato and Roasted Tomatillo Salsa

RAW TOMATILLO SALSA

18 tomatillos, halved
2 tablespoons finely chopped
  onion
2 cloves garlic
4 serrano chiles, seeded and
  finely chopped
pinch of sugar
5 sprigs cilantro (coriander),
  finely chopped
sea salt

REGION: ALL REGIONS
PREPARATION TIME: 10 MINUTES
SERVES: 4

Lightly mash the tomatillos in a mortar, add the onion, garlic, and chiles, and mix well. Season to taste with salt, stir in the sugar, and sprinkle with the cilantro (coriander).

  Serve with meat, fish, or poultry or with tacos.

Note: This salsa may also be processed in a food processor or blender, but reserve the cilantro to sprinkle over it when serving.

GREEN SALSA WITH AVOCADO

2½ oz/60 g jalapeño chiles,
  coarsely chopped
3 tablespoons finely chopped
  white onion
9 tomatillos
½ cup (1 oz/25 g) coarsely
  chopped cilantro (coriander)
1 avocado, peeled, pitted, and
  diced
sea salt

REGION: ALL REGIONS
PREPARATION TIME: 10 MINUTES
MAKES: 1½ CUPS (13½ FL OZ/375 ML)

Pour ½ cup (4½ fl oz/125 ml) water into a food processor or blender, add the chiles and onion, and process until smooth. Add the tomatillos and cilantro (coriander) and process briefly again. Season to taste with salt, pour into a bowl, and gently stir in the avocado. Taste and adjust the seasoning, if necessary.

  Serve this salsa with meat, fish, or poultry or use with tacos.

BORRACHA SALSA

※

BORRACHA SALSA

8 pasilla chiles, dry-roasted
2 cloves garlic, dry-roasted
1 onion, finely chopped
½ cup (4 fl oz/120 ml) freshly-
    squeezed orange juice
1 cup pulque (or beer with 3
    tablespoons tequila)
salt
⅓ cup queso anejo or Parmesan
    cheese, to garnish

REGION: ALL REGIONS
PREPARATION TIME: 10 MINUTES
MAKES 2 CUPS (9 FL OZ/250 ML)

Put the chiles in a small bowl, add enough hot water to cover, and soak for 15 minutes. Drain.

Process chiles, garlic, onion, and orange juice in a processor or blender and process until smooth. Gradually add the pulque and mix well. Season to taste, then stir in the onions and garnish with the cheese.

VINAGRETA ECHALLOT

※

SHALLOT VINAIGRETTE

1 shallot, dry-roasted
1 teaspoon Dijon mustard
½ cup (4½ fl oz/125 ml)
    balsamic vinegar
1½ cups (13½ fl oz/375 ml)
    extra-virgin olive oil
½ teaspoon sea salt
pepper

REGION: MEXICO CITY
PREPARATION TIME: 10 MINUTES
MAKES: 2 CUPS (16 FL OZ/475 ML)

Put the shallot, mustard, and vinegar into a food processor or blender and process until thoroughly combined. Season with the sea salt and pepper to taste. With the motor running, gradually pour in the oil through the feeder tube until smooth and combined. Store in the refrigerator.

Serve this vinaigrette with fish or poultry.

VINAGRETA DE JALAPEÑO

✻

JALAPEÑO VINAIGRETTE

½ cup (4½ fl oz/125 ml) apple cider vinegar
1 cup (9 fl oz/250 ml) corn oil
5 tablespoons extra-virgin olive oil
1 tablespoon honey
1 teaspoon dried oregano
8 scallions (spring onions), finely chopped or sliced
2–3 pickled jalapeño chiles, seeded and finely chopped
sea salt and pepper

REGION: ALL REGIONS
PREPARATION TIME: 10 MINUTES
COOKING TIME: 15 MINUTES
MAKES: 2 CUPS (16 FL OZ/475 ML)

Pour the vinegar, corn oil, olive oil, and honey into a bowl and stir with a balloon whisk until thoroughly combined. Whisk in the oregano, then add the scallions (spring onions) and chiles. Season to taste with salt and pepper and whisk again lightly.

Serve this sauce with seafood, poultry, or meat terrines.

X NI PEK

✻

HABANERO FRESH SALSA

2 tomatoes, seeded and chopped
1 small red onion, finely chopped
3 tablespoon chopped cilantro (coriander)
½ habanero chile, deveined and chopped
3 tablespoons sour orange juice
sea salt to taste

REGION: YUCATÁN
PREPARATION TIME: 10 MINUTES, PLUS 30 MINUTES STANDING TIME
MAKES: 2 CUPS (16 FL OZ/475 ML)

Combine all the ingredients and adjust the seasoning to taste. Let stand in the refrigerator at least 30 minutes.

VINAGRETA CITRICOS

✳

CITRUS VINAIGRETTE

2¼ cups (18 fl oz/535 ml)
 orange juice
¼ cup (2 fl oz/60 ml) soy sauce
4 tablespoons lemon juice 2
 cloves garlic
¼ teaspoon ground cumin,
 roasted
½ teaspoon dried oregano
½ teaspoon paprika
¼ teaspoon pepper
½ cup (4½ fl oz/125 ml) extra-
 virgin olive oil
sea salt

REGION: ALL REGIONS
PREPARATION TIME: 10 MINUTES
COOKING TIME: 15 MINUTES
MAKES: 2½ CUPS (18 FL OZ/535 ML)

Add the orange juice to a small saucepan and
bring to a boil, reduce the heat, and simmer for
about 10 minutes or until the orange juice has
reduced to 1 cup (9 fl oz/250 ml). Allow to cool.

Put the orange juice, soy sauce, lemon juice, garlic,
cumin, oregano, paprika, pepper, and oil, into
a food processor or blender and process until
smooth. Season to taste with salt.

Serve with any salad or seafood.

VINAGRETA DE OREGANO

✳

OREGANO VINAIGRETTE

2 tomatoes, peeled, seeded, and
 chopped
6 tablespoons extra-virgin
 olive oil
2 tablespoons sherry vinegar
1 tablespoon lemon juice
1 teaspoon Dijon mustard
½ teaspoon dried oregano
sea salt and pepper

REGION: VERACRUZ
PREPARATION TIME: 10 MINUTES
MAKES: 1½ CUPS (13½ FL OZ/375 ML)

Combine the tomatoes, olive oil, vinegar, lemon
juice, mustard, and oregano in a small bowl and
season with salt and pepper to taste. Cover with
plastic wrap (clingfilm) and store in the refrigerator
until required.

VINAGRETA DE NOPALITOS CON CAMARONES

✿

CACTUS PADDLE AND SHRIMP VINAIGRETTE

1 cup (9 fl oz/250 ml) apple cider vinegar

2 tablespoons Dijon mustard

2 cloves garlic, minced

1 cup (9 fl oz/250 ml) extra-virgin olive oil

2 scallions (spring onions), sliced

3 tablespoons chopped cilantro (coriander)

1 (12-oz/340-g) can sweet peppers, chopped

3 red bell peppers, chopped

1 lb 10 oz/750 g cactus paddles, cooked and diced

11 oz/300 g cooked shrimp (prawns)

dried oregano, to taste

sea salt and pepper

To serve:
3½ oz/100 g mushrooms, sliced
tortilla chips

REGION: CENTER
PREPARATION TIME: 10 MINUTES, PLUS 2 HOURS CHILLING
COOKING TIME: 5 MINUTES
SERVES: 6

Pour the vinegar into a saucepan and bring to a boil over medium heat. Remove from the heat, add the mustard, garlic, olive oil, spring onions (scallions), cilantro (coriander), both peppers, and cactus paddles and mix well. Add the shrimp (prawns), then season with salt, pepper, and oregano. Pour into a clean bowl, then cover with plastic wrap (clingfilm), and let stand in the refrigerator for at least 2 hours.

Just before serving, mix well, check the seasoning, and serve accompanied with the sliced mushrooms and tortilla chips.

VINAGRETA DE CHIPOTLE Y GUAJILLO

✺

CHIPOTLE AND GUAJILLO CHILE VINAIGRETTE

1 egg yolk
2 tablespoons red wine or balsamic vinegar
1 teaspoon chipotle chile paste (puree)
1 teaspoon guajillo chile pulp
½ cup (4½ fl oz/125 ml) extra-virgin olive oil
sea salt and pepper

REGION: ALL REGIONS
PREPARATION TIME: 10 MINUTES
MAKES: ¾ CUP (6 FL OZ/180 ML)

Put the egg yolk, ½ cup (4½ fl oz/125 ml) water, and the vinegar into a food processor or blender and process until combined. Add the chile paste (purée), chile pulp, and olive oil, season to taste with salt and pepper, and process again. If the vinaigrette is too thick, add a little water and process again. Taste and adjust the seasoning, if necessary.

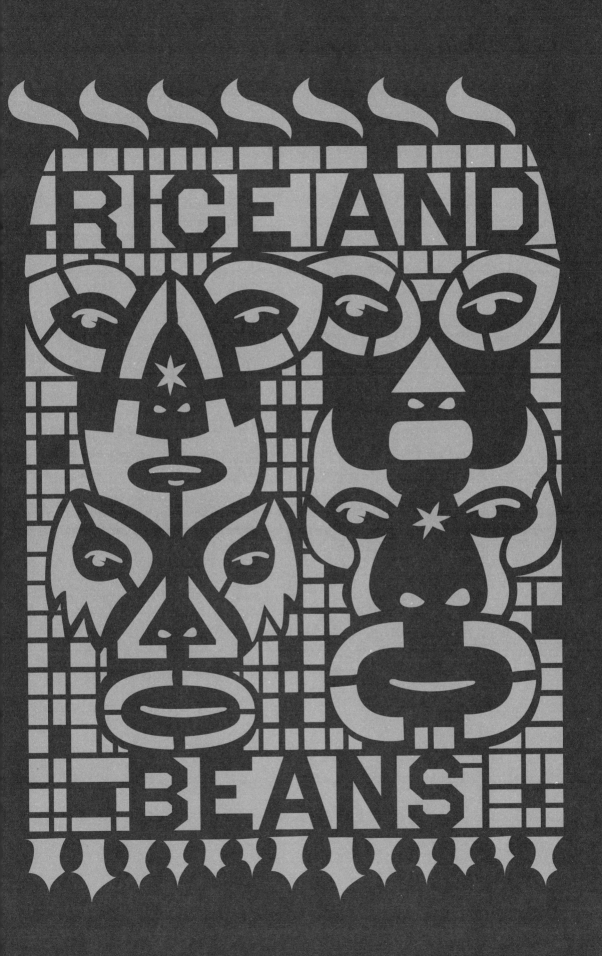

Yellow Rice

ARROZ BLANCO

WHITE RICE

2 cups (14 oz/400 g) long-grain
  rice
½ cup (4 fl oz/120 ml) corn oil
½ onion, chopped
1 clove garlic, crushed
1 sprig parsley or cilantro
  (coriander) (optional)
juice of ½ lemon
salt

REGION: ALL REGIONS
PREPARATION TIME: 10 MINUTES,
PLUS 15 MINUTES SOAKING
COOKING TIME: 25 MINUTES
SERVES: 6

Put the rice into a heatproof bowl, pour in hot water to cover, and let soak for 15 minutes. Drain well.

Heat the oil in a saucepan. Add the rice and cook over low heat, stirring occasionally, for a few minutes until it starts to change color. Drain off the oil and return the pan to the heat.

Add the onion, garlic, parsley, if using, lemon juice, a pinch of salt, and 4¼ cups (1¾ pints/1 liter) water and bring to a boil over medium heat. Reduce the heat, cover, and boil for 20 minutes.

Remove the pan from the heat. Discard the onion and parsley and fluff up the grains with a fork before serving.

ARROZ AMARILLO

YELLOW RICE

1 cup (5½ oz/160g) long-grain
  rice
3 cups (1¼ pints/750 ml)
  Chicken Stock (page 184)
12 saffron threads
½ teaspoon sea salt
½ cup (4 fl oz/120 ml) corn oil
½ onion, finely chopped
2 cloves garlic
⅔ cup (3½ oz/100g) frozen peas

REGION: CHIHUAHUA
PREPARATION TIME: 10 MINUTES, PLUS
15 MINUTES SOAKING
COOKING TIME: 35 MINUTES
SERVES: 4

Soak the rice in hot water for 15 minutes, rinse several times in cold water until water runs clear, drain well, and set aside.

Combine the chicken stock, saffron, and salt in a small saucepan and cook over low heat for 10 minutes. Set aside.

Heat the oil over medium heat in a separate saucepan, sauté the onion and garlic for 12 minutes, until browned, then remove and discard the garlic. Add the rice, stir, and cook for an additional 2 minutes. Add the chicken stock, increase to high heat, and bring to a boil. Cover and simmer for 20 minutes. Add the peas, stir, and cook for another 2 minutes. Remove from the heat, let stand for 5 minutes, then loosen the rice with a fork.

CALAMARI RICE

1 cup (7 oz/200 g) long
  grain rice
3 tablespoons olive oil
1 sprig parsley, plus
  6 tablespoons chopped
  parsley
1 large clove garlic, thinly
  sliced
½ onion, diced
1 large tomato, finely chopped
11 oz/300 g squid, cleaned,
  sliced, and ink sac(s) reserved
2 cups (16 fl oz/475 ml)
  Chicken Stock (page 184)
1 jalapeño chile, pricked all
  over with a fork (optional)
sea salt and pepper

REGION: VERACRUZ
PREPARATION TIME: 25 MINUTES, PLUS
15 MINUTES SOAKING
COOKING TIME: 30 MINUTES
SERVES: 4

Put the rice into a heatproof bowl, pour in boiling water to cover, and let soak for 15 minutes. Drain, rinse several times in cold water until the water runs clear, drain well again. Set aside.

Heat the olive oil in a medium frying pan or skillet. Add the parsley sprig and cook briefly, then remove and drain on paper towels.

Add the garlic to the skillet and cook over low heat, stirring frequently, for a few minutes but do not let it brown. Add the rice and cook, occasionally stirring gently, for a few minutes until it begins to color. Drain off the excess oil, then add the onion, tomato, chopped parsley, and squid. Snip the ink sac(s) and add the ink to the pan, then add the chicken stock and season with salt and pepper.

Bring to a boil over high heat and add the chile, if using. Reduce the heat to low, cover, and simmer for 20 minutes. Turn off the heat and let stand 5 minutes, then fluff up the rice with a fork.

Transfer the rice to a serving bowl, garnish with the fried parsley leaves, and serve immediately.

ARROZ CON FRIJOLES

✳

RICE WITH BEANS

butter, for greasing
½ quantity White Rice
  (page 521)
2 cups (12 oz/350 g) cooked
  black beans, cooking liquid
  reserved
3 poblano chiles, seeds
  removed and cut into thin
  strips
1 cup (8 fl oz/225 g) sour cream
1 cup (3½ oz/100 g) grated
  Manchego or sharp cheddar
  cheese

REGION: MORELOS
PREPARATION TIME: 25 MINUTES, PLUS
15 MINUTES SOAKING
COOKING TIME: 35 MINUTES
SERVES: 4

Preheat the oven to 400°F (200°C/Gas Mark 6). Grease an ovenproof dish with butter.

Spread a third of the rice over the bottom of the dish, cover with a third of the beans, and top with a third of the chile strips. Repeat these layers until all the ingredients have been used. Pour over the layers ½ cup (4 fl oz/120 ml) of reserved bean liquid then add the sour cream, and sprinkle with the grated cheese. Bake for about 30 minutes, until bubbling.

Remove the dish from the oven and serve immediately.

ARROZ A LA MOSTAZA

✳

MUSTARD RICE

1 cup (7 oz/200 g) long-grain
  rice
½ teaspoon cumin seeds, dry-
  roasted
½ teaspoon black peppercorns,
  dry-roasted
2–3 tomatillos, coarsely
  chopped
½ white onion, chopped
2 cloves garlic, chopped
4 tablespoons corn oil
1 tablespoon American
  mustard
1 tablespoon chopped cilantro
  (coriander)
2 carrots, diced
2 cups (16 fl oz/475 ml)
  Chicken Stock (page 184)
sea salt

REGION: TAMAULIPAS
PREPARATION TIME: 25 MINUTES, PLUS
15 MINUTES SOAKING
COOKING TIME: 30 MINUTES
SERVES: 6

Put the rice into a heatproof bowl, pour in boiling water to cover, and let soak for 15 minutes. Drain, rinse several times in cold water until the water runs clear, and drain well again. Set aside.

Grind the cumin seeds and peppercorns in a mortar with a pestle or a spice grinder. Put the tomatillos, onion, garlic, and ground spice mixture into a food processor or blender and process until thoroughly combined.

Heat the oil in a saucepan. Add the rice and cook over medium heat, occasionally stirring gently, for a few minutes until it begins to color. Drain off the excess oil and add the tomatillo mixture. Stir in the mustard, cilantro (coriander), carrots, and chicken stock, season with salt, and bring to a boil over high heat. Reduce the heat and simmer for 20 minutes, then turn off the heat and let stand 5 minutes.

Fluff up the rice with a fork, transfer to a serving plate and serve.

Green Rice

ARROZ VERDE

GREEN RICE

1 cup (7 oz/200 g) long grain
  rice
2 poblano chile, dry-roasted
1 clove garlic
½ white onion, finely chopped
2 cups (16 fl oz/475 ml)
  Chicken Stock (page 184)
5 tablespoons corn oil
4 tablespoons finely chopped
  cilantro (coriander)
chile strips, to garnish

REGION: MORELOS
PREPARATION TIME: 20 MINUTES
COOKING TIME: 25 MINUTES
SERVES: 4

Put the rice into a heatproof bowl, pour in boiling water to cover, and let soak for 15 minutes. Drain, rinse several times in cold water until the water runs clear, drain well again, and set aside.

Combine the chiles, garlic, onion, and ½ cup (4 fl oz/120 ml) chicken stock in a food processor and process until smooth.

Heat the oil in a medium saucepan over medium heat, add the rice, stir, and cook for 2 minutes or until golden. Add the chiles, stir, and then add the remaining stock. Bring to a boil, then reduce the heat, and simmer, covered, for 20 minutes. Add the cilantro (coriander), mix well, and remove from heat and let rest for 10 minutes. Fluff up the rice with a fork, garnish with chile strips, and serve immediately.

ARROZ LUZ CATALINA

LUZ CATALINA RICE

1 cup (7 oz/200 g) long grain
  rice
3 cups (1¼ pints/750 ml)
  Chicken Stock (page 184)
¼ teaspoon saffron threads,
  lightly crushed
½ cup (4 fl oz/120 ml) olive oil
2 cloves garlic, sliced
½ onion, finely chopped
1 large tomato, seeds removed
  and finely chopped
⅔ cup (3½ oz/100 g) frozen peas
1 (4 oz/110 g) can red bell
  peppers, drained and cut into
  thin strips
sea salt

REGION: CHIHUAHUA
PREPARATION TIME: 25 MINUTES, PLUS
15 MINUTES SOAKING
COOKING TIME: 35 MINUTES
SERVES: 4

Put the rice into a heatproof bowl, pour in boiling water to cover, and let soak for 15 minutes. Drain, rinse several times in cold water until the water runs clear, drain well again, and set aside.

Heat the chicken stock with the saffron and a pinch of salt in a small saucepan over medium-low heat.

Heat the oil in another saucepan. Add the garlic, stirring frequently, for a few minutes until dark brown, then remove and discard. Add the rice and cook, stirring occasionally, for a few minutes until it begins to color. Drain off the excess oil, add the onion, and cook for 5 minutes, until softened. Stir in the tomato, peas and bell pepper strips, and add the hot chicken stock mixture.

Increase the heat to high and bring to a boil. Reduce the heat to low, cover, and simmer for 20 minutes. Turn off the heat and let stand for 5 minutes, then fluff up the rice with a fork.

ARROZ CON PESCADO

❋

RICE WITH FISH

1 cup (7 oz/200 g) long grain
  rice
9 oz/250 g sea bass fillets,
  sliced
6 cloves garlic, crushed
½ cup (4 fl oz/120 ml) olive oil
½ onion, finely chopped
2 cups (16 fl oz/475 ml) Fish
  Stock (page 184)
1 jalapeño chile, chopped
2 sprigs cilantro (coriander) or
  epazote, plus extra to garnish
sea salt and pepper

REGION: VERACRUZ
PREPARATION TIME: 30 MINUTES, PLUS 15 MINUTES
SOAKING AND 1 HOUR STANDING
COOKING TIME: 40 MINUTES
SERVES: 4

Put the rice into a heatproof bowl, pour in boiling water to cover, and let soak for 15 minutes. Drain, rinse several times in cold water until the water runs clear, and drain well again. Set aside.

Brush the fish with the garlic and a pinch of salt and let stand for 1 hour.

Heat the oil in a large frying pan or skillet. Add the fish and cook quickly over medium heat, turning once, for about 5 minutes, until lightly browned. Remove the fish from the skillet. Drain off the excess oil and reserve the oil.

Pour the remaining oil from pan into a large saucepan and set over low heat. Add the onion and crushed garlic and cook, stirring occasionally, for 5 minutes, until translucent. Meanwhile, put the fish stock into another saucepan and bring to a boil over low heat.

Add the rice to the onion and garlic pan and cook, occasionally stirring gently, for a few minutes until lightly golden. Add the fish stock, increase the heat, add the chile and cilantro (coriander), season with salt and pepper, and bring back to a boil. Reduce the heat to low, cover, and cook for 20 minutes, until the rice is tender. Add the fish and cook for 5 minutes, then turn off the heat and let stand. Remove and discard the herb sprigs and fluff up the rice with a fork.

Transfer to a serving dish, sprinkle with chopped cilantro (coriander) or epazote, and serve.

ARROZ ROJO

RED RICE

REGION: ALL REGIONS
PREPARATION TIME: 25 MINUTES, PLUS
15 MINUTES SOAKING
COOKING TIME: 35 MINUTES
SERVES: 4

1 cup (7 oz/200 g) long-grain
  rice
2 tomatoes, peeled, seeded
  removed, and chopped
2 cloves garlic, coarsely
  chopped
½ onion, coarsely chopped
½ cup (4 fl oz/120 ml) olive oil
2 cups (16 fl oz/475 ml)
  Chicken Stock (page 184)
2 carrots, diced
⅓ cup (2 oz/50 g) peas
1 serrano or cuaresmeño (fresh
  jalapeño) chile, chopped
4 sprigs cilantro (coriander)
4 sprigs parsley
sea salt

Put the rice into a heatproof bowl, pour in boiling water to cover, and let soak for 15 minutes. Drain, rinse several times in cold water until the water runs clear, and drain well again. Set aside.

Put the tomatoes, garlic, and onion into a food processor or blender and process to a smooth puree.

Heat the oil in a saucepan. Add the rice and cook over medium heat, occasionally stirring gently, for a few minutes until light golden brown. Drain off the excess oil, stir in the tomato mixture, and continue cooking until the puree has been absorbed.

Pour in the chicken stock, season with salt to taste, add the carrots, peas, and chile, and stir gently. Add the cilantro (coriander) and parsley, and bring to a boil. Cover and let cook for 15–20 minutes.

Remove the pan from the heat. Remove and discard the herbs and serve the rice immediately.

ARROZ A LA TUMBADA

❋

TUMBADA RICE

1½ cups (11 oz/300 g) long
  grain rice
7 oz/200 g firm fish fillets,
  diced
all-purpose (plain) flour,
  for dusting
1 cup (9 fl oz/250 ml) corn oil
5 tomatoes, roasted
2 small onions, 1 quartered
  and 1 finely chopped
4 cloves garlic, minced
8 large shrimp (prawns), peeled
  and deveined
3 crayfish, peeled and deveined
7 oz/200 g crabmeat
3½ oz/100 g octopus, cooked
  and diced
12 small clams, scrubbed
3 cups (1¼ pints/750 ml) Fish
  Stock (page 184)
10 epazote leaves, chopped
1 jalapeño chile, thinly sliced
sea salt and pepper

REGION: VERACRUZ
PREPARATION TIME: 40 MINUTES, PLUS
15 MINUTES SOAKING
COOKING TIME: 45 MINUTES
SERVES: 6

Put the rice into a heatproof bowl, pour in boiling water to cover, and let soak for 15 minutes. Drain, rinse several times in cold water until the water runs clear, and drain well again. Set aside.

Dust the fish with flour. Heat 4 tablespoons of the oil in a frying pan or skillet over medium heat and add the fish, turning frequently, for 5–6 minutes, until browned. Remove with a slotted spoon and drain on paper towels.

Heat 4 tablespoons of the oil in a saucepan. Add the rice and cook over low heat, occasionally stirring gently, for a few minutes until light golden brown. Drain off the excess oil and add 3 cups (1¼ pints/750 ml) hot water. Reduce the heat to low, cover, and cook for 20 minutes, until the rice is tender.

Put the tomatoes and one of the onions, quartered, into a food processor or blender and process until thoroughly combined. Strain into a bowl. Heat 2 tablespoons of the remaining oil in a small saucepan, add the tomato mixture, and cook over medium-low heat for 15 minutes. Remove the pan from the heat and set aside.

Heat the remaining oil in a large frying pan or skillet. Add the garlic and cook, stirring frequently, for 2–3 minutes, then add the shrimp (prawns), crayfish, and crabmeat and season well with salt and pepper. Add the octopus, clams, tomato sauce, and fish stock and simmer for 5 minutes. Bring to a boil, add the rice, and cook for 3 minutes, then stir in the finely chopped onion, epazote, and chile. Add the fish and cook for an additional 5 minutes, just to warm the fish through.

Transfer to a serving plate and serve immediately.

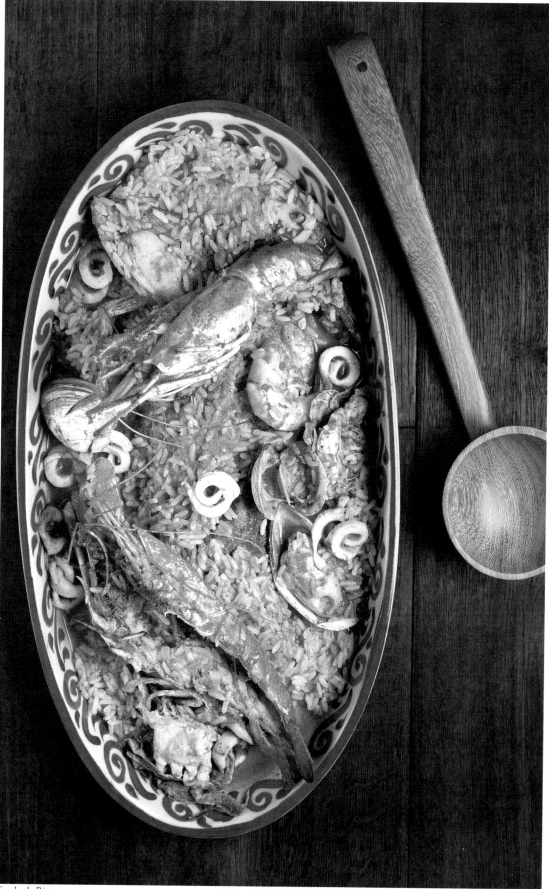

Tumbada Rice

ARROZ CREMOSA CON ELOTE

✸

RICE WITH CORN

1½ cups (11 oz/300 g) long
grain rice
3 tablespoons corn oil
1 onion, sliced
1 clove garlic, finely chopped
2 cups (16 fl oz/475 ml)
Chicken Stock (page 184)
1 cup (9 fl oz/250 ml) milk
2¼ cups (12 oz/350 g) corn
kernels
1 sprig cilantro (coriander)
2 poblano chiles, dry-roasted
and cut into thin strips
1 cup (5 oz/150 g) crumbled
queso fresco or feta cheese

REGION: BAJA CALIFORNIA
PREPARATION TIME: 25 MINUTES, PLUS
15 MINUTES SOAKING
COOKING TIME: 30 MINUTES
SERVES: 6

Put the rice into a heatproof bowl, pour in boiling water to cover, and let soak for 15 minutes. Drain, rinse several times in cold water until the water runs clear, and drain well again.

Heat 2 tablespoons of the oil in a saucepan. Add the rice, onion, and garlic and cook over medium heat, stirring frequently, for a few minutes. Do not let the garlic brown or it will become bitter. Drain off the excess oil, then add the chicken stock, milk, and corn kernels. Bring to a boil, reduce the heat to low, cover, and cook for 20 minutes. Remove the pan from the heat and let stand, still covered, for 5 minutes.

Meanwhile, heat the remaining oil in a small frying pan or skillet. Add the cilantro (coriander) and cook until they are dark green and crispy, then remove and drain on paper towels.

Fluff up the rice grains with a fork, then serve on individual plates, garnished with the chiles, cheese, and fried cilantro leaves.

SOPA ARROZ ALMEJAS

✿

RICE WITH CLAMS

1 cup (7 oz/200 g) long-grain rice
1 cup (8 fl oz/250 ml) Chicken Stock (page 184)
4 tablespoons chopped parsley
4 tablespoons chopped cilantro (coriander)
4 tablespoons chopped basil
2 poblano chiles, dry-roasted
1 Mexican pepperleaf, deveined and chopped
1 onion, finely chopped
1 clove garlic, finely chopped
2 cups (16 fl oz/450 ml) Fish Stock (page 184)
3 tablespoons corn oil
1 lb 2 oz (500 g) live clams
sea salt

REGION: NAYARIT
PREPARATION TIME: 25 MINUTES, PLUS 15 MINUTES SOAKING
COOKING TIME: 30 MINUTES
SERVES: 4

Put the rice into a heatproof bowl, pour in boiling water to cover, and let soak for 15 minutes. Drain, rinse several times in cold water until the water runs clear, and drain well again.

Pour the chicken stock, parsley, cilantro (coriander), basil, chiles, Mexican pepperleaf, onion, and garlic into a food processor and process until smooth. Strain into a bowl.

Bring the fish stock to a boil in a saucepan.

Meanwhile, heat the oil in another saucepan over medium heat. Add the rice, stir gently, and cook for 2–3 minutes until golden. Drain the oil, add the chicken stock mixture and stir. Add the fish stock and boil for 5 minutes. Reduce the heat, cover, and cook for 10 minutes or until the rice is nearly tender. Add the clams, discarding any with broken or damaged shells, and stir gently. Season to taste, cover, and cook for an additional 5 minutes or until rice is tender and clams have opened. Discard any that do not open. Serve immediately.

FRIJOLES REFRITOS

REFRIED BEANS

corn oil
1 white onion, finely chopped
1 lb/450 g cooked, strained
   black beans
120 g Panela cheese (fresh soft
   cheese) or heavy (double)
   cream cheese, grated or
   crumbled

REGION: BAJA CALIFORNIA
PREPARATION TIME: 30 MINUTES
COOKING TIME: 30 MINUTES
SERVES: 6

Heat the oil in a saucepan over medium heat, add the onion and sauté for 7 minutes, or until translucent. Add the beans, stir, and cook for 5 minutes, or until heated through. Remove from heat and mash the beans.

Serve in a service plate, giving a nice form, sprinkle on top with the cheese.

CALDILLO DE FRIJOL

BEAN STEW

1 tablespoon corn oil
7 oz (200 g) chorizo, skinned
   and coarsely chopped
2 small onions, finely chopped
3 cups (1 lb 2 oz/500 g) cooked
   black beans, cooking liquid
   reserved
4 avocado leaves
sea salt

REGION: OAXACA
PREPARATION TIME: 20 MINUTES
COOKING TIME: 30 MINUTES
SERVES: 6

Heat the oil in a saucepan. Add the chorizo and onion and cook over medium heat, stirring frequently, for 15 minutes.

Add the chorizo, onion, and beans to a food processor or blender and process into a coarse paste, adding some bean liquid, if necessary.

Return the mixture to the pan and season with salt. Add the avocado leaves, cover, and simmer for 15 minutes, adding more liquid, if necessary.

Discard the avocado leaves and serve as an accompaniment to any dish or with rice.

POT BEANS

2½ cups (1 lb 2 oz/500 g) dried
  pinto beans
2 white onions, coarsely
  chopped
1 tablespoon safflower oil
1 epazote sprig
sea salt

REGION: ALL REGIONS
PREPARATION TIME: 10 MINUTES, PLUS
12 HOURS SOAKING TIME
COOKING TIME: 2½ HOURS
SERVES: 6

In a bowl, soak the beans in cold water over night.

Drain the beans. Bring 7½ cups (60 fl oz/ 1.75 liters) water to a boil, add the beans and onions, and bring to another boi. Reduce the heat and simmer for two hours, or until they are tender.

Add the epazote, season with salt to taste, and cook for an additional 30 minutes, adding more water if necessary.

Note: In a pressure cooker they cook in 30 minutes, once they are tender add the epazote and salt, leave on for 20 minutes.

BLACK BEANS WITH GREEN BEANS AND MEMELAS

1¾ cups (12 oz/350 g) cooked
  black beans
3 cups (12 oz/350 g) green
  beans, cut into short lengths
¼ teaspoon sea salt
16 avocado leaves
4 cloves garlic
12 oz/350 g Masa Dough
  (page 36)
2¼ tablespoons butter
16 epazote leaves

REGION: OAXACA
PREPARATION TIME: 35 MINUTES
COOKING TIME: 1 HOUR 30 MINUTES
SERVES: 6

Put the black beans into a large saucepan, add water to cover, and bring to a boil. Boil vigorously for 25 minutes.

Add the green beans and simmer for an additional 30 minutes or until both beans are tender. Season with salt and simmer over low heat. Add the avocado leaves.

Combine the masa dough with the butter and salt in a bowl. Divide it into 8 pieces, shape into cylinders between the palms of your hands, and put a piece on each epazote leaf. Cover with another leaf and gently flatten to form the *memelas* (masa cakes).

Put the memelas on top of the beans in 2 layers and steam over low heat for 25 minutes, until the dough is cooked.

Remove the pan from the heat and lift out the memelas with a spatula. Divide the bean stew among 6 soup bowls, top with the memelas, and serve immediately.

FRIJOLES CHARROS

CHARROS BEANS

REGIONS: TAMAULIPAS, COAHUILA
PREPARATION TIME: 20 MINUTES
COOKING TIME: 2 HOURS 20 MINUTES
SERVES: 6

5 oz/150 g boneless pork and fatty beef, diced
¼ white onion, sliced
4 cloves garlic, finely chopped
3 tomatoes
1 tablespoon corn oil
3½ oz/100 g bacon
3½ oz/100 g chorizo, finely chopped
2–4 small green chiles, seeds removed and cut into thin strips
2¾ cups (1 lb 2 oz/300 g) cooked bayo or pinto beans
1 bunch cilantro (coriander), chopped
sea salt

Put the meat, onion, and half the garlic into a flameproof terracotta pot or a saucepan and add enough water to cover. Bring to a boil, reduce the heat, and simmer for 2 hours or until the meat is tender.

Preheat the oven to 400°F (200°C/Gas Mark 6). Put the tomatoes into a roasting pan and roast for 30 minutes. Remove the pan from the oven and let the tomatoes cool. Peel, seed, and finely chop the tomatoes.

Heat the oil in a frying pan or skillet. Add the bacon, chorizo, chopped tomatoes, chiles, remaining garlic, and beans and cook over medium heat, stirring occasionally, for about 10 minutes.

When the bean mixture has cooked, season with salt, add the meat with broth, and simmer for an additional 10 minutes, until it thickens.

Add the bacon mixture and a cilantro (coriander) sprig to the beans and simmer for an additional 10 minutes. If it dries out and begins to stick to the bottom of the pan, add a little more water.

Remove the pan from the heat and serve immediately, garnished with cilantro leaves.

Note: These beans can be served with broiled (grilled) meat. They can also be served as soup by adding a little more water.

FRIJOLES COLADOS

✳

STRAINED BEANS

3 cups (1 lb 2 oz/500 g) cooked
black beans, with their liquid
reserved
1 sprig epazote leaves
½ cup (4 oz/100 g) lard or corn
oil
2 small white onions, sliced
¼–½ habanero chile,
dry-roasted
sea salt

REGION: YUCATÁN
PREPARATION TIME: 10 MINUTES
COOKING TIME: 50 MINUTES
SERVES: 6

Put the cooked beans into a saucepan and just cover them with water. Season with salt and add the epazote. Simmer for 40 minutes, adding more liquid, if necessary. Discard the epazote.

Heat the lard in a frying pan or skillet. Add the onions and chile and cook over low heat, stirring occasionally, for 5 minutes. Add the onions and the chile to the beans and increase to medium-high heat. Simmer, stirring occasionally, until the beans are all puffy and broken in appearance but not dry.

Remove the pan from the heat and serve immediately to accompany a main dish or simply with rice for a hearty meal.

Note: You can process the beans in a food processor or blender and pass them through a strainer (sieve) before adding them to the skillet.

FRIJOLES CON XOCONOSTLES

✳

BEANS WITH XOCONOSTLES

5 xoconostles
2 tablespoons (1 oz/25 g) corn
oil
3 cups (1 lb 2 oz/500 g) cooked
black or red beans, with their
liquid reserved
2 green jalapeños, membrane
and seeds removed and diced
2 white onions, chopped
½ cup (1 oz/25 g) chopped
cilantro (coriander)

REGION: FEDERAL DISTRICT
PREPARATION TIME: 20 MINUTES
COOKING TIME: 20 MINUTES
SERVES: 6–8

Preheat the oven to 350°F (180°C/Gas Mark 4). Put the xoconostles into a roasting pan and roast for 15 minutes. Remove from oven and let cool. Peel, seed, and dice the xoconostles.

Meanwhile, heat the oil in a large saucepan over medium heat. Add the beans and just cover them with their cooking liquid. Simmer for 20 minutes.

Remove the beans from the heat and transfer to a deep serving dish. Sprinkle with the xoconostles, jalapeños, onion, and cilantro (coriander) and serve immediately.

FRIJOLES CON ELOTE

✺

CORN AND BEANS

5 green serrano chiles, dry-roasted
1 white onion, sliced and dry-roasted
1 clove garlic, dry-roasted
1 tablespoon corn oil
1½ cups (8 oz/225 g) corn kernels
2 cups (13 oz/375 g) pinto or mayacoba beans
6 tablespoons pumpkin seeds, dry-roasted
pinch of sea salt
Corn Tortillas (page 36), to serve

REGION: CHIHUAHUA
PREPARATION TIME: 35 MINUTES
COOKING TIME: 20 MINUTES
SERVES: 6

Combine the chiles, onion, and garlic in a food processor or blender and process until thoroughly combined. Heat the oil in a skillet, add the processed mixture, and cook over low heat, stirring occasionally, for about 5 minutes. Remove the pan from the heat.

Add the corn kernels and a pinch of salt to the beans and cook for another 10 minutes, then stir in the chile mixture. Remove the pan from the heat.

Divide the beans among individual plates, sprinkle with pumpkin seeds, and serve immediately with warm tortillas.

FRIJOL DE NOVIOS

✺

SWEETHEART BEANS

4 cups (2¼ lb/1 kg) canned pinto or kidney beans, liquid reserved
4 tablespoons (2 oz/50 g) lard
1 white onion, sliced
3 bay leaves
1 lb 2 oz (500 g) chorizo, skinned and chopped
4 tablespoons adobo paste
1½ teapoons dried oregano
sea salt

To serve:
4¼ oz/120 g fresh cheese
2 avocados, peeled, pitted, and sliced

REGION: PUEBLA
PREPARATION TIME: 10 MINUTES
COOKING TIME: 20 MINUTES
SERVES: 8

Place the beans in a blender and puree into a coarse paste, adding the reserved bean liquid, if necessary.

Melt half the lard in a saucepan. Add the onion and bay leaves and cook over low heat, stirring occasionally, for 5 minutes. Transfer the onion to a plate. Add the chorizo, increase the heat to medium, and cook, stirring frequently, for 8–10 minutes. Remove with a slotted spoon and put on the plate with the onion.

Melt the remaining lard in the pan, add the beans and cook, stirring occasionally, for a few minutes. Stir in the adobo paste and oregano and season to taste. Simmer gently until the beans are cooked through, then remove the pan from the heat.

Serve immediately by spooning some beans on a plate and topping them with chorizo and onions. Garnish with cheese and avocado.

QUELITES CON FRIJOLES ENTEROS

WILD GREENS WITH BEANS

3 tablespoons corn oil
1 white onion, finely chopped
1 tomato, finely chopped
2 cloves garlic, finely chopped
1 green chile, finely chopped
1 tablespoons all-purpose
  (plain) flour
1 lb 10 oz (750 g) wild greens,
  cooked and drained
1 cup (5 oz/150 g) cooked
  beans with 2 cups (16 fl oz/
  475 ml) reserved liquid
sea salt
Corn Tortillas (page 36),
  to serve

REGION: FEDERAL DISTRICT
PREPARATION TIME: 15 MINUTES
COOKING TIME: 25 MINUTES
SERVES: 6

Heat the oil in a medium pan. Add the onion and cook over low heat, stirring occasionally, for 5 minutes. Add the tomato, garlic, and chile and cooking for an additional 5 minutes. Add the flour and cook, stirring constantly, for a few minutes until lightly browned.

Stir in the wild greens, beans, and reserved cooking liquid, season with salt, and simmer for 10 minutes.

Remove the pan from the heat and divide the mixture among 6 deep soup plates. Serve immediately with warm tortillas.

AYOCOTES EN MOLE

AYOCOTE BEANS IN MOLE

2 dried guajillos chiles,
  dry-roasted
1½ cups (9 oz/250 g) ayocote
  beans
1 onion, halved, plus ½ onion,
  sliced, to garnish
4 tablespoons corn oil
1¾ cups (9 oz/250 g) diced,
  cooked pork
4 oz (125 g) Spanish sausage
4 oz (125 g) pork rinds
  (scratchings)
2 cloves garlic
sea salt
olive oil, to drizzle
oregano, to garnish

REGION: PUEBLA
PREPARATION TIME: 15 MINUTES, PLUS
30 MINUTES SOAKING
COOKING TIME: 45 MINUTES
SERVES: 6

Soak the chiles in a little warm water for 30 minutes. Drain and set aside.

Put the beans in a large saucepan, add an onion half and the oil, cover with water, and cook for 30 minutes. Add the pork, sausage, and pork rinds (scratchings), and season with salt.

Put the garlic, the other onion half, and the soaked chiles in a food processor or blender and process until smooth. Add to the beans in the pan and cook for another 15 minutes. Season with salt to taste.

Transfer the beans to a hot, deep serving dish. Garnish with a few sliced onions, drizzle with olive oil, and sprinkle over the oregano.

ROSCA BICOLOR DE FRIJOL

RED AND BLACK BEAN WREATH

1½ cups (8½ oz/240 g) cooked
   black beans
1½ cups (8½ oz/240 g) cooked
   pinto beans
9 oz/250 g good-quality
   chorizo, crumbled or finely
   chopped
1 white onion, finely chopped
2–4 marinated chipotle chiles
4 tablespoons flour, plus extra
   for dusting
olive oil, for greasing
1¼ cups (5 oz/150 g) manchego
   or chihuahua cheese, grated
tortilla chips, to serve

REGION: ALL REGIONS
PREPARATION TIME: 25 MINUTES
COOKING TIME: 1 HOUR
SERVES: 6–8

Puree the black beans into a coarse paste in a food
processor or blender. Scrape them out into a bowl
and then rinse out the food processor or blender.
Puree the pinto beans into a coarse paste and scrape
them into a second bowl. Keep the beans separate
at this point.

Preheat the oven to 350°F (180°C/Gas Mark 4).

Fry the chorizo in a pan over medium heat for
5 minutes, then drain off the excess fat, setting it
aside, and add the chopped onion. Sauté for 10
minutes, then add the chipotle chile.

In another pan, heat half of the reserved chorizo
oil over medium heat, add half the flour, and fry
for 2–3 minutes. Add the black beans, stir, and
cook for 5–10 minutes, or until they are completely
dry. Remove them from the pan and clean the pan.
Repeat the process with the pinto beans, returning
them to a separate bowl once they are fried.

Oil a crown mold with olive oil, then dust with
flour, shaking out any excess, and pour in the black
bean mixture. Spread it out until it covers the
bottom, then completely cover with half the chorizo.
Make a layer of pinto beans on top and
cover with the other half of the chorizo. Sprinkle
the cheese over the top and bake in the oven for
25 minutes. Let cool completely and tip onto
a serving plate. Serve with tortilla chips for dipping.

Red and Black Bean Wreath

✺

CASSAVA DUMPLINGS WITH BLACK BEANS

2½ lb/1 kg cassavas, peeled, diced, and ground in a food processor or blender
1 teaspoon sea salt
4 cups (1 lb 8 oz/700 g) cooked black beans, cooking liquid reserved
5 serrano chiles
2 cloves garlic
5 avocado leaves, roasted

REGION: TABASCO
PREPARATION TIME: 20 MINUTES
COOKING TIME: 20 MINUTES
SERVES: 6

Put the cassavas in a large bowl and just cover with water in a bowl. Using your hands, mix the cassavas into the water to make a dough. If necessary, add a little more water to make a dough. Add the salt, mix well, and shape the dough into 30 ¾-inch (1.5-cm) balls.

Put 1 cup (9 fl oz/250 ml) reserved bean liquid, the chiles, and garlic into a food processor or blender and process until combined. Put the beans in a saucepan, add the liquid from the food processor, and simmer for 5 minutes. Add the avocado leaves, the cassava dumplings, and more bean liquid or water to get a stewy consistency. Cover and cook for 10–15 minutes until the dumplings are glistening and cooked through (insert the tip of a knife to check).

Remove the pan from the heat and serve immediately in deep soup bowls.

✺

CHICKPEAS AND CACTUS PADDLES

7 tomatoes
3 serrano chiles
1 white onion, quartered
2 cloves garlic
3 tablespoons corn oil
5 cactus paddles, cooked and diced
½ teaspoon dried oregano
1 cup (6 oz/175 g) cooked chickpeas, cooking liquid reserved
1 sprig cilantro (coriander)
sea salt

REGION: GUANAJUATO
PREPARATION TIME: 20 MINUTES
COOKING TIME: 40 MINUTES
SERVES: 6

Put the tomatoes and chiles into a medium saucepan, add 1¼ cups (½ pint/300 ml) water, and cook over low heat for 20 minutes. Remove the pan from the heat, drain, and reserve the cooking liquid. Transfer the tomatoes and chiles to a food processor or blender, add the onion and garlic, and process until thoroughly combined. Add some of the liquid.

Heat the oil in another saucepan. Add the cactus paddles and cook for 5 minutes. Stir in the oregano.

Add the tomato mixture, 1 cup (9 fl oz/250 ml) of the reserved cooking liquid, and the chickpeas. Stir in the cilantro (coriander) and taste. Add a pinch of salt if necessary. Bring to a boil, then reduce the heat, and simmer for 15 minutes.

Remove the pan from the heat and serve.

Cassava Dumplings with Black Beans

Spinach with Chickpeas

FRIJOLES CON HUESO DE PUERCO

✴

BEANS WITH PORK BONES

3 cups (1 lb 2 oz/500 g) cooked
   black beans, cooking liquid
   reserved
1 lb 5 oz/600 g pork leg bone
   with some meat on it
½ large white onion, chopped
1 clove garlic
5 tablespoons chopped cilantro
   (coriander)
2–3 green chiles, chopped
sea salt

REGION: YUCATÁN
PREPARATION TIME: 10 MINUTES
COOKING TIME: 30 MINUTES
SERVES: 6

Put the beans in a saucepan and just cover them
with their liquid. Add water if necessary.

Add the pork bone, a pinch of salt, and the onion
and simmer for 20 minutes. Add the garlic, cilantro
(coriander), and chiles, season to taste with salt, and
simmer for an additional 10 minutes.

Remove the pan from the heat, taste, and adjust
the seasoning, if necessary. Serve immediately—
without the bone of course—to accompany a main
dish or with rice.

ESPINACAS CON GARBANZO

✴

SPINACH WITH CHICKPEAS

2 cups (12 oz/350 g) cooked
   chickpeas, drained
2¼ lb/1 kg spinach, coarse
   stems removed
½ cup (4 fl oz/120 ml) olive oil
4 cloves garlic, chopped
1 tablespoon paprika
1 tablespoon white wine
sea salt and pepper

REGION: FEDERAL DISTRICT
PREPARATION TIME: 10 MINUTES
COOKING TIME: 15 MINUTES
SERVES: 6

Put the chickpeas in a bowl and cover with half
of the olive oil. Stir well to coat the chickpeas.

Put the spinach into a saucepan, add a pinch
of salt, and cook for 5–10 minutes, until tender.
Drain well, let cool, squeeze out as much water
as possible, then chop.

Heat the remaining oil in a frying pan or skillet.
Add the garlic and cook over low heat, stirring
frequently, for a few minutes until lightly golden.
Add the chickpeas, paprika, and spinach to the
pan, mix well, and cook for 2–3 minutes. Season
to taste, add the white wine, and cook for an
additional few minutes.

Remove the pan from the heat and serve.

CHICKPEAS IN YELLOW MOLE

pinch of cumin seeds

2 tablespoons ground turmeric

¾ cup (3½ oz/100 g) masa
  harina

5½ tablespoons (2¾ oz/70 g)
  corn oil or lard

2 white onions, finely chopped

2 cloves garlic, finely chopped

3 tomatoes, chopped

6 cascabel chiles, dry-roasted

2 cups (16 fl oz/475 ml) chicken
  broth

3 cups (1 lb 2 oz/500 g) cooked
  chickpeas, drained

2 sprigs parsley, chopped, to
  garnish

sea salt

REGION: BUSCAR QUERETARO
PREPARATION TIME: 20 MINUTES
COOKING TIME: 20 MINUTES
SERVES: 6

In a small bowl, combine the cumin, turmeric, and 1 cup (9 fl oz/250 ml) water and mix well. Dissolve the masa harina in ½ cup (4 fl oz/120 ml) water and set aside.

In a large saucepan, heat the oil and sauté the onions, garlic, tomato, and chiles. Add the stock and cumin mixture, and season to taste. Bring to a boil and cook for 5 minutes, then add the masa mixture and cook until thickened.

Add the chickpeas and cook for an additional 10 minutes, adding more chicken stock to keep the chickpeas moist. Transfer to a serving platter and garnish with parsley. Serve hot.

LENTILS WITH CHORIZO

1¼ cups (9 oz/250 g) green
  lentils

pinch of sea salt

2 tablespoons corn oil

2 oz/50 g chorizo, sliced

1 white onion, chopped

1 clove garlic, chopped

1 sweet bell pepper, chopped

1 tomato, chopped

chopped parsley, to taste

REGION: ALL REGIONS
PREPARATION TIME: 15 MINUTES
COOKING TIME: 40 MINUTES
SERVES: 6

Put the lentils into a large saucepan, pour in enough water to cover, and cook over medium heat for 20–30 minutes, or until cooked. Add salt to taste.

Heat the oil in a saucepan over medium-low heat, add the chorizo and cook for 5 minutes. Remove the chorizo with a slotted spoon and set aside. Add the onion, garlic, sweet bell pepper, tomato, and parsley, and cook for 10 minutes. Add the lentils, adjust the seasoning, and cook for an additional 10 minutes. Transfer to a bowl, top with chorizo, and serve immediately.

Note: The lentils can be replaced with fava (broad) beans.

Lentils with Chorizo

TORTAS DE HABAS

✺

FAVA BEAN PATTIES

1½ cups (8 oz/225 g) cooked
   fava (broad) beans, drained
1½ cups (9 oz/250 g) cooked
   chickpeas, drained
2 eggs, lightly beaten
3 tablespoons corn oil, plus
   extra for frying
¼ white onion, finely chopped
1 tomato, chopped
4 zucchini (courgettes), finely
   chopped
sea salt

For the sauce (optional):
2 tomatoes
1 clove garlic
¼ onion
1 green chile

REGION: NAYARIT
PREPARATION TIME: 20 MINUTES
COOKING TIME: 30 MINUTES
SERVES: 6

Put the fava (broad) beans and chickpeas into a food processor or blender and process to a coarse paste. Add a little water if necessary. Transfer to a bowl, add the eggs and season with salt, and mix well. Set aside.

Heat the oil in a large frying pan or skillet over medium heat, add the onion and tomato and cook for 10 minutes. Add the zucchini (courgettes), season with salt and pepper, and simmer for 5–10 minutes, or until all the moisture has evaporated. Check the seasoning and remove from the heat. Add the bean mixture and mix well.

Take 2 tablespoons of the mixture, roll it into a ball, and flatten it into a patty. Repeat until all the mixture is used.

Put enough corn oil in a heavy saucepan to cover the bottom. Place the pan over medium heat and cook the patties, in small batches, on both sides for 2–3 minutes, or until slightly brown. Remove with a slotted spoon and drain on paper towels.

For the sauce, if using, combine all the ingredients into a food processor or blender and process until ground. Heat 1 tablespoon of corn oil in a saucepan over medium heat, then add the mixture, and fry for a few minutes. Bring to a boil, and cook for 5 minutes, stirring occasionally so it does not burn. Season with salt.

Arrange a few patties on a plate and serve with the sauce, if using.

Fava Bean Patties

PASTEL DE ELOTE

✺

CORN CAKE WITH EGGNOG SAUCE

¾ cup (7 oz/200 g) butter, plus
  extra for greasing
2½ cups (12 oz/350 g) fresh
  corn kernels
5 eggs
1 cup (7 oz/200 g) superfine
  (caster) sugar
1 teaspoon vanilla extract

For the eggnog sauce:
2 cups (¾ pint/450 ml) heavy
  (double) cream
2 egg yolks
4 tablespoons sugar
4 tablespoons brandy
½ teaspoon vanilla extract
grated fresh nutmeg, to taste

To decorate:
1 tablespoon confectioners'
  (icing) sugar
6–8 cinnamon sticks

REGION: ALL REGIONS
PREPARATION TIME: 30 MINUTES
COOKING TIME: 50 MINUTES
SERVES: 6

Preheat the oven to 350°F (180°C/Gas Mark 4).

Melt the butter and set aside to cool to room temperature. Line an 8-inch (20-cm) round cake pan with parchment paper, then grease with butter.

Put the corn kernels into a food processor or blender and process until smooth. Add the eggs, sugar, and vanilla and process until thoroughly combined. Add the melted, cooled butter and process briefly to combine.

Pour into the prepared pan and bake for 45–50 minutes or until set in the center. Remove the pan from the oven and let cool for 20 minutes.

Meanwhile, make the eggnog sauce. Put the cream, egg yolks, sugar, brandy, and vanilla extract into a bowl and stir to dissolve the sugar. (Do not process in a machine or you will get whipped cream.) Season to taste with grated nutmeg.

Turn out the cake while it is still warm and cut into slices. Pour a pool of the eggnog sauce onto each of 6–8 dessert plates, place a slice of warm cake on top, sprinkle with confectioners' (icing) sugar, and decorate with cinnamon sticks.

PANQUÉ DE NATA

✺

POUND CAKE

butter, for greasing
1¼ cups (5 oz/150 g) all-purpose
  (plain) flour, sifted, plus extra
  for dusting
4 eggs
¾ cup (5 oz/150 g) sugar
a pinch of sea salt
1 teaspoon baking powder
⅔ cup (¼ pint/150 ml) heavy
  (double) cream
2 tablespoons brandy

REGION: QUERETARO, BAJIO
PREPARATION TIME: 25 MINUTES
COOKING TIME: 45 MINUTES
SERVES: 4–6

Preheat the oven to 325°F (160°C/Gas Mark 3). Grease and flour a 10 x 4-inch (25 x 10-cm) rectangular cake pan.

Beat the eggs with the sugar and salt, then gradually add the flour and baking powder. Beat in the cream and continue beating until thickened. Stir in the brandy.

Pour into the pan and bake for about 45 minutes or until golden brown and a toothpick or skewer inserted into the center comes out clean. Let rest in the pan for 15 minutes, then cool on a wire rack.

PAN DE MUERTO ESTILO OAXAQUEÑO

OAXACAN "DAY OF THE DEAD" BREAD

2 cups (9 oz/250 g) all-purpose (plain) flour, plus extra for dusting
2 tablespoons sugar
pinch of sea salt
¾ teaspoon active dry (fast-action) yeast
1 egg
5 tablespoons milk
¼ teaspoon orange blossom extract
4 tablespoons (2 oz/50 g) butter
1 teaspoon anise seeds

To decorate:
1 egg
sesame seeds, for sprinkling

REGION: OAXACA
PREPARATION TIME: 30 MINUTES, PLUS RISING TIME
COOKING TIME: 30–45 MINUTES
MAKES: 1 LOAF

Sift the flour into a bowl and make a well in the center. Put the sugar, salt, and yeast into the well. Add the remaining ingredients and mix well. Transfer the dough to a clean work surface and knead for 10 minutes. Put the dough back into the bowl, cover with a dish towel, and let rise for 1–2 hours or until it has doubled in size.

For a classic loaf, pull the dough out gently and shape into a ball. Flatten it slightly and put it onto a baking sheet. Alternatively, shape the dough into human figures: halve the dough and shape each piece into an oval. Make a cut in each side and separate the dough to make arms. Make a cut in the middle at one end and separate the dough to make legs. Cover and let rise for 45 minutes.

Preheat the oven to 400°F (200°C/Gas Mark 6).

To decorate, beat the egg with 1 teaspoon water and brush the glaze over the loaf, then sprinkle with sesame seeds. Bake for 30–45 minutes for a round loaf or 25–30 minutes for the figures. To test if the loaf is cooked, tap the base and if it sounds hollow, it is ready. Remove from the oven and transfer to a wire rack to cool.

Note: This recipe is by the talented chef Jorge Álvarez. The classic round loaf is usually glazed with egg and sprinkled with sesame seeds. The "figures" may be painted with red food coloring once they have been baked.

PAN DE YEMA DE OAXACA

✳

OAXACAN EGG YOLK BREAD

3 teaspoons active dry
  (fast-action) yeast
8 cups (2¼ lb/1 kg) all-purpose
  (plain) flour
1 cup (9 fl oz/250 ml) sweet
  pulque or water
1¼ cups (9 oz/250 g) sugar
1 cup plus 2 tablespoons
  (9 oz/250 g) butter, melted
  and cooled, plus extra for
  greasing
18 egg yolks
1 tablespoon anise seeds

To decorate:
4 tablespoons (2 oz/50 g) butter
  or lard, melted and and
  cooled
sesame seeds

REGION: ALL REGIONS
PREPARATION TIME: 50 MINUTES, PLUS
24 HOURS RISING
COOKING TIME: 30 MINUTES
MAKES: 20

Combine the yeast, 1 cup (4 oz/120 g) flour,
4 tablespoons sugar, and the pulque in a bowl and
mix well. Cover and let sit at room temperature
for 1 hour.

Put the remaining ingredients in a large bowl
and add the yeast mixture. Bring the dough
together in the bowl and then knead well for
3–4 minutes. Cover with plastic wrap (clingfilm)
and refrigerate overnight.

Line 2 baking sheets with parchment paper.
Transfer the dough to a clean work surface and
divide into 20 pieces. Shape each into a tight ball
and place onto the baking sheets. Cover them
with a clean dish towel and let rest for 3–4 hours,
doubled in size.

Meanwhile, preheat the oven to 425°F (220°C/Gas
Mark 7).

Brush the dough with melted butter, sprinkle
with sesame seeds, and bake in the oven for
20 minutes. When you tap the bottom of a bread
it should sound hollow. If it does not, return them to
the oven to bake for another 5 minutes. Transfer
to wire racks to cool completely.

Oaxacan Egg Yolk Bread

PAN DE MANTECA

※

BUTTER BREAD

⅔ cup (¼ pint/150 ml) milk
4 cups (1 lb 2 oz/500 g)
    all-purpose (plain) flour
5 tablespoons sugar
1½ cups (11 oz/300 g) lard
    or butter
2 eggs
3¼ tablespoons active dry
    (fast-action) yeast
1 teaspoon sea salt

To glaze:
1 egg
pinch of sea salt
pinch of sugar

REGION: ALL MEXICO
PREPARATION TIME: 40 MINUTES,
PLUS 10 MINUTES RESTING
COOKING TIME: 20 MINUTES
MAKES: 15 PIECES

Put the milk into a small saucepan, bring to a boil, then let cool and set aside.

Combine the flour, sugar, yeast, eggs, salt, and milk in a food processor and beat for 10 minutes. Add the butter or lard and mix for another 5 minutes, then let rest for an additional 10 minutes.

Preheat the oven to 375°F (190°C/Gas Mark 5). Line a baking sheet with parchment paper.

Make a ball of the dough and cut it in half. Divide each half into 3 pieces. Take a piece of dough and roll it so it measures 6 inches (15 cm). Twist the strip: one end clockwise, the other end counter-clockwise. Put the strip on a baking sheet. Repeat this twice more, leaving a 1¼-inch (3-cm) space between the strips. Make 3 more strips and put them in the opposite direction, then braid the strips so that they form a lattice, leaving space for the dough to expand during cooking.

To make the glaze, combine all the ingredients with 1 tablespoon water and mix well. Glaze the dough. Bake for 15 minutes or until lightly browned.

Remove from the oven and let cool on a wire rack.

PAN DE ELOTE

CORN BREAD

6⅔ cups (2¼ lb/1 kg) corn
    kernels
3 tablespoons milk powder
3 eggs
⅔ cup (4 oz/120 g) sugar
1 teaspoon sea salt
⅔ cup (4 oz/120 g) butter
    or lard
½ teaspoon active dry
    (fast-action) yeast
¼ teaspoon ground cinnamon
corn oil, for brushing

REGION: VERACRUZ
PREPARATION TIME: 30 MINUTES
COOKING TIME: 45 MINUTES
MAKES: 8–12 PIECES

Process the corn in a food processor or blender until smooth. Add the milk powder, eggs, sugar, salt, and butter or lard and mix well, then stir in the yeast and cinnamon to form a thick mixture with no lumps.

Preheat the oven to 375°F (190°C/Gas Mark 5). Brush a 12-inch (30-cm) round cake pan with oil and line with parchment paper.

Put the dough into the prepared pan and bake for 45 minutes or until a toothpick or skewer inserted into the center of the bread comes out clean.

This bread is delicious served with coffee or atole.

SEMITAS DE ANIS

SWEET ANISEED BISCUITS

¾ cup (7 oz/200 g) butter,
    plus extra for greasing
1 tablespoon anise seeds
4 cups (1 lb 2 oz/500 g)
    all-purpose (plain) flour,
    plus extra for dusting
¼ teaspoon sea salt
1½ teaspoons baking powder
1¼ cups (9 oz/250 g) raw cane
    sugar, plus 6 tablespoons for
    sprinkling

REGION: NUEVO LEÓN, MICHOACAN, CENTRAL MEXICO
PREPARATION TIME: 30 MINUTES
COOKING TIME: 15–20 MINUTES
MAKES: 8

Preheat the oven to 350°F (180°C/Gas Mark 4). Grease 2 baking sheets with butter.

Put the anise seeds and 4 tablespoons water into a small saucepan over medium-high heat, and bring to a boil. Remove the pan from the heat, cover, and let cool.

Sift together the flour, salt, and baking powder into a mound on a work surface and make a well in the center. Put half the butter, sugar, and anise water into the well and gradually incorporate the dry ingredients with your hands to form a dough.

Knead lightly for 10 minutes and divide the dough into 8 pieces. On a lightly floured work surface, roll out each piece into a ½-inch (1-cm) thick disk. Sprinkle with sugar and put onto the prepared baking sheets. Bake for 15–20 minutes, until golden. Remove the baking sheets from the oven and transfer to wire racks to cool.

PAN DE MUERTO

✺

"DAY OF THE DEAD" BREAD

1 cup (9 fl oz/250 ml) milk

4 cups (1 lb 2 oz/500 g) plain
(all-purpose) flour

½ cup (3½ oz/100 g) sugar, plus
extra for sprinkling

1½ teaspoons active dry
(fast-action) yeast

4 eggs

½ teaspoon sea salt

1 tablespoon grated orange zest

1–2 teaspoon orange blossom
water, to taste

¾ cup (7 oz/200 g) cold butter,
diced

melted butter, for greasing
and brushing

To glaze:
1 egg, beaten
pinch of sea salt
pinch of sugar

REGION: CENTRAL MEXICO, FEDERAL DISTRICT
PREPARATION TIME: 1 HOUR, PLUS 4 HOURS RISING
COOKING TIME: 45 MINUTES
MAKES: 2 (1-LB 2-OZ/500-G) LOAVES

Bring the milk to a boil in a small saucepan over medium-high heat, then remove from heat and let cool. Set aside.

Put the flour into a large bowl and make a well. Sprinkle in the sugar and yeast and pour in the milk. Close the well by flicking flour over the milk and let it sit for 1 hour.

Add the remaining ingredients, except the melted butter, and shape into a ball. Transfer to a clean work surface and knead for 10 minutes. Add the butter and knead again for 10 minutes. Return to the bowl and cover. Let rise for 2 hours, until doubled in size.

Grease 2 baking sheets with butter. Divide the dough into 3 pieces. Take two of those pieces and roll them into tight balls and then press them gently to flatten a bit. Cover and let rise for 1 hour. Preheat the oven to 400°F (200°C/Gas Mark 6).

After 1 hour, take the remaining piece of dough and divide it into 10 little pieces. Roll 2 of these pieces into small balls and 8 of these pieces into long, thin logs.

To make the glaze, combine all the ingredients and 1 tablespoon water in a small bowl and mix well. Brush the loaves gently with the glaze. Take four of the logs and drape them in an X shape over one of the disks of dough. Repeat for the other disk of dough. Brush these with egg. Take a little ball of dough and place it on the top of one disk of dough, where the X meets. Press down gently so it sticks. Repeat for the other little ball of dough.

Glaze the dough balls and bake in the oven for 30–35 minutes or until golden. Remove from the oven and transfer to a wire rack to cool. While they are still warm, brush with melted butter and sprinkle with sugar.

"Day of the Dead" Bread

CONCHAS

SHELLS

½ cup (3½ fl oz/100ml) milk

4 cups (1 lb 2 oz/500 g)
  all-purpose (plain) flour, plus
  extra for dusting

¾ cup (5 oz/150 g) sugar

3½ teaspoons active dry
  (fast-action) yeast

⅛ teaspoon sea salt

1 tablespoon powdered milk

7 tablespoons (3½ oz/100 g)
  butter, plus extra for greasing

4 eggs, lightly beaten

oil, for oiling

For the topping:

7 tablespoons (3½ oz/100 g)
  butter

¾ cup (3½ oz/100 g)
  confectioners' (icing) sugar

¾ cup (3½ oz/100 g) all-purpose
  (plain) flour

REGION: ALL REGIONS
PREPARATION TIME: 1 HOUR, PLUS 1 HOUR RISING
COOKING TIME: 25–30 MINUTES
MAKES: 15–20

Bring the milk to a boil in a small saucepan over medium-high heat, then remove from heat and let cool. Set aside.

Combine 2 tablespoons flour, 1½ teaspoons sugar, milk, and the yeast in a small bowl and mix well. Let stand until the mixture doubles in volume.

On a clean work surface, sift together the remaining flour and the salt into a mound and make a well in the center. Add the remaining sugar, powdered milk, butter, eggs, and yeast mixture to the well and, using your fingers, gradually incorporate the dry ingredients. Knead well until a soft and elastic dough forms. Shape the dough into a ball, put it into a bowl, cover with an oiled plastic wrap (clingfilm), and let rise until doubled in volume.

Meanwhile, make the topping. Beat the butter with the sugar until light and fluffy. Add the flour and mix well to form a paste.

Grease a baking sheet with butter. Transfer the dough to a lightly floured surface, punch down (knock back), and knead briefly. Shape it into 15–20 balls, place them on the prepared baking sheet, press lightly, and brush with melted butter.

Shape 15–20 balls from the topping paste, roll out with a rolling pin into thin rounds, and then cover each dough ball, pressing carefully to stick. Dust a shell mold with flour and press it onto the paste to leave a shell imprint. Let the rolls stand until doubled in volume.

Preheat the oven to 375°F (190°C/Gas Mark 5).

Bake the bread shells for 20–25 minutes or until they are cooked through. Remove the baking sheet from the oven, transfer to a wire rack, and let cool.

Note: To make chocolate-flavored shells, replace 2 tablespoons of flour in the dough with cocoa powder.

Shells

ROSCA DE REYES

KING'S RING

20 g fresh yeast or 10 g dry
  yeast
⅓ cup (2½ oz/65 g) sugar
4½ cups (1 lb 2 oz/500 g)
  all-purpose (plain) flour, plus
  extra for dusting
3 extra large (UK large) eggs,
  lightly beaten
butter, for greasing

For the dough:
pinch of sea salt
generous 1 cup (8 oz/225 g)
  sugar
scant 1 cup (7 oz/200 g) butter
  cold, diced
4½ cups (1 lb 2 oz/500 g)
  all-purpose (plain) flour, plus
  extra for dusting
8 eggs, lightly beaten with
  2 tablespoons water
2 tablespoons orange blossom
  water
1 teaspoon grated orange zest
1 teaspoon grated lemon zest

For the topping:
¾ cup (3 oz/80 g) all-purpose
  (plain) flour
20 g sea salt
4 tablespoons (2 oz/50 g)
  butter, at room temperature
½ cup (2 oz/50 g) confectioners'
  (icing) sugar, sifted
1 egg

To decorate:
1 beaten egg
sugar, for sprinkling
candied fruit (figs, cherries,
  oranges), cut into strips
melted butter, for brushing

REGION: ALL REGIONS
PREPARATION TIME: 1 HOUR, PLUS 15 MINUTES
STANDING AND OVERNIGHT RISING
COOKING TIME: 25–30 MINUTES
SERVES: 6

Pour 4 tablespoons lukewarm water into a bowl. Add the yeast and 1 teaspoon of the sugar. Let stand for 10–15 minutes.

Put the flour, sugar, and salt into a bowl and mix well. Add the yeast mixture and eggs and mix into a rough dough. Cover and let stand for a couple of hours.

To make the dough, put the flour into a large bowl. Add the salt and stir. Add the starter dough, eggs, orange blossom water, orange and lemon zests and bring the dough together. Knead for 10 minutes. Add the butter and knead the dough for another 10 minutes until the butter is completely incorporated and the dough is shiny and elastic. Put the dough back in the bowl, cover with plastic wrap (clingfilm) and let rise for 4 hours or so, until doubled in size.

Line 2 baking sheets with parchment paper.

Divide the dough in half and shape each half into a roll, about 2 inches (5 cm) in diameter. Join the ends of each roll to make a wreath, sealing with beaten egg. Put a wreath on each baking sheet, cover with clean dish towels, and let stand for 1 hour.

Meanwhile, combine all the topping ingredients in a bowl and mix them to make a smooth paste. Cover with plastic wrap and put in the refrigerator.

Preheat the oven to 400°F (200°C/Gas Mark 6).

Brush both wreaths with beaten egg. Remove the paste from the fridge and divide it into 8 long strips. On a floury surface, use a strip to cover the seam and then evenly space the strips around the wreath. Cover the remaining strips in beaten egg and sprinkle them with a little sugar. Decorate the rest of the wreath with the candied fruit and sprinkle sugar over the top. Bake for 25–30 minutes. Check after 20 minutes or so and if the wreaths are getting too brown, cover them with aluminum foil or wax (greaseproof) paper. Remove them from the oven and carefully transfer them, on their paper, to a wire rack to cool.

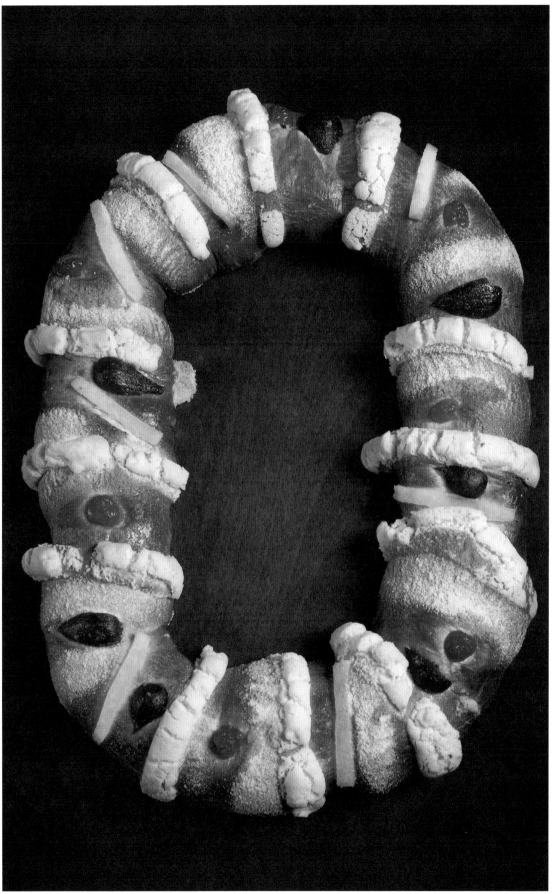

King's Ring

Campechanas

CAMPECHANAS

2½ cups (11¼ oz/320 g)
   all-purpose (plain) flour
pinch of salt
¼ teaspoon sugar
4½ oz/125 g lard or vegetable
   shortening, plus extra for
   greasing
1 cup (8 oz/225 g) caster sugar,
   for sprinkling

REGION: ALL REGIONS
PREPARATION TIME: 1 HOUR, PLUS
50 MINUTES STANDING
COOKING TIME: 25–30 MINUTES
SERVES: 6

Put 2 cups (8¾ oz/250 g) flour on a clean work surface and create a mound with a well in the center. Add ⅔ cup (5 fl oz/150 ml) water, salt and a ¼ teaspoon sugar to the well. With a spatula, mix in the flour little by little until it becomes a soft, elastic dough. Set aside.

In another bowl, cream the lard, then gradually add ½ cup (2½ oz/70 g) flour until it becomes a very soft dough. Set aside.

Grease a clean work surface with shortening and stretch out the first dough into the shape of a rectangle, about ⅛ inch (3 mm) thick.

Spread the second dough over the first dough, hold the ends of both layers together and stretch the dough into a rectangle, about 10 inches (25 cm) wide.

Spread a rolling pin with shortening or lard and stick it evenly to the rolling pin, taking care not to break it. Starting at the short end of the rectangle, carefully roll the dough loosely around the rolling pin. Using your hand, remove the dough from the pin, rub more shortening over the dough, and let stand for 20 minutes.

Preheat the oven to 375°F (190°C/Gas Mark 5) and line a baking sheet with parchment paper.

On a lightly floured surface, stretch the flatten dough so it measures 11/4 by 24 inches (3 x 60 cm) and slice the dough into 2-inch (5-cm) pieces. Press firmly and generously sprinkle with sugar.

Transfer the pieces to the baking sheet and bake for 30 minutes or until the surface of the campechanas are shiny, golden, and caramelized. Let cool completely and serve or store in an airtight container.

Note: A delicious dessert can be created by adding whipped cream and melted chocolate, or chopped fruit. Serve immediately.

CAPIROTADA DE LECHE

※

BREAD PUDDING

4¼ cups (1¾ pints/1 liter) milk
1 cup (9 fl oz/250 ml) light
   (single) cream
2 tomatoes
½ white onion, sliced
2 cloves garlic
1½ cups (11 oz/300 g) sugar
6 black peppercorns
4 cloves
3 cinnamon sticks
4 stale baguettes, cut into
   ½-inch (1-cm) disks
1 cup plus 2 tablespoons
   (9 oz/250 g) butter, melted
1 cup (2 oz/50 g) blanched
   almonds
⅓ cup (2 oz/50 g) raisins

REGION: JALISCO
PREPARATION TIME: 20 MINUTES
COOKING TIME: 1 HOUR 15 MINUTES
SERVES: 6

Preheat the oven to 400°F (200°C/Gas Mark 6).

Pour the milk and cream into a saucepan, add the tomatoes, onion, garlic, sugar, peppercorns, cloves, and cinnamon, and bring to a boil. Reduce the heat and simmer for 30 minutes, or until the tomatoes and onion are cooked. Remove the pan from the heat and strain into a bowl, pressing down on the tomatoes and the onion with the back of a spoon. Discard the contents of the strainer (sieve).

Brush the bread disks with melted butter, put them onto a baking sheet, and bake for until golden brown. Remove from the oven and reduce the oven temperature to 350°F (180°C/Gas Mark 4).

Pour the remaining butter into an ovenproof dish and cover with a layer of bread. Pour half the milk mixture evenly over it and sprinkle with half the almonds and raisins. Repeat the layers, then cover the dish with aluminum foil.

Bake for 20 minutes, then remove the aluminum foil and bake for another 10 minutes or until the top is lightly browned. Remove from the oven and serve immediately or let cool to room temperature.

Note: This traditional dish is served at Lent and "Day of the Dead."

EMPANADAS DE CALABAZA

PUMPKIN EMPANADAS

1 small pumpkin or large
butternut squash, skinned,
seeded and diced
1½ small cones piloncillo or
1½ cups (11 oz/300 g) packed
light brown (soft) sugar
4 cloves
2 cinnamon sticks

For the empanadas:
½ cup (3½ oz/100 g) granulated
sugar
3½ teaspoons active dry
(fast-action) yeast
8 cups (2¼ lb/1 kg) all-purpose
(plain) flour
½ teaspoon sea salt
1 cup plus 3 tablespoons
(9 oz/250 g) butter or lard
2 eggs, beaten
1 cup (9 fl oz/250 ml) lukewarm
milk or water

REGION: CHIHUAHUA, SONORA, DURANGO
PREPARATION TIME: 40 MINUTES, PLUS
15 MINUTES STANDING
COOKING TIME: 50 MINUTES
SERVES: 6

Put the pumpkin into a medium saucepan, add the piloncillo or brown sugar, cloves, cinnamon, and ½ cup (4 fl oz/120 ml) water, and bring to a boil. Reduce the heat and simmer for about 25 minutes, covered, until the pumpkin is tender. Remove the cloves and cinnamon stick and mash.

Remove the pan from the heat and lift out the pumpkin with a slotted spoon. Reserve the liquid.

To make the empanadas, stir 1 teaspoon of the sugar into ½ cup (4 fl oz/120 ml) lukewarm milk or milk, sprinkle the yeast over the surface, and let stand for 15 minutes.

Sift together the flour and salt into a large bowl, and add the butter or lard and remaining sugar. Stir the yeast mixture to make a smooth paste, then add it to the mixture. Stir, then add half the beaten egg. Mix well, then empty the bowl on the work surface and knead gently for a few minutes, gradually adding more milk, if necessary, to make a soft dough.

Make balls the size of walnuts from the dough by rolling them between the palms of your hands, then roll out into 4-inch (10-cm) disks with a rolling pin on a lightly floured surface.

Meanwhile, preheat the oven to 400°F (200°C/Gas Mark 6). Line a baking sheet with parchment paper. Put a spoonful of pumpkin mixture in the center of each disk, dampen the edges of the dough with beaten egg, and fold over to form a half moon shape. Gently press out all the air and seal the edges by pressing them together with the ends of a fork.

Put the empanadas onto the prepared baking sheet and bake for 20 minutes or until golden brown. Remove from the oven and let cool to room temperature before serving.

TACO DE PIÑA

PINEAPPLE TACOS

For the filling:
½ pineapple, peeled, cored, and diced
¾ cup (5 oz/150 g) sugar
a few drops of yellow food coloring (optional)
⅓ cup (2 oz/50 g) cornstarch (cornflour)

For the dough:
4 cups (1 lb 2 oz/500 g) all-purpose (plain) flour, plus extra for dusting
1 teaspoon baking powder
1 teaspoon sea salt
2¼ teaspoons active dry (fast-action) yeast
5 tablespoons white sugar
¾ cup plus 2 tablespoons (7 fl oz/200 ml) milk
½ cup plus 2 tablespoons (5 oz/150 g) cold butter, diced
5 tablespoons sour cream
1 egg yolk, beaten

REGION: FEDERAL DISTRICT
PREPARATION TIME: 50 MINUTES, PLUS 1¼ HOURS STANDING
COOKING TIME: 45 MINUTES
MAKES: 12

For the filling, combine the pineapple, sugar, and food coloring, if using, in a saucepan, and mix well. Bring to a boil, then reduce to a simmer until the pineapple is cooked and tender. Combine the cornstarch and 2 tablespoons water, add to the pan, and stir. Allow to thicken to the consistency of jam and let cool completely.

Sift together the flour, baking powder, and salt in a large bowl. Make a well in the center and sprinkle in the yeast and the sugar. Pour over ½ cup (3½ fl oz/100 ml) of the milk and let sit for 15 minutes. Add the butter and sour cream and work them into the flour gently with your hands to form a crumb-like texture. Add more milk gradually, as needed, to bring everything together into a soft dough—you should not have to use all the milk. Work the dough as little as possible so it does not get tough. Cover it with a clean dish towel and let it sit for 1 hour.

Lightly flour a clean work surface, divide the dough in half and roll out one half into a 15-inch (30-cm) square. Cut into 4 equal strips, then cut each strip into 6 equal pieces.

Spoon a little pineapple mixture into the centre of each rectangle and fold both corners of the long sides and press down towards the center. Do the same with the rest of the rectangles.

Preheat the oven to 400°F (200°C/Gas Mark 6). Brush with egg yolk and bake the tacos for 20 minutes, or until golden. Transfer to a wire rack to cool completely.

Pineapple Tacos

DRINKS AND

DESSERTS

RICE AND COCONUT HORCHATA

1 cup (7 oz/200 g) white rice
1 large cinnamon stick
1 cup (9 fl oz/250 ml)
   condensed milk
1 cup (9 fl oz/250 ml)
   evaporated milk
1 cup (9 fl oz/250 ml) coconut
   milk
1 cup (9 fl oz/250 ml) milk
1¼ cups (9 oz/250 g) ground
   almonds
1 cup (7 oz/200 g) sugar

To serve:
ice
ground cinnamon

REGION: GULF, YUCATÁN
PREPARATION TIME: 10 MINUTES, PLUS
OVERNIGHT SOAKING
SERVES: 4

Rinse the rice, then put it into a heatproof bowl, add the cinnamon stick, and cover it with boiling water. Let soak overnight. Put the mixture into a blender, add the condensed milk, evaporated milk, coconut milk, and milk, and process until the rice and the cinnamon are thoroughly pulverized. Strain and add the ground almonds and blend again. Pour the mixture into a large bowl and add 6¼ cups (50 fl oz/1.5 liters) water and check for sweetness. Add sugar to taste. Chill, then strain the horchata through a fine strainer (sieve) or cheesecloth (muslin) before serving.

Pour into glasses over ice, sprinkle with ground cinnamon, and serve.

HOT FRUIT PUNCH

6 tejocotes or yellow plums
4 guavas, halved
2 apples, cored and cut into
   wedges
3 tamarind fruits, seeded
2 sugar canes, peeled, split into
   quarters, and diced
1 cup (5 oz/150 g) raisins
1 cup (4 oz/120 g) prunes
1 large cinnamon stick
brown sugar, to taste
rum or brandy, to serve

REGION: ALL REGIONS
PREPARATION TIME: 10 MINUTES
COOKING TIME: 40 MINUTES
SERVES: 6

Pour 8 cups (3¼ pints/1.8 liters) water into a large saucepan and bring to a boil over medium heat. Add the tejocotes, guavas, apples, tamarind, sugar canes, raisins, prunes, cinnamon, and brown sugar, and bring back to a boil, stirring gently to dissolve the sugar. Reduce the heat and simmer for 30 minutes, until all the fruits are tender. Taste again and add more sugar, if desired. Remove from the heat and serve in a mug with rum or brandy.

Rice and Coconut Horchata

JUGO ANTI-COLESTEROL

ANTI-CHOLESTEROL JUICE

2 pineapple slices, skinned and
coarsely chopped
2 stalks celery, coarsely chopped
3 small oranges, peeled and
coarsely chopped
juice of 1 grapefruit
1 small tender cactus paddles,
coarsely chopped
2 sprigs cactus paddles

REGION: ALL REGIONS
PREPARATION TIME: 5 MINUTES
SERVES: 2

Put all the ingredients into a food processor or
blender and process until completely smooth.
Pour into glasses and drink immediately.

PALOMA

PALOMA

juice of 1 lime
1 tablespoon sea salt
3 tablespoons tequila
4 tablespoons
sparkling water
⅔ cup (¼ pint/150 ml)
grapefruit juice
ice cubes, to serve

REGION: ALL REGIONS
PREPARATION TIME: 5 MINUTES
SERVES: 1

Brush the rim of a glass with lime juice. Spread out
the salt on a small plate and dip the rim of the glass
into it to coat.

Put ice cubes into the glass and add the remaining
ingredients, finishing off with the sparkling water.
Stir and serve immediately.

AGUA DE JAMAICA

HIBISCUS FLOWER WATER

1 cup (3½ oz/100 g) dried
hibiscus flowers
ice, to serve
sugar, to taste

REGION: ALL REGIONS
PREPARATION TIME: 5 MINUTES
COOKING TIME: 15 MINUTES
SERVES: 6

Put the hibiscus flowers into a saucepan, pour in
4¼ cups (1¾ pints/1 liter) water, bring to a boil over
medium heat, and simmer for 10 minutes and let
cool down. Strain into a large measuring cup (jug)
and add sugar to taste. Stir to dissolve. Dilute with
more water—up to 10 cups (2 pints/2½ liters). Taste
and add more sugar, if necessary.

JUGO VERDE

✳

GREEN JUICE

juice of 1 lemon
½ cup (1 oz/25 g) parsley
1 stalk celery, coarsely chopped
5 spinach leaves
1 cucumber, skin on, seeded, and chopped
2 apples, cored and coarsely chopped

REGION: ALL REGIONS
PREPARATION TIME: 8 MINUTES
SERVES: 2

Put all the ingredients into a food processor or blender and process until completely smooth. Pour into glasses and drink immediately.

LICUADO DE AGUACATE CON MIEL

✳

HONEY AVOCADO SMOOTHIE

2 avocados, peeled, pitted, and coarsely chopped
6¼ cups (2½ pints/1.5 liters) milk
5 teaspoons honey
crushed ice, to serve (optional)

REGION: CENTRAL MEXICO
PREPARATION TIME: 8 MINUTES
SERVES: 6

Put the avocados, milk, 3–4 teaspoons honey, and the crushed ice, if using, into a food processor or blender and process until completely smooth. Taste and add more honey, if desired. Serve in large chilled glasses.

JUGO ANTIGRIPAL

✳

ANTIFLU TONIC

juice of 4 limes
juice of 9 oranges
juice of 3 grapefruits
4 guavas, chopped
4 pineapple slices, chopped
⅔ cup (¼ pint/150 ml) honey

REGION: ALL MEXICO
PREPARATION TIME: 5 MINUTES
SERVES: 6

Pour the lemon, orange, and grapefruit juices into a food processor or blender, add the guavas and pineapple slices, and process until completely smooth. Add the honey and process again. Strain into glasses and serve immediately.

Note: Do not strain the tonic if you want to include more fiber in your diet.

LAGARTIJA

LAGARTIJA

2–3 cups (16 fl oz–2¼ pints/
 475–750 ml) crushed ice
juice of 2 small limes
¾ cup (6 fl oz/175 ml) tequila
8 mint leaves
1½ cups (12 oz/350 ml) orange
 juice
¼ cup (2 fl oz/60 ml) green
 crème de menthe

For the syrup:
½ cup (3½ oz/100 g) sugar
½ cup (3½ fl oz/100 ml) aged
 mezcal

To garnish:
6 slices lemon
6 sprigs mint

REGION: ALL REGIONS
PREPARATION TIME: 5 MINUTES
SERVES: 4

To make the syrup, combine the sugar and ½ cup
(4 fl oz/120 ml) water in a saucepan, heat gently,
and stir until the sugar has dissolved. Bring to a
boil, without stirring, and boil for 2 minutes or until
clear. Remove the pan from the heat and let cool.

Put all the ingredients into a food processor or
blender and process until completely smooth. Add
the syrup and sweeten to taste. Pour into highball
glasses and garnish each with a slice of lemon and
a sprig of mint and serve.

AGUAS DE FRUTA FRESCA

FRESH FRUIT WATER

1 cup (9 fl oz/250 ml) fruit
 juice or pulp (melon, guava,
 mango, papaya, pineapple, or
 strawberry)
sugar (optional)

REGION: ALL REGIONS
PREPARATION TIME: 5 MINUTES
SERVES: 6

Put the fruit and 2 cups (16 fl oz/475 ml) water
into a food processor or blender and process
until completely smooth. Strain it through a fine
strainer (sieve) or cheesecloth (muslin), taste, and
add sugar, if desired.

Note: Every little *fonda*, or cafe, serves a three-course
set lunch (soup, main dish, and dessert) with a glass
of the *agua del dia* (water of the day) to accompany
the meal.

Fresh Fruit Water

Tamarind Water

TAMARIND
WATER

1 lb 2 oz/500 g fresh tamarind
   pods
sugar, to taste

REGION: ALL REGIONS
PREPARATION TIME: 20 MINUTES, PLUS 2 HOURS
STANDING AND 1 HOUR CHILLING
COOKING TIME: 20 MINUTES
SERVES: 6

Open the tamarind pods, remove the thick skin and discard.

Pressing the soft peels of the pods between your fingers, remove the seeds and discard. Process the pulp with some of the soaked liquid until smooth. Strain into a large container, add 1 cup sugar, stir to dissolve, and adjust the moment of water and sugar.

MILK ATOLE
WITH FRUIT

5 tablespoons cornstarch
   (corn flour)
1 cup (9 fl oz/250 ml) fruit pulp
sugar, to taste
5 cups (2 pints/1.2 liters) milk
chopped nuts, to garnish

REGION: ALL REGIONS
PREPARATION TIME: 10 MINUTES, PLUS
5 MINUTES STANDING
COOKING TIME: 30 MINUTES
SERVES: 2

Mix the cornstarch (cornflour) with 1 cup (9 fl oz/250 ml) water in a bowl and let stand for 5 minutes.

Meanwhile, put the fruit pulp into a saucepan, add sugar to taste, and heat gently until partly cooked. Add the milk and cornstarch mixture and cook until thickened.

Serve hot, sprinkled with chopped nuts.

Note: If you are using fruit pulp from acidic fruit, such as guava, orange, or pineapple, add a pinch of baking soda (bicarbonate of soda) before adding the milk to prevent it from curdling.

WATER ATOLE WITH FRUIT AND PILONCILLO

¾ cup (3 oz/80 g) Masa Dough
   (page 36)
2 cups (11–12 oz/300–350 g)
   prepared fruit (orange,
   pineapple, strawberries,
   guavas, or blackberries)
1 small cone of piloncillo
pinch of sea salt

REGION: ALL REGIONS
PREPARATION TIME: 10 MINUTES, PLUS
10 MINUTES STANDING
COOKING TIME: 30 MINUTES
SERVES: 6-8

Put the masa dough into a bowl, add 2 cups
(16 fl oz/475 ml) water, and mix well and let sit for
10 minutes while you deal with the fruit.

Put the fruit into a food processor or blender,
pour in 4¼ cups (1¾ pints/1 liter) water, and process
until completely smooth. Strain into a saucepan,
stir in the piloncillo, and bring to a boil. Reduce
the heat and simmer, stirring frequently, for 10
minutes. Pass the dough and water mixture through
a strainer (sieve), retaining the water and adding it to
the pan with the fruit. Discard the remaining dough.
Simmer, stirring continuously, for another
15 minutes, until thick. Add a pinch of salt, give it
a stir, and ladle immediately into mugs. Drink for
breakfast on cold mornings, or in the evenings with
sweet rolls or tamales.

Note: This recipe can also be made with milk. Reduce
the quantity of water to 2 cups (16 fl oz/475 ml) and
use 4¼ cups (1¾ pints/1 liter) milk. Add a pinch of
baking soda (bicarbonate of soda) before adding the
dough and omit the salt.

VAMPIRE JUICE

juice of 4 beets (beetroots)
3 cups (1¼ pints/750 ml)
   carrot juice
3 cups (1¼ pints/750 ml)
   orange juice
⅔ cup (¼ pint/150 ml)
   lemon juice
3 stalks celery
crushed ice, to taste

REGION: ALL REGIONS
PREPARATION TIME: 15 MINUTES
SERVES: 6

Pour all the juices into a food processor or blender,
add the celery and ice, and process until thoroughly
combined. Serve in glasses and drink immediately.

Water Atole with Fruit and Piloncillo

CHOCOLATE CON LECHE

✳

HOT CHOCOLATE

3½ oz/100 g dark Mexican
  chocolate, chopped
6¼ cups (50 fl oz/1.5 liters) milk
1 cinnamon stick (optional)

REGION: OAXACA
PREPARATION TIME: 10 MINUTES
COOKING TIME: 20 MINUTES
SERVES: 6

Put the chocolate into a saucepan, add the milk and cinnamon stick, and heat gently, stirring until the chocolate has melted.

As the mixture begins to bubble in the pan, reduce the heat and simmer for a few minutes.

Transfer 1 cup (9 fl oz/250 ml) of the chocolate to a bowl and whisk with an electric mixer until it is foamy, then pour into a mug. Whisk and pour the remaining chocolate milk in the same way. Serve immediately.

CAFÉ DE OLLA

✳

CLAY POT COFFEE

⅓ cup (2 oz/60 g) brown sugar
1 cinnamon stick
1 clove
3 whole allspice berry
3 whole black pepper
3 strips orange zest, white part
  removed
6 tablespoons ground coffee

REGION: ALL REGIONS
PREPARATION TIME: 5 MINUTES
COOKING TIME: 10 MINUTES, PLUS
10 MINUTES STANDING
SERVES: 6

Pour 8 cups (3½ pints/2 liters) water into a large saucepan (traditionally this would have been made of clay). Add the piloncillo or brown sugar, spices, and orange peel and bring to a boil. When the sugar has dissolved and the mixture is fragrant, remove the pot from the heat. Stir in the coffee, cover the pan, and let stand for 10 minutes.

Ladle the coffee into cups. You can also serve it with *piquete*, with a dash of tequila, rum, or brandy. Alternatively, simply serve it black. Drink this coffee with breakfast or in the afternoon with a sweet bread.

Hot Chocolate

Champurrado

CHAMPURRADO

3½ oz/100 g) masa harina
1 cinnamon stick
pinch of salt
1 big cone piloncillo or
    1 packed cup (7 oz/200 g)
    soft brown sugar
5 oz/450 g semi-sweet (dark)
    chocolate

REGION: ALL REGIONS
PREPARATION TIME: 5 MINUTES
COOKING TIME: 25–30 MINUTES
SERVES: 8–10

Put the masa harina and 2 cups (16 fl oz/475 ml) of cold water into a large bowl and mix well.

Put the cinnamon stick, piloncillo, salt, and 4¼ cups (1¾ pints/1 liter) water into a large saucepan and bring to a boil, reduce to a simmer, then add the masa mixture and stir continuously until thick and slightly translucent. Add the chocolate and continue stirring until the chocolate is completely dissolved and integrated. Serve hot.

MARGARITA

1½ tablespoons lime juice, plus
    extra for brushing
1 tablespoon sea salt
handful of ice cubes
4 tablespoons tequila
1½ tablespoons triple sec liqueur
1½ tablespoons natural syrup
1 slice lime, to decorate

REGION: ALL REGIONS
PREPARATION TIME: 5 MINUTES
SERVES: 1

Brush the rim of a cocktail glass with lime juice. Spread out the salt on a small plate and dip the rim of the glass into it to coat. Set aside in the refrigerator.

Put some ice into a cocktail shaker and add the remaining ingredients. Cover and shake vigorously until a mist forms on the outside of the shaker. Strain into the prepared cocktail glass and decorate with a slice of lime.

MEXICAN BLOODY MARY

3 tablespoons tequila
5 tablespoons tomato juice
juice of 1 lemon
3 drops Tabasco sauce
½ teaspoon Worcestershire
    sauce
sea salt and pepper
6 stalks celery, to serve

REGION: ALL REGIONS
PREPARATION TIME: 5 MINUTES
SERVES: 6

Put the tequila, tomato juice, lemon juice, Tabasco, and Worcestershire sauce into a pitcher (jug) and stir with a long spoon until thoroughly combined. Season to taste with salt and pepper. Pour into long glasses over ice and garnish with a celery stalk.

Note: This cocktail originated in France but it has been adapted in Mexico by replacing the vodka with tequila.

CHELADA

juice of 1 lemon or lime
1 dash Maggi Seasoning
1 dash Worcestershire sauce
1 dash Tabasco sauce
1 bottle dark beer
sea salt and pepper

REGION: ALL REGIONS
PREPARATION TIME: 5 MINUTES
SERVES: 1

Brush the rim of a beer glass with lemon juice. Spread out 1 tablespoon of salt in a small plate and dip the rim of the glass into it to coat.

Put ice into the glass and add the remaining lemon juice, all-purpose seasoning, Worcestershire sauce, and Tabasco sauce. Season with salt and pepper, and mix well with a long spoon. Add the beer, then serve immediately.

SANGRITA

1 cup (8 fl oz/250 ml) tomato
   juice
⅔ cup (5 fl oz/150 ml) orange
   juice
1½ tablespoons lime juice
½–1 teaspoon medium-hot
   chili powder
dash of Worcestershire sauce
dash of Tabasco sauce
sea salt and pepper

REGION: ALL REGIONS
PREPARATION TIME: 5 MINUTES
SERVES: 4

Pour the tomato juice, orange juice, and lime juice into a pitcher (jug). Add the chili powder, Worcestershire sauce, and Tabasco sauce and adjust the seasoning to taste. Stir well and chill in the refrigerator before serving.

Note: Sangrita is traditionally served as an accompaniment to tequila. The tequila and the sangria are served side by side in identical glasses and you take little sips of them in turn. If you want a thicker mixture, add tomato paste (puree).

MICHELADA

juice of 1 lemon
1 tablespoon sea salt
1 bottle dark beer
 slice of lemon, to decorate

REGION: ALL REGIONS
PREPARATION TIME: 5 MINUTES
SERVES: 1

Brush the rim of a beer glass with lemon juice. Spread out the salt on a small plate and dip the rim of the glass into it to coat. Pour the remaining lemon juice into the glass, add ice, if using, and pour in the beer. Garnish with a slice of lemon and serve.

Michelada

PINOLE DE LUJO

✳

LUXURY PINOLE

9 oz (250 g) dried corn
1 cup (3½ oz/100 g) blanched
  almonds
4 tablespoons ground
  cinnamon
sugar, to taste

REGION: TABASCO, FEDERAL DISTRICT, PUEBLA
PREPARATION TIME: 10 MINUTES
COOKING TIME: 15 MINUTES
MAKES: 2 CUPS (16 FL OZ/475 ML)

Toast the corn and almonds on a dry ridged grill (griddle) pan for about 15 minutes, until they are golden but not dark brown. Be careful not to scorch them. Remove from the griddle and put them into a food processor or blender. Add the cinnamon and process into a powder. Add sugar to taste.

Note: In Tabasco, pinole is used to make drinks, and in the center of the country is used more like sweet powder.

ALEGRIAS

✳

ALEGRIAS

½ cup (3½ oz/100 g) raw sugar
⅓ cup (3 oz/75 g) honey
4 drops each anise and vanilla
  extract
2 cups (2 oz/50 g) puffed
  amaranth
¼ cup (1¼ oz/35 g) peanuts,
  toasted
¼ cup (1¼ oz/35 g) pecans
¼ cup (1½ oz/40 g) almonds
¼ cup (1½ oz/40 g) raisins

REGION: ALL REGIONS
PREPARATION TIME: 10 MINUTES, PLUS
2 HOURS SETTING
COOKING TIME: 5 MINUTES
SERVES: 6

Line a rectangular cake pan with parchment paper or aluminum foil.

Put the sugar into a saucepan, add 4 tablespoons water, and heat gently, stirring until the sugar has dissolved. Remove the pan from the heat, stir in the honey, and add the anise and vanilla extracts, then stir in the amaranth until combined.

Combine the nuts and raisins in a bowl and mix. Add the mixture to the pan and spread out to even. Add the amaranth mixture into the prepared mold and press down with the back of the spoon. Smooth the surface with damp fingers, cover with plastic wrap and use a chopping board or any flat surface to press the amaranth. Let stand for 2 hours until set.

Turn out the set mixture from the pan and discard the lining. Cut into squares or rectangles.

Note: Alegrias may be covered with melted chocolate, nuts and raisins.

Alegrias

SEVILLE ALMOND COOKIES

1¾ cups (8 oz/225 g) all-purpose (plain) flour
½ cup (2 oz/50 g) ground almonds, lightly toasted
½ cup (3½ oz/100 g) white sugar
1 tablespoon ground cinnamon
1 teaspoon ground anise
1 egg yolk
½ cup (3½ oz/100 g) lard or vegetable shortening

REGION: ALL REGIONS
PREPARATION TIME: 45 MINUTES, PLUS 30 MINUTES RESTING
COOKING TIME: 1 HOUR 10 MINUTES
MAKES: 48

Spread out the flour on a baking sheet and bake, stirring occasionally for about 30 minutes, until lightly toasted. Remove the flour from the oven and let cool completely.

Transfer the cooled flour into a bowl, add the ground almonds, sugar, cinnamon, and anise, and mix well, then add the egg yolk and fat. With your fingers, rub in the fat and mix well to form a ball of dough. Wrap in plastic wrap (clingfilm) and let rest in the refrigerator for 30 minutes.

Preheat the oven to 325°F (160°C/Gas Mark 3).

Roll or press out the dough to about ½ inch (1 cm) thick and stamp out small disks with a cookie cutter. Carefully lift the disks onto a baking sheet and bake for 30–40 minutes or until lightly browned.

Remove from the oven, sprinkle the sugar, and let the cookies cool completely.

WALNUT BRITTLE

4¼ cups (1¾ pints/1 liter) milk
2½ cups (1 lb 2 oz/500 g) sugar
pinch of baking soda (bicarbonate of soda)
2¼ cups (9 oz/250 g) walnuts
butter, for greasing

REGION: JALISCO
PREPARATION TIME: 5 MINUTES
COOKING TIME: 1 HOUR 10 MINUTES
MAKES: 12

Gently heat the milk and sugar in a saucepan, preferably a copper pan, stirring continuously until the sugar has completely dissolved. Bring the milk to boiling point and reduce the heat.

Add the baking soda (bicarbonate of soda) and walnuts, and cook, stirring continuously, for about 1 hour, until the milk caramelizes and the spoon leaves a trail on the bottom of the pan.

Remove the pan from the heat and pour the mixture onto a cold marble slab or into a greased shallow baking pan and spread quickly with a spatula (palette knife). Let cool completely.

When it has set, cut the brittle into rounds and rectangles, and serve.

Note: The walnuts can be replaced with pumpkin seeds or peanuts.

CAPIROTADA MICHOACANA

※

MICHOACAN BREAD PUDDING

2 cups (2¼ lb/1 kg) packed
  brown sugar or piloncillo
4 tablespoons ground
  cinnamon
⅔ cup (¼ pint/150 ml) butter or
  olive oil, plus extra
  for brushing
1 large stale baguette, sliced
1¼ cups (5 oz/150 g) crumbled
  cotija or feta cheese
⅔ cup (3½ oz/100 g) raisins
¾ cup (3½ oz/100 g) chopped
  walnuts or peanuts

REGION: MICHOACAN
PREPARATION TIME: 20 MINUTES
COOKING TIME: 45 MINUTES
SERVES: 6

Put the sugar, cinnamon, and 2 cups (16 fl oz/475 ml) water into a saucepan and bring to a boil, stirring until the sugar has dissolved completely. Boil for another 10 minutes, without stirring, until thick and translucent. Remove the pan from the heat.

Heat 3 tablespoons of the oil in a skillet or frying pan, add slices of bread to fill the pan in a single layer, and cook over medium-high heat for 2–3 minutes on each side until lightly colored. Remove with a spatula (fish slice), and drain on paper towels.

Preheat the oven to 325°F (160°C/Gas Mark 3). Brush an ovenproof dish with oil or butter.

Put a layer of bread in the bottom of the dish and spoon over some syrup. Add a layer of crumbled cheese, raisins, and walnuts, and spoon over more syrup. Continue making alternating layers in this way until all the ingredients have been used. Finish with cheese, nuts, and raisins.

Bake for 30 minutes or until golden. Remove from the oven and serve immediately. Serve it at room temperature.

ANTE COLIMENSE

CAKE FROM COLIMA

4¼ cups (1¾ pints/1 liter) milk
2 cups (5 oz/150 g) dry
  unsweetened (desiccated)
  coconut
½ cup (3½ oz/100 g) sugar
pinch of sea salt
6 eggs, lightly beaten
4 oz/120 g pound cake,
  crumbled
grated zest of 6 limes
5 candied limes, quartered

For the caramel:
½ cup (3½ oz/100 g) sugar
5 lemon candies

For the sauce:
2 cups (16 fl oz/475 ml) milk
6 egg yolks
¾ cup (5 oz/150 g) sugar
grated zest of 1 lime
½ cup (4 fl oz/120 ml) brandy

REGION: PACIFIC, NAYARIT
PREPARATION TIME: 30 MINUTES, PLUS
15 STANDING
COOKING TIME: 1 HOUR 20 MINUTES
SERVES: 6

Bring the milk to a boil, then remove from the heat and stir in the coconut. Let stand for 20 minutes.

Bring the coconut milk back to a boil, add the sugar and a pinch of salt, reduce the heat, and simmer for 5 minutes. Remove the pan from the heat and let cool. Add the eggs, crumbled cake, and lime zest, and beat until creamy.

Preheat the oven to 400°F (200°C/Gas Mark 6).

To make the caramel, put the sugar, lemon candies, and 4 tablespoons water into a saucepan and heat gently, stirring. Bring to a boil and boil for a few minutes without stirring, until golden brown. Remove the pan from the heat.

Pour the syrup into a bundt pan and tilt to coat it evenly. Put the candied lemon quarters into the pan, smooth side down, then carefully add the coconut mixture. Cover with parchment paper and aluminum foil. Stand the pan in a roasting pan and pour in boiling water to come about halfway up the sides. Bake for 45 minutes.

To make the sauce, pour the milk into a saucepan and bring just to a boil, then immediately remove from the heat. Beat the egg yolks with the sugar in a bowl, then gradually stir in the hot milk. Pour the mixture back into the pan and bring to a boil, stirring continuously. Simmer gently for a few minutes, stirring continuously, until thickened. Remove the pan from heat and stir in the lemon zest and brandy.

Remove the cake from the oven and remove from the pan. Serve cold or warm with the sauce.

Northern Fritters

BUÑUELOS NORTEÑOS DE RODILLA

✻

NORTHERN FRITTERS

½ teaspoon anise seeds
½ small tequesquite stone
4 cups (1 lb 2 oz/500 g)
    all-purpose (plain) flour
½ teaspoon salt
½ cup (3½ oz/100 g) sugar
1½ tablespoons vegetable
    shortening or lard
3 eggs, lightly beaten
½ cup (4 fl oz/120 ml) tepid
    milk
vegetable oil, for deep-frying

To serve:
molasses
½ cup (2 oz/50 g) grated
    Chihuahua or mild cheddar
    cheese, if using

REGIONS: CHIHUAHUA, DURANGO,
PREPARATION TIME: 50 MINUTES
COOKING TIME: 30 MINUTES
SERVES: 6

Put the anise seeds, tequesquite, and 1 cup
(9 fl oz/250 ml) water into a saucepan and bring
to a boil. Boil until the tequesquite dissolves, then
remove the pan from the heat, and let stand for
15 minutes.

Sift together the flour and salt into a mound on
a clean work surface, and make a well in the center.
Add the sugar and lard and mix well, then add the
vegetable shortening, eggs and flavored water, being
careful not to add any sediment. Mix thoroughly,
gradually adding enough milk to make a soft but not
sticky dough. Knead well.

Sit down, cross your legs, and cover with your
knee with a kitchen cloth. Carefully stretch
a dough to make a thin disk. Put the fritters on
a clean dish towel on a work surface as you finish
stretching them.

Heat the oil in a deep fryer to 350°F (180°C) or
until a cube of day-old bread browns in 30 seconds.
Add the fritters to the hot oil in batches, and cook
until golden brown. Remove from the pan and drain
on paper towels.

Put the fritters into a dish, drizzle with molasses,
and sprinkle with grated cheese, if using. Serve.

COCHINITOS DE PILONCILLO

❋

PILONCILLO PIGLETS

For the sugar syrup:

1 large cone piloncillo or ⅔ cup
   (4½ oz/130 g) packed brown
   sugar
6 tablespoons (3 oz/90 g)
   butter, at room temperature,
   plus extra for greasing
   (optional)
⅓ cup (2¾ oz/70 g) packed
   brown sugar
½ cup (3½ oz/100 g) honey
1 egg
3¼ cups (14 oz/400 g)
   all-purpose (plain) flour,
   sifted, plus extra for dusting
1 tablespoon baking powder
½ teaspoon sea salt
½ teaspoon ground anise

REGION: CENTRAL MEXICO
PREPARATION TIME: 30 MINUTES, PLUS
5 MINUTES RESTING
COOKING TIME: 20 MINUTES
MAKES: 12

Put the piloncillo into a small, deep saucepan, add 4 tablespoons water, and bring to a boil, stirring until the sugar has dissolved. Boil, without stirring, until syrupy and reduced by about one-third. Remove the pan from the heat and let cool slightly.

Grease a baking sheet or line it with nonstick parchment paper.

Beat the butter, brown sugar, and honey until smooth. Beat in the egg. Stir in the cooled sugar syrup, then lightly fold in the flour, baking powder, salt, and anise. Shape the dough into a ball, wrap it in plastic wrap (clingfilm), and let it rest for 5 minutes in the refrigerator.

Roll out the dough to ⅛ inch (3 mm) thick on a lightly floured work surface. Stamp out little pig shapes with a novelty cookie cutter. Place on the prepared baking sheet and bake for 10 minutes or until cooked and lightly browned.

Remove the baking sheet from the oven and transfer the pigs to a wire rack to cool.

Note: The piglets are very traditional with a cup of "atole" or black coffee.

Piloncillo Piglets

ANTE COLONIAL DE PIÑA

✳

COLONIAL PINEAPPLE CAKE

⅔ fresh pineapple, peeled, cored and coarsely grated

1¾ cups (12 oz/350 g) sugar

5 tablespoons white wine or dry sherry

¾ cup (3 oz/80 g) chopped almonds

⅓ cup (1½ oz/40 g) chopped almonds, lightly toasted

¾ cup (3 oz/80 g) pine nuts

2½ tablespoons pine nuts, lightly toasted

5 egg whites

2 tablespoons confectioners' (icing) sugar

½ teaspoon ground cinnamon

1 pre-made cake

REGION: PUEBLA, FEDERAL DISTRICT
PREPARATION TIME: 35 MINUTES
COOKING TIME: 45 MINUTES
SERVES: 6–8

Put the pineapple and ¾ cup (5 oz/150 g) of the sugar into a heavy saucepan and cook over low heat for 30 minutes or until thick like jam. Remove the pan from the heat.

Put the remaining sugar into a small saucepan, add 1 cup (9 fl oz/250 ml) water, and bring to a boil over low heat, stirring continuously until the sugar has dissolved completely. Boil without stirring for an additional 2–3 minutes until syrupy, then remove from heat. Measure ¾ cup (6 fl oz/175 ml) into a bowl and stir in the wine.

Preheat 400°F (200°C/Gas Mark 6)

Put the cake on an ovenproof platter. Pour over some of the wine syrup, then add a layer of the pineapple mixture. Combine the almonds and pine nuts in a separate bowl and sprinkle them over the pineapple. Repeat the layers, ending with the pineapple mixture.

Whisk the egg whites in a grease-free bowl until soft peaks form, then add the confectioners' (icing) sugar and whisk again. Spread the meringue over the cake and top with more pineapple jam, to taste.

Bake for a few minutes until the topping is golden brown. Stir the cinnamon into the nut mixture, then sprinkle over the cake. Serve warm or at room temperature.

BUÑUELOS CON MIEL

✺

FRITTERS WITH SYRUP

1 teaspoon baking powder
pinch of sea salt
2 star anise pods
4½ cups (1¼ lb/500 g) all-
   purpose (plain) flour, plus
   extra for dusting
1 teaspoon baking powder
3 eggs, lightly beaten
½ cup (4 oz/120 g) melted
   butter
vegetable oil, for deep-frying
2½ cups (1 lb 2 oz/500 g) raw
   sugar
1 cinnamon stick

REGION: ALL REGIONS
PREPARATION TIME: 50 MINUTES, PLUS
1 HOUR STANDING
COOKING TIME: 45 MINUTES
SERVES: 6

Bring 1 cup (8 fl oz/250 ml) water to a boil in a saucepan. Add the tomatillo husks, salt, and one star anise pod and simmer for 10 minutes. Remove the pan from the heat and strain the flavored liquid into a bowl.

Sift together the flour and baking powder into a mound on a clean work surface, and make a well in the center. Put the eggs and melted butter into the well and begin to incorporate the dry ingredients with your hands, gradually adding the flavored liquid, a little at a time. Knead to make a smooth, elastic dough. Shape the dough into a ball, cover, and let stand for 1 hour in a warm place.

Heat the oil in a deep fryer to 350°F (180°C) or until a cube of day-old bread browns in 30 seconds.

Roll pieces of the dough into small balls between the palms of your hands, then roll out into disks on a lightly floured surface. Add the disks to the hot oil, in batches if necessary, and cook until golden. Remove and drain on paper towels, and let cool.

To make the syrup, put the raw sugar, the remaining star anise and the cinnamon stick into a saucepan, pour in 2 cups (16 fl oz/475 ml) water, and bring to a boil, stirring until the sugar has dissolved completely. Boil, without stirring, for a few minutes until syrupy, then remove from the heat and let cool.

Put the fritters onto a serving plate, pour the syrup over them, and serve at room temperature.

COCADAS

※

COCONUT COOKIES

butter, for greasing
4 egg yolks
½ cup (4 fl oz/120 ml) milk
1½ cups (11 oz/300 g) sugar
2 cinnamon sticks
½ cup (4 fl oz/120 ml) coconut
    water
grated flesh of 1 large fresh
    coconut
few drops of yellow food
    coloring
crystallized lime, to garnish

REGION: PUEBLA, FEDERAL DISTRICT
PREPARATION TIME: 20 MINUTES
COOKING TIME: 40 MINUTES
SERVES: 6

Preheat the oven to 475°F (240°C/Gas Mark 9). Line a baking sheet with parchment paper and grease with butter. Grease the inside of a 2-inch (5-cm) diameter cookie cutter.

Combine the egg yolks and milk in a bowl, whisk together, then strain into a bowl.

Combine the sugar, cinnamon, and coconut water in a medium saucepan over medium heat and stir until the sugar has dissolved. Add the grated coconut, reduce the heat to medium-low, and cook, stirring continuously, for 10–15 minutes, until the coconut is slightly translucent. Add the yellow food coloring and stir continuously until the mixture is nearly dry.

Gradually stir in the egg mixture, reduce the heat to low and stir continuously until you can see the bottom of the pan. Remove the pan from the heat and let cool slightly. Discard the cinnamon sticks.

Transfer half of the coconut mixture to a bowl, add 1–2 drops of yellow food coloring, and mix well.

Put the prepared cookie cutter onto the prepared baking sheet. Put a tablespoon of the yellow coconut mixture into the cookie cutter and press down gently. Continue making cookies in this way until both colors of the coconut mixture have been used.

Bake for 15 minutes or until the cookies are lightly browned. Remove from the oven and let cool before serving. Top each with a crystallized lime.

Coconut Cookies

ARROZ CON LECHE AL PERFUME DE COCO

※

RICE WITH COCONUT MILK

3 cups (9 oz/250 g) grated fresh
  coconut
1½ cups (12 fl oz/350 ml) milk
1 cup (7 oz/200 g) long grain
  rice
1 cinnamon stick
1¾ cups (12 oz/350 g) sugar
2 egg yolks, lightly beaten
3 tablespoon raisins, to
  decorate

REGION: GUERRERO
PREPARATION TIME: 30 MINUTES, PLUS
15 MINUTES SOAKING
COOKING TIME: 30 MINUTES
SERVES: 6

Put the coconut and milk into a food processor
or blender and process until the coconut is finely
ground. Strain the milk into a bowl.

Put the rice into a heatproof bowl, pour in hot
water to cover, and let soak for 15 minutes. Drain,
rinse with cold water, and drain again.

Combine the rice, cinnamon stick, and 2 cups
(16 fl oz/475 ml) water in a saucepan and bring
to a boil over medium-high heat. Stir, reduce to
a simmer, and cook for 15 minutes, or until the
liquid has been absorbed. Add the coconut milk
and sugar and cook over medium heat, stirring
frequently, for 5 minutes, until the rice is tender.

Reduce the heat to low, add the egg yolks, and
stir quickly so the yolks don't scramble. Mix the
yolks with a little bit of the hot rice, mix well, add
some more and return to the pot with the rice. Cook
the rice, stirring continuously, for a few minutes
until thickened.

Remove the pan from the heat, spoon the rice
into 6 individual cups and decorate with the raisins.
Serve warm or chilled.

BUDÍN DE ELOTE
※
CORN PUDDING

5 tablespoons (2½ oz/65 g)
  butter, plus extra for greasing
3 tablespoons bread crumbs
2⅓ cups (12 oz/350 g) fresh
  corn kernels
1 teaspoon sugar
½ cup (120 ml/4 fl oz) whole
  milk
3 extra-large (UK large) eggs
sea salt
whipped cream, to serve

REGION: CENTRAL MEXICO
PREPARATION TIME: 30 MINUTES
COOKING TIME: 35 MINUTES
SERVES: 6

Preheat the oven to 300°F (150°C/Gas Mark 2).
Grease a shallow 12-inch- (30-cm-) square cake pan
with butter and sprinkle with the bread crumbs.

Put the corn kernels into a food processor or
blender and process until smooth.

Combine the butter, sugar, and salt to taste in
a bowl and beat until fluffy. Gradually add the milk,
corn puree, and the eggs, one at a time, until all the
ingredients are well mixed.

Pour the batter into the prepared pan and bake
for 45 minutes or until it is golden and the edges are
beginning to separate from the side of the pan.

Gently shake the pan and the center should be
set. If not, return it back to the oven until its set.

CAJETA DE MEMBRILLO

✳

QUINCE JELLY

10 large quinces, peeled and
quartered
sugar (see method)

REGION: ALL REGIONS
PREPARATION TIME: 1 HOUR, PLUS
OVERNIGHT DRAINING
COOKING TIME: 1 HOUR 10 MINUTES
SERVES: 6

Seed the quinces and put the seeds into a cheesecloth (muslin) bag or in a square of cheesecloth tied with kitchen string.

Put the quinces and the seeds into a large saucepan, add enough water to cover, and bring to a boil. Reduce the heat and simmer over low heat for 1 hour, or until tender. Add more water if necessary. Remove the pan from the heat, discard the seeds, and let cool. Transfer to a colander set over a bowl and let stand, covered, overnight.

Remove the quinces from the colander and press them through a fine strainer (sieve) lined with cheesecloth. Measure the quince mixture in a large measuring cup (jug); for each 1 cup (9 fl oz/250 ml) of quince mixture, add 1 cup (7 oz/200 g) sugar to the fruit and mix well.

Put the quince and sugar mixture into a copper or stainless steel saucepan. Cook over low heat, stirring continuously, to dissolve the sugar completely, and then bring to a rapid simmer. Simmer, stirring frequently, for about 10 minutes. Use a candy (sugar) thermometer to check the setting point of 230°F (110°C). Alternatively, remove the pan from the heat to prevent overcooking and put a little of the jelly on a plate that you have put in the freezer to chill. If it does not come off the plate easily when pushed with your finger, the jelly is ready.

Remove the pan from the heat and carefully pour the hot jelly into a terrine mold lined with wax (greaseproof) paper. Let cool and set. Once cold and set, turn it out, wrap securely in wax (greaseproof) paper and aluminum foil, and store in a cool, dark place. It will keep for months. Serve in slices as a dessert or to accompany cheese.

FLAN DE CAJETA CON QUESO

❈

CRÈME CARAMEL WITH CHEESE

1 cup (7 oz/200 g) sugar

3 eggs

1 teaspoon vanilla extract

½ cup (3½ oz/100 g) cream cheese

1½ cups (12 fl oz/350 ml) evaporated milk

1¾ cups (14 fl oz/400 ml) condensed milk

sliced strawberries, to decorate

REGION: MEXICO CITY
PREPARATION TIME: 15 MINUTES
COOKING TIME: 1 HOUR 10 MINUTES
SERVES: 6

Preheat the oven to 400°F (200°C/Gas Mark 6). Place a 1½-quart (2½-pint/1.5-liter) ovenproof mold or 6 individual ramekins into the oven while you melt the sugar.

Melt the sugar in a wide saucepan over low heat. When the sugar begins to dissolve, increase the heat to medium-low and heat for about 10 minutes, until the sugar has completely dissolved and the syrup has turned brown. If any sugar crystals remain, keep it on the heat until dissolved. Working quickly, and with oven mitts (gloves) on, remove the mold or ramekins from the oven and scrape the caramel syrup into the mold or ramekins. Pick up the mold and tilt it so the syrup coats the sides and bottom completely. Set aside.

Put the eggs, vanilla, cream cheese, evaporated milk, and condensed milk into a food processor or blender and process for a few minutes until smooth. Pour through a sieve (strainer) into the prepared mold or ramekins and cover with aluminum foil.

Put the mold or ramekins into a roasting pan and pour enough boiling water to come halfway up the sides. Bake in the oven for 60 minutes, until set. Insert a knife in the flan—if it comes out clean, it is set.

Remove the pan from the oven, lift out the mold or ramekins, and let cool. Get a serving plate ready, then dip the flan in a sink full of warm water for just a few seconds and put the plate on top. Turn it over to release the flan, letting the caramel drizzle all over it. Decorate with the sliced strawberries and serve.

Crème Caramel with Cheese

PASTEL DE GARBANZOS

✻

CHICKPEA CAKE

½ cup (2 oz/50 g) butter,
  softened, plus extra for
  greasing
all-purpose (plain) flour, for
  dusting
2½ cups (1 lb/450 g) drained
  canned chickpeas, rinsed
8 eggs
2 cups (14 oz/400 g) sugar
1 teaspoon baking powder
grated zest of 1 lemon

For the lemon sauce:
1 cup (7 oz/200g) sugar
1 tablespoon cornstarch
  (cornflour)
2 tablespoons (1 oz/25 g) butter
4 tablespoons lemon juice

REGION: ALL MEXICO
PREPARATION TIME: 30 MINUTES, PLUS
15 MINUTES STANDING
COOKING TIME: 1 HOUR 5 MINUTES
SERVES: 6

Preheat oven to 350°F (180°C/Gas Mark 4). Grease and flour 9½-inch/24-cm mold.

Remove and discard the skins from the chickpeas, put them into a food processor or blender, and process to a puree. Transfer the puree to a bowl.

Add the eggs and beat until smooth and combined. Beat in the sugar, baking powder, butter, and lemon zest. Pour into the prepared mold and bake for 1 hour or until a toothpick (cocktail stick) inserted into the center of the cake comes out clean.

Remove the mold from the oven, put it on a wire rack, and let stand for 15 minutes. Remove the cake from the mold and place it on the wire rack.

To make the lemon sauce, put the sugar and cornstarch (cornflour) into a small saucepan and stir. Add 1 cup (9 fl oz/250 ml) boiling water, stir, and cook over medium heat, stirring continuously, for 5 minutes or until translucent and slightly thickened. Remove the pan from heat and stir in the butter and lemon juice. Pour into a sauceboat. Adjust seasoning.

Place the cake onto a serving plate and serve warm with the lemon sauce.

PUDIN DE AMARANTO

✺

AMARANTH PUDDING

2 cups (16 fl oz/475 ml) milk
½ cup (3½ oz/100 g) sugar
½ cup (3 oz/80 g) semolina
  or polenta
½ cup (3 oz/80 g) amaranth
½ cup (4 oz/120 g) butter, plus
  extra for greasing
8 egg yolks
6 egg whites
custard sauce or fruit sauce,
  to serve

For the candy powder:
1 cup (7 oz/200 g) sugar
5 lemon candies

REGION: CENTRAL MEXICO
PREPARATION TIME: 40 MINUTES
COOKING TIME: 1 HOUR 10 MINUTES
SERVES: 6–8

Line a baking sheet with parchment paper. To make the candy powder, put the sugar, lemon candies, and 1 tablespoon water into a saucepan and heat gently over low heat, stirring continuously, until the sugar and lemon candies have dissolved completely. Boil, without stirring, for several minutes until thick, golden, and syrupy. Remove the pan from the heat, pour the syrup onto the prepared baking sheet, spread out with a spatula, and let cool.

Break up the cooled syrup, put the pieces into a food processor or a blender, and process briefly to a powder.

Put the milk and sugar into a saucepan over medium heat and stir until the sugar has dissolved completely. Bring to a simmer and gradually add the semolina and amaranth. Cook, stirring continuously, for 20–30 minutes, until thickened.

Remove the pan from the heat and stir in the butter and egg yolks, then let cool.

Preheat the oven to 475°F (240°C Gas Mark 9). Grease a 12-inch (30-cm) square cake pan with butter and sprinkle the bottom with the candy powder.

Whisk the egg whites in a grease-free bowl until they form stiff peaks. Gently fold the egg whites into the semolina mixture.

Pour the mixture into the prepared cake pan and put the pan inside a roasting pan filled halfway with boiling water. Bake for 30 minutes.

Remove the pan from the oven. Serve hot with custard or fruit sauce.

Caramel Gelatin with Drunken Sauce

GELATINA DE CAJETA CON SALSA ENVINADA

❋

CARAMEL GELATIN WITH DRUNKEN SAUCE

4 tablespoons powdered gelatin
1 cup (8 fl oz/250 ml) milk
pinch of salt
¾ cup plus 2 tablespoons
   (7 fl oz/200 ml) caramel
½ cup (4½ fl oz/125 ml)
   whipping cream

For the sauce:
1 cup (9 fl oz/250 ml) heavy
   (double) cream
1 cup (9 fl oz/250 ml) caramel
½ cup (4 fl oz/120 ml) brandy
   or tequila
edible flower, to decorate
   (optional)

REGION: CENTRAL MEXICO
PREPARATION TIME: 30 MINUTES, PLUS 5 MINUTES
STANDING AND 4 HOURS CHILLING
COOKING TIME: 25 MINUTES
SERVES: 6

Pour ½ cup (4 fl oz/120 ml) water into a small bowl, sprinkle the gelatin over it, and let stand for 5 minutes, until spongy.

Pour the milk, salt, and ¼ cup plus 2 tablespoons (3½ fl oz/100 ml) water into a food processor or blender and process to combine. With the motor running, gradually add the caramel through the feeder tube or hole in the lid. Process until the caramel is completely dissolved.

Pour the mixture into a saucepan and bring to a boil over medium heat, stirring continuously. Add the gelatin mixture and cream and whisk with a balloon whisk until the gelatin dissolves.

Remove the pan from the heat and let cool slightly. Pour the mixture into individual molds or a single mold and chill in the refrigerator until set.

To make the sauce, heat the cream in a small saucepan over medium heat. Add the caramel and cook, stirring continuously, until thoroughly mixed. Remove the pan from the heat, stir in the brandy, and let cool.

Dip the bottom of the molds in hot water. Place an upturned plate over the mold and, holding them together, invert to turn out the gelatin. Spoon the sauce over the gelatin and decorate with caramelized nuts, if using.

Zucchini (Courgette) Cake

PASTEL DE CALABACITA

✳

ZUCCHINI CAKE

butter, for greasing
1 cup (4 oz/120 g) all-purpose
  (plain) flour, plus extra for
  dusting
1 teaspoon baking powder
½ teaspoon baking soda
  (bicarbonate of soda)
¼ teaspoon sea salt
3 eggs
1 cup (7 oz/200 g) sugar
1½ cups (7 oz/200 g) grated
  zucchini (courgettes)
2 teaspoons ground cinnamon
2 teaspoons vanilla extract
¾ cup (6 fl oz/175 ml) corn oil
1 cup (4 oz/120 g) chopped nuts
1 cup (5 oz/150 g) pineapple
  chunks
candied pineapple, to garnish

REGION: ALL REGIONS
PREPARATION TIME: 20 MINUTES
COOKING TIME: 1 HOUR
SERVES: 8

Preheat the oven to 350°F (180°C/Gas Mark 4). Grease and flour a 9 x 5 x 3-inch (23 x 13 x 7.5-cm) loaf pan or 8 mini cake pans. Sift together the flour, baking powder, baking soda (bicarbonate of soda), and salt into a bowl and set aside.

Beat the eggs and sugar until the mixture turns white. Stir in the zucchini (courgettes), cinnamon, vanilla, and oil until thoroughly combined. Add the sifted flour mixture and stir in gently until it is just mixed in. Do not overmix it.

Pour the batter into the prepared pan(s) and sprinkle the nuts and pineapple on top. Bake for 45–60 minutes (25–30 minutes for mini cake pans), or until a toothpick (cocktail stick) inserted into the center of the cake comes out clean.

Remove the pan(s) from the oven and let cool for 20–30 minutes. Turn it out on a wire rack and serve warm or at room temperature. Sprinkle the candied pineapple over the cake(s).

Corn Cake

PASTEL DE ELOTE

CORN CAKE

REGION: GENERAL
PREPARATION TIME: 30 MINUTES
COOKING TIME: 50 MINUTES
SERVES: 6

- ¾ cup plus 2 tablespoons (7 oz/200 g) butter, plus extra for greasing
- all-purpose (plain) flour for dusting
- 2½ cups (14 oz/400 g) corn kernels
- 5 eggs
- 1 cup (7 oz/200 g) superfine (caster) sugar
- 1 teaspoon vanilla extract

To decorate:
- confectioners' (icing) sugar, for dusting

Preheat the oven to 350°F (180°C/Gas Mark 4).

Melt the butter and set aside to cool to room temperature. Line an 8-inch (20-cm) round cake pan with parchment paper, then grease with a little of the butter.

Put the corn kernels into a food processor or blender and process until smooth. Add the eggs, sugar, and vanilla and process until thoroughly combined. Add the melted, cooled butter and process briefly to combine.

Pour the batter into the prepared pan and bake for 45–50 minutes or until set in the center. Remove the pan from the oven and let cool for 20 minutes.

Meanwhile, make the eggnog sauce. Put the cream, egg yolks, sugar, brandy, and vanilla extract into a bowl and stir to dissolve the sugar. (Do not process in a machine or you will get whipped cream.) Season to taste with grated nutmeg.

Turn out the cake while it is still warm and cut into slices and sprinkle with confectioners' (icing) sugar.

PASTEL TRES LECHES

✳

THREE-MILK CAKE

butter, for greasing
2½ cups (10 oz/275 g)
   all-purpose (plain) flour,
   plus extra for dusting
1 tablespoon baking powder
8 extra large (UK large) eggs,
   separated
1½ cups (9 oz/230 g) extra fine
   sugar
1 tablespoon vanilla extract
4 tablespoons milk
2 cups (1 lb/450 g) strawberries,
   hulled and halved, plus extra
   for garnish

For the cream:
1 (14-oz/395-g) can condensed
   milk
1 (5-oz/150-ml) can evaporated
   milk
generous ½ cup (5 fl oz/150 ml)
   light (single) cream
3 egg yolks
1–2 tablespoons brandy

For the topping:
3 egg whites
½ cup (3½ oz/100 g) extra fine
   sugar
juice of ½ lemon
2 tablespoons corn (golden)
   syrup

REGION: ALL MEXICO
PREPARATION TIME: 50 MINUTES, PLUS
10 MINUTES STANDING
COOKING TIME: 40 MINUTES
SERVES: 8

Preheat the oven to 350°F (180°C/Gas Mark 4). Grease and line an 11-inch (28-cm) round cake pan. Sift together the flour and baking powder into a bowl and set aside.

Whisk the egg yolks with the sugar and vanilla until ribbons form. Gently fold in the flour and baking powder mixture, alternating with the milk.

Whisk the egg whites in a grease-free bowl until they form stiff peaks, then fold into the mixture. Pour the batter into the prepared cake pan. Bake for 30–40 minutes or until a toothpick (cocktail stick) inserted into the center of the cake comes out clean.

Meanwhile, make the cream. Put all the ingredients into a food processor or blender and process until combined.

Remove the pan from the oven and let cool. Turn out onto a plate, slice cake in half, into two layers. Add the strawberries on top of one layer, and then place the second layer on top. Pour the cream over it while is still warm.

To make the topping, put the egg whites, sugar, lemon juice, and syrup in a heatproof bowl set over a pan of barely simmering water. Do not let the base of the bowl touch the surface of the water. Whisk vigorously until the mixture is fluffy, then remove the bowl from the pan, and continue whisking until a meringue forms.

Cover the cake with the meringue using a spatula and brown the tips of the meringue with a culinary blow torch. Add strawberries, if using. Serve with the cream.

Three-Milk Cake

PASTEL DE ZAPOTE NEGRO

※

BLACK SAPOTE CAKE

butter, for greasing
2¾ cups (12 oz/350 g) flour, plus extra for dusting
½ cup (2 lb/900 g) black sapote pulp
4 tablespoons packed brown sugar
5 tablespoons orange juice
2 tablespoons lemon juice
1 ripe banana, mashed
1½ cups (11 oz/300 g) sugar
¼ teaspoon sea salt
1½ teaspoons baking soda (bicarbonate of soda)
1½ teaspoons ground cinnamon
4 eggs, beaten
¾ cup (6 fl oz/175 ml) corn oil
¾ cup (4 oz/120 g) golden raisins (sultanas)
⅔ cup (2¾ oz/70 g) pumpkin seeds, toasted

REGION: FEDERAL DISTRICT
PREPARATION TIME: 30 MINUTES
COOKING TIME: 1 HOUR
SERVES: 6

Preheat the oven to 375°F (190°C/Gas Mark 5). Grease and flour two 6-inch (15-cm) round cake pans.

Combine the sapote pulp, brown sugar, orange juice, and lemon juice in a bowl and mix well. Add the mashed banana and sugar.

Sift together the flour, salt, baking soda (bicarbonate of soda), and cinnamon in a separate bowl. Gradually fold the dry ingredients into the wet mixture. Stir in the eggs, oil, golden raisins (sultanas), and pumpkin seeds.

Divide the batter between the prepared pans. Bake for 45–60 minutes or until firm to the touch.

Remove the pans from the oven, turn out the cakes onto a wire rack, and let cool. Slice and serve.

HELADO DE AGUACATE Y MIEL

AVOCADO AND HONEY ICE CREAM

4¼ cups (1¾ pints/1 liter) milk
1 cup (7 oz/200 g) sugar
1 cup (9 oz/250 g) honey
⅔ cup (5 oz/150 g) corn (golden) syrup or liquid glucose
pinch of sea salt
5 avocados
juice of 1–2 lemons
20 g ice cream stabilizer

REGION: ALL REGIONS
PREPARATION TIME: 1 HOUR, PLUS 4½ HOURS FREEZING
COOKING TIME: 20 MINUTES
SERVES: 6

In a small pan, mix together the stabilizer with sugar.

Combine the milk, sugar, honey, syrup, salt, stabilizer mixture, and 4¼ cups (1¾ pints/1 liter) water in a saucepan and bring to a boil over medium heat. Boil for 5 minutes, then remove the pan from heat and let cool.

Once the milk mixture has cooled, peel and pit the avocados. Put the cooled mixture, avocados, and half the lemon juice into a food processor or blender and process until thoroughly combined. Taste and add more lemon juice, if necessary.

Spoon the mixture into an ice cream maker and freeze according to the manufacturer's instructions. If you do not have an ice cream maker, pour the mixture into a freezerproof container and put in the freezer for 1–1½ hours, until semifrozen. Remove from freezer, transfer the ice cream to a bowl, and beat vigorously to break up the ice crystals. Return it to the container and freeze for 1 hour. Remove from the freezer and beat vigorously as before. Return to the container, cover, and freeze until firm.

Remove ice cream from the freezer and transfer to the refrigerator 20 minutes before serving to soften.

HELADO DE PÉTALOS DE ROSA

❊

ROSE PETAL ICE CREAM

1 cup (9 fl oz/250 ml) milk
1 cup (9 fl oz/250 ml) heavy (double) cream
¾ cup (5 oz/150 g) sugar
1½ cups (1 oz/25 g) rose petals, plus extra to decorate
1–2 drops red food coloring (optional)
½–1 teaspoon rose water (optional)

REGION: ALL REGIONS
PREPARATION TIME: 40 MINUTES, PLUS 4½ HOURS FREEZING
COOKING TIME: 10 MINUTES
SERVES: 6

Put the milk, cream, and sugar into a saucepan and cook over medium heat, stirring continuously, until the sugar has dissolved.

Put the rose petals into a bowl and pour over the hot milk mixture. Let cool completely.

Put the rose petal mixture into a food processor or blender and process until smooth. Pass the mixture through a strainer (sieve) into a bowl. Stir in 1–2 drops red food coloring, if using, and then add the rose water, drop by drop, to taste.

Freeze the mixture in an ice cream maker according to the manufacturer's instructions. If you do not have an ice cream maker, pour the mixture into a freezerproof container and freeze for 1–1½ hours, until semifrozen. Remove from freezer, transfer the ice cream to a bowl, and beat vigorously to break up the ice crystals. Return to the container and freeze for 1 hour. Remove from the freezer and beat vigorously as before. Return to the container, cover, and freeze until firm.

Remove the ice cream from the freezer and transfer to the refrigerator 20 minutes before serving to soften. Serve with rose petals.

MOUSSE HELADO DE LIMON

✺

FROZEN LIME MOUSSE

butter for greasing
¾ cup plus 2 tablespoons
    (6 oz/175 g) sugar, plus extra
    for sprinkling
juice of 2½ limes
3 eggs, separated
2 cups (16 fl oz/475 ml) heavy
    (double) cream, chilled

For the citrus mixture:
juice of 5 oranges
1 sprig thyme
juice of 5 tangerines
juice of 2 limes
juice of 1 grapefruit
1 cup plus 2 tablespoons
    (8 oz/225 g) sugar

To decorate:
1 tangerine, segmented with
    the membranes removed
1 grapefruit, segmented with
    the membranes removed
1 orange, segmented with the
    membranes removed

REGION: FEDERAL DISTRICT
PREPARATION TIME: 40 MINUTES, PLUS
6 HOURS FREEZING
COOKING TIME: 20 MINUTES
SERVES: 6

Butter 6 ramekins and sprinkle with sugar.

Put 4 tablespoons water and 4 tablespoons sugar into a small saucepan and heat gently over medium heat, stirring until the sugar has dissolved. Remove the pan from heat and stir in the lemon or lime juice.

Put the egg yolks and 2 tablespoons sugar into a heatproof bowl set over a saucepan of barely simmering water and whisk until pale and firm.

Whisk in ½ cup (4 fl oz/120 ml) of the lime syrup and continue whisking until light and fluffy. Remove the bowl from heat.

Whip the cream in a separate bowl until it forms soft peaks.

In another bowl, beat the egg whites with the remaining sugar until stiff peaks are formed.

Fold the cream and egg yolk mixture together then gently fold in the whites.

Spoon the mixture into the prepared ramekins and put in the freezer for 6 hours, until frozen.

To make the citrus mixture, put the orange juice and thyme in a small saucepan and boil for 3 minutes. Add the tangerine juice, lime juice, grapefruit juice, and sugar. Heat gently to dissolve the sugar, then remove the pan from the heat. Strain into a bowl and let cool.

To serve, quickly dip the bottoms of the ramekins in hot water. Put a deep plate, upside down, over a ramekin, and, holding them together, invert it, and turn out the mousse. Repeat with the remaining ramekins. Carefully pour 4 tablespoons of the citrus mixture around each mousse. Decorate with the tangerine, grapefruit, and orange segments and serve.

DATE AND
NUT FUDGE

2 tablespoons (1 oz/25 g)
  butter, plus extra for greasing
1 cup (9 fl oz/250 ml) milk
½ cup (4 fl oz/120 ml) runny
  honey
½ cup (3½ oz/100 g) sugar
¼ teaspoon sea salt
2¼ cups (9 oz/250 g) chopped
  walnuts
3 cups (1 lb 2 oz/500 g) dried
  dates, pitted and chopped
1 tablespoon vanilla extract

REGION: SOUTH BAJA, CALIFORNIA
PREPARATION TIME: 30 MINUTES
COOKING TIME: 15 MINUTES
SERVES: 6

Grease a 9-inch (23-cm) square cake pan with butter.

Combine the milk, honey, sugar, and salt in a saucepan, bring to a boil, and stir until the sugar has dissolved. Reduce the heat and simmer, stirring continuously, for 15 minutes. Stir in the walnuts and dates and remove the pan from the heat.

Stir in the butter and vanilla, pour the mixture into the prepared cake pan, and let cool completely. When the fudge is set, cut it into squares.

SWEET BEAN
PUDDING

3⅔ cups (1 lb 2 oz/500 g)
  cooked black beans
4¼ cups (1¾ pints/1 liter) milk
½ vanilla bean (pod)
½ cup (3½ oz/100 g) sugar
pinch of sea salt
½ cup (4 fl oz/120 ml) sherry
4 tablespoons chopped
  almonds

REGION: CENTRAL MEXICO
PREPARATION TIME: 10 MINUTES
COOKING TIME: 20 MINUTES
SERVES: 6

Put the beans into a food processor or blender and process until pureed. Add the milk and process again, then strain into a bowl.

Scrape the vanilla from the bean (pod). In a bowl, combine the bean mixture, sugar, vanilla bean (pod), salt, and sherry into a saucepan and cook over medium heat, stirring continuously, for about 20 minutes, until the spoon leaves a trail when pulled across the bottom of the pan.

Remove the pan from the heat and transfer the mixture to a serving platter. Sprinkle with the chopped almonds and serve warm in bowls.

DULCE DE GUAYABA DE DURANGO

DURANGO GUAVA CANDY

11 oz/300 g guavas

2 egg yolks

1 tablespoon cornstarch
(cornflour)

4¼ cups (1¾ pints/1 liter) milk

¼ teaspoon baking soda
(bicarbonate of soda)

1½ cups (11 oz/300 g) sugar

6 candied figs, cut into
thin strips

REGION: DURANGO
PREPARATION TIME: 25 MINUTES
COOKING TIME: 35 MINUTES
SERVES: 6

Put the guavas in a blender with the milk and process until smooth. Pass them through a strainer (sieve) into a saucepan. Add the cornstarch (cornflour), baking soda (bicarbonate of soda), and sugar. Cook over low heat, stirring continuously with a wooden spoon, for about 35 minutes. Pour some of the hot milk over the egg yolks whisking to temper them. Pour the yolk mixture back into hot milk, stirring constantly until the spoon leaves a trail on the base of the pan.

Remove the pan from the heat and continue stirring until cooled. Serve in dishes and garnish with candied fig strips.

DULCE DE MANGO

MANGO MERINGUE PUDDINGS

4 large mangoes, peeled, pitted,
and coarsely chopped

2 cups (16 fl oz/475 ml) milk

3 eggs, separated

1¾ cups (12 oz/350 g) sugar

4 tablespoons confectioners'
(icing) sugar

REGION: VERACRUZ
PREPARATION TIME: 25 MINUTES
COOKING TIME: 25–30 MINUTES
SERVES: 6

Put the mangoes and milk into a food processor or blender and process until combined. Add the egg yolks and the sugar and process briefly again.

Pour the mixture into a saucepan and cook over low heat, stirring continuously with a wooden spoon for about 10 minutes, or until the spoon leaves a trail on the bottom of the pan. Spoon into 6 bowls.

Beat the egg whites with the confectioners' (icing) sugar until shiny and stiff. Spoon the mixture on top of the mango pudding in the bowls. Serve warm or cold.

QUINCES WITH CREAM

3 quinces, peeled, halved, and cored
1 large green apple, peeled and grated
1¼ cups (9 oz/250 g) sugar
1 lemon
2 cloves
4 drops red food coloring
1 cup (8 oz/225 g) heavy (double) cream, cream cheese, or mascarpone

REGION: COAHUILA
PREPARATION TIME: 15 MINUTES
COOKING TIME: 30 MINUTES
SERVES: 6

Put the quinces into a wide saucepan and fill the cavity of each quince with grated apple. Sprinkle 1 tablespoon sugar on top of each quince and pour 5 cups (2 pints/1.2 liters) water into the pan, and add the cloves and 4 drops food coloring. Bring to a boil, then reduce the heat to low, cover, and simmer for 25 minutes or until the quinces are soft and the syrup is thick.

Remove the pan from the heat and let cool.

Lightly whip the cream or cheese. Plate the quinces, top each with a spoon of cream or cheese, and serve.

WALNUT CANDY

1 (14-oz/400-g) can condensed milk
¾ teaspoon vanilla extract
1 tablespoon sugar
1 tablespoon butter
¾ cup (3½ oz/100 g) walnuts

REGION: COAHUILA
PREPARATION TIME: 15 MINUTES
COOKING TIME: 12 MINUTES
SERVES: 6

Combine the condensed milk, vanilla, sugar, and butter in a saucepan over low heat, without stirring, for about 12 minutes or until thickened.

Remove the pan from the heat and let cool.

DULCE DE PLATON DE MAIZ AZUL

※

SWEET BLUE CORN PLATTER

2 cups (11 oz/300 g) blue corn
  kernels
½ teaspoon tequesquite
4¼ cups (1¾ pints/1 liter) milk
1 cinnamon stick
1¾ cups (12 oz/350 g) sugar
1 tablespoon orange blossom
  water
1 teaspoon ground cinnamon

REGION: ALL REGIONS
PREPARATION TIME: 30 MINUTES, PLUS
OVERNIGHT STANDING
COOKING TIME: 1½ HOURS
SERVES: 6

Combine the corn, tequesquite, and 4¼ cups
(1¾ pints/1 liter) water into a saucepan, bring
to a boil over medium-high heat, and boil for
5 minutes. Remove the pan from the heat and
let stand overnight in a cool place.

Meanwhile, combine the milk and cinnamon
stick in a small saucepan, bring to a boil, and then
remove from the heat. Let stand overnight in a
cool place.

The next day, drain the corn, rinse under cold
running water, and drain again. Put it into a food
processor or blender and process until fine. Mix the
processed corn with 4¼ cups (1¾ pints/1 liter) water
and drain, then mix with 2 cups (16 fl oz/475 ml)
water and drain again.

Put it into a saucepan and bring to a boil, stirring
continuously, then add the milk, cinnamon stick,
and 1½ cups (11 oz/300 g) of the sugar. Reduce the
heat to low and simmer, stirring occasionally, for
about 1 hour or until the spoon leaves a trail on the
bottom of the pan. Add the orange blossom water,
bring to a boil, and remove the pan from the heat.
Discard the cinnamon stick.

Combine the ground cinnamon with the
remaining sugar in a bowl. Pour the corn mixture
onto a platter and sprinkle with the cinnamon and
sugar mixture to serve.

WINTER FRUIT DESSERT

1¼ cups (9 oz/250 g) dark
  brown sugar
1 large cinnamon stick
12 large tejocotes
6 large guavas, seeded
4 sugar cane pieces, peeled and
  cut into strips
3 oranges, peeled and sliced
vanilla ice cream, to serve

REGION: ALL MEXICO
PREPARATION TIME: 10 MINUTES
COOKING TIME: 30 MINUTES
SERVES: 6

Bring 4¼ cups (1¾ pints/1 liter) water to a boil in
a saucepan, add the sugar and cinnamon, and
bring back to a boil. Stir until the sugar has
dissolved completely, then boil for several minutes
until syrupy.

Add the tejocotes, guavas, sugar cane, and
oranges and cook for 15 minutes or until the
tejocotes are tender. Remove the pan from heat
and let cool.

Serve cold with a scoop of vanilla ice cream.

CHICKPEA BRITTLE

⅔ cup (4 oz/120 g) dark brown
  sugar
½ cup (3½ oz/100 g) dried
  chickpeas, dry-roasted and
  ground

REGION: GUERRERO
PREPARATION TIME: 15 MINUTES
COOKING TIME: 30 MINUTES
SERVES: 6

Put the sugar and ½ cup (4 fl oz/120 ml) water into
a saucepan over medium-low heat and stir until the
sugar has dissolved completely. Turn up the heat and
simmer, without stirring, until thickened and syrupy.
If you have a candy (sugar) thermometer, it should
read 250°F (130°C). Alternatively, if you drop a little
of the mixture into a glass of cold water, it should
turn into a little ball with distinct edges.

Pour in the ground chickpeas and mix quickly.
Remove the pan from the heat and carefully pour
the mixture onto a clean, heatproof work surface.
Fold it over and over carefully with a spoon or a
scraper, working quickly, then flatten to about ⅛ inch
(3 mm) and smooth with a wet spoon or scraper.

Using a wet knife or scraper, cut it into squares
and let dry.

ROLLO DE DATIL Y NUEZ

DATE AND WALNUT ROLL

1 cup (9 fl oz/250 ml) milk
1½ cups (11 oz/300 g) sugar
36 dried dates, pitted
1½ cups (6 oz/175 g) walnuts
confectioners' (icing) sugar,
  for dusting

REGION: CHIHUAHUA
PREPARATION TIME: 30 MINUTES
COOKING TIME: 30 MINUTES
SERVES: 6

Heat the milk and sugar in a heavy saucepan over medium heat and stir until the sugar is completely dissolved. Bring to a boil, stirring continuously. If you have a candy (sugar) thermometer, it should read 250°F (130°C). Alternatively, if you drop a little of the mixture into a glass of cold water, it should turn into a little ball with distinct edges.

Remove the pan from the heat and quickly stir in the dates and nuts.

Lightly dampen a kitchen towel and sprinkle it with confectioners' (icing) sugar. Spread the date and nut mixture in a strip on the dish towel and then roll it up in the dish towel, using the towel to help you form a log shape about 2 inches (5 cm) in diameter. Let cool and then remove it from the dish towel.

Roll it again in confectioners' sugar, slice, and serve.

DULCE DE ZAPOTE NEGRO

BLACK SAPOTE DESSERT

2¼ lb/1 kg black zapotes,
  peeled and seeded
½ cup (4 fl oz/120 ml) orange
  or tangerine juice
3 tablespoons lemon juice
3 tablespoons honey

To serve (optional):
whipped cream
eggnog

REGION: OAXACA, CAMPECHE, VERACRUZ
PREPARATION TIME: 30 MINUTES, PLUS
1-2 HOURS STANDING
SERVES: 6

Put the sapotes into a food processor or blender and process to a smooth puree. Add the orange juice, lemon juice, and honey, and process briefly again to mix.

Transfer to a bowl and let stand for 1–2 hours, then chill in the refrigerator, if desired.

Serve at room temperature or chilled, by itself or with whipped cream and eggnog.

Note: To make a smoother consistency, pass the mixture through a strainer (sieve) to remove any remaining fibers or peel residue.

MANJAR BLANCO CON LECHE DE COCO

✳

YUCATÁN COCONUT MILK PUDDING

flesh of 3 coconuts, peeled
  and coarsely chopped
1¼ cups (9 oz/250 g) long grain
  rice
⅔ cup (5 oz/150 g) sugar
ground cinnamon, for
  sprinkling

REGION: YUCATÁN
PREPARATION TIME: 25 MINUTES, PLUS 4 HOURS
SOAKING, AND CHILLING
COOKING TIME: 10 MINUTES
SERVES: 6

Put the coconut flesh and 1 cup (9 fl oz/250 ml) water into a food processor or blender and process. Pour the mixture into a fine strainer (sieve) set over a bowl and press out as much liquid as possible. Pour the contents of the strainer into a second bowl, add 2¼ cups (18 fl oz/500 ml) water, and repeat. Set aside to strain.

In a bowl, combine the rice and just enough water to cover and mix. Let soak for at least 4 hours. Transfer the rice and water mixture to a food processor or blender and process to a smooth, thick mixture. Strain the processed rice into the coconut milk, stir, and strain into a pan through a fine sieve (strainer). Add the sugar and heat gently to dissolve the sugar completely. The mixture should have a consistency like thick cream.

Remove the pan from the heat and spoon the mixture into a big serving bowl or 6 individual dessert bowls. Sprinkle generously with cinnamon, cover with plastic wrap (clingfilm) and let cool, then chill in the refrigerator before serving.

MANGOS A LA CANELA

✳

MANGOES WITH CINNAMON

6 large mangoes, peeled
1 cup (7 oz/200 g) sugar
1 cinnamon stick
cream or vanilla ice cream,
  to serve

REGION: TAMAULIPAS
PREPARATION TIME: 20 MINUTES, PLUS COOLING
COOKING TIME: 30 MINUTES
SERVES: 6

Put the mangoes, sugar, and cinnamon stick into a saucepan, add enough water just to cover, and bring to a simmer, stirring, until the sugar has dissolved. Simmer for another 25 minutes.

Remove the mangoes from the pan with a slotted spoon and let cool. Return the pan to the stove and bring the liquid to a boil. Reduce it by at least half until thick and syrupy. Slice the mangoes off the pits and distribute the slices over six plates. Drizzle with hot or cold syrup and serve with cream or vanilla ice cream.

CAMOTE ACHICALADO

PURPLE SWEET POTATO WITH SYRUP

2¼ lb/1 kg purple sweet potatoes, rinsed and dried
2 big cones of piloncillo or 2½ cups (1 lb 2 oz/500 g) packed brown sugar
1 cinnamon stick
whipped cream or vanilla ice cream (optional)

REGION: QUERETARO
PREPARATION TIME: 5 MINUTES, PLUS 24 HOURS SUN DRYING
COOKING TIME: 1½–2 HOURS
SERVES: 6

Preheat the oven to 425°F (220°C/Gas Mark 7). Pierce the sweet potatoes all over with a fork, put them on baking sheet, and bake for 1½–2 hours.

When the potatoes are nearly ready, put the piloncillo or sugar, cinnamon stick, and ½ cup (4 fl oz/120 ml) water into a saucepan and heat gently over medium heat, stirring until the sugar has dissolved. Bring to a boil, without stirring, for a few minutes until thick and syrupy. Remove the pan from the heat.

Remove the potatoes from the oven, evenly distribute them between 6 shallow serving bowls, and coat with some of the syrup. Serve warm or cold. Alternatively, slice the sweet potatoes and serve with the syrup and whipped cream or vanilla ice cream.

CALABAZA EN TACHA

CANDIED PUMPKIN

2½ cups (1 lb 2 oz/500 g) dark brown sugar or piloncillo
juice of 1 large orange
2 large cinnamon sticks
3¼ lb (1.5 kg) pumpkin, seeded and cut into pieces
vanilla ice cream or cream, to serve

REGION: PUEBLA
PREPARATION TIME: 10 MINUTES
COOKING TIME: 1 HOUR 5 MINUTES
SERVES: 6–8

Put the piloncillo or sugar, orange juice, and cinnamon sticks into a large saucepan, pour in 1 cup (9 fl oz/250 ml) water, and bring to a boil. Add a layer of pumpkin pieces, skin sides downward, then add the remaining pumpkin, skin sides uppermost.

Simmer for 1 hour or until the pumpkin is cooked and well steeped in syrup. Remove the pan from the heat and let cool. Remove and discard the cinnamon sticks.

Serve with vanilla ice cream or cream.

POACHED XOCONOSTLES

2¼ lb/1 kg xoconostles, peeled and halved
4-inch (10-cm) cinnamon stick
3 star anise pods
10 allspice berries
1¼ cups (9 oz/250 g) sugar
grated zest of 1 lemon
3 drops of food red coloring (optional)

REGION: CENTRAL MEXICO
PREPARATION TIME: 20 MINUTES
COOKING TIME: 50 MINUTES
SERVES: 6

Scoop out the seeds from the xonocostles and set aside. Combine the seeds, cinnamon stick, star anise pods, and allspice berries in a piece of cheesecloth (muslin) and tie securely with kitchen string.

Combine the xonocostle, sugar, lemon zest, spice bag, and 3 cups (1¼ pints/750 ml) water in a heavy saucepan and bring to a boil. Reduce the heat and simmer for about 20 minutes, until the xonocostle is translucent.

Remove the spice bag, squeezing out any liquid into the pan. Add the red food coloring, if using, and stir. Remove the pan from the heat and let cool.

Remove the xoconostle with a slotted spoon and place them in a pretty serving bowl. Return the pan to the heat, bring to a boil, then simmer for 15–20 minutes, until the liquid is the consistency of a light syrup. Drizzle the syrup over the xoconostles and serve warm or cold.

CANDIED FIGS

24 green figs
½ cup (4 fl oz/120 ml) lemon juice
3¾ cups (1 lb 10 oz/750 g sugar
2 fig leaves
4¼ cups (1¾ pints/1 liter whipped cream, to serve

REGION: YUCATÁN
PREPARATION TIME: 5 MINUTES
COOKING TIME: 25 MINUTES
SERVES: 6

Bring the figs and enough water to cover them to a boil in a medium saucepan and boil for 8 minutes. Drain, cool, and soak in lemon juice.

Combine the sugar and 2½ cups (1 pint/600 ml) water, bring to a boil, and simmer until syrupy. Add the figs and fig leaves, bring back to a boil, and cook for 5–6 minutes. Remove from heat, plate, and serve with whipped cream.

Poached Xoconostles

BORRACHITOS DE COCO Y PIÑA AL MEZCAL

❋

DRUNKEN COCONUT AND PINEAPPLE CAKE

¾ cup (2 oz/50 g) all-purpose (plain) flour
¼ teaspoon baking powder
5½ tablespoons (2¾ oz/70 g) butter, diced
1 cup (4 oz/120 g) confectioners' (icing) sugar
3 eggs
4 tablespoons almond meal
1 cup (3 oz/80 g) finely grated unsweetened coconut

For the syrup:
½ cup (3½ oz/100 g) sugar
½ cup (3½ fl oz/100 ml) aged mezcal

To decorate:
4 tablespoons (2 oz/50 g) butter
4 tablespoons sugar
1 small ripe pineapple, peeled, cored, and sliced
½ cup (3½ fl oz/100 ml) heavy (double) cream
4 tablespoons confectioners' (icing) sugar
8 raspberries, blackberries, or strawberries

REGION: MEXICO CITY, PUEBLA
PREPARATION TIME: 1 HOUR
COOKING TIME: 40 MINUTES
SERVES: 8

Preheat the oven to 350°F (180°C/Gas Mark 4). Line an 8½-inch (22-cm) cake pan or 8 individual cake pans with parchment paper.

Sift together the flour and baking powder into a bowl.

Beat together the butter and confectioners' (icing) sugar in another bowl until pale and fluffy. Add the eggs, one at a time, beating well after each addition. Add the ground almonds and grated coconut and beat well. Add the flour mixture in batches and beat until all the ingredients have been incorporated.

Spoon the batter into the pan(s) and bake for about 30 minutes for the large one (or 20 minutes for the individual cake pans), or until golden brown and a wooden toothpick (cocktail stick) inserted into the center comes out clean.

Meanwhile, make the syrup. Combine the sugar and ½ cup (4 fl oz/120 ml) water in a saucepan, heat gently, and stir until the sugar has dissolved completely. Bring to a boil, without stirring, and boil for 2 minutes or until clear. Remove the pan from the heat and let cool.

Remove the cake pan(s) from the oven, turn out the cake(s), and let cool. Combine ½ cup (3½ fl oz/100 ml) of the cooled syrup with the mescal and drizzle over the cake(s) to make them *borracho* (drunk).

For the decoration, combine the butter and sugar in a saucepan and cook over medium heat, covered, until caramel colored. Add the pineapple slices and cook a few minutes on each side to caramelize. Remove the pan from the heat. Cover and set aside.

Beat the cream with the confectioners' sugar in a bowl until it forms soft peaks. To serve, top the cake(s) with pineapple slices and spoon over the cream. Decorate with berries of choice.

Drunken Coconut and Pineapple Cake

PUCHAS QUERÉTANAS DE SANTA ROSA

✻

DOUGHNUTS FROM THE CONVENT OF SANTA ROSA

10 egg yolks
2 tablespoons sugar
pinch of ground anise
2 tablespoons (1 oz/25 g)
   butter or lard
¼ teaspoon tequesquite
4 tablespoons eau de vie
3⅔ cups (1 lb/450 g) all-purpose
   (plain) flour
1 egg white
5⅔ cups (1½ lb/700 g)
   confectioners' (icing) sugar
   colored sprinkles, to decorate

REGION: QUERETARO
PREPARATION TIME: 1 HOUR, PLUS
10 MINUTES STANDING
COOKING TIME: 40 MINUTES
SERVES: 6

Whisk the egg yolks until thick enough for the beaters to leave a ribbon trail when lifted. Beat in the sugar and anise, then add the butter, a little at a time. Dissolve the tequesquite in the eau de vie in a small bowl and strain into the mixture to remove any lumps.

Gradually stir in the flour, a little at a time, to make a smooth dough. Knead lightly and let stand for 10 minutes.

Preheat the oven to 350°F (180°C/Gas Mark 4). Line a baking sheet with parchment paper.

Divide the dough into 1-oz (25-g) pieces and shape them into doughnuts. Put them on the prepared baking sheet and bake for 25 minutes, then turn them over, and bake for an additional 15 minutes, until lightly browned.

Meanwhile, make a glaze. Whisk the egg white in a bowl, then gradually whisk in the sugar. Keep beating until the glaze has the consistency that you want.

Remove the baking sheet from the oven and let cool for 5 minutes. Spoon the glaze over the doughnuts and top with the colored sprinkles. Let set before serving.

JAMONCILLO DE PEPITA DE CALABAZA

PUMPKIN SEED FUDGE

3½ cups (14 oz/400 g) hulled
green pumpkin seeds, ground
5 cups (2¼ lb/1 kg) sugar, plus
extra for sprinkling
1 teaspoon ground cinnamon
1–2 drops of red food coloring
(optional)

REGION: PUEBLA
PREPARATION TIME: 20 MINUTES
COOKING TIME: 45 MINUTES
SERVES: 6

Put the ground pumpkin seeds and 1 cup (9 fl oz/250 ml) water into a bowl and stir well.

Put the sugar and 2 cups (16 fl oz/475 ml) water into a saucepan and heat gently, stirring until the sugar has dissolved completely. Bring to a boil, and continue to boil, without stirring, until the temperature measures 217–221°F (103–105°C) on a candy (sugar) thermometer, or the mixture makes a short, easily broken thread when 2 teaspoons dipped in it and lifted out are gently pulled apart.

Add the pumpkin seed mixture and cook over low heat, stirring continuously, until the spoon leaves a trail on the bottom of the pan. Remove the pan from the heat and stir in the cinnamon.

Divide the mixture in half. If you are using the food coloring, add it to one half of the mixture and stir well.

Sprinkle 2 boards with sugar and spread out the pumpkin seed mixtures separately on them to a thickness of about ¾ inch (2 cm). Let cool completely before lifting off with a spatula (fish slice).

Cut into cubes and then serve both colors on one plate.

MANGATE

MANGO PUDDING

2 cups (14 oz/400 g)
sugar
2 cups (16 fl oz/475 ml)
mango puree
2 teaspoons liquid pectin

REGION: BAJA CALIFORNIA SUR
PREPARATION TIME: 20 MINUTES
COOKING TIME: 40 MINUTES
SERVES: 6

Put 1½ cups (11 oz/300 g) of the sugar and the mango puree into a saucepan and cook over low heat, stirring continuously, for 10 minutes, until the sugar is completely dissolved.

Combine the remaining sugar and pectin in a bowl and pour into the pan. Heat gently to dissolve the sugar, bring to a simmer, and stir continuously with a wooden spoon for about 30 minutes, until the spoon leaves a trail on the bottom of the pan.

Remove the pan from the heat, pour the mixture into a jelly mold, and let cool. Turn out onto a plate to serve.

LIMONES RELLENOS

✳

STUFFED CANDIED LIMES

10 limes
5 cups (2¼ lb/1 kg) sugar
few drops of green food
   coloring

For the filling:
2 cups (6 oz/175 g) grated
   coconut
1 cup (7 oz/200 g) sugar

REGION: ALL REGIONS
PREPARATION TIME: 30 MINUTES, PLUS 2 DAYS
SOAKING AND 1 DAY STANDING
COOKING TIME: 40 MINUTES
SERVES: 10

Cut the tops off the limes and scoop out the flesh with a spoon without piercing the peels. Put them into a bowl, pour in cold water to cover, and let soak for 2 days, changing the water daily.

Drain the lime shells and put them into a saucepan. Pour in water to cover and bring to a boil. Boil for 5 minutes, then drain and rinse with cold water.

Put the sugar into a saucepan, add 4¼ cups (1¾ pints/1 liter) water, and gently heat, stirring continuously until the sugar has dissolved completely. Bring to a boil, without stirring, for 5 minutes, until syrupy, then add the green food coloring. Reduce the heat, add the lime shells, and cook for 15 minutes. Remove the pan from the heat, drain, and let cool.

To make the filling, combine the coconut with the sugar in a saucepan. Cook over low heat, stirring frequently, until the sugar has melted and the coconut is soft and almost translucent.

Remove the pan from the heat and let cool slightly. Fill the candied shells with the mixture and let stand for 1 day before serving.

Stuffed Candied Limes

JERICALLA

✸

CINNAMON EGG CUSTARD

2 cups (16 fl oz/475 ml) milk
½ cup (3½ oz/100 g) sugar
1 cinnamon stick
6 egg yolks

REGION: CENTRAL MEXICO
PREPARATION TIME: 30 MINUTES, PLUS
OVERNIGHT CHILLING
COOKING TIME: 1½ HOURS
SERVES: 6

Pour the milk into a medium saucepan, add the sugar and cinnamon, and bring to a boil over medium heat, stirring until the sugar has dissolved completely. Boil for 5 minutes, then remove the pan from the heat and let cool.

Preheat the oven to 400°F (200°C/Gas Mark 6).

Remove and discard the cinnamon stick. Put the egg yolks into a large bowl. Pour in some of the hot milk mixture, beating all the while with a wire balloon whisk. Then return the egg yolk and milk mixture to the pan with the milk, beat it well, and continue to cook until thickened. Strain and pour into ramekins, then cover with aluminum foil.

Place the ramekins in a roasting pan filled halfway with hot water and bake for 1 hour. Top up the water level, if necessary. Remove the foil and leave in the oven for an additional 15 minutes, or until browned.

Remove the roasting pan from the oven and lift out the ramekins. Let cool, then chill in the refrigerator overnight.

TUNAS AL ANIS

✸

PRICKLY PEARS WITH ANISE

12 prickly pears, peeled and
   sliced
½ cup (4 fl oz/120 ml) sweet
   anise liqueur
½ cup (3½ oz/100 g) sugar
ground cinnamon, for
   sprinkling
vanilla ice cream or cream,
   to serve

REGION: FEDERAL DISTRICT
PREPARATION TIME: 15 MINUTES, PLUS
1 HOUR CHILLING
SERVES: 6

Put the prickly pears onto a serving platter. Sprinkle first with the anise liqueur and then with the sugar. Cover with plastic wrap (clingfilm) and chill in the refrigerator for 1 hour.

Remove the platter from the refrigerator and uncover. Sprinkle with cinnamon and serve with vanilla ice cream or cream.

MANJAR REAL DE GUAYABA

❋

ROYAL GUAVA PUDDING

2¼ lb (1 kg) guavas, unpeeled
⅔ cups (¼ pint/150 ml)
  evaporated milk
1 cup (4 oz/120 g) blanched
  almonds
1½ cup (11 oz/300 g) sugar, plus
  extra to decorate
1 cinnamon stick
2 cloves
3 egg yolks
4 tablespoons white wine
2 tablespoons cornstarch
  (cornflour)
5 drops red food coloring
  (optional)
ground cinnamon, to decorate

REGION: CENTRAL MEXICO
PREPARATION TIME: 35 MINUTES
COOKING TIME: 55 MINUTES
SERVES: 6

Combine the guavas and 1 cup (9 fl oz/250 ml) water in a large saucepan, bring to a boil, and reduce the heat. Simmer for 20–30 minutes, until tender. Remove the pan from the heat, crush the guavas with a potato masher, and pass through a strainer (sieve). Let cool.

Combine the evaporated milk with 2¼ cups (17 fl oz/500 ml) water. Pour the mixture into a food processor or blender, add the almonds, and process to a fine paste.

Pour the almond milk, sugar, cinnamon, and cloves into a saucepan and heat gently until the sugar is completely dissolved. Increase the heat and boil rapidly until reduced by half. Remove the pan from the heat.

Lightly beat the egg yolks with the wine and cornstarch (cornflour) in a bowl. Gradually whisk in the almond milk mixture. Remove and discard the cinnamon and cloves, then add the crushed guavas. Pour the mixture into a saucepan and cook for about 10 minutes, until thickened. Gradually stir in the food coloring, if using, until the mixture is pale pink.

Remove the pan from the heat and let cool slightly. Transfer to a serving bowl, sprinkle with sugar and cinnamon, and serve at room temperature.

MOUSSE DE GUAYABA

GUAVA MOUSSE

1 tablespoon powdered gelatin
 or 2 sheets (leaves) gelatin
1½ cups (12 fl oz/350 ml) milk
5 tablespoons sugar
zest of ½ lemon
pinch of salt
3 eggs, separated
1 cup (9 fl oz/250 ml) guava
 puree, strained and cooked
1 cup (9 fl oz/250 ml) heavy
 (double) cream

REGION: FEDERAL DISTRICT
PREPARATION TIME: 45 MINUTES, PLUS 5 MINUTES
SOAKING AND 6 HOURS CHILLING
COOKING TIME: 15 MINUTES
SERVES: 6–8

Rinse a mold, shaking out the excess, and put
it in the freezer.

Put the gelatin into a bowl with 4 tablespoons of
water. Let it soak for 5 minutes. If using sheet (leaf)
gelatin, remove it with your hands after 5 minutes
and squeeze it over the bowl. Discard the water. Stir.

Put the milk, sugar, lemon zest, and salt into
a saucepan and heat gently to dissolve the sugar
completely. Remove the pan from the heat.

Lightly beat the egg yolks in a heatproof bowl,
stir in a little of the hot milk, whisking
continuously. Pour the egg mixture back into the
pan and simmer gently, whisking constantly, until
slightly thickened. Do not boil.

Add the gelatin and stir until it has dissolved
completely. Add the guava puree and stir well.
Remove from the heat and let cool.

Whisk the cream in a bowl until soft peaks form.
Whisk the egg whites in another, grease-free bowl
until soft peaks form. Gently fold the egg whites into
the guava mixture, then fold in the cream.

Remove the mold from the freezer and spoon
the guava mousse into it. Chill in the refrigerator
for 4 hours.

To serve, remove the mold from the refrigerator
and dip the bottom briefly into hot water. Put an
upturned plate over the top of the mold and, holding
them together, invert to turn out the mousse.

NICUATOLE DE ALMENDRAS

✳

CORN AND ALMOND PUDDING

6½ cups (2¼ lb/1 kg) cooked corn kernels

6¼ cups (2½ pints/1.5 liters) milk

1 cinnamon stick

1½ cups (11 oz/300g) sugar

pinch of sea salt

2½ cups (9 oz/250 g) ground almonds

corn oil, for greasing

red sugar (sugar with a few drops of red food coloring), chokecherry, or red fruit sauce, to serve

REGION: OAXACA
PREPARATION TIME: 30 MINUTES, PLUS 3 HOURS STANDING AND CHILLING
COOKING TIME: 45 MINUTES
SERVES: 6

Put the corn kernels into a food processor or blender and process to the texture of light (single) cream. Add water, if required. Strain through a fine strainer (sieve) into a bowl and discard the contents of the strainer.

Combine the milk, cinnamon, sugar, and salt in a saucepan and heat gently until the sugar has dissolved. Gradually add the corn cream, a little at a time, stirring continuously until it has thickened. Add the ground almonds and continue to simmer, stirring continuously, until the spoon leaves a trail on the bottom of the pan. Meanwhile, lightly grease a roasting pan.

Remove the pan from the heat, taste, and add a pinch of salt, if needed. Pour into the prepared roasting pan and let cool. Cover with plastic wrap (clingfilm) so it does not form a skin. When cold, chill in the refrigerator for several hours or overnight until set.

Cut the dessert into 2-inch (5-cm) squares and decorate with sprinkled red sugar, or chokecherry or red fruit sauce, and serve.

MELADO DE PAPAYA

✺

PAPAYA DESSERT

3 tablespoons limestone
2¼ lb (1 kg) papayas, peeled,
   seeded, and cut into thick
   slices
15–20 fresh fig leaves
2 cups (16 fl oz/475 ml) honey
thinly pared zest of 2 lemons,
   cut into thin strips
1 cinnamon stick

To serve: (optional)
grated Gruyere cheese, brown
   sugar, vanilla ice cream,
   or cream

REGION: YUCATAN, TABASCO
PREPARATION TIME: 30 MINUTES, PLUS 1 HOUR
STANDING AND 2 HOURS CHILLING
COOKING TIME: 1 HOUR 20 MINUTES
SERVES: 6–8

Dissolve the limestone in 2 cups (16 fl oz/475 ml) water in a bowl, pour it over the papaya, and add enough water to cover the fruit. Let stand for 1 hour.

Line the bottom of a wide saucepan with half of the fig leaves.

Drain the papaya and rinse thoroughly with cold water. Put the papaya into the prepared pan, add the honey, the lemon strips, and cinnamon stick. Cover with the remaining fig leaves and then with parchment paper. Make a hole in the center of the paper to let steam escape during cooking.

Cook the fruit over low heat for 1 hour or until tender. Remove the pan from the heat and let cool completely, then chill in the refrigerator.

Spoon the papaya onto a serving platter and pour over the juice. Garnish with cheese, brown sugar, vanilla ice cream, or cream, if using.

Papaya Dessert

Sweet Corn Tamales

TAMAL DE CHARALES

SWEET CORN TAMALES

8 fresh white corn on the cobs
½ teaspoon ground cinnamon
1 tablespoon anise seeds
½ cup (3½ oz/100 g) butter
1 cup (7 oz/200 g) grated raw
   sugar (piloncillo) or packed
   brown sugar
½ teaspoon sea salt
sour cream, to serve
sliced lime, to serve
mild red chile, sliced, to serve

REGION: MICHOACAN
PREPARATION TIME: 1 HOUR, PLUS
15 MINUTES SOAKING
COOKING TIME: 1 HOUR
SERVES: 6

Remove the husks from the corn without damaging them, and separate the leaves. Put them into a heatproof bowl, pour enough hot water to cover, and let soak for 15 minutes. Cut the kernels from the cob, reserving the milky liquid that is sometimes exuded). Put half of the kernels and any reserved liquid into a food processor or blender and process. Transfer to a bowl. Put the remaining kernels into the food processor or blender and process, then add the cinnamon, anise seeds, butter, sugar, and salt and process briefly again. Transfer the mixture to the bowl and beat to a smooth dough.

Rinse the husks well. Fill each leaf with a generous tablespoon of the dough, down the center of the leaves, then close and roll it gently to secure it. You have to do this immediately, because the mixture tends to separate as it stands.

Place the tamales vertically in a steamer and cook over high heat, topping up with boiling water as necessary, for 1 hour or until firm to the touch. Remove the tamales from the heat and let stand 1–2 hours, until set. Serve with sour cream, lime, and chile.

TAMALES DE CHOCOLATE

❋

CHOCOLATE TAMALES

12 corn husks
¾ cup (9 oz/250 g) butter
1 cup (6 oz/175 g) sugar
2 eggs, separated
1¾ cups (7 oz/200 g) masa harina
1¼ cups (7 oz/200 g) rice flour
1 cup (3½ oz/100 g) unsweetened cocoa powder
2 teaspoons baking powder
¼ teaspoon salt
¾ cup (3 oz/80 g) ground almonds
1¾ cups (9 oz/250 g) blackberries
5 oz/150 g semisweet (dark) chocolate, broken into small pieces
5 tablespoons blackberry jam
1½ teaspoons vanilla extract

REGION: NUEVO LEÓN
PREPARATION TIME: 30 MINUTES, PLUS 20 MINUTES SOAKING
COOKING TIME: 35 MINUTES
SERVES: 6

Soak the corn husks in boiling water for 15 minutes, until softened, then drain.

Beat the butter in a bowl until soft, then beat in the sugar and salt until the mixture is light and fluffy. Beat in the egg yolks, one at a time, making sure that the first has been fully incorporated before adding the next. In a separate bowl, sift together the masa harina, flour, cocoa powder, and baking powder, then fold in the ground almonds and stir the flour mixture into the sugar and egg mixture until it is completely incorporated.

Whisk the egg whites in a grease-free bowl until they form soft peaks, then fold them into the flour and sugar mixture, making sure they are completely incorporated.

Put a few tablespoons of the batter on each corn husk leaf and spread it out. Top with a few blackberries and pieces of chocolate. Roll up the husks from a long side to enclose the filling and tie the ends with string.

Bring water in a steamer to the boil and put on the steamer basket. Place the tamales seam side down in the steamer basket and put on the lid. Cook for 40 minutes, check the water level occasionally and top up with boiling water, if necessary.

Meanwhile, combine the blackberry jam, vanilla extract, and 1 tablespoon water in a small pan and cook over medium heat until melted and combined. Remove the tamales from the steamer and serve immediately with the blackberry sauce.

TAMALES DE PIÑA Y COCO

✻

PINEAPPLE COCONUT TAMALES

⅓ pineapple, grated and juice
 reserved
1¼ cups (9 oz/250 g) sugar
1 cinnamon stick
1½ cups (3½ oz/100 g) dried
 (desiccated) coconut
2 egg yolks
1 handful corn husks

For the dough:
1 cup (7 oz/200 g) lard or
 butter
½ cup (4 oz/120 g) sugar
4¼ cups (1 lb 2 oz/500 g) masa
 harina
1½ teaspoons baking power
¼ teaspoon sea salt
½ cup (4 fl oz/120 ml) milk
4 tablespoons (2 oz/50 g)
 butter, melted

REGION: VERACRUZ
PREPARATION TIME: 30 MINUTES, PLUS
15 MINUTES SOAKING
COOKING TIME: 1¾ HOURS
SERVES: 6

Soak the corn husks in boiling water for 15 minutes, until softened, then drain. Set aside.

Put the pineapple and ⅔ cup (4 oz/120 g) sugar into a heavy saucepan and cook over medium heat, stirring, until the sugar has dissolved. Bring to a boil and boil for 20 minutes, until the mixture reaches the setting point of jam—220°F (105°C) on a candy (sugar) thermometer. Remove the pan from the heat and let cool.

Pour 1 cup (9 fl oz/250 ml) water into a pan, add the remaining sugar, and the cinnamon stick. Cook over medium heat, stirring, until the sugar has dissolved, then bring to a boil for 5 minutes. Add the coconut, reduce the heat, and simmer for about 3 minutes or until the coconut appears translucent. Remove the pan from the heat and let cool slightly. Rapidly stir a tablespoon of the hot mixture into the egg yolks in a heatproof bowl, then stir the egg yolk mixture back into the pan. Return to low heat and cook, stirring constantly, for 3 minutes or until the mixture thickens. Remove from the heat and let cool completely.

To prepare the dough, beat the lard with the sugar until fluffy. Fold in the masa harina, baking powder, and salt and add enough milk to make a soft, smooth dough. Fold in the pineapple mixture. Put a corn husk in your hand and place 1 heaping tablespoon of the dough in a rectangle toward the wider end of the husk, spoon 1 tablespoon of the coconut filling in the middle of the dough, close by joining the 2 edges of the husk together, and roll it up. Fold the thin side over the filled end. Repeat with the rest of the husks and the masa and filling. Stand the tamales vertically in a steamer and cook over medium heat for 1 hour or until the dough can easily be separated from the husk.

Remove the steamer from the heat and let the tamales rest for 20 minutes before serving.

TAMALES DE FRESA

✺

STRAWBERRY TAMALES

1 cinnamon stick
5 eggs
½ cup (2 oz/50 g) all-purpose (plain) white flour
⅔ cup (5 oz/150 g) sugar
pinch of salt
1 cup (9 fl oz/250 ml) milk
2 cups (10 oz/300 g) strawberries, washed, dry and crushed or finely chopped
3 drops of red food coloring (optional)
20 corn husk, soaked in hot water for 15 minutes or until tender and drained well

For the dough:
2 cups (350 g/12 oz) lard or butter
1½ cups (11 oz/300 g) sugar
9 cups (2¼ lb/1 kg) masa harina
2 cups (16 fl oz/450 ml) milk
1 tablespoon baking powder
½ teaspoon salt

REGION: CENTRAL MEXICO
PREPARATION TIME: 15 MINUTES, PLUS 20 MINUTES STANDING
COOKING TIME: 1½ HOURS
MAKES: 20

To make the filling, pour 1 cup (9 fl oz/250 ml) water into a small pan, add the cinnamon stick, and bring to a boil. Continue to boil until the mixture has reduced to 4 tablespoons. Discard the cinnamon. Put the water, milk, eggs, flour, sugar, and salt into a food processor or blender and process until smooth. Pour the mixture into a pan and heat, stirring constantly, for 10 minutes or until thickened and cooked. Remove the pan from the heat and let cool. It should look and taste like pastry cream but much thicker. When the mixture has cooled completely, gently stir in the crushed strawberries and the food coloring, if using. Set aside.

To make the dough, beat together the lard or butter and sugar for 5 minutes until light and fluffy. Gradually add the masa harina, milk, baking powder, and salt and continue beating for 5 minutes until the ingredients are thoroughly combined and the dough is fluffy and spreadable. Let the dough rest for 10 minutes, check the amount of liquid and add as much as needed.

Spread 2 tablespoons of the dough on the wider end of a corn husk, then place 1 heaping tablespoon of the filling on top, then roll up and fold in the ends of the husk. Make all the tamales in the same way.

Place the tamales upright in a prepared steamer and cook over high heat, adding more boiling water as necessary, for 1 hour or until the dough easily comes off the husk. Remove from heat and let the tamales stand for 20 minutes before eating.

Strawberry Tamales

MIKEL ALONSO AND BRUNO OTEIZA

BIKO
PRESIDENTE MASARYK 407
MEXICO CITY
MEXICO

Chefs Bruno Oteiza and Mikel Alonso trained Together in San Sebastian before they opened the high-acclaimed restaurant Biko in 2007. An inventive marriage of Spanish and Mexican flavors, dishes combine the traditions of Basque cuisine, while using forward-thinking techniques. Oteiza has also hosted a Spanish program called *Cocina con Bruno Oteiza*.

CANGREJO ENTRE PIELES

CRAB STEW

PREPARATION TIME: 30 MINUTES
COOKING TIME: 55 MINUTES
SERVES: 4

For the stewed crab:
1 onion, finely chopped
2 carrot, finely chopped
⅔ cup (5 fl oz/150 ml) olive oil
1 tomato, finely chopped
¾ oz/20 g diced green olives
1 teaspoon capers, plus extra
  to garnish
½ chile, finely chopped
¾ oz/20 g piquillo pepper,
  finely chopped
9 oz/250 g crabmeat
salt

For the caper puree:
2 teaspoons capers
¾ cup (2½ oz/70 g) flaked
  almonds
½ chile, finely chopped
⅓ oz/10 g cilantro (coriander)
4 teaspoons chili vinegar
2 tablespoons fried onion
½ cup (3½ fl oz/100 ml) extra
  virgin olive oil

For the tomato skins:
2 small tomatoes
2 oz/50 g piquillo peppers
½ teaspoon agar agar

For the stewed crab, fry the onion and the carrots in the olive oil. Add the rest of the evenly sliced vegetables, and sauté for 15 minutes. Add the crab and cook for 20 minutes.

Blend all the ingredients for the caper puree.

Liquidize the tomatoes, pequillo peppers and scant ½ cup (3½ fl oz/100 ml) water. Strain and boil for 15 minutes, then dissolve the agar agar into this mixture and smooth out onto a tray. Cut to the desired size and then place on wax (greaseproof) paper and let dry.

Stripe the plate with the caper puree, garnish with the almonds, capers, olive, and the chile. Place 2 oz/50 g of the crab on the plate and cover with the tomato skin.

PESCADO PIPIÁN
✻
FISH IN SAUCE

2¼/1 kg fresh white fish fillets
1 red radish, thinly sliced

For the salsa de verdolaga:
½ onion, chopped
1 clove garlic
1 cup (9 fl oz/250 ml) fish stock
7 oz/200 g verdolaga stems
¼ cup (2 fl oz/60 ml) heavy
  (double) cream
4 teaspoons olive oil
½ teaspoon vinegar
salt

For the radish air:
2 oz/50 g red radish
1 g oregano
4 teaspoons olive oil
1 cup (9 fl oz/250 ml) vinegar
1 teaspoon lecithin
salt and pepper

For the pipian sauce:
2 tomatillos
⅓ cup (1½ oz/40 g) pumpkin
  seeds
1 oz/25 g broiled (grilled)
  tortilla
⅓ onion
2 cloves garlic
¼ oz/8 g cilantro (coriander)
3 g epazote
1 g radish leaf
4 lettuce leaves
2 teaspoons cider vinegar
scant 1 cup (7 fl oz/200 ml)
  porrusalda (Basque potato
  soup)

PREPARATION TIME: 35 MINUTES
COOKING TIME: 60 MINUTES
SERVES: 4

For the radish sheets, keep the thinly sliced radishes in ice water.

Sauté the onion, garlic, and half of the verdolaga stems. Add fish stock and reduce by a third. Put the mixture, the other half of the verdolago stems, cream, olive oil, vinegar, and salt into a food processor or blender and process until smooth. Strain, add a pinch of salt, then check the sourness and the thickness of the sauce.

For the radish air, blend all ingredients, but the lecithin together, and ½ teaspoon water. Mix well and strain. Season and generate the air with lecithin.

For the pipian, broil (grill) all the ingredients, except the herbs and liquids. Blend everything together and season. Refry the puree in oil. Preheat the oven to 350°F (180°C/Gas Mark 4). Place the fish in an ovenproof dish and pour over the sauce. Cook for 15 minutes.

When cooked, transfer some of the sauce to a plate, then carefully place the fish on top. Garnish with the radish air, radishes sheets and verdolaga salsa.

JASON DEBRIERE

TACOMBI
267 ELIZABETH STREET
NEW YORK, NY
USA

Jason de Briere's work at Five Points Restaurant and Barbuto gave him a strong sense of awareness for local and sustainable produce and humanely raised animals. Born on the balmy beaches of the Yucatan in 2006, Tacombi began selling tacos out of a converted VW bus in Playa del Carmen. That same bus has been parked in New York City since 2010, when Tacombi at Fonda Nolita was established. Tacombi then open its doors to the Flatiron neighborhood with Café el Presidente, an all-day café and dining room with an in house tortilleria, juice bar, and bakery.

RED SALSA

10 Roma or plum tomatoes
3 jalapeño chiles
3 cloves garlic
¼ cup (½ oz/15 g) chopped cilantro (coriander)
1 red onion, diced
juice of 1 lime
sea salt and pepper

PREPARATION TIME: 10 MINUTES
COOKING TIME: 10 MINUTES
SERVES: 6–8

Roast the tomatoes under a broiler (grill) until the skins are charred and blackened. Dry-roast the jalapeño chiles and garlic, then remove the stems from the jalapeños. For added heat, leave the seeds in. Set aside.

Crush the jalapeños, garlic, and cilantro (coriander) in a molcajete or mortar and pestle. Smash or puree the tomatoes and add to the jalapeño mixture. Stir in the diced red onion and lime juice. Season with salt and pepper.

PICKLED RED ONION

2 allspice berries
pinch of dried oregano
1 teaspoon salt
1 tablespoon sugar
scant 2 cups (15 fl oz/450 ml) apple cider vinegar
juice of 2 limes
2 red onions, thinly sliced

PREPARATION TIME: 5 MINUTES, PLUS
1 HOUR COOLING
COOKING TIME: 10 MINUTES
SERVES: 6–8

Combine all the ingredients except the red onion in a non-reactive pot and bring to a boil. Let simmer for 5 minutes. Bring back to a boil and pour the mixture over the sliced red onion. Let cool at room temperature.

MOLE CAMERONES

✻

SHRIMP MOLE

8 poblano chiles, dry-roasted
1 onion, sliced into rings
1 head garlic
sea salt and pepper
1½ lb/680 g fresh shrimp
  (prawns), shelled and
  deveined
oil, for oiling
fresh tortillas, to serve
2 tablespoons apple cider
  vinegar

To garnish
pickled red onion (page 650)
cilantro (coriander)

PREPARATION TIME: 20 MINUTES, PLUS
15 MINUTES SOAKING
COOKING TIME: 15 MINUTES
SERVES: 6–8

In a small bowl, add the chiles and enough hot water to cover them and soak for 15 minutes.

To make the sauce, dry-roast the onion and garlicy and puree the mixture with the chiles and some of the hydrating liquid until smooth. Season with salt and pepper to taste.

Toss the shrimp (prawns) with salt and pepper, and then with the mole sauce. Be sure to coat it well. Oil a hot ridged (griddle) pan and sauté the shrimp until just cooked through. Serve on fresh tortillas and garnish with pickled red onion and cilantro (coriander).

TACOS DE MAIZ Y POBLANO

✻

CHILE AND CORN TACOS

8 ears fresh corn
olive oil (optional)
6 fresh poblano chiles
1 teaspoon dried epazote
2 tablespoons grapeseed oil
scant 1 cup (8¼ fl oz/235 ml)
  crema fresca
4 oz/120 g cotija cheese, plus
  extra to garnish
salt and freshly ground black
  pepper
fresh tortillas, to serve

PREPARATION TIME: 10 MINUTES
COOKING TIME: 20 MINUTES
SERVES: 6–8

Char the corn before removing from the cob on a broiler (grill) on a griddle. Remove the corn kernels from the cob and set aside.

Roast the poblano chile over an open flame. Remove the skins and seeds and slice into thin strips.

In a large frying pan or skillet, heat the oil over medium heat and add the corn, chiles, and epazote for 3–4 minutes. Stir in the crema fresca and cotija cheese. Season with salt and pepper to taste. Serve on fresh tortillas, garnished with a sprinkling of cotija cheese.

TACOS DE BACALAO

✳

SALT COD TACOS

2 lb/900 g cod fillet, skinned and deboned
kosher salt
3¾ cups (945 ml/1⅔ pints) whole milk
3 cloves garlic, smashed
2 arbol chiles
2 tablespoons dried Mexican oregano
2 tablespoons dried epazote
2 pasilla chiles
red salsa or mole
fresh tortillas, to serve

To garnish
pickled red onion (page 650)
cilantro (coriander)

PREPARATION TIME: 10 MINUTES, PLUS 48 HOURS SALTING AND 6 HOURS SOAKING
COOKING TIME: 20 MINUTES
SERVES: 6–8

Completely cover the fish with salt and place in a perforated, nonreactive container for 48 hours. Keep a container underneath the fish to catch the water that is extracted during the salting process. After 48 hours, remove and scrape the salt (and chiles, if used) off the fish. Rinse with water and submerge in clean water, soaking for 6 hours (changing the water three times over this period).

In a nonreactive saucepan, add the fish, milk, 3¾ cups (30 fl oz/900 ml) water, garlic, arbol chile, oregano, and epazote. Keep over low heat until the fish is cooked through, being careful not to boil, because it makes the texture of the fish like sawdust. When the fish is cooked through, remove and let cool. The texture should be flaky.

Gently flake the fish into a bowl and toss with red salsa or mole. Enjoy on a fresh tortilla with pickled red onion and cilantro (coriander).

ANDREW LOGAN

MAMASITA
11 COLLINS STREET
MELBOURNE, VICTORIA
AUSTRALIA

Andrew climbed up the ranks until 2010, when was appointed Executive Chef of The Newmarket Hotel, which has been a driving force in Melbourne's new wave Latin American food scene for the past three years. Since July 2013, Andrew has been Mamasita's Head Chef cooking up authentic Mexican cuisine.

PANCITA DE CERDO

GUAJILLO PORK BELLY

For the pork side (belly):
6½ lb (3 kg) pork side (belly), skin on and bones removed

For the pickled red onion:
scant ½ cup (7 fl oz/200 ml) red wine vinegar
5 black peppercorns
1 bay leaf
1 cup (7 oz/200 g) superfine sugar
4½ Spanish onions, cut to ¼-inch (½-cm) slices
2 red chiles, split
3½ tablespoons dried oregano

For the guajillo stock:
12 guajillo chiles, dry-roasted
1 large onion, chopped
10 cloves garlic, chopped
4 teaspoons oil
1 tablespoon cumin seeds, toasted and ground
8½ cups (3½ pints/2 liters) pork stock
sea salt and pepper

1¼ cups (9 oz/250 g) superfine (caster) sugar

PREPARATION TIME: 30 MINUTES, PLUS 1-3 DAYS STANDING AND 6-8 HOURS CHILLING
COOKING TIME: 3 HOURS 40 MINUTES
SERVES: 10-12

For the pickled red onion, bring the vinegar, peppercorns, and bay leaf to a boil, then gradually add the sugar until dissolved. Put into a jar, the onion, red chile, and oregano. Strain the hot pickle over the onion and let sit for 1–3 days.

For the guajillo stock, heat the oil in a saucepan, sauté the onion and garlic for 10 minutes, or until caramelized. Add the cumin and cook for another 2 minutes. Add the chiles and stock, bring to a boil, and cook for 20 minutes, until the chiles are rehydrated. Blend and pass through a strainer (sieve), then season.

Lay the side (belly) in gastro tray lined with baking parchment. Cover with the guajillo stock, and another sheet of baking parchment. Seal with aluminum foil and cover with a flat tray or lid. Cook for 2½ hours at 350°F (175°C/Gas Mark 3). The meat should be tender but not falling apart, and a knife should slide in easily. Strain the sauce.

Transfer and press the bellies between trays lined with baking parchment. Wrap well with plastic wrap (clingfilm) and refrigerate for 6–8 hours. Remove the skin and excess top layer fat and cut into bite-size pieces.

For the glaze, put the stock and sugar into a saucepan and reduce by a third, or until it coats the back of a spoon. Coat each piece of pork with the glaze, reheat in the oven for 10 minutes. Add the additional guajillo glaze and serve.

BARRAMUNDI CON CHILE ESCABECHE

✺

BARRAMUNDI WITH PICKLED CHILES

1 (6½ lb/3 kg) whole
   barramundi, cleaned and
   filleted with skin on
2 white onions, sliced
scant ½ cup (3½ fl oz/100 ml)
   lime juice
¾ teaspoons salt

For the pickles:
scant 1 cup (7 fl oz/200 ml) red
   wine vinegar
5 black peppercorns
1 bay leaf
scant 1 cup (7 fl oz/200 ml)
   superfine (caster) sugar
13–14 fresh poblano chiles, cut
   into ½-inch (1-cm) thick slices
2 red chiles, halved lengthwise
3½ tablespoons Mexican
   oregano

For the pasilla adobo:
10 pasilla chiles, seeded
1 red chile, chopped
1 teaspoon allspice berries
2¼ teaspoon Mexican oregano
1 teaspoon cumin
1 white onion, halved
2 cloves garlic, chopped
½ cup (2½ oz/75 g) raisins
½ cup (4 fl oz/120 ml) red wine
   vinegar
3½ tablespoons honey
4¼ cups (34 fl oz/1 liter)
   chicken stock
black pepper

For the puffed amaranth:
4 tablespoons organic
   amaranth

PREPARATION TIME: 30 MINUTES, PLUS 15 MINUTES
SOAKING, 1–3 DAYS STANDING AND 2 HOURS PICKLING
COOK TIME: 1 HOUR 10 MINUTES
SERVES: 6

Preheat the oven to 425°F (220°C/Gas Mark 7).

Divided the fish into 6 portions, season both sides, and more generously on the skin side. Roast the fish skin-side down in a nonstick saucepan until the skin is crisp. Transfer to a baking tray and bake for 10 minutes. Flip the fish and roast until the skin is crisp. Drain on paper towels.

For the pasilla adobo, dry-roast the chiles and soak for 15 minutes in enough boiling water to cover. Puree. Dry-roast the onion with the skin on until blackened, then cool, peel, and coarsely chop. Toast and grind all the spices.

In a large saucepan, sauté the onion, chopped garlic, and chiles until soft, then add the spices, oregano, and raisins and cook out until fragrant, about 3 minutes. Add the pureed chiles and cook for 20 minutes over low heat. Add the red wine vinegar, honey, and chicken stock, then cook until reduced and season. Puree and pass through a fine strainer.

For the pickles, add the the vinegar, peppercorn, and bay leaf to a saucepan and bring to a boil. Add the sugar and heat until dissolved, cool, and then strain. Put the poblanos, red chiles, oregano and pickling liquid in a jar. Let stand for at least a day, 2–3 days is better. Set aside.

In a bowl, combine the onions, lime juice, ½ cup (4 fl oz/120 ml) pickling liquid and salt and mix well. Pickle for 2 hours and only enough to eat the same day, because the onions will be past their best after 6–8 hours. Drain the onions after 2 hours.

For the puffed amaranth, heat a dry heavy saucepan over medium-high heat and add the amaranth. Once the grains start to pop, remove from the heat immediately to avoid burning them.

Plate the fish and serve with the pasilla adobo, puffed amaranth, pickled chiles, and onions.

MOUSSE DE CHOCOLATE CONGELADO

❄

FROZEN CHOCOLATE MOUSSE

For the chocolate mousse:
5 cups (1 lb 10 oz/750 g)
    Mexican drinking chocolate,
    Abuelita or Ibarra brand
1⅔ cups (13 oz/375 g) butter
18 eggs, separated
¾ cup (5 oz/150 g) superfine
    (caster) sugar

For the dulce con leche:
1 can condensed milk

For the sesame praline:
1⅓ cups (7 oz/200 g) sesame
    seeds
1 cup (7 oz/200 g) superfine
    (caster) sugar

For the roasted figs:
1 cup (7 oz/200 g) superfine
    (caster) sugar
10 ripe black figs

PREPARATION TIME: 20 MINUTES, PLUS OVERNIGHT
FREEZING AND 2 HOURS COOLING
COOKING TIME: 4 HOURS
SERVES: 9

Melt the chocolate and butter in a heatproof saucepan of simmering water.

Whisk together the yolks and ¼ cup (2 oz/50 g) sugar and cook over a double boiler to form a thick sabayon. Combine the chocolate mix and sabayon when they are both at the same temperature (about 113°F/45°C). Let cool to room temperature.

Whisk the egg whites and remaining sugar to soft peaks. Fold the whites into the chocolate in small amounts at a time. The mix should be light and fluffy. Pour the mixture into baking parchment-lined molds. We used terrine molds or rectangular plastic containers. Freeze at least overnight. Keep in the freezer until serving.

For the dulce de leche, remove the label from the can and place can in a suitable size saucepan. Fill the pan with water until the can is almost covered. Be sure not to fully submerge. Cover and simmer for 3 hours, checking every 30 minutes and refilling the pot with hot water as required. Remove the can from the water and place directly in the refrigerator.

Once cool, remove the lid and use as required.

For the sesame praline, in a heavy saucepan, toast the seeds until honey colored, stirring constantly. Remove from the heat and cool.

Make a dry caramel (347°F/175°C) in a similar heavy pan and reintroduce the seeds to the caramel. Immediately onto a nonstick silpat mat otherwise the caramel will burn in the hot pot.

Cool down to room temperature. Do not place in the refrigerator otherwise the caramel will sweat. Break into pieces and pulse in a food processor until a coarse grainy texture is obtained.

For the figs, preheat the oven to 425°F (220°C/ Gas Mark 7). Halve the figs and lay on a baking parchment-lined roasting pan. Dust with sugar lightly and roast for 5 minutes until the sugar has dissolved and the figs have softened. Serve immediately.

THOMASINA MIERS

WAHACA
66 CHANDOS PLACE
COVENT GARDEN
LONDON
UNITED KINGDOM

Masterchef winner Thomasina Miers is cofounder of the successful London Mexican restaurant Wahaca, which looks to the markets of Mexico for inspiration and pairs the flavors of Mexico with ingredients that British farmers can produce on home soil, to create a constantly evolving, seasonal menu. In addition to overseeing the restaurant, Miers has presented various cookery shows on television and radio, authored numerous cookbooks, and supports responsibly-sourced cooking.

WINTER TACOS WITH CREAMY GREENS

1½ lb/700 g winter greens
sea salt and pepper
4 potatoes, diced
2–3 tablespoons olive oil
2 shallots, finely chopped
1 jalapeño chile, finely chopped
4 cloves garlic, finely chopped
1¼ cups (10 fl oz/300 ml) crème fraîche
2 heaping tablespoons chopped tarragon
½ cup (4 fl oz/120 ml) white wine

To serve
grated Pecorino cheese
1 radish, sliced (optional)

PREPARATION TIME: 15 MINUTES
COOKING TIME: 15 MINUTES
SERVES: 4

Separate the leaves from the stems, wash in a sink of cold water, and finely shred. Bring a saucepan of water to a boil and season well with salt. When it is boiling, add the greens and blanch for 5 minutes until the leaves have softened. Remove the leaves with a slotted spoon and add the potatoes to the boiling water. Cook the potatoes for about 5 minutes, until they are soft.

Meanwhile, heat the olive oil in a skillet or frying pan and cook the shallots, chile, and garlic over medium heat until they have softened, seasoning well with salt and pepper. Add the greens and continue cooking for 5 minutes. By this stage, the potatoes should be cooked. Drain them and add them to the greens with the crème fraîche, tarragon, and white wine. Bring to a simmer and cook gently for a few minutes to reduce the cream. Check for seasoning.

Serve the greens in a warm bowl at the table, sprinkled generously with grated Pecorino and sliced radish.

SOPA DE TORTILLA

❋

TORTILLA SOUP

3 tablespoons lard or olive oil
2 onions, sliced
3 cloves garlic, sliced
¾ cup (3½ oz/100 g) fine
    cornmeal (polenta)
1 tablespoon chopped smoked
    chipotle chiles in adobo
2 (14-oz/400-g) cans plum
    tomatoes
1 tablespoon brown sugar
1 teaspoon dried oregano or
    1 tablespoon fresh
sea salt and pepper
6¼ cups (2½ pints/1.5 liters)
    chicken or vegetable stock

To garnish
1 ripe Hass avocado
lemon or lime juice
1¼ cups (10 fl oz/300 ml)
    vegetable oil (which can be
    reused)
2 corn tortillas or 2 chapatis
2 ancho chiles, seeded and
    stems removed
¾ cup (3½ oz/100 g) feta cheese,
    crumbled
a small handful of cilantro
    (coriander) leaves, chopped
½ cup (4 fl oz/120 ml) sour
    cream

PREPARATION TIME: 15 MINUTES
COOKING TIME: 40 MINUTES
SERVES: 6

Heat the lard or oil in a large saucepan, add the onions, and sweat over medium heat for 10–15 minutes, until the onion is completely soft before adding the garlic. Add the cornmeal (polenta) and continue cooking for 5 minutes before adding the chipotles, the tomatoes, sugar, oregano, and seasoning. Cook for another 5 minutes, add the stock, and simmer for another 10 minutes. Process in a food processor or blender until the soup is smooth. Warm over low heat for at least 5 minutes before serving.

Meanwhile, assemble all the garnishes for the soup. Halve the avocado, remove the pit, peel, and dice the flesh, sprinkling with a little lemon or lime juice to stop it from discoloring.

Heat the vegetable oil in a deep skillet or frying pan and cut the flat breads into thin, short 1¼-inch (3-cm) strips. Tear up the ancho chiles into coarse pieces. Test the oil and, when it is shimmering hot (and makes a tortilla strip sizzle), add the strips and cook until crisp and golden. Remove the pieces with a slotted spoon on a plate lined with paper towels, then fry the ancho chile pieces until they have puffed up. This takes only a few seconds, so watch them like a hawk and try not to burn them or you will lose their lovely sweetness. Serve the soup in bowls with all the garnishes laid out in small bowls or on plates so that people can help themselves at the table.

Note: You can also add a rehydrated ancho chile to the soup base for a rich, earthy flavor.

FIDEUS SECO

✳

SPICY CRAB NOODLES

14 oz/400 g vermicelli or angel
hair pasta
½ cup (4 fl oz/120 ml) olive oil
4 baby shallots, finely chopped
4 Serrano or other fresh green
chiles, finely chopped
2 (14-oz/400-g) cans plum
tomatoes
pinch of ground allspice
2 tablespoons baby capers
2 bay leaves
sea salt and pepper
good pinch of sugar
2¼ cups (18 fl oz/500 ml)
chicken or fish stock

To serve
4–5 tablespoons sweet chipotle
paste
11 oz/300 g dressed crab
lime wedges
small container of sour cream
handful of chopped (cilantro)
coriander

PREPARATION TIME: 10 MINUTES
COOKING TIME: 45 MINUTES
SERVES: 6

In a heavy skillet, frying pan, or paella dish, fry the vermicelli in the olive oil, stirring from time to time, for a few minutes until they turn a rich golden color. Transfer to a strainer (sieve), draining the vermicelli on paper towels and putting the oil back into the pan.

Over medium heat, sweat the shallots and chiles for about 10 minutes, until the shallots are translucent and starting to break down, then add the tomatoes, allspice, capers, and bay leaves. Season with salt, pepper, and a good pinch of sugar, and simmer for 15–20 minutes until the flavors develop and you have a rich tomato sauce.

About 15 minutes before you are ready to eat, pour the stock into the tomato sauce, bring to a simmer, and cook for 5 minutes over medium–high heat. Stir the noodles into the sauce and simmer gently until the liquid is absorbed and the noodles are tender.

Serve on plates with the crab, a good spoonful of the chipotle paste on top, wedges of lime, a dollop of sour cream, and lots of cilantro (coriander).

TERRINA DE CHOCOLATE Y CANELA

✻

CHOCOLATE AND CINNAMON PARFAIT

1¾ cups (12 oz/350 g) sugar

1 tablespoon vanilla extract, preferably homemade

6 tablespoons cocoa powder

½ teaspoon ground cinnamon

good pinch of sea salt

3½ oz/100 g semisweet dark chocolate (at least 60% cocoa solids), broken into small pieces

8 egg yolks

2¼ cups (18 fl oz/500 ml) heavy (double) cream

4 tablespoons añejo (aged) tequila or dark rum

PREPARATION TIME: 40 MINUTES, PLUS 30 MINUTES COOLING AND 2 HOURS FREEZING
COOK TIME: 20 MINUTES
SERVES: 8

Cover the sugar with 1½ cups (12 fl oz/350 ml) boiling water and stir to dissolve. Set aside a scant ¼ cup (1½ fl oz/50 ml) and store the rest. Stir in the vanilla extract.

Put the cocoa powder, cinnamon, and salt in a nonstick saucepan, add a tiny amount of the reserved sugar syrup, and stir vigorously with a wooden spoon, slowly adding enough of the remaining syrup to produce a smooth chocolate paste. Gradually stir in the rest of the sugar syrup over gentle heat, stirring from time to time for about 15 minutes, or until the cocoa comes up to simmering point. Simmer, stirring all the time, for 5 minutes before taking the mixture off the heat and adding the chocolate. Stir until the chocolate has completely melted, then cool until it feels lukewarm on your lip.

In the meantime, put the egg yolks into a mixer and beat for 5–10 minutes, until they are pale and fluffy. Beat in the chocolate mix, little by little, until it is fully incorporated. Be careful—if you add it too quickly, it will scramble the yolks. Transfer the mixture to a bowl suspended over a saucepan of simmering water. Stir until thick enough to coat the back of a wooden spoon, or it has reached 185°F/85°C. Make sure you stir continuously so that the eggs don't scramble.

Transfer the chocolate syrup back to the mixer and beat on full speed for 1 minute, on medium speed for 4 minutes, and on low speed for 5 minutes, until it has thickened and increased in volume. Transfer to a large bowl and cool in a sink of iced cold water for at least 30 minutes.

Once the chocolate syrup has cooled, whip the cream to soft peaks (be careful not to overwhip). Fold a quarter of the cream into the chocolate syrup and when that's fully incorporated, fold in another quarter. Fold in the tequila or rum and then the rest of the cream until you have a smooth mixture.

Transfer to a shallow freezerproof container, cover, and freeze for at least 2 hours. Remove from the freezer 20 minutes before serving.

ENRIQUE OLVERA

PUJOL
FRANCISCO PETRARCA 254
MEXICO CITY
MEXICO

Enrique Olvera began his career at the Culinary Institute of America before he returned to Mexico City in 2000 and opened Pujol—the first Mexican restaurant to be featured in San Pelligrino's World's 50 Best Restaurants. Olvera creates dishes using the indigenous ingredients of Mexico and experimenting with both contemporary and classic technique.

His culinary triumphs are led by an obsession for detail, carefully considered ingredients, and well-articulated flavor constructions, along with a constant exploration of Mexico's gastronomic potential. He also runs the New York tortilleria Cosme and has published two books, *UNO* and *En la Milpa*.

OCTOPUS TATEMADO

1 bay leaf
2 onions
pinch of old spice pepper
1 (3¼–4½ lb/1.5–2 kg) octopus, cleaned
1 head garlic
1 habanero chile, membrane and seeds removed
scant ½ cup (3½ fl oz/100 ml) grapeseed oil
salt

For the guacamole:
2 scallions (spring onions), finely chopped
1 Serrano chile, membrane and seeds removed and finely chopped
2 avocados
juice of 2 limes
sea salt

PREPARATION TIME: 15 MINUTES
COOK TIME: 1 HOUR
SERVES: 4

In a stockpot, combine 6.5 quarts (13 pints/ 7.5 liters) water, bay leaf, 1 onion, pepper and salt and bring to a boil. Holding the octopus firm with kitchen tongs, plunge into the water, and then remove immediately. Repeat 3 times. Add the octopus to the water and cook for 45 minutes or until it is soft to the touch. Turn off the heat and let cool in the pan until lukewarm.

Preheat the oven to 400°F (200°C/Gas Mark 6).

Quarter the remaining onion. Dry-roast the onion, garlic, and chiles. Transfer to a food processor or blender and gradually add the grapeseed oil until well combined and the texture is smooth. Set aside.

For the guacamole, remove the skin from the avocado, pit, and dice. Combine the scallions (spring onions), chile, avocado, and lime juice in a food processor and blend until smooth. Season with salt.

To finish, cut the tentacles from the octopus, brush them with the sauce, and place them on a broiler (grill). Broil (grill) for 1 minute on each side. Serve on a plate with the guacamole.

MAIZ CON CAFE Y MAYONESA CHICATANA

✳

BABY CORN WITH COFFEE AND CHICATANA ANT MAYONNAISE

4 baby corns in husk
  (preferably aged 1 month)

For the chicatana ant
  mayonnaise:
4 oz/125 g chicatana ants,
  heads and tails removed
1 egg yolk
½ cup (4½ fl oz/130 ml)
  grapeseed oil
½ cup (4½ fl oz/130 ml)
  vegetable oil
juice of 1 lime
1 puya chile, dry-roasted
  and ground
1 tablespoon ristretto, cooled
salt
4 wooden skewers

For the corn husk salt:
corn husks
½ cup (5 oz/150 g) sea salt
bottle gourge (optional)

PREPARATION TIME: 30 MINUTES
COOK TIME: 30 MINUTES
SERVES: 4

Wash the corn and remove only half the husks from the corn. Set the detached husks aside.

Wrap the attached husks around the corn to protect the kernels. Cook over a comal or flat griddle (grill) over medium-high heat until the husks are charred. Place the charred corn in a sealed container to steam and cook, conserving the corn water.

Preheat the oven to 350°F (180°C/Gas Mark 4).

Toast the ants in a sauté pan over medium-low heat, then let cool completely and grind into a powder. To make the mayonnaise, place the egg yolk in a glass bowl and whisk. Combine the grapeseed and vegetable oils in a bowl and add them a little at a time, alternating with the lime juice, until the mixture begins to thicken and lighten. Gradually add all the oil and continue mixing until incorporated. Season the mayonnaise with the ant powder, ground chile, ristretto, and salt.

For the corn husk salt, take the reserved husks and fill them with the salt, making little wraps. Bake in the oven until dark brown. Blend and pass through a strainer (sieve).

To finish, remove the corn from the container and peel, removing the silk but keeping the husks attached. Fold back the husks and secure by tying a knot. Insert a wooden skewer at the base of each cob.

Roll the corn cob in the ant mayonnaise, and season with the corn husk salt, and place them inside a bottle gourd, if using, or in a small baking pan. Using a smoking gun, smoke the corn with husks. Serve immediately.

CHILEATOLE COLIFLOR CON VENERA

✳

CHILEATOLE ROASTED CAULIFLOWER WITH BAY SCALLOPS

1 head cauliflower, chopped into large pieces and trimmings reserved
2 tablespoons olive oil, for drizzling
sea salt
4 tablespoons grapeseed oil
1 scallion (spring onion), sliced
1 serrano chile, membrane and seeds removed and sliced
8 bay scallops, cleaned and halved
juice from 1 lime
10 cilantro (coriander) leaves

For the chileatole
2 oz/50 g sea salt
2 white heirloom corn on the cobs, shucked and corn husks reserved
10 epazote leaves, plus extra for infusing
½ clove garlic
1 oz/28 g white onion
sea salt
1 guero chile

PREPARATION TIME: 15 MINUTES
COOK TIME: 4 HOURS 40 MINUTES
SERVES: 4

Preheat the oven to 350°F (180°C/Gas Mark 4). Place the chopped cauliflower on a baking sheet and drizzle with olive oil and salt. Cover with aluminum foil and bake for 20 minutes. Remove the foil and bake for another 8 minutes, until golden.

To make the chileatole, bring 2 cups (16 fl oz/ 475 ml) water to a simmer, add the salt, and blanch the cauliflower trimmings for 2 minutes or until they begin to soften. Set aside.

Bring 2 cups (16 fl oz/475 ml) water to a slow boil over medium heat and add the corn, epazote leaves, garlic, and onion for 20 minutes. Add the cauliflower trimmings and cook for another 20 minutes or until the corn is cooked through.

Transfer half the ingredients and 2 cups (16 fl oz/ 475 ml) of the cooking liquid into a food processor or blender and process until smooth. Strain through a strainer (sieve). Repeat with the remaining ingredients and cooking liquid. Season with salt to taste. Before serving, steep with more epazote leaves and the chile for a few minutes, and then strain again.

Wash the reserved corn husks and pat them dry. Put the washed husks onto a 9 x 13-inch (23 x 33-cm) baking sheet and bake at 350°F (180°C/Gas Mark 4) until golden.

Place the husks and grapeseed oil in a plastic bag and sous-vide at 150°F/65°C for 4 hours. Strain the liquid and set it aside.

Place the scallion (spring onion) and chile in a bowl of cold water. Season with the scallion (spring onion), chile, lime juice, cilantro (coriander), salt, and a few drops of the corn-infused oil.

To finish, arrange the scallops in the middle of a serving plate, place some of the roasted cauliflower around the scallops, and pour the chileatole over the top. Serve hot or cold depending on the season.

HUGO ORTEGA

HUGO'S
**1600 WESTHEIMER
HOUSTON, TX
USA**

Chef Hugo Ortega was raised in Mexico City and Puebla, Mexico, where he learned to cook from his mother and grandmother, a revered *mole* maker. At the age of 17, Ortega left Mexico for Houston, where he began his career in the restaurant industry as a dishwasher at Backstreet Cafe and eventually became the executive chef and owner. In 2002, he and his wife opened Hugo's, his second restaurant, which specializes in regional Mexican cuisine. Chef Hugo was a finalist for Best Chef: Southwest at the 2012 and 2013 James Beard Awards, and has published two cookbooks: *Hugo Ortega's Street Food of Mexico* and *Backstreet Kitchen: Seasonal Recipes from Our Neighborhood Cafe.*

CEVICHE DE HUACHINANGO

RED SNAPPER CEVICHE

6 oz/175 g red snapper fillets, cut into ½-inch (1-cm) cubes
1 tablespoon finely diced white onion
juice of 6 limes
1 tomato, seeded and finely chopped
½ jalapeño chile, membrane and seeds removed and finely chopped
2 tablespoons chopped cilantro (coriander), plus 4 sprigs to garnish, divided
1 tablespoon pitted green olives, sliced
1½ teaspoons olive oil
½ teaspoon sea salt
½ avocado, peeled, pitted, and diced, plus 8 slices to garnish
totopos, to serve (optional)

PREPARATION TIME: 15 MINUTES, PLUS 1½ HOURS MARINATING
SERVES: 4

Combine the snapper, onion, and lime juice in a large glass or ceramic bowl and gently stir to combine. (Make sure the snapper floats freely in the lime juice to ensure thorough and even marinating.) Cover with plastic wrap (clingfilm) and refrigerate for 1 hour 30 minutes. Strain and discard the lime juice.

In a separate bowl, combine the tomato, chile, chopped cilantro (coriander), olives, and olive oil, and toss to combine. Add the snapper and salt and toss. Fold in the diced avocado before serving. Serve in 4 chilled martini glasses. Garnish and serve with totopos, if using.

GUISADO DE CAZUELA CON CARNE A LA MEXICANA

✻

BEEF STEW

1½ lb/700 g stewing beef, cut
    into large chunks
2½ small white onions, plus
    extra to garnish
2 cloves garlic
1 bay leaf
1½ teaspoons kosher salt
4 tablespoons olive oil
4 cloves garlic, minced
½ whole jalapeño chile,
    membrane and seeds
    removed and minced
4 tomatoes, cut into wedges
½ poblano chile, dry-roasted
    and and cut into thin strips
½ teaspoon dried oregano
pinch of ground cumin
pinch of ground cloves
½ small bunch of cilantro
    (coriander), coarsely chopped
8 tortillas, warmed

PREPARATION TIME: 15 MINUTES
COOKING TIME: 3 HOURS
SERVES: 4–8

Cut 1 onion into quarters. In a large saucepan, combine the stewing meat, onion, garlic, bay leaf, salt, and enough water to cover. Bring to a boil over high heat, reduce the heat, and simmer for about 2½ hours, or until meat is fork tender. Strain and reserve 4 tablespoons of the liquid. Place the meat in an airtight container and the liquid in a separate container and store both in the refrigerator. This can be prepared up to 2 days before assembling.

Heat the olive oil in a saucepan over medium heat for 2 minutes. Slice the remaining onion. Add the cooked stew meat and let brown for about 3 minutes, then add the onion and cook for about 3 minutes, or until it is translucent. Add the garlic and jalapeño and cook for another 2 minutes. Reduce the heat, add the tomatoes and poblano strips, and cook for an additional 3 minutes, until the tomatoes release their juices. Add the 4 tablespoons reserved liquid and bring to a boil for 3–4 minutes. Reduce the heat and add the oregano, cumin, ground cloves, and half the amount of cilantro (coriander). Simmer for another 3–4 minutes, stirring occasionally.

Place a ladleful of stew on each tortilla. Garnish with the remaining cilantro and finely chopped onion and serve.

TAMALES DE DULCE

✳

SWEET TAMALES WITH RUM RAISINS

For the tamales
½ cup (3 oz/75 g) raisins
3 tablespoons white rum
3 cups (14 oz/375 g) masa
  harina
2 teaspoons baking powder
1¼ cups (9 oz/250 g) granulated
  sugar
1 cup (8 oz/225 g) lard
¼ teaspoon kosher salt
2 teaspoons vanilla extract
6 drops of red food coloring
  (optional)
Corn husks as needed,
  softened in warm water
chocolate caliente, to serve
  (optional)

PREPARATION TIME: 40 MINUTES
COOK TIME: 1 HOUR
MAKES: 16–20 PIECES

For the tamales, put the raisins, rum, and ½ cup (4 fl oz/120 ml) water into a small saucepan over high heat. Bring to a full boil, then remove immediately from the heat. Strain the raisins and transfer to a bowl to cool completely before using.

Using a mixer fitted with a paddle attachment, add the masa harina, baking powder, sugar, lard, salt, vanilla, and food coloring, if using, to the bowl. Mix on medium speed for 1 minute to incorporate the ingredients. While on medium speed, gradually add 2 cups (16 fl oz/475 ml) water. Increase the speed to high and mix for 6 minutes. Fold in the raisins.

Working one at a time, place each corn husk, or two depending on size, in the palm of your hand with the point end facing away from you. Scoop 4 tablespoons masa into the center and spread into a rectangle, ¾ inch (2 cm) from the top and ¼ inch (5 mm) from the bottom. Fold in the sides of the husk to the center, enclosing the masa. Fold up the point, forming a small bundle. Secure each bundle by loosely tying a thin strip of husk around the center of the tamal. Place the tamales in a steamer, covered with a clean, damp paper towel, then the lid, and cook about 40 minutes–1 hour.

To serve, place the warm tamales on a platter and accompany with chocolate caliente, if using.

JOSÉ ANDRÉS

OYAMEL
401 7ᵀᴴ STREET NW
WASHINGTON, DC
USA

José Andrés is an internationally recognized culinary innovator, author, educator, television personality, and chef/owner of ThinkFoodGroup. He has appeared in the *Time*'s 100 Most Influential list and was awarded "Outstanding Chef" by the James Beard Foundation. He is renowned for his refined approach to world cuisines—at Oyamel, in Washington, D.C., and China Poblano in Las Vegas, José offers Mexico's thriving food culture in an authentic and modern environment.

CEVICHE DE ATUN

TUNA CEVICHE

For the coconut dressing:
3 tablespoons lime juice
½ teaspoon chopped ginger
1 tablespoon Dijon mustard
1 cup (9 fl oz/250 ml) coconut milk
½ cup (4 fl oz/120 ml) canola (rapeseed) oil
sea salt and pepper

For the ceviche:
6 oz/175 g fresh, sushi-grade tuna, diced into ¼-inch (5-mm) cubes
½ cup diced jicama
2 tablespoons finely chopped red onion
1 teaspoon finely chopped Serrano chile, seeded
2 tablespoons chopped chives
salt
2 avocados

To garnish:
extra virgin olive oil
cilantro (coriander)
crushed corn nuts

PREPARATION TIME: 20 MINUTES
SERVES: 4

For the coconut dressing, combine the lime juice, ginger, mustard, coconut milk, and pepper in a food process or blender and pulse a few times to combine. With the blender running, slowly add the oil in a steady steam to emulsify. Season with salt to taste. Set aside.

For the ceviche, combine the tuna, jicama, red onion, chile, and chives in a bowl. Add ½ cup (4 fl oz/120ml) dressing and gently toss to combine. Adjust seasoning with salt to taste.

Slice the avocados in half and, with a large tablespoon, separate the flesh from the skin by slowly inserting the spoon through one side, down the middle, and out the other side to detach the flesh.

Slice the avocado into as many slices as possible widthwise, running your knife under hot water every few slices to keep the flesh from sticking to the blade. Fan out the avocado slices gently with your palm.

Divide the ceviche evenly into the center of four plates and cover each with sliced avocado. Season the avocado slices with a pinch or two of salt and garnish with extra coconut dressing, a drizzle of olive oil, cilantro (coriander), and crushed corn nuts.

TACOS DE CARNITAS DE PUERCO

※

STEWED PORK TACOS

For the salsa verde:
9 tomatillos, coarsely chopped
¼ white onion, coarsely chopped
2 cloves garlic
½ bunch of cilantro (coriander), coarsely chopped
juice from ¼ lime
¼ avocado, diced
salt

For the tacos:
4 cloves garlic, crushed
1 bay leaf
1 cup (9 fl oz/250 ml) freshly squeezed lime juice
2 oranges, sliced
1½ tablespoons kosher salt
2 lb/900 g pork shoulder, cut into 2-inch (5-cm) pieces
2 cups (16 fl oz/475 ml) olive oil
12-oz (350-ml) bottle dark malt beer, such as Negra Modelo
1 (14-oz/395-g) can condensed milk
16 corn tortillas, preferably fresh
1 small white onion, diced
4 tablespoons finely chopped cilantro (coriander)
2 limes, cut into 8 wedges

PREPARATION TIME: 30 MINUTES, PLUS 24 HOURS MARINATING
COOK TIME: 1½–2 HOURS
MAKES: 16 TACOS

For the salsa verde, put all of the ingredients into a food processor or blender and pulse until they are just pureed but not overblended. Season the salsa with salt to taste, and store in the refrigerator until ready to use.

For the tacos, in a large bowl, combine the crushed garlic, bay leaf, 4 tablespoons lime juice, orange slices, and the salt to make the marinade. Add the marinade to a large, resealable plastic bag with the pork and toss gently with your hands to make that the pork is fully coated in the marinade. Marinate the pork in the refrigerator for 24 hours.

In a large saucepan, combine the oil, beer, condensed milk, the orange slices from the marinade, and the remaining ¾ cup (6 fl oz/175 ml) lime juice and bring to a boil. Once boiling, lower the heat to a simmer and add the pork. Cook until the pork is fork tender, 1½–2 hours. When the pork is done, use two forks to shred the pork and store in the cooled braising liquid.

To assemble the tacos, drain 1½ tablespoons stewed pork and place into the center of a tortilla. Top the pork with a tablespoon of the salsa verde, a teaspoon of diced white onion, a teaspoon of minced cilantro (coriander), and a ¼ lime wedge. Repeat with the rest of the tortillas to make 16 tacos.

Note: If pork lard is readily accessible, use 1 cup (8 oz/225 g) pork lard and 1 cup (9 fl oz/250 ml) oil.

BISTEC A LA PIMIENTA CON SALSA DE 9 CHILES

✳

STEAK WITH 9 CHILE SAUCE

For the salsa:
4 ancho chiles, dry-roasted
8 mulato chiles, dry-roasted
3 chipotle morita chiles, dry-roasted
2 chipotle meco chiles, dry-roasted
1 tablespoon pequin chile, dry-roasted
12 árbol chiles
8 pasilla de Oaxaca chiles
6 guajillo chiles
5 cascabel chiles
3 cloves garlic, dry-roasted
1 tablespoon sherry vinegar
4 cups (1⅔ pints/950 ml) beef stock
4 tablespoons extra-virgin olive oil
salt

For the Bistec:
½ lb 8 oz/225 g baby or fingerling potatoes, cleaned and halved
3 tablespoons olive oil, plus extra for drizzling
1 tablespoon butter
1 large onion, diced
10 pieces allspice
25 black peppercorns
4 (4-oz/120-g) pieces hanger, skirt, or flank steak
sea salt
4 tablespoons sherry vinegar
1 tablespoon chopped parsley, plus extra to garnish

PREPARATION TIME: 25 MINUTES, PLUS 10 MINUTES SOAKING AND 15 MINUTES STANDING
COOK TIME: 1 HOUR
SERVES: 4

Place the dry-roasted chiles in a bowl, add enough boiling water to cover, and soak for 10 minutes.

Place the chiles, ¾ cup (6 fl oz/175 ml) of their soaking liquid, the roasted garlic, pequin chile, sherry vinegar, and beef stock in a blender and puree until smooth. Heat the olive oil in a small sauté pan over high heat until smoking hot. Carefully because the oil will splatter, add the chile paste and cook, stirring continuously, until the sauce is shiny and smoky, about 15 minutes. Season with salt, to taste.

For the bistec, preheat the oven to 375°F (190°C/Gas Mark 5). Toss the potatoes with 2 tablespoons of olive oil and roast in the oven until golden brown, about 30 minutes. Meanwhile, melt the butter in a small sauté pan and add the onions. Cook the onions over low heat until caramelized, about 20–30 minutes.

Place the allspice and black peppercorns in a coffee or spice grinder and puree until fine. Rub each piece of hanger steak all over with about 1 tablespoon of the rub and let them sit for 15 minutes before broiling (grilling). Preheat the broiler (grill) to medium–high heat and broil (grill) the steaks until medium-rare, about 4–5 minutes each side. Season the cooked steaks with salt to taste, and let rest for 5 minutes.

Heat 1 tablespoon of oil in a small sauté pan over medium–high heat and add the roasted potatoes and caramelized onions. Add the sherry vinegar and the parsley and cook until the vinegar is reduced, about 5 minutes. Season with salt to taste and slice against the grain.

To plate, spoon about 3 tablespoons of the salsa into the center of four plates. Top the salsa with the onions and potatoes. Place the sliced hanger steak on top of the potatoes and onions. Finish each plate with a pinch of sea salt, drizzle of olive oil, and dash of parsley.

SEAN PRENTER

MEXICANO
2/209-211 OCEAN ST
NARRABEEN
AUSTRALIA

After spending his early years training in some of Sydney's best restaurants including Beach Road Palm Beach and Cottage Point Inn, Sean Prenter spent five years in Japan at Las Chicas and Gravity Worx. Eventually Prenter's eyes turned to Mexican cuisine and he launched his first establishment, Mexicano, in Narabeen beach. The menu offers Sean's take on modern and street-style dishes served in a Tapas-style environment. Flour tortillas are rolled daily and fresh corn tortillas are pressed to order. The menu encompasses Sydney's finest seafood in ceviches to slow-braised beef briskets and chargrilled smoky achiote chicken. The small buzzing restaurant also serves its famous frozen Margarita, jalepeno Margarita on the rocks, and a huge supply of tequila and mezcal.

FLAN DE 3 HORES

❋

3-HOUR FLAN

scant ½ cup (3 oz/80 g) superfine (caster) sugar, for the caramel
3 whole eggs
1 egg yolk
1 (14 oz/395 g) can condensed milk
1 vanilla bean (pod), seeds scraped out
2½ cups (14 fl oz/395 ml) whole milk
¼ cup (1 oz/30 g) good quality cocoa powder

For the chocolate soil:
½ cup (3½ oz/100 g) superfine (caster) sugar
scant 1 cup (3½ oz/100 g) almond meal
½ cup (2¼ oz/60 g) flour
scant ½ cup (2 oz/50 g) cocoa powder
⅓ cup (2¾ oz/70 g) butter, melted

PREPARATION TIME: 10 MINUTES
COOK TIME: 3 HOURS 20 MINUTES, PLUS OVERNIGHT COOLING
SERVES: 6

For the chocolate soil, preheat the oven to 325°F (160°C/Gas Mark 3). Mix all the ingredients together. Spread evenly onto a baking tray lined with parchment paper and bake for 20 minutes, stirring every 5 minutes. Cool and store.

Preheat the oven to 225°F (110°C/Gas Mark ¼).

Heat the superfine (caster) sugar in a small saucepan over medium to high heat for about 10 minutes until it reaches a caramel colour and reaches 250°F (120°C/Gas Mark ½). Carefully pour to line a 8 x 6-inch (20 x 15-cm) flan mold. Cool.

In a bowl, mix the eggs, yolks, condensed milk, and vanilla together with a whisk. Add the milk then strain through a strainer twice to remove any egg membrane and air bubbles. Pour the egg mix into the flan mold, then place in a shallow tray half filled with water. Add a temperature gauge/ meat thermometer and cover tightly with foil. Bake for 3 hours, or until the temperature gauge reads 181°F/83°C. Cool, then refrigerate overnight for best results.

Run a knife around the edge of the flan, then remove from the mold and slice into bars. Serve on top of the chocolate soil.

FISH TACOS WITH CHIPOTLE MAYO AND CUCUMBER SALSA

7 oz/200 g flathead, cod or
   gurnard fillets
all-purpose (plain) flour, for
   dusting
salt

For the slaw:
1 carrot, finely shredded
5 oz/150 g Savoy cabbage,
   finely shredded
4 tablespoons Chipotle Mayo
   (page 671)
1 mango, peeled and diced
2 radishes, thinly sliced
cilantro (coriander), to garnish
lime wedges, to serve

For the beer batter:
¾ cup (6 fl oz/170 ml) cold beer
½ teaspoon salt
½ teaspoon baking soda
   (bicarbonate of soda)
scant 1 cup (3½ oz/100 g) all-
   purpose (plain) flour

For the cucumber salsa:
⅓ cup (2½ fl oz/75 ml) coconut
   vinegar
generous ⅓ cup (2¾ oz/75 g)
   superfine (caster) sugar
½ baby cucumber, finely diced
1 golden shallot, finely sliced
1 small red chile, finely sliced

For the flour tortillas:
generous 1¼ cups (5 oz/155 g)
   bakers flour
2 tablespoons duck fat
¼ teaspoon salt
oil for deep frying

PREPARATION TIME: 30 MINUTES, PLUS
10 MINUTES RESTING
COOKING TIME: 15 MINUTES
SERVES: 4

For the beer batter, in a bowl, mix the beer, salt, baking soda (bicarbonate of soda) and scant ½ cup (3½ fl oz/100 ml) iced water together. Add the flour and mix with your hand to form a lumpy batter. Do not overmix or the batter will be tough.

For the cucumber salsa, in a pot, bring the coconut vinegar, sugar and scant ½ cup (3½ fl oz/100 ml) water to a boil. Cool, then add the diced cucumber, golden shallot, and chiles.

For the slaw, combine all the ingredients in a bowl and mix well. Add the chipotle mayo and mix well.

For the flour tortillas, mix all the ingredients together, including 6 tablespoons hot water and work until smooth and elastic, about 3 minutes by machine or 5 minutes by hand. Divide into ¾-oz (20-g) portions and roll into balls. Rest for 10 minutes then flatten and roll out into flat tortillas with a rolling pin. Cook in a non-stick pan or Mexican comal for 30 seconds on each side, or until puffed and cooked.

Salt and flour the flathead fish, then dip into the batter and deep-fry for 2 minutes until golden brown. Remove and drain on paper towels.

Reheat the flour tortillas on a hot chargrill for best results, then place on a serving plate and top with the slaw mix, then the fish, a spoonful of chipotle mayonnaise, followed by the mango, salsa, radishes, and cilantro (coriander). Serve with lime wedges.

Note: Flathead is a Sand dwelling fish that is found in Lakes and the Ocean. Cod, latchet or gurnard are good substitutes.

MAIZ CON QUESO MAYONESA CHIPOTLE

✳

GRILLED CORN WITH CHIPOTLE MAYO CHEESE

4 corns on the cob
generous ¾ cup (3½ oz/100 g)
   grated kefalograviera cheese

For the chipotle mayo:
2 eggs
½ teaspoon Dijon mustard
½ tablespoon white vinegar
1 heaped teaspoon salt
2¼ oz/60 g smoked chipotle
   chiles in adobo
scant ¼ cup (1¾ fl oz/50 ml)
   fresh lime juice
2 tablespoons superfine (caster)
   sugar
2¼ cups (18 fl oz/500 ml)
   vegetable oil

For the corn spice:
2 guajillo chiles, dry-roasted
1 pasilla chile, dry-roasted
1 teaspoon smoked paprika
½ teaspoon cayenne pepper
zest of 2 limes
½ teaspoon cumin seeds
2 teaspoons pepitas,
   dry-roasted
2 teaspoons sea salt

To serve
banana leaf
lime wedges

PREPARATION TIME: 15 MINUTES, PLUS
30 MINUTES SOAKING
COOKING TIME: 15-20 MINUTES
SERVES: 4

Soak 4 bamboo skewers for at least 30 minutes.

For the mayonnaise, combine the eggs, mustard, vinegar, salt, chipotle, lime juice, sugar, and scant ½ cup (3½ fl oz/100 ml) water for 1 minute to emulsify. Slowly add the vegetable oil in a steady stream until it is all incorporated and emulsified.

For the corn spice, combine all the ingredients in a spice grinder and grind to a powder.

Pierce the corn with the soaked skewer and broil (grill) for 15–20 minutes, turning frequently. Remove from heat, brush with the chipotle mayo, then sprinkle with cheese, and the spice. Serve on a banana leaf with a few lime wedges.

MIGUEL RAVAGO

FONDA SAN MIGUEL
2330 WEST NORTH LOOP BOULEVARD
AUSTIN, TX
USA

In 1975, Miguel cofounded Fonda San Miguel in Austin with Tom Gilliland. Under Miguel's culinary guidance, Fonda San Miguel has set the definitive standard in Texas for authentic regional cuisine from Mexico's interior. In addition to his stewardship of the restaurant, Miguel coauthored *Cocina de la Familia* with Marilyn Tausend in 1997, which won a Julia Child cookbook award in 1998 and has also been published in Spanish. He is a longtime member of the International Association of Culinary Professionals.

VERACRUZ-STYLE CEVICHE SOUP

1 lb/450 g skinned black drum
  or redfish fillets, cut into
  1.2-inch (1-cm) cubes
juice of 8 large limes
4–5 pickled jalapeños, drained
2 medium tomatoes, seeded
  and chopped
¼ cup (2 fl oz/60 ml) olive oil
½ teaspoon dried Mexican
  oregano
½ teaspoon sea salt
½ teaspoon ground black
  pepper
leaf lettuce, for lining dish
avocado slices
lime wedges

PREPARATION TIME: 15 MINUTES,
5-12 HOURS MARINATING
SERVES: 6

Place the fish cubes in a nonreactive bowl and pour the lime juice over them; toss to coat well. Cover the bowl with plastic wrap (clingfilm) and refrigerate for at least 5 hours, or overnight. Stir occasionally with a wooden spoon.

Chop the jalapeños and add them to the fish, along with the tomatoes, oil, and seasonings. Toss well and drain. Serve chilled in a bowl or footed glass lined with lettuce leaves and garnish with avocado slices and lime wedges.

CHILES RELLENOS DE POLLO

✺

CHILES STUFFED WITH CHICKEN

4 oz/120 g piloncillo, grated
1 small cinnamon stick
⅔ cup (5 fl oz/150 ml) cider
   vinegar
½ teaspoon sea salt
8 large ancho chiles, slit open
   lengthwise, seeded and
   deveined

For the chicken picadillo:
½ cup (4 fl oz/120 ml) mild
   olive oil
½ white onion, finely chopped
2 tablespoons minced garlic
8 Roma tomatoes, diced
¼ teaspoon dried thyme
2 small bay leaves
2 tablespoons capers
½ cup (90 g/3¼ oz) pitted
   Manzanilla olives, chopped
½ cup (2¾ oz/75 g) raisins
2 lb/900 g finely chopped or
   ground (minced) chicken
1 teaspoon sea salt
½ cup (2 oz/50 g) slivered
   (flaked) almonds
¼ cup (⅓ oz/10 g) chopped
   cilantro (coriander) leaves
¼ cup (⅓ oz/10 g) chopped
   parsley leaves
1 tablespoon minced mint
   leaves

For the cream sauce:
2 cups (16 fl oz/475 ml) sour
   cream
½ cup (3 oz/80 g) minced white
   onion
¼ cup (⅓ oz/10 g) firmly packed
   cilantro (coriander) leaves,
   minced
½ teaspoon coarse sea salt

PREPARATION TIME: 20 MINUTES
COOKING TIME: 1 HOUR 10 MINUTES, PLUS
8 MINUTES SOAKING
SERVES: 8

Prepare the chicken picadillo. In a medium saucepan, heat ¼ cup (2 fl oz/60 ml) of the olive oil over medium heat and lightly fry the onion until wilted and translucent, about 4–5 minutes. Add the garlic and cook for an additional 1 minute. Add the tomatoes, thyme, and bay leaves, reduce the heat to a simmer, and cook for 15 minutes. Add the capers, olives, and raisins and cook for an additional 10 minutes, stirring often.

Meanwhile, in a heavy 12-inch (30-cm) skillet or frying pan or sauté pan, heat the remaining ¼ cup (2 fl oz/60 ml) of the oil over high heat until smoking. Add the chicken and cook over high heat until the chicken is dry, stirring constantly. Add the salt and the hot tomato sauce, then reduce the heat, and simmer for an additional 5 minutes. Stir in the almonds and fresh herbs, then remove from the heat, and let cool.

To prepare the chiles, combine 4 cups (1⅔ pints/ 950 ml) water, the piloncillo, cinnamon, vinegar, and salt in a small nonreactive saucepan. Bring to a boil, reduce the heat, and simmer until the piloncillo has dissolved, about 5 minutes. Add the chiles, cover, remove from the heat immediately, and set aside to soak for 8 minutes. Carefully transfer the chiles, one by one, onto paper towels to drain.

Preheat the oven to 350°F/180°C/Gas mark 4. Lightly grease a 13 x 9-inch (33 x 23-cm) baking dish. Stuff each chile with a portion of the cooled chicken picadillo and arrange in the prepared baking dish. Cover with foil and bake in the preheated oven for 15–20 minutes, or until the filling is heated through.

While the chiles are baking, prepare the cream sauce for the anchos rellenos. Combine the sour cream and onion in a 2-quart (3½-pint/2-liter) non-reactive saucepan. Bring to a boil and boil for 8 minutes, then strain. Add the cilantro and salt. Keep warm.

Remove the baked chiles from the oven and serve in a pool of warm sauce. Serve immediately.

FLAN ALMENDRADO

✳

ALMOND FLAN

¾ cup (5 oz/150 g) sugar

⅔ cup (2¼ oz/60 g) blanched, slivered (flaked) almonds

1½ (21 oz/600 g) cans sweetened condensed milk

1 cup (9 fl oz/250 ml) whole milk

3 whole eggs

3 egg yolks

1 teaspoon Mexican vanilla extract

PREPARATION TIME: 10 MINUTES
COOKING TIME: 1 HOUR 20 MINUTES
MAKES: 8–12 SLICES

Preheat the oven to 350°F/180°C/Gas mark 4. Place an oven rack directly in the middle position. Put the sugar in a round 9 x 3-inch (23 x 7.5-cm) cake pan (tin). Using a heavy oven mitt (glove) or tongs, place the pan directly over medium heat to caramelize the sugar. Heat until the sugar liquefies, about 3–5 minutes, stirring occasionally with a wooden spoon. Do not touch the melted sugar—it will cause serious burns. When the hot liquid in the pan is a golden brown color, remove from the heat and set aside on a rack to cool and harden.

In a blender, combine the almonds, condensed milk, whole milk, eggs, yolks, and vanilla and process on medium speed until well blended. Pour the custard mixture over the prepared caramel. Place the cake pan in a larger, deeper pan and pour about 1 inch (2.5 cm) of hot water around the cake pan to make a water bath. Cover the flan loosely with a foil tent and place the larger pan on the middle rack of the preheated oven. Bake for 1 hour 15 minutes, or until the flan is set in the center (it will no longer jiggle). Remove from the oven and cool on a rack at room temperature. Refrigerate until thoroughly chilled, at least 1 hour.

To serve, run a knife or thin spatula around the edge of the flan to release it from the sides of the pan. Place a 10-inch (25-cm) (or larger) serving platter on top of the pan. Turn the platter over and gently remove the cake pan, leaving the flan on the serving platter. Using a flexible spatula, scrape up as much of the caramel as possible from the bottom of the pan and pour over the flan. Cut into triangular wedges and serve.

ALEX STUPAK

EMPELLON COCINA
105 1ST AVENUE
NEW YORK, NY
USA

Alex Stupak, formerly the pastry chef at Alinea and wd~50, is one of Food & Wine's Best New Chefs 2013 and chef-owner of the James Beard-award nominated restaurant, Empellón Cocina. In 2010, Alex opened the restaurant he was dreaming of rather than the one he was groomed for: Empellón Taquería in New York and in less than a year later, he opened Empellón Cocina. Standing behind the philosophy that both defines and is defined by Empellón, which means "to push" in Spanish, Alex pushes himself and his team to explore the flavors of Mexican cuisine.

SALSA BORRACHA

BORRACHA SALSA

4 pasilla Oaxaca chiles, seeds and membranes removed
4 cloves garlic, unpeeled
8 tomatillos, peeled
1 small white onion, minced
½ cup (4 fl oz/120 ml) cider vinegar
1 tablespoon salt
1 tablespoon sugar
2 tablespoons mezcal

PREPARATION TIME: 15 MINUTES, PLUS SOAKING TIME
COOKING TIME: 25 MINUTES
MAKES: ABOUT 1 QUART (1¾ PINTS/ 1 LITER)

Heat a cast-iron skillet or frying pan over medium heat and cook the chiles until they begin to smoke. Remove from the skillet and place in a bowl filled with cool water for 1 hour, or until soft.

Roast the garlic cloves in the skillet or pan until the skin is charred and the garlic is soft. Set aside until they are cool enough to handle. Roast the tomatillos in the skillet or pan until they turn olive green with black spots and begin to steam, turning them from time to time until they are cooked through. Set aside.

Drain the chiles and transfer to a molcajete or mortar and pestle. Peel the roasted garlic cloves and crush with the chiles in the molcajete or mortar until they form a paste. Coarsely chop the tomatillos and add to the garlic-chile mixture in the molcajete. Continue to pound the mixture, making sure it remains chunky. Add the minced onion, vinegar, salt, sugar, and mezcal. Stir the salsa together with a spoon. Taste the salsa and adjust the seasoning if needed. Serve.

CHILAQUILES

CHILAQUILES

PREPARATION TIME: 10 MINUTES
COOKING TIME: 10 MINUTES
SERVES: 4

12 tortillas
1 quart (1¾ pints/1 liter) canola (rapeseed) oil, for frying
salt
1 tablespoon olive oil
8 oz/225 g hen of the woods mushrooms or any mushroom of your choice, chopped into bite-size pieces
1 recipe Salsa Borracha (page 675)
¼ cup (1¼ oz/30 g) crumbled queso fresco
¼ cup (2 fl oz/60 ml) cream
1 small white onion, sliced into thin rings
about 30 cilantro (coriander) leaves

Cut the tortillas into ½-inch (1-cm) strips and then cut the strips crosswise into squares.

In a 4-quart (8-pint/4½-liter) Dutch oven (casserole) fitted with a candy (sugar) thermometer, heat the canola (rapeseed) oil to 325°F/160°C. Fry the tortilla squares until golden and crisp, about 2 minutes. Drain on a plate lined with paper towels and season with salt. Set aside

In a frying pan or skillet, heat the olive oil over medium heat and briefly sauté the mushrooms. Season with salt. Add the salsa to the pan and bring to a simmer. Add the tortilla chips and briefly simmer.

Transfer the chilaquiles to a serving platter. Garnish with queso fresco and cream. Place the onion slices and cilantro (coriander) leaves over the chilaquiles and serve immediately.

FIDEO SECO CON CHORIZO

✺

TOASTED VERMICELLI NOODLES WITH CHORIZO

12 oz/350 g dried angel hair
  pasta
2 tablespoons butter
4 oz/120 g crumbled Mexican
  chorizo
6 cloves garlic, minced
1 cup (5 oz/150 g) tomato paste
2 cups (16 fl oz/475 ml) chicken
  stock
½ cup (2¾ oz/75 g) cooked or
  canned black beans
kosher salt
½ cup (4 fl oz/120 ml) Mexican
  cream or crème fraîche
4 tablespoons grated cotija
  cheese
36 cilantro (coriander) leaves
24 thin slices of red radish
4 tablespoons minced white
  onion
1 teaspoon dried Mexican
  oregano

PREPARATION TIME: 15 MINUTES
COOKING TIME: 30 MINUTES
SERVES: 4

Place the dried angel hair pasta in a bowl and, using your hands, break into approximately 1-inch (2.5-cm) pieces.

In a saucepan over medium heat, melt the butter until slightly brown. Place the pasta in the saucepan and stir to coat with the brown butter. Continue to cook the pasta until it has turned a light brown color. Transfer the pasta back into the empty bowl and set aside.

Place the crumbled Mexican chorizo into the same saucepan and let it brown and render over medium heat.

Add the minced garlic to the chorizo and cook for 4 minutes. Add the tomato paste and cook until reduced and thickened. Add the chicken stock and black beans and bring the mixture to a simmer. Season to taste with kosher salt.

Combine the toasted angel hair pasta into the saucepan with the black beans and continue to simmer while stirring constantly. Cook the pasta until the noodles are barely tender and the liquid has been absorbed. Add the cream to the noodles and adjust the seasoning, if necessary.

Lay out 4 warmed plates and place a generous serving of noodles onto each plate. Garnish each plate with the cotija cheese, cilantro (coriander) leaves, red radish slices, minced white onion, and Mexican oregano.

HELADO DE NARANJA CON CARAMELO

✺

ORANGE ICE WITH MEZCAL TOFFEE

For the orange ice base
2 sheets gelatin
2¼ cups (18 fl oz/500 ml)
  freshly squeezed orange juice
8 g agar agar

For the Mezcal Toffee
2 cups (14 oz/400 g) sugar
3½ oz (100 g) glucose
scant ½ cup (3½ fl oz/100 ml)
  cream
1¾ cups (14 fl oz/400 ml)
  mezcal
1 teaspoon salt

Equipment for forming the
  capsules
4 x 1½ x 3¼-inch (4 x 8-cm)
  acetate rectangles
8 x 1¼ x 1¼-inch (3 x 3-cm)
  acetate rectangles
desk tape

PREPARATION TIME: 1 HOUR, PLUS 14 HOURS FREEZING
COOKING TIME: 20 MINUTES
SERVES: 4

In a bowl filled with cold water, place the gelatin sheets and let bloom, about 3 minutes. In another bowl, whisk the orange juice and agar agar to combine. In a saucepan over medium heat, bring the orange juice to a boil and add the gelatin sheets.

Fill a bowl with ice water; place a smaller bowl over it and cool the mixture down in the ice bath. As the mixture cools, it will form a firm gel. Once firm, using your hands to break it into pieces. Transfer to a blender and puree until smooth.

For the toffee, in a saucepan over medium heat, combine the sugar, glucose, and scant 1 cup (7 fl oz/200 ml) water and bring to a boil. Continue cooking until the mixture is a light brown caramel. Remove the mixture from the heat and add the cream followed by the mezcal. Return the saucepan to the heat and gently simmer until the caramel dissolves. Whisk in the salt and transfer the mixture to an ice bath to cool before placing in the freezer.

To form the capsules, on a flat sheet tray, arrange four of the 1¼-inch (3-cm) acetate squares in a row.

Place a small dollop of the Orange Ice Base on each acetate piece and spread it across the acetate using a small spatula. On another tray, place four 1½ x 3½-inch (4 x 8-cm) acetate rectangles in a row. Place a dollop of Orange Ice Base on each piece and spread evenly across each with the spatula.

Lift one of the acetate rectangles up by the short ends. Meet the ends to form a cylinder and tape them together.

Place the cylinder vertically on top of one of the smaller acetate pieces. Repeat this process with the remaining three acetate rectangles and place the cylinders in a freezer for 4 hours.

Oplace a small dollop of the Orange Ice Base on each of the remaining acetate and spread it evenly across with the spatula. Once the cylinders are frozen fill each one with Mezcal Toffee. Invert the remaining four acetate onto the cylinders and place in the freezer again for 8 hours, or overnight.

Peel the acetate away from each cylinder. Place the cylinders in small serving bowls and serve immediately.

JORGE VALLEJO

QUINTONIL
NEWTON 55
FEDERAL DISTRICT
MEXICO

Quintonil's culinary offering asserts modern Mexican cooking's true flavors and forms. At the helm are Jorge Vallejo—a young Mexican chef with a series of career highlights and recognitions behind him—and his wife, Alejandra Flores. Jorge works closely with local producers to create a fresh take on home cooking. "Come in a customer, leave as a friend" is the philosophy that encapsulates the restaurant's ultimate goal. Quintonil is a distinguished and notable restaurant in Mexico's restaurant scene.

CREMA DE QUESO

CREAM OF HEBRA CHEESE, PORK SIDE, AND PLANTAIN SOUP

For the pork side (belly):
1 small white onion, chopped
1 teaspoon cloves
pepper
1 bay leaf
7 oz/200 g pork side (belly)

For the cream of cheese soup:
14 oz/400 g tortilla, toasted
10 oz/280 g hebra cheese, crumbled
5/160 g whipping cream
15 oz/440 ml milk

8½ oz/240 g plantain, peeled and diced
1½ oz/40 g banana leaf ash
½ xcatic chile
2 limes
pinch oregano
salt
½ onion, sliced
4 g edible flowers, to garnish
spring onion, to garnish

PREPARATION TIME: 5 MINUTES, PLUS OVERNIGHT MARINATING
COOK TIME: 3 HOURS 10 MINUTES
SERVES: 4

For the pork side (belly), combine the onion, cloves, pepper, and bay leaves in a blender. Let the pork marinate overnight in a vacuum bag.

Preheat the oven to 230°F (110°C/Gas Mark ¼) and bake the pork for 3 hours. Set aside.

For the soup, in a large saucepan, combine all the ingredients over medium heat. When the cheese melts and the tortilla is soft, transfer to a food processor or blender and process for 10 minutes. Reheat in a saucepan.

Place the diced plantain, pork side (belly), cilantro (coriander), banana leaf ash, onion rings, and ixcatic in a serving dish. Pour the cheese soup on top. Garnish with the flowers and sliced spring onions.

HUAUZONTLES

✸

HUAUZONTLES WITH CUADRO DE CHIAPAS CHEESE AND TOMATO SOFRITO SALSA

17 fl oz/480 ml tomato and habanero chile salsa (see below)
17 oz/280 g huauzontles
3 oz/80 g breading (see below)
3½ oz/100 g chiapas cheese

For the tomato and habanero chile salsa:
22½ oz/640 g guaje tomatoes, blanched, peeled and blanching liquid reserved
3 oz/80 g white onion
½ habanero chile
3 tablespoons vegetable oil
3¼ oz92 g cuadro cheese
xanthan gum

For the breading:
1½ egg whites
½ egg yolk
a pinch baking powder
1½ teaspoons salt
1 oz/30 g huauzontles
1 teaspoon all-purpose (plain) flour

For the salsa, grind the tomato and raw onion together. Lightly sauté the whole habanero chiles in the vegetable oil until they begin to smolder; then add the already ground mixture. Reduce over high heat by one half and use a blender to mix with the cheese. Texturize with xanthan gum. Finally, strain through a fine-mesh strainer.

For the breading, beat the egg whites into peaks, add the yolks, baking powder, and salt. Gently fold the flour and huauzontles into the mix. Heat oil on the stove at medium to high heat and add several half tablespoons (one by one) of the mix to the oil to make the huauzontle "clouds." Flip the "clouds" around after 10 seconds. Remove from oil after another 15 seconds, place on absorbent paper to drain.

Blanch huauzontles in boiling water with a pinch of salt. Spoon the tomato and chile salsa on a plate then add the blanched huauzontles followed by the crumbled cheese. Top with 10 breaded huauzontles "clouds."

NOPALES HELADO

❋

CACTUS ICE-CREAM

½ cup (4 fl oz/120 ml) lime juice
2½ oz/75 g sugar
1 oz/25 g sorbet stabilizer
⅓ oz/10 g salt
120 g cactus paddles, coarsely
  chopped

PREPARATION TIME: 45 MINUTES, PLUS
3 HOURS REFRIGERATING TIME
SERVES: 4

Strain lime juice through a fine mesh strainer (sieve) and into a large bowl. Add sugar and stabilizer and refrigerate for 3 hours.

Place the cactus paddles in a container and add enough water to cover. For each liter of water, add ⅓ oz/10 g of salt, mix well, and refrigerate for 3 hours. Rinse the cactus under plenty of water until it is no longer viscous.

Put the cactus paddles and 3½ fl oz/100 ml of water in a blender and puree until smooth. Strain through a cone strainer (sieve). Combine with the lime juice and mix thoroughly. Finally, process mix in an ice-cream or sorbet maker for 15 minutes or until stable. Place the sorbet in a container inside a freezer until it is served.

BIBLIOGRAPHY

A book of this nature requires an extensive amount of research and many days have been dedicated to the development of these recipes. The following books have been tremendous resources for inspiration and I'd like to express my gratitude to the authors and publishers who have contributed to recording this wonderful cuisine. In addition, I'd also like to acknowledge the resources and recipes from doña Luz Catalina Arronte de Carrillo, Gerardo Vazquez Lugo, Jorge Alvarez, and Raul Traslosheros.

Banrural Voluntariado Nacional. *Comida Familiar* series. Mexico City: Banrural, 1987–1988.

Carrillo Arronte, Margarita. *Tamales y Atoles Mexicanos.* Mexico City: Larousse Mexico, 2013.

Chapa, Gerardo. *Cien Salsas.* Mexico City: 2013.

Gironella De'Angeli , Alicia. *Larousse de la Cocina Mexicana.* Mexico City: Larousse, 2006.

Gironella De'Angeli, Alicia and Jorge De'Angeli. *Larousse de la Cocina Mexicana,* vol. 1–3. Mexico City: Ediciones Larousse, 2007.

Cocina Indigena y Popular. Mexico City: Consejo Nacional para la Cultura y las Artes, 1999.

Guzmán de Vasquez Colmenares, Ana Maria. *Tradiciones Gastronomicas Oaxaqueñas.* Oaxaca: A. M. Guzmán de Vasquez Colmenares, 1982

Kennedy, Diana. *The Art of Mexican Cooking.* New York: Bantam, 1989.

Kennedy, Diana. *From My Mexican Kitchen Techniques and Ingredients.* New York: Potter, 2003.

Kennedy, Diana. *Oaxaca al Gusto.* San Pedro Garza García, Nuevo León: Plenus, 2008.

Luengas, Arnulfo. *La Cocina del Banco Nacional de Mexico.* Mexico City: Fomento Cultural Banamex, 2000.

Muñoz Zurita, Ricardo. *Larousse Diccionario Enciclopedico de la Gastronomia Mexicana.* Mexico City: Ediciones Larousse, 2013.

Muñoz Zurita, Ricardo. *Verde en la Cocina Mexicana.* Mexico City: Fundacion Herdez, 1999.

Quintana, Patricia. *El Gran Libro de los Antojitos Mexicanos.* Mexico City: Oceano De Mexico, 2003.

Quintana, Patricia. *Puebla: La Cocina de Los Angeles.* Puebla: Hospital para el Nino Poblano, 1992.

Rios Szalay, Adalberto, Christina Barros, and Prisciliano Jiménez. *Paranguas Hogar De Manjares Michoacanos.* Barcelona: Lunwerg, 2007.

Stoopen, Maria. *La Cocina Veracruzana (Veracruz en la cultura).* Veracruz: Gobierno del Estado de Veracruz, 1992.

Titita, Carmen. *Alquimias y Atmosferas del Sabor.* Mexico City: Tiempo imaginario, 2001

INGREDIENTS

AUSTRALIA

AZTEC PRODUCTS
8A ADINA COURT
TULLAMARINE
VICTORIA 3043
WWW.AZTECMEXICAN.COM.AU

CHILE MOJO
381 MAGILL ROAD
ST. MORRIS
SOUTH AUSTRALIA 5068
WWW.CHILEMOJO.COM.AU

CASA IBERICA
25 JOHNSTON ST
FITZROY
VICTORIA 3065
WWW.CASAIBERICADELI.COM.AU

MONTEREY MEXICAN FOODS
UNIT 6/340 HOXTON PARK ROAD
PRESTONS
NEW SOUTH WALES 2171
WWW.MONTEREYFOODS.COM.AU

UNITED KINGDOM

COOL CHILE CO.
GREEN MARKET
BOROUGH MARKET
LONDON BRIDGE
LONDON SE1 9AL
WWW.COOLCHILE.CO.UK

MEXGROCER
UNIT 9A
BRITANNIA ESTATES
LEAGRAVE ROAD
LUTON LU3 1RJ
WWW.MEXGROCER.CO.UK

THE SPICE SHOP
1 BLENHEIM CRESCENT
LONDON W11 2EE
WWW.THESPICESHOP.CO.UK

LUPE PINTOS
313 GREAT WESTERN ROAD
GLASGOW G4 9HR
WWW.LUPEPINTOS.COM

NORTH AMERICA

EL BURRITO MERCADO
175 CESAR CHAVEZ STREET
ST. PAUL
MINNESOTA 55107
WWW.ELBURRITOMERCADO.COM

EL MERCADO LATINO
1514 PIKE PLACE
SEATTLE
WASHINGTON 98101
WWW.LATINMERCHANT.COM

MI PUEBLO FOOD CENTER
1775 STORY ROAD
SAN JOSE
CALIFORNIA 95122
WWW.MIPUEBLO.COM

PLAZA FIESTA
4166 BUFORD HIGHWAY NE
ATLANTA
GEORGIA 30345
WWW.PLAZAFIESTA.NET

ZARAGOZA MEXICAN DELI & GROCERY
215 AVENUE A
NEW YORK
NEW YORK 10009

ONLINE

ALEGRO FOODS
WWW.ALEGROFOODS.COM

EL CIELO
WWW.ELCIELO.COM.AU

MEX GROCER
WWW.MEXGROCER.COM

MY MEXICAN PANTRY
WWW.MYMEXICANPANTRY.COM

MY MEXICAN SHOP
WWW.MYMEXICANSHOP.IE

SOUS CHEF
WWW.SOUSCHEF.CO.UK

CERAMICS AND TEXTILES

AUSTRALIA

LOS ANDES
287 VICTORIA STREET
WEST MELBOURNE
VICTORIA 3003
WWW.LOSANDES.COM.AU

THE MEXICAN SHOP
69 UNLEY ROAD
PARKSIDE
SOUTH AUSTRALIA 5063
WWW.THEMEXICANSHOP.NET

RUSTICO MEXICANO
UNIT 23/284 MUSGRAVE ROAD
COOPERS PLAINS
QUEENSLAND 4108
WWW.MEXICANHANDCRAFTS.COM.AU

UNITED KINGDOM

CASA MEXICO
1 WINKLEY STREET
LONDON E2 6PY
WWW.CASAMEXICO.CO.UK

MILAGROS
61 COLUMBIA ROAD
LONDON E2 7RG
WWW.MILAGROS.CO.UK

OTOMÍ
7 CLIFTON ARCADE
BOYCES AVENUE
BRISTOL
BS8 4AA
WWW.OTOMI.CO.UK

NORTH AMERICA

QUE CHULA
510 MONROE SE
ALBUQUERQUE
NEW MEXICO 87108
WWW.QUECHULASTYLE.COM

TALAVERA CERAMICS
1801 UNIVERSITY AVENUE
BERKELEY
CALIFORNIA 94703
WWW.TALAVERACERAMICS.COM

TALAVERA EMPORIUM
107 CONCHO STREET
SAN ANTONIO
TEXAS 78207
WWW.TALAVERAEMPORIUM.COM

ONLINE

AMOR Y LOCURA
WWW.AMORYLOCURA.COM

DIRECT FROM MEXICO
WWW.DIRECTFROMMEXICO.COM

LA FUENTE IMPORTS
WWW.LAFUENTE.COM

MEXICAN POTTERY ART
WWW.MEXICANPOTTERY-ART.COM

THE MEXICAN RUG COMPANY
WWW.MEXICANRUGCOMPANY.CO.UK

MI PATRIA
WWW.MIPATRIA.COM

NOVICA
WWW.NOVICA.COM

GLOSSARY

A

ACHIOTE SEED PASTE Achiote (sometimes called annatto) seeds impart a yellow color and a subtle taste likened to saffron. Recipes for the paste typically combine the seeds with lime, allspice berries, garlic and salt. Varieties include red achiote paste (recado rojo) and black achiote paste (recado negro).

ACITRÓN DE BIZNAGA Crystallized cactus pieces. Use candied pineapple as a substitute.

ADOBERO CHEESE A soft, cow's milk cheese, very similar to Queso Fresco. Use feta or a mild cheddar as a substitute.

ADOBO Marinade.

AGUARDIENTE A term for strong alcoholic liquors.

AL PASTOR Marinated fillets of meat stacked on a spit and roasted in front of a vertical fire. Once the meat is lightly browned, it is shaved off and put into tacos "al pastor," shepherd style.

ALUBIA BEANS Small white beans. Use cannellini beans as a substitute.

AMARANTH The seeds of the amaranth plant are enjoyed in the same way as a grain. They are gluten free and considered a health food. You can use quinoa as a substitute. Puffed amaranth seeds can be replaced with quinoa pops or puffed rice.

AÑEJO CHEESE Aged cheese made from skimmed goat's or cow's milk and coated in paprika. Use romano as a substitute.

ANTOJITOS Appetizers or street food, which are central to Mexican food culture. Usually antojitos have a corn base, are fried, and accompanied with a chile sauce. Examples include esquita (toasted or boiled corn kernels with various toppings), and sope (rounds of corn dough with raised edges to hold a topping).

ATE Concentrated fruit paste made from various fruits: quince, guava, pineapple, cherry, or lime.

AVOCADO LEAVES Can be used in dried or fresh form, to wrap food or to flavor stews. Use fennel as a substitute if chopped or banana or maguey leaves if used as wrappers. Aguacatillo are a smaller variety.

B

BARBACOA In Mexico, the term "barbeque" typically refers to the traditional method of cooking or steaming meat in its own juice.

BERROS Watercress.

BLACK SAPOTE Also known as chocolate pudding fruit. A fruit with a rich, sweet flavor and a dark brown flesh hence the alternative name. It is often used as a healthy alternative for chocolate. Use persimmon or plum as a substitute.

BOLILLO Crusty bread rolls, similar to baguettes.

BORRACHO Translates as "drunk" and used to describe sauces featuring alcohol.

BROCHETTE Skewer.

BUÑUELOS Deep-fried doughnuts made of a thin batter with a sweet or savory filling and often soaked in syrup.

BUTTERFISH Type of mild white fish. Use sea bass or other white fish as a substitute.

C

CABUCHES Flowers from the biznaga cactus. Similar in taste to artichoke.

CACAHUATE Peanut.

NOPALES Cactus paddles. Though fresh ones are preferable, they can be bought tinned too. Use okra, green beans or green peppers as a substitute. To prepare, put the cactus paddles in a copper pot (to prevent them from discolouring), add enough water to cover them, and bring to a boil. Add a teaspoon of salt and cook over high heat for 40 minutes or until the cactus paddles turn bright green again. Drain in a strainer (sieve) and immediately cover with a dish towel to draw the slime. Set aside for 20 minutes, then prepare as instructed in the recipe.

CAL Slaked lime (calcium oxide) used in the nixtamalization process.

CALABAZA EN TACHA Pumpkin candied in piloncillo syrup.

CALABACITAS Zucchini (courgette).

CALDO A clear broth.

CAMBRAY ONIONS Spring onions or scallions.

CAMBRAY PINEAPPLE A variety of pineapple, which is grown in Mexico.

CAMOTE Yam or sweet potato. The young leaves and shoots are sometimes eaten as greens.

CAZUELA Large, clay casserole dish.

CECINA Thin slices of dried pork. Cecina blanca is seasoned with salt; cecina enchilada is smothered with chile paste.

CEVICHE Fish cured in citrus juice. Served cold or at room temperature.

CHALUPA Crisp, deep-fried oval tortilla with raised edges covered with beans, sauces, meats and cheese.

CHAPULINE Fried grasshopper.

CHARALES Tiny fish, eaten dried or deep-fried. Use whitebait as a substitute.

CHAYA A large-leafed, green vegetable. Use spinach or chard as a substitute.

CHAYOTE A vegetable belonging to the same gourd family as squash. Use zucchini (courgette) as a substitute.

CHICHARRÓN Pork rinds (scratchings).

CHIHUAHUA CHEESE Also known as Menonita. A semi-soft, mild, cow's milk cheese. Use mild cheddar or Monterey Jack as a substitute.

CHILAQUILES Totopos tossed with a salsa and other ingredients and topped with cheese or sour cream.

CHILMOLE A spicy paste made from habanero peppers and spices.

CHINTEXTLE A Oaxacan sauce or paste, characterized by its smoky flavor and made with Oaxacan or pasilla chile. Typically spread on tortillas.

CHOKECHERRY Small red fruits with a sour, bitter flavor. The stones are poisonous so avoid consumption. Use red currants or sour cherries as a substitute.

CHOCHOYOTES Small, corn dough dumplings cooked in soups or moles.

CIRUELA CRIOLLA Translates to Creole plums. Use regular plums as a substitute.

COMAL A flat, round griddle of unglazed pottery or metal used for dry frying.

COTIJA CHEESE A salty, hard cheese made from cow's milk. Use parmesan or feta as a substitute.

CREMA Thick, acidulated dairy cream. Use crème fraiche or sour cream as a substitute.

E

EAU DE VIE A colorless brandy made from fermented fruit.

EMPANADA Turnover filled with sweet or savory fillings.

ENCHILADA Tortilla which are rolled into cylinders or folded in half with a filling inside and bathed in sauce.

EPAZOTE Herb, otherwise known as wormseed or Jesuit's tea, used to flavor beans, corn and other dishes. Epazote becomes a purple color when exposed to light. Use parsley or cilantro as a substitute, through both are lacking in bitterness.

ESCABECHE Fish or chicken which has been marinated in an acidic mixture and then fried.

ESCAMOL Giant ant egg.

ESMEDREGAL Also known as jack fish. Use another white fish as a substitute.

F

FARMER'S CHEESE Pressed, firm cottage cheese. Use feta as a substitute.

FIG LEAVES Used for wrapping ingredients. Use banana leaves, lemon or lime leaves as a substitute.

FLOR DE CALABAZA Zucchini (courgette) flower.

FLOR DE JAMAICA Hibiscus flower.

FLOR DE MAYO BEANS Rose-colored, delicate, smoked flavor. Use pinto beans as a substitute.

G

GORDITAS Small pasties or pockets made of a thick corn exterior and filled with meat, seafood, or vegetables.

GUISADO A type of stew.

GUSANOS DE MAGUEY Worms from the maguey plant that are dried and smoked.

H

HIERBAS DE OLOR Aromatic herbs, like oregano, thyme, marjoram and bay leaf, sold in tiny bundles.

HOMINY Otherwise known as hominy. Dried, nixtamalized corn kernels.

HORCHATA Blended rice and water drink flavored with cinnamon and sugar.

HOJA SANTA Also called Mexican pepperleaf. A native plant with heart-shaped leaves and an anise flavor. Used in moles, stews and tamales, or to wrap chicken and fish when steamed. Use Thai basil as a substitute.

HUAZONTLE Aztec broccoli. Use purple sprouting broccoli as a substitute.

HUITLACOCHE Also known as cuitlacoch or corn smut. A fungus that grows on corn, which is eaten as a filling for tortilla based foods and soups.

J

JAMONCILLO A sweet made from piloncillo and coconut. Similar to fudge.

JICAMA Also known as Mexican yam. A root vegetable with a sweet flavor and eaten cooked or raw.

JOCOQUE Fermented milk product with the consistency of sour cream and a slightly acidic taste. Use salted buttermilk, sour cream, yogurt or crema as a substitute.

L

LARD Pig fat in rendered and unrendered form. Essential for most tamales and for adding flavor to many dishes.

LONGANIZA A long Spanish sausage made of minced pork meat and similar to chorizo.

M

MACHACA Shredded, marinated and dried beef or pork that is similar to jerky.

MAGUEY LEAVES A cousin to the Tequila blue agave, the maguey is also known as the century plant. Its leaves can be used to wrap and flavor meat. It can be substituted with banana leaves.

MAMEY A fruit with a very sweet and delicate taste. Use papaya as a substitute.

MARQUESOTE A type of sweet bread.

MASA A dough made from masa harina.

MASA HARINA Dehydrated, nixtamalized corn dough which is mixed with water to reconstitute it. It's finely ground for making tortillas or coarsely ground for tamales.

MAYACOBA BEANS Small beans with a yellow color. Use pinto beans as a substitute.

METATE A pre-Hispanic grinding stone consisting of a large stone base with a shallow depression in it.

METATE CHOCOLATE Chocolate ground on the metate.

MEXICAN PINK PINE NUTS A Mexican variety of pine nut. Substitute with another type of pine nut.

MEZCAL Liquor distilled from the maguey (agave) plant. Mezcal reposado is aged mezcal.

MIXIOTE A pit-barbqued meat dish wrapped in maguey leaves. Use parchment paper as a substitute.

MOLE Generic name for numerous sauces and the dishes based on these sauces. The term is most often associated with thick, brownish-red sauces, though the term is much broader than that. The base of all moles is chiles. Some examples include mole amarillo, mole coloradito, mole verde, and the best known, mole poblano.

N

NATA Cream. Usually refers to the membrane that forms on top of heated milk.

NOGADA Walnut sauce. Most common in *Chiles en Nogada* (page 396).

O

OLLA Clay pot or stockpot.

MEXICAN OREGANO A type of oregano. Use marjoram or European oregano as a substitute (though use a little less).

P

PANELA CHEESE Soft, creamy, cow's milk cheese. Use ricotta or paneer as a substitute.

PAPALO A Mexican herb also known as Bolivian coriander. Use an increased amount of cilantro (coriander) as a replacement.

PILONCILLO Unrefined brown sugar.

PINEAPPLE VINEGAR Fermented pineapple peelings used to make a vinegar with a light pineapple flavor. Use apple cider vinegar as a substitute.

PIMIENTOS Large, red peppers with a sweeter taste than bell peppers.

PIPIÁN Stew or sauce made with pumpkin or sesame seeds.

PLANTAIN LEAVES Fresh plantain leaves used for wrapping tamales and meat and for lining pans.

POMPANO Medium-flavored white fish. Use mullet, mahi-mahi, red snapper or mackerel as a substitute.

PORGY Also known as sea bream.

POZOLE A soup or stew made from corn kernels with many regional variations.

PRICKLY PEAR Cactus fruit. The prickly pear is sweeter than the xoconostle. Use heavy gardening gloves to hold the prickly pears when you do this as they have tiny almost invisible prickles that will get you!

PULQUE Alcoholic drink made from the fermented sap of the maguey plant.

PUMPKIN SEEDS Used in moles, pipanes, sweets.

PURPLE AYOCOTE BEANS Purple runner beans. Use green runner beans as a substitute.

PURSLANE Green leafy plant, also known as pig weed. Use watercress or rocket as a substitute.

Q

QUESADILLAS A corn or flour tortilla filled with meat, seafood, or vegetables, folded into a half-moon, and fried until crisp.

QUESO CORAZON A regional, fresh, white cheese shaped like a heart. Use paneer or ricotta as a substitute.

QUESO REQUESÓN A creamy cheese made from whey. Use ricotta as a substitute.

R

RECADO NEGRO Charred dried chile and spice paste.

ROMERITOS A wild plant with a flavor like spinach and a similar appearance to rosemary. Use baby spinach as a substitute.

S

SAFFLOWER OIL An oil with a high smoke point which is good for deep-frying. Use rapeseed or corn oil as a substitute.

SOUR ORANGE Seville oranges, which by the way, have a thick, wrinkled peel like those from Yucatán or make a mixture of: 1 part of regular orange juice, 2 parts of lime juice and 1 part of grapefruit juice,

SAPODILLA A tropical fruit with a flavor like caramelized pear. Use pear or apricot as a substitute.

SOURSOP Also known as guanabana. The fruit is from the same family as the paw paw and has been likened to pineapple and bananas in its flavor but with an acidic edge. Use pineapple or papaya as a substitute.

SUGAR CANE VINEGAR Vinegar made from fermented sugar cane and less sour than other vinegars. Use white wine vinegar or cider vinegar as a substitute.

T

TACO Fresh tortilla wrapped around filling such as beans, shredded meat or fish with salsa and other trimmings.

TAMARIND CONCENTRATE A thick, dark paste or block with a sweet-sour tamarind flavor.

TASAJO Thinly sliced strips of beef that are either salted or dried.

TEJOCOTE A fruit resembling the crab apple. In general the fruit is cooked before consumption. Use kumquat, plum or apple as a substitute.

TEPARY BEANS Small beans native to southwest US and Mexico. Use pinto or red kidney beans as a substitute.

TEQUESQUITE A mineral salt used for two key purposes: to help green ingredients, such as nopales, retain their color; and to leaven the corn masa for tamales. Use baking powder or bicarbonate of soda as a substitute for leavening.

TLACOYO Fried or grilled, flattened pocket of masa dough filled with beans or cheese. Often served with soups or stews.

TOMATILLO A small, green, and sour vegetable from the gooseberry family. Used in soups, sauces and moles. To dry-roast, place the whole tomatillo on an ungreased comal or griddle and cook over medium heat until fairly soft and the skin is patched with brown.

TOSTADA An open-faced taco or a very crisp pizza, the tostada has toppings spread over a toasted or fried tortilla base.

TOTOMOXTLE Corn husks which are used for tamale wrappers. Use baking parchment as a substitute.

TOTOPO Triangular piece of toasted tortilla.

X

XOCONOSTLE A cactus fruit similar to the prickly pear to look at but with a different taste. The xoconostle is prized for its more acidic flesh and that the seeds are clustered in the centre of the fruit rather than scattered throughout it.

XONEQUI A green leafy vegetable. Use spinach or Swiss chard as a substitute.

Y

YUCA Root vegetable, also known as cassava, with brown skin and white flesh. Substitute for sweet potato.

COOKING TERMS

BLANCH To partially cook fruit, vegetables or nuts briefly in boiling water to make them softer or easier to peel.

BLISTER To expose meat or vegetables etc. to a high heat so that the skin bubbles and blackens.

DEEP-FRY To cook in plenty of hot oil or fat over high heat. Olive or vegetable oil may be used for deep-frying, although olive oil has a lower smoke point than oils such as groundnut. Margarine and butter are not suitable as they tend to burn. Lard may not be advisable for dietary reasons.

DEVEIN To remove the black threadlike intestinal tract of a shrimp (prawn) or the tissue under the stem of a chile to which the seeds are attached.

DISCOLORATION When fruit and vegetables are cut and the flesh oxidises. Can be counteracted by adding vinegar or lemon juice to the fruit or vegetable.

DRY-ROAST To expose vegetables, spices, seeds, etc. to high heat in a heavy-based pan to intensify their flavor. Rough roasting times:
Avocado leaves: 2–3 minutes
Garlic and fresh chiles: 5–10 minutes
Onions, tomatoes, and tomatillos: 10–15 minutes
Whole spices: 1–2 minutes (until aromatic)

DRY-ROAST CHILES All poblano and other fresh chiles need to be roasted over a direct flame, then put in a plastic bag which is then wrapped with a kitchen towel. Let the chiles sweat for a few minutes, then remove the skin, membranes, and seeds. For dry chiles, remove seeds and membranes, then soak in water for several minutes.

EMULSIFY To mix two liquids of different densities, such as oil and vinegar or lemon juice, by whisking them together. The resulting mixture is unstable and the ingredients will separate again after a while.

FILLET To remove fillets of raw or cooked fish from the bones. A very sharp, flexible knife is required for raw fish.

FLAKE To break up cooked fish into large chunks with your fingers.

GARNISH To decorate single plates or serving dishes of savory ingredients with cut vegetables, herb sprigs, lemon slices or other garnishes to make them look attractive and to achieve a visual balance between the various shapes and colors and to enhance the flavour of the ingredients.

GLAZE To evenly brush pastry or dough with either milk, egg, or a mix of both, to give a shiny, golden appearance once baked. It can also apply to meats and vegetables coated in a shiny sauce.

GRIND To crush or break whole spices, vegetables, etc. into fine powder or paste.

HULL To remove the inedible stem from a fruit or vegetable.

INFUSE To soak ingredients to soak in a liquid or spice mix, such as wine, liqueur or seasoning, for a specified period.

KNEAD To mix solid and liquid ingredients by 'working them' for varying lengths of time by hand, with a spatula or with an electric mixer fitted with dough hooks. Pasta and yeast doughs are kneaded vigorously, whereas pastry dough is kneaded lightly.

MOLCAJETE Stone bowl like a mortar used to grind chiles and spices and to make salsas.

MOLINO A grinding mill

PARBOIL To partially boil rice or vegetables until they start to soften but before they are fully cooked.

PARING KNIFE A small knife used for intricate work such as peeling and coring.

PIT To remove the stone from a fruit, such as an avocado or mango.

POACH To cook eggs by breaking them into boiling water and cooking them for a few minutes. Fish, meat and poultry may also be poached in gently simmering water or stock.

PUREE To reduce a solid, semi-solid substance or mixture to a semi-liquid or smooth cream using a food processor or blender.

REDUCE To make a liquid, such as a stock or sauce, thicker and more concentrated by heating it for longer and therefore decreasing the amound of liquid.

REST To allow the gluten in a dough to relax, making it more elastic.

RUB IN To combine flour and a fat, such as butter or lard, by gently rubbing the ingredients together with your fingertips until the mixture resembles breadcrumbs.

SAUTE To cook meat, fish or vegetables in a frying pan or saute pan with oil or butter until the ingredients are lightly browned and cooked through.

SCORE To slice a piece of meat or fish without cutting all the way through, giving a bigger surface area for flavours to penetrate.

SEAL To create a caramelized crust on meat or fish by searing it in a pan on a high temperature.

SEED To remove the seeds from a fruit or vegetable, first cutting it in half then scraping out the seeds with a spoon or the tip of a knife.

SHELL To remove the outer casing from a vegetable, such as a broad beans

SHRED To cut ingredients, such as cabbage and lettuce, into very thin strips.

SHUCK To remove the husk from an ear of corn or the shell from an oyster.

SKIN To remove the skin from a fish or meat by sliding a sharp, flexible knife between the skin and the flesh.

STAND To leave ingredients mixed in a bowl for a short time to allow the flavours to combine. When there is acidity in the mixture, such as lemon juice or vinegar, the ingredients will also tenderize.

STRAIN To pour a mixture through a strainer (sieve) to separate the liquid from any solids.

TORTILLA PRESS A utensil with flatten tortilla dough into thin rounds. Sheets of plastic are often used to line the plates to prevent the dough from sticking.

Any important body of work is never done by only one person—it always involves the work of a team and this book is no exception. First and foremost, I would like to thank my beloved husband Angel, who always thought, until the last day of his life, that I was the best cook on Earth, and had encouraged me to do this book.

To Ricardo and Luzka, my parents, who made me the person I am today and taught me my love for Mexico. To *abuelita* Quica, my beloved grandmother for teaching me the secrets of good food.

I'd like to extend my gratitude to the Phaidon team who have been kind, enthusiastic, helpful and attentive: Emilia, Emma, Michelle, Ellie, and Orla.

A special recognition to Mauro, my sous chef who is always ready to support me And I cannot close this page without a heartfelt thank you to my team whom have always given me unconditional support and affection: Sarita, Chabelita, Alejandra, Gaby, Octavio, and Salvador.

A very special recognition goes to Jane Mason who has been a great help and who always believed in me—this book would not be possible without her contribution.

PHAIDON PRESS LIMITED
REGENT'S WHARF
ALL SAINTS STREET
LONDON N1 9PA

PHAIDON PRESS INC.
65 BLEECKER STREET
NEW YORK, NY 10012

WWW.PHAIDON.COM

FIRST PUBLISHED 2014
© 2014 PHAIDON PRESS LIMITED

ISBN: 978 07148 6752 6

A CIP CATALOGUE RECORD FOR THIS BOOK
IS AVAILABLE FROM THE BRITISH LIBRARY.

COMMISSIONING EDITOR: EMILIA TERRAGNI
PROJECT EDITOR: MICHELLE LO
CONSULTANT EDITOR: JANE MASON
PRODUCTION CONTROLLER: VANESSA TODD-HOLMES

DESIGNED BY BARBARA SAYS
PHOTOGRAPHS BY FIAMMA PIACENTINI

PRINTED IN CHINA

RECIPE NOTES

Unless otherwise stated, eggs and individual vegetables and fruits, such as onions and apples, are assumed to be medium.

Unless otherwise stated, pepper is freshly ground black pepper.

Cooking times are for guidance only, as individual ovens vary. If using a fan oven, follow the manufacturer's instructions concerning oven temperatures.

Exercise a high level of caution when following recipes involving any potentially hazardous activity, including the use of high temperatures, open flames, and when deep-frying. In particular, when deep-frying, add food carefully to avoid splashing, wear long sleeves, and never leave the pan unattended.

Some recipes include raw or very lightly cooked eggs, meat, or fish, and fermented products. These should be avoided by the elderly, infants, pregnant women, convalescents, and anyone with an impaired immune system.

Insects should only be purchased from reliable sources and kept as fresh as possible. Live insects should be stored in a refrigerator for 30–60 minutes prior to cooking.

When no quantity is specified, for example of oils, salts, and herbs used for finishing dishes, quantities are discretionary and flexible.

Both metric and imperial measures are used in this book. Follow one set of measurements throughout, not a mixture, as they are not interchangeable.

All spoon and cup measurements are level, unless otherwise stated. 1 teaspoon = 5ml; 1 tablespoon = 15 ml. Australian standard tablespoons are 20 ml, so Australian readers are advised to use 3 teaspoons in place of 1 tablespoon when measuring small quantities.